BARRON'S

PSAT/ NMSQT®

PSAT/NATIONAL MERIT SCHOLARSHIP QUALIFYING TEST

13TH EDITION

Sharon Weiner Green
Former Instructor in English
Merritt College
Oakland, California

Ira K. Wolf, Ph.D.
President, PowerPrep, Inc.
Former High School Teacher,
College Professor, and
University Director of
Teacher Preparation

BARRON'S

All inquiries should be addressed to:
Barron's Educational Series, Inc.
250 Wireless Boulevard
Hauppauge, NY 11788
www.barronseduc.com

Library of Congress Catalog Card No. 2006042694

ISBN 13: 978-0-7641-3360-2
ISBN 10: 0-7641-3360-8

Library of Congress Cataloging-in-Publication Data
Green, Sharon, 1939–
    Barron's how to prepare for the PSAT/NMSQT: PSAT/National Merit
Scholarship Qualifying Test/Sharon Weiner Green, Ira K. Wolf.—13th ed.
        p.   cm.
    ISBN-13: 978-0-7641-3360-2
    ISBN-10: 0-7641-3360-8 (alk. paper)
    1. Preliminary Scholastic Assessment Test—Study guides.   2. National
Merit Scholarship Qualifying Test—Study guides.   I. Title: How to prepare for
the PSAT/NMSQT.   II. Title: PSAT/NMSQT.   III. Title: PSAT/National
Merit Scholarship Qualifying Test.   IV. Wolf, Ira K.   V. Title.

LB2353.56.B76 2006
378.1'662–dc22

                                                    2006042694

PRINTED IN THE UNITED STATES OF AMERICA
9 8 7 6 5 4 3 2 1

Contents

Preface   v

Acknowledgments   vi

PART ONE   INTRODUCTION

1 The PSAT/National Merit Scholarship Qualifying Test   **3**

Some Basic Questions Answered   3

Sample PSAT Questions   6

After the PSAT/NMSQT   21

2 How to Approach the PSAT/NMSQT   **22**

Test-Taking Tactics   22

Reducing Anxiety   23

Guessing   24

PART TWO   DIAGNOSE YOUR PROBLEM

3 A Diagnostic Test   **29**

Examination   33

Answer Key and Explanations   53

PART THREE   CRITICAL READING

4 The Sentence Completion Question   **67**

Tips for Handling Sentence Completion Questions   67

Sentence Completion Exercises   70

5 Improving Critical Reading Comprehension   **78**

Long-Range Strategy   78

Tips for Handling Critical Reading Questions   79

Practice Reading Exercises   92

6 Building Your Vocabulary   **106**

Long-Range Strategy   106

PSAT High-Frequency Word List   107

Basic Word List   109

Basic Word Parts   157

PART FOUR   MATHEMATICS

7 Introduction to the Mathematics Sections   **175**

8 Tactics and Strategies   **182**

9   Review of PSAT Mathematics   194

Section A: Basic Arithmetic Concepts   194
Section B: Fractions and Decimals   203
Section C: Percents   208
Section D: Ratios and Proportions   212
Section E: Averages   216
Section F: Polynomials   219
Section G: Solving Equations and Inequalities   224
Section H: Word Problems   229
Section I: Lines and Angles   233
Section J: Triangles   237
Section K: Quadrilaterals   244
Section L: Circles   250
Section M: Solid Geometry   255
Section N: Coordinate Geometry   259
Section O: Basic Probability   265
Section P: Sequences   268
Section Q: Interpretation of Data   271
Section R: Functions   279

PART FIVE   WRITING SKILLS

10   Improving Written Expression   285

Tips for Handling Improving Sentence Questions   286
Tips for Handling Identifying Sentence Error Questions   289
Tips for Handling Improving Paragraph Questions   290
Common Grammar and Usage Errors   291
Practice Exercises   294

PART SIX   TEST YOURSELF

11   Six Model Tests   305

Test A   307
Test B   339
Test C   373
Test D   407
Test E   441
Test F   475

Index   509

Preface

Welcome to the Thirteenth Edition of *Barron's PSAT/NMSQT*. Today's PSAT, like the SAT, has changed. If you are preparing for the *new* PSAT, this is the book you need.

This Thirteenth Edition updates America's leading book focused on the PSAT. Along with the best of the time-tested features of earlier editions, today's Thirteenth Edition provides much, much more.

It clears up misconceptions you may have about the test—although there's a Writing Skills section, you *don't* have to write an essay!—and gives you a brief rundown of the entire test.

It features seven full-length sample tests modeled on the PSAT in length and difficulty, seven crucial "dress rehearsals" for the day you walk into the examination room.

It prepares you for the Writing Skills section, teaching you how to spot errors and polish rough drafts so that you can shine on the PSAT and eventually on the SAT.

It briefs you on vocabulary-in-context and reading comprehension questions, giving you key tips on how to tackle these important verbal question types.

It takes you step by step through the double reading passages, showing you how to work your way through a pair of reading passages without wasting effort or time.

It introduces you to the non-multiple-choice questions in the Mathematics section, teaching you shortcuts to solving problems and entering your own answers on a sample grid.

It offers you advice on how (and when) to use a calculator in dealing with both multiple-choice and "grid-in" questions.

It contains a separate chapter that reviews every math topic you need to know.

It gives you the 300-word PSAT High Frequency Word List, 300 vital words that have been shown by computer analysis to occur and reoccur on actual published PSATs, plus Barron's PSAT Basic Word List, more than 1,300 words that you'll want to master as you work to build a college-level vocabulary. (For quick review, there's also a list of Basic Word Parts.)

Most important, it teaches you the special tactics and strategies essential for scoring high on the PSAT.

No other book tells you as much about the test. No other book offers you as many questions modeled on the PSAT.

The PSAT is your chance to get yourself set for the all-important SAT. It's also your chance to qualify for some of the nation's most prestigious college scholarships. Go for your personal best; take the time to learn how to prepare for the PSAT.

This Thirteenth Edition of *Barron's PSAT/NMSQT* is evidence of Barron's on-going commitment to make this publication America's outstanding PSAT study guide.

Acknowledgments

The authors gratefully acknowledge all those sources who granted permission to use materials from their publications:

Pages 8, 89–90: From *Summer of '49* by David Halberstam, © 1989 by David Halberstam. Reprinted by permission of HarperCollins Publishers Inc.

Pages 8, 90: From *Take Time for Paradise,* © 1989 by the Estate of A. Bartlett Giamatti.

Pages 34–35: From *Life Nature Library: The Forest* by Peter Farb and the editors of Time-Life Books, © Time-Life Books Inc., pp. 75–76.

Page 36: From *Bury My Heart at Wounded Knee* by Dee Brown, © 1976 by Dee Brown, pp. xi–xiii. Reprinted by permission of Henry Holt & Co., Inc.

Pages 41–42: From *Modern Dancer's Primer for Action,* by Martha Graham, © 1941 by PUP. Reprinted by permission of Princeton University Press.

Page 42: From *The Chez Panisse Menu Cookbook* by Alice Waters, © 1982 by Alice L. Waters. Used by permission of Random House, Inc.

Pages 81–82, 84, 87–88: From "The Odds Are You're Innumerate" by John Allen Paulos in *The New York Times Book Review,* © by the New York Times Co., January 1, 1989, pp. 16–17. Reprinted by permission.

Pages 98–99: From "The Birth of Massive Stars" by Michael Zelik in *Scientific American Inc.,* April 1978.

Pages 101–102: From *The English Novel: Form and Function* by Dorothy Van Ghent, © 1953, 1981. Holt, Rinehart and Winston, Inc.

Page 104: From *Rodents: Their Lives and Habitats* by Peter W. Haney. Published by David and Charles Publishers.

Page 310: From *King Solomon's Ring* by Konrad Z. Lorenz, © 1952, Harper & Row, pp. 128–129.

Page 311: Excerpts from *Renaissance to Modern Tapestries in The Metropolitan Museum of Art* (pp. 4–6) by Edith Appleton Standen. © 1987, the Metropolitan Museum of Art. Reprinted courtesy of the Metropolitan Museum of Art.

Pages 316–317: From "Yonder Peasant, Who Is He?" by Mary McCarthy in *Memories of a Catholic Girlhood,* © 1948 and 1975, p. 57. Reprinted with permission of Harcourt Brace & Co.

Page 317: From *Reinventing Womanhood* by Caroline G. Heilbrun, © 1979. Reprinted with permission of W. W. Norton & Company, Inc., pp. 56–57.

Pages 342–343: From *Composing a Life* by Mary Catherine Bateson, © 1990, pp. 1–2 and 4–7. Reprinted with permission of Penguin Books.

Pages 344–345: From "Chapter 3. Overview" by Darlene Clark Hine, from *The Eyes on the Prize Civil Rights Reader* by Clayborne Carson et al., © 1991 by Blackside Inc. Used by permission of Viking Penguin, a division of Penguin Putnam Inc.

Page 350: From *The Greenpeace Book of Dolphins* edited by John May, © 1990. Reprinted by permission of Greenpeace.

Pages 377–378: From "Huge Conservation Effort Aims to Save Vanishing Architect of the Savannah" by William K. Stevens, © 2001 by the New York Times Co. Reprinted by permission.

Pages 383–384: From "Let's Say You Wrote Badly This Morning" by David Huddle in *The Writing Habit,* University Press of New England, Hanover, N.H., 1994.

Page 384: From "My Two One-Eyed Coaches" by George Garrett. *Virginia Quarterly Review,* V. 63, N. 2.

Pages 411–412: From "W. E. B. Du Bois: Protagonist of the Afro-American Protest" in *Black Leaders of the Twentieth Century* edited by John Hope Franklin and August Meier, by permission of University of Illinois Press, © 1982.

Pages 417–418: From *The Soul of the Night* by Chet Raymo, © 1985, pp. 68–70. With permission of the author.

Pages 444–445: From "The Tornado" by John T. Snow in *Scientific American Inc.,* April 1984, pp. 41–42.

PSAT/NMSQT TEST TIME:
2 HOURS AND 10 MINUTES

Section 1
Critical Reading
    sentence completions
    short-paragraph reading comprehension
    long-passage reading comprehension
	25 minutes	24 questions

1-MINUTE BREAK		
Section 2 Mathematical Reasoning multiple-choice	25 minutes	20 questions
1-MINUTE BREAK		

Section 3
Critical Reading
    sentence completions
    short-paragraph reading comprehension
    long-passage reading comprehension
	25 minutes	24 questions

5-MINUTE BREAK		

Section 4
Mathematical Reasoning
    multiple-choice
    student-produced response (grid-in)
	25 minutes	18 questions

1-MINUTE BREAK		

Section 5
Writing Skills
    identifying sentence errors
    improving sentences
    improving paragraphs
	30 minutes	39 questions

PART ONE

Introduction

▶ **CHAPTER 1** : **The PSAT/National Merit Scholarship Qualifying Test**

▶ **CHAPTER 2** : **How to Approach the PSAT/NMSQT**

► CHAPTER 1
The PSAT/National Merit Scholarship Qualifying Test

Your plan to take the PSAT/NMSQT is perhaps your first concrete step toward planning a college career. The PSAT/NMSQT and the SAT—what do they mean to you? When do you take them? What sort of hurdles do you face? How do these tests differ from the tests you ordinarily face in school? In this chapter we answer these basic questions so that you will be able to move on to the following chapters and concentrate on preparing yourself for this test.

SOME BASIC QUESTIONS ANSWERED

Why is the test called the PSAT/NMSQT?

The "P" in PSAT stands for "preliminary." So first and foremost the PSAT is the Preliminary SAT. As such, its major functions are to familiarize students with the types of questions that are on the SAT and to help students assess their strengths and weaknesses.

The PSAT also serves as the National Merit Scholarship Qualifying Test (NMSQT). Approximately 50,000 students nationally gain recognition in the NMSQT competition by their scores on the PSAT.

What is the PSAT/NMSQT?

The SAT: Reasoning Test is a standardized test designed to measure your ability to do college work. As explained above, the PSAT/NMSQT is the first step in getting ready for the SAT. It is given once a year, in mid-October. Most schools administer the exam on a Saturday; some, however, give it on a weekday.

While many students take the test "for practice" as sophomores, most students take it only once, in their junior year.

The test consists of five sections: two test critical reading skills, two test mathematical reasoning skills, and one tests writing skills. The time allowed for each of the reading and math sections is twenty-five minutes; the time allowed for the writing skills section is thirty minutes.

What are Merit Scholarships?

Merit Scholarships are prestigious national awards that carry with them a chance for solid financial aid. Conducted by NMSC, an independent, nonprofit organization with offices at 1560 Sherman Avenue, Suite 200, Evanston, Illinois 60201-4897, the Merit Program today is supported by grants from over 600 corporations, private foundations, colleges and universities, and other organizations. The top-scoring PSAT/NMSQT participants in every state are named Semifinalists. Those who advance to Finalist standing by meeting additional requirements compete for one-time National Merit $2000 Scholarships and renewable, four-year Merit Scholarships, which may worth as much as $10,000 a year for four years.

What is the National Achievement Scholarship Program for Outstanding Black Students?

This program is aimed at honoring and assisting promising African American high school students throughout the country. It is also administered by NMSC. Students who enter the Merit Program by taking the PSAT/NMSQT and who are also eligible to participate in the Achievement program mark a space on their test answer sheets asking to enter this competition as well. Top-scoring African American students in each of the regions established for the competition compete for nonrenewable National Achievement $2000 Scholarships and for four-year Achievement Scholarships supported by many colleges and corporate organizations.

Note: To be considered for this program, you *must* mark the appropriate space on your answer sheet.

How can the PSAT/NMSQT help me?

If you are a high school junior, it will help you gauge your potential scores on the SAT that you will take in the spring. It will give you some idea of which colleges you should apply to in your senior year. It will give you access to scholarship competitions. It will definitely give you practice in answering multiple-choice questions, where timing is an important factor.

In addition, you may choose to take advantage of the College Board's Student Search Service. This service is free for students who fill out the biographical section of the PSAT/NMSQT. If you fill out this section, you will receive mail from colleges and search programs.

How do I apply for this test?

You apply through your school. Fees, when required, are collected by your school. Fee waivers are available for students whose families cannot afford the test fee; if this applies to you, talk to your counselor.

The test is given in October. In December the results are sent to your school and to the scholarship program that you indicated on your answer sheet in the examination room. Your school will send you your score report.

What makes the PSAT different from other tests?

The PSAT is trying to measure your ability to reason using facts that are part of your general knowledge or facts that are included in your test booklet. You are not required to recall any history or literature or science. You are not even required to recall most math formulas—they are printed right in the test booklet.

Your score depends upon how many correct answers you get within a definite period of time. You can't go too slowly; however, accuracy is even more important than speed. You have to pace yourself so that you don't sacrifice speed to gain accuracy (or sacrifice accuracy to gain speed).

The biggest mistake most students make is to answer too many questions. It is better to answer fewer questions correctly, even if you have to leave some out at the end of a section.

How is the PSAT different from the SAT?

The PSAT is a mini-version of the SAT. For most students, it serves as a practice test. The PSAT takes two hours and ten minutes, whereas the SAT takes more than three and a half hours. You have to answer fewer reading, math, and writing skills questions on the PSAT than you do on the SAT; however, the questions are similar in level of difficulty.

The PSAT, unlike the SAT, has *no* essay-writing section. *You do not have to write an essay*. Your school may recommend that you participate in the College Board's practice essay-writing program, *Score Write*. However, your participation in *Score Write* will *not* affect your PSAT score.

How is the PSAT scored?

The PSAT has three parts: critical reading, math, and writing skills. On each part you will receive a score between 20 and 80, and a combined Selection Index, which is the sum of your three scores. For example, if your score report listed scores of 53 in critical reading, 61 in math, and 48 in writing skills, your Selection Index would be 53 + 61 + 48 = 162. For each individual score, as well as the Selection Index, you will receive a percentile ranking that shows how your scores compare with those of the other students who took the PSAT the same day you did.

Because SAT scores range from 200 to 800, many students multiply their PSAT scores by 10 to make them look like SAT scores. So, if you earned the scores given in the previous paragraph, you might say that your PSAT score was a 1620.

How are the results of your PSAT/NMSQT reported?

About six to eight weeks after the test, you will receive, through your school, the following:

1. an official score report that includes:
   a) the answer you gave for each question
   b) the correct answer for each question
   c) the difficulty level of each question
   d) a Selection Index, which is used to determine eligibility for NMSC programs
2. a copy of the original test booklet that you used in the examination room

Can I do anything if I miss the test but still want to participate in scholarship competitions?

If you fail to take the PSAT/NMSQT because you were ill or involved in an emergency, you still may be able to qualify for a National Merit or National Achievement Scholarship. You need to contact the NMSC to find out about alternative testing arrangements that would enable you to take part in the National Merit competitions.

If you are of Hispanic descent, you need to contact the National Hispanic Scholar Recognition Program run by the College Board. You can arrange to be considered for this program by communicating with The College Board, Suite 600, 1233 20th Street NW, Washington, DC 20036.

The purpose of this section is to familiarize you with the kinds of questions that appear on the PSAT by presenting questions like those on recent PSATs. Knowing what to expect when you take the examination is an important step in preparing for the test and succeeding in it.

The directions that precede the various types of questions are similar to those on the PSAT. For all except the student-produced response questions, you are to choose the best answer and fill in the corresponding blank on the answer sheet.

CRITICAL READING

The Critical Reading sections consist of forty-eight questions to be answered in fifty minutes. A typical test might be made up of thirteen sentence completion questions, eight short-passage critical reading questions, and twenty-seven long-passage critical reading questions.

SENTENCE COMPLETIONS

Select the best answer to the following questions.

Sentence Completion Directions

Each of the following sentences contains one or two blanks; these blanks indicate that a word or set of words has been left out. Below the sentence are five words or phrases, lettered A through E. Select the word or set of words that best completes the sentence.

EXAMPLE:

Fame is ----; today's rising star is all too soon tomorrow's washed-up has-been.

(A) rewarding   (B) gradual   (C) essential
(D) spontaneous   (E) transitory

Ⓐ Ⓑ Ⓒ Ⓓ ●

1. Folk dancing is ---- senior citizens, and it is also economical; they need neither great physical agility nor special accoutrements to enjoy participating in the dance.

   (A) bewildering to   (B) costly for   (C) foreign to
   (D) appropriate for   (E) impracticable for

2. Holding her infant son, the new mother felt an ---- greater than any other joy she had known.

   (A) affluence   (B) incentive   (C) assurance
   (D) incredulity   (E) elation

3. The author contended that his insights were not ---- but had been made independently of others.

   (A) derivative   (B) esoteric   (C) fallacious
   (D) hypothetical   (E) concise

4. Suspicious of the ---- actions of others, the critic Edmund Wilson was in many ways a ---- man, unused to trusting anyone.

   (A) altruistic . . cynical
   (B) questionable . . contrite
   (C) generous . . candid
   (D) hypocritical . . cordial
   (E) benevolent . . dauntless

5. Although Roman original contributions to government, jurisprudence, and engineering are commonly acknowledged, the artistic legacy of the Roman world continues to be judged widely as ---- the magnificent Greek traditions that preceded it.

   (A) an improvement on   (B) an echo of
   (C) a resolution of   (D) a precursor of
   (E) a consummation of

6. ---- though she appeared, her journals reveal that her outward maidenly reserve concealed a passionate nature unsuspected by her family and friends.

   (A) Effusive   (B) Suspicious   (C) Tempestuous
   (D) Domineering   (E) Reticent

7. Crabeater seal, the common name of *Lobodon carcinophagus*, is ----, since the animal's staple diet is not crabs, but krill.

   (A) a pseudonym   (B) a misnomer
   (C) an allusion   (D) a digression
   (E) a compromise

Answer Explanations

Sentence Completion Questions

1. *D* *Because* senior citizens don't need great physical agility to enjoy folk dancing, it is an *appropriate* activity for them.

2. *E* If the missing word is an emotion greater than *any other joy*, then it too must be a form of joy. *Elation* is a feeling of great joy.

3. *A* If the author got his insights independently, then he did not get or derive them from the insights of other people. In other words, his insights were not *derivative*.

4. *A* Someone given to distrusting the motives and actions of others is by definition *cynical*. Such a person would question even the *altruistic*, unselfish deeds of others, suspecting there to be ulterior motives for these charitable acts.

5. *B* The view of Rome's contributions to government, law, and engineering is wholly positive: these original additions to human knowledge are generally acknowledged or recognized. *In contrast*, Rome's original contributions to art are *not* recognized; they are seen as just an *echo* or imitation of the art of ancient Greece.

   Note that *Although* sets up the contrast here.

6. *E* Her outward appearance was one of "maidenly reserve" (self-restraint; avoidance of intimacy). Thus, she seemed to be *reticent* (reserved; disinclined to speak or act freely), even though she actually felt things passionately.

7. *B* Because these seals eat far more krill than crabs, it *misnames* them to call them crabeater seals. The term is thus a *misnomer*, a name that's wrongly applied to someone or something.

   Beware of eye-catchers. Choice A is incorrect. A *pseudonym* isn't a mistaken name; it's a false name that an author adopts.

CRITICAL READING

Your ability to read and understand the kind of material found in college texts and the more serious magazines is tested in the critical reading section of the PSAT/NMSQT. There are two types of passages on the test, short passages and long passages. Short passages are approximately 100 words in length; long passages generally range from 400–850 words. You may be asked to find the central thought of a passage, interpret just what the author means by a specific phrase or idea, determine the meaning of individual words from their use in the text, evaluate the special techniques the author uses to achieve his or her effects, or analyze the author's mood and motivation. You will also be asked to answer two or three questions that compare the viewpoints of two passages on the same subject. You can expect to spend most of your verbal testing time reading the passages and answering the critical reading questions.

Critical Reading Directions

The passage below is followed by questions based on its content. The correct answer may be <u>stated outright</u> or merely <u>suggested</u> in the passage and in any introductory or footnoted material included.

Questions 8 and 9 are based on the following passage.

"Ladybug, ladybug, fly away home. Your house is on fire; your children do roam." Few farmers would seek to chase away ladybugs, or ladybird
Line beetles, with this familiar children's rhyme, for
5 ladybugs are known as the farmer's friend. Clusters of ladybugs are often gathered and sold to farmers, who employ them to control the spread of insect pests. In 1888, for example, when California's orange orchards were threatened by
10 an outbreak of cottony-cushion scale, farmers imported the Australian ladybird beetle to devour the scale. In less than two years, the ladybugs had saved the orchards.

8. The quotation in the opening lines of the passage primarily serves to

   (A) alert the ladybugs to an actual danger
   (B) introduce the passage's subject informally
   (C) demonstrate a common misapprehension
   (D) provide a critical literary allusion
   (E) diminish the importance of ladybird beetles

9. As used in line 12, the word "scale" most likely refers to

   (A) a form of cotton
   (B) a variety of insect
   (C) a type of orange
   (D) a plant nutrient
   (E) a measure of weight

The questions that follow the two passages in this section relate to the content of both and to their relationship. The correct response may be <u>stated outright</u> or merely <u>suggested</u> in the passages and in any introductory or footnoted material included.

Questions 10–16 are based on the following passages.

The following passages are excerpted from books on America's national pastime, baseball.

Passage 1

DiMaggio had size, power, and speed. McCarthy, his longtime manager, liked to say that DiMaggio might have stolen 60 bases a season if
Line he had given him the green light. Stengel, his
5 new manager, was equally impressed, and when DiMaggio was on base he would point to him as an example of the perfect base runner. "Look at him," Stengel would say as DiMaggio ran out a base hit, "he's always watching the ball. He isn't watching
10 second base. He isn't watching third base. He knows they haven't been moved. He isn't watching the ground, because he knows they haven't built a canal or a swimming pool since he was last there. He's watching the ball and the outfielder, which is
15 the one thing that is different on every play."

DiMaggio complemented his natural athletic ability with astonishing physical grace. He played the outfield, he ran the bases, and he batted not just effectively but with rare style. He would glide
20 rather than run, it seemed, always smooth, always ending up where he wanted to be just when he wanted to be there. If he appeared to play effortlessly, his teammates knew otherwise. In his first season as a Yankee, Gene Woodling, who played
25 left field, was struck by the sound of DiMaggio chasing a fly ball. He sounded like a giant truck horse on the loose, Woodling thought, his feet thudding down hard on the grass. The great, clear noises in the open space enabled Woodling to
30 measure the distances between them without looking.

He was the perfect Hemingway hero, for Hemingway in his novels romanticized the man who exhibited grace under pressure, who withheld
35 any emotion lest it soil the purer statement of his deeds. DiMaggio was that kind of hero; his grace and skill were always on display, his emotions always concealed. This stoic grace was not achieved without a terrible price: DiMaggio was a man
40 wound tight. He suffered from insomnia and ulcers. When he sat and watched the game he chainsmoked and drank endless cups of coffee. He was ever conscious of his obligation to play well. Late in his career, when his legs were bothering him
45 and the Yankees had a comfortable lead in a pennant race, columnist Jimmy Cannon asked him why he played so hard—the games, after all, no longer meant so much. "Because there might be somebody out there who's never seen me play
50 before," he answered.

Passage 2

Athletes and actors—let actors stand for the set of performing artists—share much. They share the need to make gestures as fluid and economical as possible, to make out of a welter of choices the
55 single, precisely right one. They share the need for thousands of hours of practice in order to train the body to become the perfect, instinctive instrument to express. Both athlete and actor, out of that abundance of emotion, choice, strategy, knowl-
60 edge of the terrain, mood of spectators, condition of others in the ensemble, secret awareness of injury or weakness, and as nearly an absolute *concentration* as possible so that all externalities are integrated, all distraction absorbed to the self,
65 must be able to change the self so successfully that it changes us.

When either athlete or actor can bring all these skills to bear and focus them, then he or she will achieve that state of complete intensity and
70 complete relaxation—complete coherence or integrity between what the performer wants to do and what the performer has to do. Then, the performer is free; for then, all that has been learned, by thousands of hours of practice and discipline
75 and by repetition of pattern, becomes natural. Then, intellect is upgraded to the level of an instinct. The body follows commands that precede thinking.

When athlete and artist achieve such self-
80 knowledge that they transform the self so that we are re-created, it is finally an exercise in power. The individual's power to dominate, on stage or field, invests the whole arena around the locus of performance with his or her power. We draw from
85 the performer's energy, just as we scrutinize the performer's vulnerabilities, and we criticize as if we were equals (we are not) what is displayed. This is why all performers dislike or resent the audience as much as they need and enjoy it. Power
90 flows in a mysterious circuit from performer to spectator (I assume a "live" performance) and back, and while cheers or applause are the hoped-for outcome of performing, silence or gasps are the most desired, for then the moment has
95 occurred—then domination is complete, and as the performer triumphs, a unity rare and inspiring results.

10. In Passage 1, Stengel is most impressed by DiMaggio's

  (A) indifference to potential dangers
  (B) tendency to overlook the bases in his haste
  (C) ability to focus on the variables
  (D) proficiency at fielding fly balls
  (E) overall swiftness and stamina

11. It can be inferred from the content and tone of Stengel's comment (lines 7–15) that he would regard a base runner who kept his eye on second base with

  (A) trepidation   (B) approbation
  (C) resignation   (D) exasperation
  (E) tolerance

12. The phrase "a man wound tight" (lines 39–40) means a man

  (A) wrapped in confining bandages
  (B) living in constricted quarters
  (C) under intense emotional pressure
  (D) who drank alcohol to excess
  (E) who could throw with great force

13. Which best describes what the author is doing in the parenthetical comment "let actors stand for the set of performing artists" [lines 51–52]?

  (A) indicating that actors should rise out of respect for the arts
  (B) defining the way in which he is using a particular term
  (C) encouraging actors to show tolerance for their fellow artists
  (D) emphasizing that actors are superior to other performing artists
  (E) correcting a misinterpretation of the role of actors

14. To the author of Passage 2, freedom for performers depends on

  (A) their subjection of the audience
  (B) their willingness to depart from tradition
  (C) the internalization of all they have learned
  (D) their ability to interpret material independently
  (E) the absence of injuries or other weaknesses

15. The author's attitude toward the concept of the equality of spectators and performers (lines 83–87) is one of

  (A) relative indifference
  (B) mild skepticism
  (C) explicit rejection
  (D) strong embarrassment
  (E) marked perplexity

16. The author of Passage 2 would most likely react to the characterization of DiMaggio presented in lines 43–50 by pointing out that DiMaggio probably

  (A) felt some resentment of the spectator whose good opinion he supposedly sought
  (B) never achieved the degree of self-knowledge that would have transformed him
  (C) was unaware that his audience was surveying his weak points
  (D) was a purely instinctive natural athlete
  (E) was seldom criticized by his peers

Answer Explanations

Critical Reading Questions

8. *B* Rather than launch immediately into a formal discussion of the beneficial qualities of ladybugs or ladybird beetles, the author chooses to *introduce the subject informally* by quoting a familiar nursery rhyme.

9. *B* Cottony-cushion scale is just one of the insect pests combatted by ladybird beetles. The correct answer is Choice B, *a variety of insect*.

10. *C* Stengel's concluding sentence indicates that DiMaggio watches "the one thing that is different on every play." In other words, DiMaggio *focuses on the variables*, the factors that change from play to play.

11. *D* The sarcastic tone of Stengel's comment suggests that he would be *exasperated* or irritated by a base runner who had his eye on second base when he should have been watching the ball and the outfielder.

12. *C* Look at the sentences following this phrase. They indicate that DiMaggio was a man *under intense emotional pressure*, one who felt so much stress that he developed ulcers and had problems getting to sleep.

13. *B* The author is taking a moment away from his argument to make sure the reader knows exactly who the subjects of his comparison are. He is not simply comparing athletes and actors. He is comparing athletes and *all* performing artists, "the set of performing artists," to use his words. Thus, in his side comment, he is *defining* how he intends to use the word *actors* throughout the discussion.

14. *C* Performers are free when all they have learned becomes so natural, so internalized, that it seems instinctive. In other words, freedom depends on *the internalization* of what they have learned.

15. *C* The author bluntly states that we spectators are not the performers' equals. Thus, his attitude toward the concept is one of *explicit rejection*.

16. *A* Passage 1 indicates DiMaggio always played hard to live up to his reputation and to perform well for anyone in the stands who had never seem him play before. Clearly, he wanted the spectators to have a good opinion of him. Passage 2, however, presents a more complex picture of the relationship between the performer and his audience. On the one hand, the performer needs the audience, needs its good opinion and its applause. On the other hand, the performer also resents the audience, resents the way spectators freely point out his weaknesses and criticize his art. Thus, the author of Passage 2 might well point out that DiMaggio *felt some resentment* of the audience, whom he hoped to impress with his skill.

MATHEMATICS

There are two types of questions on the Mathematics portion of the PSAT:

1. multiple-choice questions   **2.** grid-in questions

Examples of both types will be given in this chapter. In Chapter 8, you will learn several important strategies for handling all math questions. The math questions are in Sections 2 and 4 of the PSAT. You are allotted twenty-five minutes to complete each section.

- Section 2 has twenty multiple-choice questions (Questions 1–20)
- Section 4 has eight multiple-choice questions (Questions 21–28) followed by ten grid-in questions (Questions 29–38).

Within each group, the questions are presented approximately in order of increasing difficulty. In fact, on the score report, which you will receive about seven weeks after taking the PSAT, each question will be rated E (Easy), M (Medium), or H (Hard), depending on how many students answered that question correctly. A typical ranking of the math questions would be as follows:

	Easy	Medium	Hard
Section 2: Multiple-choice	1–6	7–14	15–20
Section 4: Multiple-choice	21–22	23–25	26–28
Section 4: Grid-in	29–31	32–35	36–38

As a result, the amount of time you spend on any one question will vary greatly. We will discuss this in detail in Chapter 2, when you learn the best way to pace yourself and how to make educated guesses.

MULTIPLE-CHOICE QUESTIONS

Twenty-eight of the thirty-eight mathematics questions on the PSAT are multiple-choice questions. Although you have certainly taken multiple-choice tests before, the PSAT uses a few different types of questions in these sections, and you must become familiar with all of them. By far, the most common type of question is one in which you are asked to solve a problem. The straightforward way to answer such a question is to do the necessary work, get the solution, then look at the five choices and choose the one that corresponds to your answer. In Chapter 8 we will discuss other techniques for answering these questions, but for now let's look at a couple of examples.

EXAMPLE 1

What is the average (arithmetic mean) of −2, −1, 0, 1, 2, 3, and 4?

(A) 0   (B) $\frac{3}{7}$ (C) 1   (D) $\frac{7}{6}$ (E) $\frac{7}{2}$

To solve this problem requires only that you know how to find the average of a set of numbers. Ignore the fact that this is a multiple-choice question. *Don't even look at the choices.*

- Calculate the average by adding the 7 numbers and dividing by 7.

- $\dfrac{-2 + -1 + 0 + 1 + 2 + 3 + 4}{7} = \dfrac{7}{7} = 1.$

- Now look at the five choices. Find 1, listed as Choice C, and blacken in C on your answer sheet.

EXAMPLE 2

Emily was born on Wednesday, April 15, 1987. Her sister Erin was born exactly 1200 days later. On what day of the week was Erin born?

(A) Tuesday (B) Thursday (C) Friday (D) Saturday (E) Sunday

Again, you are not helped by the fact that this question is a multiple-choice question. You need to determine the day of the week on which Erin was born and then select the choice that matches your answer.

- The 7 days keep repeating in exactly the same order: 1 day after Emily was born was a Thursday, 2 days after Emily was born was a Friday, and so on. Make a table.

	Thurs.	Fri.	Sat.	Sun.	Mon.	Tues.	Wed.
Days after Emily was born	1 8 and so on.	2 9	3 10	4 11	5 12	6 13	7 14

- Note that whenever the number of days is a multiple of 7 (7, 14, 21, . . . , 70, . . .) a whole number of weeks has gone by, and it is again a Wednesday.
- If 1200 were a multiple of 7, the 1200th day would be a Wednesday.
- Is it? To find out, use your calculator: $1200 \div 7 = 171.4285\ldots$
- 1200 days is <u>not</u> a whole number of weeks; it is a little more than 171 weeks.
- Since $171 \times 7 = 1197$, the 1197th day completes the 171st week and hence is a Wednesday.
- The 1198th day starts the next week. It is a Thursday; the 1199th day is a Friday; and the 1200th day is a Saturday.
- The answer is D.

NOTE: Did you notice that the solution didn't use the fact that Emily was born on April 15, 1987? This is unusual. Occasionally, but not often, a PSAT problem contains extraneous information.

In contrast to Examples 1 and 2, some questions *require* you to look at all five choices in order to find the answers. Consider Example 3.

EXAMPLE 3

For any numbers a and b: let the operation ☺ be defined by $a ☺ b = a^2 + b^2$. Which of the following is *not* equal to $6 ☺ 8$?

(A) $-10 ☺ 0$ (B) $-8 ☺ -6$ (C) $9 ☺ \sqrt{19}$ (D) $(6 ☺ 9) - (4 ☺ 1)$
(E) $2(3 ☺ 4)$

The words *which of the following* alert you to the fact that you are going to have to examine each of the five choices and determine which of them satisfies the stated condition—in this case, that it is *not* equal to $6 ☺ 8$.

Do not be concerned that you have never seen the symbol "☺" used this way before. No one has. On the PSAT there is always at least one question that uses a symbol that the test makers have made up. All you have to do is read the question very carefully and follow the directions exactly. In this case we have: $6 ☺ 8 = 6^2 + 8^2 = 36 + 64 = 100$.

Now check each of the five choices, and find the one that is *not* equal to 100.

(A) $-10 ☺ 0 = (-10)^2 + 0^2 = 100 + 0 = 100$
(B) $-8 ☺ -6 = (-8)^2 + (-6)^2 = 64 + 36 = 100$
(C) $9 ☺ \sqrt{19} = 9^2 + (\sqrt{19})^2 = 81 + 19 = 100$
(D) $(6 ☺ 9) - (4 ☺ 1) = (6^2 + 9^2) - (4^2 + 1^2) = (36 + 81) - (16 + 1) =$
$117 - 17 = 100$
(E) $2(3 ☺ 4) = 2(3^2 + 4^2) = 2(9 + 16) = 2(25) = 50$, which is *not* equal to 100.

So, the correct answer is E.

Another kind of multiple-choice question that appears on the PSAT is the Roman numeral-type question. These questions actually consist of three statements labeled I, II, and III. The five answer choices give various possibilities for which statement or statements are true. Here is a typical example.

EXAMPLE 4

In $\triangle ABC$, $AB = 3$ and $BC = 4$. Which of the following could be the perimeter of $\triangle ABC$?

  I. 8
 II. 12
III. 16

(A) I only   (B) II only   (C) I and II only   (D) II and III only   (E) I, II, and III

- To solve this problem, examine each statement independently.
  - I. Could the perimeter be 8? If it were, then the third side would be 1. But in any triangle, the smallest side must be greater than the difference of the other two sides. So, the third side must be *greater* than $4 - 3 = 1$. It cannot equal 1. I is false.
  - II. Could the perimeter be 12? That is, could the third side be 5? Yes. The three sides could be 3, 4, and 5. In fact, the most common right triangle to appear on the PSAT is a 3-4-5 right triangle. II is true.
  - III. Could the perimeter be 16? If it were, then the third side would be 9. But in any triangle, the largest side must be less than the sum of the other two sides. So, the third side must be less than $4 + 3 = 7$. It cannot equal 9. III is false.
- Only statement II is true. The answer is B.

GRID-IN QUESTIONS

Ten of the forty mathematics questions on the PSAT are what the College Board calls Student-Produced Response Questions. These are the only questions on the PSAT that are not multiple-choice. Since the answers to these questions are entered on a special grid, they are usually referred to as *grid-in* questions. Except for the method of entering your answer, this type of question is probably the one with which you are most familiar. In your math class, most of your homework problems and test questions require you to determine an answer and write it down, and this is what you will do on the grid-in problems. The only difference is that once you have figured out an answer, it must be recorded on a special grid, such as the one shown, so that it can be read by a computer. Here is a typical grid-in question.

EXAMPLE 5

John has a rectangular garden in his backyard. He decides to enlarge it by increasing its length by 20% and its width by 30%. If the area of the new garden is a times the area of the original garden, what is the value of a?

Solution. From the wording of the question, it is clear that the answer does not depend on the actual original dimensions. Therefore, pick an easy value. For example, assume that the original garden is a square whose sides are 10. Since 20% of 10 is 2 and 30% of 10 is 3, then the new garden is a 12 by 13 rectangle. Therefore, the area of the original garden is 100, and the area of the new garden is 156. So $156 = a(100)$, and $a = 1.56$.

To enter this answer, you write 1.56 in the four spaces at the top of the grid and blacken in the appropriate circle under each space. In the first column, under the 1, blacken the oval marked 1; in the second column, under the decimal point, blacken the oval with the decimal point; in the third column, under the 5, blacken the oval marked 5; and finally, in the fourth column, under the 6, blacken in the oval marked 6.

Note that the only symbols that appear in the grid are the digits from 0 to 9, a decimal point, and a fraction bar (/). The grid does not have a minus sign, so *answers to grid-in problems can never be negative*. In Chapter 7, you will read suggestions for the best way to fill in grids. You will also learn the special rules concerning the proper way to grid-in fractions, mixed numbers, and decimals that won't fit in the grid's four columns. When you take the diagnostic test in Chapter 3, just enter your answers exactly as was done in Example 5.

THE USE OF CALCULATORS ON THE PSAT

There isn't a single question on the PSAT for which a calculator is required. In fact, for most questions a calculator is completely useless. There are several questions, however, for which a calculator *could* be used, and since calculators are permitted, you should definitely bring one with you when you take the PSAT. As you go through the hundreds of practice math questions in this book, you should have available the calculator you intend to take to the test, and you should use it whenever you think it is appropriate. You will probably use it more at the beginning of your review because, as you go through this book, you will learn more and more strategies to help you solve problems easily without doing tedious calculations.

If you forget to bring a calculator to the actual test, you will not be able to use one, since none will be provided, and you will not be allowed to share one with a friend. For exactly the same reason, be sure that you have new batteries in your calculator or that you bring a spare, because if your calculator fails during the test, you will have to finish without one.

What Calculator Should You Use?

Almost any four-function, scientific, or graphing calculator is acceptable. Since you don't "need" a calculator at all, you don't "need" any particular type. There is absolutely no advantage to having a graphing calculator, but we do recommend a scientific calculator, since it is occasionally useful to have parentheses keys, ( ); a reciprocal key, $\frac{1}{x}$; and an exponent key, y^x or $^\wedge$. All scientific calculators have these features. If you tend to make mistakes working with fractions, you might want to get a calculator that can do fractional arithmetic. With such a calculator, for example, you can add $\frac{1}{3}$ and $\frac{1}{5}$ by entering 1/3 + 1/5; the readout will be 8/15, not the decimal 0.5333333. Some, but not most, scientific calculators have this capability.

CAUTION: Do not buy a new calculator right before you take the PSAT. The best advice is to use a calculator you are completely familiar with—the one you always use in your math class. If you don't have one or want to get a different one, *buy it now* and become familiar with it. Do all the practice exams in this book with the same calculator you intend to bring to the test.

When Should Calculators Be Used?

If you have strong math skills and are a good test-taker, you will probably use your calculator infrequently, if at all, since, for one thing, strong math students can do a lot of basic arithmetic just as accurately, and faster, in their heads or on paper than with a calculator. A less obvious but more important point is that students who are good test-takers will realize that many problems can be solved without doing any calculations at all (mental, written, or with a calculator); they will solve those problems in less time than it takes to pick a calculator up. On the other hand, if you are less confident about your mathematical ability or your test-taking skills, you will probably find your calculator a useful tool.

NOTE: Throughout this book, this icon ▦ will be placed next to a problem where the use of a calculator is recommended. As you will see, this judgment is very subjective. Sometimes a question can be answered in a few seconds with no calculations whatsoever, *if* you see the best approach. In that case, the use of a calculator would *not* be recommended. If you don't see the easy way, however, and have to do some arithmetic, you may prefer to use a calculator.

Let's look at two sample questions on which some students would use calculators frequently, others less frequently, and still others not at all.

EXAMPLE 1

If $16 \times 25 \times 36 = (4a)^2$, what is the value of a?

(A) 6 (B) 15 (C) 30 (D) 36 (E) 60

(i) Heavy calculator use: WITH A CALCULATOR multiply: $16 \times 25 \times 36 = 14400$. Observe that $(4a)^2 = 16a^2$, and so $16a^2 = 14,400$. WITH A CALCULATOR divide: $a^2 = 14,400 \div 16 = 900$. Finally, WITH A CALCULATOR take the square root: $a = \sqrt{900} = 30$. The answer is C.

(ii) Light calculator use: Immediately notice that you can "cancel" the 16 on the left-hand side with the 4^2 on the right-hand side. WITH A CALCULATOR: multiply $25 \times 36 = 900$, and WITH A CALCULATOR take the square root of 900.

(iii) No calculator use: Cancel the 16 and the 4^2. Notice that $25 = 5^2$ and $36 = 6^2$; so $a^2 = 5^2 \times 6^2 = 30^2$, and $a = 30$.

EXAMPLE 2 (GRID-IN)

If the length of a diagonal of a rectangle is 15, and if one of the sides is 9, what is the perimeter?

Whether or not you intend to use your calculator, the first thing to do is to draw a diagram.

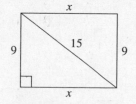

(i) Heavy calculator use: By the Pythagorean theorem, $x^2 + 9^2 = 15^2$. Observe that $9^2 = 81$, and WITH A CALCULATOR evaluate: $15^2 = 225$. Then WITH A CALCULATOR subtract: $225 - 81 = 144$. So, $x^2 = 144$. Hit the square root key on your calculator to get $x = 12$. Finally, WITH A CALCULATOR add to find the perimeter: $9 + 12 + 9 + 12 = 42$.

(ii) Light calculator use: Everything is the same as in (i) except *some* of the calculations can be done mentally: finding the square root of 144 and adding to find the perimeter.

(iii) No calculator use: *All of the calculations* are done mentally, or, better yet, *no calculations are done at all*, because you immediately see that each half of the rectangle is a 9-12-15 right triangle (a 3-4-5 right triangle in which each side was multiplied by 3), and you add up the sides in your head.

Here are three final comments on the use of calculators:

1. The reason that calculators are of limited value on the PSAT is that no calculator can *do* mathematics. *You* have to know the mathematics and the way to apply it. A calculator cannot tell you whether to multiply or divide or that on a particular question you should use the Pythagorean theorem.

2. No PSAT problem ever requires tedious calculations. However, if you don't see how to avoid calculating, just do it—*don't spend a lot of time looking for a shortcut that will save you a little time!*

3. Most students use calculators more than they should, but if you can solve a problem with a calculator that you might otherwise miss, use the calculator.

WRITING SKILLS

The Writing Skills section consists of thirty-nine questions to be answered in thirty minutes. A typical test might be made up of fourteen identifying sentence error questions, twenty improving sentence questions, and five improving paragraph questions.

IDENTIFYING SENTENCE ERROR

The identifying sentence error questions test your ability to spot faults in usage and sentence structure.

Identifying Sentence Error Directions

The sentences in this section may contain errors in grammar, usage, choice of words, or idioms. There is either just one error per sentence, or the sentence is correct. Some words or phrases are underlined and lettered; everything else in the sentence is correct.

If an underlined word or phrase is incorrect, choose that letter; if the sentence is correct, select <u>No error</u>. Then blacken the appropriate space on your Answer Sheet.

EXAMPLE:

The region has a climate <u>so severe that</u> plants
                              A

<u>growing there</u> rarely <u>had been</u> more than twelve
      B   C

inches <u>high</u>. <u>No error</u>
        D   E

SAMPLE ANSWER:

Ⓐ Ⓑ ● Ⓓ Ⓔ

---

1. Despite the fact that <u>some states</u> have resisted,
   <u>A</u>   <u>B</u>

   the Congress <u>have passed</u> legislation <u>permitting</u>
                    C   D

   highway speed limits to 65 miles per hour on

   rural Interstates. <u>No error</u>
                          E

2. Mohandas Gandhi, <u>to who</u> the title "Father of
                        A

   Passive Resistance" <u>may be given</u>, <u>bravely led</u> the
                            B   C

   nationalist movement in India <u>against</u> British
                                     D

   rule. <u>No error</u>
             E

3. Joe DiMaggio, <u>whose</u> style was one of
                    A

   <u>quiet excellence</u>, was consistently the New York
         B

   Yankees' <u>outstanding player</u> <u>during</u> his thirteen
                 C   D

   years on the team. <u>No error</u>
                          E

4. When Ms. Rivera <u>was</u> <u>truly</u> happy, she does not
                       A   B

   <u>constantly</u> complain <u>that</u> she has no purpose in
       C   D

   life. <u>No error</u>
             E

Answer Explanations

1. *C* Error in subject-verb agreement. The antecedent, *Congress*, is singular. Change *have passed* to *has passed*.

2. *A* Error in case. Change *who* to *whom*. It is the object of the preposition *to*.

3. *E* Sentence is correct.

4. *A* Error in sequence of tenses. The sentence should read: *When Ms. Rivera is truly happy, she does not complain.*

IMPROVING SENTENCE QUESTIONS

The improving sentence questions test your ability to select the wording that makes the strongest sentence—the clearest, the smoothest, the most compact.

Improving Sentence Directions

Some or all parts of the following sentences are underlined. The first answer choice, (A), simply repeats the underlined part of the sentence. The other four choices present four alternative ways to phrase the underlined part. Select the answer that produces the most effective sentence, one that is clear and exact, and blacken the appropriate space on your answer sheet. In selecting your choice, be sure that it is standard written English and that it expresses the meaning of the original sentence.

EXAMPLE:

The first biography of author Eudora Welty came out in 1998, and she was eighty-nine years old at the time.

(A) and she was eighty-nine years old at the time
(B) at the time when she was eighty-nine
(C) upon becoming an eighty-nine year old
(D) when she was eighty-nine
(E) at the age of eighty-nine years old

SAMPLE ANSWER:

Ⓐ Ⓑ Ⓒ ● Ⓔ

---

5. More than any animal, the wolverine exemplifies the unbridled ferocity of "nature red in tooth and claw."

   (A) More than any animal
   (B) More than any other animal
   (C) More than another animal
   (D) Unlike any animal
   (E) Compared to other animals

6. The reviewer knew that Barbara Cartland had written several Gothic novels, she didn't remember any of their titles.

   (A) novels, she didn't remember any of their titles
   (B) novels, however she didn't remember any of their titles
   (C) novels, their titles, however, she didn't remember
   (D) novels without remembering any of their titles
   (E) novels, but she remembered none of their titles

7. I think the United States will veto the resolution imposing sanctions against Israel regardless of the desires of the Arab nations for strong action.

   (A) regardless of the desires of the Arab nations
   (B) irregardless of the Arab nations' desires
   (C) regardless of the Arab nations desires
   (D) irregardless of the Arab nation's desires
   (E) mindful of the desires of the Arab nations

Answer Explanations

5. *B* Choice B includes the necessary word *other*, which makes the comparison correct. Choice D changes the meaning of the sentence by its implication that the wolverine is *not* an animal.

6. *E* Choices A, B, and C are run-on sentences. Choice D changes the meaning of the sentence by implying that it was Barbara Cartland who could not remember the titles.

7. *A* *Irregardless* in Choices B and D is incorrect. Also, in Choices C and D, the case of *nations* is incorrect. The correct form of the plural possessive case of *nation* is *nations'*. Choice E changes the meaning of the sentence; in fact, it reverses it.

IMPROVING PARAGRAPH QUESTIONS

The improving paragraph questions test your ability to polish an essay by combining sentences or manipulating sentence parts. You may need to arrange sentences to improve the essay's logical organization or to pick evidence to strengthen the writer's argument.

Improving Paragraph Directions

The passage below is the unedited draft of a student's essay. Some of the essay needs to be rewritten to make the meaning clearer and more precise. Read the essay carefully.

The essay is followed by questions about changes that might improve all or part of its organization, development, sentence structure, use of language, appropriateness to the audience, or use of standard written English. Choose the answer that most clearly and effectively expresses the student's intended meaning. Indicate your choice by filling in the corresponding space on the answer sheet.

---

[1] As people grow older, quite obviously, the earth does too. [2] And with the process of the earth aging, we must learn to recycle. [3] The idea of using things over and over again to conserve our supply of natural resources is a beautiful one. [4] Those who don't see how easy it is to recycle should be criticized greatly.

[5] As we become more aware of the earth's problems, we all say "Oh, I'd like to help." [6] However, so few really do get involved. [7] Recycling is a simple, yet effective place to start. [8] Taking aluminum cans to the supermarket to be recycled is an ingenious idea. [9] It attracts those who want the money (5 cents a can), and it is also a convenient place to go to. [10] In addition, in almost every town, there is a Recycling Center. [11] I know that there are separate bins for paper, bottles, cans, etc. [12] This is a convenient service to those

who recycle. [13] It is so easy to drive a few blocks to a center to drop off what needs to be recycled. [14] This is just another simple example of how easy it really is to recycle and to get involved. [15] Those who don't see its simplicity should be criticized for not doing their part to help make the world a better place.

[16] When I go to other people's houses and see aluminum cans in the garbage, I can honestly say I get enraged. [17] Often I say, "Why don't you just recycle those cans instead of throwing them out?" [18] What makes me even more angry is when they say "We have no time to recycle them." [19] Those people, I feel, should be criticized for not recycling in the past and should be taught a lesson about our earth and how recycling can conserve it.

---

8. Which of the following most effectively expresses the underlined portion of sentence 2 below?

   And *with the process of the earth aging, we must learn to recycle.*

   (A) with the aging process of the earth
   (B) the process of the earth's aging
   (C) as the earth ages
   (D) with the aging earth's process
   (E) as the process of the earth's aging continues

9. Considering the essay as a whole, which of the following best explains the main purpose of the second paragraph?

   (A) to explain the historical background of the topic
   (B) to provide a smooth transition between the first and third paragraphs
   (C) to define terms introduced in the first paragraph
   (D) to give an example of an idea presented in the first paragraph
   (E) to present a different point of view on the issue being discussed

10. Which of the sentences below most effectively combines sentences 10, 11, and 12?

   (A) Recycling centers offer recyclers convenience by providing separate bins for paper, bottles, and cans and by being located in almost every town.
   (B) Recycling centers, located in almost every town, serve recyclers by providing convenient bins to separate paper, bottles, and cans.
   (C) Almost every town has a recycling center with separate bins for paper, bottles, and cans, and this is a convenient service for people who want to recycle.
   (D) People who want to recycle will find recycling centers in almost every town, providing a convenient separation of paper, bottles, and cans into bins.
   (E) For the convenience of recyclers, separate bins for paper, bottles, and cans are provided by almost every town's recycling center.

Answer Explanations

8. *C* This question asks you to find an alternative to a rather awkward group of words, composed of two phrases, *with the process* and *of the earth aging*. The second is graceless and ungrammatical. It should have read *of the earth's aging*, because in standard usage, nouns and pronouns modifying gerunds are usually written as possessives. Knowing what it should have been, however, is not much help in answering the question. You still must select from the five alternatives the one best way to express the essay writer's idea. In the context of the whole sentence, two of the choices, B and D, make no sense at all. A also borders on incomprehensibility. Left with C and E, the better choice is C because it is more concise and it expresses exactly what the writer intended.

9. *D* To answer this question, you need to have read the whole essay. You also need to know the way individual paragraphs function in an essay—any essay. Here, all five choices describe legitimate uses of a paragraph, but they don't all apply to this particular essay. Choices A, C, and E can be quickly discarded. Choice B is a possibility because in a unified essay every paragraph (except the first and last) in some sense serves as a bridge between paragraphs. Because the second paragraph is the longest in the essay, however, its main function is probably more than transitional. In fact, it develops by example an idea originating in the first paragraph—how easy it is to recycle. Therefore, D is the best choice.

10. *B* In a series of short sentences, every idea carries equal weight. By combining short sentences, writers may emphasize the important ideas and subordinate the others. To answer this question, then, you have to decide which idea expressed by the three sentences ought to be emphasized. Since two of the sentences (11 and 12) refer to the convenient arrangement of recycling centers, that's the point to stress. In the context of the whole essay, the other sentence (10), which pertains to the location of recycling centers, contains less vital information. Usually, the main point of a sentence is contained in the main, or independent, clause, and secondary ideas are found in subordinate, or dependent, clauses.

With that principle in mind, read each of the choices. A and C give equal weight to the location and convenience of recycling centers. D stresses the location rather than the convenience. E subordinates properly but changes the meaning. Therefore, B is the correct answer. In B, information about the location of recycling centers is contained in a subordinate clause included parenthetically inside the main clause.

After the scores of the PSAT/NMSQT are received, you, your parents, and your guidance counselor can begin to make plans for college. Here are some Barron's reference books that will be very helpful to you.

BARRON'S SAT, by Sharon Weiner Green and Ira K. Wolf. *This classic of college entrance examinations includes a diagnostic test as well as seven complete simulated exams that enable you to practice under exact* SAT *format and test conditions; all model tests have answer keys and answer explanations. Critical Reading practice includes selected and graded word lists, definitions, and vocabulary tests. Mathematical Reasoning practice reviews necessary math from arithmetic through high school algebra and geometry and features the grid-in questions included on the* SAT. *Writing Skills review includes common grammar and usage errors. Testing tactics and strategies are featured.* 2006, 23rd Edition.

NEW SAT—MATH WORKBOOK, by Lawrence Leff. *This all-new workbook is geared to today's test-takers' needs. Practice exercises contain hundreds of multiple-choice questions, quantitative comparisons, and grid-in questions with answers. Lesson topics include calculators, the new Student-Produced Response Question type, and a wide array of math subjects related to the* SAT. 2005, 3rd Edition.

NEW SAT—CRITICAL READING WORKBOOK, by Mitchel Weiner and Sharon Weiner Green. *A companion to the Math Workbook—this workbook provides hundreds of practice exercises and diagnostic tests for intensive review of vocabulary, sentence completion, and reading comprehension. Suggested study plan and 1,000 questions plus 10 complete model verbal aptitude tests prepare students to score high on college boards, admission, placement, and scholarship examinations where word usage and understanding are tested.* 2005, 11th Edition.

BARRON'S PROFILES OF AMERICAN COLLEGES. *Searching studies of more than 1,600 regionally accredited four-year American colleges and universities give the prospective student a preview of his or her relationship to a particular college—based on its facilities, outstanding features and programs, admission requirements, costs, available financial aid, extracurricular activities, programs and major offerings, degrees awarded, enrollment, religious affiliation, housing facilities, social and honorary societies, and religious or other regulations for student life. The comprehensive and detailed information on each college will be of tremendous help to guidance counselors, college-bound students, and their families.* 2004, 26th Edition.

BASIC WORD LIST, by Samuel C. Brownstein, Mitchel Weiner, and Sharon Weiner Green. *This effective vocabulary builder presents more than 2,000 words that all students should know to prepare for the* SAT, ACT, *and other standardized college entrance and college level exams. Each new word is defined and placed in a model sentence. Practice vocabulary exercises and a review of word prefixes and roots are included.* 1997, 3rd Edition.

ESSAYS THAT WILL GET YOU INTO COLLEGE, by Daniel Kaufman, Chris Dowhan, and Amy Burnham. *Over fifty model essays that have worked for applicants, with advice, discussion, and commentary, reveal the secrets of successful essay writing.* 2003, 2nd Edition.

HOT WORDS FOR THE SAT I, by Linda Carnevale. *This book includes hundreds of words focused on preparing students for the* SAT, *with definitions, samples, and explanations, as well as with quizzes.* 2004, 2nd Edition.

► CHAPTER 2
How to Approach the PSAT/NMSQT

TEST-TAKING TACTICS

What tactics can help me when I take the PSAT?

1. Memorize the directions given in this book for each type of question. These are only slightly different from the exact words you'll find on the PSAT you'll take. During the test, do not waste even a few seconds reading any directions or sample questions.

2. Know the test. The number and kinds of questions should break down roughly as follows:

   48 Critical Reading Questions (2 sections, 25 minutes each)
   13 sentence completion questions
   8 short-paragraph critical reading questions
   27 long-paragraph critical reading questions

   38 Math Questions (2 sections, 25 minutes each)
   28 standard multiple-choice questions
   10 student-produced response (grid-in) questions

   39 Writing Skills Questions (1 section, 30 minutes)
   20 improving sentence questions
   14 identifying sentence errors questions
   5 improving paragraph questions

3. Expect easy questions at the beginning of many sets of the same question type. Within these sets (except for the reading comprehension and writing skills questions), the questions progress from easy to difficult. In other words, the first sentence completion question in a set will be easier than the last sentence completion in that set. Similarly, the first grid-in question will be much easier than the last grid-in question.

4. Take advantage of the easy questions to boost your score. Remember, each question is worth the same number of points. Whether it is easy or difficult, whether it takes you ten seconds or two minutes to answer, you get the same number of points for each question you answer correctly. Your job is to answer as many questions as you possibly can without rushing ahead so fast that you make careless errors or lose points for failing to give some questions enough thought. So take enough time to get those easy questions right!

5. *First* answer all the easy questions; *then* tackle the hard ones if you have time. You know that the questions in each segment of the test get harder as you go along (except for the reading comprehension and writing skills questions). But there's no rule that says you have to answer the questions in order. You're allowed to skip. So, if the last three sentence completion questions are driving you crazy, move on to the short reading passages right away. Test-wise students know when it's time to move on.

6. Eliminate as many wrong answers as you can. Deciding between two choices is easier than deciding among five. Whenever you guess, every answer choice you eliminate improves your chances of guessing correctly.

7. Change answers only if you have a reason for doing so. Don't give in to last-minute panic. It's usually better for you not to change your answers on a sudden hunch or whim.

8. Because calculators are permitted in the test room, bring along a calculator that you are comfortable using. No question on the test will *require* the use of a calculator, but it may be helpful for some questions. Almost any standard calculator will do: four-function, scientific, and graphing calculators all are allowed.

9. Remember that you are allowed to write anything you want in your test booklet. Circle questions you skip, and put big question marks next to questions you answer but are unsure about. In sentence completion questions, circle or underline key words such as *although*, *therefore*, *not*, and so on. In reading passages, circle key words and underline or put a mark in the margin next to any major point. On math questions, mark up diagrams, adding lines when necessary. And, of course, use all the space provided to solve the problem. In short, write anything that will help you, using whatever symbols you like. But remember, the only thing that counts is what you enter on your answer sheet. No one will ever see anything that you write in your test booklet.

10. Be careful not to make any stray marks on your answer sheet. This test is graded by a machine, and a machine cannot tell the difference between an accidental mark and a filled-in answer. When the machine sees two marks instead of one, the answer is marked wrong.

11. Check frequently to make sure you are answering the questions in the right spots. No machine is going to notice that you made a mistake early in the test, that you answered question 4 in the space for question 5, and that all your following answers are in the wrong place. One way to avoid this problem is to mark your answers in your test booklet and transfer them to your answer sheet by blocks.

12. Line up your test book with your answer sheet. Whether you choose to fill in the answers question by question or in blocks, you will do so most efficiently if you keep your test book and your answer sheet aligned.

13. Be particularly careful in marking the student-produced responses on the math grid. Before you fill in the appropriate blanks in the grid, write your answer at the top of the columns. Then go down each column and make sure you fill in the right spaces.

14. Don't get bogged down on any one question. By the time you get to the actual PSAT, you should have a fair idea of how much time to spend on each question. If a question is taking too long, leave it and go on to the next question. This is no time to try to show the world that you can stick to a job no matter how long it takes. All the machine that grades the test will notice is that after a certain point you didn't have any correct answers.

REDUCING ANXIETY

How can I prevent PSAT anxiety from setting in?

1. The best way to prepare for any test you ever take is to get a good night's sleep before the test so that you are well rested and alert.

2. Eat breakfast for once in your life. You have a full morning ahead of you; you should have a full stomach as well.

3. Allow plenty of time for getting to the test site. Taking a test is pressure enough. You don't need the extra tension that comes from worrying about whether you will get there on time.

4. Be aware of the amount of time the test is going to take. There are five sections. They will take two hours and ten minutes total. Add to that a five-minute break after the third section, one-minute breaks between the others, plus thirty minutes

for paper pushing. If the test starts at 8:00 A.M., don't make a dentist appointment for 11:00. You can't possibly get there on time, and you'll just spend the last half hour of the test worrying about it.

5. The College Board tells you to bring two sharpened No. 2 pencils to the test. Bring four. They don't weigh much, and this might be the one day in the decade when two pencil points decide to break. Bring full-size pencils, not little stubs. They are easier to write with, and you might as well be comfortable.

6. Speaking of being comfortable, wear comfortable clothes. This is a test, not a fashion show. Aim for the layered look. Wear something light, but bring a sweater. The test room may be hot, or it may be cold. You can't change the room, but you can put on the sweater.

7. Bring an accurate watch. You need one. The room in which you take the test may not have a clock, and some proctors are not very good about posting the time on the blackboard. Don't depend on them. Each time you begin a test section, write down in your booklet the time according to your watch. That way you will always know how much time you have left.

8. Smuggle in some quick energy in your pocket—trail mix, raisins, a candy bar. Even if the proctors don't let you eat in the test room, you can still grab a bite en route to the restrooms during the five-minute break. Taking the test can leave you feeling drained and in need of a quick pickup—bring along your favorite comfort food.

9. There will be a break after the third section. Use this period to clear your thoughts. Take a few deep breaths. Stretch. Close your eyes and imagine yourself floating or sunbathing. In addition to being under mental pressure, you're under physical pressure from sitting so long in an uncomfortable seat with a No. 2 pencil clutched in your hand. Anything you can do to loosen up and get the kinks out will ease your body and help the oxygen get to your brain.

10. Most important of all, remember: very little, if anything, is riding on the result of this test. If you do poorly, no one will know; your PSAT scores are not reported to the colleges to which you plan to apply. So relax!

GUESSING

If you don't know the answer to a question on the PSAT, should you guess?

There is a lot of controversy surrounding the issue of guessing, and if you ask several people for advice, you will surely get conflicting answers. However, the answer to the above question is very simple: In general, *it pays to guess*. To understand why this is so and why so many people are confused about it, you must understand how the PSAT is scored.

On each portion of the PSAT, every question is worth exactly the same amount: one point. A correct answer to a reading comprehension question for which you might have to reread a whole paragraph is worth no more than a correct answer to a sentence completion that you can answer in a few seconds. You get no more credit for a correct answer to the hardest math question than you do for the easiest. For each question that you answer correctly, you receive one raw score point. Your total raw scores on the Mathematics, Critical Reading, and Writing Skills sections are then converted to scaled scores between 20 and 80.

Consider the following scenario. Suppose that working very slowly and carefully you answer only twenty-three of the forty-eight questions on the Critical Reading part of the PSAT but get each of them correct. Your raw score would be 23, and that would be converted to a scaled score of about 51—an above-average score, even though you left out more than half of the questions. If that were the whole story, then you should take the last minute of the test and quickly fill in an answer to each of the other twenty-five questions. Since each question has five choices, you should get about one-fifth of them right. Surely, you would get *some* of them right—most likely between four and six. Say you get five of them right. Then your raw score would go from 23 to 28, and your scaled score would now be about 56. Your Critical Reading score would increase 5 points (50 SAT points) thanks to one minute of wild guessing! Clearly, this is not what the College Board wants to happen. To counter this, an adjustment is made (the so-called *guessing penalty*) to your scores for wrong answers that makes it unlikely that you will profit from wild guessing.

The penalty for each incorrect answer on the Critical Reading sections is a reduction of $\frac{1}{4}$ of a point. What effect would this penalty have in the example just discussed? Recall that by wildly guessing at twenty-five questions, you got five right and twenty wrong. Those five extra right answers caused your raw score to go up by five points. But now you lose $\frac{1}{4}$ of a point for each of the twenty problems you missed—a total reduction of $\frac{20}{4} = 5$ points. So you broke even: you gained five points and lost five points. Your raw score and hence your scaled score didn't change at all.

Notice that the guessing *penalty* didn't actually penalize you. It prevented you from making a big gain that you didn't deserve, but it didn't punish you by lowering your score. It's not a very harsh penalty after all.

Educated guessing, on the other hand, can have an enormous effect on your score; it **can increase** it dramatically! Let's look at what we mean by educated guessing and see how it can improve your score on the PSAT.

Consider the following sentence completion question.

In Victorian times, countless Egyptian mummies were ground up to produce dried mummy powder, hailed by quacks as a near-magical ----, able to cure a wide variety of ailments.

(A) toxin   (B) diagnosis   (C) symptom   (D) panacea   (E) placebo

Clearly, what is needed is a word such as *medicine*—something capable of curing ailments. Let's assume that you know that *toxin* means poison; so you immediately eliminate A. You also know that although *diagnosis* and *symptom* are medical terms, neither means a medicine or a cure; so you eliminate B and C. You now know that the correct answer must be D or E, but unfortunately you have no idea what *panacea* or *placebo* means. You *could* guess, but you don't want to be wrong; after all, there's that penalty for incorrect answers. So, should you leave it out? Absolutely not. *You must guess!* We'll explain why and how in a moment, but first let's look at one more example, this time a math one.

From 2000 to 2005 the number of students participating in a school's community service program increased by 25%. If the number of participants in 2005 was *P*, how many students participated in 2000?

(A) 0.75*P*   (B) 0.80*P*   (C) 1.20*P*   (D) 1.25*P*   (E) 1.50*P*

Even if you are not very good at percent problems (especially when they involve letters!), you should realize that since participation in the program increased, the number of students who participated in 2000 must be *less than P*. So you know the answer must be A or B. What do you do? Do you guess and risk incurring the guessing penalty, or do you leave it out because you have no idea which answer is correct? *You must guess!*

Suppose that you are still working slowly and carefully on the Critical Reading sections, and that of the forty-eight questions, you are sure of the answers to twenty-three of them; in fifteen of them you are able to eliminate three of the choices, but you have no idea which of the remaining two choices is correct; and the remaining ten questions you don't even look at. You already know what would happen if you guessed wildly on the last ten questions—you would probably break even. But what about the fifteen questions you narrowed down to two choices? If you guess on those, you should get about half right and half wrong. Is that good or bad? *It's very good!* Assume you got seven right and eight wrong. For the seven correct answers you would receive 7 points, and for the eight incorrect answers, you would lose $\frac{8}{4} = 2$ points. This is a net gain of 5 raw score points, for which your critical reading score would go from 51 to 56 (that's 50 SAT points!). It would be a shame to throw away those points just because you were afraid of the guessing penalty.

Occasionally, you can even eliminate four of the five choices! Suppose that in the sentence completion above, you realize that you do know what *placebo* means and that it can't be the answer. You still have no idea about *panacea*, and so you may be hesitant to answer a question with a word you never heard of, but you *must*. If in the math question above, only one of the choices were smaller than *P*, it would have to be correct. Don't leave it out because you can't verify the answer directly. You must choose the only answer you haven't eliminated.

What if you can't eliminate three or four of the choices? You should guess if you can eliminate even one choice. Remember, guessing wildly—when you can't eliminate anything—you break even. If you can eliminate anything at all, you come out ahead by guessing.

PART TWO

Diagnose Your Problem

▶ **CHAPTER 3 : A Diagnostic Test**

► CHAPTER 3
A Diagnostic Test

This chapter offers a simulated PSAT/NMSQT test. The purpose is to provide you with a fairly accurate evaluation of what your score would be without any special preparation. Take this test, following directions for time allowances for each of the sections. Then score your answers and evaluate the results using the self-rating guides provided. Consult the explanations of answers for all test items that you failed to answer correctly.

You will then be in a position to approach your review program realistically and allot your time for study. You will know which type of questions you have to practice, which topics in mathematics require your review, which of your verbal skills require concentrated study, and which writing skills need improvement.

SIMULATE TEST CONDITIONS TOTAL TIME: 2 HOURS, 10 MINUTES*

Find a quiet place to work, in order to simulate examination conditions. Keep an accurate record of your time. If you complete one section before the suggested time has elapsed, check your work over rather than start the next section. Don't be worried, however, if you are not able to answer all questions in the allotted time. This may also occur on the actual test. No one is expected to know the answers to all questions on any of these tests. Read the questions carefully. Work carefully and rapidly. Do not spend too much time on questions that seem difficult for you. If time permits, go back to the ones you left out.

Except for the ten student-produced response questions in the second math section, the questions are all multiple-choice with a penalty imposed for wrong answers. Your score on each part is determined by the number of correct answers minus one-fourth of the number of incorrectly marked answers. Omitted answers do not count. Work rapidly and carefully. Do not waste time on questions that contain difficult or unfamiliar material. Do not guess wildly, but make educated guesses whenever you can. You may sometimes eliminate certain possible answers to a question because of your general knowledge, and despite your inability to explain by good reasoning why you choose a specific answer, you may feel that it is the correct one. Such a shrewd guess may be right, and you should therefore give that answer.

*Not counting the short breaks between the sections (see page viii).

Answer Sheet
A DIAGNOSTIC TEST

Each mark should completely fill the appropriate space, and should be as dark as all other marks. Make all erasures complete. Traces of an erasure may be read as an answer.

Section 1 — Critical Reading
25 minutes

1 Ⓐ Ⓑ Ⓒ Ⓓ Ⓔ
2 Ⓐ Ⓑ Ⓒ Ⓓ Ⓔ
3 Ⓐ Ⓑ Ⓒ Ⓓ Ⓔ
4 Ⓐ Ⓑ Ⓒ Ⓓ Ⓔ
5 Ⓐ Ⓑ Ⓒ Ⓓ Ⓔ
6 Ⓐ Ⓑ Ⓒ Ⓓ Ⓔ
7 Ⓐ Ⓑ Ⓒ Ⓓ Ⓔ
8 Ⓐ Ⓑ Ⓒ Ⓓ Ⓔ
9 Ⓐ Ⓑ Ⓒ Ⓓ Ⓔ
10 Ⓐ Ⓑ Ⓒ Ⓓ Ⓔ
11 Ⓐ Ⓑ Ⓒ Ⓓ Ⓔ
12 Ⓐ Ⓑ Ⓒ Ⓓ Ⓔ
13 Ⓐ Ⓑ Ⓒ Ⓓ Ⓔ
14 Ⓐ Ⓑ Ⓒ Ⓓ Ⓔ
15 Ⓐ Ⓑ Ⓒ Ⓓ Ⓔ
16 Ⓐ Ⓑ Ⓒ Ⓓ Ⓔ
17 Ⓐ Ⓑ Ⓒ Ⓓ Ⓔ
18 Ⓐ Ⓑ Ⓒ Ⓓ Ⓔ
19 Ⓐ Ⓑ Ⓒ Ⓓ Ⓔ
20 Ⓐ Ⓑ Ⓒ Ⓓ Ⓔ
21 Ⓐ Ⓑ Ⓒ Ⓓ Ⓔ
22 Ⓐ Ⓑ Ⓒ Ⓓ Ⓔ
23 Ⓐ Ⓑ Ⓒ Ⓓ Ⓔ
24 Ⓐ Ⓑ Ⓒ Ⓓ Ⓔ

Section 2 — Math
25 minutes

1 Ⓐ Ⓑ Ⓒ Ⓓ Ⓔ
2 Ⓐ Ⓑ Ⓒ Ⓓ Ⓔ
3 Ⓐ Ⓑ Ⓒ Ⓓ Ⓔ
4 Ⓐ Ⓑ Ⓒ Ⓓ Ⓔ
5 Ⓐ Ⓑ Ⓒ Ⓓ Ⓔ
6 Ⓐ Ⓑ Ⓒ Ⓓ Ⓔ
7 Ⓐ Ⓑ Ⓒ Ⓓ Ⓔ
8 Ⓐ Ⓑ Ⓒ Ⓓ Ⓔ
9 Ⓐ Ⓑ Ⓒ Ⓓ Ⓔ
10 Ⓐ Ⓑ Ⓒ Ⓓ Ⓔ
11 Ⓐ Ⓑ Ⓒ Ⓓ Ⓔ
12 Ⓐ Ⓑ Ⓒ Ⓓ Ⓔ
13 Ⓐ Ⓑ Ⓒ Ⓓ Ⓔ
14 Ⓐ Ⓑ Ⓒ Ⓓ Ⓔ
15 Ⓐ Ⓑ Ⓒ Ⓓ Ⓔ
16 Ⓐ Ⓑ Ⓒ Ⓓ Ⓔ
17 Ⓐ Ⓑ Ⓒ Ⓓ Ⓔ
18 Ⓐ Ⓑ Ⓒ Ⓓ Ⓔ
19 Ⓐ Ⓑ Ⓒ Ⓓ Ⓔ
20 Ⓐ Ⓑ Ⓒ Ⓓ Ⓔ

Section 3 — Critical Reading
25 minutes

25 Ⓐ Ⓑ Ⓒ Ⓓ Ⓔ
26 Ⓐ Ⓑ Ⓒ Ⓓ Ⓔ
27 Ⓐ Ⓑ Ⓒ Ⓓ Ⓔ
28 Ⓐ Ⓑ Ⓒ Ⓓ Ⓔ
29 Ⓐ Ⓑ Ⓒ Ⓓ Ⓔ
30 Ⓐ Ⓑ Ⓒ Ⓓ Ⓔ
31 Ⓐ Ⓑ Ⓒ Ⓓ Ⓔ
32 Ⓐ Ⓑ Ⓒ Ⓓ Ⓔ
33 Ⓐ Ⓑ Ⓒ Ⓓ Ⓔ
34 Ⓐ Ⓑ Ⓒ Ⓓ Ⓔ
35 Ⓐ Ⓑ Ⓒ Ⓓ Ⓔ
36 Ⓐ Ⓑ Ⓒ Ⓓ Ⓔ
37 Ⓐ Ⓑ Ⓒ Ⓓ Ⓔ
38 Ⓐ Ⓑ Ⓒ Ⓓ Ⓔ
39 Ⓐ Ⓑ Ⓒ Ⓓ Ⓔ
40 Ⓐ Ⓑ Ⓒ Ⓓ Ⓔ
41 Ⓐ Ⓑ Ⓒ Ⓓ Ⓔ
42 Ⓐ Ⓑ Ⓒ Ⓓ Ⓔ
43 Ⓐ Ⓑ Ⓒ Ⓓ Ⓔ
44 Ⓐ Ⓑ Ⓒ Ⓓ Ⓔ
45 Ⓐ Ⓑ Ⓒ Ⓓ Ⓔ
46 Ⓐ Ⓑ Ⓒ Ⓓ Ⓔ
47 Ⓐ Ⓑ Ⓒ Ⓓ Ⓔ
48 Ⓐ Ⓑ Ⓒ Ⓓ Ⓔ

For each question in this section, select the best answer from among the choices given and fill in the corresponding circle on the answer sheet.

> **Directions**
>
> Each sentence below has one or two blanks, each blank indicating that something has been omitted. Beneath the sentence are five words or sets of words labeled A through E. Choose the word or set of words that, when inserted in the sentence, best fits the meaning of the sentence as a whole.
>
> **EXAMPLE:**
>
> Medieval kingdoms did not become constitutional republics overnight; on the contrary, the change was ----.
>
> (A) unpopular   (B) unexpected
> (C) advantageous   (D) sufficient   (E) gradual
>
> Ⓐ Ⓑ Ⓒ Ⓓ ●

1. For Miro, art became a ---- ritual: paper and pencils were holy objects to him, and he worked as though he were performing a religious rite.

   (A) superficial   (B) sacred   (C) banal
   (D) cryptic   (E) futile

2. Many Wright scholars, striving for accurate reconstructions of the architect's life, have been ---- by the palpable ---- and smoke screens of Wright's autobiography.

   (A) delighted..truths   (B) amazed..facts
   (C) vexed..errors   (D) confused..precision
   (E) entertained..omissions

3. A certain ---- in Singer's prose always keeps one at arm's length from his protagonist's emotions.

   (A) detachment   (B) lyricism   (C) fluency
   (D) brevity   (E) rhythm

4. The books' topics are no less varied than their bindings, for their prolific author has ---- specialization as energetically as some of his colleagues have ---- it.

   (A) resisted..pursued
   (B) admired..supported
   (C) endorsed..accepted
   (D) defended..attacked
   (E) repudiated..deliberated

5. The mayfly is an ---- creature: its adult life lasts little more than a day.

   (A) elegant   (B) ephemeral   (C) idiosyncratic
   (D) impulsive   (E) omnivorous

> **Directions**
>
> Each of the passages below precedes two questions based on its content. Answer the questions following each passage on the basis of what is stated or implied in that passage.

Questions 6 and 7 are based on the following passage.

It was not until modern scholarship uncovered the secret of reading Middle English that we could understand that Chaucer, far from being a
Line rude versifier, was a perfectly accomplished tech-
5 nician, and that his verse is rich in music and elegant to the highest degree. Chaucer's own urbane personality is a delight to encounter in his books. He is avowedly a bookworm, yet few poets observe nature with more freshness and delight. He is a
master of genial satire, but can sympathize with
10 true piety and goodness with as much pleasure as he attacks the hypocritical.

6. The paragraph suggests that Chaucer was underrated for a time because
   (A) people looked down upon him as a mere technician
   (B) he was secretive about the language in which he composed his verse
   (C) people lacked the knowledge to appreciate his poetic technique
   (D) readers were not drawn to the works of a bookworm
   (E) his satire proved too gentle to suit the taste of the average reader

GO ON TO NEXT PAGE ▶

7. The word "rude" (line 4) most nearly means
   (A) impertinent   (B) brusque
   (C) tactless   (D) inconsiderate
   (E) unpolished

Questions 8 and 9 are based on the following passage.

Knighthoods are not what they used to be.
Members of the press have had a field day with the
recent knighting of Mick Jagger, rock and roll's
Line perennial bad boy. Though Sir Mick, as he is now
5 to be called, is not the first rock and roller to be
dubbed a knight—Sir Elton John was knighted in
1997, Sir Paul McCartney in 1996—he is the most
notorious. One reporter even quipped that Jagger's
trip to Buckingham Palace was not his first experi-
10 ence with royal hospitality: in 1967 he had spent a
night in Her Majesty's Prison, Brixton, convicted
of drug possession.

8. The reaction of the press to the news of Jagger's
knighting (line 2) can best be characterized as one
of
   (A) indifference
   (B) disappointment   (C) outrage
   (D) envy   (E) glee

9. The phrase "royal hospitality" (line 10) is being
used
   (A) literally
   (B) ironically
   (C) colloquially
   (D) descriptively
   (E) objectively

Directions

Each passage below is followed by questions based on
its content. Answer the questions following each passage on the basis of what is stated or implied in that
passage and in any introductory material that may be
provided.

Questions 10–15 are based on the following passage.

*The world's tropical rain forests contain varieties of
plant and animal life found nowhere else on earth. The
following passage presents background information on
the epiphytes and their relatives the strangler trees,
fascinating specimens of rain forest plant life.*

The great trees furnish support for much of
the other plant life of the forest. Climbers are
abundant, much more so than elsewhere. Greedy
Line for light, they have various adaptations for hoist-
5 ing themselves to the upper canopy—some are
twiners, others are equipped with tendrils, hooks
or suckers. An entire group of plants is unfitted to

start low and climb high to reach the light. These
are epiphytes, plants that grow on trees without
10 parasitizing them or deriving any advantage except a platform near the sun. They are extraordinarily common. However, in order to grow close
to the sunlight, they have had to pay a price—they
have lost their root connection with the forest
15 floor and its abundant moisture. For soil, they
must often make do with the small amounts of
debris that lodge in crannies in the trees, with
dust from the atmosphere and organic matter and
seeds deposited by ants that often nest in the roots
20 of epiphytes—a small but vital source of humus
and minerals. So well have these plants managed
to create their own environment that the spoonfuls of soil in which they grow do not differ significantly from normal soil in microbiological
25 processes.
Some of the epiphytes have developed remarkable adaptations for conserving water. Many
are encased in a waxy layer that retards evapora-
tion. The roots of some orchids have a spongy
30 tissue that not only soaks up water but also carries

GO ON TO NEXT PAGE ▶

on photosynthesis. The staghorn fern accumulates water-holding humus in a sort of bucket structure at the base of its leaves. The large group of tropical plants known as bromeliads are living cisterns—
35 their long branching leaves spring from the same place around the stem, and overlap so tightly at their bases that they can hold water, as much as four-and-a-half quarts in a large plant. These bromeliad tanks become a center of life, holding
40 breeding frogs, snails and aquatic insects, all of which add to the supply of nutrients in the water. Hairs at the base of the leaves line the tank and perform the job of absorbing water and nutrients, making the bromeliad independent of a root con-
45 nection with the soil.

The problems of living in the dark rain forest, and the unusual efforts made to rise into the sun, are best symbolized by the strangler trees. They achieve their place in the sun by stealth. The
50 strangler begins life as an epiphyte, its seed germinating high up in the fork of a large tree. The seedling puts out two kinds of roots: one seizes the branch and serves as a grapple to hold the plant in place, and the other dangles like a cable, growing

55 steadily closer to the soil. Until it makes contact with the ground, the strangler grows like any other epiphyte, obtaining small quantities of water and nutrients from the debris in the tree crevice. But once the descending root reaches the soil its
60 source of supply is increased enormously and the plant's growth quickens. It sprouts more leaves high in the canopy and grows upward toward a sunlit window between the leaves; a maze of additional feeding cables descends to the soil and even-
65 tually the supporting tree is encased in a network of them. It was once thought that the strangler kills the forest giant by the simple process of enwrapping it and preventing its trunk from expanding, but it is now known that it actually squeezes
70 its host to death. As the hold tightens, the strangler's roots thicken to a marked degree, preparing for the time when it will need props to stand by itself in the sunlight it has captured. The host finally expires, thoroughly encased inside the
75 "trunk" (actually the fused roots) of the strangler tree which now stands on its own pedestal as a member of the high forest canopy.

---

10. According to the passage, epiphytes are particularly adapted to

(A) the floor of the tropical rain forest
(B) a sunless environment
(C) the dissipation of rainwater
(D) drawing sustenance from a host
(E) the retention of liquid

11. It can be inferred from the passage that one of the following is true of epiphytes.

(A) They lack root systems.
(B) They do not require large amounts of soil for growth.
(C) They are incapable of photosynthesis.
(D) They are hard to perceive in the dense rain forest canopy.
(E) They need different nutrients than other plants do.

12. The passage can best be described as

(A) enthusiastic exhortation
(B) sophisticated analysis
(C) straightforward description
(D) indirect exposition
(E) forceful argument

13. The author states all of the following about the strangler tree EXCEPT

(A) It eventually becomes self-supporting.
(B) Its feeding cables ascend toward the forest canopy.
(C) Its roots extend far from its point of germination.
(D) It undergoes a rapid growth spurt.
(E) Its roots become conspicuously larger.

14. The word "marked" in line 71 means

(A) noticeable
(B) branded
(C) graded
(D) doomed
(E) unique

15. Which of the following does the passage suggest about the strangler tree?

(A) It needs only a small supply of nutrients for full growth.
(B) All its roots seek the forest floor.
(C) It outgrows its need for its host.
(D) It is killed by the forest giant that supports it.
(E) It eventually sheds its feeder cables.

GO ON TO NEXT PAGE ▶

Questions 16–24 are based on the following passage.

The passage below is excerpted from the introduction to Bury My Heart at Wounded Knee, *written in 1970 by the Native American historian Dee Brown.*

Since the exploratory journey of Lewis and Clark to the Pacific Coast early in the nineteenth century, the number of published accounts de-
Line scribing the "opening" of the American West has
5 risen into the thousands. The greatest concentration of recorded experience and observation came out of the thirty-year span between 1860 and 1890—the period covered by this book. It was an incredible era of violence, greed, audacity, senti-
10 mentality, undirected exuberance, and an almost reverential attitude toward the ideal of personal freedom for those who already had it.

During that time the culture and civilization of the American Indian was destroyed, and out of
15 that time came virtually all the great myths of the American West—tales of fur traders, mountain men, steamboat pilots, goldseekers, gamblers, gunmen, cavalrymen, cowboys, harlots, missionaries, schoolmarms, and homesteaders. Only occa-
20 sionally was the voice of the Indian heard, and then more often than not it was recorded by the pen of a white man. The Indian was the dark menace of the myths, and even if he had known how to write in English, where would he have found a
25 printer or a publisher?

Yet they are not all lost, those Indian voices of the past. A few authentic accounts of American western history were recorded by Indians either in pictographs or in translated English, and some
30 managed to get published in obscure journals, pamphlets, or books of small circulation. In the late nineteenth century, when the white man's curiosity about Indian survivors of the wars reached a high point, enterprising newspaper re-
35 porters frequently interviewed warriors and chiefs and gave them an opportunity to express their opinions on what was happening in the West. The quality of these interviews varied greatly, depending upon the abilities of the interpreters, or upon
40 the inclination of the Indians to speak freely. Some feared reprisals for telling the truth, while others delighted in hoaxing reporters with tall tales and shaggy-dog stories. Contemporary newspaper statements by Indians must therefore be
45 read with skepticism, although some of them are masterpieces of irony and others burn with outbursts of poetic fury.

Among the richest sources of first-person statements by Indians are the records of treaty
50 councils and other formal meetings with civilian and military representatives of the United States government. Isaac Pitman's new stenographic system was coming into vogue in the second half of the nineteenth century, and when Indians spoke
55 in council a recording clerk sat beside the official interpreter.

Even when the meetings were in remote parts of the West, someone usually was available to write down the speeches, and because of the slow-
60 ness of the translation process, much of what was said could be recorded in longhand. Interpreters quite often were half-bloods who knew spoken languages but seldom could read or write. Like most oral peoples they and the Indians depended upon
65 imagery to express their thoughts, so that the English translations were filled with graphic similes and metaphors of the natural world. If an eloquent Indian had a poor interpreter, his words might be transformed to flat prose, but a good in-
70 terpreter could make a poor speaker sound poetic.

Most Indian leaders spoke freely and candidly in councils with white officials, and as they became more sophisticated in such matters during the 1870's and 1880's, they demanded the right to
75 choose their own interpreters and recorders. In this latter period, all members of the tribes were free to speak, and some of the older men chose such opportunities to recount events they had witnessed in the past, or sum up the histories of their
80 peoples. Although the Indians who lived through this doom period of their civilization have vanished from the earth, millions of their words are preserved in official records. Many of the more important council proceedings were published in
85 government documents and reports.

Out of all these sources of almost forgotten oral history, I have tried to fashion a narrative of the conquest of the American West as the victims experienced it, using their own words whenever
90 possible. Americans who have always looked westward when reading about this period should read this book facing eastward.

This is not a cheerful book, but history has a way of intruding upon the present, and perhaps
95 those who read it will have a clearer understanding of what the American Indian is, by knowing what he was. They may learn something about their own relationship to the earth from a people who were true conservationists. The Indians knew
100 that life was equated with the earth and its resources, that America was a paradise, and they could not comprehend why the intruders from the East were determined to destroy all that was Indian as well as America itself.

GO ON TO NEXT PAGE ▶

16. A main concern of the author in this passage is to

    (A) denounce the white man for his untrustworthiness and savagery
    (B) evaluate the effectiveness of the military treaty councils
    (C) argue for the improved treatment of Indians today
    (D) suggest that Indian narratives of the conquest of the West are similar to white accounts
    (E) introduce the background of the original source materials for his text

17. In line 4, the quotation marks around the word "opening" serve to

    (A) emphasize the author's belief that the conquest of the West took place much earlier
    (B) demonstrate the uniqueness of the author's choice of words
    (C) indicate the author's disagreement with a term in common use
    (D) emphasize the need for the word to be stressed when it is spoken aloud
    (E) criticize the rapid growth in number of these published accounts

18. The word "concentration" in line 5 means

    (A) memory
    (B) attention
    (C) diligence
    (D) imprisonment
    (E) cluster

19. According to the passage, nineteenth-century newspaper accounts of interviews with Indians are variable in quality for which of the following reasons?

    I. Lack of skill on the part of the translators
    II. The tendency of the reporters to overstate what they were told by the Indians
    III. The Indians' misgivings about possible retaliations

    (A) I only
    (B) III only
    (C) I and II only
    (D) I and III only
    (E) I, II, and III

20. The author's tone in describing the Indian survivors can best be described as

    (A) skeptical   (B) detached   (C) elegiac
    (D) obsequious   (E) impatient

21. The author is most impressed by which aspect of the English translations of Indian speeches?

    (A) Their vividness of imagery
    (B) Their lack of frankness
    (C) The inefficiency of the process
    (D) Their absence of sophistication
    (E) Their brevity of expression

22. The word "flat" in line 69 means

    (A) smooth   (B) level   (C) pedestrian
    (D) horizontal   (E) unequivocal

23. The author most likely suggests that Americans should read this book facing eastward

    (A) in an inappropriate attempt at levity
    (B) out of respect for Western superstitions
    (C) in order to read by natural light
    (D) because the Indians came from the East
    (E) to identify with the Indians' viewpoint

24. The phrase "equated with" in line 100 means

    (A) reduced to an average with
    (B) necessarily tied to
    (C) numerically equal to
    (D) fulfilled by
    (E) differentiated by

IF YOU FINISH IN LESS THAN 25 MINUTES, YOU MAY CHECK YOUR WORK ON THIS SECTION ONLY. DO NOT TURN TO ANY OTHER SECTION IN THE TEST.

STOP

> ### Multiple-Choice Directions
>
> For each question in this section, determine which of the five choices is correct, and blacken that choice on your answer sheet. You may use any blank space on the page for your work.
>
> NOTES:
> - You may use a calculator whenever you believe it will be helpful.
> - Use the diagrams provided to help you solve the problems. Unless you see the phrase
>
>   <u>Note:</u> Figure not drawn to scale
>
> under a diagram, it has been drawn as accurately as possible. Unless it is stated that a figure is three dimensional, you may assume that it lies in a plane.
>
> ### Reference
>
>
>
> $A = \pi r^2$
> $C = 2\pi r$
> $A = \ell w$
> $A = \frac{1}{2}bh$
> $V = \ell wh$
> $V = \pi r^2 h$
> $c^2 = a^2 + b^2$
> **Special Right Triangles**
>
> Number of degrees in a circle: 360
> Sum of the measures, in degrees, of the three angles of a triangle: 180

1. If $4x = 12$, then $12x =$
    (A) 4   (B) 6   (C) 24   (D) 36   (E) 48

2. Which of the following numbers has the same digit in the hundreds and hundredths places?
    (A) 3300.0033   (B) 3335.3553   (C) 3353.5353
    (D) 3357.3573   (E) 3357.7533

3. In the figure above, what is the value of x?
    (A) 50   (B) 60   (C) 70   (D) 110
    (E) It cannot be determined from the information given.

4. For how many integers n is it true that $n^2 - 10$ is negative?
    (A) 5   (B) 6   (C) 7   (D) 10
    (E) More than 10

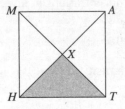

5. In the figure above, *MATH* is a square. If $MX = 3$, what is the area of the shaded triangle?
    (A) $\frac{9}{4}$ (B) $\frac{9\sqrt{3}}{4}$ (C) 4.5   (D) 9   (E) 18

6. If $7x + 5 = 74$, what is the value of $\sqrt{7x - 5}$?
    (A) 7   (B) 8   (C) 9   (D) 10   (E) 11

7. How many primes less than 100 are divisible by 3?
    (A) none   (B) 1
    (C) more than 1 but less than 33
    (D) 33   (E) more than 33

8. If $f(x) = x^2 - 2^x$, what is the value of $f(3)$?

(A) −17 (B) −1 (C) 0 (D) 1 (E) 17

9. If Michael can paint $\frac{2}{5}$ of a room each hour, how many rooms can he paint in h hours?

(A) $\frac{2h}{5}$ (B) $\frac{5h}{2}$ (C) $h - \frac{2}{5}$ (D) $\frac{2}{5h}$ (E) $\frac{5}{2h}$

10. If $x^2 + 1 = 50$, which of the following could be the value of $x + 1$?

(A) −8 (B) −6 (C) $\sqrt{50}$ (D) 6 (E) 7

11. Evelyn's average (arithmetic mean) on her six math tests this marking period is 80. Fortunately for Evelyn, her teacher drops each student's lowest grade; doing so raises Evelyn's average to 90. What was her lowest grade?

(A) 20 (B) 25 (C) 30 (D) 40 (E) 50

12. For how many prime numbers p is $p + 1$ also a prime?

(A) None (B) 1 (C) 2 (D) 3
(E) More than 3

Questions 13 and 14 refer to the following definition.

$\boxed{W \quad X \quad Y \quad Z}$ is a *number bar* if $W + Z = X + Y$ and $2W = 3X$.

13. If $\boxed{3 \quad X \quad Y \quad 7}$ is a *number bar*, what is the value of Y?

(A) 0 (B) 2 (C) 4 (D) 6 (E) 8

14. If $\boxed{W \quad X \quad Y \quad W}$ is a *number bar*, $Y =$

(A) $\frac{3}{4}W$ (B) W (C) $\frac{4}{3}W$ (D) $3W$ (E) $4W$

15. If m is an integer, which of the following could be true?

   I. $\frac{16}{m}$ is an odd integer
   II. $\frac{m}{16}$ is an odd integer
   III. $16m$ is an odd integer

(A) I only (B) II only (C) III only
(D) I and II only (E) I, II, and III

16. What is the volume, in cubic inches, of a cube whose surface area is 60 square inches?

(A) $10\sqrt{10}$ (B) $15\sqrt{15}$ (C) $60\sqrt{60}$
(D) 1000 (E) 3375

17. In rectangle $PQRS$, diagonal PR makes a 60° angle with side PS. If $PR = 10$, what is the area of the rectangle?

(A) $25\sqrt{2}$ (B) $25\sqrt{3}$ (C) 48
(D) 50 (E) 100

18. If $25 - 2\sqrt{x} = 7$, then $x =$

(A) −81 (B) 9 (C) 36 (D) 49 (E) 81

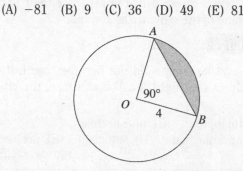

19. In the figure above, the radius of circle O is 4, and m$\angle AOB = 90°$. What is the perimeter of the shaded region?

(A) $4 + 2\pi$ (B) $4\sqrt{2} + \pi$
(C) $4\sqrt{2} + 2\pi$ (D) $4\sqrt{3} + \pi$
(E) $4\sqrt{3} + 2\pi$

20. Because her test turned out to be more difficult than she intended it to be, a teacher decided to adjust the grades by deducting only half the number of points a student missed. For example, if a student missed 20 points, she received a 90 instead of an 80. Before the grades were adjusted Mary's grade was G. What was her grade after the adjustment?

(A) $50 + \frac{G}{2}$ (B) $\frac{1}{2}(100 - G)$ (C) $100 - \frac{G}{2}$
(D) $\frac{100 - G}{2}$ (E) $G + 25$

IF YOU FINISH IN LESS THAN 25 MINUTES, YOU MAY CHECK YOUR WORK ON THIS SECTION ONLY. DO NOT TURN TO ANY OTHER SECTION IN THE TEST.

STOP

For each question in this section, select the best answer from among the choices given and fill in the corresponding circle on the answer sheet.

Directions

Each sentence below has one or two blanks, each blank indicating that something has been omitted. Beneath the sentence are five words or sets of words labeled A through E. Choose the word or set of words that, when inserted in the sentence, best fits the meaning of the sentence as a whole.

EXAMPLE:

Medieval kingdoms did not become constitutional republics overnight; on the contrary, the change was ----.

(A) unpopular   (B) unexpected
(C) advantageous   (D) sufficient   (E) gradual

Ⓐ Ⓑ Ⓒ Ⓓ ●

---

25. Feeling ---- about her latest victories, the tennis champion looked smugly at the row of trophies on her mantelpiece.

    (A) downcast   (B) agitated   (C) indifferent
    (D) complacent   (E) philosophical

26. Normally an individual thunderstorm lasts about 45 minutes, but under certain conditions the storm may ----, becoming ever more severe, for as long as four hours.

    (A) wane   (B) moderate   (C) persist
    (D) vacillate   (E) disperse

27. The newest fiber-optic cables that carry telephone calls cross-country are made of glass so ---- that a piece 100 miles thick is clearer than a standard windowpane.

    (A) fragile   (B) immaculate   (C) tangible
    (D) transparent   (E) iridescent

28. Her employers could not complain about her work because she was ---- in the ---- of her duties.

    (A) derelict..performance
    (B) importunate..observance
    (C) meticulous..postponement
    (D) assiduous..execution
    (E) hidebound..conception

29. Decorated in ---- style, his home contained bits and pieces of furnishings from widely divergent periods, strikingly juxtaposed to create a unique decor.

    (A) an aesthetic   (B) a lyrical   (C) a traditional
    (D) an eclectic   (E) a perfunctory

30. Equipped with mechanisms that deliberately delay sprouting, woodland seeds often seem strangely ---- to germinate.

    (A) prone   (B) reluctant   (C) qualified
    (D) prolific   (E) modified

31. Soap operas and situation comedies, though given to distortion, are so derivative of contemporary culture that they are inestimable ---- the attitudes and values of our society in any particular decade.

    (A) contradictions of   (B) antidotes to
    (C) indices of   (D) prerequisites for
    (E) determinants of

32. Although eighteenth-century English society as a whole did not encourage learning for its own sake in women, nonetheless it illogically ---- women's sad lack of education.

    (A) palliated   (B) postulated
    (C) decried   (D) brooked
    (E) vaunted

GO ON TO NEXT PAGE ▶

Questions 33 and 34 are based on the following passage.

One of the world's most celebrated crusaders for social justice and peace is South Africa's Archbishop Desmond Tutu. Despite his prominence, however, Archbishop Tutu has always made time for his people. On the day in 1984 that he was named winner of the Nobel Peace Prize, reporters and photographers mobbed the seminary where he was staying. A press conference was hastily set up. Just as it was to begin, the archbishop's student assistant entered the courtyard, returning from a family funeral. Leaving the microphones and cameras behind, the archbishop went to comfort her. The world press could wait; her grief could not.

33. The anecdote about Archbishop Tutu serves primarily to demonstrate his
(A) fame   (B) anguish   (C) distraction
(D) compassion   (E) peacefulness

34. In line 3, "prominence" most nearly means
(A) projection   (B) high altitude
(C) land elevation   (D) emphasis   (E) renown

Questions 35 and 36 are based on the following passage.

Although most of the world's active volcanoes are located along the edges of the great shifting plates that make up Earth's surface, there are more than 100 isolated areas of volcanic activity far from the nearest plate boundary. Geologists call these volcanic areas hot spots. Lying deep in the interior of a plate, hot spots or intra-plate volcanoes are sources of magma, the red-hot, molten material within the earth's crust. These intra-plate volcanoes often form volcanic chains, trails of extinct volcanoes. Such volcanic chains serve as landmarks signaling the slow but relentless passage of the plates.

35. The term "hot spot" is being used in the passage
(A) rhetorically   (B) colloquially
(C) technically   (D) ambiguously
(E) ironically

36. The author regards the assumption that the plates making up the earth's surface move as
(A) tentative   (B) accurate
(C) discredited   (D) unanimous   (E) relative

Questions 37–48 are based on the following passages.

In Passage 1, the author, the dancer-choreographer Martha Graham, draws on her experience as a dancer to generalize about her art. In Passage 2, the author, California chef Alice Waters, presents her approach to cooking, as practiced at her restaurant, Chez Panisse.

Passage 1

I am a dancer. My experience has been with dance as an art.

Each art has an instrument and a medium. The instrument of the dance is the human body; the medium is movement. The body has always been to me a thrilling wonder, a dynamo of energy, exciting, courageous, powerful; a delicately balanced logic and proportion. It has not been my aim to evolve or discover a new method of dance training, but rather to dance significantly. To dance significantly means "through the medium of discipline and by means of a sensitive, strong instrument, to bring into focus unhackneyed movement: a human being."

I did not want to be a tree, a flower, or a wave. In a dancer's body, we as audience must see *ourselves*, not the imitated behavior of everyday actions, not the phenomena of nature, not exotic creatures from another planet, but something of the miracle that is a human being, motivated, disciplined, concentrated.

Technique and training have never been a substitute for that condition of awareness which is talent, for that complete miracle of balance which is genius, but it can give plasticity and tension, freedom and discipline, balancing one against the other. It can awaken memory of the race through muscular memory of the body. Training and technique are means to strength, to freedom, to spontaneity.

Contrary to popular belief, spontaneity as one sees it in dance or in theater, is not wholly dependent on emotion at that instant. It is the condition of emotion objectified. It plays that part in theater that light plays in life. It illumines. It excites. Spontaneity is essentially dependent on energy,

GO ON TO NEXT PAGE ▶

upon the strength necessary to perfect timing. It is the result of perfect timing to the Now. It is not essentially intellectual or emotional, but is nerve reaction.

To me, the acquirement of nervous, physical, and emotional concentration is the one element possessed to the highest degree by the truly great dancers of the world. Its acquirement is the result of discipline, of energy in the deep sense. That is why there are so few great dancers.

A great dancer is not made by technique alone any more than a great statesman is made by knowledge alone. Both possess true spontaneity. Spontaneity in behavior, in life, is due largely to complete health; on the stage to a technical use—often so ingrained by proper training as to seem instinctive—of nervous energy. Perhaps what we have always called intuition is merely a nervous system organized by training to perceive.

Passage 2

Flexibility is an essential component of good cooking. You should never feel locked in to a recipe or a menu unless it involves a basic principle regarding procedure or technique such as those involved in breadmaking and pastry. I don't ever want to write anything in this book that is so precise that the reader must invoke great powers of concentration on every last detail in order to ensure the success of a recipe or a dinner; ingredients are simply too variable. I want to *suggest* the expected taste; I want to *suggest* the appearance of the complete dish; I want to *suggest* the combination of ingredients; and I want to *suggest* the overall harmony and balance of the meal. Then it will be up to you to determine the correct balance and

composition. Perhaps the garlic is sharp and strong and you will use it sparingly in a particular presentation, or you may find the garlic to be sweet and fresh and you will want to use twice as much!

Learn to trust your own instincts. A good cook needs only to have positive feelings about food in general, and about the pleasures of eating and cooking. I have known some cooks who did not seem to discover pleasure and gratification in things culinary. At the restaurant, I look for employees who are interested in working in the kitchen for reasons above and beyond those of simply needing a job, any job. This applies equally to the home cook: a cook who dislikes food is a bad cook. Period. Even an ambivalent cook is a bad cook. Yet a person who responds to the cooking processes and the mound of fresh ingredients with a genuine glow of delight is likely to be, or become, a very good cook indeed. Technical skills can be acquired and perfected along the way, but dislike or ambivalence toward food cannot always be overcome.

In the early stages of my culinary pursuits, I cooked as I had seen cooking done in France. I copied some of the more traditional cooks, and I stayed within the bounds they had laid out so carefully because I didn't trust my own instincts yet. Having imitated their styles, I found that with time and experience, their fundamental principles had become a part of my nature and I began to understand why they had done certain things in a particular way. Then I could begin to develop a different and more personal style based on the ingredients available to me here in California.

---

37. Graham rejects movement in dance that is

(A) jerky   (B) spontaneous   (C) brief
(D) trite   (E) natural

38. In saying that she "did not want to be a tree, a flower, or a wave" (line 15), Graham

(A) emphasizes that dancers must express their humanity
(B) reveals an innate discomfort with natural phenomena
(C) suggests a budding desire to imitate other phenomena
(D) conveys a sense of unsatisfied longings
(E) indicates impatience with how long such transformations take

39. The word "plasticity" in line 25 means

(A) nervous energy
(B) strength and endurance
(C) mobility and pliancy
(D) organic coherence
(E) muscular memory

40. According to Graham, most people believe that spontaneous theatrical moments

(A) are the product of disciplined rehearsal and training
(B) happen only because the actor is gripped by a sudden emotion
(C) are dependent on the audience's willingness to suspend their disbelief
(D) depends upon the quickness of the actor's reaction time
(E) are more objective than subjective

GO ON TO NEXT PAGE ▶

41. Graham attempts to clarify the function of spontaneity in dance or theater (lines 34–35) by means of

(A) a digression
(B) an analogy
(C) a hypothesis
(D) an anecdote
(E) a quotation

42. In Passage 2, Waters is discussing cooking from the point of view of

(A) a chef on the verge of opening her own restaurant
(B) someone uninformed about traditional methods of French cuisine
(C) an accomplished practitioner of the culinary arts
(D) a gifted home cook and collector of recipes
(E) a professional determined to outstrip her competitors

43. Waters uses the example of the garlic (lines 71–75) to show

(A) the variability of ingredients
(B) the importance of every last detail
(C) her insistence on fresh ingredients
(D) the need to be a flexible shopper
(E) her preference for strong flavors

44. In writing her cookbook, Waters is trying to

(A) anticipate any pitfalls those using her recipes might run into
(B) provide precise measurements for her readers to follow
(C) limit herself to basic principles and procedures
(D) dictate the spices going into each meal
(E) allow scope for the reader's own culinary initiative

45. To Waters, to produce superior results, the cook must possess

(A) an excellent sense of smell
(B) first-rate technical skills
(C) the finest kitchen equipment
(D) detailed recipes to follow
(E) a love of her medium

46. In lines 81–84 Waters indicates she seeks restaurant employees who share her

(A) level of expertise
(B) classical French training
(C) enjoyment of culinary processes
(D) willingness to work long hours
(E) respect for tradition

47. In these passages, both Graham and Waters are

(A) examining their consciences
(B) presenting their artistic creeds
(C) criticizing their opponents
(D) analyzing their impact on their fields
(E) reassessing their chosen professions

48. Waters and Graham seem alike in that they both

(A) have an abundant supply of nervous energy
(B) benefited from extensive classical training
(C) occasionally distrust their own instincts
(D) are passionately involved with their art
(E) believe in maintaining a positive attitude

IF YOU FINISH IN LESS THAN 25 MINUTES, YOU MAY CHECK YOUR WORK ON THIS SECTION ONLY. DO NOT TURN TO ANY OTHER SECTION IN THE TEST.

STOP

Multiple-Choice Directions

For questions 21–28, determine which of the five choices is correct, and blacken that choice on your answer sheet. You may use any blank space on the page for your work.

NOTES:
- You may use a calculator whenever you believe it will be helpful.
- Use the diagrams provided to help you solve the problems. Unless you see the phrase

<u>Note:</u> Figure not drawn to scale

under a diagram, it has been drawn as accurately as possible. Unless it is stated that a figure is three dimensional, you may assume that it lies in a plane.

Reference

$A = \pi r^2$
$C = 2\pi r$

$A = \ell w$

$A = \frac{1}{2}bh$

$V = \ell wh$

$V = \pi r^2 h$

$c^2 = a^2 + b^2$

Special Right Triangles

Number of degrees in a circle: 360
Sum of the measures, in degrees, of the three angles of a triangle: 180

---

21. If $7d + 5 = 5d + 7$, what is the value of d?

(A) -1 (B) 0   (C) 1   (D) 5   (E) 7

22. In the figure above, what is the value of $a + b + c$?

(A) 210   (B) 220   (C) 240   (D) 270   (E) 280

Questions 23 and 24 refer to the following definition.

For all integers a and b, *let the operation* ✛ *be defined by*:

$$a ✛ b = a, \text{ if } a + b \text{ is even;}$$
$$a ✛ b = b, \text{ if } a + b \text{ is odd.}$$

23. What is the value of $-5 ✛ 5$?

(A) 10   (B) 5   (C) 0   (D) -5 (E) -10

24. If $a \neq b$ and $a ✛ b = 10$, which of the following could be true?

   I. $a + b$ is even
   II. $a + b$ is odd
   III. $b ✛ a = 10$

(A) I only   (B) II only   (C) III only
(D) I and II only   (E) I, II, and III

25. If $5\sqrt{x} + 1 = 46$, what is the value of x?

(A) 1   (B) 3   (C) 9   (D) 81   (E) 729

26. If $x^2 = y^2$, which of the following must be true?

(A) $x = y$ (B) $x = -y$ (C) $y = |x|$
(D) $x = |y|$ (E) $|x| = |y|$

27. A bag contains 4 red, 5 white, and 6 blue marbles. Sarah begins removing marbles from the bag at random, one at a time. What is the least number of marbles she must remove to be sure that she has at least one of each color?

(A) 3   (B) 6   (C) 9   (D) 12   (E) 15

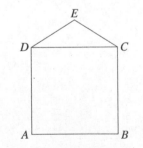

Note: Figure not drawn to scale

28. In the figure above, $ED = EC$, the area of square $ABCD$ is 100, and the area of $\triangle DEC$ is 10. Find the distance from A to E.

(A) 11   (B) 12   (C) $\sqrt{146}$
(D) 13   (E) $\sqrt{44}$

GO ON TO NEXT PAGE ▶

Student-Produced Response Directions

In questions 29–38, first solve the problem, and then enter your answer on the grid provided on the answer sheet. The instructions for entering your answers follow.

- First, write your answer in the boxes at the top of the grid.
- Second, grid your answer in the columns below the boxes.
- Use the fraction bar in the first row or the decimal point in the second row to enter fractions and decimals.

Write your answer in the boxes

Answer: $\frac{8}{15}$ Answer: 1.75   Answer: 100

Grid-in your answer

Either position is acceptable

- Grid only one space in each column.
- Entering the answer in the boxes is recommended as an aid in gridding but is not required.
- The machine scoring your exam can read only what you grid, so you **must grid-in your answers correctly to get credit.**
- If a question has more than one correct answer, grid-in only one of them.
- The grid does not have a minus sign; so no answer can be negative.
- A mixed number *must* be converted to an improper fraction or a decimal before it is gridded. Enter $1\frac{1}{4}$ as $\frac{5}{4}$ or 1.25; the machine will interpret 11/4 as $\frac{11}{4}$ and mark it wrong.

- **All decimals must be entered as accurately as possible.** Here are three acceptable ways of gridding

$$\frac{3}{11} = 0.272727\ldots$$

- Note that rounding to .273 is acceptable because you are using the full grid, but you would receive **no credit** for .3 or .27, because they are less accurate.

---

29. If $5 - w = 4.99$, then what is the value of w?

30. If, in the figure above, $a:b:c = 5:7:12$, what is the value of c?

31. If $xy = 30$ and $x = -6$, what is the value of $x^2 - y^2$?

32. If 25% of x equals 35% of x, what is 45% of x?

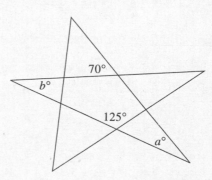

Note: Figure not drawn to scale

33. In the figure above, if $a = 30$, what is the value of b?

GO ON TO NEXT PAGE ▶

45

34. The first term of a sequence is 2. Starting with the second term, each term is 1 more than 2 times the preceding term. How many terms of this sequence are less than 100?

35. In the correctly worked out addition problem below, each letter represents a different digit. What is the number *ABC*?

$$\begin{array}{r} 2B \\ 4B \\ + 6B \\ \hline ABC \end{array}$$

36. If circle *O* has its center at $(1, 1)$, and line *l* is tangent to circle *O* at $P(4, -4)$, then what is the slope of *l*?

37. What is the height, in feet, of a rectangular box whose width and length are 5 feet and 7 feet, respectively, and whose total surface area is 298 square feet?

38. A group charters three identical buses and occupies $\frac{4}{5}$ of the seats. After $\frac{1}{4}$ of the passengers leave, the remaining passengers use only two of the buses. What fraction of the seats on the two buses are now occupied?

IF YOU FINISH IN LESS THAN 25 MINUTES, YOU MAY CHECK YOUR WORK ON THIS SECTION ONLY. DO NOT TURN TO ANY OTHER SECTION IN THE TEST.

STOP

Improving Sentence Directions

Some or all parts of the following sentences are underlined. The first answer choice, (A), simply repeats the underlined part of the sentence. The other four choices present four alternative ways to phrase the underlined part. Select the answer that produces the most effective sentence, one that is clear and exact, and blacken the appropriate space on your answer sheet. In selecting your choice, be sure that it is standard written English and that it expresses the meaning of the original sentence.

EXAMPLE:

The first biography of author Eudora Welty came out in 1998, <u>and she was eighty-nine years old at the time</u>.

(A) and she was eighty-nine years old at the time
(B) at the time when she was eighty-nine
(C) upon becoming an eighty-nine year old
(D) when she was eighty-nine
(E) at the age of eighty-nine years old

SAMPLE ANSWER:

Ⓐ Ⓑ Ⓒ ● Ⓔ

1. <u>If he was to decide to go to college</u>, I, for one, would recommend that he plan to go to Yale.

   (A) If he was to decide to go to college
   (B) If he were to decide to go to college
   (C) Had he decided to go to college
   (D) In the event that he decides to go to college
   (E) Supposing he was to decide to go to college

2. <u>Except for you and I, everyone brought</u> a present to the party.

   (A) Except for you and I, everyone brought
   (B) With the exception of you and I, everyone brought
   (C) Except for you and I, everyone had brought
   (D) Except for you and me, everyone brought
   (E) Except for you and me, everyone had brought

3. <u>Had I realized how close</u> I was to failing, I would not have gone to the party.

   (A) Had I realized how close
   (B) If I would have realized how close
   (C) Had I had realized how close
   (D) When I realized how close
   (E) If I realized how close

4. <u>Being a realist</u>, I could not accept his statement that supernatural beings had caused the disturbance.

   (A) Being a realist
   (B) Due to the fact that I am a realist
   (C) Being that I am a realist
   (D) Being as I am a realist
   (E) Realist that I am

5. Having finished the marathon in record-breaking time, <u>the city awarded him its Citizen's Outstanding Performance Medal</u>.

   (A) the city awarded him its Citizen's Outstanding Performance Medal
   (B) the city awarded the Citizen's Outstanding Performance Medal to him
   (C) he was awarded the Citizen's Outstanding Performance Medal by the city
   (D) the Citizen's Outstanding Performance Medal was awarded to him
   (E) he was awarded by the city the Citizen's Outstanding Performance Medal

6. <u>The football team's winning its first game of the season</u> excited the student body.

   (A) The football team's winning its first game of the season
   (B) The football team having won its first game of the season
   (C) Having won its first game of the season, the football team
   (D) Winning its first game of the season, the football team
   (E) The football team winning its first game of the season

7. Anyone interested in the use of computers can learn much <u>if you have access to</u> a copy of *PC Magazine* or of *MacUser*.

   (A) if you have access to
   (B) if he or she has access to
   (C) if access is available to
   (D) by access to
   (E) from access to

GO ON TO NEXT PAGE ▶

8. I have <u>to make dinner, wash the dishes, do my homework, and then relaxing</u>.

   (A) to make dinner, wash the dishes, do my homework, and then relaxing

   (B) to make dinner, washing the dishes, my homework, and then relaxing

   (C) to make dinner, wash the dishes, doing my homework, and then relax

   (D) to prepare dinner, wash the dishes, do my homework, and then relaxing

   (E) to make dinner, wash the dishes, do my homework, and then relax

9. The climax <u>occurs when he asks who's</u> in the closet.

   (A) occurs when he asks who's

   (B) is when he asks who's

   (C) occurs when he is asking who's

   (D) is when he is asking who's

   (E) occurs when he asked who's

10. Setting up correct bookkeeping procedures <u>is important to any new business, it helps</u> to obtain the services of a good accountant.

   (A) is important to any new business, it helps

   (B) are important to any new business, it

   (C) is important to any new business, therefore, try

   (D) is important to any new business; it helps

   (E) are important to any new business, so try

11. The grocer <u>hadn't hardly any of those kind</u> of canned goods.

   (A) hadn't hardly any of those kind

   (B) hadn't hardly any of those kinds

   (C) had hardly any of those kind

   (D) had hardly any of those kinds

   (E) had scarcely any of those kind

12. <u>Having stole the money, the police searched the thief</u>.

   (A) Having stole the money, the police searched the thief.

   (B) Having stolen the money, the thief was searched by the police.

   (C) Having stolen the money, the police searched the thief.

   (D) Having stole the money, the thief was searched by the police.

   (E) Being that he stole the money, the police searched the thief.

13. Juan broke his <u>hip, he has not and possibly never will be able to run</u> the mile again.

   (A) hip, he has not and possibly never will be able to run

   (B) hip; he has not been able to run and possibly never will be able to run

   (C) hip; he has not and possibly never will be able to run

   (D) hip, he has not been and possibly never would be able to run

   (E) hip; he has not and possibly will never be able to run

14. I came late to class <u>today; the reason being that</u> the bus broke down.

   (A) today; the reason being that

   (B) today, the reason being that

   (C) today because

   (D) today;

   (E) today; since

15. Young children's fevers are <u>erratic, furthermore they can spike unpredictably, and, just as unpredictably, can subside</u>.

   (A) erratic, furthermore they can spike unpredictably, and, just as unpredictably, can subside

   (B) erratic; nevertheless, they can spike unpredictably, and, just as unpredictably, they can subside

   (C) erratic, and can spike unpredictably, and, just as unpredictable, they can subside

   (D) erratic: they can spike unpredictably, and, just as unpredictably, can subside

   (E) erratic, they can spike just as unpredictably as they can subside

16. <u>Of all the characters in *A Christmas Carol*, sweet and saintly Tiny Tim is the more beloved</u>.

   (A) Of all the characters in *A Christmas Carol*, sweet and saintly Tiny Tim is the more beloved.

   (B) Of all the characters in *A Christmas Carol*, sweet and saintly Tiny Tim was the more beloved.

   (C) In *A Christmas Carol*, of all the characters, sweet and saintly Tiny Tim is the more beloved.

   (D) Of all the characters in *A Christmas Carol*, sweet and saintly Tiny Tim is the most beloved

   (E) Sweet and saintly Tiny Tim is more beloved than all the characters in *A Christmas Carol*.

GO ON TO NEXT PAGE ▶

17. The history of the past quarter century illustrates how a president may increase his power to act aggressively in international <u>affairs, and he does not consider the wishes of Congress.</u>

(A) affairs, and he does not consider the wishes of Congress

(B) affairs, therefore he did not consider the wishes of Congress

(C) affairs without considering the wishes of Congress

(D) affairs, but he does not consider what Congress wishes

(E) affairs, and he may not have considered the wishes of Congress

18. With the exception of a few publications like *The New York Times*, American newspapers tend to ignore world news <u>unless the event to be reported immediately affects American citizens.</u>

(A) unless the event to be reported immediately affects American citizens

(B) unless the event being reported immediately effects American citizens

(C) except the event to be reported has immediately affected American citizens

(D) unless the event immediately to be reported affecting American citizens

(E) unless the immediate event they reported affects American citizens

19. When he was a war correspondent during the Spanish Civil War (1936–1939), the American novelist Ernest <u>Hemingway has written movingly about the struggle</u> of the Republican forces against General Francisco Franco's Nationalist troops.

(A) Hemingway has written movingly about the struggle

(B) Hemingway has written while moving about the struggle

(C) Hemingway has written movingly from the struggle

(D) Hemingway has been writing movingly about the struggle

(E) Hemingway wrote movingly about the struggle

20. Fearful that Rome's hungry, restless throngs might grow unruly, Roman <u>emperors catered to the masses, providing the mob with bread</u> and circuses.

(A) emperors catered to the masses, providing the mob with bread

(B) emperors catered to the masses, provided that the mob with bread

(C) emperors catered for the masses, providing the mob with bread

(D) emperors catered to the masses, they provided the mob with bread

(E) emperors catered for the masses by providing the mob with bread

Identifying Sentence Error Directions

The sentences in this section may contain errors in grammar, usage, choice of words, or idioms. There is either just one error per sentence, or the sentence is correct. Some words or phrases are underlined and lettered; everything else in the sentence is correct.

If an underlined word or phrase is incorrect, choose that letter; if the sentence is correct, select <u>No error</u>. Then blacken the appropriate space on your Answer Sheet.

EXAMPLE:

The region has a climate <u>so severe that</u> plants
                                    A

<u>growing there</u> rarely <u>had been</u> more than twelve
     B   C

inches <u>high.</u> <u>No error</u>
         D   E

SAMPLE ANSWER:

Ⓐ Ⓑ ● Ⓓ Ⓔ

21. <u>In order to</u> conserve valuable gasoline, motorists
         A

<u>had ought to</u> check their speedometers <u>while</u>
       B   C

driving along the highways <u>since it is very easy to</u>
                                D

exceed 55 miles per hour while driving on open

roads. <u>No error</u>
          E

22. The book <u>must</u> be old, <u>for</u> its cover <u>is torn</u> <u>bad.</u>
                    A   B   C   D

<u>No error</u>
    E

23. <u>Not one</u> of the children <u>has ever sang</u> <u>in public</u>
         A   B   C

<u>before.</u> <u>No error</u>
     D   E

GO ON TO NEXT PAGE ▶

24. Neither you nor $\underset{A}{I}$ can realize the $\underset{B}{affect}$ his behavior $\underset{C}{will\ have}$ on his chances $\underset{D}{for\ promotion}$.

$\underset{E}{No\ error}$

25. The $\underset{A}{apparently}$ $\underset{B}{obvious\ solution\ to}$ the problem was overlooked by $\underset{C}{many\ of}$ $\underset{D}{}$ the contestants.

$\underset{E}{No\ error}$

26. After he $\underset{A}{had\ drank}$ the warm milk, he began $\underset{B}{}$ to feel sleepy $\underset{C}{}$ and $\underset{D}{finally\ decided}$ to go to bed.

$\underset{E}{No\ error}$

27. $\underset{A}{Without\ hardly}$ a moment's delay, the computer began $\underset{B}{to\ print\ out}$ the $\underset{C}{}$ $\underset{D}{answer\ to}$ the problem.

$\underset{E}{No\ error}$

28. $\underset{A}{Of}$ the two candidates for this newly $\underset{B}{formed}$ government position, Ms. Rivera is the

$\underset{C}{most\ qualified}$ $\underset{D}{because}$ of her experience in the field. $\underset{E}{No\ error}$

29. Diligence and honesty $\underset{A}{as\ well\ as}$ $\underset{B}{being\ intelligent}$ $\underset{C}{are}$ qualities that personnel directors look for $\underset{D}{when}$ they interview applicants. $\underset{E}{No\ error}$

30. Neither the San Francisco earthquake $\underset{A}{or}$ the $\underset{B}{subsequent}$ fire $\underset{C}{was}$ able to destroy the $\underset{D}{spirit}$ of the city dwellers. $\underset{E}{No\ error}$

31. The $\underset{A}{impatient\ customer}$ had $\underset{B}{scarcely\ enough}$ money $\underset{C}{to\ pay}$ the clerk $\underset{D}{at}$ the checkout counter.

$\underset{E}{No\ error}$

32. The $\underset{A}{principal}$ of equal justice $\underset{B}{for\ all}$ is $\underset{C}{one}$ of the cornerstones of the democratic $\underset{D}{way\ of\ life}$.

$\underset{E}{No\ error}$

33. Although alchemy anticipated science in its belief

$\underset{A}{that}$ physical reality was $\underset{B}{determined\ by}$ an

$\underset{C}{unvarying}$ set of natural laws, the alchemist's

experimental method $\underset{D}{was\ not\ hardly}$ scientific.

$\underset{E}{No\ error}$

34. $\underset{A}{If}$ anyone $\underset{B}{calls}$ while the delegates are in conference, tell $\underset{C}{them}$ the chairman will

$\underset{D}{return\ the\ call}$ after the meeting. $\underset{E}{No\ error}$

GO ON TO NEXT PAGE ▶

Improving Paragraph Directions

The passage below is the unedited draft of a student's essay. Some of the essay needs to be rewritten to make the meaning clearer and more precise. Read the essay carefully.

The essay is followed by five questions about changes that might improve all or part of its organization, development, sentence structure, use of language, appropriateness to the audience, or use of standard written English. Choose the answer that most clearly and effectively expresses the student's intended meaning. Indicate your choice by filling in the corresponding space on the answer sheet.

[1] There are many reasons making it cruel to keep animals penned up in zoos for the sole purpose of letting families gawk at caged creatures. [2] There has to be a better reason to imprison animals than merely to allow visitors to drop a quarter into a food dispenser so that one can feed the monkeys or the elephant. [3] One might argue that it is educational. [4] If someone is so dumb that they don't know what a zebra looks like, they should pull out an encyclopedia and look it up. [5] Humans have no right to pull animals from their natural environment and to seal their fate forever behind a set of cold metal bars. [6] Animals need to run free and live, but by putting them in zoos we are disrupting and disturbing nature.

[7] Then there is the issue of sanitary conditions for animals at the zoo. [8] When the animals have been at the zoo for a while they adopt a particular lifestyle. [9] They lounge around all day, and they're fed at a particular time. [10] They get used to that. [11] That means that they would never again be able to be placed back in their natural environment. [12] They would never survive. [13] And if they reproduce while in captivity, the offspring are born into an artificial lifestyle. [14] After a few generations the animals become totally different from their wild and free ancestors, and visitors to the zoo see animals hardly resembling the ones living in their natural habitat.

[15] The vicious cycle should be stopped before it is too late. [16] The whole idea of a zoo is cruel. [17] If zoos are not cruel and if, as some people say, they serve a useful purpose, then why not put homo sapiens on display, too?

35. Which is the most effective revision of the underlined segment of sentence 1 below?

    There are many reasons making it cruel to keep animals penned up in zoos for the sole purpose of letting families gawk at caged creatures.

    (A) Many reasons exist for the cruelty of keeping animals penned up in zoos
    (B) It is a cruel practice to keep animals penned up in zoos
    (C) The reasons are numerous to object to the cruelty experienced by animals locked in cages
    (D) There are several reasons for it being cruel toward animals to lock them up in zoos
    (E) Locking up animals in zoos a cruel practice especially

36. Taking sentence 3 into account, which of the following is the most effective revision of sentence 4?

    (A) Reading about animals in the encyclopedia rather than studying them first hand.
    (B) In the encyclopedia you can gain more information about zebras and other animals.
    (C) Viewing the animal in a zoo is clearly more informative than looking at a picture in a book.
    (D) Doesn't everyone know what a zebra looks like, even little children?
    (E) But if someone is so dumb that they don't know what a zebra looks like, they should look it up in an encyclopedia.

GO ON TO NEXT PAGE ▶

37. Which of the following reasons most accurately describes the author's intention in the selection of words used in the underlined segment of sentence 5 below?

Humans have no right to pull animals from their natural environment and <u>to seal their fate forever behind a set of cold metal bars</u>.

(A) to inform the reader that animals in the zoo live in cages

(B) to propose a solution to the plight of animals in the zoo

(C) to arouse in the reader an emotional response to the problem

(D) to appeal to the reader to weigh both sides of the issue

(E) to convince the reader that animals don't enjoy being in the zoo

38. Which of the following revisions of sentence 7 is the best topic sentence for paragraph 2?

(A) Life in captivity causes animals to change.

(B) No one favors zoos that deliberately try to change the lifestyle of animals in captivity.

(C) Living conditions for animals in the zoo are ordinarily harsh and cruel.

(D) Living in the zoo, conditions for animals affect them permanently.

(E) Life in the zoo for animals is not a bowl of cherries.

39. Which revision most effectively combines sentences 10, 11, and 12?

(A) Because they would never be able to survive again back in their natural environment, they grow used to being fed.

(B) Having grown used to regular feedings, the animals would be unable to survive back in their native environment.

(C) Growing accustomed to that, placing them back in their native habitat and being unable to survive on their own.

(D) They, having gotten used to being fed regularly, in their natural environment would never survive.

(E) Being unable to survive back in their natural environment, the animals have grown accustomed to regular feedings.

IF YOU FINISH IN LESS THAN 30 MINUTES, YOU MAY CHECK YOUR WORK ON THIS SECTION ONLY. DO NOT TURN TO ANY OTHER SECTION IN THE TEST.

STOP

52 ▶ **CHAPTER 3 / A Diagnostic Test**

Answer Key

Section 1 Critical Reading

1. B
2. C
3. A
4. A
5. B
6. C
7. E
8. E
9. C
10. E
11. B
12. C
13. B
14. A
15. C
16. E
17. C
18. E
19. D
20. C
21. A
22. C
23. E
24. B

Section 2 Mathematics

1. D
2. C
3. C
4. C
5. C
6. B
7. B
8. D
9. A
10. B
11. C
12. B
13. E
14. C
15. D
16. A
17. B
18. E
19. C
20. A

Section 3 Critical Reading

25. D
26. C
27. D
28. D
29. D
30. B
31. C
32. C
33. D
34. E
35. C
36. B
37. D
38. A
39. C
40. B
41. B
42. C
43. A
44. E
45. E
46. C
47. B
48. D

Section 4 Mathematics

21. C
22. B
23. D
24. D
25. D
26. E
27. D
28. D

31. 11

32. 0

33. 40

34. 6

35. 126

36. 3/5

or .6

29. .01

30. 90

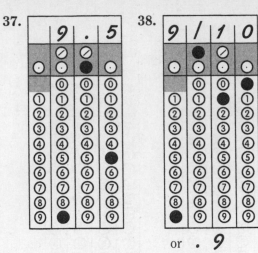

37.

38.

or $\cdot 9$

Section 5 Writing Skills

1. B	9. A	17. C	25. E	33. D
2. D	10. D	18. A	26. B	34. C
3. A	11. D	19. E	27. A	35. B
4. A	12. B	20. A	28. C	36. C
5. C	13. B	21. B	29. B	37. C
6. A	14. C	22. D	30. A	38. A
7. B	15. D	23. B	31. E	39. B
8. E	16. D	24. B	32. A	

Scoring Chart—Diagnostic Test

Critical Reading Sections

Section 1: 24 Questions (1–24)

Number correct	_____	(A)
Number omitted	_____	(B)
Number incorrect	_____	(C)
$\frac{1}{4}$ (C)	_____	(D)
(A) − (D)	_____	Raw Score I

Section 3: 24 Questions (25–48)

Number correct	_____	(A)
Number omitted	_____	(B)
Number incorrect	_____	(C)
$\frac{1}{4}$ (C)	_____	(D)
(A) − (D)	_____	Raw Score II

Total Critical Reading Raw Score
Raw Scores I + II _____

Mathematics Sections

Section 2: 20 Questions (1–20)

Number correct	_____	(A)
Number omitted	_____	(B)
Number incorrect	_____	(C)
$\frac{1}{4}$ (C)	_____	(D)
(A) − (D)	_____	Raw Score I

Section 4: First 8 Questions (21–28)

Number correct	_____	(A)
Number omitted	_____	(B)
Number incorrect	_____	(C)
$\frac{1}{4}$ (C)	_____	(D)
(A) − (D)	_____	Raw Score II

Section 4: Next 10 Questions (29–38)
Number correct _____ Raw Score III

Total Mathematical Raw Score
Raw Scores I + II + III _____

NOTE: In each section (A) + (B) + (C) should equal the number of questions in that section.

Writing Skills Section

Section 5: 39 Questions (1–39)

Number correct	_____	(A)
Number omitted	_____	(B)
Number incorrect	_____	(C)
$\frac{1}{4}$ (C)	_____	(D)

Writing Skills Raw Score
(A) − (D) _____

Evaluation Chart

Study your score. Your raw score is an indication of your probable achievement on the PSAT/NMSQT. As a guide to the amount of work you need or want to do with this book, study the following.

	Raw Score		Self-rating
Critical Reading	*Mathematics*	*Writing*	
42–48	35–38	33–39	Superior
37–46	30–34	28–32	Very good
32–36	25–29	23–27	Good
26–35	21–24	17–22	Above average
20–25	17–20	12–16	Average
12–19	10–16	7–11	Below average
less than 12	less than 10	less than 7	Inadequate

Answer Explanations

Section 1 Critical Reading

1. *B* For Miro, art was holy or *sacred*. Note how the second clause clarifies what kind or ritual art became for Miro.

2. *C* The key term here is "smoke screen," something designed to obscure or mislead. How would accuracy-loving scholars react to an autobiography filled with misleading remarks? They would be *vexed* (annoyed) by the smoke screens and other misleading *errors*.

3. *A* To be kept "at arm's length" from someone's emotions is to feel an emotional distance between you and that person. Singer's own quality of uninvolvement or *detachment* makes the reader feel distant from his main character.

4. *A* Break down the sentence. The prolific (highly productive) author has written many different books, bound in many different bindings. The fact that the books' topics vary as much as their bindings indicates the author has not specialized in any one topic. Instead, he has *resisted* or fought specialization as strongly as some other writers have *pursued* it.

5. *B* If the mayfly's adult life lasts for such a short time, it clearly is an *ephemeral* (short-lived, fleeting) creature. Note how the second clause clarifies what the author means by *ephemeral*.

6. *C* The opening sentence states that Chaucer was considered a "rude versifier" until scholars learned to understand his technique. This suggests that people's failure to understand just what Chaucer was doing caused them to undervalue his poetic skill.

7. *E* A "rude versifier" is someone who composes rude (crude and *unpolished*) verse.

8. *E* Reporters "have had a field day" commenting on the controversial knighting. In other words, they have had an occasion for unrestrained ridicule and hilarity, to which their response has been one of pure *glee* (high-spirited delight, often prompted by a malicious joy in someone else's discomfiture).

9. *C* Consider that the original instance of royal hospitality to which the reporter refers is a night in a prison cell. Does that sound hospitable to you? Clearly, the reporter is using the phrase *ironically*, in an amusingly surprising way.

10. *E* The second paragraph discusses the various methods epiphytes adopt in order to retain or conserve moisture.

Choice A is incorrect. Epiphytes have lost their root connection with the forest floor. Choice B is incorrect. Epiphytes seek the sun; they are not adapted to a sunless environment. Choice C is incorrect. Epiphytes have developed ways to conserve rainwater, not to dissipate or squander it. Choice D is incorrect. Epiphytes are not parasites; they do not derive nourishment ("sustenance") from the tree trunks to which they attach themselves.

11. *B* The first paragraph states that epiphytes grow in "spoonfuls" of soil. We can infer from this that they do not need particularly large amounts of soil for growth.

Choice A is incorrect. Although epiphytes have lost their root connection with the forest floor, they do possess root systems. Choice C is incorrect. The passage states that the roots of some orchids carry on photosynthesis; epiphytes clearly are not incapable of photosynthesis. Choice D is incorrect. Nothing in the passage suggests epiphytes are hard to spot. Choice E is incorrect. Epiphytes have "managed to create their own environment" so well that the soil in which they grow does not differ significantly from normal soil in microbiological processes. This fact does not suggest that their need for nutrients differs from that of plants that grow in normal soil.

12. *C* Epiphytes are described in a straightforward, direct manner.

Choice A is incorrect. The author is not exhorting or urging anyone to do anything. Choice B is incorrect. The author is not analyzing epiphytes, that is, thoroughly studying each of the individual features that comprise these plants in order to understand their structure. He is simply saying what they are like. Choice D is incorrect. The author is being direct rather than indirect in presenting what he knows about epiphytes. Choice E is incorrect. The author is not being particularly forceful in his presentation; neither is he presenting an argument.

13. *B* The strangler tree's feeding cables do not ascend toward the canopy; they descend to the forest floor. You can double-check your answer by using the process of elimination.

The strangler tree eventually stands on its own pedestal or supports itself. You can eliminate Choice A. One set of the strangler tree's roots (the "feeding cable") extends all the way from high up in the fork of the host tree down to the forest floor. You can eliminate Choice C.

When the feeder cable reaches the soil, the plant's growth quickens. You can eliminate Choice D. The strangler's roots "thicken to a marked degree," becoming *conspicuously larger*. You can eliminate Choice E. Only Choice B is left. It is the correct answer.

14. *A* The roots thicken to a marked or *noticeable* degree, eventually growing thick enough to support the strangler tree.

15. *C* The concluding sentence states that the host expires and the strangler tree stands on its own pedestal of thickened roots (its original feeding cables, now fused together). Thus, the strangler tree has *outgrown its need for its host*.

16. *E* Throughout the passage the author presents and comments on the nature of the original documents that form the basis for his historical narrative. Thus, it is clear that a major concern of his is to *introduce* these "sources of almost forgotten oral history" to his readers.

Choice A is incorrect. The author clearly regrets the fate of the Indians. However, he does not take this occasion to denounce or condemn the white man. Choice B is incorrect. While the author discusses the various treaty councils, he does not evaluate or judge how effective they were. Choice C is incorrect. The author never touches on the current treatment of Indians. Choice D is incorrect. The author indicates no such thing.

17. *C* Because Brown looks on the conquest of the West from a Native American perspective, he views it as the tragic destruction of Indian civilization rather than as the heroic opening of new, uncivilized territory by European civilization. Thus, by putting quotation marks around the word "opening," Brown indicates his *disagreement with* the notion of "the opening of the West," *a term in common use* in typical narratives of the period.

18. *E* Of all the thousands of published descriptions of the opening of the West, the greatest concentration or *cluster* of accounts date from the period of 1860 to 1890.

19. *D* You can arrive at the correct choice by the process of elimination.

Statement I is true. The passage states that the quality of the interviews depended on the interpreters' abilities. Inaccuracies could creep in because of the translators' lack of skill. Therefore, you can eliminate Choice B.

Statement II is untrue. The passage indicates that the Indians sometimes exaggerated, telling the reporters tall tales. It does not indicate that the reporters in turn overstated what they had been told. Therefore, you can eliminate Choices C and E.

Statement III is true. The passage indicates that the Indians sometimes were disinclined to speak the whole truth because they feared reprisals (retaliation) if they did. Therefore, you can eliminate Choice A.

Only Choice D is left. It is the correct answer.

20. *C* Brown speaks of the Indians who lived through the "doom period of their civilization," the victims of the conquest of the American West. In doing so, his tone can best be described as *elegiac*, expressing sadness about their fate and lamenting their vanished civilization.

21. *A* In the fifth paragraph Brown comments upon the "graphic similes and metaphors of the natural world" found in the English translations of Indian speeches. Thus, he is impressed by their *vividness of imagery*.

22. *C* Commenting about inadequate interpreters who turned eloquent Indian speeches into "flat" prose, Brown is criticizing the translations for their *pedestrian*, unimaginative quality.

23. *E* Brown has tried to create a narrative of the winning of the West from the victims' perspective. In asking his readers to read the book facing eastward (the way the Indians would have been looking when they first saw the whites headed west), he is asking them metaphorically to look at things from the Indians' point of view.

24. *B* In the sentence immediate preceding the one in which this phrase appears, Brown calls the Indians "true conservationists." Such conservationists know that life is *necessarily tied to* the earth and to its resources and that by destroying these resources by imbalancing the equation, so to speak, you destroy life itself.

Section 2 Mathematics

For many problems, the explanation provides a reference to one or more **KEY FACTS** from Chapter 9. These are the mathematical facts that you need to solve that problem. If a solution refers to **KEY FACT J2**, for example, the solution depends on the second **KEY FACT** discussed in Section J of Chapter 9.

For some problems, an alternative solution, indicated by two asterisks (**), follows the first solution. When this occurs, usually one of the solutions is the direct mathematical one and the other is based on one of the tactics discussed in Chapters 8 and 9.

1. *D* $4x = 12 \Rightarrow x = 3 \Rightarrow 12x = 36$.

2. *C* Just look at each number carefully. The hundreds place is the third from the left of the decimal point and the hundredths place is the second to the right of the decimal point: 3353.5353.

3. *C* In the figure at the right, by **KEY FACT J1**, $x + y + z = 180$, and by **KEY FACT I2**, $y = 60$ and $z = 50$. Therefore,
$$x = 180 - (50 + 60) = 180 - 110 = 70.$$

4. *C* The expression $n^2 - 10$ is negative whenever $n^2 < 10$. This is true for all integers between -3 and 3 inclusive: $-3, -2, -1, 0, 1, 2, 3$—7 in all.

5. *C* By **KEYFACT J6**, triangle *MAX* is a 45-45-90 right triangle, so
$$MX = 3 \Rightarrow AX = 3 \Rightarrow$$
area of $\triangle MAX = \frac{1}{2}(3)(3) = 4.5$,
which is also the area of the shaded triangle.

$MX = 3 \Rightarrow MT = 6$. By **KEY FACT K6, the area of a square equals $\frac{d^2}{2}$, where d is the length of a diagonal. So the area of *MATH* square is $\frac{1}{2}(6)^2 = 18$. Then the area of the shaded triangle is $18 \div 4 = 4.5$.

6. *B* $7x + 5 = 74 \Rightarrow 7x = 69 \Rightarrow 7x - 5 = 64 \Rightarrow \sqrt{7x - 5} = \sqrt{64} = 8$. (Note that, since the given equation and what you want both involve $7x$, you should *not* solve for x.)

7. *B* There is only one prime divisible by 3, namely 3.

8. *D* $3^2 - 2^3 = 9 - 8 = 1$.

9. *A* Just multiply: $\frac{2}{5}(h) = \frac{2h}{5}$.

Use **TACTIC 8-2 and pick an easy-to-use number for *h*: 2, for example. Michael can paint $\frac{2}{5}$ of a room in the first hour and another $\frac{2}{5}$ of a room in the second hour, for a total of $\frac{4}{5}$ of a room. Check the choices. Only $\frac{2h}{5}$ equals $\frac{4}{5}$ when $h = 2$.

10. *B* $x^2 + 1 = 50 \Rightarrow x^2 = 49 \Rightarrow x = 7$ or $x = -7$. Therefore, $x + 1 = 8$ or $x + 1 = -6$. Since 8 is not one of the choices, the answer is -6.

11. *C* On her 6 tests combined, Evelyn earned a total of $6 \times 80 = 480$ points (see **KEY FACT E1**). The total of her 5 best grades is $5 \times 90 = 450$ points. So, her lowest grade was $480 - 450 = 30$.

Assume that Evelyn's 5 best grades were each 90. Then each one has a deviation of 10 points above the average of 80, and the total deviation above 80 is $5 \times 10 = 50$ points. Therefore, her one bad grade must have been 50 points below 80 (see **KEY FACT E2).

12. *B* Of the two consecutive integers *p* and *p* + 1, one is odd and one is even. Since 2 is the only even prime number, there is only one possibility:
$p = 2$ and $p + 1 = 3$. ($p = 1$ and $p + 1 = 2$ does *not* work, because 1 is *not* a prime number.)

13. *E* Since $W = 3$ and $2W = 3X$, then
$$3X = 6 \Rightarrow X = 2.$$
Therefore, $3 + 7 = 2 + Y \Rightarrow Y = 10 - 2 = 8$.

14. *C* Here $Z = W$. So by definition of a number bar, $W + Z = X + Y \Rightarrow 2W = X + Y$; but the definition also states that $2W = 3X$, so $X = \frac{2}{3}W$. Therefore,
$$2W = \frac{2}{3}W + Y \Rightarrow Y = \frac{4}{3}W.$$

15. *D* Check each statement. If $m = 16$, then $\frac{16}{m} = 1$, an odd integer. (I is true.) Eliminate B and C. Could $\frac{m}{16}$ be an odd integer? Sure, it could be any odd integer; for example, if $m = 16$, $\frac{m}{16} = 1$, and if $m = 80$, $\frac{m}{16} = 5$. (II is true.) Eliminate A. Check III: could $16m$ be odd? No, the product of 16 and any integer is even. (III is false.) Eliminate E. Only statements I and II are true.

16. *A* By **KEY FACT M2**, if *e* is the edge of the cube, the surface area, *A*, is $6e^2$ and the volume, *V*, is e^3. Then
$$A = 6e^2 = 60 \Rightarrow e^2 = 10 \Rightarrow e = \sqrt{10} \Rightarrow$$
$$V = \left(\sqrt{10}\right)^3 = \left(\sqrt{10}\right)\left(\sqrt{10}\right)\left(\sqrt{10}\right) = 10\sqrt{10}.$$

17. *B* *PR* is the hypotenuse of a 30-60-90 right triangle. By **KEY FACT J11**, *PS*, the leg opposite the 30° angle, is 5 (half the hypotenuse), and *SR* is $5\sqrt{3}$. So the area of the rectangle is $5 \times 5\sqrt{3} = 25\sqrt{3}$.

18. *E* $25 - 2\sqrt{x} = 7 \Rightarrow -2\sqrt{x} = -18 \Rightarrow \sqrt{x} = 9 \Rightarrow$ $x = 9^2 = 81.$

19. *C* Since each radius is 4, $OA = OB$ and $\triangle AOB$ is an isosceles right triangle. So by **KEY FACT J5**, $AB = 4\sqrt{2}$. The length of arc AB is $\frac{90}{360} = \frac{1}{4}$ of the circumference, which by **KEY FACT L4** is $2\pi(4) = 8\pi$; so the length of arc $AB = 2\pi$. The perimeter of the region, then, is $4\sqrt{2} + 2\pi$.

20. *A* If Mary earned a grade of G on the test, she missed $(100 - G)$ points. In adjusting the grades, the teacher decided to deduct only half that number: $\frac{100-G}{2}$. So Mary's new grade was $100 - \left(\frac{100-G}{2}\right) = 100 - 50 + \frac{G}{2} = 50 + \frac{G}{2}$.

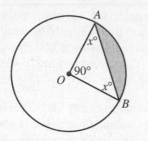

Section 3 Critical Reading

25. *D* The key word here is *smugly*. The tennis champion is smug or *complacent* about her victories.

26. *C But* signals a contrast. Normally thunderstorms last for a short time. However, sometimes they last or *persist* for a long time. Note the effect of the phrase "becoming ever more severe." If the storm keeps on getting worse, it is not *waning* (declining), *moderating* (becoming less severe), *vacillating* (wavering), or *dispersing* (being scattered).

27. *D* Why is this 100-mile-thick piece of glass clearer than a standard windowpane? *Because* the glass is exceptionally *transparent*. The "so . . . that" structure signals cause and effect.

28. *D* The *assiduous* or diligent *execution* (performance) of one's job would give one's employer no cause for complaint. Note the signal word *because* indicating the sentence's cause and effect structure.

29. *D* Something *eclectic* is by definition composed of items drawn from many different sources. In this case, the style of interior decoration is eclectic.

30. *B* One expects seeds to germinate or sprout within a relatively short period of time. However, for woodland seeds, the process takes longer than normal; the seeds seem strangely *reluctant* to sprout.

31. *C* Because these shows are highly derivative of (stem from) our culture, they reflect what our culture is like. Thus, they are good *indices* (indi-cators or signs) of our culture's attitudes and values. *Indices* is the plural form of *index*.

32. *C* Given that English society didn't encourage women to get an education, you would expect it not to care that women were uneducated. However, English society was illogical: it *decried* or expressed its disapproval of women's lack of education.

33. *D* The passage depicts Archbishop Tutu's *compassion*, his feeling for someone in need that leads him to ignore the importunate demands of the press. Choice B is incorrect: it is the distressed student assistant who feels grief or anguish, not the archbishop.

34. *E* The archbishop's prominence is his fame or *renown*.

35. *C* The author uses the term "hot spot" to indicate a geological phenomenon; she uses the term *technically*, as it is used by geologists.
Choice B is incorrect. In its informal, or colloquial, sense, a hot spot is a nightclub.

36. *B* In explaining hot spots, the author speaks confidently of "great shifting plates that make up Earth's surface" and "the slow but relentless passage" of the plates. Thus, she clearly agrees with the assumption that the plates move, viewing it as *accurate*.

37. *D* Graham's goal is "to bring into unhackneyed movement." Thus, she rejects movement in dance that is hackneyed or *trite*.

38. *A* Graham insists that, in the dancer's body, the audience must see themselves, "something of the miracle that is a human being." In rejecting the idea of their imitating natural phenomena (trees, flowers, waves), she emphasizes that dancers must embody or *express their humanity*.

39. *C* Graham is pairing opposite qualities that are held in balance by training and technique. Thus, technique and training give freedom and its opposite, discipline; tension and its opposite, plasticity (*mobility and pliancy*).

40. *B* What do most people believe? Most people believe that spontaneity in dance or in theater *is wholly dependent on emotion at that moment*. That is what Graham refers to as the "popular belief." It is the belief that spontaneous theatrical moments *happen only because the actor is gripped by a sudden emotion*.

41. *B* Graham draws an *analogy* or comparison between the function of spontaneity in dance or theater and that of light in life.

42. *C* Waters is an experienced cook and restaurateur, an *accomplished practitioner of the culinary arts*.

You can determine the answer to this question by using the process of elimination. Waters is not a cook on the verge of opening a restaurant or simply a gifted home cook; she has run her own restaurant for years, long enough to have developed criteria for hiring employees (lines 81–84). Therefore, you can eliminate Choices A and D. She is not uninformed about traditional methods of French cooking; she served her culinary apprenticeship in France.

You can eliminate Choice B. Though she is a professional, there is nothing in the passage to suggest that she is set on outstripping her competition. You can eliminate Choice E. Only Choice C is left; it is the correct answer.

43. *A* Sometimes sharp and strong, sometimes sweet and fresh, garlic varies in quality. Waters uses the example of the garlic to show the *variability of ingredients*.

44. *E* Waters stresses that she is only making suggestions and that it is up to the reader to "determine the correct balance and composition" of the meal. Thus, she is trying to *allow scope* (room) *for the reader's own culinary initiative*.

45. *E* Waters states firmly that "a person who responds to the cooking processes and the mound of fresh ingredients with a genuine glow of delight is likely to be, or become, a very good cook indeed." Thus, to be a good cook, one who will produce superior results, one must have *a love of one's medium* (material for artistic expression; in this case, food).

46. *C* Waters is looking for employees who will take great personal satisfaction in what they are doing, people who enjoy the *culinary processes*.

47. *B* Waters and Graham are expressing their belief as artists in spontaneity, in flexibility, in energy, in joy. They are *presenting their artistic creeds*.

48. *D* Graham and Waters resemble one another in their marked enthusiasm and love for their work. Both clearly *are passionately involved with their art*.

Section 4 Mathematics

MULTIPLE-CHOICE QUESTIONS

For many problems, the explanation provides a reference to one or more **KEY FACTS** from Chapter 9. These are the mathematical facts that you need to solve that problem. If a solution refers to **KEY FACT J2**, for example, the solution depends on the second **KEY FACT** discussed in Section J of Chapter 9.

For some problems, an alternative solution, indicated by two asterisks (**), follows the first solution. When this occurs, usually one of the solutions is the direct mathematical one and the other is based on one of the tactics discussed in Chapters 8 and 9.

21. *C* Solve the given equation using the six-step method discussed in Section 9-G.
$$7d + 5 = 5d + 7 \Rightarrow$$
$$2d + 5 = 7 \Rightarrow 2d = 2 \Rightarrow d = 1.$$

**Use TACTIC 8-1. Test the answer choices, starting with C.

22. *B* The unmarked angle opposite the 60° angle also measures 60° (**KEY FACT I4**), and the sum of the measures of all six angles in the diagram is 360° (**KEY FACT I3**). Then,
$$360 = a + b + c + 20 + 60 + 60 =$$
$$a + b + c + 140.$$

Subtracting 140 from each side, we get $a + b + c = 220$.

23. *D* Since $-5 + 5 = 0$, and 0 is an even integer, $-5 \div\!\!\!\cdot 5 = -5$.

24. *D* Since $10 \div\!\!\!\cdot 2 = 10$ (10 + 2 is even), I is true; and since $1 \div\!\!\!\cdot 10 = 10$ (1 + 10 is odd), II is true.

$$a \div\!\!\!\cdot b = b \div\!\!\!\cdot a \Rightarrow a = b$$

which by the given information is impossible. III is false. Statements I and II only are true.

25. *D* $5\sqrt{x} + 1 = 46 \Rightarrow 5\sqrt{x} = 45 \Rightarrow \sqrt{x} = 9 \Rightarrow x = 81$.

26. *E* If $y = 1$, then x could be 1 or -1; so neither Choice A nor Choice B is correct. If $x = 1$ and $y = -1$, Choice C is wrong, and if $y = 1$ and $x = -1$, Choice D is wrong. Only Choice E is correct.

$$x^2 = y^2 \Rightarrow x^2 - y^2 = 0 \Rightarrow (x - y)(x + y) = 0 \Rightarrow$$
$$x - y = 0 \text{ or } x + y = 0 \Rightarrow$$
$$x = y \text{ or } x = -y \Rightarrow |x| = |y|$$

27. *D* If Sarah were really unlucky, what could go wrong in her attempt to get one marble of each color? Well, her first 11 picks *might* yield 6 blue marbles and 5 white ones. But then the twelfth marble would be red, and she would have at least one of each color. The answer is 12.

28. *D* Draw in segment $EXY \perp AB$. Then $XY = 10$ since it is the same length as a side of the square. EX is the height of $\triangle ECD$, whose base is 10 and whose area is 10. So $10 = \frac{1}{2}(10)(EX) \Rightarrow EX = 2 \Rightarrow EY = 12$.

Since $\triangle ECD$ is isosceles, $DX = 5$; so $AY = 5$. Finally, recognize $\triangle AYE$ as a 5-12-13 right triangle, or use the Pythagorean theorem to find the hypotenuse, AE, of the triangle:

$$(AE)^2 = 5^2 + 12^2 = 25 + 144 = 169,$$

so $AE = 13$.

GRID-IN QUESTIONS

29. *(.01)* First, add w to each side of the given equation, and then subtract 4.99: $5 - w = 4.99 \Rightarrow 5 = 4.99 + w \Rightarrow w = .01$.

30. *(90)* In a ratio problem write the letter x after each number (**TACTIC D-1**). Then $a = 5x$, $b = 7x$, and $c = 12x$; and since, by **KEY FACT J1**, the sum of the measures of the angles of a triangle is 180°:

$$5x + 7x + 12x = 180 \Rightarrow 24x = 180 \Rightarrow$$
$$x = 7.5. \text{ So } c = 12x = 12(7.5) = 90.$$

31. *(11)* $xy = 30$ and $x = -6 \Rightarrow -6y = 30 \Rightarrow y = -5$; so $x^2 - y^2 = 36 - 25 = 11$.

32. *(0)* If $a \neq b$ and $ax = bx$, then x must be 0. Therefore,

$$25\% \text{ of } x = 35\% \text{ of } x \Rightarrow$$
$$x = 0 \Rightarrow 45\% \text{ of } x = 0.$$

33. *(40)* Consider the diagram below in which several additional angles have been labeled and repeatedly use **KEY FACTS I2, I4,** and **J1**.

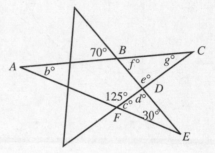

Since $125 + c = 180$, then $c = 55$; so in $\triangle DEF$, $55 + 30 + d = 180 \Rightarrow d = 95$. Also, since vertical angles are equal, $e = 95$ and $f = 70$. Then in $\triangle BCD$,

$$95 + 70 + y = 180 \Rightarrow g = 15.$$

Finally, in $\triangle CAF$,

$$15 + 125 + b = 180 \Rightarrow b = 40.$$

34. *(6)* Write out the first few terms being careful to follow the directions. The first term is 2. The second term is 1 more than 2 times the first term: $2(2) + 1 = 5$. The third term is 1 more than 2 times the second term: $2(5) + 1 = 11$. Continuing in this way, you find that the terms less than 100 are: 2, 5, 11, 23, 47, 95. There are 6 of them.

35. *(126)* In the tens column, $2 + 4 + 6 = 12$; so if nothing was carried from the units column, $A = 1$ and $B = 2$. In fact, this works, because if $B = 2$, the units column adds up to 6, and $ABC = 126$.

36. $\left(\frac{3}{5} \text{ or } .6\right)$ A quick sketch can eliminate a few choices and guard against carelessness. From the diagram, we see that the slope of l is positive (**KEY FACT N5**), and so we can eliminate choices A and B. By **KEY FACT N4**, the slope of $\overline{OP}$ is $\frac{-4-1}{4-1} = \frac{-5}{3}$. Since $\overline{OP} \perp l$, by **KEY FACT N6**, the slope of l is the negative reciprocal of $-\frac{5}{3}$ or $\frac{3}{5}$.

37. (9.5) By **KEY FACT M2**, the surface area of a rectangular box is given by $A = 2(\ell w + wh + \ell h)$. Replacing w by 5, ℓ by 7, and A by 298, we get
$$298 = 2(35 + 5h + 7h) = 70 + 24h.$$
Therefore, $24h = 228$ and $h = 9.5$.

38. $\left(\frac{9}{10} \text{ or } .9\right)$ If there are x seats on each bus, then the group is using $\frac{4}{5}(3x) = \frac{12}{5}x$ seats. After $\frac{1}{4}$ of the passengers get off, $\frac{3}{4}$ of them, or $\frac{3}{1\,4}\left(\frac{12}{5}^{3}x\right) = \frac{9}{5}x$ remain. The fraction of the $2x$ seats now being used on the two buses is
$$\frac{\frac{9}{5}x}{2x} = \frac{\frac{9}{5}}{2} = \frac{9}{10}.$$

**To avoid working with x, assume there are 20 seats on each bus. At the beginning, the group is using 48 of the 60 seats on the three buses $\left[\frac{4}{5}(60) = 48\right]$. When 12 people left $\left[\frac{1}{4}(48) = 12\right]$, the 36 remaining people used $\frac{36}{40} = \frac{9}{10}$ of the 40 seats on two buses.

Section 5 Writing Skills

1. *B* Choice B corrects the misuse of the subjunctive.

2. *D* Choice D corrects the error in the case of the pronoun. Choice E corrects the error in case but introduces an error in tense.

3. *A* The clause is correct.

4. *A* Sentence is correct.

5. *C* Error in modification and word order. Choice C corrects the dangling participle.

6. *A* Sentence is correct.

7. *B* This corrects the unnecessary switch in the pronouns, *anyone–you*.

8. *E* Error in parallelism. *Relax* matches *make*, *wash*, and *do*.

9. *A* Sentence is correct.

10. *D* Comma splice. The run-on sentence is corrected by the use of a semicolon.

11. *D* Error in following conventions. Choice D corrects the double negative *hadn't hardly* and the misuse of *those* with *kind*.

12. *B* Error in modification and word order. Choice B corrects the dangling participle and the misuse of *stole* for *stolen*.

13. *B* Comma splice. In Choice B, the run-on sentence is corrected by the use of a semicolon, and the omission of the past participle *been* is also corrected.

14. *C* Errors in following conventions. Choice C expresses the author's meaning directly and concisely. All other choices are either indirect or ungrammatical.

15. *D* Incorrect conjunction. The conjunction *furthermore* fails to link the two clauses logically. Choice D corrects the error by eliminating the incorrect conjunction and substituting a colon to separate the two main clauses. (A colon may separate two main clauses when the second explains the first. In Choice D, the second clause ["they . . . subside"] explains in what way young children's fevers are erratic.)

16. *D* Error in degree of comparison. Because there are many characters in *A Christmas Carol,* you must describe Tiny Tim as the *most* beloved of them all.

17. *C* Wordiness. Choice C eliminates the unnecessary words.

18. *A* Sentence is correct.

19. *E* Error in sequence of tenses. Because Hemingway worked as a correspondent at a definite time in the past (during the Spanish Civil War), the verb should be in the past tense ("wrote"), not the present perfect tense ("has written").

20. *A* Sentence is correct.

21. *B* Error in diction. Change *had ought* to *ought*.

22. *D* Adjective and adverb confusion. Change *bad* to *badly*.

23. *B* Error in tense. Change *has sang* to *has sung*.

24. *B* Error in diction. Change *affect* to *effect*.

25. *E* Sentence is correct.

26. *B* Error in verb. Change *had drank* to *had drunk*.

27. *A* Error in diction. Since *without hardly* is a double negative, change *without hardly* to either *without* or *with hardly*.

28. *C* Error in comparison of modifiers. Incorrect use of the superlative. Change *most* to *more*.

29. *B* Error in parallelism. Change *being intelligent* to *intelligence*.

30. *A* Error in diction. Change *or* to *nor*.

31. *E* Sentence is correct.

32. *A* Error in diction. Change *principal* to *principle*.

33. *D* Double negative. Do not combine *hardly* with *not*. Either say the alchemist's method was not scientific, or say that it was hardly scientific.

34. *C* Error in agreement. Change *them* to *him* or *her*.

35. *B* Choice A is awkwardly constructed. The phrase *for the cruelty of keeping animals* is cumbersome. Moreover, the sentence suggests that cruelty to animals can be justified—the opposite of what the writer intended to say.
Choice B states the idea clearly and economically. It is the best answer.
Choice C is wordy and awkwardly expressed.
Choice D is wordy and awkwardly expressed.
Choice E, which lacks a main verb, is a sentence fragment.

36. *C* Choice A is a sentence fragment. It lacks a main verb.

Choice B contradicts the idea that zoos can be educational.
Choice C accurately develops the idea introduced in sentence 3 that zoos can be educational. It is the best answer.
Choice D is irrelevant to the idea in sentence 3.
Choice E is written with a hostile and inappropriate tone.

37. *C* Choice A is not the best answer because most readers probably know that zoos house animals in cages. Moreover, highly charged language is not ordinarily used merely to pass along information.
Choice B is unrelated to the words in question.
Choice C is the best answer. The choice of words is meant to shock and disturb the reader.
Choice D suggests that the author is trying to be objective, but the words in question are hardly objective.
Choice E describes the purpose of the entire essay but not the particular words in question.

38. *A* Choice A introduces the main idea of the paragraph. It is the best answer.
Choice B raises an issue not mentioned in the remainder of the paragraph. Thereofre, it is not a good topic sentence of the paragraph.
Choice C contains an idea not discussed in the paragraph. The paragraph focuses on how animals behave in captivity, not on living conditions at the zoo.
Choice D contains a dangling modifier. The phrase *Living in the zoo*s should modify *animals* instead of *conditions*.
Choice E contains a frivolous cliché that is not consistent with the tone of the essay.

39. *B* Choice A is grammatically correct, but it reverses the cause-effect relationship stated by the original sentences.
Choice B accurately and economically conveys the ideas of the original sentences. It is the best answer.
Choice C is a sentence fragment. It lacks a main verb. The -ing forms of verbs (e.g., *growing, placing, being*) may not be used as the main verb without a helping verb, as in *was growing, is placing*, and so on.
Choice D is grammatically correct but stylistically awkward mainly because the subject *They* is too far removed from the verb *would . . . survive*.
Choice E is virtually meaningless because the cause-effect relationship has been reversed.

PART THREE

Critical Reading

Verbal Reasoning

► **CHAPTER 4** : **The Sentence Completion Question**

► **CHAPTER 5** : **Improving Critical Reading Comprehension**

► **CHAPTER 6** : **Building Your Vocabulary**

► CHAPTER 4
The Sentence Completion Question

The sentence completion questions ask you to choose the best way to complete a sentence from which one or two words have been omitted. These questions test a combination of reading comprehension skills and vocabulary. You must be able to recognize the logic, style, and tone of the sentence so that you can choose the answer that makes sense in this context. You must also be able to recognize the way words are normally used. At some time in your schooling, you have probably had a vocabulary assignment in which you were asked to define a word and use it in a sentence of your own. In this part of the PSAT, you have to use the words in sentences that are given to you. Once you understand the implications of a sentence, you should be able to choose the answer that will make the sentence clear, logical, and stylistically consistent.

The sentences cover a wide variety of topics of the sort you have probably encountered in your general reading. However, this is not a test of your general knowledge. You may feel more comfortable if you are familiar with the topic the sentence is discussing, but you should be able to handle any of the sentences using your understanding of the English language.

TIPS FOR HANDLING SENTENCE COMPLETION QUESTIONS

1. Before you look at the answer choices, read the sentence and think of words you know that might make sense in the context. You may not come up with the exact word, but you *may* come up with a synonym.

2. Don't be hasty in picking an answer. Test each answer choice, substituting it for the missing word. That way you can satisfy yourself that you have selected the answer that best fits.

3. In double-blank sentences, eliminate answer pairs by testing their first words. Read through the entire sentence. Then insert the first word of each answer pair in the first blank of the sentence. Ask yourself whether this particular word makes sense in this blank. If the initial word of an answer pair makes no sense in the sentence, you can eliminate that answer pair.

4. If you're having vocabulary trouble, look for familiar parts—prefixes, suffixes, and roots—in unfamiliar words.

5. Watch out for negative words and words telling how long something lasts. Only a small change makes these two sentences very different in meaning:

    They were not lovers.
    They were not often lovers.

6. Look for words or phrases that indicate a contrast between one idea and another—words like *although, however, despite,* or *but.* In such cases an antonym or near-antonym for another word in the sentence may provide the correct answer.

7. Look for words or phrases that indicate similarities—words like *in the same way, in addition,* and *also.* In such cases, a synonym or near-synonym for another word in the sentence may provide the correct answer.

8. Look for words or phrases that indicate that one thing causes another—words like *because, since, therefore,* or *thus.*

EXAMPLE 1

See how the first tip works in dealing with the following sentence:

The psychologist set up the experiment to test the rat's ----; he wished to see how well the rat adjusted to the changing conditions it had to face.

Even before you look at the answer choices, you can figure out what the answer *should* be.

Look at the sentence. A psychologist is trying to test some particular quality or characteristic of a rat. What quality? How do you get the answer?

Look at the second part of the sentence, the part following the semicolon (the second clause, in technical terms). This clause defines or clarifies what the psychologist is trying to test. He is trying to see how well the rat *adjusts*. What words does this suggest to you? *Flexibility* possibly, or *adaptability* comes to mind. Either of these words could logically complete the sentence's thought.

Here are the five answer choices given:

(A) reflexes   (B) communicability   (C) stamina   (D) sociability   (E) adaptability

The best answer clearly is *adaptability,* Choice E.

EXAMPLE 2

When you're racing the clock, you feel like marking down the first correct-sounding answer you come across. *Don't.* You may be going too fast.

Because the enemy had a reputation for engaging in sneak attacks, we were ---- on the alert.

(A) frequently   (B) furtively   (C) evidently   (D) constantly   (E) occasionally

A hasty reader might be content with Choice A, *frequently,* but *frequently* is not the best fit. The best answer is Choice D, *constantly,* because "frequent" periods of alertness would not be enough to provide the necessary protection against sneak attacks that could occur at any time. "Constant" vigilance is called for: the troops would have to be always on the alert.

EXAMPLE 3

Dealing with double-blank sentences can be tricky. It helps to test the first word of each answer pair when you're narrowing things down.

The opossum is ---- venom of snakes in the rattlesnake subfamily and thus views the reptiles not as ---- enemies but as a food source.

(A) vulnerable to . . natural   (B) indicative of . . mortal
(C) impervious to . . lethal   (D) sensitive to . . deadly
(E) defenseless against . . potential

Look at the first word of each answer pair. Do any of these words make no sense in the context? The sentence is talking about the way opossums react to rattlesnake poison. What words seem possible? Opossums could be *vulnerable* to this poison, capable of being hurt by it. They could be *sensitive* to it, excessively affected by it. They could be *defenseless* against it, wholly unable to protect themselves from the poison. They could even be *impervious* to it, unaffected by it. But *indicative* of it? The word makes no sense. You can eliminate Choice B.

Now examine the second half of the sentence. Opossums look on rattlesnakes as a food source; they eat rattlers. What makes it possible for them to do so? They can do so *because* they're *impervious* to the poison (that is, unharmed by it). That's the reason they can treat the rattlesnake as a potential source of food and not as a *lethal* or deadly enemy. The correct answer is Choice C.

Note the cause-and-effect signal *thus*. The nature of the opossum's response to the venom explains why it can look on a dangerous snake as an easy prey.

EXAMPLE 4

After a tragedy, many people claim to have had a ---- of disaster.

(A) taste (B) dislike (C) presentiment (D) context (E) verdict

Use your knowledge of word parts to enable you to deal with unfamiliar words in sentence completion questions.

Take the unfamiliar word *presentiment*. Break it down into parts. A sentiment is *a feeling* (the root *sens* means *feel*). *Pre-* means *before*. A *presentiment* is something *you feel before* it happens, a foreboding. Your best answer is Choice C.

EXAMPLE 5

Watch out for *not:* it's easy to overlook, but it's a key word.

Madison was not ---- person and thus made few public addresses; but those he made were memorable, filled with noble phrases.

(A) a reticent (B) a stately (C) an inspiring (D) an introspective
(E) a communicative

What would happen if you overlooked *not* in this question? Probably you'd wind up choosing Choice A: Madison was a *reticent* (quiet; reserved) man. *For this reason* he made few public addresses.

Unfortunately, you'd have gotten things backward. The sentence isn't telling you what Madison was like. It's telling you what he was not like. And he was not a *communicative* person; he didn't express himself freely. However, when he did get around to speaking in public, he had valuable things to say.

EXAMPLE 6

We expected him to be jubilant over his victory, but he was ---- instead.

(A) triumphant (B) adult (C) morose (D) talkative (E) culpable

Watch for words that indicate contrast: *although, however, despite,* or *but.*

But suggests that the winner's expected reaction contrasts with his actual one. Instead of being *jubilant* (extremely joyful), he is sad. The correct answer is Choice C, *morose.*

EXAMPLE 7

The simplest animals are those whose bodies are least complex in structure and that do the things done by all animals, such as eating, breathing, moving, and feeling, in the most ---- way.

(A) haphazard (B) bizarre (C) advantageous (D) primitive (E) unique

The transition word *and* signals you that the writer intends to develop the concept of simplicity introduced in the sentence. You should know from your knowledge of biology that *primitive* life forms were simple in structure and that the more complex forms evolved later. Choice C may seem possible. However, to secure the most *advantageous* way of conducting the activities of life, the animal would have to become specialized and complex. Thus, Choice D (*primitive*) is best, because it is the only choice that develops the idea of simplicity.

EXAMPLE 8

Because his delivery was ----, the effect of his speech on the voters was nonexistent.

(A) halting (B) plausible (C) moving (D) respectable (E) audible

Watch for words that show a cause-and-effect relationship: *because, since, therefore,* or *thus.*

What sort of delivery would cause a speech to have no effect? Obviously, you would not expect a moving or eloquent delivery to have such a sorry result. A *halting* or stumbling speech, however, would normally have little or no effect. Thus, Choice A is best.

The two exercises that follow will give you an indication of your ability to handle these sentence completion questions. Scoring may be interpreted as follows:

43 TO **50**—EXCELLENT
35 TO **43**—SUPERIOR
27 TO **34**—SATISFACTORY
21 TO **26**—AVERAGE
0 TO **20**—UNSATISFACTORY

SENTENCE COMPLETION EXERCISES

EXERCISE A

Each of the following sentences contains one or two blanks; these blanks indicate that a word or set of words has been left out. Below the sentence are five words or phrases, lettered A through E. Select the word or set of words that best completes the sentence.

1. Although the play was not praised by the critics, it did not ---- thanks to favorable word-of-mouth comments.

   (A) succeed (B) translate (C) function
   (D) close (E) continue

2. Perhaps because something in us instinctively distrusts such displays of natural fluency, some readers approach John Updike's fiction with ----.

   (A) indifference (B) suspicion (C) veneration
   (D) recklessness (E) bewilderment

3. We lost confidence in him because he never ---- the grandiose promises he had made.

   (A) forgot about (B) reneged on (C) tired of
   (D) delivered on (E) retreated from

4. Because the hawk is ---- bird, farmers try to keep it away from their chickens.

   (A) a migratory (B) an ugly (C) a predatory
   (D) a reclusive (E) a huge

5. We were amazed that a man who had been heretofore the most ---- of public speakers could, in a single speech, electrify an audience and bring them cheering to their feet.

   (A) enthralling (B) accomplished
   (C) pedestrian (D) auspicious (E) masterful

6. If you are trying to make a strong impression on your audience, you cannot do so by being understated, tentative, or ----.

   (A) hyperbolic (B) restrained
   (C) argumentative (D) authoritative
   (E) passionate

7. Despite the mixture's ---- nature, we found that by lowering its temperature in the laboratory we could dramatically reduce its tendency to vaporize.

   (A) resilient (B) volatile (C) homogeneous
   (D) insipid (E) acerbic

8. No other artist rewards the viewer with more sheer pleasure than Miró: he is one of those blessed artists who combine profundity and ----.

   (A) education (B) wisdom (C) faith
   (D) fun (E) depth

9. Some Central Intelligence Agency officers have ---- their previous statements denying any involvement on their part with the rebel network and are now revising their earlier testimony.

   (A) justified (B) recanted (C) repeated
   (D) protracted (E) heeded

10. New concerns about growing religious tension in northern India were ---- this week after at least fifty people were killed and hundreds were injured or arrested in rioting between Hindus and Moslems.

(A) lessened   (B) invalidated   (C) restrained
(D) dispersed   (E) fueled

11. In a happy, somewhat boisterous celebration of the origins of the United States, the major phase of the Constitution's Bicentennial got off to ---- start on Friday.

(A) a slow   (B) a rousing   (C) a reluctant
(D) an indifferent   (E) a quiet

12. In a revolutionary development in technology, several manufacturers now make biodegradable forms of plastic: some plastic six-pack rings, for example, gradually ---- when exposed to sunlight.

(A) harden   (B) stagnate   (C) inflate
(D) propagate   (E) decompose

13. To alleviate the problem of contaminated chicken, the study panel recommends that the federal government shift its inspection emphasis from cursory bird-by-bird visual checks to a more ---- random sampling for bacterial and chemical contamination.

(A) rigorous   (B) perfunctory   (C) symbolic
(D) discreet   (E) dubious

14. To the dismay of the student body, the class president was ---- berated by the principal at a school assembly.

(A) ignominiously   (B) privately
(C) magnanimously   (D) fortuitously
(E) inconspicuously

15. Although Barbara Tuchman never earned a graduate degree, she nonetheless ---- a scholarly career as a historian noted for her vivid style and ---- erudition.

(A) interrupted . . deficient
(B) relinquished . . immense
(C) abandoned . . capricious
(D) pursued . . prodigious
(E) followed . . scanty

16. When Frazer's editors at Macmillan tried to ---- his endless augmentations, he insisted on a type size so small and a page so packed as to approach illegibility; and if that proved ----, thinner paper.

(A) protract . . unwarranted
(B) expurgate . . satisfactory
(C) reprimand . . irrelevant
(D) restrict . . insufficient
(E) revise . . idiosyncratic

17. Baldwin's brilliant *The Fire Next Time* is both so eloquent in its passion and so searching in its ---- that it is bound to ---- any reader.

(A) bitterness . . embarrass
(B) romanticism . . appall
(C) candor . . unsettle
(D) indifference . . disappoint
(E) conception . . bore

18. Unlike other examples of ---- verse, Milton's *Lycidas* does more than merely mourn for the death of Edward King; it also denounces corruption in the church in which King was ordained.

(A) satiric   (B) elegiac   (C) free
(D) humorous   (E) didactic

19. We now know that what constitutes practically all of matter is empty space: relatively enormous ---- in which revolve infinitesimal particles so small that they have never been seen or photographed.

(A) crescendos   (B) enigmas
(C) conglomerates   (D) abstractions   (E) voids

20. The officers threatened to take ---- if the lives of their men were ---- by the conquered natives.

(A) liberties . . irritated
(B) measures . . enhanced
(C) pains . . destroyed
(D) reprisals . . endangered
(E) affront . . enervated

21. Despite his ---- appearance, he was chosen by his employer for a job that required neatness and polish.

(A) unkempt   (B) impressive
(C) prepossessing   (D) aloof   (E) tardy

22. The ---- remarks of the speaker annoyed the audience because they were lengthy as well as meaningless.

(A) lugubrious   (B) sarcastic   (C) pithy
(D) inane   (E) pungent

23. He was so ---- in meeting the payments on his car that the finance company threatened to seize the automobile.

(A) dilatory   (B) mercenary   (C) solvent
(D) diligent   (E) compulsive

24. The earthquake created some damage, but the tidal wave that followed was more devastating because it ---- many villages.

(A) bypassed   (B) absorbed   (C) desiccated
(D) congested   (E) inundated

25. The insurance company rejected his application for accident insurance because his ---- occupation made him a poor risk.

   (A) desultory (B) haphazard (C) esoteric
   (D) hazardous (E) peripatetic

26. Since we had been promised a definite answer to our proposal, we were ---- by his ---- reply.

   (A) pleased . . equivocal
   (B) vexed . . negative
   (C) annoyed . . noncommital
   (D) delighted . . dilatory
   (E) baffled . . decided

27. Because she had a reputation for ---- we were surprised and pleased when she greeted us so ----.

   (A) insolence . . informally
   (B) insouciance . . cordially
   (C) graciousness . . amiably
   (D) arrogance . . disdainfully
   (E) querulousness . . affably

28. The child was so spoiled by her indulgent parents that she pouted and became ---- when she did not receive all of their attention.

   (A) discreet (B) suspicious (C) elated
   (D) sullen (E) tranquil

29. Just as disloyalty is the mark of the renegade, ---- is the mark of the ----.

   (A) timorousness . . hero
   (B) temerity . . coward
   (C) avarice . . philanthropist
   (D) cowardice . . craven
   (E) vanity . . flatterer

30. He became quite overbearing and domineering once he had become accustomed to the ---- shown to soldiers by the natives; he enjoyed his new sense of power and self-importance.

   (A) disrespect (B) apathy (C) deference
   (D) culpability (E) enmity

31. The ---- of time had left the castle ----; it towered above the village, looking much as it must have done in Richard the Lion-Hearted's time.

   (A) repairs . . destroyed
   (B) remoteness . . alone
   (C) lack . . defended
   (D) status . . lonely
   (E) ravages . . untouched

32. One of the most ---- educators in New York's history, Dr. Shalala ignited a controversy in 1984 by calling the city public schools a "rotten barrel" in need of ---- reform.

   (A) disputatious . . little
   (B) outspoken . . systemic
   (C) caustic . . partial
   (D) indifferent . . pretentious
   (E) sycophantic . . superficial

33. The reasoning in this editorial is so ---- that we cannot see how anyone can be deceived by it.

   (A) coherent (B) astute (C) cogent
   (D) specious (E) dispassionate

34. The ---- of evidence was on the side of the plaintiff since all but one witness testifed that his story was correct.

   (A) paucity (B) propensity (C) accuracy
   (D) brunt (E) preponderance

35. Because Inspector Morse could not contain his scorn for the police commissioner, he was imprudent enough to make ---- remarks about his superior officer.

   (A) ambiguous (B) dispassionate
   (C) unfathomable (D) interminable
   (E) scathing

36. Modern architecture has discarded ---- trimming on buildings and has concentrated on an almost Greek simplicity of line.

   (A) flamboyant (B) austere
   (C) inconspicuous (D) aesthetic
   (E) derivative

37. If you are seeking ---- that will resolve all our ailments, you are undertaking an impossible task.

   (A) a precedent (B) a panacea
   (C) an abstraction (D) a direction
   (E) a contrivance

38. I have no ---- motive in offering this advice; I seek no personal advantage or honor.

   (A) nominal (B) altruistic (C) incongruous
   (D) disinterested (E) ulterior

39. This park has been preserved in all its ---- wildness so that visitors in future years may see how people lived during the eighteenth century.

   (A) hedonistic (B) prospective (C) esoteric
   (D) untrammeled (E) pristine

40. Though she was theoretically a friend of labor, her voting record in Congress ---- that impression.

   (A) implied (B) created (C) confirmed
   (D) belied (E) maintained

41. The orator was so ---- that the audience became ----.

    (A) soporific .. drowsy
    (B) inaudible .. elated
    (C) pompous .. bombastic
    (D) dramatic .. affable
    (E) convincing .. moribund

42. If you carry this ---- attitude to the conference, you will ---- any supporters you may have at this moment.

    (A) belligerent .. delight
    (B) truculent.. alienate
    (C) conciliatory .. defer
    (D) supercilious .. attract
    (E) flippant .. consolidate

43. The ---- pittance the widow receives from the government cannot keep her from poverty.

    (A) magnanimous (B) indulgent
    (C) meticulous (D) munificent
    (E) scanty

44. Harriman, Kennan, and Acheson were part of that inner ---- of the American diplomatic establishment whose distinguished legacy ---- U.S. foreign policy to this day.

    (A) circle . . . grieves
    (B) sanctum . . . absorbs
    (C) core . . . dominates
    (D) life . . . biases
    (E) coterie . . . exacerbates

45. The young man was quickly promoted when his employers saw how ---- he was.

    (A) indigent (B) indifferent (C) assiduous
    (D) lethargic (E) cursory

46. Because it arrives so early in the season, before many other birds, the robin has been called the ---- of spring.

    (A) hostage (B) autocrat (C) compass
    (D) newcomer (E) harbinger

47. Shy and hypochondriacal, Madison was uncomfortable at public gatherings; his character made him a most ---- lawmaker and practicing politician.

    (A) conscientious (B) unlikely (C) fervent
    (D) gregarious (E) effective

48. The tapeworm is an example of ---- organism, one that lives within or on another creature, deriving some or all of its nutriment from its host.

    (A) a hospitable (B) an exemplary
    (C) a parasitic (D) an autonomous
    (E) a protozoan

49. In place of the more general debate about abstract principles of government that most delegates probably expected, the Constitutional Convention put ---- proposals on the table.

    (A) theoretical (B) vague (C) concrete
    (D) tentative (E) redundant

50. Overindulgence ---- character as well as physical stamina.

    (A) strengthens (B) stimulates (C) debilitates
    (D) maintains (E) provides

EXERCISE B

    Each of the following sentences contains one or two blanks; these blanks indicate that a word or set of words has been left out. Below the sentence are five words or phrases, lettered A through E. Select the word or set of words that best completes the sentence.

51. The scientist maintains that any hypothesis must explain what has already been discovered and must be constantly ---- by future findings.

    (A) confirmed (B) invalidated
    (C) disregarded (D) equaled
    (E) reversed

52. Being cynical, he was reluctant to ---- the ---- of any kind act until he had ruled out all possible secret, uncharitable motives.

    (A) question .. benevolence
    (B) acknowledge .. wisdom
    (C) credit .. unselfishness
    (D) endure .. loss
    (E) witness .. outcome

53. In view of the interrelationships among a number of the African-American leaders treated in this anthology, there is inevitably a certain amount of ---- among some of the essays presented here.

(A) overlapping   (B) inaccuracy
(C) pomposity   (D) exaggeration
(E) objectivity

54. Hellman was not an ---- woman and thus was hard to get to know; nevertheless, many made the attempt, attracted by her wit and celebrity.

(A) enigmatic   (B) eccentric   (C) astute
(D) extroverted   (E) eminent

55. Most Antarctic animals ---- depend on the tiny shrimplike krill, either feeding on them directly, like the humpback whale, or consuming species that feed on them.

(A) seldom   (B) ultimately   (C) preferably
(D) immediately   (E) marginally

56. Truculent in defending their rights of sovereignty under the Articles of Confederation, the newly formed states ---- constantly.

(A) apologized   (B) digressed   (C) conferred
(D) acquiesced   (E) squabbled

57. If the *Titanic* had hit the iceberg head on, its watertight compartments might have saved it from ----, but it swerved to avoid the iceberg, and in the collision so many compartments were opened to the sea that disaster was ----.

(A) foundering. . inevitable
(B) sinking . . escaped
(C) damage . . limited
(D) buoyancy . . unavoidable
(E) collapse . . averted

58. Written in an amiable style, the book provides a comprehensive overview of European wines that should prove inviting to both the virtual ---- and the experienced connoisseur.

(A) prodigal   (B) novice   (C) zealot
(D) miser   (E) glutton

59. The sugar dissolved in water ----; finally all that remained was an almost ---- residue on the bottom of the glass.

(A) quickly . . lumpy
(B) immediately . . fragrant
(C) gradually . . imperceptible
(D) subsequently . . glassy
(E) spectacularly . . opaque

60. Traffic speed limits are set at a level that achieves some balance between the danger of ---- speed and the desire of most people to travel as quickly as possible.

(A) marginal   (B) normal   (C) prudent
(D) inadvertent   (E) excessive

61. Although the economy suffers downturns, it also has strong ---- and self-correcting tendencies.

(A) unstable
(B) recidivist
(C) inauspicious
(D) recuperative
(E) self-destructive

62. Since Cyrano de Bergerac did not wish to be under an obligation to any man, he refused to be a ---- of Cardinal Richelieu.

(A) skeptic   (B) mentor   (C) protegé
(D) benefactor   (E) predecessor

63. The members of the religious sect ostracized the ---- who had abandoned their faith.

(A) coward   (B) suppliant   (C) litigant
(D) recreant   (E) proselyte

64. I am not attracted by the ---- life of the ----, always wandering through the countryside, begging for charity.

(A) proud . . almsgiver
(B) noble . . philanthropist
(C) affluent. . mendicant
(D) natural . . philosopher
(E) peripatetic . . vagabond

65. They fired upon the enemy from behind trees, walls, and any other ---- point they could find.

(A) conspicuous   (B) definitive   (C) vantage
(D) exposed   (E) indefensible

66. We need more men and women of culture and enlightenment; we have too many ---- among us.

(A) visionaries   (B) students   (C) philistines
(D) pragmatists   (E) philosophers

67. It is foolish to vent your spleen on ---- object; still, you make ---- enemies that way.

(A) an inanimate . . fewer
(B) an immobile . . bitter
(C) an interesting . . curious
(D) an insipid . . dull
(E) a humane . . more

68. After the Japanese attack on Pearl Harbor on December 7, 1941, Japanese-Americans were ---- of being spies for Japan, although there was no ---- to back up this viewpoint.

(A) acquitted . . buttress
(B) tired . . witness
(C) reminded . . reason
(D) suspected . . evidence
(E) exonerated . . money

69. More than one friendly whale has nudged a boat with such ---- that passengers have been knocked overboard.

(A) enthusiasm   (B) lethargy   (C) hostility
(D) serenity   (E) animosity

70. Chaotic in conception but not in ----, Kelly's canvases are as neat as the proverbial pin.

(A) conceit   (B) theory   (C) execution
(D) origin   (E) intent

71. After having worked in the soup kitchen feeding the hungry, the volunteer began to see her own good fortune as ---- and her difference from the ---- as chance rather than destiny.

(A) an omen . . homeless
(B) a fluke . . impoverished
(C) a threat . . destitute
(D) a reward . . indigent
(E) a lie . . affluent

72. Some students are ---- and want to take only the courses for which they see immediate value.

(A) theoretical   (B) impartial   (C) pragmatic
(D) idealistic   (E) opinionated

73. Unlike the Shakespearean plays that lit up the English stage, the "closet dramas" of the nineteenth century were meant to be ---- rather than ----.

(A) seen . . acted   (B) read . . staged
(C) quiet . . raucous   (D) sophisticated . . urbane
(E) produced . . performed

74. Japan's industrial success is ---- in part to its tradition of group effort and ----, as opposed to the emphasis on personal achievement that is a prominent aspect of other industrial nations.

(A) responsive . . independence
(B) related . . introspection
(C) equivalent . . solidarity
(D) subordinate . . individuality
(E) attributed . . cooperation

75. I was so bored with the verbose and redundant style of Victorian novelists that I welcomed the change to the ---- style of Hemingway.

(A) prolix   (B) consistent   (C) terse
(D) logistical   (E) florid

76. As ---- head of the organization, he attended social functions and civic meetings but had no ---- in the formulation of company policy.

(A) titular . . voice
(B) hypothetical . . vote
(C) former . . pride
(D) nominal . . competition
(E) actual . . say

77. Her listeners enjoyed her ---- wit but her victims often ---- at its satire.

(A) lugubrious . . suffered
(B) caustic . . laughed
(C) kindly . . smarted
(D) subtle . . smiled
(E) trenchant . . winced

78. It is only to the vain that all is vanity; and all is ---- only to those who have never been ---- themselves.

(A) arrogance . . proud of
(B) deception . . sincere with
(C) cowardice . . afraid for
(D) indolence . . bored by
(E) solitude . . left to

79. No act of ---- was more pronounced than his refusal of any rewards for his discovery.

(A) abeyance   (B) submission   (C) egoism
(D) denunciation   (E) abnegation

80. The evil of class and race hatred must be eliminated while it is still in an ---- state; otherwise it may grow to dangerous proportions.

(A) amorphous   (B) embryonic
(C) uncultivated   (D) overt
(E) independent

81. She is a pragmatist, as ---- to base her future on impractical dreams as she would be to build a castle on shifting sand.

(A) determined   (B) disinclined   (C) quick
(D) apt   (E) diligent

82. Aimed at curbing European attempts to seize territory in the Americas, the Monroe Doctrine was a warning to ---- foreign powers.

(A) pertinacious   (B) credulous   (C) remote
(D) overt   (E) predatory

83. Although Josephine Tey was arguably as good a mystery writer as Agatha Christie, she was clearly far less ---- than Christie, having written only six books in comparison to Christie's sixty.

(A) coherent   (B) prolific   (C) equivocal
(D) pretentious   (E) gripping

84. The systems analyst hesitated to talk to strangers about his highly specialized work, fearing it was too ---- for people uninitiated in the computer field to understand.

(A) intriguing   (B) derivative   (C) frivolous
(D) esoteric   (E) rudimentary

85. Through her work at the Center for the Family in Transition, Wallerstein has come to see divorce not as a single circumscribed event but as ---- of changing family relationships—as a process that begins during the failing marriage and extends over many years.

(A) a continuum   (B) an episode   (C) a parody
(D) a denial   (E) a curtailment

86. A code of ethics governing the behavior of physicians during epidemics did not exist until 1846, when it was ---- by the American Medical Association.

(A) rescinded   (B) promulgated
(C) presupposed   (D) depreciated
(E) implied

87. Both *China Beach* and *Tour of Duty* reflect the way dissent has become ---- in America; what were radical antiwar attitudes in the 1960s are now ---- TV attitudes.

(A) domesticated . . mainstream
(B) obsolete . . militant
(C) meaningful . . unfashionable
(D) sensationalized . . trite
(E) troublesome . . conventional

88. MacDougall's former editors remember him as a ---- man whose ---- and exhaustive reporting was worth the trouble.

(A) domineering . . wearisome
(B) congenial . . pretentious
(C) popular . . supercilious
(D) fastidious . . garbled
(E) cantankerous . . meticulous

89. Americans have always been rightfully ---- unnecessary government coercion, feeling that the government should use its powers sparingly.

(A) disarmed by   (B) chary about
(C) dependent on (D) amenable to
(E) enthusiastic about

90. Lavish in visual beauty, the film *Lawrence of Arabia* also boasts ---- of style: it knows how much can be shown in a shot, how much can be said in a few words.

(A) nonchalance   (B) economy   (C) autonomy
(D) frivolity   (E) arrogance

91. We must try to understand his momentary ----, for he has ---- more strain and anxiety than any among us.

(A) outcry . . described
(B) senility . . understood
(C) vision . . forgotten
(D) generosity . . desired
(E) aberration . . undergone

92. He is ---- opponent; you must respect and fear him at all times.

(A) a redoubtable   (B) a disingenuous
(C) a pugnacious   (D) an insignificant
(E) a craven

93. Your ---- tactics may compel me to cancel the contract as the job must be finished on time.

(A) dilatory   (B) offensive   (C) repugnant
(D) infamous   (E) confiscatory

94. The mind of a bigot is like the pupil of the eye: the more light you pour upon it, the more it will ----.

(A) blink   (B) veer   (C) stare   (D) reflect
(E) contract

95. In the North American tribes, men were the representational artists; women, on the other hand, traditionally ---- abstract, geometrical compositions.

(A) decried   (B) shunned   (C) devised
(D) impaired   (E) prefigured

96. By its very nature, printmaking was judged ---- the aims of most Impressionist painters, who believed that its technical procedures ---- spontaneity and failed to render the transient appearance of nature.

(A) antithetical to . . defeated
(B) indicative of . . enhanced
(C) conducive to . . increased
(D) warranted by . . encouraged
(E) incumbent on . . bypassed

97. Breaking with established artistic and social conventions, Dali was ---- genius whose heterodox works infuriated the traditionalists of his day.

(A) a derivative   (B) an iconoclastic
(C) an uncontroversial   (D) a venerated
(E) a trite

98. Dr. Smith cautioned that the data so far are not sufficiently ---- to warrant dogmatic assertions by either side in the debate.

(A) hypothetical   (B) tentative
(C) controversial   (D) unequivocal
(E) imponderable

99. Mr. Wilson sets out only the broad contours of a new policy agenda, leaving it to others to ---- specific initiatives.

(A) ignore   (B) mold   (C) apprehend
(D) forestall   (E) regret

100. The concept of individual freedom grew from political and moral convictions that were to ----- the closed and ---- world of feudalism into a more open and dynamic society.

(A) galvanize . . vibrant
(B) convert . . irreverent
(C) transform . . hierarchical
(D) recast . . vital
(E) merge . . unregulated

Answer Key

EXERCISE A

1. *D*	18. *B*	35. *E*
2. *B*	19. *E*	36. *A*
3. *D*	20. *D*	37. *B*
4. *C*	21. *A*	38. *E*
5. *C*	22. *D*	39. *E*
6. *B*	23. *A*	40. *D*
7. *B*	24. *E*	41. *A*
8. *D*	25. *D*	42. *B*
9. *B*	26. *C*	43. *E*
10. *E*	27. *E*	44. *C*
11. *B*	28. *D*	45. *C*
12. *E*	29. *D*	46. *E*
13. *A*	30. *C*	47. *B*
14. *A*	31. *E*	48. *C*
15. *D*	32. *B*	49. *C*
16. *D*	33. *D*	50. *C*
17. *C*	34. *E*	

EXERCISE B

51. *A*	68. *D*	85. *A*
52. *C*	69. *A*	86. *B*
53. *A*	70. *C*	87. *A*
54. *D*	71. *B*	88. *E*
55. *B*	72. *C*	89. *B*
56. *E*	73. *B*	90. *B*
57. *A*	74. *E*	91. *E*
58. *B*	75. *C*	92. *A*
59. *C*	76. *A*	93. *A*
60. *E*	77. *E*	94. *E*
61. *D*	78. *B*	95. *C*
62. *C*	79. *E*	96. *A*
63. *D*	80. *B*	97. *B*
64. *E*	81. *B*	98. *D*
65. *C*	82. *E*	99. *B*
66. *D*	83. *B*	100. *C*
67. *A*	84. *D*	

► CHAPTER 5
Improving Critical Reading Comprehension

Now more than ever, doing well on the critical reading questions can make the difference between success and failure on the PSAT. The most numerous questions in each verbal section, they are also the most time-consuming and the ones most likely to bog you down. However, you can handle them, and this chapter will show you how.

LONG-RANGE STRATEGY

Read, Read, Read!
Just do it.

There is no substitute for extensive reading as a preparation for the PSAT and for college work. The only way to build up your proficiency in reading is by reading books of all kinds. As you read, you will develop speed, stamina, and the ability to comprehend the printed page. But if you want to turn yourself into the kind of reader the colleges are looking for, you must develop the habit of reading—closely and critically—every day.

Challenge yourself. Don't limit your reading to light fiction or popular biographies. Branch out a bit. Try to develop an interest in as many fields as you can. Sample some of the serious magazines: *The New Yorker, Smithsonian, Natural History, National Geographic, Newsweek, Time, The New York Review of Books, Harper's Magazine.* In these magazines you'll find articles on literature, music, science, philosophy, history, the arts—the whole range of fields touched on by the PSAT. If you take time to acquaint yourself with the contents of these magazines, you won't find the subject matter of the reading passages on the examination so strange.

Learn your strengths and weaknesses as a reader. Are you a slow but steady reader, able to work your way through hard material if you're given enough time? Are you a superfast reader, able to skim entire pages in barely any time at all? Are you a careful reader or a careless one?

Students often ask whether it is better to read the passage first or the questions first. The answer is, it depends on the passage, and *it depends on you*. If you are a superfast reader faced with one of the 100-word short reading passages, you may want to head for the questions first. It all depends on how good your visual memory is and on how good at scanning you are. Try this approach. As you read each question, be on the lookout for key words, either in the question itself or among the answer choices. Then run your eye down the passage, looking for those key words or their synonyms. (That's called *scanning*.) When you locate your key word, read that sentence and a couple of sentences around it and see whether you can confidently answer the question on the basis of just that portion of the passage. Then check to see whether your answer is correct.

If you're not a speed demon at reading, this may not be the best approach for you. If that's the case, your best move is to skim the whole passage before you read the questions. Only you can decide which method suits you best.

TIPS FOR HANDLING CRITICAL READING QUESTIONS

1. Tackle the short passages before the long ones. Consider them a warm-up for the longer passages that follow.

2. Tackle passages with familiar subjects before passages with unfamiliar ones. It is hard to concentrate when you read about something wholly unfamiliar to you. Give yourself a break. In each section, first tackle the reading passage that interests you or deals with topics in which you are well grounded. Then move on to the other passage. You'll do better that way.

3. If you are stumped by a tough reading question, do not skip the other questions on that passage. The critical reading questions following each passage are not arranged in order of difficulty. They tend to be arranged sequentially: questions on paragraph 1 come before questions on paragraph 2. So try all the questions on the passage. That tough question may be just one question away from one that's easy for you.

4. Read as rapidly as you can with understanding, but do not force yourself. Do not worry about the time element. If you worry about not finishing the test, you will begin to take shortcuts and miss the correct answer in your haste.

5. As you read the italicized introductory material preceding the passage and tackle the passage's opening sentences, try to anticipate what the passage will be about. Ask yourself who or what the author is talking about.

6. Read purposefully. As you continue reading, try to identify what *kind* of writing this is, what *techniques* are being used, who its intended *audience* may be, and what *feeling* (if any) the author has toward his subject. Try to retain names, dates, and places for quick reference later. In particular, try to remember where in the passage the author makes *major points*. Then, when you start looking for the phrase or sentence that will justify your choice of answer, you may be able to save time by going back to that section of the passage immediately without having to reread the entire selection.

7. Read any footnotes to clarify terms that appear in the passage. Use this information to answer the questions.

8. When you tackle the questions, *go back to the passage* to verify each answer choice. Do not rely on your memory alone, and, above all, do not ignore the passage and just answer questions on the basis of other things you've read. Remember, the questions are asking you about what *this* author has to say about the subject, not about what some other author you once read said about it in another book.

9. Use the line references in the questions to be sure you've gone back to the correct spot in the passage. Many reading passages on the PSAT tend to be long. Fortunately, the lines are numbered, and the questions often refer you to specific lines in the passage by number. It takes less time to locate a line number than to spot a word or phrase. Use the line numbers to orient yourself in the text.

10. When dealing with the double passages, tackle them one at a time. The questions are organized sequentially: questions about Passage 1 come before questions about Passage 2. So, do things in order. *First* read Passage 1; then jump straight to the questions and answer all those based on Passage 1. *Next* read Passage 2; then answer all the questions based on Passage 2. *Finally*, tackle the two or three questions that refer to *both* passages. Go back to both passages as needed.

   Occasionally a couple of questions referring to *both* passages will precede the questions focusing on Passage 1. Do not let this minor hitch throw you. Use your common sense. You've just read the first passage. Skip the one or two questions on both passages, and head for those questions about Passage 1. Answer them. Then read Passage 2. Answer the questions on Passage 2. Finally, go back to those questions you skipped and answer them and any other questions at the end of the set that refer to *both* passages. Remember, however: whenever you skip from question to question or from passage to passage, *be sure you're filling in the right spaces on your answer sheet.*

11. When the questions ask about specific information in the passage, do not expect to find it stated in exactly the same words. If the question is

According to the passage, widgets are
(A) good (B) bad (C) indifferent
(D) pink (E) purple

Ⓐ Ⓑ Ⓒ Ⓓ Ⓔ

do not expect to find a sentence in the passage that says, "Widgets are bad." However, you may well find a sentence that says, "Widgets are wholly undesirable and have a strongly negative influence." That is close enough to tell you that the answer must be B.

12. When you read, watch for key words that indicate how a passage is being developed.

Equality or continuity of ideas (one idea is equal in importance to another, or continues a thought expressed earlier): *again, also, and, another, as well as, besides, first, furthermore, likewise, moreover, in addition.*

Contrast or change of topic: *although, despite, in spite of, instead of, notwithstanding, regardless, nevertheless, on the other hand, however.*

Conclusion: *accordingly, as a result, hence, in conclusion, in short, therefore, thus, consequently.*

13. Be on the lookout for *all-inclusive words*, such as *always, at all times,* and *entirely,* and for negative or limiting words, such as *only, never, no, none, except,* and *but.*

14. Watch out for words or phrases in the question that can alert you to the kind of question being asked. Just as it will help you to know the directions for the sentence completion questions on the PSAT, it will also help you to familiarize yourself with the major types of critical reading questions on the test. If you can recognize just what a given question is asking for, you'll be better able to tell which particular reading tactic to apply.

PSAT Critical Reading Questions Test Your Ability To

➤ determine the meaning of individual words from their context
➤ paraphrase or interpret specific information in the text
➤ analyze or find the central thought of a passage
➤ find implications and draw inferences from the text
➤ evaluate or make judgments about the techniques, logic, and applications of the text

Determining the Meanings of Individual Words from Their Context

If you have ever looked into a dictionary, you are well aware that many words have more than one meaning: a *run* in a baseball game is not the same thing as a *run* in a nylon stocking. Generally, the word is a common one that's being used in a specific, sometimes uncommon way; you must figure out its exact meaning as used by the author.

Read the following passage and try the vocabulary-in-context questions based upon it.

The following passage is taken from an article on mathematical and scientific illiteracy published in The New York Times *in January 1989, as Ronald and Nancy Reagan left the White House.*

The abstractness of mathematics is a great obstacle for many intelligent people. Such people may readily understand narrative particulars, but
Line strongly resist impersonal generalities. Since
5 numbers, science, and such generalities are intimately related, this resistance can lead to an almost willful mathematical and scientific illiteracy. Numbers have appeal for many only if they're associated with them personally—hence
10 part of the attraction of astrology, biorhythms, Tarot cards and the I Ching, all individually customized "sciences."

Mathematical illiteracy and the attitudes underlying it provide in fact a fertile soil for the
15 growth of pseudoscience. In "Pseudoscience and Society in Nineteenth-Century America," Arthur Wrobel remarks that belief in phrenology, homeopathy, and hydropathy was not confined to the poor and the ignorant, but pervaded much
20 of 19th-century literature. Such credulity is not as extensive in contemporary literature, but astrology is one pseudoscience that does seem to engage a big segment of the reading public. Literary allusions to it abound, appearing in everything from
25 Shakespeare to Don DeLillo's "Libra." A 1986 Gallup poll showed that 52 percent of American teenagers subscribe to it, as does at least 50 percent of the nation's departing First Couple.

Given these figures, it may not be entirely
30 inappropriate to note here that no mechanism through which the alleged zodiacal influences exert themselves has ever been specified by astrologers. Gravity certainly cannot account for these natal influences, since even the gravitational
35 pull of the attending obstetrician is orders of magnitude greater than that of the relevant planet or planets. Nor is there any empirical evidence; top astrologers (as determined by their peers) have failed repeatedly to associate personality profiles
40 with astrological data at a rate higher than that of chance. Neither of these fatal objections to astrology, of course, is likely to carry much weight with literate but innumerate people who don't estimate magnitudes or probabilities, or who are over-
45 impressed by vague coincidences yet unmoved by overwhelming statistical evidence.

1. The word "confined" in line 18 means

(A) enclosed   (B) jailed (C) isolated
(D) restricted (E) preached

ANALYSIS OF QUESTION 1

Your best bet in answering vocabulary-in-context questions is to tackle them the way you do sentence completion questions. First, read the sentence, blocking out the word in quotes. Think of words you know that might make sense in the context. Then test each answer choice, substituting it in the sentence for the word in quotes. Ask yourself whether this particular answer choice makes sense in this specific context. In question 1, for example, the original sentence states that "belief . . . was not __ to the poor and the ignorant, but pervaded much of 19th-century literature." Nonscientific belief was widespread in the 19th century; it pervaded or spread throughout the literature of the period. Therefore, it was not *restricted* or confined to poor, ignorant people, but had spread to the well-to-do, literate classes.

Note that *many* of the answer choices could be good substitutes for "confined" *in other contexts*. For example, if the sentence were "The dog catcher *confined* dozens of stray animals in the pound," Choice A, *enclosed*, would be the best word to substitute. Your job is to spot which meaning of the word works this time.

See how well you do with another vocabulary-in-context question on the same passage.

2. As used in line 22, "engage" most nearly means

(A) hire   (B) reserve   (C) attract
(D) confront   (E) interlock

ANALYSIS OF QUESTION 2

Again, look at the sentence, blocking out the key word. "Astrology . . . does seem to __ a big segment of the reading public." What word would make sense in the context? Summarize the situation here. The author is reacting to the strong hold astrology has on the reading public. Despite its being a pseudoscience, astrology has managed to *attract* or involve many members of the reading public. The correct answer is Choice C.

Try one more vocabulary-in-context question on this passage.

3. The term "subscribe to" in line 27 means

(A) sign up for   (B) agree with   (C) write about
(D) suffer from   (E) pay for

ANALYSIS OF QUESTION 3

"52 percent of American teenagers __ it, as does at least 50 percent of the nation's departing First Couple." The author has been talking about how many people have been attracted or drawn to astrology. Many of these people have been more or less won over by it: they accept it as a valid belief. Thus, the teenagers (and the Reagans) who *subscribe to* astrology *agree with* it, acquiescing to its doctrines. Once again, you've found a word that makes sense in context.

Paraphrasing or Interpreting Specific Information in the Text

In interpreting a text, you are doing what a translator does in dealing with a passage in a foreign language. Your job is to turn the original text into understandable, familiar prose. In the process, you have to do several things. You have to explain the meaning of key phrases or idioms in the passage. You have to resolve any possible ambiguities in the text, making sure that the author's meaning is absolutely clear. In other words, sentence by sentence, you have to answer the question, "Just what is this person telling me?"

Questions testing your ability to understand significant information in the text often take the following forms:

- According to the author, what is the reason for . . .
- To the author, Emily Dickinson's poetry was . . .
- The "crucial question" referred to in line 33 is the . . .

In answering these questions, you must be certain that the answer you select is in the passage. You must find a word or sentence or group of sentences that justifies your choice. You must not pick an answer just because it agrees with your personal opinions or with information on the subject that you've gotten from other sources.

The following questions based on the passage on mathematical and scientific illiteracy all require you to clarify the meaning of the text. Again, be sure to go back to the passage to verify your answer choice.

The following passage is taken from an article on mathematical and scientific illiteracy published in The New York Times *in January 1989, as Ronald and Nancy Reagan left the White House.*

The abstractness of mathematics is a great obstacle for many intelligent people. Such people may readily understand narrative particulars, but
Line strongly resist impersonal generalities. Since
5 numbers, science, and such generalities are intimately related, this resistance can lead to an almost willful mathematical and scientific illiteracy. Numbers have appeal for many only if they're associated with them personally—hence part of the
10 attraction of astrology, biorhythms, Tarot cards and the I Ching, all individually customized "sciences."

Mathematical illiteracy and the attitudes underlying it provide in fact a fertile soil for the
15 growth of pseudoscience. In "Pseudoscience and Society in Nineteenth-Century America," Arthur Wrobel remarks that belief in phrenology, homeopathy, and hydropathy was not confined to the poor and the ignorant, but pervaded much of
20 19th-century literature. Such credulity is not as extensive in contemporary literature, but astrology is one pseudoscience that does seem to engage a big segment of the reading public. Literary allusions to it abound, appearing in everything from
25 Shakespeare to Don DeLillo's "Libra." A 1986 Gallup poll showed that 52 percent of American teenagers subscribe to it, as does at least 50 percent of the nation's departing First Couple.

Given these figures, it may not be entirely
30 inappropriate to note here that no mechanism through which the alleged zodiacal influences exert themselves has ever been specified by astrologers. Gravity certainly cannot account for these natal influences, since even the gravitational
35 pull of the attending obstetrician is orders of magnitude greater than that of the relevant planet or planets. Nor is there any empirical evidence; top astrologers (as determined by their peers) have failed repeatedly to associate personality profiles
40 with astrological data at a rate higher than that of chance. Neither of these fatal objections to astrology, of course, is likely to carry much weight with literate but innumerate people who don't estimate magnitudes or probabilities, or who are overimpressed
45 by vague coincidences yet unmoved by overwhelming statistical evidence.

4. Which of the following best summarizes the reason given in lines 1–7 for the extent of mathematical and scientific illiteracy today?

(A) Many intelligent people dislike the intimacy of the connection between numbers and science.

(B) Many otherwise intelligent people have difficulty dealing with impersonal, abstract concepts.

(C) Intelligent people prefer speaking in generalities to narrating particular incidents.

(D) Few people are able to appreciate the benefits of an individually customized science.

(E) People today no longer cherish their personal associations with numbers.

ANALYSIS OF QUESTION 4

In lines 1 and 2, the author states that the abstractness of mathematics is a problem for many intelligent people. People resist dealing with abstractions ("impersonal generalities"). However, to work in science or math, you must deal with abstractions: numbers, science, and abstractions are "intimately connected." *Because* many otherwise intelligent people have difficulty dealing with impersonal, abstract concepts, these people wind up mathematically and scientifically illiterate. That, according to the author, is the reason for much of the mathematical and scientific illiteracy we see today. The correct answer is Choice B.

5. According to the author, "phrenology, homeopathy, and hydropathy" (lines 17–18) are all

(A) scholarly allusions   (B) pseudosciences
(C) branches of astrology   (D) forms of society
(E) mechanisms

ANALYSIS OF QUESTION 5

Phrenology, homeopathy, and hydropathy are three beliefs mentioned in a book titled *Pseudoscience and Society in Nineteenth-Century America*. Throughout the passage the author is being critical of various beliefs he categorizes as unscientific. He groups such beliefs together as *pseudosciences*, false sciences in which many otherwise intelligent individuals believe. Phrenology is the belief that the shape of your skull indicates your character traits and mental abilities. Homeopathy is the belief that you can cure a disease by giving someone ill minute doses of a substance that would produce in someone healthy symptoms similar to those of the disease. Hydropathy is the belief that you can cure a disease by giving someone ill huge amounts of water (both internally and externally). To the author, all three beliefs are *pseudosciences.*

Note the phrase "to the author." The question is not asking you what *you* think about phrenology, homeopathy, and hydropathy. It is asking you what *the author* thinks of these beliefs.

6. The "figures" referred to in line 29 are the

(A) pseudosciences
(B) literary references
(C) prominent political leaders
(D) numbers involved in calculating horoscopes
(E) statistics concerning believers in astrology

ANALYSIS OF QUESTION 6

The paragraph immediately preceding line 29 gives the percentage of American teenagers who go along with astrology. It also refers to the well-known fact that Nancy Reagan (half of "the nation's departing First Couple") accepts the tenets of astrology (she followed the advice of astrologers in setting up her husband's engagements during his presidency) and that her husband may possibly believe in it as well. Thus, the figures referred to are *statistics concerning believers in astrology.*

7. The term "innumerate" (line 43) is best interpreted to mean

(A) various in kind
(B) too numerous to count
(C) scientifically sophisticated
(D) unable to use mathematics
(E) indifferent to astrology

ANALYSIS OF QUESTION 7

The author contrasts the word "innumerate" with the word "literate." Since *illiterate* means unable to read, *innumerate* must mean unable to use mathematics.

You can use your knowledge of word parts to answer this question. *In-* means not; *numer-* means number. *Innumerate* means not having numbers, unable to use numbers. Watch out, however, for eyecatchers. The word *innumerable* means uncountable, too many, or too numerous to count.

Analyzing or Finding the Central Thought of a Passage

Questions that test your ability to find the central thought of a passage often take the following forms:

- Which of the following best states the theme of the passage?
- The main idea of this passage may be best expressed as . . .
- In the second paragraph of the passage, the author primarily stresses that . . .
- The passage illustrates . . .
- The author's purpose in writing this passage is . . .

When asked to find the central thought, be sure to check the opening and summary sentence of each paragraph. Authors frequently provide readers with a sentence that expresses a paragraph's main idea succinctly. Although such *topic sentences* may appear anywhere in the paragraph, readers customarily look for them in the opening or closing sentences.

Note: In PSAT reading passages, topic sentences are frequently implied rather than stated directly. If you cannot find a topic sentence, ask yourself these questions:

- Who or what is this passage about?
- What aspect of this subject is the author talking about?
- What is the author trying to get across about this aspect of the subject?

You'll be on your way to locating the passage's central thought.

The two questions following the passage ask you to determine the author's main idea. Try them.

The following passage is taken from an article on mathematical and scientific illiteracy published in The New York Times *in January 1989, as Ronald and Nancy Reagan left the White House.*

The abstractness of mathematics is a great obstacle for many intelligent people. Such people may readily understand narrative particulars, but
Line strongly resist impersonal generalities. Since
5 numbers, science, and such generalities are intimately related, this resistance can lead to an almost willful mathematical and scientific illiteracy. Numbers have appeal for many only if they're associated with them personally—hence part of
10 the attraction of astrology, biorhythms, Tarot cards and the I Ching, all individually customized "sciences."

Mathematical illiteracy and the attitudes underlying it provide in fact a fertile soil for the
15 growth of pseudoscience. In "Pseudoscience and Society in Nineteenth-Century America," Arthur Wrobel remarks that belief in phrenology, homeopathy, and hydropathy was not confined to the poor and the ignorant, but pervaded much of
20 19th-century literature. Such credulity is not as extensive in contemporary literature, but astrology is one pseudoscience that does seem to engage a big segment of the reading public. Literary allusions to it abound, appearing in everything from
25 Shakespeare to Don DeLillo's "Libra." A 1986 Gallup poll showed that 52 percent of American teenagers subscribe to it, as does at least 50 percent of the nation's departing First Couple.

Given these figures, it may not be entirely
30 inappropriate to note here that no mechanism through which the alleged zodiacal influences exert themselves has ever been specified by astrologers. Gravity certainly cannot account for these natal influences, since even the gravitational
35 pull of the attending obstetrician is orders of magnitude greater than that of the relevant planet or planets. Nor is there any empirical evidence; top astrologers (as determined by their peers) have failed repeatedly to associate personality profiles
40 with astrological data at a rate higher than that of chance. Neither of these fatal objections to astrology, of course, is likely to carry much weight with literate but innumerate people who don't estimate magnitudes or probabilities, or who are over-
45 impressed by vague coincidences yet unmoved by overwhelming statistical evidence.

8. In the final paragraph of the passage, the author stresses that

    (A) astrologers are working to discover the mechanisms through which the zodiac affects human lives

    (B) the planets are able to influence people in mysterious, imperceptible ways

    (C) top astrologers strive to maintain accurate personality profiles of their clientele

    (D) astrologers have been unable to corroborate their theories scientifically

    (E) astrologers are more mechanically minded than mathematically literate

ANALYSIS OF QUESTION 8

The author spends the final paragraph debunking the claims of astrologers. To their claim that the planets in the heavens at the time of one's birth influence one's destiny, he retorts that the attending physician exerts more gravitational pull on the infant than the distant planets do. To their claim that astrological data can be used to predict personality types, he retorts that no valid correlation exists between astrological predictions and the results of scientifically legitimate personality profiles. Throughout the paragraph, he stresses that *astrologers have been unable to corroborate their theories scientifically.*

9. The author's primary purpose throughout the passage is to

    (A) contrast astrology and other contemporary pseudosciences with phrenology, homeopathy, and hydropathy

    (B) trace the development of the current belief in astrology to its nineteenth-century roots

    (C) apologize for the rise of mathematical and scientific illiteracy in the present day

    (D) relate mathematical illiteracy to the prevalence of invalid pseudoscientific beliefs today

    (E) disprove the difficulty of achieving universal mathematical and scientific literacy

ANALYSIS OF QUESTION 9

Consider the opening sentences of the three paragraphs and the concluding sentence of the third paragraph. "The abstractness of mathematics is a great obstacle for many intelligent people." "Mathematical illiteracy and the attitudes underlying it provide in fact a fertile soil for the growth of pseudoscience." "Given these figures, it may not be entirely inappropriate to note here that no mechanism through which the alleged zodiacal influences exert themselves has ever been specified by astrologers." "Neither of these fatal objections to astrology, of course, is likely to carry much weight with literate but innumerate people who don't estimate magnitudes or probability, or who are overimpressed by vague coincidences yet unmoved by overwhelming statistical evidence." Throughout the passage the author is discussing mathematical illiteracy and demonstrating how it *relates to the prevalence* (widespread acceptance) of astrology and other *invalid pseudoscientific beliefs today*.

Choice A is incorrect. While the author mentions phrenology and the other pseudosciences, he never contrasts them with or differentiates them from astrology. Choice B is incorrect. While the author spends a good deal of the passage discussing astrology, his chief purpose is to use it as an example of a contemporary pseudoscientific belief, not to trace its nineteenth-century connections. Choice C is incorrect; the author is irked by the state of mathematical and scientific illiteracy today, not apologetic about it. Choice E is incorrect; it is unsupported by the passage.

PART THREE / Critical Reading

Finding Implications and Drawing Inferences from the Text

Questions that ask you to draw inferences often begin in one of the following ways:

- It can be inferred from the passage that . . .
- The author implies that . . .
- The passage suggests that . . .
- It can be argued that . . .
- The author would most likely . . .
- The author probably considers . . .

Inference questions require you to use your own judgment. You are drawing a conclusion *based on what you have read in the text*. When asked to draw an inference, think about what the passage logically suggests. You must not take anything directly stated in the passage as an inference. Instead, you must look for clues in the passage that you can use in coming up with your own conclusion. Then you should choose as your answer a statement that logically develops the information the author has provided.

Turn once more to the mathematical illiteracy passage for some practice in finding the implications of an author's words.

The following passage is taken from an article on mathematical and scientific illiteracy published in The New York Times *in January 1989, as Ronald and Nancy Reagan left the White House.*

The abstractness of mathematics is a great obstacle for many intelligent people. Such people may readily understand narrative particulars, but
Line strongly resist impersonal generalities. Since
5 numbers, science, and such generalities are intimately related, this resistance can lead to an almost willful mathematical and scientific illiteracy. Numbers have appeal for many only if they're associated with them personally—hence part of the
10 attraction of astrology, biorhythms, Tarot cards and the I Ching, all individually customized "sciences."

Mathematical illiteracy and the attitudes underlying it provide in fact a fertile soil for the
15 growth of pseudoscience. In "Pseudoscience and Society in Nineteenth-Century America," Arthur Wrobel remarks that belief in phrenology, homeopathy, and hydropathy was not confined to the poor and the ignorant, but pervaded much of
20 19th-century literature. Such credulity is not as extensive in contemporary literature, but astrology is one pseudoscience that does seem to engage a big segment of the reading public. Literary allusions to it abound, appearing in everything from
25 Shakespeare to Don DeLillo's "Libra." A 1986 Gallup poll showed that 52 percent of American teenagers subscribe to it, as does at least 50 percent of the nation's departing First Couple.

Given these figures, it may not be entirely
30 inappropriate to note here that no mechanism through which the alleged zodiacal influences exert themselves has ever been specified by astrologers. Gravity certainly cannot account for these natal influences, since even the gravitational
35 pull of the attending obstetrician is orders of magnitude greater than that of the relevant planet or planets. Nor is there any empirical evidence; top astrologers (as determined by their peers) have failed repeatedly to associate personality profiles
40 with astrological data at a rate higher than that of chance. Neither of these fatal objections to astrology, of course, is likely to carry much weight with literate but innumerate people who don't estimate magnitudes or probabilities, or who are over-
45 impressed by vague coincidences yet unmoved by overwhelming statistical evidence.

Here is a straightforward inference question on the passage.

10. The author most likely regards the lack of empirical evidence for astrology as

(A) an oversight on the part of the astrologers
(B) a key argument against its validity
(C) a flaw that will be corrected in time
(D) the unfortunate result of too small a sampling
(E) a major reason to keep searching for fresh data

ANALYSIS OF QUESTION 10

The final sentence of the passage characterizes these absences of empirical evidence as "fatal objections to astrology." In general, the author sees astrology as invalid, a pseudoscience, not a real science. If he were faced with empirical experimental data supporting astrological theory, he probably would have a hard time rejecting it so sharply. Thus, he most likely regards the lack of empirical, observable evidence for astrology as *a key argument against its validity*.

Other inference questions ask you to draw conclusions about the author's attitude toward the topic, overall mood, or tone of voice. What does the author's choice of words imply about his feelings about the topic? Such inference questions often take the following forms:

• The author's attitude toward . . . is . . .
• The author regards the idea that . . . with . . .
• The author's tone in the passage . . .

Try the following two questions that ask you to interpret the author's emotional state.

11. The author's attitude toward astrology can best be described as one of

(A) grudging respect (B) amused tolerance
(C) open disdain (D) disguised hostility
(E) puzzled fascination

ANALYSIS OF QUESTION 11

The author states that people who believe in astrology are the sort who are "overimpressed by vague coincidences." In his opinion, astrology as a science is fatally flawed, and he looks down on those innumerate souls who continue to believe in it. Thus, his attitude is one of *open disdain* or contempt.

12. The author's tone in referring to the nation's departing First Couple can best be described as

(A) respectful   (B) nostalgic   (C) negative
(D) mocking   (E) effusive

ANALYSIS OF QUESTION 12

In saying that *at least* 50 percent of the Reagans subscribes to a belief in astrology, the author is making a little joke. He is referring to Nancy Reagan's dependence on astrologers and, at the same time, implying that 100 percent of the Reagans, that is, the first lady *and* the president, may believe in a subject he considers nonsensical. Even the term *First Couple* has a mocking ring. The correct answer is Choice D.

Evaluating the Techniques, Logic, and Applications of the Text

Among the more challenging critical reading questions on the new PSAT are ones that ask you to make judgments about the techniques the author uses, to evaluate the logic of his or her argument, and to infer how what is said in this passage might apply in other situations.

Questions concerning the author's technique often have the following wording:

- Which of the following best describes the development of this passage?
- In presenting the argument, the author does all of the following EXCEPT . . .
- The relationship between the second paragraph and the first paragraph can best be described as . . .
- In the passage, the author makes the central point primarily by . . .

Questions concerning the author's logic or the applications of his or her remarks frequently are worded as follows:

- With which of the following statements would the author be in strongest agreement?
- The author's argument would be most weakened by the discovery of which of the following?
- The author's contention would be most clearly strengthened if which of the following were found to be true?

Again, look at the passage on mathematical illiteracy to answer questions on the author's logic and techniques.

The following passage is taken from an article on mathematical and scientific illiteracy published in The New York Times *in January 1989, as Ronald and Nancy Reagan left the White House.*

The abstractness of mathematics is a great obstacle for many intelligent people. Such people may readily understand narrative particulars, but
Line strongly resist impersonal generalities. Since
5 numbers, science, and such generalities are intimately related, this resistance can lead to an almost willful mathematical and scientific illiteracy. Numbers have appeal for many only if they're associated with them personally—hence
10 part of the attraction of astrology, biorhythms, Tarot cards and the I Ching, all individually customized "sciences."

Mathematical illiteracy and the attitudes underlying it provide in fact a fertile soil for the
15 growth of pseudoscience. In "Pseudoscience and Society in Nineteenth-Century America," Arthur Wrobel remarks that belief in phrenology, homeopathy, and hydropathy was not confined to the poor and the ignorant, but pervaded much of
20 19th-century literature. Such credulity is not as extensive in contemporary literature, but astrology is one pseudoscience that does seem to engage a big segment of the reading public. Literary allusions to it abound, appearing in everything from
25 Shakespeare to Don DeLillo's "Libra." A 1986 Gallup poll showed that 52 percent of American teenagers subscribe to it, as does at least 50 percent of the nation's departing First Couple.

Given these figures, it may not be entirely
30 inappropriate to note here that no mechanism through which the alleged zodiacal influences exert themselves has ever been specified by

astrologers. Gravity certainly cannot account for these natal influences, since even the gravitational
35 pull of the attending obstetrician is orders of magnitude greater than that of the relevant planet or planets. Nor is there any empirical evidence; top astrologers (as determined by their peers) have failed repeatedly to associate personality profiles
40 with astrological data at a rate higher than that of chance. Neither of these fatal objections to astrology, of course, is likely to carry much weight with literate but innumerate people who don't estimate magnitudes or probabilities, or who are over-
45 impressed by vague coincidences yet unmoved by overwhelming statistical evidence.

13. The author's point about the popularity of astrology is made through both

(A) personal testimony and generalizations
(B) assertions and case histories
(C) comparisons and anecdotes
(D) statistics and literary references
(E) observation and analogy

ANALYSIS OF QUESTION 13

Familiarize yourself with the technical terms commonly used to describe a passage's organization: *analogies, assertions, allusions*. You need to know the meaning of these terms and of others you'll encounter in the course of taking our model PSATs.

In this instance, the author offers as evidence of astrology's popularity both *literary references* (allusions to Don DeLillo's *Libra* and to Shakespeare) and *statistics* based on Gallup poll figures.

14. Which of the following would most weaken the author's assumption that mathematical and scientific literacy would make people less likely to believe in a pseudoscience such as astrology?

(A) Assertions by professional astrologers that astrology has a firm scientific basis in astronomy
(B) Anecdotal reports that an individual astrologer has been known to use a calculator in computing horoscopes
(C) Poll results showing that the percentage of American teenagers believing in astrology has radically decreased since 1989
(D) Evidence that the majority of practicing astrologers have also taught mathematics or a scientific discipline
(E) A statement by ex-president Reagan denying that he has ever believed in astrology

ANALYSIS OF QUESTION 14

If we assume that people who have professionally taught math or science are therefore not mathematically and scientifically illiterate and if we also assume that practicing astrologers believe in astrology, then *evidence that the majority of practicing*

astrologers have also taught mathematics or a scientific discipline would clearly weaken the author's assumption that mathematical and scientific literacy would make people less likely to believe in astrology.

15. With which of the following statements would the author be most likely to disagree?

(A) Phrenology may be of some interest to sociologists and cultural historians, but it has no real value as a scientific discipline.
(B) A rigorous training in mathematics would benefit young people by equipping them to estimate magnitudes and probabilities.
(C) People were somewhat less apt to be taken in by pseudoscientific claims in the nineteenth century than they are today.
(D) Despite the weight of the evidence against astrology, scientifically illiterate individuals will continue to believe in it.
(E) Determining biorhythms and computing astrological horoscopes may require people to perform some mathematical calculations.

ANALYSIS OF QUESTION 15

You can answer this question by using the process of elimination.

The key word here is "disagree." Examine each statement in turn, asking yourself whether it does or does not reflect the author's point of view. Eliminate every answer choice with which the author would agree. Phrenology is one of the pseudosciences mentioned in the second paragraph; clearly, the author would agree *it has no real value as a scientific discipline* or field of study. You can eliminate Choice A.

In the concluding sentence of the passage, the author mentions the failure to estimate magnitudes and probabilities as a characteristic of innumerate, mathematically illiterate people. He wishes people to be mathematically *literate*; therefore, he would agree that *a rigorous training in mathematics* that enabled them to estimate magnitudes and probabilities *would benefit young people*. You can eliminate Choice B.

In the second paragraph, the author states that belief in various pseudosciences "pervaded much of the 19th-century literature"; it was widespread in earlier days. He then asserts that "such credulity is not as extensive in contemporary literature." In other words, the author contends that people are somewhat *less* apt to be taken in by pseudoscientific claims *today* than they were a century ago. This directly contradicts what is stated in Choice C, which must be the correct answer.

Double-check yourself. Test the other two answer choices.

In lines 41–46, the author states directly that the "fatal objections to astrology" he has just pointed out are unlikely to convince the innumerate, scientifically illiterate believers in astrology that the powers of the zodiac are nonexistent. Clearly, the author would agree that *scientifically illiterate individuals will continue to believe* in astrology despite the evidence. You can eliminate Choice D.

The author asserts that the only numbers that appeal to some people are ones with personal associations—numbers connected to individual biorhythms or astrological horoscopes, for example. Given this personal connection with numbers, even nonmathematically inclined individuals might wind up having *to perform mathematical computations*, though ones the author would consider of doubtful value. You can eliminate Choice E.

Only Choice C is left. As you suspected, it is the correct answer.

Dealing with the Double Passage

If the Double-Passage section has you worried, relax. It's not that formidable, especially if you deal with it our way.

Look at a typical double passage. First you'll see a few lines in italics introducing both passages. Then will come the two passages. Their lines will be numbered as if they were one enormous passage: if PASSAGE 1 ends on line 42, PASSAGE 2 will begin on line 43. However, they are two separate passages, and you should tackle them one at a time. Remember, the questions are organized sequentially: questions about PASSAGE 1 will come before questions about PASSAGE 2. Therefore, as soon as you finish reading PASSAGE 1, you should skip to the questions and try to answer the three to five questions based on PASSAGE 1. Then you should read PASSAGE 2 and answer the three to five questions based on that passage. (The line numbers in the questions will help you spot where the questions on PASSAGE 1 end and those on PASSAGE 2 begin.) At that point you'll have done everything possible to maximize your score and will be ready to tackle the final two to three questions that ask you to evaluate both passages.

The following set of paired passages is the same set that appeared in Chapter 1. The questions following the paired passages, however, will be new to you. See how well you do in dealing with this mix of the different question types you're likely to face on the PSAT.

The following passages are excerpted from books on America's national pastime, baseball.

Passage 1

DiMaggio had size, power, and speed. McCarthy, his longtime manager, liked to say that DiMaggio might have stolen 60 bases a season if
Line he had given him the green light. Stengel, his
5 new manager, was equally impressed, and when DiMaggio was on base he would point to him as an example of the perfect base runner. "Look at him," Stengel would say as DiMaggio ran out a base hit, "he's always watching the ball. He isn't watching
10 second base. He isn't watching third base. He knows they haven't been moved. He isn't watching the ground, because he knows they haven't built a canal or a swimming pool since he was last there. He's watching the ball and the outfielder, which is
15 the one thing that is different on every play."

DiMaggio complemented his natural athletic ability with astonishing physical grace. He played the outfield, he ran the bases, and he batted not just effectively but with rare style. He would glide
20 rather than run, it seemed, always smooth, always ending up where he wanted to be just when he wanted to be there. If he appeared to play effortlessly, his teammates knew otherwise. In his first season as a Yankee, Gene Woodling, who played
25 left field, was struck by the sound of DiMaggio chasing a fly ball. He sounded like a giant truck horse on the loose, Woodling thought, his feet thudding down hard on the grass. The great, clear noises in the open space enabled Woodling to
30 measure the distances between them without looking.

He was the perfect Hemingway hero, for Hemingway in his novels romanticized the man who exhibited grace under pressure, who withheld
35 any emotion lest it soil the purer statement of his deeds. DiMaggio was that kind of hero; his grace and skill were always on display, his emotions always concealed. This stoic grace was not achieved without a terrible price: DiMaggio was a man
40 wound tight. He suffered from insomnia and ulcers. When he sat and watched the game he chain-

smoked and drank endless cups of coffee. He was ever conscious of his obligation to play well. Late in his career, when his legs were bothering him

45 and the Yankees had a comfortable lead in a pennant race, columnist Jimmy Cannon asked him why he played so hard—the games, after all, no longer meant so much. "Because there might be somebody out there who's never seen me play

50 before," he answered.

Passage 2

Athletes and actors—let actors stand for the set of performing artists—share much. They share the need to make gestures as fluid and economical as possible, to make out of a welter of choices the

55 single, precisely right one. They share the need for thousands of hours of practice in order to train the body to become the perfect, instinctive instrument to express. Both athlete and actor, out of that abundance of emotion, choice, strategy, knowl-

60 edge of the terrain, mood of spectators, condition of others in the ensemble, secret awareness of injury or weakness, and as nearly an absolute *concentration* as possible so that all externalities are integrated, all distraction absorbed to the self,

65 must be able to change the self so successfully that it changes us.

When either athlete or actor can bring all these skills to bear and focus them, then he or she will achieve that state of complete intensity and

70 complete relaxation—complete coherence or integrity between what the performer wants to do and what the performer has to do. Then, the performer is free; for then, all that has been learned, by thousands of hours of practice and discipline

75 and by repetition of pattern, becomes natural. Then, intellect is upgraded to the level of an instinct. The body follows commands that precede thinking.

When athlete and artist achieve such self-

80 knowledge that they transform the self so that we are re-created, it is finally an exercise in power. The individual's power to dominate, on stage or field, invests the whole arena around the locus of performance with his or her power. We draw from

85 the performer's energy, just as we scrutinize the performer's vulnerabilities, and we criticize as if we were equals (we are not) what is displayed. This is why all performers dislike or resent the audience as much as they need and enjoy it. Power

90 flows in a mysterious circuit from performer to spectator (I assume a "live" performance) and back, and while cheers or applause are the hoped-for outcome of performing, silence or gasps are the most desired, for then the moment has

95 occurred—then domination is complete, and as the performer triumphs, a unity rare and inspiring results.

1. Stengel's comments in lines 7–15 serve chiefly to
   (A) point up the stupidity of the sort of error he condemns
   (B) suggest the inevitability of mistakes in running bases
   (C) show it is easier to spot problems than to come up with answers
   (D) answer the criticisms of DiMaggio's base-running
   (E) modify his earlier position on DiMaggio's ability

2. In line 25, the word "struck" most nearly means
   (A) halted   (B) slapped   (C) afflicted
   (D) enamored   (E) impressed

3. By quoting Woodling's comment on DiMaggio's running (lines 26–31), the author most likely intends to emphasize
   (A) his teammates' envy of DiMaggio's natural gifts
   (B) how much exertion went into DiMaggio's moves
   (C) how important speed is to a baseball player
   (D) Woodling's awareness of his own slowness
   (E) how easily DiMaggio was able to cover territory

4. In the last paragraph of Passage 1, the author acknowledges which negative aspect of DiMaggio's heroic stature?
   (A) his overemphasis on physical grace
   (B) his emotional romanticism
   (C) the uniformity of his performance
   (D) the obligation to answer the questions of reporters
   (E) the burden of living up to his reputation

5. The author makes his point about DiMaggio's prowess through all the following EXCEPT
   (A) literary allusion   (B) quotations
   (C) personal anecdotes   (D) generalization
   (E) understatement

6. The phrase "stand for" in line 51 means
   (A) tolerate   (B) represent   (C) advocate
   (D) withstand   (E) surpass

7. The phrase "bring all these skills to bear" in lines 67–68 means
   (A) come to endure   (B) carry toward
   (C) apply directly   (D) cause to behave
   (E) induce birth

8. Why, in line 91, does the author of Passage 2 assume a "live" performance?

(A) His argument assumes a mutual involvement between performer and spectator that can occur only when both are present.

(B) He believes that televised and filmed images give a false impression of the performer's ability to the spectators.

(C) He fears the use of "instant replay" and other broadcasting techniques will cause performers to resent spectators even more strongly.

(D) His argument dismisses the possibility of combining live performances with filmed segments.

(E) He prefers audiences not to have time to reflect about the performance they have just seen.

9. Which of the following attributes of the ideal athlete mentioned in Passage 2 is NOT illustrated by the anecdotes about DiMaggio in Passage 1?

(A) knowledge of the terrain
(B) secret awareness of injury or weakness
(C) consciousness of the condition of other teammates
(D) ability to make gestures fluid and economical
(E) absolute powers of concentration

10. Which of the following statements is best supported by a comparison of the two excerpts?

(A) Both excerpts focus on the development of a specific professional athlete.

(B) The purpose of both excerpts is to compare athletes with performing artists.

(C) The development of ideas in both excerpts is similar.

(D) Both excerpts examine the nature of superior athletic performance.

(E) Both excerpts discuss athletic performance primarily in abstract terms.

Double-Passage Answer Key

1. *A*	5. *E*	9. *C*
2. *E*	6. *B*	10. *D*
3. *B*	7. *C*	
4. *E*	8. *A*	

Answer Explanations

1. *A* Stengel's sarcastic comments about the mistakes DiMaggio *doesn't* make indicate just how dumb he thinks it is to look down at the ground when you should have your attention on the outfielder and the ball. Clearly, if one of his players made such an error, Stengel's response would be to say, "What's the matter, stupid? Are you afraid you're going to fall in a canal down there?"

2. *E* Woodling was struck, or *impressed,* by the sound of DiMaggio's running; he found the impact of DiMaggio's feet hitting the ground noteworthy.

3. *B* Note the context of the reference to Woodling. In the sentence immediately preceding, the author says that, if DiMaggio "appeared to play effortlessly, his teammates knew otherwise." The author then introduces a comment by Woodling, one of DiMaggio's teammates. Woodling knew a great deal of effort went into DiMaggio's playing: he describes how DiMaggio's feet pounded as he ran. Clearly, the force of DiMaggio's running is mentioned to illustrate *how much exertion went into DiMaggio's moves.*

4. *E* In the final paragraph, the author describes DiMaggio pushing himself to play hard despite his injuries. DiMaggio does so because he is trying to live up to the image his public has of him. He feels *the burden of living up to his reputation.*

5. *E* You can answer this technique question by using the process of elimination. The author makes a *literary allusion,* or reference, to the novels of Ernest Hemingway. He *quotes* the comments of Casey Stengel and of DiMaggio himself. He cites an *anecdote,* or story, about Gene Woodling's first impression of DiMaggio. He makes *generalizations*—general statements—about DiMaggio ("He was the perfect Hemingway hero . . ."). However, he always expresses himself emphatically, using strong, extremely positive words to describe his subject; he never uses any *understatements.*

6. *B* At this point, the questions on Passage 2 begin. In this brief aside, the author is defining how he intends to use a word. He wishes to use the word *actors* to stand for, or *represent,* all other performers. This way every time he makes his comparison between athletes and performers he

won't have to list all the various sorts of performing artists (actors, dancers, singers, acrobats, clowns) who resemble athletes in their need for physical grace, extensive rehearsal, and total concentration.

7. *C* The author has been describing the wide range of skills a performer utilizes in crafting an artistic or athletic performance. It is by taking these skills and *applying them purposefully* and with concentration to the task at hand that the performer achieves his or her goal.

8. *A* While a spectator may feel powerfully involved with a filmed or televised image of a performer, the filmed image is unaffected by the spectator's feelings. Thus, for power to "flow in a mysterious circuit" from performer to spectator *and back*, the assumption is that both performer and spectator *must be present* in the flesh.

9. *C* Though DiMaggio's teammates clearly were aware of *his* condition (as the Woodling anecdote illustrates), none of the anecdotes in Passage 1 indicate or even imply that DiMaggio was specifically *conscious of his teammates'*

condition. You can answer this question by using the process of elimination. In running bases, DiMaggio never lets himself be distracted by looking at the bases or down at the ground; as Stengel says, he knows where they are. Clearly, he *knows the terrain*. You can eliminate Choice A. When DiMaggio's legs are failing him late in his career, he still pushes himself to perform well for the fan in the stands who hasn't seen him play before. In doing so, he takes into account his *secret awareness* of his legs' weakness. You can eliminate Choice B. Gliding rather than running, always smooth, never wasting a glance on inessentials, DiMaggio clearly exhibits *fluidity and economy* in his movements. You can eliminate Choice D. Running bases, DiMaggio always keeps his eye on the ball and the outfielder; he *concentrates absolutely* on them. You can eliminate Choice E. Only Choice C is left. It is the correct answer.

10. *D* Though one passage presents an abstract discussion of the nature of the ideal athlete and the other describes the achievements and character of a specific superior athlete, both passages *examine the nature of superior athletic performance.*

PRACTICE READING EXERCISES

On the following pages are five groups of reading exercises. The passages tend to get somewhat more difficult as you go along. You will find the correct answers at the end of the chapter.

EXERCISE A

Although patience is the most important quality a treasure hunter can have, the trade demands a certain amount of courage, too. I have
Line my share of guts, but make no boast about
5 ignoring the hazards of diving. As all good divers know, the business of plunging into an alien world with an artificial air supply as your only link to the world above can be as dangerous as stepping into a den of lions. Most of the danger rests within the
10 diver himself.

The devil-may-care diver who shows great bravado underwater is the worst risk of all. He may lose his bearings in the glimmering dim light which penetrates the sea and become separated
15 from his diving companions. He may dive too deep, too long and suffer painful, sometimes fatal, bends.

He may surface too quickly and force his lungs to squeeze their supply of high pressure air
20 into his blood stream, causing an embolism—a bubble of air in the blood—which often kills. He may become trapped in a submarine rockslide, get lost in an underwater cave, or be chopped to bits by a marauding shark. These are not occasional

25 dangers such as crossing a street in busy traffic. They are always with you underwater. At one time or another I have faced all of them except bends and embolism, which can be avoided by common sense and understanding of human physical limits
30 beneath the surface.

Once, while salvaging brass from the sunken hulk of an old steel ship, I brushed lightly against a huge engine cylinder, which looked as if it were as solid as it was on the day the ship was launched.
35 Although the pressure of my touch was hardly enough to topple a toy soldier, the heavy mass of cast iron collapsed, causing a chain reaction in which the rest of the old engine crumbled. Tons of iron dropped all around me. Sheer luck saved me
40 from being crushed. I have been wary of swimming around steel shipwrecks ever since.

1. The title that best expresses the central point of this passage is

(A) Alien Adventures
(B) The Wrong Kind of Courage
(C) The Successful Skindiver
(D) Underwater Perils
(E) Hunting Treasure the Hard Way

2. The passage most probably appeared in

(A) a short story
(B) an autobiographical article
(C) a diver's logbook
(D) an article in an encyclopedia
(E) a manual of skin diving instructions

3. Which of the following does the author NOT do?

(A) define a term   (B) give an example
(C) make a comparison   (D) pose a question
(E) list a possibility

4. The word "sheer" (line 39) most nearly means

(A) steep   (B) pure   (C) sharp
(D) filmy   (E) abrupt

Intuition is not a quality which everyone can
understand. As the unimaginative are miserable
about a work of fiction until they discover what
Line flesh-and-blood individual served as the model for
5 the hero or heroine, so even many scientists doubt
scientific intuition. They cannot believe that a
blind person can see anything that they cannot
see. They rely utterly on the celebrated inductive
method of reasoning: the facts are to be exposed,
10 and we are to conclude from them only what we
must. This is a very sound rule—for mentalities
that can do no better. But it is not certain that the
really great steps are made in this plodding fashion. Dreams are made of quite other stuff, and if
15 there are any left in the world who do not know
that dreams have remade the world, then there is
little that we can teach them.

5. The primary purpose of this passage is to

(A) denounce the unimaginative snobbery of
scientists
(B) correct a misconception about the nature
of dreams
(C) argue against the use of inductive reasoning
(D) explain the importance of intuition in
science
(E) show how challenging scientific research
can be

6. The author's attitude toward those who rely
solely on the inductive method of reasoning
can best be described as

(A) condescending   (B) approving
(C) indignant   (D) ambivalent
(E) hypocritical

7. The word "exposed" in line 9 means

(A) bared to the elements
(B) laid open to danger
(C) held up to ridicule
(D) unmasked
(E) made known

8. The phrase "the really great steps" (lines
12–13) most likely refers to

(A) extremely large paces
(B) vast distances
(C) grandiose fantasies
(D) major scientific advances
(E) broadly interpreted measures

Too many parents force their children into
group activities. They are concerned about the
child who loves to do things alone, who prefers a
Line solitary walk with a camera to a game of ball. They
5 want their sons to be "good fellows" and their
daughters "social mixers." In such foolish fears lie
the beginnings of the blighting of individuality,
the thwarting of personality, the stealing of the
wealth of one's capital for living joyously and well
10 in a confused world. What America needs is a new
army of defense, manned by young men and
women who, through guidance and confidence,
encouragement and wisdom, have built up values
for themselves and away from crowds and
15 companies.

9. According to the passage, too many parents
push their children to be

(A) unnecessarily gregarious
(B) foolishly timorous
(C) pointlessly extravagant
(D) acutely individualistic
(E) financially dependent

10. The primary point the author wishes to make is
that

(A) young people need time to themselves
(B) group activities are harmful to children
(C) parents knowingly thwart their children's
personalities
(D) independent thinking is of questionable
value
(E) America needs universal military training

11. The author puts quotation marks around the
words "good fellows" and "social mixers" to indicate that he

(A) is using vocabulary that is unfamiliar to
the reader
(B) intends to define these terms later in
course of the passage
(C) can readily distinguish these terms from
one another
(D) prefers not to differentiate roles by secondary factors such as gender
(E) refuses to accept the assumption that
these are positive values

12. By "the wealth of one's capital for living joyously and well in a confused world" (lines 8–10), the author most likely means

(A) the financial security that one attains from one's individual professional achievements and overanalyzing it

(B) the riches that parents thrust upon children who would far prefer to be left alone to follow their own inclinations

(C) the hours spent in solitary pursuits that enable one to develop into an independent, confident adult

(D) the happy memories of childhood days spent in the company of true friends

(E) the profitable financial and personal contacts young people make when they engage in group activities

"Sticks and stones can break my bones,
But names will never harm me."

No doubt you are familiar with this childhood
Line rhyme; perhaps, when you were younger, you fre-
5 quently invoked whatever protection it could offer
against unpleasant epithets. But like many popular slogans and verses, this one will not bear too
close scrutiny. For names will hurt you. Sometimes you may be the victim, and find yourself an
10 object of scorn, humiliation, and hatred just because other people have called you certain names.
At other times you may not be the victim, but
clever speakers and writers may, through name
calling, blind your judgment so that you will fol-
15 low them in a course of action wholly opposed to
your own interests or principles. Name calling can
make you gullible to propaganda which you might
otherwise readily see through and reject.

13. The author's primary purpose in quoting the rhyme in lines 1–2 is to

(A) remind readers of their childhood vulnerabilities

(B) emphasize the importance of maintaining one's good name

(C) demonstrate his conviction that only physical attacks can harm us

(D) affirm his faith in the rhyme's ability to shield one from unpleasant epithets

(E) introduce the topic of speaking abusively about others

14. By "this one will not bear too close scrutiny" (lines 7–8), the author means that

(A) the statement will no longer seem valid if you examine it too closely

(B) the literary quality of the verse does not improve on closer inspection

(C) people who indulge in name-calling are embarrassed when they are in the spotlight

(D) the author cannot stand having his comments looked at critically

(E) a narrow line exists between analyzing a slogan and overanalyzing it

15. According to the passage, name calling may make you more susceptible to

(A) poetic language   (B) biased arguments
(C) physical abuse   (D) risky confrontations
(E) offensive epithets

16. The author evidently believes that slogans and verses frequently

(A) appeal to our better nature

(B) are disregarded by children

(C) are scorned by unprincipled speakers

(D) represent the popular mood

(E) oversimplify a problem

It takes no particular expert in foods, or even a
glutton, to know that no meal on the table ever is
as good as the meal in the oven's roasting pan or
Line the stove's covered kettle. There is something
5 about the furtive lifting of the lid and the opening
of the door that is better than all sauces and
gravies. Call it the surprise appetizer. Call it, also,
that one gesture which the proprietor of the
kitchen hates above all others, which brings forth
10 the shortest, most succinct sentences with the
word "meddling" in them. Yet it is essentially a
friendly gesture, one based on good will, and not
on its more general misconstruction, curiosity. It
is quite proper, to state the case flatly, to say that a
15 little quiet investigation of what is cooking is simply an attempt to share the good things of life. It is
possible to state that, but it will take more than a
statement to convince the cook that it is not an
act of interference. The kitchen has special laws.

17. The author maintains that cooks

(A) feel proprietary about their domain

(B) readily share the good things they create

(C) avoid making friendly gestures to strangers

(D) exercise care in lifting hot pan lids

(E) tend to be unusually laconic

18. We can infer that the tone of the short sentences to which the author refers (line 10) is

(A) admonitory (B) tentative
(C) nonchalant
(D) cordial (E) serious

19. The word "flatly" in line 14 means

(A) evenly (B) horizontally
(C) without animation
(D) without qualification
(E) lacking flavor

20. The author's tone in the concluding sentence can best be described as

(A) bitterly resentful (B) mildly ironic
(C) thoroughly respectful
(D) openly bewildered
(E) quietly curious

EXERCISE B

There are exceptions to the rule of male insects being smaller than the females, and some of these exceptions are intelligible. Size and strength
Line would be an advantage to the males which fight
5 for the possession of the females, and in these cases, as with the stag beetle (Lucanus), the males are larger than the females. There are, however, other beetles which are not known to fight together, of which the males exceed the females
10 in size. The meaning of this fact is not known, but in some of these cases, as with the huge Dynastes and Megasoma, we can at least see that there would be no necessity for the males to be smaller than the females in order to be matured before
15 them, for these beetles are not short-lived, and there would be ample time for the pairing of the sexes.

1. The paragraph preceding this one most likely

(A) discusses a generalization about the size of insects
(B) develops the idea that male insects do not live long after maturity
(C) emphasizes the natural belligerence of beetles
(D) dispels some misconceptions about insect behavior
(E) indicates the enormous variety of species of beetle

2. According to the author, the male Lucanus is particularly

(A) adaptable (B) strong (C) massive
(D) belligerent (E) long-lived

3. According to the author, which of the following is true?

(A) Male insects are always smaller than females.
(B) In a given species nature provides differences between the sexes to ensure successful reproduction.
(C) Size and strength protect females from the attacks of other females.
(D) Longevity is characteristic of the Dynastes and Megasoma.
(E) In the stag beetle, the females are larger than the males.

4. The word "pairing" in line 16 means

(A) lining up together (B) physical resemblance
(C) full development (D) comparison
(E) mating

All museum adepts are familiar with examples of *ostrakoi,* the oystershells used in balloting in ancient Athens. As a matter of fact, these "oyster-
Line shells" are usually shards of pottery, conveniently
5 glazed to enable the voter to express his wishes in writing. In the Agora a great number of these have come to light, bearing the thrilling name Themistocles. Into rival jars were dropped the ballots for or against his banishment. On account
10 of the huge vote taken on that memorable day, it was to be expected that many ostrakoi would be found, but the interest of this collection is that a number of these ballots are inscribed in an *identical* handwriting. There is nothing mysterious
15 about it! The Boss was on the job, then as now. He prepared these ballots and voters cast them—no doubt for the consideration of an obol or two. *The ballot box was stuffed.*

How the glory of the American boss is dimin-
20 ished! A vile imitation, he. His methods as old as Time!

5. The author evidently assumes that the reader

    (A) would have voted in favor of Themistocles' banishment

    (B) is familiar with the story of Themistocles

    (C) knows that the ostrakoi were usually made of clay

    (D) approves of the methods used by the Boss

    (E) prefers Greek customs to American ones

6. We can infer from lines 14–18 that the Boss most likely was

    (A) a leader facing banishment

    (B) a corrupt politician

    (C) an Athenian voter

    (D) a counter of ballots

    (E) an American employer

7. What additional information would undermine the author's conclusion that the ballot box was stuffed?

    (A) Educated people in ancient Greece cultivated a highly individualistic style of penmanship.

    (B) A public scribe was assigned to write Themistocles' name on the ballots of illiterate voters.

    (C) Women, children, and slaves traditionally were denied the right to vote.

    (D) More than two jars were used for the historic vote on Themistocles' banishment.

    (E) Far fewer ostrakoi have been found than museumgoers would generally expect.

8. The author's attitude toward the alleged ballot-stuffing can best be described as

    (A) detached   (B) indignant   (C) approving
    (D) defensive   (E) cynical

Good American English is simply good English, English that differs little in pronunciation, vocabulary, and occasionally in idiom
Line from English as spoken in London or South
5 Africa, but which differs no more than our physical surroundings, our political and social institutions, and other circumstances that are reflected in language. It rests upon the same basis as that which the standard speech of England rests upon—the
10 usage of reputable speakers and writers throughout the country. No American student of language is so provincial as to hope, or wish, that the American standard may some day be adopted in England. Nor does he or she share the views of
15 such in England as think that we would do well to take our standard ready-made from them. The American student will be content with the opinion of Henry Bradley that "the wiser sort among us will not dispute that Americans have acquired the
20 right to frame their own standards of correct English on the usage of their best writers and speakers."

9. The word "rests" in line 8 means

    (A) reposes   (B) remains   (C) is present
    (D) is based   (E) lingers

10. The author considers good American English to be

    (A) appropriate for use in America

    (B) superior to the English spoken in South Africa

    (C) inferior to the English in use in England

    (D) too idiomatic to find general acceptance

    (E) suitable as a standard for all English-speaking countries

11. According to the author, correctness in language is determined by

    (A) the will of the majority of those who speak that language

    (B) the dominant social and political structures

    (C) those who wish to standardize the language

    (D) the practice of the most respected communicators

    (E) unique geographical considerations

12. The word "frame" in line 20 means

    (A) devise   (B) border   (C) incriminate
    (D) line up visually   (E) enunciate distinctly

It takes no calendar to tell root and stem that the calm days of mid-summer are here. Last spring's sprouted seed comes to fruit. None of
Line these things depends on a calendar of the days and
5 months. They are their own calendar, marks on the span of time that reaches far back into the shadows of time. The mark is there for all to see, in every field and meadow and treetop, as it was last year and ten years ago and when the centuries
10 were young.

    The time is here. This is that point in the great continuity when these things happen, and will continue to happen year after year. Any summer arrives at this point, only to lead on to the next
15 and the next, and so to summer again. These things we can count on; these things will happen again and again, so long as the earth turns.

13. By "It takes no calendar to tell root and stem that the calm days of mid-summer are here" (lines 1–2), the author means that

    (A) plants respond to the changing seasons naturally

    (B) no calendar can exactly pinpoint the summer solstice

    (C) trees sink their roots deeply into the soil in mid-summer

    (D) the tranquillity of mid-summer seems timeless

    (E) calendars are more useful during the fall harvest season

14. We can infer from the passage that the author

    (A) does not possess a calendar
    (B) is a very elderly person
    (C) is writing in mid-summer
    (D) dislikes urban life
    (E) welcomes breaks in continuity

15. The author's mood can best be described as one of

    (A) keen frustration
    (B) fear of the forces of nature
    (C) regret at the rapid passage of time
    (D) moderate pessimism
    (E) serene confidence

16. The word "count" in line 16 means

    (A) include   (B) depend   (C) represent
    (D) check over   (E) have merit

      Most people do not think of fishes and other
marine animals as having voices, and of those who
are aware of the fact that many of them can
Line "speak," few understand that these "conversations"
5 have significance. Actually, their talk may be as
meaningful as much of our own. For example,
some sea animals use their "voices" to locate their
food in the ocean expanses; others, to let their fellows know of their whereabouts; and still others,
10 as a means of obtaining mates. Sometimes,
"speaking" may mean the difference between life
and death to a marine animal. It appears in some
cases that when a predator approaches, the prey
depends on no more than the sounds it makes to
15 escape.
      Fish sounds are important to human beings
also. By listening to them we can learn a great deal
about the habits of the creatures that make them,
the size of the schools they form, the patterns of
20 their migrations, and the nature of the environments in which they live. We can also apply this
information to the more effective utilization of the
listening posts we have set up to detect enemy
submarines. A knowledge of fish sounds can avoid

25 confusion and unneeded effort when a "new"
sound is picked up and the sound sentry must
decide whether or not to call an alert.

17. The author's primary purpose in the passage is to

    (A) define a technical term
    (B) describe a natural process
    (C) explain the usefulness of a phenomenon
    (D) indicate the adaptations marine animals make
    (E) record the results of an experiment

18. Which of the following sentences is *best* supported by the information given?

    (A) Noises produced by fish are apparently random.
    (B) Fish noises are used by fishermen to increase their catch.
    (C) Fish noises can be utilized to tell whether or not a submarine is nearby.
    (D) Fish noises can puzzle users of submarine-detection equipment.
    (E) Fish noises are inaudible underwater.

19. Which of the following statements can *best* be inferred from the information given?

    (A) Fish noises cannot be transmitted through air.
    (B) Hearing is more acute in fishes than in people.
    (C) The chief use of "fish voices" is to enable one fish to communicate with another fish.
    (D) The significance of some fish voices has been studied.
    (E) Fishes can be surprisingly noisier than people.

20. The phrase "picked up" in line 26 means

    (A) put in good order
    (B) learned by experience
    (C) brought into range of reception
    (D) taken into an automobile or ship
    (E) obtained casually

EXERCISE C

      For the sad state of criticism the writers must
hold themselves much to blame. Literary artists,
concerned solely in the creation of a book or story
Line as close to perfection as their powers will permit,
5 are generally quiet individuals, contemplative,
retiring. On occasion they can be influenced to
anger by some grievous social wrong that calls for
desperate remedy. But mostly they are prone to sit
in their towers reflecting on the absurdities of a
10 foolish world, asking only to be left alone with

their labor. Never aggressive in their own interest,
seeking only peace, they lay themselves open to
aggression. Thus they do not see the enemy who
has stolen into the shadows at the rear of their re-
15 treat and is slowly scaling the walls. Such has been
the course of events. While the artists have slept,
the critical dwarfs have appeared. They have
evolved a new language, written out a new set of
definitions. Black is white, and white is black. The
20 ugly and the nauseous are beautiful; the beautiful
is nightmare.

1. According to the passage, literary artists are inclined to
   (A) ignore what is happening around them
   (B) be perpetually aroused by social injustices
   (C) slight the work involved in writing
   (D) welcome the onset of aggression
   (E) accept criticism gladly

2. Which best captures the meaning of the word "powers" in line 4?
   (A) delegated authority   (B) physical energies
   (C) written statements   (D) intellectual abilities
   (E) political ascendancy

3. The word "retiring" in line 6 means
   (A) departing from office
   (B) tending toward fatigue
   (C) withdrawing from contact
   (D) receiving a pension
   (E) going to bed

4. Through his comments about the critical dwarfs in lines 17–21, the author wishes to convey the impression that critics
   (A) deserve praise for their linguistic originality
   (B) lack the intellectual stature of those they criticize
   (C) appreciate the fundamental oneness of apparent opposites
   (D) are as able as writers to scale the literary heights
   (E) are less hostile than the authors who look down upon them

5. According to the passage, the critics' standards of criticism are
   (A) a natural outgrowth of former standards
   (B) a complete reversal of accepted standards
   (C) an invaluable guide to the literary artist
   (D) a source of suggestions of new topics to write about
   (E) the result of the artists' neglect of good writing

When there is no distance between people, the only way that anyone can keep his or her distance is by a code of etiquette that has acceptance in a
Line community. Manners are the antidote to adjust-
5 ment to the group. They make social intercourse possible without any forfeit of one's personal dignity. They are armor against invasion of privacy; they are the advance patrols that report whether one should withdraw or advance into intimacy.
10 They are the friendly but noncommittal gestures of civilized people. The manners of crowded countries are, I believe, always more formal than those of open countries (as they are, for example, in Europe and Japan), and it may be that we are seeing

15 a rising concern about American manners precisely because we encounter more people in closer quarters than we ever have before. We feel the need to find ways in which to be part of the group without selling out our privacy or our individuality for a
20 mess of adjustment.

6. The title that best expresses the idea of this passage is
   (A) The Function of Politeness
   (B) Invasions of Privacy
   (C) Reasons for Social Relationships
   (D) The Need for Complete Privacy
   (E) American Manners

7. According to the author, manners serve to
   (A) facilitate relationships among people
   (B) preserve certain ceremonies
   (C) help people to make friends quickly
   (D) reveal character traits
   (E) assist in pleasing one's friends

8. By stating that manners "are armor against invasion of privacy" (line 7), the author wishes to convey that manners
   (A) protect one from physical danger
   (B) are a cold, hard barrier separating people
   (C) allow us to vent our aggressions safely
   (D) shield one from unwanted intrusions
   (E) enable us to guard our possessions

9. The author suggests that in Europe good manners are
   (A) informal
   (B) excessive
   (C) essential
   (D) ignored
   (E) individual

10. In the course of the passage, the author does all of the following EXCEPT
   (A) state a possibility
   (B) use a metaphor
   (C) cite an example
   (D) make a parenthetical remark
   (E) pose a question

One simple physical concept lies behind the formation of the stars: gravitational instability. The concept is not new; Newton first perceived it
Line late in the seventeenth century.
5   Imagine a uniform, static cloud of gas in space. Imagine then that the gas is somehow disturbed so that one small spherical region becomes a little denser than the gas around it so that the small region's gravitational field becomes slightly

10 stronger. It now attracts more matter to it and its gravity increases further, causing it to begin to contract. As it contracts its density increases, which increases its gravity even more, so that it picks up even more matter and contracts even fur-
15 ther. The process continues until the small region of gas finally forms a gravitationally bound object.

11. The primary purpose of the passage is to

(A) demonstrate the evolution of the meaning of a term
(B) depict the successive stages of a phenomenon
(C) establish the pervasiveness of a process
(D) support a theory considered outmoded
(E) describe a static condition

12. The word "disturbed" in line 6 means

(A) hindered   (B) perplexed   (C) disarranged
(D) pestered   (E) thickened

13. It can be inferred from the passage that the author views the information contained within it as

(A) controversial but irrefutable
(B) speculative and unprofitable
(C) uncomplicated and traditional
(D) original but obscure
(E) sadly lacking in elaboration

14. The author provides information that answers which of the following questions?

I. How does the small region's increasing density affect its gravitational field?
II. What causes the disturbance that changes the cloud from its original static state?
III. What is the end result of the gradually increasing concentration of the small region of gas?

(A) I only   (B) II only   (C) I and II only
(D) I and III only   (E) I, II, and III

15. Throughout the passage, the author's manner of presentation is

(A) argumentative   (B) convoluted
(C) discursive   (D) expository
(E) hyperbolic

Unlike the carefully weighed and planned compositions of Dante, Goethe's writings have always the sense of immediacy and enthusiasm. He was a
Line constant experimenter with life, with ideas, and
5 with forms of writing. For the same reason, his works seldom have the qualities of finish or formal beauty which distinguish the masterpieces of Dante and Virgil. He came to love the beauties of classicism, but these were never an essential
10 part of his make-up. Instead, the urgency of the moment, the spirit of the thing, guided his pen. As

a result, nearly all his works have serious flaws of structure, of inconsistencies, of excesses and redundancies and extraneities.
15 In the large sense, Goethe represents the fullest development of the romanticist. It has been argued that he should not be so designated because he so clearly matured and outgrew the kind of romanticism exhibited by Wordsworth, Shelley,
20 and Keats. Shelley and Keats died young; Wordsworth lived narrowly and abandoned his early attitudes. In contrast, Goethe lived abundantly and developed his faith in the spirit, his understanding of nature and human nature, and his
25 reliance on feelings as man's essential motivating force. The result was an all-encompassing vision of reality and a philosophy of life broader and deeper than the partial visions and attitudes of other romanticists. Yet the spirit of youthfulness, the
30 impatience with close reasoning or "logic-chopping," and the continued faith in nature remained his to the end, together with an occasional waywardness and impulsiveness and a disregard of artistic or logical propriety which savor strongly of
35 romantic individualism. Since so many twentieth-century thoughts and attitudes are similarly based on the stimulus of the Romantic Movement, Goethe stands as particularly the poet of the modern man as Dante stood for medieval
40 man and as Shakespeare for the man of the Renaissance.

16. The word "close" in line 30 means

(A) nearby   (B) intimate   (C) fitting tightly
(D) strictly logical   (E) nearly even

17. A main concern of the passage is to

(A) describe the history of romanticism until its decline
(B) suggest that romantic literature is similar to Shakespearean drama
(C) argue that romantic writings are more fully developed than classical works
(D) compare Goethe with twentieth-century writers and poets
(E) explain the ways in which Goethe embodied the romantic spirit

18. A characteristic of romanticism NOT mentioned in this passage is its

(A) elevation of nature
(B) preference for spontaneity
(C) modernity of ideas
(D) unconcern for artistic decorum
(E) simplicity of language

19. It can be inferred from the passage that classicism has which of the following characteristics?

    I. sensitivity toward emotional promptings
    II. emphasis on formal aesthetic standards
    III. meticulous planning of artistic works

    (A) II only   (B) III only   (C) I and II
    (D) II and III   (E) I, II, and III

20. The author's attitude toward Goethe's writings is best described as

    (A) unqualified endorsement
    (B) lofty indifference
    (C) reluctant tolerance
    (D) measured admiration
    (E) undisguised contempt

EXERCISE D

    To keep clear of concealment, to keep clear of the need of concealment, to do nothing which you might not do out on the middle of Boston Common at noonday—I cannot say how more and
5 more it seems to me the glory of a young person's life. It is an awful hour when the first necessity of hiding anything comes. The whole life is different thenceforth. When there are questions to be feared and eyes to be avoided and subjects which must
10 not be touched, then the bloom of life is gone. Put off that day as long as possible. Put it off forever if you can.

1. The author regards the occasion when one first must conceal something as

    (A) anticlimactic   (B) insignificant
    (C) fleeting   (D) momentous
    (E) enviable

2. The author's tone throughout the passage can best be described as

    (A) hostile   (B) condescending   (C) playful
    (D) serious   (E) impersonal

3. Which of the following does the author recommend to his audience?

    I. to deny the necessity of aging
    II. to act in an aboveboard manner
    III. to rationalize one's misconduct

    (A) I only   (B) II only   (C) I and II only
    (D) II and III only   (E) I, II, and III

    Most people want to know how things are made. They frankly admit, however, that they feel completely at sea when it comes to understanding how a piece of music is made. Where a composer
5 begins, how he manages to keep going—in fact, how and where he learns his trade—all are shrouded in impenetrable darkness. The composer, in short, is a figure of mystery, and the composer's workshop an unapproachable ivory tower.
10   One of the first things lay persons want to hear about is the part inspiration plays in composing. They find it difficult to believe that composers are not much preoccupied with that question, that composing is as natural for the composer as eating
15 or sleeping. Composing is something that the composer happens to have been born to do; and because of that, it loses the character of a special virtue in the composer's eyes.

    The composer, therefore, does not say to himself:
20 "Do I feel inspired?" He says to himself: "Do I feel like composing today?" And if he feels like composing, he does. It is more or less like saying to himself: "Do I feel sleepy?" If you feel sleepy, you go to sleep. If you don't feel sleepy, you stay
25 up. If the composer doesn't feel like composing, he doesn't compose. It's as simple as that.

4. The author of the passage indicates that creating music is an activity that is

    (A) difficult   (B) rewarding   (C) inspirational
    (D) fraught with anxiety   (E) instinctive

5. When considering the work involved in composing music, the lay person often

    (A) exaggerates the difficulties of the composer in commencing work
    (B) minimizes the mental turmoil that the composer undergoes
    (C) is unaware that a creative process is involved
    (D) loses the ability to enjoy the composition
    (E) loses the ability to judge the work apart from the composer

6. The author's approach toward the subject is

    (A) highly emotional   (B) casually informative
    (C) negative in tone   (D) deeply philosophical
    (E) consciously prejudiced

    John Greenleaf Whittier was the "Quaker-Puritan" scion of Massachusetts farmers. For this frail young man, however, farm life was too tough an existence. His early interest in books and legends
5 led him toward journalism, with poetry a pleasant side line. He became a Quaker firebrand and agitator, the politician among abolitionists, and a gadfly to New England Congressmen during the original "Great Debate." His impassioned prose and poetry

10 against slavery were often directed at a clergy whose acceptance of it he fought as a Quaker and a Christian.

Only after the Civil War, when emancipation had been at least nominally won, did the aging
15 Whittier emerge as the genial, easygoing "folk-bard" remembered today. Until recently the prominence given this last phase of his literary life by scholarly circles has obscured his earlier contributions to American literature and political
20 freedom and tolerance.

7. The primary purpose of this passage is to

(A) denounce a social injustice
(B) evaluate a writer's poetic style
(C) explain a nineteenth-century literary fashion
(D) correct a misconception about an individual
(E) argue against political involvement

8. The author's attitude toward Whittier's early career as a firebrand can best be described as one of

(A) wary skepticism (B) moral censure
(C) reluctant tolerance (D) objective neutrality
(E) open approbation

9. It can be inferred from the passage that New England Congressmen during the time of the "Great Debate" most likely thought of Whittier as

(A) a cordial teller of tales
(B) an antiabolitionist
(C) an annoying critic
(D) a virtuous Quaker
(E) a literary scholar

10. On the basis of the passage, which of the following opinions can appropriately be attributed to Whittier?

(A) The aim of literature is to entertain the reading public rather than to advocate a particular cause.
(B) Emancipation can occur only with the full cooperation of the slave owners, who thus must be won over gently.
(C) A poet must devote himself to his art, forsaking worldly claims in favor of aesthetic values.
(D) It is particularly reprehensible for Christian ministers to tolerate an institution as immoral as slavery.
(E) There is no place in the church for disharmony and strife, for the church is the temple of the Lord.

We were about a quarter mile away when quiet swept over the colony. A thousand or more heads periscoped. Two thousand eyes glared. Save for our
Line wading, the world's business had stopped. A thou-
5 sand avian personalities were concentrated on us, and the psychological force of this was terrific. Contingents of home-coming feeders, suddenly

aware of four strange specks moving across the lake, would bank violently and speed away. Then
10 the chain reaction began. Every throat in that rookery let go with a concatenation of wild, raspy, terrorized trumpet bursts. With all wings now fully spread and churning, and quadrupling the color mass, the birds began to move as one, and
15 the sky was filled with the sound of judgment day.

11. The author's primary purpose in this passage is to

(A) explain a natural catastrophe
(B) issue a challenge
(C) denounce an expedition
(D) evoke an experience
(E) demonstrate a thesis

12. According to the passage, when they first noticed the visitors, the birds of the colony

(A) flew away
(B) churned their wings
(C) became very still
(D) set up a series of cries
(E) glared at the homecoming birds

13. The "four strange specks" (line 8) are

(A) wild birds
(B) animal predators
(C) intruding humans
(D) unusual clouds
(E) diners heading homeward

14. The word "bank" in line 9 means

(A) cover (B) heap up (C) count on
(D) tip laterally (E) reserve carefully

15. The response of the visitors to the episode described in this passage was probably one of

(A) impatience (B) fear (C) anger
(D) sadness (E) awe

With Meredith's *The Egoist* we enter into a critical problem that we have not yet before faced in these studies. That is the problem offered by a
Line writer of recognizably impressive stature, whose
5 work is informed by a muscular intelligence, whose language has splendor, whose "view of life" wins our respect, and yet for whom we are at best able to feel only a passive appreciation which amounts, practically, to indifference. We should be
10 unjust to Meredith and to criticism if we should, giving in to the inertia of indifference, simply avoid dealing with him and thus avoid the problem along with him. He does not "speak to us," we might say; his meaning is not a "meaning for us";
15 he "leaves us cold." But do not the challenge and the excitement of the critical problem as such lie in that ambivalence of attitude which allows us to

recognize the intelligence and even the splendor of Meredith's work, while, at the same time, we
20 experience a lack of sympathy, a failure of any enthusiasm of response?

16. According to the passage, the work of Meredith is noteworthy for its elements of

(A) sensibility and artistic fervor
(B) ambivalence and moral ambiguity
(C) tension and sense of vitality
(D) brilliance and linguistic grandeur
(E) wit and whimsical frivolity

17. The word "informed" in line 5 means

(A) notified   (B) permeated   (C) disclosed
(D) acquainted   (E) incriminated

18. Meredith's chief flaw as a writer is that

(A) his writing fails to excite the reader
(B) his works have fallen out of fashion
(C) he retreated into ineffectual passivity
(D) he should have been a poet rather than a novelist
(E) his novels lack any genuine meaning

19. It can be inferred from the passage that the author finds the prospect of appraising Meredith's work critically to be

(A) counterproductive   (B) highly formidable
(C) somewhat tolerable   (D) markedly unpalatable
(E) clearly invigorating

20. It can be inferred from the passage that the author would be most likely to agree with which of the following statements about the role of criticism?

(A) Its chief task should be to make our enjoyment of the things that feed the mind as conscious as possible.
(B) It should be a disinterested attempt to learn and propagate the best that is known and thought in the world.
(C) It should enable us to go beyond personal prejudice to appreciate the virtues of works not to our own tastes.
(D) It should dwell upon virtues rather than imperfections, ignoring such defects as irrelevant.
(E) It should strive both to purify literature and to elevate the literary standards of the reading public.

EXERCISE E

For all of e.e. cummings's typographical innovations, he was an old-fashioned poet. He wrote about death and love, the graces of nature and the
Line disgraces of civilization. He implored beautiful
5 ladies for their favors and wittily thanked them afterwards. He distrusted power and satirized people in power. He adored Paris and said so in random lines as taking as any in English about that lovely city. He valued childhood and described its inno-
10 cence with wide-open-eyed clarity. He adored puns and practiced them like an Elizabethan.

In all this he was an old-fashioned poet. Even his typography, which seemed so modern, was ancient in intention. Cummings revered Latin and
15 Greek verse and understood that English, for all its excellences, had never achieved the concision and special effects available to the interlocking syntaxes of those inflected languages. In his poems he wanted to make many things happen simulta-
20 neously. He wanted to catch action in words and yet keep it shivering. He wanted words to merge as impressions in the mind do. He wanted to reach backward and forward, pulling past and future into a present instant. To do this he used punctuation
25 like a second language. This was not an innovation so much as a thorough realization of a lost art.

1. Throughout the passage, the author's primary purpose is to

(A) emphasize cummings's revolutionary technique
(B) account for cummings's choice of subject matter
(C) contrast cummings with foreign poets
(D) provide specific examples of cummings's verse
(E) correct a misconception about cummings's poetry

2. As used in line 8, "taking" most nearly means

(A) grasping   (B) pleasing   (C) selective
(D) resounding   (E) ironic

3. It can be inferred from the passage that the Elizabethans

(A) believed in the value of practice
(B) were contemporaries of cummings
(C) employed modern typography
(D) enjoyed playing with words
(E) lacked childlike vision

4. Cummings admired classical verse for its

(A) succinctness   (B) piety   (C) lyricism
(D) euphony   (E) profundity

5. By "He wanted to catch action in words and yet keep it shivering" (lines 20–21), the author means that cummings

(A) hoped to evoke a sense of terror in the reader
(B) wished to preserve the act's excitement and vitality
(C) was shaken by the prospect of verbal criticism
(D) believed that it was simple to capture a moment poetically
(E) preferred the poetry of action to the poetry of contemplation

Rocks which have solidified directly from molten materials are called igneous rocks. Igneous rocks are commonly referred to as primary
Line rocks because they are the original source of
5 material found in sedimentaries and metamorphics. Igneous rocks compose the greater part of the earth's crust, but they are generally covered at the surface by a relatively thin layer of sedimentary or metamorphic rocks. Igneous rocks are dis-
10 tinguished by the following characteristics: (1) they contain no fossils; (2) they have no regular arrangement of layers; and (3) they are nearly always made up of crystals.

Sedimentary rocks are composed largely of
15 minute fragments derived from the disintegration of existing rocks and in some instances from the remains of animals. As sediments are transported, individual fragments are assorted according to size. Distinct layers of such sediments as gravels,
20 sand, and clay build up, as they are deposited by water and occasionally wind. These sediments vary in size with the material and the power of the eroding agent. Sedimentary materials are laid down in layers called strata.
25 When sediments harden into sedimentary rocks, the names applied to them change to indicate the change in physical state. Thus, small stones and gravel cemented together are known as conglomerates; cemented sand becomes sand-
30 stone; and hardened clay becomes shale. In addition to these, other sedimentary rocks such as limestone frequently result from the deposition of dissolved material. The ingredient parts are normally precipitated by organic substances, such as
35 shells of clams or hard skeletons of other marine life.

Both igneous and sedimentary rocks may be changed by pressure, heat, solution, or cementing action. When individual grains from existing rocks
40 tend to deform and interlock, they are called metamorphic rocks. For example, granite, an igneous rock, may be metamorphosed into a gneiss or a schist. Limestone, a sedimentary rock, when subjected to heat and pressure may become marble, a
45 metamorphic rock. Shale under pressure becomes slate.

6. The primary purpose of the passage is to

(A) explain the factors that may cause rocks to change in form
(B) show how the scientific names of rocks reflect the rocks' composition
(C) present a new hypothesis about the nature of rock formation
(D) define and describe several diverse kinds of rocks
(E) explain why rocks are basic parts of the earth's structure

7. The word "state" in line 27 means

(A) mood   (B) pomp   (C) territory
(D) predicament   (E) condition

8. According to the passage, igneous rocks are characterized by

(A) their inability to be changed by heat or pressure
(B) the wealth of fossils they incorporate
(C) their granular composition
(D) their relative rarity
(E) their lack of regular strata

9. The passage contains information that would answer which of the following questions?

I. Which elements form igneous rocks?
II. What produces sufficient pressure to alter a rock?
III. Why is marble called a metamorphic rock?

(A) I only   (B) III only   (C) I and II only
(D) II and III only   (E) I, II, and III

10. Which of the following methods is NOT used by the author?

(A) precise examples
(B) classification and discussion
(C) specific enumeration
(D) observation and hypothesis
(E) cause and effect

The oldest adult human skull yet found belongs to the lowest grade of *Homo erectus*, and to the Australoid line. It is known as Pithecanthropus
Line (Ape-Man) Number 4, because it was the fourth
5 of its kind to be found. All four were unearthed in river banks in central Java. Number 4 is about 700,000 years old, and Numbers 1, 2, and 3 between 600,000 and 500,000. We know this because tektites—small, glassy nodules from outer space—
10 were found in the same beds as the first three, and the beds containing Number 4 lay underneath the tektite bed, along with the bones of a more ancient group of animals. These tektites have been picked up in large numbers in Java, the Philippines, and
15 Australia, where they all fell in a single celestial shower. Their age—approximately 600,000 years—has been accurately measured in several

laboratories by nuclear chemical analysis, through
the so-called argon-potassium method.

20   Pithecanthropus Number 4 consists of the
back part of a skull and its lower face, palate, and
upper teeth. As reconstructed by Weidenreich, it is
a brutal-looking skull, with heavy crests behind
four powerful neck muscle attachments, a large
25 palate, and large teeth, as in apes. The brain size of
this skull was about 900 cubic centimeters;
modern human brains range from about 1,450 cc.
The brains of apes and Australopithecines are about
350 to 650 cc. So Pithecanthropus Number 4 was
30 intermediate in brain size between apes and living
men.

     This fragmentary skull was not the only find
made in the beds it lay in. Nearby were found the
cranial vault of a two-year-old baby, already differ-
35 ent from those of living infants, and a piece of
chinless adult lower jaw. Two other jaws have been
discovered in the same deposits which were much
larger than any in the world certainly belonging to
Homo erectus. They are called Meganthropus (Big
40 Man) and may have belonged to a local kind of
Australopithecine, but this is not certain. If so,
Homo erectus coexisted with, or overlapped, the
Australopithecines in Java as well as in South
Africa, which implies that man did not originate
45 in either place, but somewhere in between.

11. According to the passage, tektites are

    (A) customarily found with the bones of animals
    (B) undersized lumps of a glasslike substance
    (C) a step in the evolutionary process
    (D) equal in age to Ape-Man Number 4
    (E) dissolved in a solution of argon-potassium

12. Scientists are certain that Pithecanthropus Number 4 is older than Pithecanthropus Numbers 1, 2,
and 3 because

    (A) it was discovered later than the others
    (B) it was found in the company of tektites
    (C) its age was measured by nuclear chemical
       analysis
    (D) it was located below the tektite layer
    (E) its skull is larger in cranial capacity

13. According to the passage, archaeological study
of Pithecanthropus skulls involves which of the
following?

    I. measurement of cranial capacity
   II. piecing together of bone fragments
  III. comparison with analogous primate skulls

    (A) I only   (B) II only   (C) I and II only
    (D) II and III only   (E) I, II, and III

14. The word "vault" in line 34 means

    (A) a running jump
    (B) a curved ceiling over a room or hall
    (C) a strongbox for safeguarding valuables
    (D) an arched roof of a cavity
    (E) a burial chamber

15. The author does all of the following EXCEPT

    (A) approximate an age
    (B) define a term
    (C) cite an authority
    (D) describe an object
    (E) make a comparison

     A few species demonstrate conditions which
are neither complete hibernation nor aestivation.
Instead of going into a long "sleep" during the
Line most adverse season, they become torpid for a few
5 hours each day. This kind of behavior is known in
other animals—bats become torpid during day-
time, and hummingbirds at night. The first time I
appreciated this phenomenon was while working
with fat mice (*Steatomys*) in Africa. These mice,
10 incidentally, have a most appropriate name, for
their bodies are so full of fat they resemble little
furry balls. Fat storage as a method of survival has
rebounded to some extent as far as the fat mice are
concerned. They are regarded as a succulent deli-
15 cacy by many African tribes who hunt them with
great tenacity; when captured, the mice are skew-
ered and fried in their own fat. A captive fat mouse
was once kept without food or water for thirty-six
days; at the end of that time it had lost a third of
20 its weight but appeared quite healthy. During the
dry season, some captives spent the day in such a
deep state of torpor that they could be roughly
handled without waking. The body temperature
was a couple of degrees above room temperature
25 and the respiration was most irregular, several
short pants being followed by a pause of up to
three minutes. Just before dusk the mice woke up
of their own accord and respired normally. In this
case the torpid state was not induced by shortage
30 of food or abnormal temperatures. The forest dor-
mouse of southern Asia and Europe also undergoes periods of torpidity during the day; this
species has been recorded as having pauses of up
to seventeen minutes between breaths. There is
35 also a record of a leaf-eared mouse of the Peruvian
desert which became torpid under severe
conditions.

16. The primary focus of the passage is on
   (A) the inhumane treatment of laboratory specimens
   (B) irregularities of respiration in mammals
   (C) conditions that induce rodents to hibernate
   (D) rodent species that exhibit brief periods of dormancy
   (E) the similarities among rodent species

17. The word "rebounded" in line 13 means
   (A) recovered from discouragement
   (B) sprung back from ill health
   (C) had a negative impact
   (D) rapidly gained hold
   (E) been rejected

18. The tone of the passage can best be described as
   (A) apologetic   (B) facetious   (C) exhortatory
   (D) authoritative   (E) ironic

19. This passage would most likely appear in which of the following types of publications?
   (A) a geographical atlas
   (B) a history of African exploration
   (C) a textbook on rodent biology
   (D) a guide to the care of laboratory animals
   (E) a general-interest periodical

20. It can be inferred that in the paragraph preceding this passage the author most likely discussed
   (A) his initial journey to Africa
   (B) the problems caused by sleep deprivation
   (C) other types of dormant states
   (D) the physical appearance of rodents
   (E) methods for measuring rodent respiration

Answer Key—Reading

EXERCISE A

1. D	8. D	15. B
2. B	9. A	16. E
3. D	10. A	17. A
4. B	11. E	18. A
5. E	12. C	19. D
6. A	13. E	20. B
7. E	14. A	

EXERCISE B

1. A	8. E	15. E
2. D	9. D	16. B
3. D	10. A	17. C
4. E	11. D	18. D
5. B	12. A	19. D
6. B	13. A	20. C
7. B	14. C	

EXERCISE C

1. A	8. D	15. D
2. D	9. C	16. D
3. C	10. E	17. E
4. B	11. B	18. E
5. B	12. C	19. D
6. A	13. C	20. D
7. A	14. D	

EXERCISE D

1. D	8. E	15. E
2. D	9. C	16. D
3. B	10. D	17. B
4. E	11. D	18. A
5. A	12. C	19. E
6. B	13. C	20. C
7. D	14. D	

EXERCISE E

1. E	8. E	15. C
2. B	9. B	16. D
3. D	10. D	17. C
4. A	11. B	18. D
5. B	12. D	19. C
6. D	13. E	20. C
7. E	14. D	

► CHAPTER 6
Building Your Vocabulary

Recognizing the meaning of words is essential to comprehending what you read. The more you stumble over unfamiliar words in a text, the more you have to take time out to look up words in your dictionary, the more likely you are to wind up losing track of what the author has to say.

To succeed in college, you must develop a college-level vocabulary. You must familiarize yourself with technical words in a wide variety of fields, mastering each field's special vocabulary. You must learn to use these words, and reuse them until they become second nature to you. The time you put in now learning vocabulary-building techniques for the PSAT will pay off later on and not just on the PSAT.

LONG-RANGE STRATEGY

There is only one effective long-range strategy for vocabulary building: READ.

Read—widely and well. Sample different fields—physics, art history, political science, geology—and different styles. Extensive reading is the one sure way to make your vocabulary grow.

As you read, however, take some time to acquaint yourself specifically with the kinds of words you must know to do well on the PSAT. No matter how little time you have before the test, you still can familiarize yourself with the sort of vocabulary you will be facing on the PSAT. First, look over the 300 words you will find on our PSAT high-frequency word list (page 118): each of these 300 words, ranging from everyday words such as *ample* and *meek* to less commonly known ones such as *esoteric* and *pervasive* has appeared (as answer choices or as question words) at least four times in PSATs in the past two decades.

Next, proceed to master these high-frequency words. First check off the words you think you know. Then *look up all 300 words and their definitions in our abridged basic word list* (pages 120–167). Pay particular attention to the words you thought you knew. See whether any of them are defined in an unexpected way. If they are, make a special note of them. As you know from the preceding chapters, the PSAT often stumps students with questions based on unfamiliar meanings of familiar-looking words.

Not only will looking over the high-frequency word list reassure you that you *do* know some PSAT-type words; but also it may well help you on the actual day of the test. These words have turned up on recent tests; some of them may appear on the test you take.

Examine the abridged basic word list as well. Even before the College Board began publishing its own PSAT sample examinations, the basic word list was unique in its ability to reflect and often predict the actual vocabulary appearing on the PSAT. Today, thanks to our ongoing research and computer analysis of published PSAT materials, we believe our basic word list is the best in the field.

For this book, we have selected the most important 1,300 words of the master list. Most students preparing for the PSAT/NMSQT have little time in which to study and don't feel up to facing the 3,500-word SAT list. We want you to have a tool that will be useful to you, both now and when you study for the SAT in the coming year. We hope this compact list will be the tool you need.

A Plan for Using the Word List

For those of you who wish to work your way through the word list and feel the need for a plan, we recommend that you follow the procedure described below in order to use the lists most profitably:

1. Allot a definite time each day for the study of a list.
2. Devote at least one hour to each list.
3. First, go through the list looking at the short, simple-looking words (six letters at most). Mark those you don't know. In studying, pay particular attention to them.
4. Go through the list again looking at the longer words. Pay particular attention to words with more than one meaning and familiar-looking words that have unusual definitions that come as a surprise to you. Many tests make use of these secondary definitions.
5. List unusual words on index cards so that you can shuffle and review them from time to time. (Study no more than five cards at a time.)
6. Use the illustrative sentences in the list as models and make up new sentences of your own.

For each word, the following is provided:

- The word (printed in heavy type)
- Its part of speech (abbreviated)
- A brief definition
- A sentence illustrating the word's use

Whenever appropriate, related words are provided, together with their parts of speech.

The forty-eight word lists are arranged in alphabetical order.

PSAT HIGH-FREQUENCY WORD LIST

absolve	aspire	composure	demean
abstract	assert	compromise	denounce
accessible	assumption	condone	depict
acclaim	authentic	confirm	deplete
accommodate	autonomous	conformity	deplore
acknowledge	aversion	confront	derision
acrimony	banal	congenial	derivative
adversary	beneficial	conscientious	detached
adverse	benign	consistency	deterrent
aesthetic	betray	consolidation	didactic
affable	brittle	contentious	diffident
affinity	buoyant	convention	digression
alleviate	candor	convoluted	discernible
altruistic	captivate	corrosion	disclaimer
ambiguous	caricature	curtail	disclose
ambivalence	censor	dawdle	discord
amenable	chronicle	dearth	discrepancy
ample	circumspect	debilitate	disgruntled
antagonism	cite	decorous	disinterested
apathy	cliché	decry	dismiss
apprehension	coalesce	defamation	disparage
apprenticeship	collaborate	deference	disparate
appropriate	compliance	defiance	dispatch
aristocracy	component	degenerate	dispel

disperse
dissent
dissipate
distinction
divulge
docile
doctrine
dogmatic
eclectic
eclipse
elated
elicit
elusive
embellish
endorse
enhance
enigma
entice
enumerate
ephemeral
erode
erratic
erroneous
esoteric
espouse
esteem
excerpt
exemplary
exonerate
expedite
exploit
facilitate
fallacious
farce
fastidious
fawning
feasible
fervor
flippant
forthright
frail
frivolous
garrulous
generate
genre
gluttonous
gratify
gregarious
hackneyed
hamper
hindrance

hostility
hypocritical
hypothetical
iconoclastic
immutable
impede
imperceptible
implacable
implement
implication
impromptu
incarcerate
incongruity
inconsequential
inconsistency
incorporate
indict
indifferent
induce
industrious
inept
infallible
ingenious
ingenuous
ingrate
inherent
initiate
innate
innocuous
inscrutable
insightful
intangible
integrity
intricacy
introspective
irony
judicious
languid
larceny
lethargic
loathe
malice
meek
meticulous
misconception
misrepresent
mock
monarchy
monotony
mutability
naïveté

nocturnal
nonchalance
nostalgia
notorious
nurture
obnoxious
obscure
opaque
optimist
orator
ostentatious
outmoded
pacifist
pacify
paradox
patronize
pedantic
perjury
perpetual
pervasive
pessimism
petulant
phenomena
philanthropist
plagiarize
potency
pragmatic
precedent
predator
premise
premonition
presumptuous
prevail
prey
profound
proliferation
prolific
prologue
prominent
promote
prophetic
prosperity
provocative
prudent
ramble
random
recluse
refute
rejuvenate
relinquish
renown

reprehensible
repudiate
reserved
resignation
resolution
resolve
restraint
retain
reticent
reverent
ruthless
satirize
scrutinize
seclusion
serenity
sever
severity
singular
skeptical
steadfast
stoic
stratagem
subdued
subversive
superficial
superfluous
suppress
surpass
susceptible
suspend
sustain
symmetry
synthesis
taciturn
tedious
temper
temperament
termination
thwart
toxic
transcendent
transparent
trepidation
turbulence
urbane
utopia
vacillate
versatile
volatile
voracious
wary

The abridged Basic Word List follows. *Do not let this list overwhelm you.* You do not need to memorize every word.

The present word list derives from our standard 3,500-word list, published in *Barron's How to Prepare for the SAT*. Ever since this list first appeared in 1954, countless students have reported that working with these words has helped them immensely in taking all kinds of college entrance and scholarship tests. The list has been used with profit by people preparing for civil service examinations, placement tests, and promotional examinations in many fields. Above all, it has been used with profit by students studying for the SAT and the PSAT.

An entry preceded by a bullet (•) is a High-Frequency Word.

WORD LIST 1

abase – accommodate

abase V. lower; humiliate. Defeated, Queen Zenobia was forced to *abase* herself before the conquering Romans, who forced her to march before the emperor Aurelian in the procession celebrating his triumph.

abate V. subside; decrease; lessen. Rather than leaving immediately, they waited for the storm to *abate*. abatement, N.

abdicate V. renounce; give up. When Edward VIII *abdicated* the British throne to marry the woman he loved, he surprised the entire world. When the painter Gauguin *abdicated* his family responsibilities to run off to Samoa, he surprised no one at all.

aberration N. deviation from the expected or the normal; mental irregularity or disorder. Survivors of a major catastrophe are likely to exhibit *aberrations* of behavior because of the trauma they have experienced. aberrant, ADJ. and N.

abet V. encourage; aid. She was accused of aiding and *abetting* the drug dealer by engaging in a money-laundering scheme to help him disguise his illegal income. abettor, N.

abeyance N. suspended action. The deal was held in *abeyance* until her arrival.

abject ADJ. hopeless and crushed; servile and spiritless; wretched. On the streets of New York, the homeless live in *abject* poverty, lying huddled in doorways to find shelter from the wind.

abrade V. wear away by friction; scrape; erode. The sharp rocks *abraded* the skin on her legs; so she put iodine on her *abrasions*.

abscond V. depart secretly to avoid capture. The teller who *absconded* with the bonds was not captured until someone recognized him from his photograph on *America's Most Wanted*.

absolute ADJ. complete; totally unlimited; certain. Although the king of Siam was an *absolute* monarch, he did not want to behead his unfaithful wife without *absolute* evidence of her infidelity.

• **absolve** V. pardon (an offense); free from blame. The father confessor *absolved* him of his sins. absolution, N.

abstain V. refrain; hold oneself back voluntarily from an action or practice (especially one regarded as improper or unhealthy). After considering the effect of alcohol on his athletic performance, he decided to *abstain* from drinking while he trained for the race. abstinence, N.; abstinent or abstemious, ADJ.

• **abstract** ADJ. theoretical; not concrete; nonrepresentational. To him, hunger was an *abstract* concept; he had never missed a meal.

abstruse ADJ. obscure; profound; difficult to understand. She carries around *abstruse* works of philosophy, not because she understands them but because she wants her friends to think she does.

accelerate V. move faster. In our science class, we learn how falling bodies *accelerate*.

• **accessible** ADJ. easy to approach; obtainable. We asked our guide whether the ruins were *accessible* on foot.

accessory N. additional object; useful but not essential thing. The *accessories* she bought cost more than the dress. also ADJ.

• **acclaim** V. applaud; announce with great approval. The NBC sportscasters *acclaimed* every American victory in the Olympics and lamented every American defeat. acclamation, acclaim, N.

accolade N. award of merit. In the world of public relations, a Clio is the highest *accolade* an advertising campaign can receive.

• **accommodate** V. provide lodgings. Mary asked the room clerk whether the hotel would be able to *accommodate* the tour group on such short notice. accommodations, N.

• **accommodate** V. oblige or help someone; adjust or bring into harmony; adapt. Mitch always did everything possible to *accommodate* his elderly relatives, from driving them to medical appointments to helping them with paperwork. accommodating, ADJ. (secondary meaning)

accomplice N. partner in crime. Because he had provided the criminal with the lethal weapon, he was arrested as an *accomplice* in the murder.

• **acknowledge** V. recognize; admit. Although Ira *acknowledged* that the Beatles' tunes sounded pretty dated nowadays, he still preferred them to the punk rock songs his nephews played.

acquittal N. declaration of innocence; deliverance from a charge. His *acquittal* by the jury surprised those who had thought him guilty. acquit, V.

• **acrimony** N. bitterness of words or manner. The candidate attacked his opponent with great *acrimony*. acrimonious, ADJ.

acumen N. mental keenness. His business *acumen* helped him to succeed where others had failed.

adamant ADJ. hard; inflexible. Bronson played the part of a revenge-driven man, *adamant* in his determination to punish the criminals who had destroyed his family. adamancy, N.

adapt V. alter; modify. Some species of animals have become extinct because they could not *adapt* to a changing environment.

addiction N. compulsive, habitual need. His *addiction* to drugs caused his friends much grief.

adhere V. stick fast to. I will *adhere* to this opinion until someone comes up with solid proof that I am wrong. adhesive, ADJ.

adjacent ADJ. adjoining; neighboring; close by. Philip's best friend Jason lived only four houses away, close but not immediately *adjacent*.

adjudicate V. pass legal judgment on; sit in judgment. Do you trust Judge Judy to *adjudicate* disputes impartially?

admonish V. warn; scold. The preacher *admonished* his listeners to change their wicked ways. admonition, N.

adroit ADJ. skillful; nimble. The juggler's admirers particularly enjoyed his *adroit* handling of difficult balancing tricks.

adulation N. flattery; admiration. The rock star relished the *adulation* she received from her groupies and yes-men.

adulterate V. make impure by adding inferior or tainted substances. It is a crime to *adulterate* foods without informing the buyer; when consumers learned that the manufacturer had *adulterated* its apple juice by mixing it with water, they protested vigorously.

• **adversary** N. opponent. "Aha!" cried Holmes. "Watson, I suspect this delay is the work of my old *adversary* Professor Moriarty." adversarial, ADJ.

• **adverse** ADJ. unfavorable; hostile. The recession had a highly *adverse* effect on Father's investment portfolio: he lost so much money that he could no longer afford the butler and the upstairs maid. adversity, N.

adversity N. poverty; misfortune. We must learn to meet *adversity* gracefully.

advocate V. urge; plead for. Noted abolitionists such as Frederick Douglass and Sojourner Truth *advocated* the eradication of the Southern institution of slavery. also N.

• **aesthetic** ADJ. artistic; dealing with or capable of appreciation of the beautiful. The beauty of Tiffany's stained glass appealed to Alice's *aesthetic* sense. aesthete, N.

• **affable** ADJ. easily approachable; warmly friendly. Accustomed to cold, aloof supervisors, Nicholas was amazed by how *affable* his new employer was.

affected ADJ. artificial; pretended; assumed in order to impress. His *affected* mannerisms—his "Harvard" accent, his air of boredom, his flaunting of obscure foreign words—irritated many of us who had known him before he had gone away to school. affectation, N.

• **affinity** N. kinship; attraction to. She felt an *affinity* with all who suffered; their pains were her pains. Her brother, in contrast, had an *affinity* for political wheeling and dealing; he manipulated people shamelessly, not caring who got hurt.

affirmation N. positive assertion; confirmation; solemn pledge by one who refuses to take an oath. Despite Tom's *affirmations* of innocence, Aunt Polly still suspected he had eaten the pie. affirm, V.

affix V. add on; fasten; attach. First the registrar had to *affix* her signature to the license; then she had to *affix* her official seal.

affluence N. wealth; prosperity; abundance. Galvanized by his sudden, unexpected *affluence*, the lottery winner dashed out to buy himself a brand new Ferrari. affluent, ADJ.

affront V. insult; offend. Accustomed to being treated with respect, Miss Challoner was *affronted* by Vidal's offensive behavior.

aggregate V. gather; accumulate. Before the Wall Street scandals, dealers in so-called junk bonds managed to *aggregate* great wealth in short periods of time. aggregation, N.

agility N. nimbleness. The acrobat's *agility* amazed and thrilled the audience. agile, ADJ.

agitate V. stir up; disturb. Her fiery remarks further *agitated* the already angry mob.

alacrity N. cheerful promptness. Phil and Dave were raring to get off to the mountains; they packed up their ski gear and climbed into the van with *alacrity*.

alias N. an assumed name. John Smith's *alias* was Bob Jones. also ADV.

alienate V. make hostile; separate. Her attempts to *alienate* the two friends failed because they had complete faith in each other.

• **alleviate** V. relieve; lessen. This should *alleviate* the pain; if it does not, we will use stronger drugs.

alloy V. mix; make less pure; lessen or moderate. Our delight at the victory was *alloyed* by our concern for the pitcher, who injured his pitching arm in the game.

allude V. refer indirectly. Try not to mention divorce in John's presence because he will think you are *alluding* to his marital problems with Jill.

allure V. entice; attract. *Allured* by the song of the sirens, the helmsman steered the ship toward the reef. also N.

allusion N. indirect reference. When Amanda said to the ticket scalper, "One hundred bucks? What do you want, a pound of flesh?," she was making an *allusion* to Shakespeare's *Merchant of Venice*.

aloft ADV. upward. The sailor climbed *aloft* into the rigging. To get into a loft bed, you have to climb *aloft*.

aloof ADJ. apart; reserved; standoffish. People thought James was a snob because he remained *aloof* while all the rest of the group conversed.

altercation N. noisy quarrel; heated dispute. In that hot-tempered household, no meal ever came to a peaceful conclusion; the inevitable *altercation* occasionally even ended in blows.

• **altruistic** ADJ. unselfishly generous; concerned for others. The star received no fee for appearing at the benefit; it was a purely *altruistic* act. altruism, N.

amalgam N. mixture of different elements; alloy. In character, King Gustav was a strange *amalgam* of hard-headed practicality and religious zeal. amalgamate, V.

• **ambiguous** ADJ. unclear or doubtful in meaning. The proctor's *ambiguous* instructions thoroughly confused us; we didn't know which columns we should mark and which we should leave blank. ambiguity, N.

• **ambivalence** N. having contradictory or conflicting emotional attitudes. Torn between loving her parents one minute and hating them the next, she was confused by the *ambivalence* of her feelings. ambivalent, ADJ.

ambulatory ADJ. able to walk; not bedridden. Jonathan was a highly *ambulatory* patient; not only did he refuse to be confined to bed, but also he insisted on riding his skateboard up and down the halls.

ameliorate V. improve; make more satisfactory. Carl became a union organizer because he wanted to join the fight to *ameliorate* working conditions in the factory.

• **amenable** ADJ. readily managed; willing to give in; agreeable; submissive. A born snob, Wilbur was *amenable* to any suggestions from those he looked up to, but he resented advice from his supposed inferiors. Unfortunately, his incorrigible snobbery was not *amenable* to improvement.

amiable ADJ. agreeable; lovable; warmly friendly. In *Little Women*, Beth is the *amiable* daughter whose loving disposition endears her to all who have dealings with her.

amorous ADJ. moved by sexual love; loving. "Love them and leave them" was the motto of the *amorous* Don Juan.

amorphous ADJ. formless; lacking shape or definition. As soon as we have decided on our itinerary, we shall send you a copy; right now, our plans are still *amorphous*.

• **ample** ADJ. abundant. Bond had *ample* opportunity to escape. Why did he let us catch him?

amplify V. broaden or clarify by expanding; intensify; make stronger. Charlie Brown tried to *amplify* his remarks, but he was drowned out by jeers from the audience. Lucy, however, used a loudspeaker to *amplify* her voice and drowned out all the hecklers.

anachronism N. something regarded as outmoded; something or someone misplaced in time. In today's world of personal copiers and fax machines, the old-fashioned mimeograph machine is clearly an *anachronism*; even the electric typewriter seems *anachronistic* next to a laptop PC.

analogy N. similarity; parallelism. A well-known *analogy* compares the body's immune system with an army whose defending troops are the lymphocytes or white blood cells. *Analogies* are useful, but you can't take them too far: cells, after all, are not soldiers; there is no boot camp for lymphocytes.

anarchist N. person who seeks to overturn the established government; advocate of abolishing authority. Denying she was an *anarchist*, Katya maintained she wished only to make changes in our government, not to destroy it entirely.

anarchy N. absence of governing body; state of disorder. For weeks China was in a state of *anarchy*, with soldiers shooting down civilians in the streets and rumors claiming that Premier Deng was dead. Foreigners fleeing the country reported conditions were so *anarchic* that it was a miracle they escaped.

ancillary ADJ. serving as an aid or accessory; auxiliary. In an *ancillary* capacity Doctor Watson was helpful; however, Holmes could not trust the good doctor to solve a perplexing case on his own. also N.

animated ADJ. lively; spirited. Jim Carrey's facial expressions are highly *animated:* when he played Ace Ventura, he looked practically rubber-faced.

animosity N. active enmity. Mr. Fang incurred the *animosity* of the party's rulers because he advocated limitations of their power.

anomaly N. irregularity; something out of place or abnormal. A bird that cannot fly is an *anomaly.* A classical harpist in the middle of a heavy metal band is *anomalous;* she is also inaudible.

• **antagonism** N. hostility; active resistance. Barry showed his *antagonism* toward his new stepmother by ignoring her whenever she tried talking to him. antagonistic, ADJ.

antecedents N. preceding events or circumstances that influence what comes later; ancestors or early background. Susi Bechhofer's ignorance of her Jewish background had its *antecedents* in the chaos of World War II. Smuggled out of Germany and adopted by a Christian family, she knew nothing of her birth and *antecedents* until she was reunited with her family in 1989.

anticlimax N. letdown in thought or emotion. After the fine performance in the first act, the rest of the play was an *anticlimax.* anticlimactic, ADJ.

antipathy N. aversion; dislike. Tom's extreme *antipathy* for disputes keeps him from getting into arguments with his temperamental wife. Noise in any form is *antipathetic* to him. Among his particular *antipathies* are honking cars, boom boxes, and heavy metal rock.

antiquated ADJ. obsolete; outdated. Accustomed to editing his papers on word processors, Philip thought typewriters were too *antiquated* for him to use.

antiseptic N. substance that prevents infection. It is advisable to apply an *antiseptic* to any wound, no matter how slight or insignificant. also ADJ.

antithesis N. contrast; direct opposite of or to. This tyranny was the *antithesis* of all that he had hoped for, and he fought it with all his strength.

• **apathy** N. lack of caring; indifference. A firm believer in democratic government, she could not understand the *apathy* of people who never bothered to vote. She wondered whether they had ever cared or whether they had always been *apathetic.*

aplomb N. poise; assurance. Gwen's *aplomb* in handling potentially embarrassing moments was legendary around the office; when one of her clients broke a piece of her best crystal, she coolly picked up her own goblet and hurled it into the fireplace.

apocryphal ADJ. untrue; made up. To impress his friends, Tom invented *apocryphal* tales of his adventures in the big city.

apostate N. one who abandons his religious faith or political beliefs. Because he switched from one party to another, his former friends shunned him as an *apostate.*

append V. attach. I shall *append* this chart to my report. When you *append* a bibliography to a text, you have just created an *appendix.*

• **apprehension** N. fear; discernment; capture. The tourist refused to drive his rental car through downtown Miami because he felt some *apprehension* that he might be carjacked.

• **apprenticeship** N. time spent as a novice learning a trade from a skilled worker. As a child, Pip had thought it would be wonderful to work as Joe's *apprentice;* now he hated his *apprenticeship* and scorned the blacksmith's trade.

• **appropriate** ADJ. fitting or suitable; pertinent. Madonna spent hours looking for a suit that would be *appropriate* to wear at a summer wedding.

• **appropriate** V. acquire; take possession of for one's own use; set aside for a special purpose. The ranchers *appropriated* lands that had originally been intended for Indian use. In response, Congress *appropriated* additional funds for the Bureau of Indian Affairs.

arable ADJ. fit for growing crops. The first settlers wrote home glowing reports of the New World, praising its vast acres of *arable* land ready for the plow.

arbiter N. a person with power to decide a dispute; judge. As an *arbiter* in labor disputes, she is skillful: she balances the demands of both sides and hands down rulings with which everyone agrees. As an *arbiter* of style, however, she is worthless: she wears such unflattering outfits that no woman in her right mind would imitate her.

arbitrary ADJ. unreasonable or capricious; randomly selected without any reason; based solely on one's unrestricted will or judgment. The coach claimed the team lost because the umpire made some *arbitrary* calls.

archipelago N. group of closely located islands. When Gauguin looked at the map and saw the *archipelagoes* in the South Seas, he longed to visit them.

arduous ADJ. hard; strenuous. Bob's *arduous* efforts had sapped his energy. Even using a chain saw, he found chopping down trees an *arduous,* time-consuming task.

aria N. operatic solo. At her Metropolitan Opera audition, Marian Anderson sang an *aria* from the opera *Norma.*

arid ADJ. dry; barren. The cactus has adapted to survive in an *arid* environment.

• **aristocracy** N. hereditary nobility; privileged class. Americans have mixed feelings about hereditary *aristocracy:* we say all men are created equal, but we describe people who bear themselves with grace and graciousness as natural *aristocrats.*

arrogance N. pride; haughtiness. Convinced that Emma thought she was better than anyone else in the class, Ed rebuked her for her *arrogance*.

articulate ADJ. effective; distinct. Her *articulate* presentation of the advertising campaign impressed her employers. also V.

ascendancy N. controlling influence. President Marcos failed to maintain his *ascendancy* over the Philippines. He was overthrown by the forces of Corazon Aquino when she *ascended* to power.

ascetic ADJ. practicing self-denial; austere. The wealthy, self-indulgent young man felt oddly drawn to the strict, *ascetic* life led by members of some monastic orders. also N.

• **aspire** V. seek to attain; long for. Because he *aspired* to a career in professional sports, Philip enrolled in a graduate program in sports management. aspiration, N.

assail V. assault. He was *assailed* with questions after his lecture.

• **assert** V. state strongly or positively; insist on or demand recognition of (rights, claims, etc). When Jill *asserted* that nobody else in the junior class had such an early curfew, her parents *asserted* themselves, telling her that if she didn't get home by nine o'clock, she would be grounded for the week. assertion, N.

assiduous ADJ. diligent. It took Rembrandt weeks of *assiduous* labor before he was satisfied with his self-portrait. assiduity, N.

assuage V. ease or lessen (pain); Jilted by Jane, Dick tried to *assuage* his heartache by indulging in ice cream.

• **assumption** N. something taken for granted; taking over or taking possession of. The young princess made the foolish *assumption* that the regent would not object to her *assumption* of power. assume, V.

assurance N. promise or pledge; certainty; self-confidence. When Guthrie gave Guinness his *assurance* rehearsals were going well, he spoke with such *assurance* that Guinness felt relieved. assure, V.; assured, ADJ.

astute ADJ. wise; shrewd; keen. As tutor, she made *astute* observations about how to take multiple-choice tests. She was an *astute* observer: she noticed every tiny detail and knew exactly how important each one was.

asylum N. place of refuge; safety. Fleeing persecution, the political refugee sought *asylum* in the United States.

atrophy V. waste away. After three months in a cast, Stan's biceps had *atrophied* somewhat; however, he was sure that if he pumped iron for a while he would soon build it up.

attain V. reach or accomplish; gain. It took Bolingbroke years to *attain* his goal of gaining the throne.

attentive ADJ. watching carefully; considerate; thoughtful. Spellbound, the *attentive* audience watched the final game of the match, never taking their eyes from the ball. Stan's *attentive* daughter slipped a sweater over his shoulders without distracting his attention from the game.

attire N. clothing (especially, splendid clothes). At the Academy Awards ceremony, the television host commented on the highly fashionable *attire* worn by the nominees. also N.

attribute N. essential quality. His outstanding *attribute* was his kindness.

attribute V. ascribe or credit (to a cause); regard as characteristic of a person or thing. I *attribute* Andrea's success in science to the encouragement she received from her parents.

attrition N. gradual decrease in numbers; reduction in the work force without firing employees; wearing away of opposition by means of harassment. In the 1960s urban churches suffered from *attrition* as members moved from the cities to the suburbs. Rather than fire staff members, church leaders followed a policy of *attrition*, allowing elderly workers to retire without replacing them.

audacity N. boldness. Luke could not believe his own *audacity* in addressing the princess. Where did he get the nerve?

augment V. increase. Armies *augment* their forces by calling up reinforcements; teachers *augment* their salaries by taking odd jobs. Lexy *augments* her salary by working in a record store. Her *augmentation* of wealth has not been great; however, she has *augmented* her record collection considerably.

aura N. distinctive atmosphere; luminous glow. Radiant with happiness, the bride seemed surrounded by an *aura* of brightness.

auspicious ADJ. favoring success; fortunate. With favorable weather conditions, it was an *auspicious* moment to set sail. Prospects for trade were good: under such promising *auspices* we were bound to thrive. Thomas, however, had doubts: a paranoid, he became suspicious whenever conditions seemed *auspicious*.

austere ADJ. forbiddingly stern; severely simple and unornamented. The headmaster's *austere* demeanor tended to scare off the more timid students, who never visited his study willingly. The room reflected the man, for it was *austere* and bare, like a monk's cell, with no touches of luxury to moderate its *austerity*.

• **authentic** ADJ. genuine. The art expert was able to distinguish the *authentic* van Gogh painting from the forged copy. authenticate, V.

authoritative ADJ. having the weight of authority; overbearing and dictatorial. Impressed by the young researcher's well-documented presentation, we accepted her analysis of the experiment as *authoritative*.

• **autonomous** ADJ. self-governing. This island is a colony; however, in most matters, it is *autonomous* and receives no orders from the mother country. The islanders are an independent lot and would fight to preserve their *autonomy*.

autopsy N. examination of a dead body; postmortem. The medical examiner ordered an *autopsy* to determine the cause of death. also V.

avarice N. greediness for wealth. King Midas is a perfect example of *avarice*, for he was so greedy that he wished everything he touched would turn to gold.

averse ADJ. reluctant. The reporter was *averse* to revealing the sources of his information.

• **aversion** N. firm dislike. Bert had an *aversion* to yuppies; Alex had an *aversion* to punks. Their mutual *aversion* was so great that they refused to speak to one another.

avert V. prevent; turn aside. "Watch out!" she cried, hoping to *avert* an accident. She *averted* her eyes from the dead cat on the highway.

avid ADJ. greedy; eager for. Abner was *avid* for pleasure and partied with great *avidity*.

awe N. solemn wonder. The tourists gazed with *awe* at the tremendous expanse of the Grand Canyon.

babble V. chatter idly. The little girl *babbled* about her dolls and pets.

badger V. pester; annoy; harass. Madge was forced to change her telephone number because she was *badgered* by obscene phone calls.

baffle V. frustrate; perplex. The new code *baffled* the enemy agents.

balk V. foil or thwart; stop short; refuse to go on. When the warden learned that several inmates were planning to escape, he took steps to *balk* their attempt. However, he *balked* at punishing them by shackling them to the walls of their cells.

• **banal** ADJ. hackneyed; commonplace; trite; lacking originality. The hack writer's worn-out clichés made his comic sketch seem *banal*. He even resorted to the *banality* of having someone slip on a banana peel!

bane N. cause of ruin; curse. Lucy's little brother was the *bane* of her existence: his attempts to make her life miserable worked so well that she could have fed him some ratsbane for having such a *baneful* effect.

bastion N. stronghold; something seen as a source of protection. The villagers fortified the town hall, hoping this improvised *bastion* could protect them from the guerrilla raids.

begrudge V. resent. I *begrudge* every minute I have to spend attending meetings; they're a complete waste of time.

beguile V. mislead or delude; cheat; pass time. With flattery and big talk of easy money, the con men *beguiled* Kyle into betting his allowance on the shell game. Broke, Kyle *beguiled* himself during the long hours by playing solitaire.

belie V. contradict; give a false impression of. His coarse, hard-bitten exterior *belied* his underlying sensitivity.

benefactor N. gift giver; patron. In later years Scrooge became Tiny Tim's *benefactor* and gave him many gifts.

• **beneficial** ADJ. helpful; advantageous; useful. Tiny Tim's cheerful good nature had a *beneficial* influence on Scrooge's disposition.

beneficiary N. person entitled to benefits or proceeds of an insurance policy or will. In Scrooge's will, he made Tiny Tim his *beneficiary*. Everything he left would go to the benefit of young Tim.

benevolent ADJ. generous; charitable. Mr. Fezziwig was a *benevolent* employer, who wished to make Christmas merrier for young Scrooge and his other employees.

• **benign** ADJ. kindly; favorable; not malignant. Though her *benign* smile and gentle bearing made Miss Marple seem a sweet little old lady, in reality she was a tough-minded, shrewd observer of human nature. benignity, N.

bestial ADJ. beastlike; brutal. According to legend, the werewolf was able to abandon its human shape to take on a *bestial* form.

bestow V. confer. The president wished to *bestow* great honors upon the hero.

• **betray** V. be unfaithful; reveal (unconsciously or unwillingly). The spy *betrayed* his country by selling military secrets to the enemy. When he was taken in for questioning, the tightness of his lips *betrayed* his fear of being caught.

biased ADJ. slanted; prejudiced. Because the judge played golf regularly with the district attorney's father, we feared he might be *biased* in the prosecution's favor. bias, N.

bizarre ADJ. fantastic; violently contrasting. The plot of the novel was too *bizarre* to be believed.

bland ADJ. soothing; mild; dull. Unless you want your stomach lining to be eaten away, stick to a *bland* diet. blandness, N.

blandishment N. flattery. Despite the salesperson's *blandishments*, the customer did not buy the outfit.

blare N. loud, harsh roar; screech. I don't know which is worse: the steady *blare* of a teenager's boom box deafening your ears or a sudden blaze of flashbulbs dazzling your eyes.

blasphemy N. irreverence; sacrilege; cursing. In my father's house, the Dodgers were the holiest of holies; to cheer for another team was to utter words of *blasphemy*. blasphemous, ADJ.

blatant ADJ. flagrant; conspicuously obvious; loudly offensive. To the unemployed youth from Dublin, the "No Irish Need Apply" placard in the shop window was a *blatant* mark of prejudice.

blithe ADJ. gay; joyous; carefree. Without a care in the world, Beth went her *blithe,* light-hearted way.

bloat V. expand or swell (with water or air); puff up with conceit. Constant flattery from his hangers-on *bloated* the heavyweight champion's already sizable ego.

boisterous ADJ. rough and noisy; rowdy; stormy. The unruly crowd of demonstrators became even more *boisterous* when the mayor tried to quiet them.

bolster V. support; reinforce. The debaters amassed file boxes full of evidence to *bolster* their arguments.

boon N. blessing; benefit. The recent rains that filled our empty reservoirs were a *boon* to the whole community.

boundless ADJ. unlimited; vast. Mike's energy was *boundless:* the greater the challenge, the more vigorously he tackled the job.

bountiful ADJ. abundant; graciously generous. Thanks to the good harvest, we had a *bountiful* supply of food, and we could be as *bountiful* as we liked in distributing food to the needy.

bourgeois ADJ. middle class; selfishly materialistic; dully conventional. Technically, anyone who belongs to the middle class is *bourgeois,* but, given the word's connotations, most people resent it if you call them that.

boycott V. refrain from buying or using. In an effort to stop grape growers from using pesticides that harmed the farm workers' health, Cesar Chavez called for consumers to *boycott* grapes.

brackish ADJ. somewhat salty. Following the stream, we noticed its fresh, springlike water grew increasingly *brackish* as we drew nearer to the bay.

brandish V. wave around; flourish. Alarmed, Doctor Watson wildly *brandished* his gun until Holmes told him to put the thing away before he shot himself.

breach N. breaking of contract or duty; fissure; gap. Jill sued Jack for *breach* of promise, claiming he had broken his promise to marry her. They found a *breach* in the enemy's fortifications and penetrated their lines. also V.

brevity N. conciseness. Since you are charged for every transmitted word, *brevity* is essential when you send a telegram or cablegram.

brine N. salt water; seawater (as opposed to fresh). If you pack a peck of peppers in *brine,* what do you get? A peck of pickled peppers! briny, ADJ.

• **brittle** ADJ. easily broken; difficult. My employer's self-control was as *brittle* as an eggshell. Her *brittle* personality made it difficult for me to get along with her.

brochure N. pamphlet. This free *brochure* on farming was issued by the Department of Agriculture.

brusque ADJ. blunt; abrupt. Jill was offended by Jack's *brusque* reply; he had no right to be so impatient with her.

bungle V. mismanage; blunder. Don't botch this assignment, Bumstead; if you *bungle* the job, you're fired!

• **buoyant** ADJ. able to float; cheerful and optimistic. When the boat capsized, her *buoyant* life jacket kept Jody afloat. Scrambling back on board, she was still in a *buoyant* mood, certain that despite the delay she'd win the race. buoyancy, N.

burgeon V. bloom; develop rapidly; flourish. From its start as a small Seattle coffeehouse, Starbucks seemed to *burgeon* almost overnight into a major national chain.

bustle V. move about energetically; teem. David and the children *bustled* about the house getting in each other's way as they tried to pack for the camping trip.

buttress V. support or prop up. The government is considering price supports to *buttress* the declining economy. The huge cathedral walls were supported by flying *buttresses.* also N.

cajole V. coax; wheedle. Jill tried to *cajole* Jack into buying her a fur coat, but no matter how much she coaxed him, he wouldn't give in to her *cajolery.*

calamity N. disaster; misery. As news of the *calamity* spread, offers of relief poured in to the stricken community. calamitous, ADJ.

calligraphy N. beautiful writing; excellent penmanship. In the Middle Ages, before a novice scribe was allowed to copy an important document, he had to spend years practicing *calligraphy.*

callous ADJ. hardened; unfeeling. Carl had worked in the hospital for so many years that he was *callous* to the suffering in the wards. It was as if he had a *callus* on his soul.

camaraderie N. good-fellowship. What Ginger loved best about her job was the sense of *camaraderie* she and her coworkers shared.

• **candor** N. frankness; open honesty. Jack can carry *candor* too far: when he told Jill his honest opinion of her, she nearly slapped his face. Instead of being so *candid,* try keeping your opinions to yourself.

canine ADJ. related to dogs; doglike. Some days the *canine* population of Berkeley seems almost to outnumber the human population.

cant N. insincere, hypocritical speech; "pious" talk; jargon of thieves. Shocked by news of the minister's extramarital love affairs, the worshippers dismissed his talk about the sacredness of marriage as mere *cant. Cant* is a form of hypocrisy: those who can, pray; those who can't, pretend.

capricious ADJ. unpredictable; fickle. The storm was *capricious:* it changed course constantly. Jill was *capricious,* too: she changed boyfriends almost as often as she changed clothes.

caption N. title; chapter heading; text under illustration. The capricious *captions* that accompany "The Far Side" cartoons are almost as funny as the pictures. also V.

• **captivate** V. charm; fascinate. Although he was predisposed to dislike Elizabeth, Darcy found himself *captivated* by her charm and wit.

cardiac ADJ. pertaining to the heart. Since no one in his family had ever had *cardiac* problems, Bill was unconcerned about the possibility of a heart attack.

• **caricature** N. distortion; burlesque. The *caricatures* he drew always emphasized a personal weakness of the people he burlesqued. also V.

carping ADJ. finding fault. A *carping* critic is a nit-picker, someone who loves to point out flaws. carp, V.

caste N. one of the hereditary classes in Hindu society; social stratification; prestige. She bore a mark on her forehead signifying she was a Brahmin, a member of the highest *caste*.

castigation V. punishment, severe criticism. Sensitive to even mild criticism, Virginia Woolf could not bear the *castigation* that she met in certain reviews. castigate, V.

casualty N. serious or fatal accident. The number of *casualties* on this holiday weekend was high.

catacomb N. subterranean cemetery; underground passageway. Londoners refer to their *catacomb-*like subway system as the Underground.

catastrophe N. calamity; disaster. The 1906 San Francisco earthquake was a *catastrophe* that destroyed most of the city.

caustic ADJ. burning; sarcastically biting. The critic's *caustic* review humiliated the actors, who resented his cutting remarks.

cede V. yield (title, territory) to; surrender formally. Eventually the descendants of England's Henry II were forced to *cede* their French territories to the King of France.

• **censor** N. inspector overseeing public morals; official who prevents publication of offensive material. Because certain passages in his novel *Ulysses* had been condemned by the *censor,* James Joyce was unable to publish the novel in England for many years.

censure V. blame; criticize. Though I don't blame Tony for leaving Tina, I do *censure* him for failing to pay child support.

cerebral ADJ. pertaining to the brain or intellect. The content of philosophical works is *cerebral* in nature and requires much thought.

cessation N. stopping. The airline workers threatened a *cessation* of all work if management failed to meet their demands. cease, V.

chafe V. warm by rubbing; make sore (by rubbing). Chilled, he *chafed* his hands before the fire. The collar of his school uniform *chafed* Tom's neck, but not as much the school's strict rules *chafed* his spirit. also N.

chaff N. husks and stems left over when grain has been threshed; worthless, leftover by-products. When you separate the wheat from the *chaff,* be sure you throw out the *chaff.*

chagrin N. vexation (caused by humiliation or injured pride); disappointment. Embarrassed by his parents' shabby, working-class appearance, Doug felt their visit to his school would bring him nothing but *chagrin.* Someone filled with *chagrin* doesn't grin: he's too mortified.

chameleon N. lizard that changes color in different situations. Like the *chameleon,* the candidate assumed the political thinking of every group he met.

chaotic ADJ. in utter disorder. He tried to bring order into the *chaotic* state of affairs. chaos, N.

charlatan N. quack; pretender to knowledge. When they realized that the Wizard didn't know how to get them back to Kansas, Dorothy and her friends were sure they'd been duped by a *charlatan.*

chary ADJ. cautious; sparing or restrained about giving. A prudent, thrifty, New Englander, DeWitt was as *chary* of investing money in junk bonds as he was *chary* of paying people unnecessary compliments.

chasm N. abyss. They could not see the bottom of the *chasm.*

chastise V. punish physically; scold verbally. "Spare the rod and spoil the child," Miss Watson said, grabbing her birch wand and proceeding to *chastise* poor Huck thoroughly.

chauvinist N. blindly devoted patriot. *Chauvinists* cannot recognize any faults in their country, no matter how flagrant they may be. Likewise, a male *chauvinist* cannot recognize how biased he is in favor of his own sex, no matter how flagrant that may be.

chicanery N. trickery; deception. Those sneaky lawyers misrepresented what occurred, made up all sorts of implausible alternative scenarios to confuse the jurors, and in general depended on *chicanery* to win the case.

choreography N. art of representing dances in written symbols; arrangement of dances. Merce Cunningham has begun to use a computer in designing *choreography:* a software program allows him to compose arrangements of possible moves and to view them immediately onscreen.

chronic ADJ. long established (as a disease). The doctors were finally able to attribute his *chronic* headaches and nausea to traces of formaldehyde gas in his apartment.

• **chronicle** V. report; record (in chronological order). The gossip columnist was paid to *chronicle* the latest escapades of the socially prominent celebrities. also N.

circumscribe V. limit; confine. Although I do not wish to *circumscribe* your activities, I must insist that you complete this assignment before you start anything else.

• **circumspect** ADJ. prudent; cautious. Investigating before acting, she tried always to be *circumspect*.

• **cite** V. quote; refer to; commend. Because Virginia could *cite* hundreds of biblical passages from memory, her pastor *cited* her for her studiousness. citation, N.

clairvoyant ADJ., N. having foresight; fortune-teller. Cassandra's *clairvoyant* warning was not heeded by the Trojans. clairvoyance, N.

clandestine ADJ. secret. After avoiding their chaperone, the lovers had a *clandestine* meeting.

claustrophobia N. fear of being shut in. If Santa Claus got stuck in a chimney and couldn't get out, would he wind up suffering from *claustrophobia*?

clemency N. disposition to be lenient; mildness, as of the weather. The lawyer was pleased when the case was sent to Judge Smith's chambers because Smith was noted for her *clemency* toward first offenders. We decided to eat dinner in the garden to enjoy the unexpected *clemency* of the weather.

• **cliché** N. phrase dulled in meaning by repetition. High school compositions are often marred by such *clichés* as "strong as an ox."

climactic ADJ. relating to the highest point. When Jack reached the *climactic* portions of the book, he could not stop reading. climax, N.

clique N. small exclusive group. Fitzgerald wished that he belonged to the *clique* of popular athletes and big men on campus who seemed to run Princeton's social life.

• **coalesce** V. combine; fuse. The brooks *coalesced* into one large river. When minor political parties *coalesce*, their *coalescence* may create a major coalition.

coalition N. association; union. Jesse Jackson's Rainbow *Coalition* brought together people of many different races and creeds.

cogitate V. think over. *Cogitate* on this problem; the solution will come.

coincidence N. two or more things occurring at the same time by chance. Was it just a *coincidence* that John and she had chanced to meet at the market for three days running, or was he deliberately trying to seek her out? coincident, ADJ.

• **collaborate** V. work together. Two writers *collaborated* in preparing this book.

colossal ADJ. huge. Radio City Music Hall has a *colossal* stage.

collusion N. conspiring in a fraudulent scheme. The swindlers were found guilty of *collusion*. collude, V.

comely ADJ. attractive; agreeable. I would rather have a poor but *comely* wife than a rich and homely one.

commiserate V. feel or express pity or sympathy for. Her friends *commiserated* with the widow.

compact ADJ. tightly packed; firm; brief. His short, *compact* body was better suited to wrestling than to basketball.

compact N. agreement; contract. The signers of the Mayflower *Compact* were establishing a form of government.

comparable ADJ. similar. People whose jobs are *comparable* in difficulty should receive *comparable* pay.

compatible ADJ. harmonious; in harmony with. They were *compatible* neighbors, never quarreling over unimportant matters. compatibility, N.

compile V. assemble; gather; accumulate. We planned to *compile* a list of the words most frequently used on SAT I examinations. compilation, N.

complacent ADJ. self-satisfied; smug. Feeling *complacent* about his latest victories, he looked smugly at the row of trophies on his mantelpiece. complacency, N.

complement V. complete; make perfect. The waiter recommended a glass of port to *complement* the cheese. also N.

• **compliance** N. readiness to yield; conformity in fulfilling requirements. Bill was so bullheaded that we never expected his easy *compliance* to our requests. As an architect, however, Bill recognized that his design for the new school had to be in *compliance* with the local building code.

• **component** N. element; ingredient. I wish all the *components* of my stereo system were working at the same time.

• **composure** N. mental calmness. Even the latest work crisis failed to shake her *composure*.

compress V. close; squeeze; contract. She *compressed* the package under her arm.

• **compromise** V. adjust or settle by making mutual concessions; endanger the interests or reputation of. Sometimes the presence of a neutral third party can help adversaries *compromise* their differences. Unfortunately, your presence at the scene of the dispute *compromises* our claim to neutrality in this matter. also N.

compute V. reckon; calculate. He failed to *compute* the interest; so his bank balance was not accurate.

concerted ADJ. mutually agreed on; done together. All the Girl Scouts made a *concerted* effort to raise funds for their annual outing. When the movie star appeared, his fans let out a *concerted* sigh.

concise ADJ. brief but comprehensive. The instructions were *concise* and to the point: they included every necessary detail and not one word more. Precision indicates exactness; *concision* indicates compactness. To achieve *conciseness,* cut out unnecessary words.

concoct V. prepare by combining; make up in concert. How did the inventive chef ever *concoct* such a strange dish? concoction, N.

concurrent ADJ. happening at the same time. In America, the colonists were resisting the demands of the mother country; at the *concurrent* moment in France, the middle class was sowing the seeds of rebellion. The two revolutionary movements took place *concurrently.*

condescend V. act conscious of descending to a lower level; patronize. Though Jill was a star softball player in college, when she played a pickup game at the local park she never *condescended* to her teammates or acted as if she thought herself superior to them. condescension. N.

condole V. express sympathetic sorrow. Bill's friends gathered to *condole* with him over his loss. Those unable to attend the funeral sent letters of *condolence.*

• **condone** V. overlook voluntarily; forgive. Although she had excused Huck for his earlier escapades, Widow Douglas refused to *condone* his latest prank.

confine V. shut in; restrict. The terrorists had *confined* their prisoner in a small room. However, they had not chained him to the wall or done anything else to *confine* his movements further. confinement, N.

• **confirm** V. corroborate; verify; support. I have several witnesses who will *confirm* my account of what happened.

conflagration N. great fire. In the *conflagration* that followed the 1906 earthquake, much of San Francisco burned to the ground.

• **conformity** N. agreement or compliance; actions in agreement with prevailing social customs. In *conformity* with the bylaws of the Country Dance and Song Society, I am submitting a petition nominating Susan Murrow as president of the society. Because Kate had always been a rebellious child, we were surprised by her *conformity* to the standards of behavior prevalent at her new school.

• **confront** V. face someone or something; encounter, often in a hostile way. Fearing his wife's hot temper, Stanley was reluctant to *confront* her about her skyrocketing credit card bills.

congeal V. freeze; coagulate. His blood *congealed* in his veins as he saw the dreaded monster rush toward him.

• **congenial** ADJ. pleasant; friendly. My father loved to go out for a meal with *congenial* companions.

connotation N. suggested or implied meaning of an expression. Foreigners frequently are unaware of the *connotations* of the words they use.

consensus N. general agreement. Every time the garden club members had nearly reached a *consensus* about what to plant, Mistress Mary, quite contrary, disagreed.

consequence N. self-importance; pomposity. Convinced of his own importance, the actor strutted about the dressing room with such an air of *consequence* that it was hard for his valet to keep a straight face. consequential, ADJ.

• **consistency** N. harmony of parts; dependability; uniformity; degree of thickness. Holmes judged puddings and explanations on their *consistency*: he liked his puddings without lumps and his explanations without contradictions or improbabilities. consistent, ADJ.

console V. lessen sadness or disappointment; give comfort. When her father died, Marius did his best to *console* Cosette.

• **consolidation** N. unification; process of becoming firmer or stronger. The recent *consolidation* of several small airlines into one major company has left observers of the industry wondering whether room still exists for the "little guy" in aviation. consolidate, V.

conspicuous ADJ. easily seen; noticeable; striking. Janet was *conspicuous* both for her red hair and for her height.

constituent N. resident of a district represented by an elected official. The congressman received hundreds of letters from angry *constituents* after the Equal Rights Amendment failed to pass.

constraint N. compulsion; repression of feelings. There was a feeling of *constraint* in the room because no one dared to criticize the speaker. constrain, V.

contagion N. infection. Fearing *contagion,* the health authorities took great steps to prevent the spread of the disease.

contempt N. scorn; disdain. The heavyweight boxer looked on ordinary people with *contempt,* scorning them as weaklings who couldn't hurt a fly. We thought it was *contemptible* of him to be *contemptuous* of people for being weak.

contention N. claim; thesis. It is our *contention* that, if you follow our tactics, you will boost your score on the PSAT. contend, V.

- **contentious** ADJ. quarrelsome. Disagreeing violently with the referees' ruling, the coach became so *contentious* that they threw him out of the game.

context N. writings preceding and following the passage quoted. Because these lines are taken out of *context,* they do not convey the message the author intended.

contingent ADJ. dependent on; conditional. Cher's father informed her that any increase in her allowance was *contingent* on the quality of her final grades. contingency, N.

contingent N. group that makes up part of a gathering. The New York *contingent* of delegates at the Democratic National Convention was a boisterous, sometimes rowdy lot.

contortion N. twisting; distortion. Watching the *contortions* of the gymnast as he twisted and heaved his body from one side to the other of the pommel horse, we were awed by his strength and flexibility.

contrite ADJ. penitent. Her *contrite* tears did not influence the judge when he imposed sentence.

- **convention** N. social or moral custom; established practice. Flying in the face of *convention,* George Sand shocked society by taking lovers and wearing men's clothes.

converge V. approach; tend to meet; come together. African-American men from all over the United States *converged* on Washington to take part in the historic Million Man march.

convert N. one who has adopted a different religion or opinion. On his trip to Japan, though the president spoke at length about the merits of American automobiles, he made few *converts* to his beliefs. also V.

conviction N. judgment that someone is guilty of a crime; strongly held belief. Even her *conviction* for murder did not shake Peter's *conviction* that Harriet was innocent of the crime.

- **convoluted** ADJ. complex and involved; intricate; winding; coiled. Talk about twisted! The new tax regulations are so *convoluted* that even my accountant can't unravel their mysteries.

cordial ADJ. gracious; heartfelt. Our hosts greeted us at the airport with a *cordial* welcome and a hearty hug.

corroborate V. confirm; support. Though Huck was quite willing to *corroborate* Tom's story, Aunt Polly knew better than to believe either of them.

- **corrosion** N. destruction by chemical action. The *corrosion* of the girders supporting the bridge took place so gradually that no one suspected any danger until the bridge suddenly collapsed. corrode, V.

cosmic ADJ. pertaining to the universe; vast. *Cosmic* rays derive their name from the fact that they bombard the earth's atmosphere from outer space. cosmos, N.

cosmopolitan ADJ. sophisticated. Her years in the capital had transformed her into a *cosmopolitan* young woman highly aware of international affairs.

countenance V. approve; tolerate. He refused to *countenance* such rude behavior on their part.

covert ADJ. secret; hidden; implied. Investigations of the Central Intelligence Agency and other secret service networks reveal that such *covert* operations can get out of control.

covetous ADJ. avaricious; eagerly desirous of. The child was *covetous* by nature and wanted to take the toys belonging to his classmates. covet, V.

cower V. shrink quivering, as from fear. The frightened child *cowered* in the corner of the room.

crass ADJ. very unrefined; grossly insensible. The film critic deplored the *crass* commercialism of moviemakers who abandon artistic standards in order to make a quick buck.

credibility N. believability. Because the candidate had made some pretty unbelievable promises, we began to question the *credibility* of everything she said.

credulity N. belief on slight evidence; gullibility; naïveté. Con artists take advantage of the *credulity* of inexperienced investors to swindle them out of their savings. credulous, ADJ.

criterion N. standard used in judging. What *criterion* did you use when you selected this essay as the prizewinner? criteria, Pl.

cryptic ADJ. mysterious; hidden; secret. Thoroughly baffled by Holmes's *cryptic* remarks, Watson wondered whether Holmes was intentionally concealing his thoughts about the crime.

culinary ADJ. relating to cooking. Many chefs attribute their *culinary* skill to the wise use of spices.

cull V. pick out; reject. Every month the farmer *culls* the nonlaying hens from his flock and sells them to the local butcher. also N.

culmination N. attainment of highest point. Her inauguration as president of the United States marked the *culmination* of her political career. culminate, V.

culpable ADJ. deserving blame. Corrupt politicians who condone the illegal activities of gamblers are equally *culpable.*

cumbersome ADJ. heavy; hard to manage. He was burdened down with *cumbersome* parcels.

curb V. restrain. The overly generous philanthropist had to *curb* his beneficent impulses before he gave away all his money and left himself with nothing.

cursory ADJ. casual; hastily done. Because a *cursory* examination of the ruins indicates the possibility of arson, we believe the insurance agency should undertake a more extensive investigation of the fire's cause.

- **curtail** V. shorten; reduce. When Elton asked Cher for a date, she said she was really sorry she couldn't go out with him, but her dad had ordered her to *curtail* her social life.

cynical ADJ. skeptical or distrustful of human motives. *Cynical* from birth, Sidney was suspicious whenever anyone give him a gift "with no strings attached." cynic, N.

dabble V. work at in a nonserious fashion; splash around. The amateur painter *dabbled* at art, but seldom produced a finished piece. The children *dabbled* their hands in the bird bath, splashing one another gleefully.

daunt V. intimidate; frighten. "Boast all you like of your prowess. Mere words cannot *daunt* me," the *dauntless* hero answered the villain.

• **dawdle** V. loiter; waste time. At the mall, Mother grew impatient with Jo and Amy because they tended to *dawdle* as they went from store to store.

• **dearth** N. scarcity. The *dearth* of skilled labor compelled the employers to open trade schools.

debase V. reduce in quality or value; lower in esteem; degrade. In *The King and I,* Anna refuses to kneel down and prostrate herself before the king, for she feels that to do so would *debase* her position, and she will not submit to such *debasement*.

• **debilitate** V. weaken; enfeeble. Michael's severe bout of the flu *debilitated* him so much that he was too tired to go to work for a week.

decadence N. decay or decline, especially moral; self-indulgence. We named our best-selling ice cream flavor "chocolate *decadence*" because only truly self-indulgent people would treat themselves to something so calorific and cholesterol laden.

decipher V. decode. I could not *decipher* the doctor's handwriting.

• **decorous** ADJ. proper. Prudence's *decorous* behavior was praised by her teachers, who wished they had a classroom full of such polite and proper little girls. decorum, N.

decoy N. lure or bait. The wild ducks were not fooled by the *decoy*. also V.

• **decry** V. express strong disapproval of; disparage. The founder of the Children's Defense Fund, Marian Wright Edelman, strongly *decries* the lack of financial and moral support for children in America today.

deducible ADJ. derived by reasoning. If we accept your premise, your conclusions are easily *deducible*.

deface V. mar; disfigure. If you *deface* a library book, you will have to pay a hefty fine.

• **defamation** N. harming a person's reputation. *Defamation* of character may result in a slander suit. If rival candidates persist in *defaming* one another, the voters may conclude that all politicians are crooks.

defeatist ADJ. attitude of one who is ready to accept defeat as a natural outcome. If you maintain your *defeatist* attitude, you will never succeed. also N.

• **deference** N. courteous regard for another's wish. In *deference* to the minister's request, please do not take photographs during the wedding service.

• **defiance** N. opposition; willingness to resist. In learning to read and write in *defiance* of his master's orders, Frederick Douglass showed exceptional courage. defy, V.

definitive ADJ. final; complete. Carl Sandburg's *Abraham Lincoln* may be regarded as the *definitive* work on the life of the Great Emancipator.

defrock V. strip a priest or minister of church authority. We knew the minister had violated church regulations, but we had not realized his offense was serious enough for people to seek to *defrock* him.

defunct ADJ. dead; no longer in use or existence. The lawyers sought to examine the books of the *defunct* corporation.

• **degenerate** V. become worse; deteriorate. As the fight dragged on, the champion's style *degenerated* until he could barely keep on his feet.

deign V. condescend; stoop. The celebrated fashion designer would not *deign* to speak to a mere seamstress; his overburdened assistant had to convey the master's wishes to the lowly workers assembling his great designs.

delete V. erase; strike out. Less is more: if you *delete* this paragraph, the composition will have more appeal.

deleterious ADJ. harmful. If you believe that smoking is *deleterious* to your health (and the surgeon general certainly does), then quit!

delineate V. portray; depict; sketch. Using only a few descriptive phrases, Jane Austen *delineates* the character of Mr. Collins so well that we can predict his every move. delineation, N.

delirium N. mental disorder marked by confusion. In his *delirium,* the drunkard saw pink panthers and talking pigs. Perhaps he wasn't *delirious;* he might just have wandered into a movie.

delusion N. false belief; hallucination. Don suffers from *delusions* of grandeur: he thinks he's a world-famous author when he's published just one paperback book.

• **demean** V. degrade; humiliate. Standing on his dignity, he refused to *demean* himself by replying to the offensive letter. If you truly believed in the dignity of labor, you would not think it would *demean* you to work as a janitor.

demeanor N. behavior; bearing. His sober *demeanor* quieted the noisy revelers.

demolish V. destroy; tear down. Before building a new hotel along the waterfront, the construction company had to *demolish* several rundown warehouses on that site. demolition, N.

demur V. object (because of doubts, scruples); hesitate. When offered a post on the board of directors, David *demurred*: he had doubts about taking on the job because he was unsure he could handle it in addition to his other responsibilities.

demure ADJ. grave; serious; coy. She was *demure* and reserved, a nice modest girl whom any young man would be proud to take home to his mother.

• **denounce** V. condemn; criticize. The reform candidate *denounced* the corrupt city officials for having betrayed the public's trust. denunciation, N.

deny V. contradict; refuse. Do you *deny* his story, or do you support what he says? How could Pat *deny* the truth of the accusation that he'd been swiping the Oreos when he'd been caught with his hand in the cookie jar? denial, N.

• **depict** V. portray. In this sensational exposé, the author *depicts* John Lennon as a drug-crazed neurotic. Do you question the accuracy of this *depiction* of Lennon?

• **deplete** V. reduce; exhaust. We must wait until we *deplete* our present inventory before we order replacements.

• **deplore** V. regret strongly; express grief over. Although Ann Landers *deplored* the disintegration of the modern family, she recognized that not every marriage could be saved.

deprecate V. express disapproval of; protest against. A firm believer in old-fashioned courtesy, Miss Post *deprecated* the unfortunate modern tendency to address new acquaintances by their first names. deprecatory, ADJ.

depreciate V. lessen in value. If you neglect this property, it will *depreciate*.

deprivation N. loss. In prison she faced the sudden *deprivation* of rights she had taken for granted: the right to stay up late reading a book, the right to privacy, the right to make a phone call to a friend.

derelict ADJ. abandoned; negligent. The *derelict* craft was a menace to navigation. Whoever abandoned it in mid harbor was *derelict* in living up to his or her responsibilities as a boat owner. dereliction, N.

• **derision** N. ridicule; mockery. Greeting his pretentious dialogue with *derision*, the critics refused to consider his play seriously. deride, V.

• **derivative** ADJ. unoriginal; derived from another source. Although her early poetry was clearly *derivative* in nature, the critics felt she had promise and eventually would find her own voice.

desecrate V. profane; violate the sanctity of. The soldiers *desecrated* the temple, shattering the altar and trampling the holy objects underfoot.

designation N. identifying name; appointment to a position or office. For years the president's home had no proper *designation*; eventually it was called the White House. Given Gary's background in accounting, his *designation* as treasurer came as no surprise to his fellow board members.

despise V. look on with scorn; regard as worthless or distasteful. Mr. Bond, I *despise* spies; I look down on them as mean, *despicable,* honorless men, whom I would cheerfully wipe from the face of the earth.

despondent ADJ. depressed; gloomy. To the dismay of his parents, William became so seriously *despondent* after he broke up with Jan that they despaired of finding a cure for his gloom. despondency, N.

desultory ADJ. aimless; haphazard; digressing at random. In prison Malcolm X set himself the task of reading straight through the dictionary; to him, reading was purposeful, not *desultory*.

• **detached** ADJ. emotionally removed; calm and objective; indifferent. A psychoanalyst must maintain a *detached* point of view and stay uninvolved with her patients' personal lives. detachment, N. (secondary meaning)

determination N. resolve; measurement or calculation; decision. Nothing could shake his *determination* that his children would get the best education that money could buy. Thanks to my pocket calculator, my *determination* of the answer to the problem took only seconds of my time.

• **deterrent** N. something that discourages; hindrance. Does the threat of capital punishment serve as a *deterrent* to potential killers? deter, V.

detrimental ADJ. harmful; damaging. The candidate's acceptance of major financial contributions from a well-known racist ultimately proved *detrimental* to his campaign, for he lost the backing of many of his early grassroots supporters. detriment, N.

deviate V. turn away from (a principle, norm); depart; diverge. Richard never *deviated* from his daily routine: every day he set off for work at eight o'clock, had his sack lunch (peanut butter on whole wheat) at 12:15, and headed home at the stroke of five.

devious ADJ. roundabout; erratic; not straightforward. The Joker's plan was so *devious* that it was only with great difficulty we could follow its shifts and dodges.

dexterous ADJ. skillful. The magician was so *dexterous* that we could not follow him as he performed his tricks.

diagnosis N. art of identifying a disease; analysis of a condition. In medical school Margaret developed her skill at *diagnosis,* learning how to read volumes from a rapid pulse or a hacking cough. diagnose, V.; diagnostic, ADJ.

dichotomy N. split; branching into two parts (especially contradictory ones). Willie didn't know how to resolve the *dichotomy* between his ambition to go to college and his childhood longing to run away to join the circus. Then he heard about Ringling Brothers Circus College, and he knew he'd found the perfect school.

• **didactic** ADJ. teaching; instructional. Pope's lengthy poem *An Essay on Man* is too *didactic* for my taste: I dislike it when poets turn preachy and moralize.

diehard N. unyielding opponent (to a measure, position, etc.). Even the popular new president could not win support for his universal health care plan from the *diehards* in his party.

• **diffident** ADJ. shy; lacking confidence; reserved. Can a naturally *diffident* person become a fast-talking, successful used car salesman?

diffuse ADJ. wordy; rambling; spread out (like a gas). If you pay authors by the word, you tempt them to produce *diffuse* manuscripts rather then brief ones. diffusion, N.

• **digression** N. wandering away from the subject. Nobody minded when Professor Renoir's lectures wandered away from their official theme; his *digressions* were always more fascinating than the topic of the day. digress, V.

dilemma N. problem; choice of two unsatisfactory alternatives. In this *dilemma,* he knew no one to whom he could turn for advice.

dilettante N. aimless follower of the arts; amateur; dabbler. He was not serious in his painting; he was rather a *dilettante*.

diligence N. steadiness of effort; persistent hard work. Her employers were greatly impressed by her *diligence* and offered her a partnership in the firm. diligent, ADJ.

dilute V. make less concentrated; reduce in strength. She preferred her coffee *diluted* with milk.

diminutive ADJ. small in size. Looking at the tiny gymnast, we were amazed that anyone so *diminutive* could perform with such power.

din N. continued loud noise. The *din* of the jackhammers outside the classroom window drowned out the lecturer's voice. also V.

dirge N. lament with music. The funeral *dirge* stirred us to tears.

disavowal N. denial; disclaiming. His *disavowal* of his part in the conspiracy was not believed by the jury. disavow, V.

• **discernible** ADJ. distinguishable; perceivable. The ships in the harbor were not *discernible* in the fog.

discerning ADJ. mentally quick and observant; having insight. Though no genius, the star was sufficiently *discerning* to tell her true friends from the countless phonies who flattered her.

• **disclaimer** N. denial of a legal claim or right; disavowal. Though reporter Joe Klein issued a *disclaimer* stating that he was *not* Anonymous, the author of *Primary Colors,* eventually he admitted that he had written the controversial novel. disclaim, V.

• **disclose** V. reveal. Although competitors offered him bribes, he refused to *disclose* any information about his company's forthcoming product. disclosure, N.

disconcert V. confuse; upset; embarrass. The lawyer was *disconcerted* by the evidence produced by her adversary.

• **discord** N. lack of harmony; conflict; Watching Tweedledum battle Tweedledee, Alice wondered what had caused this pointless *discord*.

discount V. discredit; reduce in price. Be prepared to *discount* what he has to say about his ex-wife.

• **discrepancy** N. lack of consistency; contradiction; difference. "Observe, Watson, the significant *discrepancies* between Sir Percy's original description of the crime and his most recent testimony. What do these contradictions suggest?"

discriminating ADJ. able to see differences; prejudiced. A superb interpreter of Picasso, she was sufficiently *discriminating* to judge the most complex works of modern art. [secondary meaning] discrimination, N.

discursive ADJ. digressing; rambling. As the lecturer wandered from topic to topic, we wondered what if any point there was to his *discursive* remarks.

disdain V. view with scorn or contempt. In the film *Funny Face,* the bookish heroine *disdained* fashion models for their lack of intellectual interests. also N.

disembark V. go ashore; unload cargo from a ship. Before the passengers could *disembark,* they had to pick up their passports from the ship's purser.

• **disgruntled** ADJ. discontented; sulky and dissatisfied. The numerous delays left the passengers feeling *disgruntled*. disgruntle, V.

disheveled ADJ. untidy. Your *disheveled* appearance will hurt your chances in this interview.

• **disinterested** ADJ. unprejudiced. Given the judge's political ambitions and the lawyers' financial interest in the case, the only *disinterested* person in the courtroom may have been the court reporter.

dismay V. discourage; frighten. The huge amount of work she had left to do *dismayed* her. also N.

• **dismiss** V. put away from consideration; reject. Believing in John's love for her, she *dismissed* the notion that he might be unfaithful. [secondary meaning]

• **disparage** V. belittle. A doting mother, Emma was more likely to praise her son's crude attempts at art than to *disparage* them.

• **disparate** ADJ. basically different; unrelated. Unfortunately, Tony and Tina have *disparate* notions of marriage: Tony sees it as a carefree extended love affair, while Tina sees it as a solemn commitment to build a family and a home.

disparity N. difference; condition of inequality. Their *disparity* in rank made no difference at all to the prince and Cinderella.

dispassionate ADJ. calm; impartial. Known in the company for his cool judgment, Bill could impartially examine the causes of a problem, giving a *dispassionate* analysis of what had gone wrong, and go on to suggest how to correct the mess.

• **dispatch** N. speediness; prompt execution; message sent with all due speed. Young Napoleon defeated the enemy with all possible *dispatch*; he then sent a *dispatch* to headquarters, informing his commander of the great victory. also V.

• **dispel** V. scatter; cause to vanish. The bright sunlight eventually *dispelled* the morning mist.

• **disperse** V. scatter. The police fired tear gas into the crowd to *disperse* the protesters.

disputatious ADJ. argumentative; fond of arguing. Convinced he knew more than his lawyers, Tom was a *disputatious* client, ready to argue about the best way to conduct the case.

dissemble V. disguise; pretend. Even though John tried to *dissemble* his motive for taking modern dance, we all knew he was there not to dance but to meet girls.

disseminate V. distribute; spread; scatter (like seeds). By their use of the Internet, propagandists have been able to *disseminate* their pet doctrines to new audiences around the globe.

• **dissent** V. disagree. In the recent Supreme Court decision, Justice O'Connor *dissented* from the majority opinion. also N.

dissertation N. formal essay. In order to earn a graduate degree from many of our universities, a candidate is frequently required to prepare a *dissertation* on some scholarly subject.

dissident ADJ. dissenting; rebellious. In the purge that followed the student demonstrations at Tiananmen Square, the government hunted down the *dissident* students and their supporters. also N.

• **dissipate** V. squander; waste; scatter. He is a fine artist, but we fear he may *dissipate* his gifts if he keeps wasting his time doodling on napkins.

dissuade V. persuade not to do; discourage. Since Tom could not *dissuade* Huck from running away from home, he decided to run away with him. dissuasion, N.

• **distinction** N. honor; contrast; discrimination. A holder of the Medal of Honor, George served with great *distinction* in World War II. He made a *distinction*, however, between World War II and Vietnam, which he considered an immoral conflict.

distort V. twist out of shape. It is difficult to believe the newspaper accounts of the riots because of the way some reports *distort* and exaggerate the actual events. distortion, N.

divergent ADJ. differing; deviating. Since graduating from medical school, the two doctors have taken *divergent* paths, the one going on to become a nationally prominent surgeon, the other dedicating himself to a small family practice in his hometown. divergence, N.

diverse ADJ. differing in some characteristics; various. The professor suggested *diverse* ways of approaching the assignment and recommended that we choose one of them. diversity, N.

diversion N. act of turning aside; pastime. After studying for several hours, he needed a *diversion* from work. divert, V.

• **divulge** V. reveal. No lover of gossip, Charlotte would never *divulge* anything that a friend told her in confidence.

• **docile** ADJ. obedient; easily managed. As *docile* as he seems today, that old lion was once a ferocious, snarling beast.

• **doctrine** N. teachings, in general; particular principle (religious, legal, etc.) taught. He was so committed to the *doctrines* of his faith that he was unable to evaluate them impartially.

document V. provide written evidence. She kept all the receipts from her business trip in order to *document* her expenses for the firm. also N.

• **dogmatic** ADJ. opinionated; arbitrary; doctrinal. We tried to discourage Doug from being so *dogmatic* but never could convince him that his opinions might be wrong.

dormant ADJ. sleeping; lethargic; latent. At fifty her long-*dormant* ambition to write flared up once more; within a year she had completed the first of her great historical novels.

doubtful ADJ. uncertain; undecided. From the outset, the outcome of the battle was *doubtful*: we had no certainty that we were going to win.

downcast ADJ. disheartened; sad. Cheerful and optimistic by nature, Beth was never *downcast* despite the difficulties she faced.

draconian ADJ. extremely severe. When the principal canceled the senior prom because some seniors had been late to school that week, we thought the *draconian* punishment was far too harsh for such a minor violation of the rules.

dregs N. sediment; worthless residue. David poured the wine carefully to avoid stirring up the *dregs*.

dross N. waste matter; worthless impurities. Many methods have been devised to separate the valuable metal from the *dross*.

ductile ADJ. malleable; flexible; pliable. Copper is an extremely *ductile* material: you can stretch it into the thinnest of wires, bend it, even wind it into loops.

duplicity N. double-dealing; hypocrisy. When Tanya learned that Mark had been two-timing her, she was furious at his *duplicity*.

duty N. tax on imported or exported goods. Because he was too stingy to pay the *duty* on the watch he'd bought in Switzerland, Rex foolishly tried to smuggle it through Customs.

dwindle V. shrink; reduce. The food in the lifeboat gradually *dwindled* away to nothing.

ebb V. recede; lessen. Mrs. Dalloway sat on the beach and watched the tide *ebb*. also N.

ebullient ADJ. showing excitement; overflowing with enthusiasm. Her *ebullient* nature could not be repressed; she was always bubbling over with exuberance. ebullience, N.

eccentric ADJ. irregular; odd; whimsical; bizarre. The comet veered dangerously close to the earth in its *eccentric* orbit. eccentricity, N.

• **eclectic** ADJ. composed of elements drawn from disparate sources. His style of interior decoration was *eclectic*: bits and pieces of furnishings from widely divergent periods strikingly juxtaposed to create a unique decor. eclecticism, N.

• **eclipse** V. darken; extinguish; surpass. The new stock market high *eclipsed* the previous record set in 1995.

ecstasy N. rapture; joy; any overpowering emotion. When Allison received her long-hoped-for letter of acceptance from Harvard, she was in *ecstasy*. ecstatic, ADJ.

effervescence N. inner excitement or exuberance; bubbling from fermentation or carbonation. Nothing depressed Sue for long; her natural *effervescence* soon reasserted itself. Soda that loses its *effervescence* goes flat. effervescent, ADJ., effervesce, V.

effrontery N. insolent boldness. Lady Bracknell was shocked that Jack, a man of no rank or breeding, had possessed the *effrontery* to court the daughter of a noble family.

egotistical ADJ. excessively self-centered; self-important; conceited. Typical *egotistical* remark: "But enough of this chit-chat about you and your little problems. Let's talk about what's really important: *Me!*"

egregious ADJ. notorious; gross; shocking. She was an *egregious* liar; we all knew better than to believe a word she said.

• **elated** ADJ. overjoyed; in high spirits. Grinning from ear to ear, Carl Lewis was clearly *elated* by his ninth Olympic gold medal. elation, N.

• **elicit** V. draw out (by discussion); call forth. The camp counselor's humorous remarks finally *elicited* a smile from the shy new camper.

eloquence N. expressiveness; persuasive speech. The crowds were stirred by Martin Luther King's *eloquence*. eloquent, ADJ.

elucidate V. explain; enlighten. He was called upon to *elucidate* the disputed points in his article.

• **elusive** ADJ. evasive; baffling; hard to grasp. Trying to pin down exactly when the contractors would be done remodeling the house, Nancy was frustrated by their *elusive* replies. elude, V.

emanate V. issue forth. A strong odor of sulphur *emanated* from the spring.

emancipate V. set free. At first, the attempts of the abolitionists to *emancipate* the slaves were unpopular in New England as well as in the South.

• **embellish** V. adorn. We enjoyed my mother-in-law's stories about how she came here from Russia, in part because she *embellished* the bare facts of the journey with humorous anecdotes and vivid descriptive details.

embrace V. hug; adopt or espouse; accept readily; encircle; include. Clasping Maid Marian in his arms, Robin Hood *embraced* her lovingly. In joining the outlaws in Sherwood Forest, she had openly *embraced* their cause.

empathy N. ability to identify with another's feelings, ideas, etc. What made Ann such a fine counselor was her *empathy*, her ability to put herself in her client's place and feel his emotions as if they were her own. empathize, V.

empirical ADJ. based on experience. He distrusted hunches and intuitive flashes; he placed his reliance entirely on *empirical* data.

emulate V. imitate; rival. In a brief essay, describe a person you admire, someone whose virtues you would like to *emulate*.

encumber V. burden. Some people *encumber* themselves with too much luggage when they go for short trips.

• **endorse** V. approve; support. Everyone waited to see which one of the rival candidates for the city council the mayor would *endorse*. endorsement, N. (secondary meaning).

enduring ADJ. lasting; surviving. Keats believed in the *enduring* power of great art, which would outlast its creators' brief lives. endure, V.

energize V. invigorate; make forceful and active. Rather than exhausting Maggie, dancing *energized* her.

engage V. attract; hire; pledge oneself; confront. "Your case has *engaged* my interest, my lord," said Holmes. "You may *engage* my services."

engaging ADJ. charming; attractive. Everyone liked Nancy's pleasant manners and *engaging* personality.

engender V. cause; produce. To receive praise for real accomplishments *engenders* self-confidence in a child.

engross V. occupy fully. John was so *engrossed* in his studies that he did not hear his mother call.

• **enhance** V. increase; improve. You can *enhance* your chances of being admitted to the college of your choice by learning to write well; an excellent essay can *enhance* any application.

- **enigma** N. puzzle; mystery. "What *do* women want?" asked Dr. Sigmund Freud. Their behavior was an *enigma* to him.

  enterprising ADJ. ready to undertake ambitious projects. An *enterprising* young man, Matt saw business opportunities on every side and was always eager to capitalize on them.

- **entice** V. lure; attract; tempt. She always tried to *entice* her baby brother into mischief.

- **enumerate** V. list; mention one by one. Huck hung his head in shame as Miss Watson *enumerated* his many flaws.

  enunciate V. speak distinctly. Stop mumbling! How will people understand you if you do not *enunciate*?

- **ephemeral** ADJ. short-lived; fleeting. The mayfly is an *ephemeral* creature: its adult life lasts little more than a day.

  epic N. long heroic poem, novel, or similar work of art. Kurosawa's film *Seven Samurai* is an *epic* portraying the struggle of seven warriors to destroy a band of robbers. also ADJ.

  epilogue N. short speech at conclusion of dramatic work. The audience was so disappointed in the play that many did not remain to hear the *epilogue*.

  equivocal ADJ. ambiguous; intentionally misleading. Rejecting the candidate's *equivocal* comments on tax reform, the reporters pressed him to state clearly where he stood on the issue. equivocate, V.

- **erode** V. eat away. The limestone was *eroded* by the dripping water until only a thin shell remained. erosion, N.

- **erratic** ADJ. odd; unpredictable. Investors become anxious when the stock market appears *erratic*.

- **erroneous** ADJ. mistaken; wrong. I thought my answer was correct, but it was *erroneous*.

  eschew V. avoid. Hoping to present himself to his girlfriend as a totally reformed character, he tried to *eschew* all the vices, especially chewing tobacco and drinking bathtub gin.

- **esoteric** ADJ. hard to understand; known only to the chosen few. *New Yorker* short stories often included *esoteric* allusions to obscure people and events; the implication was, if you were in the in-crowd, you'd get the reference; if you came from Cleveland, you would not.

- **espouse** V. adopt; support. She was always ready to *espouse* a worthy cause.

- **esteem** V. respect; value; Jill *esteemed* Jack's taste in music, but she deplored his taste in clothes.

  estranged ADJ. separated; alienated. The *estranged* wife sought a divorce. estrangement, N.

  ethereal ADJ. light; heavenly; unusually refined. In Shakespeare's *The Tempest,* the spirit Ariel is an *ethereal* creature, too airy and unearthly for our mortal world.

  euphemism N. mild expression used in place of an unpleasant one. Until recently, many American southerners avoided the word *bull* in polite speech, replacing it by a *euphemism,* such as *he-cow* or *male beast.*

  euphonious ADJ. pleasing in sound. *Euphonious* even when spoken, the Italian language is particularly pleasing to the ear when sung. euphony, N.

  evenhanded ADJ. impartial; fair. Do men and women receive *evenhanded* treatment from their teachers, or, as recent studies suggest, do teachers pay more attention to male students than to females?

  eventuality N. possible occurrence. The government instituted new security procedures to prepare for the *eventuality* of a terrorist attack.

  evocative ADJ. tending to call up (emotions, memories). Scent can be remarkable *evocative:* the aroma of pipe tobacco *evokes* the memory of my father; a whiff of talcum powder calls up images of my daughter as a child.

  exacting ADJ. extremely demanding. Cleaning the ceiling of the Sistine Chapel was an *exacting* task, one that demanded extremely meticulous care on the part of the restorers. exaction, N.

- **excerpt** N. selected passage (written or musical). The cinematic equivalent of an *excerpt* from a novel is a clip from a film.

  exculpate V. clear from blame. Though Sid came up with excuse after excuse to *exculpate* himself, Samantha still blamed him for his conduct.

  execute V. put into effect; carry out; put to death. The prima ballerina *executed* the pirouette so badly that the infuriated choreographer was ready to tear out his hair. execution, N.

- **exemplary** ADJ. serving as a model; outstanding. At commencement the dean praised Ellen for her *exemplary* behavior as class president.

- **exonerate** V. acquit; exculpate. The defense team feverishly sought fresh evidence that might *exonerate* its client.

  expansive ADJ. outgoing and sociable; broad and extensive; able to increase in size. Mr. Fezziwig was in an *expansive* humor, cheerfully urging his guests to join in the Christmas feast. Looking down on his *expansive* paunch, he sighed: if his belly *expanded* any further, his pants would need an *expansive* waistline.

  expedient ADJ. suitable to achieve a particular end; practical; politic. A pragmatic politician, he was guided by what was *expedient* rather than by what was ethical. expediency, N.

- **expedite** V. hasten. Because we are on a tight schedule, we hope you will be able to *expedite* the delivery of our order. expeditious, ADJ.

  explicate V. explain; interpret; clarify. Harry Levin *explicated* James Joyce's often bewildering novels with such clarity that even *Finnegan's Wake* seemed comprehensible to his students.

explicit ADJ. totally clear; definite; outspoken. Don't just hint around that you're dissatisfied: be *explicit* about what's bugging you.

• **exploit** N. deed or action, particularly a brave deed. Raoul Wallenberg was noted for his *exploits* in rescuing Jews from Hitler's forces.

exploit V. make use of, sometimes unjustly. Cesar Chavez fought attempts to *exploit* migrant farmworkers in California. exploitation, N.

expunge V. wipe out; remove; destroy. If you hit the "Delete" key by mistake, you can accidentally *expunge* an entire block of text.

expurgate V. clean; remove offensive parts of a book. The editors felt that certain passages in the book had to be *expurgated* before it could be used in the classroom.

extraneous ADJ. not essential; superfluous. No wonder Ted can't think straight! His mind is so cluttered up with *extraneous* trivia, he can't concentrate on the essentials.

extrapolate V. infer; project from known data into the unknown; make a conjecture. On the basis of what they could *extrapolate* from the results of the primaries on Super Tuesday, the networks predicted that Bob Dole would be the Republican candidate for the presidency.

extricate V. free; disentangle. The fox could not *extricate* itself from the trap.

exuberant ADJ. joyfully enthusiastic; flamboyant; lavish; abundant. I was bowled over by Amy's *exuberant* welcome. What an enthusiastic greeting!

fabricate V. build; lie. If we *fabricate* the buildings in this project out of standardized sections, we can reduce construction cost considerably. Because of Jack's tendency to *fabricate*, Jill had trouble believing a word he said.

facile ADJ. easily accomplished; ready or fluent; superficial. Words came easily to Jonathan: he was a *facile* speaker and prided himself on being ready to make a speech at a moment's notice.

• **facilitate** V. help bring about; make less difficult. Rest and proper nourishment should *facilitate* the patient's recovery.

• **fallacious** ADJ. false; misleading. Paradoxically, *fallacious* reasoning does not always yield erroneous results: even though your logic may be faulty, the answer you get may nevertheless be correct. fallacy, N.

fallible ADJ. liable to err. I know I am *fallible*, but I feel confident that I am right this time.

• **farce** N. broad comedy; mockery. Nothing went right; the entire interview degenerated into a *farce*. farcical, ADJ.

• **fastidious** ADJ. difficult to please; squeamish. Bobby was such a *fastidious* eater that he would eat a sandwich only if his mother first cut off every scrap of crust.

• **fawning** ADJ. seeking favor by cringing and flattering; obsequious. "Stop crawling around like a bootlicker, Uriah! I can't stand your sweet talk and *fawning* ways." fawn, V.

• **feasible** ADJ. practical. Is it *feasible* to build a new stadium for the Yankees on New York's West Side? Without additional funding, the project is clearly unrealistic.

feint N. trick; shift; sham blow. Fooled by his opponent's *feint*, the boxer unwisely dropped his guard. also V.

ferment N. agitation; commotion. With the breakup of the Soviet Union, much of Eastern Europe was in a state of *ferment*.

• **fervor** N. glowing ardor; intensity of feeling. At the protest rally, the students cheered the strikers and booed the dean with equal *fervor*. fervent, fervid, ADJ.

fester V. provoke keen irritation or resentment. Joe's insult *festered* in Anne's mind for days and made her too angry to speak to him.

fetid ADJ. having a foul, disgusting odor. Change the kitty litter in the cat box right now! No self-respecting cat would use a litter box with such a *fetid* smell.

fetter V. shackle. The prisoner was *fettered* to the wall.

fiasco N. total failure. Tanya's attempt to look sophisticated by smoking was a *fiasco*: she lit the wrong end of the cigarette, choked when she tried to inhale, and burned a hole in her boyfriend's couch.

fiery ADJ. easily provoked; passionate; burning. By reputation, redheads have *fiery* tempers; the least little thing can cause them to explode.

finesse N. delicate skill. The *finesse* and adroitness with which the surgeon wielded her scalpel impressed the observers in the operating theater.

finite ADJ. having an end; limited. Though Bill really wanted to win the pie-eating contest, the capacity of his stomach was *finite*, and he had to call it quits after eating only seven cherry pies.

firebrand N. hothead; troublemaker. The police tried to keep track of all the local *firebrands* when the president came to town.

fissure N. crevice. The mountain climbers secured footholds in tiny *fissures* in the rock.

fitful ADJ. spasmodic; intermittent. After several *fitful* attempts, he decided to postpone the start of the project until he felt more energetic.

fleeting ADJ. transitory; vanishing quickly. The glory of a New England autumn is *fleeting*: the first gust of wind strips the trees of their colorful leaves.

- **flippant** ADJ. lacking proper seriousness. When Mark told Mona he loved her, she dismissed his earnest declaration with a *flippant* "Oh, you say that to all the girls!" flippancy, N.

flout V. reject; mock. The headstrong youth *flouted* all authority; he refused to be curbed.

fluctuate V. waver; shift. The water pressure in our shower *fluctuates* wildly; you start rinsing yourself off with a trickle, and, two minutes later, a blast of water nearly knocks you down.

fluency N. smoothness of speech. He spoke French with *fluency* and ease.

foible N. weakness; slight fault. We can overlook the *foibles* of our friends; no one is perfect.

foliage N. masses of leaves. Every autumn before the leaves fell, he promised himself he would drive through New England to admire the colorful fall *foliage*.

forbearance N. patience. We must use *forbearance* in dealing with him because he is still weak from his illness.

foreboding N. premonition of evil. Suspecting no conspiracies against him, Caesar gently ridiculed his wife's *forebodings* about the ides of March.

foreshadow V. give an indication beforehand; portend; prefigure. In retrospect, political analysts realized that Yeltsin's defiance of the attempted coup *foreshadowed* his emergence as the dominant figure of the new Russian republic.

foresight N. ability to foresee future happenings; careful provision for the future. A shrewd investor, she had the *foresight* to buy land just before the current real estate boom.

forestall V. prevent by taking action in advance. By setting up a prenuptial agreement, the prospective bride and groom hoped to *forestall* any potential arguments about money in the event of a divorce.

forfeit V. lose; surrender. Convicted murderers *forfeit* the right to inherit anything from their victims; the law does not allow them to benefit financially from their crimes.

forgo V. give up; do without. Determined to lose weight over the summer, Michelle decided to *forgo* dessert until she could fit into a size eight again.

formidable ADJ. inspiring fear or apprehension; difficult; awe inspiring. In the film *Meet the Parents,* the hero is understandably nervous about meeting his fiancée's father, a *formidable* CIA agent.

- **forthright** ADJ. outspoken; frank. Never afraid to call a spade a spade, she was perhaps too *forthright* to be a successful party politician.

fortuitous ADJ. accidental; by chance. Though he pretended their encounter was *fortuitous,* he'd actually been hanging around her usual haunts for the past two weeks, hoping she'd turn up.

foster V. rear; encourage. According to the legend, Romulus and Remus were *fostered* by a she-wolf who raised the abandoned infants as her own. also ADJ.

- **frail** ADJ. weak. The delicate child seemed too *frail* to lift the heavy carton.

franchise N. right granted by authority; right to vote; business licensed to sell a product in a particular territory. The city issued a *franchise* to the company to operate surface transit lines on the streets for 99 years. For most of American history, women lacked the right to vote: not until the early twentieth century was the *franchise* granted to women. Stan owns a Carvel's ice cream *franchise* in Chinatown.

frantic ADJ. wild. At the time of the collision, many people became *frantic* with fear.

fraudulent ADJ. cheating; deceitful. The government seeks to prevent *fraudulent* and misleading advertising.

- **frivolous** ADJ. lacking in seriousness; self-indulgently carefree; relatively unimportant. Though Nancy enjoyed Bill's *frivolous,* lighthearted companionship, she sometimes wondered whether he could ever be serious. frivolity, N.

fugitive ADJ. fleeting or transient; elusive; fleeing. How can a painter capture on canvas the *fugitive* beauty of clouds moving across the sky? also N.

fundamental V. basic; primary; essential. The committee discussed all sorts of side issues without ever getting down to addressing the *fundamental* problem.

furtive ADJ. stealthy; sneaky. Noticing the *furtive* glance the customer gave the diamond bracelet on the counter, the jeweler wondered whether he had a potential shoplifter on his hands.

fusion N. union; coalition. The opponents of the political party in power organized a *fusion* of disgruntled groups and became an important element in the election.

futile ADJ. useless; hopeless; ineffectual. It is *futile* for me to try to get any work done around here while the telephone is ringing every thirty seconds. futility, N.

gainful ADJ. profitable. After having been out of work for six months, Brenda was excited by the prospect of *gainful* employment.

gale N. windstorm; gust of wind; emotional outburst (laughter, tears). The Weather Channel warned viewers about a rising *gale,* with winds of up to 60 miles per hour.

galvanize V. stimulate by shock; stir up; revitalize. News that the prince was almost at their door *galvanized* the ugly stepsisters into a frenzy of combing and primping.

garble V. mix up; jumble; distort. A favorite party game involves passing a whispered message from one person to another, till, by the time it reaches the last player, everyone has totally *garbled* the message.

garish ADJ. overbright in color; gaudy. She wore a gaudy rhinestone necklace with an excessively *garish* gold lamé dress.

• **garrulous** ADJ. loquacious; wordy; talkative. My Uncle Henry can outtalk any three people I know. He is the most *garrulous* person in Cayuga County. garrulity, N.

gastric ADJ. pertaining to the stomach. Clutching his stomach and grimacing broadly, the acting student feigned *gastric* distress.

gavel N. hammerlike tool; mallet. "Sold!" cried the auctioneer, banging her *gavel* on the table to indicate she'd accepted the final bid.

genealogy N. record of descent; lineage. He was proud of his *genealogy* and constantly referred to the achievements of his ancestors.

• **generate** V. cause; produce; create. In his first days in office, President Clinton managed to *generate* a new mood of optimism; we hoped he could *generate* a few new jobs.

generic ADJ. characteristic of an entire class or species. Sue knew so many computer programmers who spent their spare time playing fantasy games that she began to think that playing Dungeons & Dragons was a *generic* trait.

• **genre** N. particular variety of art or literature. Both a short story writer and a poet, Langston Hughes proved himself equally skilled in either *genre*.

genteel ADJ. well-bred; elegant. We are looking for a man with a *genteel* appearance who can inspire confidence by his cultivated manner.

germane ADJ. pertinent; bearing upon the case at hand. The lawyer objected that the witness's testimony was not *germane* to the case and should be ignored by the jury.

gibberish N. nonsense; babbling. "Did you hear that fool boy spouting *gibberish* about monsters from outer space? I never heard anything so nonsensical in all my . . ."

giddy ADJ. lighthearted; dizzy. The silly, *giddy* young girls rode ride after ride on the Tilt-a-Whirl until they were *giddy* and sick.

gingerly ADV. very carefully. To separate egg whites, first crack the egg *gingerly*, avoiding breaking the yolk.

glimmer V. shine erratically; twinkle. In the darkness of the cavern, the glowworms hanging from the cavern roof *glimmered* like distant stars.

gloss over V. explain away. No matter how hard he tried to talk around the issue, the president could not *gloss over* the fact that he had raised taxes after all.

glower V. scowl. The angry boy *glowered* at his father.

• **gluttonous** ADJ. greedy for food. The *gluttonous* boy ate all the cookies.

gorge N. small, steep-walled canyon. The white-water rafting guide warned us about the rapids farther downstream, where the river cut through a narrow *gorge*.

gorge V. stuff oneself. The gluttonous guest *gorged* himself, cramming food into his mouth as fast as he could.

grandeur N. impressiveness; stateliness; majesty. No matter how often he hiked through the mountains, David never failed to be struck by the *grandeur* of the Sierra Nevada range.

grandiose ADJ. pretentious; high-flown; ridiculously exaggerated; impressive. The aged matinee idol still had *grandiose* notions of his supposed importance in the theatrical world.

graphic ADJ. pertaining to the art of delineating; vividly described. I was particularly impressed by the *graphic* presentation of the storm.

• **gratify** V. please. Amy's success in her new job *gratified* her parents.

gratuitous ADJ. given freely; unwarranted; uncalled for. Quit making *gratuitous* comments about my driving; no one asked you for your opinion.

• **gregarious** ADJ. sociable. Typically, party-throwers are *gregarious*; hermits are not.

guile N. deceit; duplicity; wiliness; cunning. Iago uses considerate *guile* to trick Othello into believing that Desdemona has been unfaithful.

gullible ADJ. easily deceived. Overly *gullible* people have only themselves to blame if they fall for scams repeatedly. As the saying goes, "Fool me once, shame on you. Fool me twice, shame on me."

• **hackneyed** ADJ. commonplace; trite. When the reviewer criticized the movie for its *hackneyed* plot, we agreed; we had seen similar stories hundreds of times before.

• **halting** ADJ. hesitant; faltering. Novice extemporaneous speakers often talk in a *halting* fashion as they grope for the right words.

• **hamper** V. obstruct. The new mother didn't realize how much the effort of caring for an infant would *hamper* her ability to keep an immaculate house.

harangue N. noisy speech. In her lengthy *harangue*, the principal berated the offenders. also V.

harass V. to annoy by repeated attacks. When he could not pay his bills as quickly as he had promised, he was *harassed* by his creditors.

harbor V. provide a refuge for; hide. The church *harbored* illegal aliens who were political refugees.

haughtiness N. pride; arrogance. When she realized that Darcy believed himself too good to dance with his inferiors, Elizabeth took great offense at his *haughtiness*.

hazardous ADJ. dangerous. Your occupation is too *hazardous* for insurance companies to consider your application.

headstrong ADJ. stubborn; willful; unyielding. Because she refused to marry the man her parents had chosen for her, everyone scolded Minna and called her a foolish *headstrong* girl.

heckle V. harass; taunt; jeer at. The home team's fans mercilessly *heckled* the visiting pitcher, taunting him whenever he let anyone get on base.

heed V. pay attention to; consider. We hope you *heed* our advice and get a good night's sleep before the test. also N.

herculean ADJ. very strong; extremely difficult to perform; like the mythological hero Hercules. Muscles rippling, the action hero was a *herculean* figure, lifting enormous weights with ease.

heresy N. opinion contrary to popular belief; opinion contrary to accepted religion. Galileo's assertion that the earth moved around the sun directly contradicted the religious teachings of his day; as a result, he was tried for *heresy*. heretic, N.

hermetic ADJ. sealed by fusion so as to be airtight. After you sterilize the bandages, place them in a container and seal it with a *hermetic* seal to protect them from contamination by airborne bacteria.

hermit N. someone who chooses to live in solitude; recluse. Abandoning society, Thoreau chose to go off and live in the woods like a *hermit*.

hiatus N. gap; pause. Except for a brief two-year *hiatus*, during which she enrolled in the Peace Corps, Ms. Clements has devoted herself to her medical career.

hibernate V. sleep throughout the winter. Bears are one of the many species of animals that *hibernate*. hibernation, N.

hierarchy N. arrangement by rank or standing; authoritarian body divided into ranks. To be low man on the totem pole is to have an inferior place in the *hierarchy*.

• **hindrance** N. block; obstacle. Stalled cars along the highway are a *hindrance* to traffic that tow trucks should remove without delay. hinder, V.

homespun ADJ. domestic; made at home. *Homespun* wit like *homespun* cloth was often coarse and plain.

• **hostility** N. unfriendliness; hatred. Children who have been the sole objects of their parents' attention often feel *hostility* toward a new baby in the family, resenting the newcomer who has taken their place.

humane ADJ. marked by kindness or consideration. It is ironic that the *Humane* Society sometimes must show its compassion toward mistreated animals by killing them to put them out of their misery.

humble ADJ. modest; not proud. He spoke with great feeling of how much he loved his *humble* home, which he would not trade for a palace. humility, N.

husband V. use sparingly; conserve; save. Marathon runners must *husband* their energy so that they can keep going for the entire distance.

hyperbole N. exaggeration; overstatement. As far as I'm concerned, Apple's claims about the new computer are pure *hyperbole:* no machine is that good!

• **hypocritical** ADJ. pretending to be virtuous; deceiving. It was *hypocritical* of Martha to say such nice things about my poetry to me and then make fun of my verses behind my back. hypocrisy, N.

• **hypothetical** ADJ. based on assumptions or hypotheses; supposed. Suppose you are accepted by Harvard, Stanford, and Brown. Which one would you choose to attend? Remember, this is only a *hypothetical* situation. hypothesis, N.

• **iconoclastic** ADJ. attacking cherished traditions. Deeply *iconoclastic,* Jean Genet deliberately set out to shock conventional theatergoers with his radical plays.

ideology N. system of ideas of a group. For people who had grown up believing in the communist *ideology,* it was hard to adjust to capitalism.

idiom N. expression whose meaning as a whole differs from the meanings of its individual words; distinctive style. The phrase "to lose one's marbles" is an *idiom:* if I say that Joe's lost his marbles, I'm not asking you to find some for him. I'm telling you *idiomatically* that he's crazy.

idiosyncrasy N. individual trait, usually odd in nature; eccentricity. One of Richard Nixon's little *idiosyncrasies* was his liking for ketchup on cottage cheese. One of Hannibal Lecter's little *idiosyncrasies* was his liking for human flesh.

ignite V. kindle; light. When Desi crooned "Baby, light my fire," literal-minded Lucy looked around for some paper to *ignite*.

ignoble ADJ. unworthy; base in nature; not noble. Sir Galahad was so pure in heart that he could never stoop to perform an *ignoble* deed.

illuminate V. brighten; clear up or make understandable; enlighten. Just as a lamp can *illuminate* a dark room, a perceptive comment can *illuminate* a knotty problem.

illusory ADJ. deceptive; not real. Unfortunately, the costs of running the lemonade stand were so high that Tom's profits proved *illusory*.

imbalance N. lack of balance or symmetry; disproportion. To correct racial *imbalance* in the schools, school boards have bussed black children into white neighborhoods and white children into black ones.

imbibe V. drink in. The dry soil *imbibed* the rain quickly.

imbue V. permeate completely; dye thoroughly; fill. The sight of her grandparents' names inscribed on the wall of Ellis Island *imbued* Sarah with a sense of her special heritage as the descendant of immigrants.

immaterial ADJ. unimportant; irrelevant; intangible. Though Kit said it was wholly *immaterial* whether she had a birthday party or not, we wanted to throw her a party.

imminent ADJ.; near at hand; impending. Rosa was such a last-minute worker that she could never start writing a paper till the deadline was *imminent*.

immobilize V. make unable to move. For a moment, Peter's fear of snakes *immobilized* him; then the use of his limbs returned to him and he bolted from the room.

immune ADJ. resistant to; free or exempt from. Fortunately, Florence had contracted chicken pox as a child and was *immune* to it when her baby broke out in spots.

• **immutable** ADJ. unchangeable. All things change over time; nothing is *immutable*.

impair V. injure; hurt. Drinking alcohol can *impair* your ability to drive safely; if you're going to drink, don't drive.

impart V. give or convey; communicate. A born dancer, she *imparted* her love of movement to her audience with every step she took.

impartial ADJ. not biased; fair. Knowing she could not be *impartial* about her own child, Jo refused to judge any match in which Billy was competing.

impassable ADJ. not able to be traveled or crossed. A giant redwood had fallen across the highway, blocking all four lanes: the road was *impassable*.

impasse N. predicament offering no escape; deadlock; dead end. The negotiators reported they had reached an *impasse* in their talks and had little hope of resolving the deadlock swiftly.

impecunious ADJ. without money. Though Scrooge claimed he was too *impecunious* to give alms, he easily could have afforded to be charitable.

• **impede** v. hinder; block; delay. A series of accidents *impeded* the launching of the space shuttle.

impel V. drive or force onward. A strong feeling of urgency *impelled* her; if she failed to finish the project right then, she knew that she would never get it done.

• **imperceptible** ADJ. unnoticeable; undetectable. Fortunately, the stain on the blouse was *imperceptible* after the blouse had gone through the wash.

impermeable ADJ. impervious; not permitting passage through its substance. Sue chose a raincoat made of Gore-Tex because the material was *impermeable* to liquids.

impertinent ADJ. insolent; rude. His neighbors' *impertinent* curiosity about his lack of dates angered Ted. It was downright rude of them to ask him such personal questions.

imperturbable ADJ. calm; placid; composed. In the midst of the battle, the Duke of Wellington remained *imperturbable* and in full command of the situation despite the hysteria and panic all around him. imperturbability, N.

impetuous ADJ. violent; hasty; rash. "Leap before you look" was the motto suggested by one particularly *impetuous* young man.

impiety N. irreverence; lack of respect for God. When members of the youth group draped the church in toilet paper one Halloween, the minister reprimanded them for their *impiety*. impious, ADJ.

• **implacable** ADJ. incapable of being pacified. Madame Defarge was the *implacable* enemy of the Evremonde family.

• **implement** V. put into effect; supply with tools. The mayor was unwilling to *implement* the plan until she was sure it had the governor's backing. also N.

implicate V. incriminate; show to be involved. Here's the deal: If you agree to take the witness stand and *implicate* your partners in crime, the prosecution will recommend that the judge go easy in sentencing you.

• **implication** N. something hinted at or suggested. When Miss Watson said she hadn't seen her purse since the last time Jim was in the house, the *implication* was that she suspected Jim had taken it. imply, V.

implicit ADJ. understood but not stated. Jack never told Jill he adored her; he believed his love was *implicit* in his deeds.

importune V. beg persistently. Democratic and Republican phone solicitors *importuned* her for contributions so frequently that she decided to give nothing to either party.

impotent ADJ. weak; ineffective. Although he wished to break the nicotine habit, he found himself *impotent* to resist the craving for a cigarette.

• **impromptu** ADJ. without previous preparation; off the cuff; on the spur of the moment. The judges were amazed that she could make such a thorough, well-supported presentation in an *impromptu* speech.

inadvertently ADV. unintentionally; by oversight; carelessly. Judy's great fear was that she might *inadvertently* omit a question on the exam and mismark her whole answer sheet.

inane ADJ. silly; senseless. There's no point in what you're saying. Why are you bothering to make such *inane* remarks? inanity, N.

inanimate ADJ. lifeless. She was asked to identify the still and *inanimate* body.

inarticulate ADJ. speechless; producing indistinct speech. He became *inarticulate* with rage and uttered sounds without meaning.

incapacitate V. disable. During the winter, many people were *incapacitated* by respiratory ailments.

• **incarcerate** V. imprison. The civil rights workers were willing to be arrested and even *incarcerated* if by their imprisonment they could serve the cause.

incentive N. spur; motive. Mike's strong desire to outshine his big sister was all the *incentive* he needed to do well in school.

incessant ADJ. uninterrupted; unceasing. In a famous TV commercial, the frogs' *incessant* croaking goes on and on until eventually it turns into a single word: "Bud-weis-er."

incipient ADJ. beginning; in an early stage. I will go to sleep early for I want to break an *incipient* cold.

incite V. arouse to action; goad; motivate; induce to exist. In a fiery speech, Mario *incited* his fellow students to go out on strike to protest the university's anti-affirmative-action stand.

inclusive ADJ. tending to include all. The comedian turned down the invitation to join the Players' Club, saying any club that would let him in was too *inclusive*.

• **incongruity** N. lack of harmony; absurdity. The *incongruity* of his wearing sneakers with formal attire amused the observers. incongruous, ADJ.

incoherent ADJ. unintelligible; muddled; illogical. The excited fan blushed and stammered, her words becoming almost *incoherent* in the thrill of meeting her favorite rock star face to face. incoherence, N.

• **inconsequential** ADJ. insignificant; unimportant. Brushing off Ali's apologies for having broken the wine glass, Tamara said, "Don't worry about it; it's *inconsequential*."

• **inconsistency** N. state of being self-contradictory; lack of uniformity or steadiness. How are lawyers different from agricultural inspectors? While lawyers check *inconsistencies* in witnesses' statements, agricultural inspectors check *inconsistencies* in Grade A eggs. inconsistent, ADJ.

• **incorporate** V. introduce something into a larger whole; combine; unite. Breaking with precedent, President Truman ordered the military to *incorporate* blacks into every branch of the armed services. also ADJ.

incorporeal ADJ. lacking a material body; insubstantial. Although Casper the friendly ghost is an *incorporeal* being, he and his fellow ghosts make a decided impact on the physical world.

incorrigible ADJ. uncorrectable. Though Widow Douglass hoped to reform Huck, Miss Watson pronounced him *incorrigible* and said he would come to no good end.

incredulous ADJ. unwilling or unable to believe; skeptical. When Marco claimed he hadn't eaten the jelly doughnut, Joyce took one *incredulous* look at his smeared face and laughed.

incrustation N. hard coating or crust. In dry dock, we scraped off the *incrustation* of dirt and barnacles that covered the hull of the ship.

incumbent N. officeholder. The newly elected public official received valuable advice from the previous *incumbent*. also ADJ.

indefatigable ADJ. tireless. Although the effort of taking out the garbage tired Wayne out for the entire morning, when it came to partying, he was *indefatigable*.

indelible ADJ. not able to be erased. The *indelible* ink left a permanent mark on my shirt. Young Bill Clinton's meeting with President Kennedy made an *indelible* impression on the youth.

• **indict** V. charge. The district attorney didn't want to *indict* the suspect until she was sure she had a strong enough case to convince a jury. indictment, N.

• **indifferent** ADJ. unmoved or unconcerned by; mediocre. Because Consuela felt no desire to marry, she was *indifferent* to Edward's constant proposals. Not only was she *indifferent* to him personally, but she felt that, given his general silliness, he would make an *indifferent* husband.

indigenous ADJ. native. Cigarettes are made of tobacco, a plant *indigenous* to the New World.

indisputable ADJ. too certain to be disputed. In the face of these *indisputable* statements, I withdraw my complaint.

indomitable ADJ. unconquerable; unyielding. Focusing on her final vault despite her twisted ankle, gymnastics star Kerri Strug proved she had an *indomitable* will to win.

indubitable ADJ. unable to be doubted; unquestionable. Auditioning for the chorus line, Molly was an *indubitable* hit: the director fired the leading lady and hired Molly in her place!

• **induce** V. persuade; bring about. After the quarrel, Tina said nothing could *induce* her to talk to Tony again. inducement, N.

indulgent ADJ. humoring; yielding; lenient. Jay's mom was excessively *indulgent*: she bought him every Nintendo cartridge and video game on the market. She *indulged* Jay so much, she spoiled him rotten.

• **industrious** ADJ. diligent; hard-working. Look busy when the boss walks past your desk; it never hurts to appear *industrious*. industry, N.

ineffable ADJ. unutterable; unable to be expressed in speech. Looking down at her newborn daughter, Ruth felt such *ineffable* joy that, for the first time in her adult life, she had no words to convey what was in her heart.

• **inept** ADJ. lacking skill; unsuited; incompetent. The *inept* glove maker was all thumbs. ineptitude, ineptness, N.

inevitable ADJ. unavoidable. Though death and taxes are both supposedly *inevitable*, some people avoid paying taxes for years.

• **infallible** ADJ. unerring; faultless. Jane refused to believe the pope was *infallible*, reasoning: "All human beings are capable of error. The pope is a human being. Therefore, the pope is capable of error."

infamous ADJ. notoriously bad. Charles Manson and Jeffrey Dahmer are both *infamous* killers.

infer V. deduce; conclude. From the students' glazed looks, it was easy for me to *infer* that they were bored out of their minds. inference, N.

infernal ADJ. pertaining to hell; devilish. Batman was baffled: he could think of no way to hinder the Joker's *infernal* scheme to destroy the city.

infinitesimal ADJ. exceedingly small; so small as to be almost nonexistent. Making sure everyone was aware she was on an extremely strict diet, Melanie said she would have only an *infinitesimal* sliver of pie.

infraction N. violation (of a rule or regulation); breach. When Dennis Rodman butted heads with the referee, he committed a clear *infraction* of NBA rules.

• **ingenious** ADJ. clever; resourceful. Kit admired the *ingenious* way that her computer keyboard opened up to reveal the built-in CD-ROM below. ingenuity, N.

• **ingenuous** ADJ. naive and trusting; young; unsophisticated. The woodsman had not realized how *ingenuous* Little Red Riding Hood was until he heard that she had gone off for a walk in the woods with the Big Bad Wolf.

• **ingrate** N. ungrateful person. That *ingrate* Bob sneered at the tie I gave him.

ingratiate V. make an effort to become popular with others. In *All About Eve,* the heroine, an aspiring actress, wages a clever campaign to *ingratiate* herself with Margo Channing, an established star.

• **inherent** ADJ. firmly established by nature or habit. Katya's *inherent* love of justice caused her to champion anyone she considered treated unfairly by society.

inhibit V. restrain; retard or prevent. Only two things *inhibited* him from taking a punch at Mike Tyson: Tyson's left hook and Tyson's right jab. The protective undercoating on my car *inhibits* the formation of rust.

• **initiate** V. begin; originate; receive into a group. The college is about to *initiate* a program for reducing math anxiety among students.

inkling N. hint. This came as a complete surprise to me as I did not have the slightest *inkling* of your plans.

inlet N. small bay; narrow passage between islands; entrance. Seeking shelter from the gale, Drake sailed the *Golden Hind* into a protected *inlet,* where he hoped to wait out the storm.

• **innate** ADJ. inborn. Mozart's parents soon recognized young Wolfgang's *innate* talent for music.

• **innocuous** ADJ. harmless. An occasional glass of wine with dinner is relatively *innocuous* and should have no ill effect on you.

innovation N. change; introduction of something new. Although Richard liked to keep up with all the latest technological *innovations,* he didn't always abandon tried-and-true techniques in favor of something new. innovate, V.

inopportune ADJ. untimely; poorly chosen. A punk rock concert is an *inopportune* setting for a quiet conversation.

inordinate ADJ. unrestrained; excessive. She had an *inordinate* fondness for candy, eating two or three boxes in a single day.

inquisitor N. questioner (especially harsh); investigator. Fearing being grilled ruthlessly by the secret police, Masha faced her *inquisitors* with trepidation.

insatiable ADJ. not easily satisfied; greedy. Welty's thirst for knowledge was *insatiable;* she was in the library day and night.

• **inscrutable** ADJ. impenetrable; not readily understood; mysterious. Experienced poker players try to keep their expressions *inscrutable,* hiding their reactions to the cards behind a so-called poker face.

insidious ADJ. treacherous; stealthy; sly. The fifth column is *insidious* because it works secretly within our territory for our defeat.

• **insightful** ADJ. discerning; perceptive. Sol thought he was very *insightful* about human behavior, but he was actually clueless as to why people acted the way they did.

insinuate V. hint; imply; creep in. When you say I look robust, do you mean to *insinuate* that I'm getting fat?

insipid ADJ. lacking in flavor; dull. Flat prose and flat ginger ale are equally *insipid*: both lack sparkle.

insolence N. impudent disrespect; haughtiness. How dare you treat me so rudely! The manager will hear of your *insolence*. insolent, ADJ.

insolvent ADJ. bankrupt; lacking money to pay. When rumors that he was *insolvent* reached his creditors, they began to press him to pay the money he owed them. insolvency, N.

insomnia N. wakefulness; inability to sleep. He refused to join us in a midnight cup of coffee because he claimed it gave him *insomnia*.

instigate V. urge; start; provoke. Rumors of police corruption led the mayor to *instigate* an investigation into the department's activities.

insubordination N. disobedience; rebelliousness. At the slightest hint of *insubordination* from the sailors of the *Bounty,* Captain Bligh had them flogged; finally, they mutinied.

insubstantial ADJ. lacking substance; insignificant; frail. His hopes for a career in acting proved *insubstantial;* no one would cast him, even in an *insubstantial* role.

insurgent ADJ. rebellious. Because the *insurgent* forces had occupied the capital and had gained control of the railway lines, several of the war correspondents covering the uprising predicted a rebel victory.

insurrection N. rebellion; uprising. In retrospect, given how badly the British treated the American colonists, the eventual *insurrection* seems inevitable.

• **intangible** ADJ. not able to be perceived by touch; vague. Though the financial benefits of his Oxford post were meager, Lewis was drawn to it by its *intangible* rewards: prestige, intellectual freedom, the fellowship of his peers.

• **integrity** N. uprightness; wholeness. Lincoln, whose personal *integrity* has inspired millions, fought a civil war to maintain the *integrity* of the Republic, that these United States might remain undivided for all time.

interminable ADJ. endless. Although his speech lasted for only twenty minutes, it seemed *interminable* to his bored audience.

intermittent ADJ. periodic; on and off. The outdoor wedding reception had to be moved indoors to avoid the *intermittent* showers that fell all afternoon.

interrogate V. question closely; cross-examine. Knowing that the Nazis would *interrogate* him about his background, the secret agent invented a cover story that would help him meet their questions.

intimidate V. frighten. I'll learn karate and then those big bullies won't be able to *intimidate* me any more.

intransigence N. refusal of any compromise; stubbornness. When I predicted that the strike would be over in a week, I didn't expect to encounter such *intransigence* from both sides. intransigent, ADJ.

• **intricacy** N. complexity; knottiness. Philip spent many hours designing mazes of such great *intricacy* that none of his classmates could solve them. intricate, ADJ.

intrigue V. fascinate; interest. Holmes's air of reserve *intrigued* Irene Adler; she wanted to know just what made the great detective tick.

intrinsic ADJ. essential; inherent; built-in. Although my grandmother's china has little *intrinsic* value, I shall always cherish it for the memories it evokes.

• **introspective** ADJ. looking within oneself. Though young Francis of Assisi led a wild and worldly life, even he had *introspective* moments during which he examined his soul.

intrude V. trespass; enter as an uninvited person. She hesitated to *intrude* on their conversation.

intuition N. immediate insight; power of knowing without reasoning. Even though Tony denied that anything was wrong, Tina trusted her *intuition* that something was bothering him. intuitive, ADJ.

inundate V. overwhelm; flood; submerge. This semester I am *inundated* with work: you should see the piles of paperwork flooding my desk. Until the great dam was build, the waters of the Nile used to *inundate* the river valley every year.

invalidate V. discredit; nullify. The relatives who received little or nothing sought to *invalidate* the will by claiming that the deceased had not been in his right mind when he signed the document.

invective N. abuse. He had expected criticism but not the *invective* that greeted his proposal.

inviolable ADJ. secure from corruption, attack, or violation; unassailable. Batman considered his oath to keep the people of Gotham City safe *inviolable*: nothing on earth could make him break this promise.

irascible ADJ. irritable; easily angered. Pop had what people call a hair-trigger temper; he was a hot-tempered, *irascible* guy.

irksome ADJ. annoying; tedious. The petty rules and regulations Bill had to follow at work irritated him: he found them uniformly *irksome*.

• **irony** N. hidden sarcasm or satire; use of words that seem to mean the opposite of what they actually mean. Gradually his listeners began to realize that the excessive praise he was lavishing on his opponent was actually *irony;* he was in fact ridiculing the poor fool.

irrational ADJ. illogical; lacking reason; insane. Many people have such an *irrational* fear of snakes that they panic at the sight of a harmless garter snake.

irrelevant ADJ. not applicable; unrelated. No matter how *irrelevant* the patient's mumblings may seem, they give us some indications of what he has on his mind.

isolate V. keep apart; pinpoint; quarantine. The medical researchers *isolated* themselves in a remote village. Until they could *isolate* the cause of the plague and develop an effective vaccine, they had to avoid potential carriers of the disease. Anyone infected they *isolated* immediately.

itinerant ADJ. wandering; traveling. He was an *itinerant* peddler and traveled through Pennsylvania and Virginia selling his wares. also N.

jabber V. chatter rapidly or unintelligibly. Why does the fellow insist on *jabbering* away in French when I can't understand a word he says?

jargon N. language used by a special group; technical terminology; gibberish. The computer salesmen at the store used a *jargon* of their own that we simply couldn't follow; we had no idea what they were jabbering about.

jaunty ADJ. lighthearted; animated; easy and carefree. In *Singing in the Rain,* Gene Kelly sang and danced his way through the lighthearted title number in a properly *jaunty* style.

jeopardize V. endanger; imperil; put at risk. You can't give me a D in chemistry; you'll *jeopardize* my chances of getting into M.I.T. jeopardy, N.

jocose ADJ. giving to joking. The salesman was so *jocose* that many of his customers suggested that he become a stand-up comic.

jocular ADJ. said or done in jest. Although Bill knew the boss hated jokes, he couldn't resist making one *jocular* remark. jocularity, N.

• **judicious** ADJ. sound in judgment; wise. At a key moment in his life, he made a *judicious* investment that was the foundation of his later wealth.

justification N. good or just reason; defense; excuse. The jury found him guilty of the more serious charge because they could see no possible *justification* for his actions.

juxtapose V. place side by side. You'll find it easier to compare the two paintings if you *juxtapose* them.

kindle V. start a fire; inspire. One of the first things Ben learned in the Boy Scouts was how to *kindle* a fire by rubbing two dry sticks together. Her teacher's praise for her poetry *kindled* a spark of hope inside Maya.

knit V. contract into wrinkles; grow together. Whenever David worries, his brow *knits* in a frown. When he broke his leg, he sat around the house all day waiting for the bones to *knit*.

laborious ADJ. demanding much work or care; tedious. In putting together his dictionary of the English language, Doctor Johnson undertook a *laborious* task.

laconic ADJ. brief and to the point. Many of the characters portrayed by Clint Eastwood are *laconic* types, rugged men of few words.

laggard ADJ. slow; sluggish. The sailor had been taught not to be *laggard* in carrying out orders. lag, N., V.

lair N. wild animal's living place; den; hideaway. Jack London called his remote dwelling place the *Lair of the Wolf*.

lament V. grieve; express sorrow. Even advocates of the war *lamented* the loss of so many lives in combat. lamentation, N.

lampoon V. ridicule. This hilarious article *lampoons* the pretensions of some movie moguls. also N.

• **languid** ADJ. weary; feeble; listless; apathetic. The chronic invalid's most recent siege of illness left her *languid* and drooping. languor, N. languish, V.

• **larceny** N. theft. Because of the prisoner's long record of thefts, the district attorney refused to reduce the charge from grand *larceny* to petty *larceny*.

latent ADJ. potential but undeveloped; dormant; hidden. Polaroid pictures are popular at parties, because you can see the *latent* photographic image gradually appear before your eyes.

laud V. praise. The NFL *lauded* Boomer Esiason's efforts to raise money to combat cystic fibrosis. laudable, laudatory, ADJ.

leaven V. cause to rise or grow lighter; mix in something that transforms, alleviates, or enlivens. As bread dough is *leavened*, it puffs up, expanding in volume. also N.

lenience N. mildness; permissiveness. Considering the gravity of the offense, we were surprised by the *lenience* of the sentence. also leniency; lenient, ADJ.

lethal ADJ. deadly. It is unwise to leave *lethal* weapons where children may find them.

• **lethargic** ADJ. drowsy; dull. The stuffy room made her *lethargic*: she felt as if she was about to nod off.

levity N. lack of seriousness; lightness. Stop giggling and wiggling around in your seats: such *levity* is improper in church.

libel N. defamatory statement; act of writing something that smears a person's character. If Batman wrote that the Joker was a dirty, rotten, mass-murdering criminal, could the Joker sue Batman for *libel*?

lilliputian ADJ. extremely small. Tiny and delicate, the model was built on a *lilliputian* scale. also N.

linger V. loiter or dawdle; continue or persist. Hoping to see Juliet pass by, Romeo *lingered* outside the Capulet house for hours. Though Mother made stuffed cabbage on Monday, the smell *lingered* around the house for days.

loath ADJ. reluctant; disinclined. Fearing for her son's safety, the overprotective mother was *loath* to let him go on the class trip.

• **loathe** V. detest. Booing and hissing, the audience showed how much they *loathed* the wicked villain.

lofty ADJ. very high. Though Barbara Jordan's fellow students used to tease her about her *lofty* ambitions, she rose to hold one of the highest positions in the land.

longevity N. long life. When he reached 90, the old man was proud of his *longevity*.

loquacious ADJ. talkative. She is very *loquacious* and can speak on the telephone for hours.

lucid ADJ. easily understood; clear; intelligible. Her explanation was *lucid* enough for a child to grasp.

lucrative ADJ. profitable. He turned his hobby into a *lucrative* profession.

lugubrious ADJ. mournful; funereal. Gloomy Gus walked around town with a *lugubrious* expression on his face.

luminous ADJ. shining; issuing light. The sun is a *luminous* body.

lure V. entice; attract. Baiting his hook with the latest fly he had put together, Grandpa Joe swore that this new fly was so attractive that it could *lure* the wariest trout out of hiding.

lurk V. stealthily lie in waiting; slink; exist unperceived. "Who knows what evils *lurk* in the hearts of men? The Shadow knows!"

luxuriant ADJ. abundant; rich and splendid; fertile. Lady Godiva was completely covered by her *luxuriant* hair.

maelstrom N. whirlpool. The canoe was tossed about in the *maelstrom.*

magnanimous ADJ. generous. Philanthropists by definition are *magnanimous;* misers, by definition, are not. magnanimity, N.

• **malice** N. hatred; spite. Jealous of Cinderella's beauty, her wicked stepsisters expressed their *malice* by forcing her to do menial tasks.

malign V. speak evil of; bad-mouth; defame. Her hatred of her ex-husband ran so deep that she *maligned* anyone who even casually dated him.

malignant ADJ. having an evil influence; virulent. This is a *malignant* disease; we may have to use drastic measures to stop its spread.

malleable ADJ. capable of being shaped by pounding; impressionable. Gold is a *malleable* metal, easily shaped into bracelets and rings. Fagin hoped Oliver was a *malleable* lad, easily shaped into a thief.

manifest ADJ. evident; visible; obvious. Digby's embarrassment when he met Madonna was *manifest:* his ears turned bright pink, he kept scuffing one shoe in the dirt, and he couldn't look her in the eye.

marked ADJ. noticeable; targeted for vengeance. He walked with a *marked* limp, a souvenir of an old I.R.A. attack. As British ambassador, he knew he was a *marked* man.

marshal V. put in order. At a debate tournament, extemporaneous speakers have only a minute or two to *marshal* their thoughts before they address their audience.

martinet N. strict disciplinarian. Captain Bligh was a *martinet* who observed each regulation to the letter.

massive ADJ. solid or heavy; large in scope; severe. The bust of Beethoven emphasizes his high forehead and *massive* brow. The composer suffered a *massive* hearing loss that left him unable to hear the music the orchestra played.

materialism N. preoccupation with physical comforts and things. By its nature, *materialism* is opposed to idealism, for where the *materialist* emphasizes the needs of the body, the idealist emphasizes the needs of the soul. materialistic, ADJ.

maverick N. rebel; nonconformist. To the masculine literary establishment, George Sand, with her insistence on wearing trousers and smoking cigars, was clearly a *maverick* who fought her proper womanly role.

mawkish ADJ. mushy and gushy; sentimental; maudlin. Whenever Gigi and her boyfriend would sigh and get all lovey-dovey, her little brother would shout, "Yuck!," protesting their *mawkish* behavior.

maxim N. proverb; a truth pithily stated. Aesop's fables illustrate moral *maxims.*

meager ADJ. scanty; inadequate. Still hungry after his *meager* serving of porridge, Oliver Twist asked for a second helping.

mealymouthed ADJ. indirect in speech; hypocritical; evasive. Rather than tell Jill directly what he disliked, Jack made a few *mealymouthed* comments and tried to change the subject.

meander V. wind or turn in its course. Needing to stay close to a source of water, he followed every twist and turn of the stream as it *meandered* through the countryside.

mediate V. settle a dispute through the services of an outsider. King Solomon was asked to *mediate* a dispute between two women, each of whom claimed to be the mother of the same child.

mediocre ADJ. ordinary; commonplace. We were disappointed because he gave a rather *mediocre* performance in this role.

meditation N. reflection; thought. She reached her decision only after much *meditation.*

• **meek** ADJ. quiet and obedient; spiritless. Can Lois Lane see through Superman's disguise and spot the superhero masquerading as the *meek,* timorous Clark Kent?

melancholy ADJ. gloomy; morose; blue. To Eugene, stuck in his small town, a train whistle was a *melancholy* sound, for it made him think of all the places he would never get to see.

mellifluous ADJ. sweetly or smoothly flowing; melodious. What a *mellifluous* language Italian is! Even the street vendors' cries sound like little songs.

mentor N. counselor; teacher. During this very trying period, she could not have had a better *mentor,* for her adviser was sympathetic and understanding.

mercantile ADJ. concerning trade. Selling candy bars to his classmates whose parents had packed their lunch boxes with apples and carrot sticks, George clearly was destined to be a *mercantile* success.

mercenary ADJ. interested in money or gain. Andy's every act was prompted by *mercenary* motives: his first question was always, "What's in it for me?"

mercurial ADJ. capricious; changing; fickle. Quick as quicksilver to change, he was *mercurial* in nature and therefore unreliable.

mesmerize V. hypnotize; fascinate. On a long stretch of road between Fresno and Los Angeles, the open highway began to *mesmerize* Richard; he pulled over to the side of the road and rested to free himself from highway hypnosis.

• **meticulous** ADJ. excessively careful; painstaking; scrupulous. Martha Stewart, a *meticulous* housekeeper, fusses about each and every detail that goes into making up her perfect home.

migratory ADJ. wandering. The return of the *migratory* birds to the northern sections of this country is a harbinger of spring.

ministration N. act of giving care; attending to someone's needs. Red Cross founder Florence Nightingale was honored for her *ministrations* to wounded soldiers during the Crimean War.

minute ADJ. extremely small. The twins resembled one another closely; only *minute* differences set them apart.

misanthrope N. one who hates mankind. In *Gulliver's Travels,* Swift portrays human beings as vile, degraded beasts; for this reason, some critics consider him a *misanthrope.*

• **misconception** N. misunderstanding; misinterpretation. I'm afraid you are suffering from a *misconception,* Mr. Collins: I do not want to marry you at all.

misconstrue V. interpret incorrectly; misjudge. She took the passage seriously rather than humorously because she *misconstrued* the author's ironic tone.

miserly ADJ. stingy; mean. The *miserly* old man greedily counted the gold coins he had hoarded over the years.

misnomer N. wrong name; incorrect designation. His tyrannical conduct proved to us all that his nickname, King Eric the Just, was a *misnomer.*

• **misrepresent** V. give a false or incorrect impression, usually intentionally. The ad "Lovely Florida building site with water view" *misrepresented* the property, which was actually ten acres of bottomless swamp.

mitigate V. appease; moderate. Nothing Jason did could *mitigate* Medea's anger; she refused to forgive him for betraying her.

mobile ADJ. movable; not fixed. The *mobile* blood bank operated by the Red Cross visited our neighborhood today. mobility, N.

• **mock** V. ridicule; imitate, often in derision. It is unkind to *mock* anyone; it is stupid to *mock* anyone significantly bigger than you. mockery, N.

mode N. prevailing style; manner; way of doing something. The rock star had to have her hair done in the latest *mode:* frizzed, with occasional moussed spikes for variety. Henry plans to adopt a simpler *mode* of life: he is going to become a mushroom hunter and live off the land.

mollify V. soothe. The airline customer service representative tried to *mollify* the angry passenger by offering her a seat in first class.

momentous ADJ. very important. When Marie and Pierre Curie discovered radium, they had no idea of the *momentous* impact their discovery would have upon society.

• **monarchy** N. government under a single ruler. Though England today is a *monarchy,* there is some question whether it will be one in 20 years,

given the present discontent at the prospect of Prince Charles as king.

monochromatic ADJ. having only one color. Most people who are color blind actually can distinguish several colors; some, however, have a truly *monochromatic* view of a world all in shades of gray.

• **monotony** N. sameness leading to boredom. What could be more deadly dull than the *monotony* of punching numbers into a computer hour after hour?

monumental ADJ. massive; immense. Writing a dictionary is a *monumental* task; so is reading one.

moratorium N. suspension of activity; authorized period of delay (of a payment, etc.). If we declare a *moratorium* and delay collecting all debts for six months, I am sure the farmers will be able to meet their bills.

morose ADJ. ill-humored; sullen; melancholy. Forced to take early retirement, Bill acted *morose* for months; then, all of a sudden, he shook off his sullen mood and was his usual cheerful self.

morsel N. small bit of food. "No, thank you, Aunt Polly," he said. "I'm so stuffed I can't eat another *morsel.*"

mortify V. humiliate; punish the flesh. She was so *mortified* by her blunder that she ran to her room in tears.

muddle V. confuse; mix up. His thoughts were *muddled* and chaotic. also N.

mural N. wall painting. The walls of the Chicano Community Center are covered with *murals* painted in the style of Diego Rivera, the great Mexican artist.

murky ADJ. dark and gloomy; thick with fog; vague. The *murky* depths of the swamp were so dark that you couldn't tell the vines and branches from the snakes.

muse V. ponder. For a moment he *mused* about the beauty of the scene, but his thoughts soon changed as he recalled his own personal problems. also N.

• **mutability** N. ability to change in form; fickleness. Going from rags to riches and then back to rags again, the bankrupt financier was a victim of the *mutability* of fortune.

muted ADJ. silent; muffled; toned down. Thanks to the thick, sound-absorbing walls of the cathedral, only *muted* traffic noise reached the worshippers within.

mutinous ADJ. unruly; rebellious. The captain had to use force to quiet his *mutinous* crew.

myriad N. very large number. *Myriads* of mosquitoes from the swamps invaded our village every evening at twilight. also ADJ.

nadir N. lowest point. Although few people realized it, the Dow-Jones averages had reached their *nadir* and would soon begin an upward surge.

• **naïveté** N. quality of being unsophisticated; simplicity; artlessness; gullibility. Touched by the *naïveté* of sweet, convent-trained Cosette, Marius pledges himself to protect her innocence. naive, ADJ.

narrative ADJ. related to telling a story. A born teller of tales, Olsen used her impressive *narrative* skills to advantage in her story, "I Stand Here Ironing."

navigable ADJ. wide and deep enough to allow ships to pass through; able to be steered. So much sand had built up at the bottom of the canal that the waterway was barely *navigable*.

nebulous ADJ. vague; hazy; cloudy. After 20 years, she had only a *nebulous* memory of her grandmother's face.

negligence N. neglect; failure to take reasonable care. Tommy failed to put back the cover on the well after he fetched his pail of water; because of his *negligence*, Kitty fell in.

negligible ADJ. so small, trifling, or unimportant that it may be easily disregarded. Because the damage to his car had been *negligible*, Michael decided he wouldn't bother to report the matter to his insurance company.

neologism N. new or newly coined word or phrase. As we invent new devices and professions, we must also invent *neologisms* such as "microcomputer" and "astronaut" to describe them.

neophyte N. recent convert; beginner. This mountain slope contains slides that will challenge experts as well as *neophytes*.

• **nocturnal** ADJ. relating to, occurring, or active in the night. Mr. Jones obtained a watchdog to prevent the *nocturnal* raids on his chicken coops.

• **nonchalance** N. indifference; lack of concern; composure. Cool, calm, and collected under fire, James Bond shows remarkable *nonchalance* in the face of danger.

nondescript ADJ. undistinctive; ordinary. The private detective was a *nondescript* fellow with no outstanding features, the sort of person one would never notice in a crowd.

nonentity N. person or thing of no importance; nonexistence. Don't dismiss John as a *nonentity*; in his quiet way, he's very important to the firm.

• **nostalgia** N. homesickness; longing for the past. My grandfather seldom spoke of life in the old country; he had little patience with *nostalgia*. nostalgic, ADJ.

notable ADJ. conspicuous; important; distinguished. Normally *notable* for his calm in the kitchen, today the head cook was shaking, for the *notable* chef Julia Child was coming to dinner.

• **notorious** ADJ. disreputable; widely known; scandalous. To the starlet, any publicity was good publicity: if she couldn't have a good reputation, she'd settle for being *notorious*. notoriety, N.

novelty N. something new; newness. The computer is no longer a *novelty* around the office; every office has one. novel, ADJ.

novice N. beginner. Even a *novice* at working with computers can install *Barron's Computer Study Program for the SAT* by following the easy steps outlined in the user's manual.

nozzle N. projecting spout; tapering tube. Did you leave the garden hose on? I see a trail of water leaking from its *nozzle*.

nucleus N. central point or core; component of protoplasm; central part of atom. Kathryn, Lexy, and Steven formed the *nucleus* of the debate team, which eventually grew to include most of the senior class.

nullify V. to make invalid; make null or void. Once the contract was *nullified*, it no longer had any legal force.

• **nurture** V. nourish; educate; foster. The Head Start program attempts to *nurture* pre-kindergarten children so that they will do well when they enter public school. also N.

nutrient N. nourishing substance. As a budding nutritionist, Kim has learned to design diets that contain foods rich in important basic *nutrients*.

obdurate ADJ. stubborn. The manager was *obdurate* in refusing to discuss the workers' grievances.

obfuscate V. confuse; muddle; make unclear. Occasionally in talking with patients, doctors seem to use medical terms to *obfuscate* rather than to inform them about the state of their health.

objective ADJ. not influenced by emotions; fair. Even though he was her son, she tried to be *objective* about his behavior.

objective N. goal; aim. A degree in medicine was her ultimate *objective*.

obligatory ADJ. required; legally or morally binding. It is *obligatory* that books borrowed from the library be returned within two weeks.

oblique ADJ. indirect; slanting (deviating from the perpendicular or from a straight line). Casting a quick, *oblique* glance at the reviewing stand, the sergeant ordered the company to march "*Oblique* Right.*"

obliterate V. destroy completely. In the film *Independence Day* the explosion *obliterated* the White House, vaporizing it completely.

oblivion N. obscurity; forgetfulness. After a brief period of popularity, Hurston's works fell into *oblivion*; no one bothered to reprint them or even to read them any more.

oblivious ADJ. inattentive or unmindful; wholly absorbed. Deep in her book, Nancy was *oblivious* of the noisy squabbles of her brother and his friends.

• **obnoxious** ADJ. offensive; objectionable. A sneak and a tattletale, Sid was an *obnoxious* little brat.

- **obscure** ADJ. dark; vague; unclear. Even after I read the poem a fourth time, its meaning was still *obscure*. obscurity, N.

- **obscure** V. darken; make unclear. At times he seemed purposely to *obscure* his meaning, preferring mystery to clarity.

obsequious ADJ. slavishly attentive; servile; fawning; sycophantic. Why are some waiters in fancy restaurants so *obsequious*? What makes them think diners want to have people fawning all over them?

obsessive ADJ. related to thinking about something constantly; preoccupying. Ballet, which had been a hobby, began to dominate her life; her love of dancing became *obsessive*.

obsolescent ADJ. going out of use. Given how quickly computer technology changes, I've had to reconcile myself to the fact that, no matter how up-to-date a system I buy, it's practically *obsolescent* as soon as I've gotten it out of its box.

obsolete ADJ. outmoded. "Hip" is an *obsolete* expression; it went out with love beads and tie-dye shirts.

obtrude V. push (oneself or one's ideas) forward or intrude; butt in; stick out or extrude. Because Fanny was reluctant to *obtrude* her opinions about child raising upon her daughter-in-law, she kept a close watch on her tongue. obtrusive, ADJ.

offensive ADJ. attacking; insulting; distasteful. Getting into street brawls is no minor matter for professional boxers, who are required by law to restrict their *offensive* impulses to the ring.

officious ADJ. meddlesome; excessively pushing in offering one's services. After her long flight, Jill just wanted to nap, but the *officious* bellboy was intent on showing her all the special features of the deluxe suite.

olfactory ADJ. concerning the sense of smell. A wine taster must have a discriminating palate and a keen *olfactory* sense, for a good wine appeals both to the taste buds and to the nose.

ominous ADJ. threatening. Those clouds are *ominous*; they suggest a severe storm is on the way.

omnivorous ADJ. eating both plant and animal food; devouring everything. Some animals, including man, are *omnivorous* and eat both meat and vegetables; others are either carnivorous or herbivorous.

- **opaque** ADJ. not transparent; impenetrable to light. The *opaque* window shade kept the sunlight out of the room. opacity, N.

opportunist N. individual who sacrifices principles for expediency by taking advantage of circumstances. Forget ethics! He's such an *opportunist* that he'll vote in favor of any deal that will give him a break.

opprobrium N. public disgrace or reproach; vilification. How did the Republicans manage to turn the once-honored name of "liberal" into a term of *opprobrium?*

opt V. decide in favor of; choose. Given the choice between the movie and the folk dance, Sharon *opted* to go to the dance.

- **optimist** N. person who looks on the good side. The pessimist says the glass is half empty; the *optimist* says it is half full.

opulence N. extreme wealth; luxuriousness; abundance. The glitter and *opulence* of the ballroom took Cinderella's breath away. opulent, ADJ.

- **orator** N. public speaker. The abolitionist Frederick Douglass was a brilliant *orator* whose speeches brought home to his audience the evils of slavery.

ordeal N. severe trial or affliction. June was so painfully shy that it was an *ordeal* for her to speak up when the teacher called on her in class.

ornate ADJ. excessively or elaborately decorated. The furnishings of homes shown on *Lifestyles of the Rich and Famous* tend to be highly *ornate*.

- **ostentatious** ADJ. showy; pretentious; trying to attract attention. Trump's latest casino in Atlantic City is the most *ostentatious* gambling palace in the East: it easily outglitters its competitors. ostentation, N.

outlandish ADJ. bizarre; peculiar; unconventional. The eccentric professor who engages in markedly *outlandish* behavior is a stock figure in novels with an academic setting.

- **outmoded** ADJ. no longer stylish; old-fashioned. Unconcerned about keeping in style, Lenore was perfectly happy to wear *outmoded* clothes as long as they were clean and unfrayed.

outwit V. outsmart; trick. By disguising himself as an old woman, Holmes was able to *outwit* his pursuers and escape capture.

overbearing ADJ. bossy; arrogant; decisively important. Certain of her own importance and of the unimportance of everyone else, Lady Bracknell was intolerably *overbearing* in her manner. "In choosing a husband," she said, "good birth is of *overbearing* importance; compared to that, neither wealth nor talent signifies."

overt ADJ. open to view. According to the United States Constitution, a person must commit an *overt* act before he or she may be tried for treason.

- **pacifist** N. one opposed to force; antimilitarist. Shooting his way through the jungle, Rambo was clearly not a *pacifist*.

- **pacify** V. soothe; make calm or quiet; subdue. Dentists criticize the practice of giving fussy children sweets to *pacify* them.

painstaking ADJ. expending or showing diligent care and great effort. The new high-frequency word list is the result of *painstaking* efforts on the part of our research staff.

palatable ADJ. agreeable; pleasing to the taste. Neither Jack's underbaked opinions nor his overcooked casseroles were *palatable* to me.

pallid ADJ. pale; wan. Because his occupation required that he work at night and sleep during the day, he had an exceptionally *pallid* complexion.

panacea N. cure-all; remedy for all diseases. Some people claim that vitamin C is a *panacea* that can cure everything from cancer to the common cold.

pandemonium N. wild tumult. When the ships collided in the harbor, *pandemonium* broke out among the passengers.

parable N. short tale illustrating a moral principle. In the *parable* of the good shepherd, Jesus encourages his followers to seek those who have strayed from the flock.

• **paradox** N. something apparently contradictory in nature; statement that looks false but is actually correct. Richard presents a bit of a *paradox,* for he is a card-carrying member of both the National Rifle Association and the relatively pacifist American Civil Liberties Union.

paragon N. model of perfection. The class disliked him because the teacher was always pointing him out as a *paragon* of virtue.

paramount ADJ. foremost in importance; supreme. Proper nutrition and hygiene are of *paramount* importance in adolescent development and growth.

parched ADJ. extremely dry; very thirsty. The *parched* desert landscape seemed hostile to life.

parody N. humorous imitation; spoof; takeoff; travesty. The show *Forbidden Broadway* presents *parodies* spoofing the year's new productions playing on Broadway.

partial ADJ. incomplete; having a liking for something. In this issue we have published only a *partial* list of contributors because we lack space to acknowledge everyone. I am extremely *partial* to chocolate eclairs.

partisan ADJ. one-sided; prejudiced; committed to a party. On certain issues of principle, she refused to take a *partisan* stand but let her conscience be her guide. also N.

partition V. divide into parts. Before their second daughter was born, Jason and Lizzie decided each child needed a room of her own, and so they *partitioned* a large bedroom into two small but separate rooms. also N.

passive ADJ. not active; acted upon. Mahatma Gandhi urged his followers to pursue a program of *passive* resistance rather than resort to violence and acts of terrorism.

passport N. legal document identifying the bearer as a citizen of a country and allowing him or her to travel abroad. In arranging your first trip abroad, be sure to allow yourself enough time to apply for and receive your *passport*: you won't be allowed to travel without one.

pastoral ADJ. rural; simple and peaceful; idyllic; relating to shepherds. Tired of city living, David dreamed of moving to the country and enjoying the tranquillity of *pastoral* life.

• **patronize** V. support; act superior toward; be a customer of. Penniless artists hope to find some wealthy art lover who will *patronize* them. If a wine steward *patronized* me because he saw I knew nothing about fine wine, I'd refuse to *patronize* his restaurant.

paucity N. scarcity; lack. They closed the restaurant because the *paucity* of customers made it a losing proposition to operate.

• **pedantic** ADJ. showing off learning; bookish. Leavening his decisions with humorous, down-to-earth anecdotes, Judge Walker was not at all the *pedantic* legal scholar. pedant, N.

pedestrian ADJ. ordinary; unimaginative. Unintentionally boring, he wrote page after page of *pedestrian* prose. (secondary meaning)

peerless ADJ. having to equal; incomparable. To his admirers, the reigning operatic tenor of his generation, Luciano Pavarotti, was *peerless*; no one could compare with him.

pendulum N. suspended body that swings freely. Watching the swinging *pendulum* of the grandfather clock, Johnny swayed from side to side, echoing its movement.

penitent ADJ. feeling regret or sorrow for one's offenses; repentant. When he realized the enormity of his crime, he became remorseful and *penitent*. also N.

perceptive ADJ. insightful; aware; wise. Although Maud was a generally *perceptive* critic, she had her blind spots: she could never see flaws in the work of her friends.

perdition N. damnation; complete ruin. Praying for salvation, young Steven feared he was damned to eternal *perdition*.

peremptory ADJ. demanding and leaving no choice. From Jack's *peremptory* knock on the door, Jill could tell he would not give up until she let him in.

perfidious ADJ. treacherous; disloyal. When Caesar realized that Brutus had betrayed him, he reproached his *perfidious* friend. perfidy, N.

perfunctory ADJ. superficial; not thorough; lacking interest, care, or enthusiasm. Giving the tabletop only a *perfunctory* swipe with her dust cloth, Betty promised herself she'd clean it more thoroughly tomorrow.

• **perjury** N. false testimony while under oath. Rather than lie under oath and perhaps be indicted for *perjury*, the witness chose to take the Fifth

Amendment, refusing to answer any questions on the grounds that he might incriminate himself.

permutation N. transformation; rearrangement of elements. I'm pretty sure Ted's phone number ends in 5236 or some *permutation* of those digits.

pernicious ADJ. very destructive. Crack cocaine has had a *pernicious* effect on urban society: it has destroyed families, turned children into drug dealers, and increased the spread of violent crimes.

perpetrate V. commit an offense. Only an insane person could *perpetrate* such a horrible crime.

• **perpetual** ADJ. everlasting. Ponce de León hoped to find the legendary fountain of *perpetual* youth. perpetuity, N.

perpetuate V. make something last; preserve from extinction. Some critics attack *The Adventures of Huckleberry Finn* because they believe Twain's book *perpetuates* a false image of blacks in this country.

peruse V. read with care. After the conflagration that burned down her house, Joan closely *perused* her home insurance policy to discover exactly what benefits her coverage provided her. perusal, N.

• **pervasive** ADJ. pervading; spread throughout every part. Despite airing them for several hours, she could not rid her clothes of the *pervasive* odor of mothballs that clung to them. pervade, V.

perverse ADJ. stubbornly wrongheaded; wicked and perverted. When Jack was in a *perverse* mood, he would do the opposite of whatever Jill asked him. When Hannibal Lecter was in a *perverse* mood, he ate the flesh of his victims.

• **pessimism** N. belief that life is basically bad or evil; gloominess. Considering how well you have done in the course so far, you have no real reason for such *pessimism* about your final grade.

• **petulant** ADJ. touchy; peevish. If you'd had hardly any sleep for three nights and people kept on phoning and waking you up, you'd sound pretty *petulant*, too.

• **phenomena** N. Pl. observable facts or events. We kept careful records of the *phenomena* we noted in the course of these experiments.

• **philanthropist** N. lover of mankind; doer of good. In his role as *philanthropist* and public benefactor, John D. Rockefeller Sr., donated millions to charity; as an individual, however, he was a tight-fisted old man.

phlegmatic ADJ. not easily excited to action or emotional displays; calm; sluggish. The nurse was a cheerful but *phlegmatic* person, untroubled by sudden emergencies.

pious ADJ. devout; religious. The challenge for church members today is how to be *pious* in the best sense, that is, to be devout without becoming hypocritical or sanctimonious. piety, N.

pique V. provoke or arouse; annoy. "I know something *you* don't know," said Lucy, trying to *pique* Ethel's interest.

pique N. irritation; resentment. She showed her *pique* at her loss by refusing to appear with the other contestants at the end of the competition.

pivotal ADJ. crucial; key; vital. The new "smart weapons" technology played a *pivotal* role in the quick resolution of the war with Iraq.

placate V. pacify; conciliate. The store manager, trying to *placate* the angry customer, offered to replace the damaged merchandise or to give back her money right away.

placid ADJ. calm; peaceful. Looking at the storm-tossed waters of the lake, Bob wondered why they ever called it Lake *Placid*.

• **plagiarize** V. steal another's ideas and pass them off as one's own. The teacher could tell that the student had *plagiarized* parts of his essay; she could recognize whole paragraphs straight from *Barron's Book Notes*.

platitude N. trite remark; commonplace statement. In giving advice to his son, old Polonius expressed himself only in *platitudes;* every word out of his mouth was commonplace.

plausible ADJ. having a show of truth but open to doubt; specious. Your mother made you stay home from school because she needed you to program the VCR? I'm sorry, you'll have to come up with a more *plausible* excuse than that.

plethora N. excess; overabundance. She offered a *plethora* of excuses for her shortcomings.

pliable ADJ. flexible; yielding; adaptable. In remodeling the bathroom, we have replaced all the old, rigid lead pipes with new, *pliable* copper tubing.

plight N. condition, state (especially a bad state or condition); predicament. Loggers, unmoved by the *plight* of the spotted owl, plan to keep on logging whether or not they ruin the owl's habitat.

pluck N. courage. Even the enemies of young Indiana Jones were impressed by the boy's *pluck* in trying to rescue the archaeological treasure they had stolen. plucky, ADJ.

plunder N. loot; takings from a raid. Rubbing his hands with glee, the robber gloated over his ill-gotten *plunder*. also V.

podium N. pedestal; raised platform. The audience applauded as the conductor made his way to the *podium*.

polemical ADJ. aggressive in verbal attack; disputatious. Lexy was a master of *polemical* rhetoric; she should have worn a T-shirt with the slogan "Born to Debate."

ponderous ADJ. weighty; unwieldy. His humor lacked the light touch; his jokes were always *ponderous*.

pore V. study deeply; stare. In doing research on the SAT, we *pored* over back issues of *Scientific American* to locate articles from which reading passages had been excerpted.

porous ADJ. full of pores; like a sieve. Dancers like to wear *porous* clothing because it allows the ready passage of air.

portend V. foretell; presage. The king did not know what these omens might *portend* and asked his soothsayers to interpret them.

portly ADJ. stout; corpulent. The salesclerk diplomatically referred to the overweight customer as not fat but *portly*.

posterity N. descendants; future generations. We hope to leave a better world to *posterity*.

• **potency** N. power; effectiveness; influence. Looking at the expiration date on the cough syrup bottle, we wondered whether the medication still retained its *potency*. potent, ADJ.

potentate N. monarch; sovereign. The *potentate* spent more time at Monte Carlo than he did at home on his throne.

practical ADJ. based on experience; useful. He was a *practical* man, opposed to theory.

• **pragmatic** ADJ. practical (as opposed to idealistic); concerned with the practical worth or impact of something. This coming trip to France should provide me with a *pragmatic* test of the value of my conversational French class.

prairie N. vast, level, or slightly rolling tract of grassland. The *prairie* is "big sky" country: your views are unobstructed by buildings or trees.

prate V. speak foolishly; boast idly. Let us not *prate* about our qualities; rather, let our virtues speak for themselves.

prattle V. babble. Baby John *prattled* on and on about the cats and his ball and the Cookie Monster.

preamble N. introductory statement. In the *preamble* to the Constitution, the purpose of the document is set forth.

precarious ADJ. uncertain; risky. Saying the stock would be a *precarious* investment, the broker advised her client against purchasing it.

• **precedent** N. something preceding in time that may be used as an authority or guide for future action. If I buy you a car for your sixteenth birthday, your brothers will want me to buy them cars when they turn sixteen, too; I can't afford to set such an expensive *precedent*.

precipitate ADJ. rash; premature; abrupt; hasty; sudden. Though I was angry enough to resign on the spot, I had enough sense to keep myself from quitting a job in such a *precipitate* fashion.

precipitous ADJ. steep; overhasty. This hill is difficult to climb because it is so *precipitous*; one slip, and our descent will be *precipitous* as well.

preclude V. make impossible; eliminate. Because the band was already booked to play in Hollywood on New Year's Eve, that booking *precluded* their accepting the New Year's Eve gig in London they were offered.

precursor N. forerunner. Though Gray and Burns share many traits with the Romantic poets who followed them, most critics consider them *precursors* of the Romantic movement, not true Romantics.

• **predator** N. creature that seizes and devours another animal; person who robs or exploits others. Not just cats, but a wide variety of *predators*—owls, hawks, weasels, foxes—catch mice for dinner. A carnivore is by definition *predatory*, for it *preys* on weaker creatures.

predetermine V. predestine; settle or decide beforehand; influence markedly. Romeo and Juliet believed that Fate had *predetermined* their meeting. Bea gathered estimates from caterers, florists, and stationers so that she could *predetermine* the costs of holding a catered buffet. Philip's love of athletics *predetermined* his choice of a career in sports marketing.

predilection N. partiality; preference. Although my mother wrote all sorts of poetry over the years, she had a definite *predilection* for occasional verse.

preeminent ADJ. outstanding; superior. The king traveled to Boston because he wanted the *preeminent* surgeon in the field to perform the operation.

preempt V. head off; forestall by acting first; appropriate for oneself; supplant. Hoping to *preempt* any attempts by the opposition to make educational reform a hot political issue, the candidate set out her own plan to revitalize the public schools. preemptive, ADJ.

prelate N. church dignitary. The archbishop of Moscow and other high-ranking *prelates* visited the Russian Orthodox seminary.

• **premise** N. assumption; postulate. Acting on the *premise* that there's no fool like an old fool, P. T. Barnum hired a 90-year-old clown for his circus.

• **premonition** N. forewarning. We ignored these *premonitions* of disaster because they appeared to be based on childish fears.

preposterous ADJ. absurd; ridiculous. When he tried to downplay his youthful experiments with marijuana by saying he hadn't inhaled, we all thought, "What a *preposterous* excuse!"

prescience N. ability to foretell the future. Given the current wave of Japan bashing, it does not take *prescience* for me to foresee problems in our future trade relations with Japan.

preside V. act as president or chairman; exercise control. When the club president cannot attend a meeting, the vice president will *preside* over that session.

prestige N. impression produced by achievements or reputation. Many students want to go to Harvard College not for the education offered but for the *prestige* of Harvard's name.

• **presumptuous** ADJ. taking liberties; overstepping bounds; nervy. I thought it was *presumptuous* of Mort to butt into Bishop Tutu's talk with Mrs. Clinton and ask them for their autographs; I wouldn't have had the nerve.

pretentious ADJ. ostentatious; pompous; making unjustified claims; overly ambitious. None of the other prizewinners are wearing their medals; isn't it a bit *pretentious* of you to wear yours?

• **prevail** V. triumph; predominate; prove superior in strength, power, or influence; be current. A radical committed to social change, Reed had no patience with the conservative views that *prevailed* in the America of his day. prevalent, ADJ.; prevailing, ADJ.

prevaricate V. lie. Some people believe that to *prevaricate* in a good cause is justifiable and regard their false statement as a "white lie."

• **prey** N. target of a hunt; victim. In *Stalking the Wild Asparagus*, Euell Gibbons has as his *prey* not wild beasts but wild plants. also V.

privation N. hardship; want. In his youth, he knew hunger and *privation*.

procrastinate V. postpone; delay or put off. Looking at four years of receipts and checks he still had to sort through, Bob was truly sorry he had *procrastinated* for so long and not finished filing his taxes long ago.

prodigal ADJ. wasteful; reckless with money. Don't be so *prodigal* spending my money; when you've earned some money, you can waste it as much as you want! also N.

prodigious ADJ. marvelous; enormous. Watching the champion weight lifter heave the weighty barbell to shoulder height and then boost it overhead, we marveled at his *prodigious* strength.

prodigy N. highly gifted child; extraordinary accomplishment or event. Menuhin was a *prodigy*, performing wonders on his violin when he was barely eight years old.

profane V. violate; desecrate; treat unworthily. The members of the mysterious Far Eastern cult sought to kill the British explorer because he had *profaned* the sanctity of their holy goblet by using it as an ashtray. also ADJ.

profligate N. dissipated; wasteful; wildly immoral. Although surrounded by wild and *profligate* companions, she nevertheless managed to retain some sense of decency.

• **profound** ADJ. deep; not superficial; complete. Freud's remarkable insights into human behavior caused his fellow scientists to honor him as a *profound* thinker. profundity, N.

profusion N. overabundance; lavish expenditure; excess. Freddy was so overwhelmed by the *profusion* of choices on the menu that he knocked over his wine glass and soaked his host. He made *profuse* apologies to his host, the waiter, the busboy, the people at the next table, and the man in the men's room giving out paper towels.

progenitor N. ancestor. The Roth family, whose *progenitors* emigrated from Germany early in the nineteenth century, settled in Peru, Illinois.

• **proliferation** N. rapid growth; spread; multiplication. Times of economic hardship inevitably encourage the *proliferation* of countless get-rich-quick schemes. proliferate, V.

• **prolific** ADJ. abundantly fruitful. My editors must assume I'm a *prolific* writer: they expect me to revise six books this year!

• **prologue** N. introduction (to a poem or play). In the *prologue* to *Romeo and Juliet*, Shakespeare introduces the audience to the feud between the Montagues and the Capulets.

prolong V. make longer; draw out; lengthen. In their determination to discover ways to *prolong* human life, doctors fail to take into account that longer lives are not always happier ones.

• **prominent** ADJ. conspicuous; notable; sticking out. Have you ever noticed that Prince Charles's *prominent* ears make him resemble the big-eared character in *Mad* comics?

promontory N. high point of land jutting out into a body of water; headland. They erected a lighthouse on the *promontory* to warn approaching ships of their nearness to the shore.

• **promote** V. help to flourish; advance in rank; publicize. Founder of the Children's Defense Fund, Marian Wright Edelman ceaselessly *promotes* the welfare of young people everywhere.

promulgate V. proclaim a doctrine or law; make known by official publication. When Moses came down from the mountaintop all set to *promulgate* God's commandments, he was shocked on discovering his followers worshipping a golden calf.

prone ADJ. inclined to; prostrate. She was *prone* to sudden fits of anger.

propagate V. multiply; spread. Since bacteria *propagate* more quickly in unsanitary environments, it is important to keep hospital rooms clean.

propensity N. natural inclination. Convinced of his own talent, Sol has an unfortunate *propensity* to belittle the talents of others.

property N. quality or aspect; belongings; land. In science class we learned that each element has certain physical and chemical *properties*.

• **prophetic** ADJ. foretelling the future. I have no magical *prophetic* powers; when I predict what will happen, I base my predictions on common sense. prophesy, V.

proponent N. supporter; backer. In the Senate, *proponents* of the universal health care measure lobbied to gain additional support for the controversial legislation.

propriety N. fitness; correct conduct. Miss Manners counsels her readers so that they may behave with due *propriety* in any social situation and not embarrass themselves.

prosaic ADJ. dull and unimaginative; matter-of-fact; factual. Though the ad writers had come up with a wildly imaginative campaign to publicize the company's newest product, the head office rejected it for a more *prosaic,* down-to-earth approach.

• **prosperity** N. good fortune; financial success; physical well-being. Promising to stay together "for richer, for poorer," the newlyweds vowed to be true to one another in *prosperity* and hardship alike.

protagonist N. principal character; leading actor. Emma, the *protagonist* of Jane Austen's novel, is an overindulged young woman convinced of her ability as a matchmaker.

prototype N. original work used as a model by others. The National Air and Space Museum displays the Wright brothers' first plane, the *prototype* of all the American aircraft that came after.

protract V. prolong. Seeking to delay the union members' vote, the management team tried to *protract* the negotiations endlessly, but the union representatives saw through their strategy.

protrude V. stick out. His fingers *protruded* from the holes in his gloves. protrusion, N.

protuberance N. protrusion; bulge. A ganglionic cyst is a fluid-filled tumor that develops near a joint membrane or tendon sheath and that bulges beneath the skin, forming a *protuberance*.

provident ADJ. displaying foresight; thrifty; preparing for emergencies. In his usual *provident* manner, he had insured himself against this type of loss.

provincial ADJ. pertaining to a province; limited in outlook; unsophisticated. As *provincial* governor, Sir Henry administered the queen's law in his remote corner of Canada. Caught up in local problems, out of touch with London news, he became sadly *provincial.*

provisional ADJ. tentative. Kim's acceptance as an American Express cardholder was *provisional:* before issuing her a card, American Express wanted to check her employment record and credit history.

• **provocative** ADJ. arousing anger or interest; annoying. In a typically *provocative* act, the bully kicked sand into the weaker man's face.

proximity N. nearness. Blind people sometimes develop a compensatory ability to sense the *proximity* of objects around them.

• **prudent** ADJ. cautious; careful. A miser hoards money not because he is *prudent* but because he is greedy. prudence, N.

prune V. cut away; trim. With the help of her editor, she was able to *prune* her manuscript into publishable form.

pseudonym N. pen name. Samuel Clemens's *pseudonym* was Mark Twain.

puerile ADJ. childish; immature. Throwing tantrums? You should have outgrown such *puerile* behavior years ago.

pugnacious ADJ. combative; disposed to fight. "Put up your dukes!" he cried, making a fist to show how *pugnacious* he was.

pulverize V. crush or grind into dust. Before sprinkling the dried herbs into the stew, Michael first *pulverized* them into a fine powder.

pummel V. beat or pound with fists. Swinging wildly, Pammy *pummeled* her brother around the head and shoulders.

punctilious ADJ. laying stress on niceties of conduct or form; minutely attentive to fine points (perhaps too much so). Percy is *punctilious* about observing the rules of etiquette whenever Miss Manners invites him to stay. punctiliousness, N.

pungent ADJ. stinging; sharp in taste or smell; caustic. The *pungent* odor of ripe Limburger cheese appealed to Simone but made Stanley gag.

puny ADJ. insignificant; tiny; weak. Our *puny* efforts to stop the flood were futile.

purge V. remove or get rid of something unwanted; free from blame or guilt; cleanse or purify. The Communist government *purged* the party to get rid of members suspected of capitalist sympathies. also N.

purveyor N. furnisher of foodstuffs; caterer. As *purveyor* of rare wines and viands, he traveled through France and Italy every year in search of new products to sell.

quack N. charlatan; impostor. Do not be misled by the exorbitant claims of this *quack;* he cannot cure you. quackery, N.

quagmire N. soft wet boggy land; complex or dangerous situation from which it is difficult to free oneself. Up to her knees in mud, Myra wondered how on earth she was going to extricate herself from this *quagmire.*

qualified ADJ. limited; restricted. Unable to give the candidate full support, the mayor gave him only a *qualified* endorsement. (secondary meaning)

quandary N. dilemma. When both Harvard and Stanford accepted Lori, she was in a *quandary* as to which school she should attend.

quarry N. victim; object of a hunt. The police closed in on their *quarry*.

quarry V. dig into. They *quarried* blocks of marble out of the hillside. also N.

quell V. extinguish; put down; quiet. Miss Minchin's demeanor was so stern and forbidding that she could *quell* any unrest among her students with one intimidating glance.

quench V. douse or extinguish; assuage or satisfy. What's the favorite song of the fire department? "Baby, *Quench* My Fire!"

querulous ADJ. fretful; whining. Even the most agreeable toddlers can begin to act *querulous* if they miss their nap.

quibble N. minor objection or complaint. Aside from a few hundred teensy-weensy *quibbles* about the set, the script, the actors, the director, the costumes, the lighting, and the props, the hypercritical critic loved the play. also V.

quip N. taunt. You are unpopular because you are too free with your *quips* and sarcastic comments. also V.

quiver V. tremble; shake. The bird dog's nose twitched and his whiskers *quivered* as he strained eagerly against the leash. also N.

quiver N. case for arrows. Robin Hood reached back and plucked one last arrow from his *quiver*. (secondary meaning)

quixotic ADJ. idealistic but impractical. Simon's head is in the clouds; he constantly comes up with *quixotic*, unworkable schemes.

rabid ADJ. like a fanatic; furious. He was a *rabid* follower of the Dodgers and watched them play whenever he could go to the ball park.

raconteur N. storyteller. My father was a gifted *raconteur* with an unlimited supply of anecdotes.

rally V. call up or summon (forces, vital powers, etc.); revive or recuperate. Washington quickly *rallied* his troops to fight off the British attack. The patient had been sinking throughout the night, but at dawn she *rallied* and made a complete recovery.

• **ramble** V. wander aimlessly (physically or mentally). Listening to the teacher *ramble*, Shelby wondered whether he'd ever get to the point. also N.

rampant ADJ. growing in profusion; unrestrained. In the garden, the weeds were *rampant*: they killed all the flowers that had been planted in the spring. In the city, crime was *rampant*: the burglars and muggers were out of control.

ramshackle ADJ. rickety; falling apart. The boys propped up the *ramshackle* clubhouse with a couple of boards.

rancid ADJ. having the odor of stale fat. A *rancid* odor filled the ship's galley and nauseated the crew.

rancor N. bitterness; deep-seated hatred. Thirty years after the war, she could not let go of the past but still felt an implacable *rancor* against the foe.

• **random** ADJ. without definite purpose, plan, or aim; haphazard. Although the sponsor of the raffle claimed all winners were chosen at *random*, people had their suspicions when the grand prize went to the sponsor's brother-in-law.

rant V. rave; talk excitedly; scold; make a grandiloquent speech. When he heard that I'd totaled the family car, Dad began to *rant* at me like a complete madman.

rarefied ADJ. made less dense [of a gas]. The mountain climbers had difficulty breathing in the *rarefied* atmosphere. rarefy, V.

raucous ADJ. harsh and shrill; disorderly and boisterous. The *raucous* crowd of New Year's Eve revelers got progressively noisier as midnight drew near.

raze V. destroy completely. Spelling is important: to raise a building is to put it up; to *raze* a building is to tear it down.

reactionary ADJ. recoiling from progress; politically ultraconservative. Opposing the use of English in worship services, *reactionary* forces in the church fought to reinstate the mass in Latin.

rebuff V. snub; beat back. She *rebuffed* his invitation so smoothly that he did not realize he had been snubbed.

recalcitrant ADJ. obstinately stubborn. Donkeys are reputed to be the most *recalcitrant* of animals.

recant V. disclaim or disavow; retract a previous statement; openly confess error. Those who can, keep true to their faith; those who can't, *recant*.

recapitulate V. summarize. Let us *recapitulate* what has been said thus far before going ahead.

recession N. withdrawal; time of low economic activity. The slow *recession* of the floodwaters created problems for the crews working to restore power to the area.

reciprocate V. repay in kind. It was kind of Donna to have us over to dinner; I'd like us to *reciprocate* in some way, if we can.

• **recluse** N. hermit; loner. Disappointed in love, Miss Emily became a *recluse;* she shut herself away in her empty mansion and refused to see another living soul. reclusive, ADJ.

reconcile V. correct inconsistencies; become friendly after a quarrel. Every time we try to *reconcile* our checkbook with the bank statement, we quarrel.

However, despite these monthly lovers' quarrels, we always manage to *reconcile*.

recount V. narrate or tell; count over again. About to *recount* the latest adventure of Sherlock Holmes, Watson lost track of exactly how many cases Holmes had solved and refused to begin his tale until he'd *recounted* them one by one.

rectify V. set right; correct. You had better send a check to *rectify* your account before American Express cancels your credit card.

rectitude N. uprightness; moral virtue; correctness of judgment. The Eagle Scout was a model of *rectitude*.

recumbent ADJ. reclining; lying down completely or in part. The command "at ease" does not permit you to take a *recumbent* position.

recuperate V. recover. The doctors were worried because the patient did not *recuperate* as rapidly as they had expected.

recurrent ADJ. occurring again and again. These *recurrent* attacks disturbed us, and we consulted a physician.

redundant ADJ. superfluous; repetitious; excessively wordy. The bottle of wine I brought to Bob's was certainly *redundant:* how was I to know Bob owned a winery? In your essay, you repeat several points unnecessarily; try to be less *redundant* in the future. redundancy, N.

refine V. free from impurities; perfect. Just as you can *refine* sugar by removing bits of cane and other unwanted material, you can *refine* verse by removing awkward metaphors and polishing rough rhymes. refinement, N.

reflect V. consider or deliberate; show; mirror. Mr. Collins *reflected* on Elizabeth's rejection of his proposal. Did it *reflect* her true feelings, he wondered. Looking at his *reflection* in the mirror, he refused to believe that she could reject such a fine figure of a man.

refraction N. bending of a ray of light. Insert a stick in a glass of water and look at it carefully. It looks bent because of the *refraction* of the light by the water.

refrain V. abstain from; resist. Whenever he heard a song with a lively chorus, Sol could never *refrain* from joining in on the refrain.

refrain N. chorus. Whenever he heard a song with a lively chorus, Sol could never refrain from joining in on the *refrain*.

• **refute** V. disprove. The defense called several respectable witnesses who were able to *refute* the false testimony of the prosecution's only witness.

regress V. move backward to an earlier, generally more primitive state. Although Timmy outgrew his need for a pacifier well over a year ago, occasionally when he's tired or nervous, he *regresses* and starts sucking his thumb.

reiterate V. repeat. He *reiterated* the warning to make sure that everyone understood it.

rejoinder N. retort; comeback; reply. When someone has been rude to me, I find it particularly satisfying to come up with a quick *rejoinder*.

• **rejuvenate** V. make young again. The charlatan claimed that his elixir would *rejuvenate* the aged and weary.

relegate V. banish to an inferior position; delegate; assign. After Ralph dropped his second tray of drinks that week, the manager swiftly *relegated* him to a minor post cleaning up behind the bar.

relevant ADJ. pertinent; referring to the case in hand. How *relevant* Virginia Woolf's essays are to women writers today; it's as if Woolf in the 1930s foresaw our current literary struggles. relevancy, N.

relic N. surviving remnant; memento. Egypt's Department of Antiquities prohibits tourists from taking mummies and other ancient *relics* out of the country. Mike keeps his photos of his trip to Egypt in a box with other *relics* of his travels.

• **relinquish** V. give up something with reluctance; yield. Once you get used to fringe benefits like expense account meals and a company car, it's very hard to *relinquish* them.

relish V. savor; enjoy. Watching Peter enthusiastically chow down, I thought, "Now there's a man who *relishes* a good dinner!" also N.

reminiscence N. recollection. Her *reminiscences* of her experiences are so fascinating that she ought to write a book.

remiss ADJ. negligent. He was accused of being *remiss* in his duty when the prisoner escaped.

remnant N. remainder. I suggest that you wait until the store places the *remnants* of these goods on sale.

remonstrance N. protest; objection. The authorities were deaf to the pastor's *remonstrances* about the lack of police protection in the area. remonstrate, V.

remorse N. guilt; self-reproach. The murderer felt no *remorse* for his crime.

remunerative ADJ. compensating; rewarding. I find my new work so *remunerative* that I may not return to my previous employment. remuneration, N.

renegade N. deserter; traitor. Because he had abandoned his post and joined forces with the Indians, his fellow officers considered the hero of *Dances with Wolves* a *renegade*. also ADJ.

renounce V. abandon; disown; repudiate. Even though she knew she would be burned at the stake as a witch, Joan of Arc refused to *renounce* her belief that her voices came from God. renunciation, N.

renovate V. restore to good condition; renew. They claim that they can *renovate* worn shoes so that they look like new ones.

• **renown** N. fame. For many years an unheralded researcher, Barbara McClintock gained international *renown* when she won the Nobel Prize in physiology and medicine.

rent N. rip; split. Kit did an excellent job of mending the *rent* in the lining in her coat. rent, V.

repatriate V. return to one's own country. Although the Western powers hoped to *repatriate* the refugees swiftly, they were unable to do so because of the still dangerous conditions in the refugees' homeland.

repeal V. revoke; annul. What would the effect on our society be if we decriminalized drug use by *repealing* the laws against the possession and sale of narcotics?

repel V. drive away; disgust. At first, the Beast's ferocious appearance *repelled* Beauty, but she came to love the tender heart hidden behind that beastly exterior.

repertoire N. list of works of music, drama, etc., a performer is prepared to present. The opera company decided to include *Madame Butterfly* in its *repertoire* for the following season.

replenish V. fill up again. Before she could take another backpacking trip, Carla had to *replenish* her stock of freeze-dried foods.

• **reprehensible** ADJ. deserving blame. Shocked by the viciousness of the bombing, politicians of every party uniformly condemned the terrorists' *reprehensible* deed.

repress V. restrain; hold back; crush; suppress. Anne's parents tried to curb her impetuosity without *repressing* her boundless high spirits.

reprieve N. temporary stay. During the twenty-four-hour *reprieve*, the lawyers sought to make the stay of execution permanent. also V.

reprimand V. reprove severely; rebuke. Every time Ermengarde made a mistake in class, she was afraid that Miss Minchin would *reprimand* her and tell her father how badly she was doing in school. also N.

reproachful ADJ. expressing disapproval. He never could do anything wrong without imagining the *reproachful* look in his mother's eye.

reprove V. censure; rebuke. Though Aunt Bea at times would *reprove* Opie for inattention in church, she believed he was at heart a God-fearing lad.

• **repudiate** V. disown; disavow. On separating from Tony, Tina announced that she would *repudiate* all debts incurred by her soon-to-be ex-husband.

repulsion N. distaste; act of driving back. Hating bloodshed, she viewed war with *repulsion*. Even defensive battles distressed her, for the *repulsion* of enemy forces is never accomplished bloodlessly.

reputable ADJ. respectable. If you want to buy antiques, look for a *reputable* dealer; far too many dealers today pass off fakes as genuine antiques.

rescind V. cancel. Because of the public outcry against the new taxes, the senator proposed a bill to *rescind* the unpopular financial measure.

• **reserved** ADJ. self-controlled; careful in expressing oneself. They made an odd couple: she was outspoken and uninhibited; he was cautious and *reserved*. (secondary meaning)

• **resignation** N. patient submissiveness; statement that one is quitting a job. If Bob Cratchit had not accepted Scrooge's bullying with such *resignation*, he might have gotten up the nerve to hand in his *resignation*. resigned, ADJ.

resilient ADJ. elastic; having the power of springing back. Highly *resilient*, steel makes excellent bedsprings. resilience, N.

• **resolution** N. determination. Nothing could shake his *resolution* to succeed despite all difficulties. resolved, ADJ.

• **resolve** V. decide; settle; solve. "I have *resolved*, Watson, to travel to Bohemia to *resolve* the dispute between Irene Adler and the King. In my absence, do your best to *resolve* any mysteries that arise."

resonant ADJ. echoing; resounding; deep and full in sound. The deep, *resonant* voice of the actor James Earl Jones makes him particularly effective when he appears on stage.

respiration N. breathing. The doctor found that the patient's years of smoking had adversely affected both his lung capacity and his rate of *respiration*. respire, V.

restive ADJ. restlessly impatient; obstinately resisting control. Waiting impatiently in line to see Santa Claus, even the best-behaved children grow *restive* and start to fidget.

• **restraint** N. moderation or self-control; controlling force; restriction. Control yourself, young lady! Show some *restraint!*

resumption N. taking up again; recommencement. During summer break, Don had not realized how much he missed university life; at the *resumption* of classes, however, he felt marked excitement and pleasure. resume, V.

resurge V. rise again; flow to and fro. It was startling to see the spirit of nationalism *resurge* as the Soviet Union disintegrated into a loose federation of ethnic and national groups. resurgence, N.

• **retain** V. keep; employ. Fighting to *retain* his seat in Congress, Senator Foghorn *retained* a new manager to head his reelection campaign.

retaliation N. repayment in kind (usually for bad treatment). Because everyone knew the Princeton Band had stolen Brown's mascot, the whole Princeton student body expected some sort of *retaliation* from Brown. retaliate, V.

• **reticent** ADJ. reserved; uncommunicative; inclined to be silent. Fearing his competitors might get advance word about his plans from talkative staff members, Hughes preferred *reticent* employees to loquacious ones.

retract V. withdraw; take back. When I saw how Fred and his fraternity brothers had trashed the frat house, I decided to *retract* my offer to let them use our summer cottage for the weekend. retraction, N.

retrieve V. recover; find and bring in. The dog was intelligent and quickly learned to *retrieve* the game killed by the hunter.

retroactive ADJ. taking effect prior to its enactment (as a law) or imposition (as a tax). Because the new pension law was *retroactive* to the first of the year, even though Martha had retired in February, she was eligible for the pension.

revelry N. boisterous merrymaking. New Year's Eve is a night of *revelry*.

• **reverent** ADJ. respectful; worshipful. Though I bow my head in church and recite the prayers, sometimes I don't feel properly *reverent*. revere, V.

revoke V. cancel; retract. Repeat offenders who continue to drive under the influence of alcohol face having their driver's license permanently *revoked*.

revulsion N. sudden violent change of feeling; reaction. The feelings of many people in this country who admired dictatorships underwent *revulsion* when they realized what Hitler and Mussolini were trying to do.

rift N. opening made by splitting; open space; break in friendly relations. After the recent earthquake, geologists observed several fresh *rifts* in the Hayward hills. Through a *rift* in the dense clouds the pilot glimpsed a beacon light far below. Unsure how he had offended Jo, Laurie tried to think of some way to mend the *rift* in their friendship.

rigid ADJ. stiff and unyielding; strict; hard and unbending. By living with a man to whom she was not married, George Eliot broke Victorian society's most *rigid* rule of respectable behavior.

rigor N. severity. Many settlers could not stand the *rigors* of the New England winters.

rile V. vex; irritate. Red had a hair-trigger temper: he was an easy man to *rile*.

rivulet N. small stream. As the rains continued, the small trickle of water running down the hillside grew into a *rivulet* that threatened to wash away a portion of the slope.

rousing ADJ. lively; stirring. "And now, let's have a *rousing* welcome for TV's own Roseanne Barr, who'll lead us in a *rousing* rendition of 'The Star Spangled Banner.'"

ruddy ADJ. reddish; healthy looking. Her *ruddy* cheeks indicated that she had been spending most of her days outdoors.

rue V. regret; lament; mourn. Tina *rued* the night she met Tony and wondered how she'd ever fallen for such a jerk. rueful, ADJ.

rummage V. ransack; thoroughly search. When we *rummaged* through the trunks in the attic, we found many souvenirs of our childhood days. also N.

rupture N. act of breaking; fracture; break in harmony or peaceful relations. The *rupture* of gas lines caused by the earthquake contributed greatly to the fire that ensued.

ruse N. trick; stratagem. Because they wanted to decorate the living room for their mother's surprise birthday party, the girls tried to think of some good *ruse* to lure her out of the house for a couple of hours.

• **ruthless** ADJ. pitiless; cruel. Captain Hook was a dangerous, *ruthless* villain who would stop at nothing to destroy Peter Pan.

saboteur N. one who commits sabotage; destroyer of property. Members of the Resistance acted as *saboteurs*, blowing up train lines to prevent supplies from reaching the Nazi army.

saccharine ADJ. cloyingly sweet. She tried to ingratiate herself, speaking sweetly and smiling a *saccharine* smile.

sagacious ADJ. keen; shrewd; having insight. Holmes is far too *sagacious* to be fooled by a simple trick like that. sagacity, N.

salutary ADJ. tending to improve; beneficial; wholesome. The punishment had a *salutary* effect on the boy, for he became a model student.

sanction V. approve; ratify. Nothing will convince me to *sanction* the engagement of my daughter to such a worthless young man.

sap V. diminish; undermine. The element kryptonite has an unhealthy effect on Superman: it *saps* his strength.

sarcasm N. scornful remarks; stinging rebuke. Though Ralph tried to ignore the mocking comments of his supposed friends, their *sarcasm* wounded him deeply.

sate V. satisfy to the full; cloy. Its hunger *sated*, the lion dozed.

satiate V. satisfy fully. Having stuffed themselves until they were *satiated*, the guests were so full they were ready for a nap.

• **satirize** V. mock. Cartoonist Gary Trudeau often *satirizes* contemporary politicians; through the comments of the *Doonesbury* characters, Trudeau ridicules political corruption and folly. satirical, ADJ.

saturate V. soak thoroughly. Thorough watering is the key to lawn care: you must *saturate* your new lawn well to encourage its growth.

saunter V. stroll slowly. Too tired for his usual brisk walk, Stan *sauntered* through the park, taking time to enjoy the spring flowers.

savant N. learned scholar. Despite all her academic honors, Dr. Diamond refused to be classed as a *savant*: considering herself a simple researcher, she refused to describe herself in such grandiose terms.

savory ADJ. tasty; pleasing, attractive, or agreeable. Julia Child's recipes enable amateur chefs to create *savory* delicacies for their guests.

scamper V. run about playfully. Looking forward to the game of hide-and-seek, the children *scampered* off to find good spots in which to hide.

scanty ADJ. meager; insufficient. Thinking his helping of food was *scanty*, Oliver Twist asked for more.

scapegoat N. someone who bears the blame for others. After the *Challenger* disaster, NASA searched for *scapegoats* on whom they could cast the blame.

scavenge V. hunt through discarded materials for usable items; search, especially for food. If you need parts for an old car that the dealers no longer have in stock, try *scavenging* for odd bits and pieces at the auto wreckers' yards. scavenger, N.

schism N. division; split. Let us not widen the *schism* by further bickering.

scintillate V. sparkle; flash. I enjoy her dinner parties because the food is excellent and the conversation *scintillates*.

scrupulous ADJ. conscientious; extremely thorough. Though Alfred is *scrupulous* in fulfilling his duties at work, he is less conscientious about his obligations to his family and friends.

• **scrutinize** V. examine closely and critically. Searching for flaws, the sergeant *scrutinized* every detail of the private's uniform.

scuffle V. struggle confusedly; move off in a confused hurry. The twins briefly *scuffled*, wrestling to see which of them would get the toy. When their big brother yelled, "Let go of my Gameboy!" they *scuffled* off down the hall.

seasoned ADJ. experienced. Though pleased with her new batch of rookies, the basketball coach wished she had a few more *seasoned* players on the team. (secondary meaning)

• **seclusion** N. isolation; solitude. One moment she loved crowds; the next, she sought *seclusion*.

sect N. separate religious body; faction. As university chaplain, she sought to address universal religious issues and not limit herself to concerns of any one *sect*.

secular ADJ. worldly; not pertaining to church matters. The church leaders decided not to interfere in *secular* matters.

sedate ADJ. composed; grave. The parents were worried because they felt their son was too quiet and *sedate*.

sedition N. resistance to authority; insubordination; rebellion. Her words, though not treasonous in themselves, were calculated to arouse thoughts of *sedition*. seditious, ADJ.

seep V. leak through; trickle. After all the times we'd tried to repair the leaky roof, we were discouraged to see the water *seep* through the ceiling once again.

sensory ADJ. pertaining to the physical senses. Blasted by sound waves, dazzled by flashing lights, jostled by crowds, a newcomer to rock concerts can suffer from *sensory* overload.

sequester V. isolate; retire from public life; segregate; seclude. Banished from his kingdom, the wizard Prospero *sequestered* himself on a desert island.

serendipity N. gift for finding valuable or desirable things by accident; accidental good fortune or luck. Many scientific discoveries are a matter of *serendipity*: Newton was not sitting there thinking about gravity when the apple dropped on his head.

• **serenity** N. calmness; placidity. The *serenity* of the sleepy town was shattered by a tremendous explosion.

servile ADJ. slavishly submissive; fawning; cringing. Constantly fawning over his employer, Uriah Heep was a *servile* creature.

servitude N. slavery; compulsory labor. Born a slave, Douglass resented his life of *servitude* and plotted to escape to the North.

• **sever** V. cut; separate. Dr. Guillotin invented a machine that could neatly *sever* an aristocratic head from its equally aristocratic body.

• **severity** N. harshness; intensity; austerity; rigidity. The *severity* of Jane's migraine attack was so great that she took to her bed for a week.

shackle V. chain; fetter. In a chain gang, convicts are *shackled* together to prevent their escape. also N.

shambles N. wreck; mess; slaughterhouse. After the hurricane, the Carolina coast was a *shambles*. After the New Year's Eve party, the apartment was a *shambles*.

shimmer V. glimmer intermittently. The moonlight *shimmered* on the water as the moon broke through the clouds for a moment. also N.

shortcomings N. failures; deficiencies. Aware of his own *shortcomings* as a public speaker, the candidate worked closely with debate coaches to prepare for the coming campaign.

shrewd ADJ. clever; astute. A *shrewd* investor, he took clever advantage of the fluctuations of the stock market.

shun V. keep away from. Cherishing his solitude, the recluse *shunned* the company of other human beings.

shyster N. lawyer using questionable methods. The respectable attorney was horrified to learn that his newly discovered half brother was nothing but a cheap *shyster*.

simile N. comparison of one thing with another, using the word like or as. "My love is like a red, red rose" is a *simile*.

simplistic ADJ. oversimplified. Though Jack's solution dealt adequately with one aspect of the problem, it was *simplistic* in failing to consider various complications that might arise.

simulate V. feign; pretend. The judge ruled that the accused racketeer had *simulated* insanity and was in fact sane enough to stand trial.

• **singular** ADJ. unique; extraordinary; odd. Though the young man tried to understand Father William's *singular* behavior, he still found it odd that the old man incessantly stood on his head. singularity, N.

sinister ADJ. evil; conveying a sense of ill omen. Aware of the Penguin's *sinister* purpose, Batman wondered how he could save Gotham City from the ravages of his evil enemy.

sinuous ADJ. winding; bending in and out; not morally honest. The snake moved in a *sinuous* manner.

• **skeptical** ADJ. doubting; suspending judgment until having examined the evidence supporting a point of view. I am *skeptical* about this project; I want some proof that it can work. skepticism, N.

skulk V. move furtively and secretly. He *skulked* through the less fashionable sections of the city in order to avoid meeting any of his former friends.

slacken V. slow up; loosen. As they passed the finish line, the runners *slackened* their pace.

slag N. residue from smelting metal; dross; waste matter. The blast furnace had a special opening at the bottom to allow the workers to remove the worthless *slag*.

slapdash ADJ. haphazard; careless; sloppy. From the number of typos and misspellings I found in it, it's clear that Mario proofread the report in a remarkably *slapdash* fashion.

slather V. spread abundantly. Johnny *slathered* jelly on his toast so generously that it oozed over the edge and dripped on the clean tablecloth below.

slothful ADJ. lazy. Lying idly on the sofa while others worked, Reggie denied he was *slothful*: "I just supervise better lying down."

sluggish ADJ. slow; lazy; lethargic. After two nights without sleep, she felt *sluggish* and incapable of exertion.

smelt V. melt or blend ores, changing their chemical composition. The furnaceman *smelts* tin with copper to create a special alloy used in making bells.

smolder V. burn without flame; be liable to break out at any moment. The rags *smoldered* for hours before they burst into flame.

smuggler N. one who illegally moves goods across national borders. Suspecting Randy might be a *smuggler*, the customs inspector made a thorough search of his luggage but found nothing illicit.

sneer V. smile or laugh contemptuously; make an insulting comment or face. "I could paint better than that with both hands tied behind my back," *sneered* Marvin.

sobriety N. moderation (especially regarding indulgence in alcohol); seriousness. Neither falling-down drunks nor stand-up comics are noted for *sobriety*. sober, ADJ.

sodden ADJ. soaked; dull, as if from drink. He set his *sodden* overcoat near the radiator to dry.

solemnity N. seriousness; gravity. The minister was concerned that nothing should disturb the *solemnity* of the marriage service.

soliloquy N. talking to oneself. The *soliloquy* is a device used by the dramatist to reveal a character's innermost thoughts and emotions.

somber ADJ. gloomy; depressing; dark; drab. Dull brown and charcoal gray are pretty *somber* colors; can't you wear something bright?

somnolent ADJ. half asleep. The heavy meal and the overheated room made us all *somnolent* and indifferent to the speaker.

soporific ADJ. sleep-causing; marked by sleepiness. Professor Pringle's lectures were so *soporific* that even he fell asleep in class. also N.

sordid ADJ. vile; filthy; wretched; mean. Talk show hosts seem willing to discuss any topic, no matter how *sordid* and disgusting it may be.

spartan ADJ. avoiding luxury and comfort; sternly disciplined. Looking over the bare, unheated room with its hard cot, he wondered what he was doing in such *spartan* quarters. Only his *spartan* sense of duty kept him at his post.

spat N. quarrel. Desi and Lucy had many lovers' *spats*; however, in the end they always reconciled.

specious ADJ. seemingly reasonable but incorrect; misleading (often intentionally). To claim that, because houses and birds both have wings, both can fly, is extremely *specious* reasoning.

speculate V. theorize or ponder; assume a financial risk; gamble. Students of the stock market *speculate* that the seeds of the financier's downfall were planted when he *speculated* heavily in junk bonds.

spendthrift N. someone who wastes money. Easy access to credit encourages people to turn into *spendthrifts* who shop till they drop.

splendor N. magnificence; grandeur; brilliance. Awed by the glittering chandeliers and finely costumed courtiers, Cinderella was overwhelmed by the *splendor* of the ball.

spoke N. radiating bar supporting the rim of a wheel. The repair man at the bicycle shop took less than half an hour to fix the bent *spokes* on Bob's rear wheel.

spontaneity N. lack of premeditation; naturalness; freedom from constraint. When Betty and Jennifer met, Jen impulsively hugged her roommate-to-be, but Betty drew back, unprepared for such *spontaneity*. spontaneous, ADJ.

sporadic ADJ. occurring irregularly. Although you can still hear *sporadic* outbursts of laughter and singing outside, the big Halloween parade has passed; the party's over till next year.

spurious ADJ. false; counterfeit; forged; illogical. The hero of Jonathan Gash's mystery novels is an antique dealer who gives the reader advice on how to tell *spurious* antiques from the real thing.

spurt V. gush forth; squirt. Water suddenly *spurted* from the fountain and splashed Bert right in the face.

squabble N. minor quarrel; bickering. Children invariably get involved in petty *squabbles*; wise parents know when to interfere and when to let the children work things out on their own.

squalor N. filth; degradation; dirty, neglected state. With rusted, broken-down cars in its yard, trash piled up on the porch, and tar paper peeling from the roof, the shack was the picture of *squalor*.

squander V. waste. If you *squander* your allowance on candy and comic books, you won't have any money left to buy the new box of crayons you want.

stagnant ADJ. motionless; stale; dull. Mosquitoes commonly breed in ponds of *stagnant* water. Mike's career was *stagnant;* it wasn't going anywhere, and neither was he! stagnate, V.

staid ADJ. sober; sedate. Her conduct during the funeral ceremony was *staid* and solemn.

stalemate N. deadlock. Negotiations between the union and the employers have reached a *stalemate*: neither side is willing to budge from its previously stated position.

stalwart ADJ. strong and vigorous; unwaveringly dependable. We thought the congressman was a *stalwart* Democrat until he voted against the president's health care plan.

stamina N. strength; staying power. I doubt that she has the *stamina* to run the full distance of the marathon race.

stanza N. division of a poem. We all know the first *stanza* of the "The Star Spangled Banner." Does anyone know the last?

static ADJ. unchanging; lacking development. Why watch chess on TV? I like watching a game with action, not something *static* where nothing seems to be going on. stasis, N.

statute N. law enacted by the legislature. The *statute* of limitations sets the limits on how long you have to take legal action in specific cases.

• **steadfast** ADJ. loyal; unswerving. Penelope was *steadfast* in her affections, faithfully waiting for Ulysses to return from his wanderings.

stem V. check the flow. The paramedic used a tourniquet to *stem* the bleeding from the slashed artery.

stem from V. arise from. Morton's problems in school *stemmed from* his poor study habits.

stereotyped ADJ. oversimplified; lacking individuality; seen as a type. My chief objection to the book is that the characters are *stereotyped;* they don't come across as real people with individual quirks, fears, and dreams. stereotype, N., V.

stifle V. suppress; extinguish; inhibit. Halfway through the boring lecture, Laura gave up trying to *stifle* her yawns.

stodgy ADJ. stuffy; boringly conservative. For a young person, Winston seems remarkably *stodgy*: you'd expect someone his age to show a little more life.

• **stoic** ADJ. impassive; unmoved by joy or grief. I wasn't particularly *stoic* when I had my flu shot; I squealed like a stuck pig. also N.

stolid ADJ. dull; impassive. The earthquake shattered Stuart's usual *stolid* demeanor; trembling, he crouched on the no longer stable ground.

• **stratagem** N. deceptive scheme. Though Wellington's forces seemed to be in full retreat, in reality their withdrawal was a *stratagem* intended to lure the enemy away from its sheltered position.

strident ADJ. loud and harsh; insistent. Whenever Sue became angry, she tried not to raise her voice; she had no desire to appear *strident*.

stringent ADJ. binding; rigid; strict. Protesting that the school dress code was too *stringent*, Katya campaigned to have the rules relaxed.

stupor N. state of apathy; daze; lack of awareness. The paramedics shook the unconscious man but could not rouse him from his drunken *stupor*.

stupefy V. make numb; stun; amaze. Disapproving of drugs in general, Laura refused to take sleeping pills or any other medicine that might *stupefy* her. stupefaction, N.

• **subdued** ADJ. less intense; quieter. Bob liked the *subdued* lighting at the restaurant because he thought it was romantic. I just thought it was dimly lit.

subjective ADJ. existing in the mind, rather than in the object itself; opposite of objective; personal. Your analysis is highly *subjective*; you have permitted your emotions and your opinions to color your thinking.

sublime ADJ. exalted; noble and uplifting; utter. Lucy was in awe of Desi's *sublime* musicianship, while he was in awe of her *sublime* naïveté.

subordinate ADJ. occupying a lower rank; inferior; submissive. Bishop Proudie's wife expected all the *subordinate* clergy to behave with great deference to the wife of their superior.

subsequent ADJ. following; later. In *subsequent* lessons, we shall take up more difficult problems.

subside V. sink to a low(er) level; grow quiet, less active, or less violent. The doctor assured us that the fever would eventually *subside*.

subsidiary ADJ. supplementary; subordinate; secondary. Although this *subsidiary* evidence is relevant, it is insufficient by itself to prove your argument. also N.

substantial ADJ. ample; solid; in essentials. The scholarship represented a *substantial* sum of money.

substantiate V. establish by evidence; verify; support. These endorsements from satisfied customers *substantiate* our claim that Barron's *How to Prepare for the PSAT* is the best PSAT-prep book on the market.

subtlety N. perceptiveness; ingenuity; delicacy. Never obvious, she expressed herself with such *subtlety* that her remarks went right over the heads of most of her audience. subtle, ADJ.

• **subversive** ADJ. tending to overthrow or destroy. At first glance, the notion that styrofoam cups may actually be more ecologically sound than paper cups strikes most environmentalists as *subversive*.

succinct ADJ. brief; terse; compact. Don't bore your audience with excess verbiage: be *succinct*.

succulent ADJ. juicy; full of richness. To some people, Florida citrus fruits are more *succulent* than those from California. also N.

suffragist N. advocate of voting rights (for women). In recognition of her efforts to win the vote for women, Congress authorized coining a silver dollar honoring the *suffragist* Susan B. Anthony.

• **superficial** ADJ. trivial; shallow. Since your report gave only a *superficial* analysis of the problem, I cannot give you more than a passing grade.

• **superfluous** ADJ. excessive; unnecessary. Please try not to include so many *superfluous* details in your report; just give me the bare facts. superfluity, N.

supplant V. replace; usurp. Did the other woman actually *supplant* Princess Diana in Prince Charles's affections, or did Charles never love Diana at all?

supple ADJ. flexible; pliant. Years of yoga exercises made Grace's body *supple*.

• **suppress** V. crush; subdue; inhibit. Too polite to laugh in anyone's face, Roy did his best to *suppress* his amusement at Ed's inane remark.

surfeit V. satiate; stuff; indulge to excess in anything. Every Thanksgiving we are *surfeited* with an overabundance of holiday treats. also N.

• **surpass** V. exceed. Her PSAT scores *surpassed* our expectations.

surreptitious ADJ. secret; furtive; sneaky. Hoping to discover where Mom had hidden the Christmas presents, Tommy took a *surreptitious* peek into the master bedroom closet.

• **susceptible** ADJ. impressionable; easily influenced; having little resistance, as to a disease; receptive to. Said the patent medicine man to the extremely *susceptible* customer, "Buy this new miracle drug, and you will no longer be *susceptible* to the common cold."

• **suspend** V. defer or postpone; expel or eject; halt or discontinue; hang from above. When the judge *suspended* his sentence, Bill breathed a sigh of relief. When the principal *suspended* her from school, Wanda tried to look as if she didn't care. When the trapeze artist broke her arm, she had to *suspend* her activities: she no longer could be *suspended* from her trapeze.

• **sustain** V. experience; support; nourish. Stuart *sustained* such a severe injury that the doctors feared he would be unable to work to *sustain* his growing family.

swill V. drink greedily. Singing "Yo, ho, ho, and a bottle of rum," Long John Silver and his fellow pirates *swilled* their grog.

swindler N. cheat. She was gullible and trusting, an easy victim for the first *swindler* who came along.

sycophant N. servile flatterer; bootlicker. Fed up with the toadies and flatterers who made up his entourage, the star cried, "Get out, all of you! I'm sick to death of *sycophants!*"

• **symmetry** N. arrangement of parts so that balance is obtained; congruity. Something lopsided by definition lacks *symmetry*.

• **synthesis** N. combining parts into a whole. Now that we have succeeded in isolating this drug, our next problem is to plan its *synthesis* in the laboratory. synthesize, V.

• **taciturn** ADJ. habitually silent; talking little. The stereotypical cowboy is a *taciturn* soul, answering lengthy questions with "Yep" or "Nope."

tactile ADJ. pertaining to the organs or sense of touch. His callused hands had lost their *tactile* sensitivity.

taint V. contaminate; cause to lose purity; modify with a trace of something bad. One speck of dirt on your utensils may contain enough germs to *taint* an entire batch of preserves.

tangential ADJ. peripheral; only slightly connected; digressing. Despite Clark's attempts to distract her with *tangential* remarks, Lois kept on coming back to her main question: why couldn't he come out to dinner with Superman and her?

tantalize V. tease; torture with disappointment. Tom loved to *tantalize* his younger brother with candy; he knew the boy was forbidden to have it.

tarry V. delay; dawdle. We can't *tarry* if we want to get to the airport on time.

- **tedious** ADJ. boring; tiring. The repetitive nature of work on the assembly line made Martin's job very *tedious*. tedium, N.

- **temper** V. moderate; tone down or restrain; toughen (steel). Not even her supervisor's grumpiness could *temper* Nancy's enthusiasm for her new job.

- **temperament** N. characteristic frame of mind; disposition; emotional excess. Although the twins look alike, they differ markedly in *temperament*: Todd is calm, but Rod is excitable. Racket-throwing tennis star John McEnroe was famed for his displays of *temperament*.

temperate ADJ. restrained; self-controlled; moderate in respect to temperature. Try to be *temperate* in your eating this holiday season; if you control your appetite, you won't gain too much weight.

tempestuous ADJ. stormy; quarreling, reconciling, and quarreling again. The unhappy couple had a *tempestuous* married life.

tenet N. doctrine; dogma. The agnostic did not accept the *tenets* of their faith.

tentative ADJ. hesitant; not fully worked out or developed; experimental; not definite or positive. Unsure of his welcome at the Christmas party, Scrooge took a *tentative* step into his nephew's drawing room.

tenuous ADJ. thin; rare; slim. The allegiance of our allies is held by rather *tenuous* ties.

- **termination** N. end. Though the time for *termination* of the project was near, we still had a lot of work to finish before we shut up shop.

terrestrial ADJ. on the earth. We have been able to explore the *terrestrial* regions much more thoroughly than the aquatic or celestial regions.

terse ADJ. concise; abrupt; pithy. There is a fine line between speech that is *terse* and to the point and speech that is too abrupt.

theocracy N. government run by religious leaders. Though some Pilgrims aboard the *Mayflower* favored the establishment of a *theocracy* in New England, many of their fellow voyagers preferred a nonreligious form of government.

theoretical ADJ. not practical or applied; hypothetical. Bob was better at applied engineering and computer programming than he was at *theoretical* physics and math. While I can still think of some *theoretical* objections to your plan, you've convinced me of its basic soundness.

therapeutic ADJ. curative. Now better known for its racetrack, Saratoga Springs first gained attention for the *therapeutic* qualities of its famous "healing waters."

thrifty ADJ. careful about money; economical. A *thrifty* shopper compares prices before making major purchases.

thrive V. prosper; flourish. Despite the impact of the recession on the restaurant trade, Philip's cafe *thrived*.

- **thwart** V. baffle; frustrate. He felt that everyone was trying to *thwart* his plans and prevent his success.

tiff ADJ. minor quarrel; fit of annoyance. Whenever the Kramdens had a *tiff*, Ralph would bluster, "That's it, Alice!" and storm out of the apartment.

tiller N. handle used to move a boat's rudder (to steer). Fearing the wind might shift suddenly and capsize the skiff, Tom kept one hand on the *tiller* at all times.

timidity N. lack of self-confidence or courage. If you are to succeed as a salesman, you must first lose your *timidity* and fear of failure.

tirade N. extended scolding; denunciation; harangue. Every time the boss holds a meeting, he goes into a lengthy *tirade*, scolding us for everything from tardiness to padding our expenses.

titanic ADJ. gigantic. *Titanic* waves beat against the shore during the hurricane.

title N. right or claim to possession; mark of rank; name (of a book, film, etc.). Though the penniless Duke of Ragwort no longer had *title* to the family estate, he still retained his *title* as head of one of England's oldest families. The *title* of his autobiography was *From Riches to Rags*.

toady N. servile flatterer; yes man. Never tell the boss anything he doesn't wish to hear: he doesn't want an independent adviser, he just wants a *toady*. also V.

torpor N. lethargy; sluggishness; dormancy. Throughout the winter, nothing aroused the bear from his *torpor*: he would not emerge from hibernation until spring. torpid, ADJ.

torrent N. rushing stream; flood. Day after day of heavy rain saturated the hillside until the water ran downhill in *torrents*. torrential, ADJ.

totter V. move unsteadily; sway, as if about to fall. On unsteady feet, the drunk *tottered* down the hill to the nearest bar.

- **toxic** ADJ. poisonous. We must seek an antidote for whatever *toxic* substance he has eaten. toxicity, N.

tractable ADJ. docile; easily managed. Although Susan seemed a *tractable* young woman, she had a stubborn streak of independence that occasionally led her to defy the powers-that-be when she felt they were in the wrong.

traduce V. slander; malign. His opponents tried to *traduce* the candidate's reputation by spreading rumors about his past.

- **transcendent** ADJ. surpassing; exceeding ordinary limits; superior. Standing on the hillside watching the sunset through the Golden Gate was a *transcendent* experience for Lise: it was so beautiful it surpassed her wildest dreams.

transcribe V. copy. It took hours for the secretary to *transcribe* his shorthand notes of the conference into a form others could read.

transgression N. violation of a law; sin. Forgive us our *transgressions;* we know not what we do. transgress, V.

transient ADJ. momentary; temporary; staying for a short time. Lexy's joy at finding the perfect Christmas gift for Phil was *transient;* she still had to find presents for Roger, Laura, Allison, and Uncle Bob. Located near the airport, this hotel caters to a largely *transient* trade.

transition N. going from one state of action to another. During the period of *transition* from oil heat to gas heat, the furnace will have to be shut off.

transitory ADJ. impermanent; fleeting. Fame is *transitory*: today's rising star is all too soon tomorrow's washed-up has-been. transitoriness, N.

translucent ADJ. partly transparent. We could not recognize the people in the next room because of the *translucent* curtains that separated us.

• **transparent** ADJ. easily detected; permitting light to pass through freely. Bobby managed to put an innocent look on his face; to his mother, however, his guilt was *transparent*.

travail N. painful physical or mental labor; drudgery; torment. Like every other high school student she knew, Sherry detested the yearlong *travail* of cramming for the SAT.

trek N. travel; journey. The tribe made their *trek* farther north that summer in search of game. also V.

trenchant ADJ. cutting; keen. I am afraid of his *trenchant* wit for it is so often sarcastic.

• **trepidation** N. fear; nervous apprehension. As she entered the office of the dean of admissions, Sharon felt some *trepidation* about how she would do in her interview.

trifling ADJ. trivial; unimportant. Why bother going to see a doctor for such a *trifling,* everyday cold?

trigger V. set off. John is touchy today; say one word wrong and you'll *trigger* an explosion.

trite ADJ. hackneyed; commonplace. The *trite* and predictable situations on many television programs turn off viewers, who respond by turning off their sets.

trivial ADJ. trifling; unimportant. Too many magazines ignore newsworthy subjects and feature *trivial* gossip about celebrities.

trough N. container for feeding farm animals; lowest point (of a wave, business cycle, etc.) The hungry pigs struggled to get at the fresh swill in the *trough*. The surfer rode her board, coasting along in the *trough* between two waves.

troupe N. group of stage performers; touring company. Was Will Kemp a member of Shakespeare's *troupe* of players when they performed at the Globe?

truism N. self-evident truth. Many a *truism* is summed up in a proverb; for example, "Marry in haste, repent at leisure."

turbid ADJ. muddy; having the sediment disturbed. The water was *turbid* after the children had waded through it.

• **turbulence** N. state of violent agitation. Warned of approaching *turbulence* in the atmosphere, the pilot told the passengers to fasten their seat belts.

turgid ADJ. swollen; distended. The *turgid* river threatened to overflow the levees and flood the countryside.

turmoil N. great commotion and confusion. Lydia running off with a soldier! Mother fainting at the news! The Bennet household was in *turmoil*.

typhoon N. tropical hurricane or cyclone. If you liked *Twister,* you'll love *Typhoon!*

tyranny N. oppression; cruel government. Frederick Douglass fought against the *tyranny* of slavery throughout his entire life. tyrant, N.

ubiquitous ADJ. being everywhere; omnipresent. That Christmas "The Little Drummer Boy" seemed *ubiquitous*: Justin heard the tune everywhere he went.

ultimate ADJ. final; not susceptible to further analysis. Scientists are searching for the *ultimate* truths.

unanimity N. complete agreement. We were surprised by the *unanimity* with which members of both parties accepted our proposals. unanimous, ADJ.

unassuming ADJ. modest. He is so *unassuming* that some people fail to realize how great a man he really is.

unbecoming ADJ. unattractive; improper. What an *unbecoming* dress Mona is wearing! That girl has no color sense. At the court martial the captain was charged with conduct *unbecoming* an officer.

undermine V. weaken; sap. The recent corruption scandals have *undermined* many people's faith in the city government.

underscore V. emphasize. Addressing the jogging class, Kim *underscored* the importance to runners of good nutrition.

undulating ADJ. moving with a wavelike motion. The Hilo Hula Festival was an *undulating* sea of grass skirts.

unearth V. dig up. When they *unearthed* the city, the archaeologists found many relics of an ancient civilization.

unequivocal ADJ. plain; obvious. My answer to your proposal is an *unequivocal* and absolute "No."

unfazed ADJ. not bothered; unworried. Surrounded by armed opponents, Bond nevertheless appeared completely *unfazed* by his danger.

unfeasible ADJ. not practical or workable. Roy's plan to enlarge the living room by knocking down a couple of internal walls proved *unfeasible* when he discovered that those walls were holding up the roof.

unfounded ADJ. baseless; not based on fact. Cher feared that her boyfriend was unfaithful; fortunately, her suspicions proved to be *unfounded*.

ungainly ADJ. awkward; clumsy; unwieldy. "If you want to know whether Nick's an *ungainly* dancer, check out my bruised feet," said Nora. Anyone who has ever tried to carry a bass fiddle knows it's an *ungainly* instrument.

uniformity N. sameness; monotony. After a while, the *uniformity* of TV situation comedies becomes boring.

unintimidating ADJ. unfrightening. Though Phil had expected to feel overawed when he met Joe Montana, he found the world-famous quarterback friendly and *unintimidating*.

unique ADJ. without an equal; single in kind. You have the *unique* distinction of being the first student whom I have had to fail in this course.

universal ADJ. characterizing or affecting all; present everywhere. At first, no one shared Christopher's opinions; his theory that the world was round was met with *universal* disbelief.

unnerve V. upset; weaken. His wartime experiences left Tom badly shaken; any sudden noise could *unnerve* him, reducing him to a quivering wreck.

unprecedented ADJ. novel; unparalleled. Margaret Mitchell's book *Gone with the Wind* was an *unprecedented* success.

unravel V. disentangle; solve. With equal ease Miss Marple *unraveled* tangled balls of yarn and baffling murder mysteries.

unrequited ADJ. not reciprocated. Suffering the pangs of *unrequited* love, Olivia rebukes Cesario for his hard-heartedness.

unscathed ADJ. unharmed. Juan's parents prayed that he would come home from the war *unscathed*.

unseemly ADJ. unbecoming; indecent; in poor taste. When he put whoopie cushions on all the seats in the funeral parlor, Seymour's conduct was most *unseemly*.

unsightly ADJ. unpleasant to look at; ugly. Although James was an experienced emergency room nurse, he occasionally became queasy when faced with a particularly *unsightly* injury.

unsullied ADJ. spotlessly clean; unstained. The reputation of our school is *unsullied*, young ladies; you must conduct yourself modestly and discreetly so that you never disgrace our good name.

unwarranted ADJ. unjustified; groundless; undeserved. We could not understand Martin's *unwarranted* rudeness to his mother's guests.

upbraid V. severely scold; reprimand. Not only did Miss Minchin *upbraid* Ermengarde for her disobedience, but she hung her up by her braids from a coat rack in the classroom.

uphold V. give support; keep from sinking; lift up. Bold Sir Robin was ready to fight to the death to *uphold* the honor of his lady.

upright ADJ. honest; ethical; erect; perpendicular. An *upright* person acts straight: he does not cheat. An *upright* post stands straight: it does not lean.

uproarious ADJ. marked by commotion; extremely funny; very noisy. The *uproarious* comedy hit *Ace Ventura: Pet Detective* starred Jim Carrey, whose comic mugging provoked gales of *uproarious* laughter from audiences coast to coast.

• **urbane** ADJ. suave; refined; elegant. The courtier was *urbane* and sophisticated. urbanity, N.

usurp V. seize another's power or rank. The revolution ended when the victorious rebel general succeeded in *usurping* the throne.

• **utopia** N. ideal place, state, or society. Fed up with this imperfect universe, Don would have liked to run off to Shangri-la or some other fictitious *utopia*. utopian, ADJ.

• **vacillate** V. waver; fluctuate. Uncertain which suitor she ought to marry, the princess *vacillated*, saying now one, now the other. vacillation, N.

vacuous ADJ. empty; lacking in ideas; stupid. The politician's *vacuous* remarks annoyed the audience, who had hoped to hear more than empty platitudes.

vagabond N. wanderer; tramp. In summer, college students wander the roads of Europe like carefree *vagabonds*. also ADJ.

validate V. confirm; ratify. I will not publish my findings until I *validate* my results.

vanguard N. advance guard of a military force; forefront of a movement. When no enemy was in sight, the duke of Plaza Toro marched in the *vanguard* of his troops, but once the bullets flew above, he headed for the rear.

vantage N. position giving an advantage. They fired upon the enemy from behind the trees, walls, and any other point of *vantage* they could find.

vapid ADJ. dull and unimaginative; insipid and flavorless. "Bor-ing!" said Cheryl, as she suffered through yet another *vapid* lecture about Dead White Male Poets.

vehement ADJ. forceful; intensely emotional; with marked vigor. Alfred became so *vehement* in describing what was wrong with the Internal Revenue Service that he began jumping up and down and frothing at the mouth. vehemence, N.

veneer N. thin layer; cover. Deceived by Victor's *veneer* of sophistication, casual acquaintances failed to perceive his fundamental shallowness.

venerate V. revere. In Tibet today, the common people still *venerate* their traditional spiritual leader, the Dalai Lama.

venturesome ADJ. bold. A group of *venturesome* women were the first to scale Mt. Annapurna.

veracity N. truthfulness. Asserting his *veracity,* young George Washington proclaimed, "Father, I cannot tell a lie!"

verbose ADJ. wordy. Someone mute can't talk; someone *verbose* can hardly stop talking.

verdant ADJ. green; lush in vegetation. Monet's paintings of the *verdant* fields were symphonies in green.

verisimilitude N. appearance of truth; likelihood. Critics praised her for the *verisimilitude* of her performance as Lady Macbeth. She was completely believable.

• **versatile** ADJ. having many talents; capable of working in many fields. She was a *versatile* athlete, earning varsity letters in basketball, hockey, and track.

vertigo N. severe dizziness. When you test potential airplane pilots for susceptibility to spells of *vertigo,* be sure to hand out airsick bags.

vicarious ADJ. acting as a substitute; done by a deputy. Though Maud was too meek to talk back to anyone, she got a *vicarious* kick out of Rita's sharp retorts.

vicissitude N. change of fortune. Humbled by life's *vicissitudes,* the last emperor of China worked as a lowly gardener in the palace over which he had once ruled.

vie V. contend; compete. Politicians *vie* with one another, competing for donations and votes.

vigor N. active strength. Although he was over 70 years old, Jack had the *vigor* of a man in his prime. vigorous, ADJ.

vindicate V. clear from blame; exonerate; justify or support. The lawyer's goal was to *vindicate* her client and prove him innocent on all charges. The critics' extremely favorable reviews *vindicate* my opinion that *The Madness of King George* is a brilliant movie.

vindictive ADJ. out for revenge; malicious. Divorce sometimes brings out a *vindictive* streak in people; when Tony told Tina he wanted a divorce, she poured green Jello into the aquarium and turned his tropical fish into dessert.

virtuoso N. highly skilled artist. The child prodigy Yehudi Menuhin grew into a *virtuoso* whose *virtuosity* on the violin thrilled millions.

virulent ADJ. extremely poisonous; hostile; bitter. Laid up with a *virulent* case of measles, Vera blamed her doctors because her recovery took so long. In fact, she became quite *virulent* on the subject of the quality of modern medical care.

vise N. tool for holding work in place. Before filing its edges, the keysmith took the blank key and fixed it firmly between the jaws of a *vise.*

vivacious ADJ. animated; lively. She had always been *vivacious* and sparkling.

• **volatile** ADJ. changeable; explosive; evaporating rapidly. The political climate today is extremely *volatile*: no one can predict what the electorate will do next. Maria Callas's temper was extremely *volatile*: the only thing you could predict was that she was sure to blow up. Ethyl chloride is an extremely *volatile* liquid: it evaporates instantly.

voluble ADJ. fluent; glib; talkative. Excessively *voluble* speakers suffer from logorrhea: they run off at the mouth a lot!

voluminous ADJ. extensive; bulky; large. Despite her family burdens, she kept up a *voluminous* correspondence with her friends. A caftan is a *voluminous* garment; most people wearing one look as if they're draped in a small tent.

• **voracious** ADJ. ravenous. The wolf is a *voracious* animal, its hunger never satisfied.

vulnerable ADJ. susceptible to wounds. His opponents could not harm Achilles, who was *vulnerable* only in his heel.

waive V. give up a claim or right voluntarily; refrain from enforcing; postpone considering. Although technically prospective students had to live in Piedmont to attend high school there, occasionally the school *waived* the residence requirement in order to enroll promising athletes.

wallow V. roll in; indulge in; become helpless. The hippopotamus loves to *wallow* in pools of mud. The horror film addict loves to *wallow* in tales of blood.

wanderlust N. strong longing to go off traveling. The cowboy had a bad case of *wanderlust;* he could never settle down.

wane V. decrease in size or strength; draw gradually to an end. When lit, does a wax candle *wane*?

wanton ADJ. unrestrained; willfully malicious; unchaste. Pointing to the stack of bills, Sheldon criticized Sarah for her *wanton* expenditures. In response, Sarah accused Sheldon of making an unfounded, *wanton* attack.

warble V. sing; babble. Every morning the birds *warbled* outside her window. also N.

• **wary** ADJ. very cautious. The spies grew *wary* as they approached the sentry.

wayward ADJ. ungovernable; unpredictable; contrary. Miss Watson warned Huck that if he didn't mend his ways she would ship him off to a school for *wayward* youths.

wheedle V. cajole; coax; deceive by flattery. She knows she can *wheedle* almost anything she wants from her father.

whet V. sharpen; stimulate. The odors from the kitchen are *whetting* my appetite; I will be ravenous by the time the meal is served.

whiff N. puff or gust (of air, scent, etc.); hint. The slightest *whiff* of Old Spice cologne brought memories of George to her mind.

whimsical N. capricious; fanciful. In *Mrs. Doubtfire,* the hero is a playful, *whimsical* man who takes a notion to dress up as a woman so that he can look after his children, who are in the custody of his ex-wife. whimsy, N.

whittle V. pare; cut off bits. As a present for Aunt Polly, Tom *whittled* some clothespins out of a chunk of wood.

willful ADJ. intentional; headstrong. Donald had planned to kill his wife for months; clearly, her death was a case of deliberate, *willful* murder, not a crime of passion committed by a hasty, *willful* youth unable to foresee the consequences of his deeds.

wile N. trick intended to deceive; stratagem. At the end of the movie, the hero sees through the temptress's *wiles* and returns to his sweetheart back home.

wily ADJ. cunning; artful. She is as *wily* as a fox in avoiding trouble.

winnow V. sift; separate good parts from bad. This test will *winnow* out the students who study from those who never open a book.

withdrawn ADJ. introverted; remote. Rebuffed by his colleagues, the initially outgoing young researcher became increasingly *withdrawn*.

wither V. shrivel; decay. Cut flowers are beautiful for a day, but all too soon they *wither*.

withhold V. hold back; desist from giving; keep possession of. The tenants decided to *withhold* a portion of the rent until the landlord kept his promise to renovate the building.

wretch N. miserable person; vile, despicable person. Tina felt sorry for the poor *wretches* who stood shivering in the rain. However, she was furious with that *wretch* Tony, who stood her up.

wry ADJ. twisted; with a humorous twist. We enjoy Dorothy Parker's verse for its *wry* wit.

zeal N. eager enthusiasm. Wang's *zeal* was contagious; soon all his fellow students were busily making posters, inspired by his ardent enthusiasm for the cause. zealous, ADJ.

zenith N. highest point; culmination. When the film star's career was at its *zenith,* she was in such great demand that producers told her to name her own price.

zephyr N. gentle breeze; west wind. When these *zephyrs* blow, it is good to be in an open boat under a full sail.

BASIC WORD PARTS

In addition to reviewing the High-Frequency Word List, what other quick vocabulary-building tactics can you follow when you face a test deadline?

One good approach is to learn how to build up (and tear apart) words. You know that words are made up of other words: the *room* in which you *store* things is the *storeroom;* the person whose job is to *keep* the *books* is the *bookkeeper.*

Just as words are made up of other words, words are also made up of word parts: prefixes, suffixes, and roots. A knowledge of these word parts and their meanings can help you determine the meanings of unfamiliar words.

Most modern English words are derived from Anglo-Saxon (Old English), Latin, and Greek. Because few students nowadays study Latin and Greek (and even fewer study Anglo-Saxon!), the majority of high school juniors and seniors lack a vital tool for unlocking the meaning of unfamiliar words.

Build your vocabulary by mastering basic word parts. Learning thirty key word parts can help you unlock the meaning of over 10,000 words. Learning fifty key word parts can help you unlock the meaning of over 100,000!

COMMON PREFIXES

Prefixes are syllables that precede the root or stem and change or refine its meaning.

Prefix	Meaning	Illustration
ab, abs	from, away from	*abduct* lead away, kidnap *abjure* renounce *abject* degraded, cast down
ad, ac, af, ag, an, ap, as, as, at	to, forward	*adit* entrance *adjure* request earnestly *admit* allow entrance *accord* agreement, harmony *affliction* distress *aggregation* collection *annexation* add to *apparition* ghost *arraignment* indictment *assumption* arrogance, the taking for granted *attendance* presence, the persons present
ambi	both	*ambidextrous* skilled with both hands *ambiguous* of double meaning *ambivalent* having two conflicting emotions
an, a	without	*anarchy* lack of government *anemia* lack of blood *amoral* without moral sense
ante	before	*antecedent* preceding event or word *antediluvian* ancient (before the flood) *antenuptial* before the wedding
anti	against, opposite	*antipathy* hatred *antiseptic* against infection *antithetical* exactly opposite
arch	chief, first	*archetype* original *archbishop* chief bishop *archaeology* study of first or ancient times

Prefix	Meaning	Illustration
be	over, thoroughly	*bedaub* smear over *befuddle* confuse thoroughly *beguile* deceive, charm thoroughly
bi	two	*bicameral* composed of two houses (Congress) *biennial* every two years *bicycle* two-wheeled vehicle
cata	down	*catastrophe* disaster *cataract* waterfall *catapult* hurl (throw down)
circum	around	*circumnavigate* sail around (the globe) *circumspect* cautious (looking around) *circumscribe* limit (place a circle around)
com, co, col, con, cor	with, together	*combine* merge with *commerce* trade with *communicate* correspond with *coeditor* joint editor *collateral* subordinate, connected *conference* meeting *corroborate* confirm
contra, contro	against	*contravene* conflict with *controversy* dispute
de	down, away	*debase* lower in value *decadence* deterioration *decant* pour off
demi	partly, half	*demigod* partly divine being
di	two	*dichotomy* division into two parts *dilemma* choice between two bad alternatives
dia	across	*diagonal* across a figure *diameter* distance across a circle *diagram* outline drawing
dis, dif	not, apart	*discord* lack of harmony *differ* disagree (carry apart) *disparity* condition of inequality; difference
dys	faulty, bad	*dyslexia* faulty ability to read *dyspepsia* indigestion
ex, e	out	*expel* drive out *extirpate* root out *eject* throw out
extra, extro	beyond, outside	*extracurricular* beyond the curriculum *extraterritorial* beyond a nation's bounds *extrovert* person interested chiefly in external objects and actions
hyper	above; excessively	*hyperbole* exaggeration *hyperventilate* breathe at an excessive rate
hypo	beneath; lower	*hypoglycemia* low blood sugar
in, il, im, ir	not	*inefficient* not efficient *inarticulate* not clear or distinct *illegible* not readable *impeccable* not capable of sinning; flawless *irrevocable* not able to be called back

Prefix	Meaning	Illustration
in, il, im, ir	in, on, upon	*invite* call in *illustration* something that makes clear *impression* effect upon mind or feelings *irradiate* shine upon
inter	between, among	*intervene* come between *international* between nations *interjection* a statement thrown in
intra, intro	within	*intramural* within a school *introvert* person who turns within himself
macro	large, long	*macrobiotic* tending to prolong life *macrocosm* the great world (the entire universe)
mega	great, million	*megalomania* delusions of grandeur *megaton* explosive force of a million tons of TNT
meta	involving change	*metamorphosis* change of form
micro	small	*microcosm* miniature universe *microbe* minute organism *microscopic* extremely small
mis	bad, improper	*misdemeanor* minor crime; bad conduct *mischance* unfortunate accident *misnomer* wrong name
mis	hatred	*misanthrope* person who hates mankind *misogynist* woman-hater
mono	one	*monarchy* government by one ruler *monotheism* belief in one god
multi	many	*multifarious* having many parts *multitudinous* numerous
neo	new	*neologism* newly coined word *neophyte* beginner; novice
non	not	*noncommittal* undecided *nonentity* person of no importance
ob, oc, of, op	against	*obloquy* infamy; disgrace *obtrude* push into prominence *occlude* close; block out *offend* insult *opponent* someone who struggles against; foe
olig	few	*oligarchy* government by a few
pan	all, every	*panacea* cure-all *panorama* unobstructed view in all directions
para	beyond, related	*parallel* similar *paraphrase* restate; translate
per	through, completely	*permeable* allowing passage through *pervade* spread throughout
peri	around, near	*perimeter* outer boundary *periphery* edge *periphrastic* stated in a roundabout way
poly	many	*polygamist* person with several spouses *polyglot* speaking several languages

Prefix	Meaning	Illustration
post	after	*postpone* delay *posterity* generations that follow *posthumous* after death
pre	before	*preamble* introductory statement *prefix* word part placed before a root/stem *premonition* forewarning
prim	first	*primordial* existing at the dawn of time *primogeniture* state of being the first born
pro	forward, in favor of	*propulsive* driving forward *proponent* supporter
proto	first	*prototype* first of its kind
pseudo	false	*pseudonym* pen name
re	again, back	*reiterate* repeat *reimburse* pay back
retro	backward	*retrospect* looking back *retroactive* effective as of a past date
se	away, aside	*secede* withdraw *seclude* shut away *seduce* lead astray
semi	half, partly	*semiannual* every six months *semiconscious* partly conscious
sub, suc, suf, sug, sup, sus	under, less	*subway* underground road *subjugate* bring under control *succumb* yield; cease to resist *suffuse* spread through *suggest* hint *suppress* put down by force *suspend* delay
super, sur	over, above	*supernatural* above natural things *supervise* oversee *surtax* additional tax
syn, sym, syl, sys	with, together	*synchronize* time together *synthesize* combine together *sympathize* pity; identify with *syllogism* explanation of how ideas relate *system* network
tele	far	*telemetry* measurement from a distance *telegraphic* communicated over a distance
trans	across	*transport* carry across *transpose* reverse, move across
ultra	beyond, excessive	*ultramodern* excessively modern *ultracritical* exceedingly critical
un	not	*unfeigned* not pretended; real *unkempt* not combed; disheveled *unwitting* not knowing; unintentional
under	below	*undergird* strengthen underneath *underling* someone inferior

Prefix	Meaning	Illustration
uni	one	*unison* oneness of pitch; complete accord *unicycle* one-wheeled vehicle
vice	in place of	*vicarious* acting as a substitute *viceroy* governor acting in place of a king
with	away, against	*withhold* hold back; keep *withstand* stand up against; resist

COMMON ROOTS AND STEMS

Roots are basic words which have been carried over into English. *Stems* are variations of roots brought about by changes in declension or conjugation.

Root or Stem	Meaning	Illustration
ac, acr	sharp	*acrimonious* bitter; caustic *acerbity* bitterness of temper *acidulate* to make somewhat acid or sour
aev, ev	age, era	*primeval* of the first age *coeval* of the same age or era *medieval or mediaeval* of the middle ages
ag, act	do	*act* deed *agent* doer
agog	leader	*demagogue* false leader of people *pedagogue* teacher (leader of children)
agri, agrari	field	*agrarian* one who works in the field *agriculture* cultivation of fields *peregrination* wandering (through fields)
ali	another	*alias* assumed (another) name *alienate* estrange (turn away from another)
alt	high	*altitude* height *altimeter* instrument for measuring height
alter	other	*altruistic* unselfish, considering others *alter ego* a second self
am	love	*amorous* loving, especially sexually *amity* friendship *amicable* friendly
anim	mind, soul	*animadvert* cast criticism upon *unanimous* of one mind *magnanimity* greatness of mind or spirit
ann, enn	year	*annuity* yearly remittance *biennial* every two years *perennial* present all year; persisting for several years
anthrop	man	*anthropology* study of man *misanthrope* hater of mankind *philanthropy* love of mankind; charity
apt	fit	*aptitude* skill *adapt* make suitable or fit

Root or Stem	Meaning	Illustration
aqua	water	*aqueduct* passageway for conducting water *aquatic* living in water *aqua fortis* nitric acid (strong water)
arch	ruler, first	*archaeology* study of antiquities (study of first things) *monarch* sole ruler *anarchy* lack of government
aster	star	*astronomy* study of the stars *asterisk* starlike type character (*) *disaster* catastrophe (contrary star)
aud, audit	hear	*audible* able to be heard *auditorium* place where people may be heard *audience* hearers
auto	self	*autocracy* rule by one person (self) *automobile* vehicle that moves by itself *autobiography* story of one's own life
belli	war	*bellicose* inclined to fight *belligerent* inclined to wage war *rebellious* resisting authority
ben, bon	good	*benefactor* one who does good deeds *benevolence* charity (wishing good) *bonus* something extra above regular pay
biblio	book	*bibliography* list of books *bibliophile* lover of books *Bible* The Book
bio	life	*biography* writing about a person's life *biology* study of living things *biochemist* student of the chemistry of living things
breve	short	*brevity* briefness *abbreviate* shorten *breviloquent* marked by brevity of speech
cad, cas	to fall	*decadent* deteriorating *cadence* intonation, musical movement *cascade* waterfall
cap, capt, cept, cip	to take	*capture* seize *participate* take part *precept* wise saying (originally a command)
capit, capt	head	*decapitate* remove (cut off) someone's head *captain* chief
carn	flesh	*carnivorous* flesh-eating *carnage* destruction of life *carnal* fleshly
ced, cess	to yield, to go	*recede* go back, withdraw *antecedent* that which goes before *process* go forward
celer	swift	*celerity* swiftness *decelerate* reduce swiftness *accelerate* increase swiftness

Root or Stem	Meaning	Illustration
cent	one hundred	*century* one hundred years *centennial* hundredth anniversary *centipede* many-footed, wingless animal
chron	time	*chronology* timetable of events *anachronism* a thing out of time sequence *chronicle* register events in order of time
cid, cis	to cut, to kill	*incision* a cut (surgical) *homicide* killing of a man *fratricide* killing of a brother
cit, citat	to call, to start	*incite* stir up, start up *excite* stir up *recitation* a recalling (or repeating) aloud
civi	citizen	*civilization* society of citizens, culture *civilian* member of community *civil* courteous
clam, clamat	to cry out	*clamorous* loud *declamation* speech *acclamation* shouted approval
claud, claus, clos, clud	to close	*claustrophobia* fear of close places *enclose* close in *conclude* finish
cognosc, cognit	to learn	*agnostic* lacking knowledge, skeptical *incognito* traveling under assumed name *cognition* knowledge
compl	to fill	*complete* filled out *complement* that which completes something *comply* fulfill
cord	heart	*accord* agreement (from the heart) *cordial* friendly *discord* lack of harmony
corpor	body	*incorporate* organize into a body *corporeal* pertaining to the body, fleshly *corpse* dead body
cred, credit	to believe	*incredulous* not believing, skeptical *credulity* gullibility *credence* belief
cur	to care	*curator* person who has the care of something *sinecure* position without responsibility *secure* safe
curr, curs	to run	*excursion* journey *cursory* brief *precursor* forerunner
da, dat	to give	*data* facts, statistics *mandate* command *date* given time
deb, debit	to owe	*debt* something owed *indebtedness* debt *debenture* bond

Root or Stem	Meaning	Illustration
dem	people	*democracy* rule of the people *demagogue* (false) leader of the people *epidemic* widespread (among the people)
derm	skin	*epidermis* skin *pachyderm* thick-skinned quadruped *dermatology* study of skin and its disorders
di, diurn	day	*diary* a daily record of activities, feelings, etc. *diurnal* pertaining to daytime
dic, dict	to say	*abdicate* renounce *diction* speech *verdict* statement of jury
doc, doct	to teach	*docile* obedient; easily taught *document* something that provides evidence *doctor* learned person (originally, teacher)
domin	to rule	*dominate* have power over *domain* land under rule *dominant* prevailing
duc, duct	to lead	*viaduct* arched roadway *aqueduct* artificial waterway
dynam	power, strength	*dynamic* powerful *dynamite* powerful explosive *dynamo* engine making electrical power
ego	I	*egoist* person who is self-interested *egotist* selfish person *egocentric* revolving about self
erg, urg	work	*energy* power *ergatocracy* rule of the workers *metallurgy* science and technology of metals
err	to wander	*error* mistake *erratic* not reliable, wandering *knight-errant* wandering knight
eu	good, well, beautiful	*eupeptic* having good digestion *eulogize* praise *euphemism* substitution of pleasant way of saying something blunt
fac, fic, fec, fect	to make, to do	*factory* place where things are made *fiction* manufactured story *affect* cause to change
fall, fals	to deceive	*fallacious* misleading *infallible* not prone to error, perfect *falsify* lie
fer, lat	to bring, to bear	*transfer* bring from one place to another *translate* bring from one language to another *conifer* bearing cones, as pine trees
fid	belief, faith	*infidel* nonbeliever, heathen *confidence* assurance, belief
fin	end, limit	*confine* keep within limits *finite* having definite limits

Root or Stem	Meaning	Illustration
flect, flex	bend	*flexible* able to bend *deflect* bend away, turn aside
fort	luck, chance	*fortuitous* accidental, occurring by chance *fortunate* lucky
fort	strong	*fortitude* strength, firmness of mind *fortification* strengthening *fortress* stronghold
frag, fract	break	*fragile* easily broken *infraction* breaking of a rule *fractious* unruly, tending to break rules
fug	flee	*fugitive* someone who flees *refuge* shelter, home for someone fleeing
fus	pour	*effusive* gushing, pouring out *diffuse* widespread (poured in many directions)
gam	marriage	*monogamy* marriage to one person *bigamy* marriage to two people at the same time *polygamy* having many wives or husbands at the same time
gen, gener	class, race	*genus* group of animals with similar traits *generic* characteristic of a class *gender* class organized by sex
grad, gress	go, step	*digress* go astray (from the main point) *regress* go backwards *gradual* step by step, by degrees
graph, gram	writing	*epigram* pithy statement *telegram* instantaneous message over great distance *stenography* shorthand (writing narrowly)
greg	flock, herd	*gregarious* tending to group together, as in a herd *aggregate* group, total *egregious* conspicuously bad; shocking
helio	sun	*heliotrope* flower that faces the sun *heliograph* instrument that uses the sun's rays to send signals
it, itiner	journey, road	*exit* way out *itinerary* plan of journey
jac, jact, jec	to throw	*projectile* missile; something thrown forward *trajectory* path taken by thrown object *ejaculatory* casting or throwing out
jur, jurat	to swear	*perjure* testify falsely *jury* group of men and women sworn to seek the truth *adjuration* solemn urging
labor, laborat	to work	*laboratory* place where work is done *collaborate* work together with others *laborious* difficult
leg, lect, lig	to choose, to read	*election* choice *legible* able to be read *eligible* able to be selected

Root or Stem	Meaning	Illustration
leg	law	*legislature* law-making body *legitimate* lawful *legal* lawful
liber, libr	book	*library* collection of books *libretto* the "book" of a musical play *libel* slander (originally found in a little book)
liber	free	*liberation* the act of setting free *liberal* generous (giving freely); tolerant
log	word, study	*entomology* study of insects *etymology* study of word parts and derivations *monologue* speech by one person
loqu, locut	to talk	*soliloquy* speech by one individual *loquacious* talkative *elocution* speech
luc	light	*elucidate* enlighten *lucid* clear *translucent* allowing some light to pass through
magn	great	*magnify* enlarge *magnanimity* generosity, greatness of soul *magnitude* greatness, extent
mal	bad	*malevolent* wishing evil *malediction* curse *malefactor* evildoer
man	hand	*manufacture* create (make by hand) *manuscript* written by hand *emancipate* free (let go from the hand)
mar	sea	*maritime* connected with seafaring *submarine* undersea craft *mariner* seaman
mater, matr	mother	*maternal* pertaining to motherhood *matriarch* female ruler of a family, group, or state *matrilineal* descended on the mother's side
mit, miss	to send	*missile* projectile *dismiss* send away *transmit* send across
mob, mot, mov	move	*mobilize* cause to move *motility* ability to move *immovable* not able to be moved
mon, monit	to warn	*admonish* warn *premonition* foreboding *monitor* watcher (warner)
mori, mort	to die	*mortuary* funeral parlor *moribund* dying *immortal* not dying
morph	shape, form	*amorphous* formless, lacking shape *metamorphosis* change of shape *anthropomorphic* in the shape of man

Root or Stem	Meaning	Illustration
mut	change	*immutable* not able to be changed *mutate* undergo a great change *mutability* changeableness, inconstancy
nat	born	*innate* from birth *prenatal* before birth *nativity* birth
nav	ship	*navigate* sail a ship *circumnavigate* sail around the world *naval* pertaining to ships
neg	deny	*negation* denial *renege* deny, go back on one's word *renegade* turncoat, traitor
nomen	name	*nomenclature* act of naming, terminology *nominal* in name only (as opposed to actual) *cognomen* surname, distinguishing nickname
nov	new	*novice* beginner *renovate* make new again *novelty* newness
omni	all	*omniscient* all-knowing *omnipotent* all-powerful *omnivorous* eating everything
oper	to work	*operate* work *cooperation* working together
pac	peace	*pacify* make peaceful *pacific* peaceful *pacifist* person opposed to war
pass	feel	*dispassionate* free of emotion *impassioned* emotion-filled *impassive* showing no feeling
pater, patr	father	*patriotism* love of one's country (fatherland) *patriarch* male ruler of a family, group, or state *paternity* fatherhood
path	disease, feeling	*pathology* study of diseased tissue *apathetic* lacking feeling; indifferent *antipathy* hostile feeling
ped, pod	foot	*impediment* stumbling block; hindrance *tripod* three-footed stand *quadruped* four-footed animal
ped	child	*pedagogue* teacher of children *pediatrician* children's doctor
pel, puls	to drive	*compulsion* a forcing to do *repel* drive back *expel* drive out, banish
pet, petit	to seek	*petition* request *appetite* craving, desire *compete* vie with others

Root or Stem	Meaning	Illustration
phil	love	*philanthropist* benefactor, lover of humanity *Anglophile* lover of everything English *philanderer* one involved in brief love affairs
pon, posit	to place	*postpone* place after *positive* definite, unquestioned (definitely placed)
port, portat	to carry	*portable* able to be carried *transport* carry across *export* carry out (of country)
poten	able, powerful	*omnipotent* all-powerful *potentate* powerful person *impotent* powerless
psych	mind	*psychology* study of the mind *psychosis* mental disorder *psychopath* mentally ill person
put, putat	to trim, to calculate	*putative* supposed (calculated) *computation* calculation *amputate* cut off
quer, ques, quir, quis	to ask	*inquiry* investigation *inquisitive* questioning *query* question
reg, rect	rule	*regicide* murder of a ruler *regent* ruler *insurrection* rebellion; overthrow of a ruler
rid, ris	to laugh	*derision* scorn *risibility* inclination to laughter *ridiculous* deserving to be laughed at
rog, rogat	to ask	*interrogate* question *prerogative* privilege
rupt	to break	*interrupt* break into *bankrupt* insolvent *rupture* a break
sacr	holy	*sacred* holy *sacrilegious* impious, violating something holy *sacrament* religious act
sci	to know	*science* knowledge *omniscient* knowing all *conscious* aware
scop	watch, see	*periscope* device for seeing around corners *microscope* device for seeing small objects
scrib, script	to write	*transcribe* make a written copy *script* written text *circumscribe* write around, limit
sect	cut	*dissect* cut apart *bisect* cut into two pieces
sed, sess	to sit	*sedentary* inactive (sitting) *session* meeting

Root or Stem	Meaning	Illustration
sent, sens	to think, to feel	*consent* agree *resent* show indignation *sensitive* showing feeling
sequi, secut, seque	to follow	*consecutive* following in order *sequence* arrangement *sequel* that which follows *non sequitur* something that does not follow logically
solv, solut	to loosen	*absolve* free from blame *dissolute* morally lax *absolute* complete (not loosened)
somn	sleep	*insomnia* inability to sleep *somnolent* sleepy *somnambulist* sleepwalker
soph	wisdom	*philosopher* lover of wisdom *sophisticated* worldly wise
spec, spect	to look at	*spectator* observer *aspect* appearance *circumspect* cautious (looking around)
spir	breathe	*respiratory* pertaining to breathing *spirited* full of life (breath)
string, strict	bind	*stringent* strict *constrict* become tight *stricture* limit, something that restrains
stru, struct	build	*constructive* helping to build *construe* analyze (how something is built)
tang, tact, ting	to touch	*tangent* touching *contact* touching with, meeting *contingent* depending upon
tempor	time	*contemporary* at same time *extemporaneous* impromptu *temporize* delay
ten, tent	to hold	*tenable* able to be held *tenure* holding of office *retentive* holding; having a good memory
term	end	*interminable* endless *terminate* end
terr	land	*terrestrial* pertaining to earth *subterranean* underground
therm	heat	*thermostat* instrument that regulates heat *diathermy* sending heat through body tissues
tors, tort	twist	*distort* twist out of true shape or meaning *torsion* act of twisting *tortuous* twisting
tract	drag, pull	*distract* pull (one's attention) away *intractable* stubborn, unable to be dragged *attraction* pull, drawing quality

Root or Stem	Meaning	Illustration
trud, trus	push, shove	*intrude* push one's way in *protrusion* something sticking out
urb	city	*urban* pertaining to a city *urbane* polished, sophisticated (pertaining to a city dweller) *suburban* outside of a city
vac	empty	*vacuous* lacking content, empty-headed *evacuate* compel to empty an area
vad, vas	go	*invade* enter in a hostile fashion *evasive* not frank; eluding
veni, vent, ven	to come	*intervene* come between *prevent* stop *convention* meeting
ver	true	*veracious* truthful *verify* check the truth *verisimilitude* appearance of truth
verb	word	*verbose* wordy *verbiage* excessive use of words *verbatim* word for word
vers, vert	turn	*vertigo* turning dizzy *revert* turn back (to an earlier state) *diversion* something causing one to turn aside
via	way	*deviation* departure from the way *viaduct* roadway (arched) *trivial* trifling (small talk at crossroads)
vid, vis	to see	*vision* sight *evidence* things seen *vista* view
vinc, vict, vanq	to conquer	*invincible* unconquerable *victory* winning *vanquish* defeat
viv, vit	alive	*vivisection* operating on living animals *vivacious* full of life *vitality* liveliness
voc, vocat	to call	*avocation* calling, minor occupation *provocation* calling or rousing the anger of *invocation* calling in prayer
vol	wish	*malevolent* wishing someone ill *voluntary* of one's own will
volv, volut	to roll	*revolve* roll around *evolve* roll out, develop *convolution* coiled state

COMMON SUFFIXES

Suffixes are syllables that are added to a word. Occasionally, they change the meaning of the word; more frequently, they serve to change the grammatical form of the word (noun to adjective, adjective to noun, noun to verb).

Suffix	Meaning	Illustration
able, ible	capable of (adjective suffix)	*portable* able to be carried *interminable* not able to be limited *legible* able to be read
ac, ic	like, pertaining to (adjective suffix)	*cardiac* pertaining to the heart *aquatic* pertaining to the water *dramatic* pertaining to the drama
acious, icious	full of (adjective suffix)	*audacious* full of daring *perspicacious* full of mental perception *avaricious* full of greed
al	pertaining to (adjective or noun suffix)	*maniacal* insane *final* pertaining to the end *logical* pertaining to logic
ant, ent	full of (adjective or noun suffix)	*eloquent* pertaining to fluid, effective speech *suppliant* pleader (person full of requests) *verdant* green
ary	like, connected with (adjective or noun suffix)	*dictionary* book connected with words *honorary* with honor *luminary* celestial body
ate	to make (verb suffix)	*consecrate* to make holy *enervate* to make weary *mitigate* to make less severe
ation	that which is (noun suffix)	*exasperation* irritation *irritation* annoyance
cy	state of being (noun suffix)	*democracy* government ruled by the people *obstinacy* stubbornness *accuracy* correctness
eer, er, or	person who (noun suffix)	*mutineer* person who rebels *lecher* person who lusts *censor* person who deletes improper remarks
escent	becoming (adjective suffix)	*evanescent* tending to vanish *pubescent* arriving at puberty
fic	making, doing (adjective suffix)	*terrific* arousing great fear *soporific* causing sleep
fy	to make (verb suffix)	*magnify* enlarge *petrify* turn to stone *beautify* make beautiful
iferous	producing, bearing (adjective suffix)	*pestiferous* carrying disease *vociferous* bearing a loud voice
il, ile	pertaining to, capable of (adjective suffix)	*puerile* pertaining to a boy or child *ductile* capable of being hammered or drawn *civil* polite
ism	doctrine, belief (noun suffix)	*monotheism* belief in one god *fanaticism* excessive zeal; extreme belief

Suffix	Meaning	Illustration
ist	dealer, doer (noun suffix)	*fascist* one who believes in a fascist state *realist* one who is realistic *artist* one who deals with art
ity	state of being (noun suffix)	*annuity* yearly grant *credulity* state of being unduly willing to believe *sagacity* wisdom
ive	like (adjective suffix)	*expensive* costly *quantitative* concerned with quantity *effusive* gushing
ize, ise	make (verb suffix)	*victimize* make a victim of *rationalize* make rational *harmonize* make harmonious *enfranchise* make free or set free
oid	resembling, like (adjective suffix)	*ovoid* like an egg *anthropoid* resembling man *spheroid* resembling a sphere
ose	full of (adjective suffix)	*verbose* full of words *lachrymose* full of tears
osis	condition (noun suffix)	*psychosis* diseased mental condition *neurosis* nervous condition *hypnosis* condition of induced sleep
ous	full of (adjective suffix)	*nauseous* full of nausea *ludicrous* foolish
tude	state of (noun suffix)	*fortitude* state of strength *beatitude* state of blessedness *certitude* state of sureness

PART FOUR

Mathematics

▶ **CHAPTER 7 :** **Introduction to the Mathematics Sections**

▶ **CHAPTER 8 :** **Tactics and Strategies**

▶ **CHAPTER 9 :** **Review of PSAT Mathematics**

► CHAPTER 7
Introduction to the Mathematics Sections

Part Four consists of three chapters. This first brief chapter serves as an introduction to the mathematics part of the PSAT. Please do not skip it—take the few minutes necessary to carefully read everything in this chapter. It gives some valuable information about the organization of the math part of this book, as well as some important information about the test itself. It discusses the use of calculators on the test and explains the directions for both types of math questions.

Chapter 8 includes a discussion of all the essential tactics and strategies that good test takers need to know to do their best on the math part of the PSAT. The explanation of each tactic is followed by sample problems to solve using that particular tactic. The chapter ends with a set of exercises to test your understanding of the tactics discussed. If you master Chapter 8, you will be able to significantly improve your score on the math part of the PSAT.

Chapter 9 contains a review of the mathematics you need to know in order to do well on the PSAT, as well as hundreds of sample problems patterned on actual test questions. The chapter is conveniently divided into eighteen short sections (Section A through Section R), each on a different topic—percents, ratios, averages, triangles, circles, and so on.

WHEN TO STUDY CHAPTER 9

How much time you initially devote to Chapter 9 should depend on your math skills. If you are an excellent student who consistently earns A's in math class, you can skip the instructional parts of Chapter 9 for now. If, while doing the model tests in Part Six, you find that you keep making mistakes on certain types of problems (averages, percents, geometry, for example) or they take you too long, you should study the appropriate sections of Chapter 9. Even if your math skills are excellent and you don't need the review, you should do the sample questions in those sections; they are an excellent source of additional PSAT questions. If you know that your math skills are not very good, it is advisable to review the material in Chapter 9 and work out the problems *before* tackling the model tests in Part Six.

No matter how good you are in math, *you should carefully read Chapter 8*. In that chapter you will learn techniques for (1) getting the correct answer to problems that you don't know how to solve and (2) getting the correct answer more quickly on those that you do know how to do.

➐ AN IMPORTANT SYMBOL

Throughout the book, the symbol $\Rightarrow$ is used to indicate that one step in the solution of a problem follows *immediately* from the preceding one and that no explanation is necessary. You should read

$2x = 12 \Rightarrow x = 6$ as

$2x = 12$, *which implies that* $x = 6$, or, *since* $2x = 12$, *then* $x = 6$.

Here is a sample solution to the following problem using $\Rightarrow$:

What is the value of $3x^2 - 7$ when $x = -5$?

$x = -5 \Rightarrow x^2 = (-5)^2 = 25 \Rightarrow 3x^2 = 3(25) = 75 \Rightarrow 3x^2 - 7 = 75 - 7 = 68.$

When the reason for a step is not obvious, $\Rightarrow$ is not used; rather, an explanation is given, often including a reference to a **KEY FACT** from Chapter 9. In many solutions, some steps are explained, while others are linked by the $\Rightarrow$ symbol, as in the following example:

In the diagram at the right, if $w = 10$, what is the value of z?

- By **KEY FACT J1**, $w + x + y = 180$.
- Since $\triangle ABC$ is isosceles, $x = y$ [**KEY FACT J5**].
- Therefore, $w + 2y = 180 \Rightarrow 10 + 2y = 180 \Rightarrow 2y = 170 \Rightarrow y = 85$.
- Finally, since $y + z = 180$ [**KEY FACT I2**], $85 + z = 180 \Rightarrow z = 95$.

USE OF THE CALCULATOR

Before doing all the work in Part Four and the Model Tests in Part Five, you should reread the short discussion in Chapter 1 on the use of calculators on the PSAT. As you do the sample problems in this book, always have with you the same calculator you intend to use during the actual exam, and use it whenever you feel it is appropriate. Throughout the rest of the book, whenever the use of a calculator is recommended or whenever most students would probably use their calculator, the icon ▦ has been placed next to examples and questions. We stress that *no problem requires the use of a calculator*, but there are several for which it is helpful.

Because students' mathematical knowledge and arithmetic skills vary considerably, the decision as to when to use a calculator is very subjective. Consider the following rather easy problem. Would you use a calculator?

EXAMPLE

What is the average (arithmetic mean) of 301, 303, and 305?

Let's analyze the four possibilities.

1. Some students would use their calculator twice:
   first to add $\qquad$ $301 + 303 + 305 = 909$
   then to divide $\qquad$ $909 \div 3 = 303$
2. Others would use their calculators just once: to add the numbers. They would then divide mentally.
3. Others would not use their calculators at all, because they can add the three numbers mentally faster than they can on a calculator. (Just say to yourself: 300, 300, and 300 is 900; and $1 + 3 + 5$ is 9 more.)
4. Finally, others would not perform any calculations. Having read Section 9-E, they would know that the average of three consecutive odd integers is always the middle one: 301, **303**, 305.

NOTE that the more you use your calculator, the *longer* it takes to solve the problem. Use your calculator only when it will really save you time or if you think you will make a mistake without it. Note that although the *preferred* solution to the preceding problem did not use a calculator at all, we would have placed a calculator icon in the margin, indicating that a calculator *could* have been used.

HELPFUL HINT *In general, you should do very little arithmetic using paper and pencil. If you can't do it mentally, use your calculator. In particular, avoid long division and multiplication in which the factors have two or more digits. If you know that $15^2 = 225$, terrific; if not, it is better to use your calculator than to multiply with paper and pencil.*

DIRECTIONS FOR MATHEMATICS SECTIONS

On the first page of Section 2 (the first math section), you will see the following instructions for multiple-choice questions.

Multiple-Choice Directions

For each question in this section, determine which of the five choices is correct and blacken that choice on your answer sheet. You may use any blank space on the page for your work.

NOTES:
- You may use a calculator whenever you believe it will be helpful.
- Use the diagrams provided to help you solve the problems. Unless you see the phrase

Note: Figure not drawn to scale

under a diagram, it has been drawn as accurately as possible. Unless it is stated that a figure is three dimensional, you may assume that it lies in a plane.

On the first page of Section 4 (the second math section), you will see these exact same directions for questions 21–28.

In the middle of Section 4 of your PSAT, you will see the following directions for handling questions 29–38, the student-produced response questions, the only questions on the PSAT that are not multiple-choice. Because the answers to these questions are entered in special grids, they are usually referred to as grid-in questions.

Student-Produced Response Directions

In questions 29–38, first solve the problem, and then enter your answer on the grid provided on the answer sheet. The instructions for entering your answers follow.

- First, write your answer in the boxes at the top of the grid.
- Second, grid your answer in the columns below the boxes.
- Use the fraction bar in the first row or the decimal point in the second row to enter fractions and decimals.

- Grid only one space in each column.
- Entering the answer in the boxes is recommended as an aid in gridding but is not required.
- The machine scoring your exam can read only what you grid, so you **must grid-in your answers correctly to get credit.**
- If a question has more than one correct answer, grid-in only one of them.
- The grid does not have a minus sign; so no answer can be negative.
- A mixed number *must* be converted to an improper fraction or a decimal before it is gridded. Enter $1\frac{1}{4}$ as $\frac{5}{4}$ or 1.25; the machine will interpret 11/4 as $\frac{11}{4}$ and mark it wrong.

- **All decimals must be entered as accurately as possible.** Here are three acceptable ways of gridding

$$\frac{3}{11} = 0.272727\ldots$$

- Note that rounding to .273 is acceptable because you are using the full grid, but you would receive **no credit** for .3 or .27, because they are less accurate.

In addition to the directions for multiple-choice questions, the first page of each math section has a box labeled "Reference" that contains the following mathematical facts:

Reference

$A = \pi r^2$
$C = 2\pi r$

$A = \ell w$

$A = \frac{1}{2}bh$

$V = \ell wh$

$V = \pi r^2 h$

$c^2 = a^2 + b^2$

Special Right Triangles

Number of degrees of arc in a circle: 360
Sum of the measures, in degrees, of the angles of a triangle: 180

Many books advise that since these formulas are printed in the exam booklet, students can always look them up as needed and, therefore, don't have to learn or review them. Even the College Board's official guide, *Taking the SAT Reasoning Test*, states:

The test doesn't require you to memorize formulas. Commonly used formulas are provided in the test booklet at the beginning of each mathematical section.

This is very poor advice. During the test, you don't want to spend any of your valuable time looking up facts that you can learn now. All of these "commonly used formulas" and other important facts are presented in Chapter 9, where each of them is highlighted and identified as a "Reference Fact." As you learn and review these facts, you should commit them to memory.

INSTRUCTIONS FOR GRID-IN QUESTIONS

On the math part of the PSAT, questions 29–38 are the student-produced response questions. This is the type of question that is most familiar—you solve a problem and then write the answer on your answer sheet. The only difference is that on the PSAT, *after* you write the answer on your answer sheet, you must then enter the answer on a special grid that can be read by a computer. For this reason, these questions are usually referred to as grid-ins.

To be sure you get credit for these questions, you need to know the guidelines for gridding-in your answers. Not all of this information is given in the directions printed in the exam booklet; so you should carefully read each of the ten rules below.

Your answer sheet will have ten grids, one for each question. Each one will look like the grid shown here. After solving a problem, the first step is to write the answer in the four boxes at the top of the grid. You then blacken the appropriate space under each box. For example, if your answer to a question is 2450, you write 2450 at the top of the grid, one digit in each box, and then in each column blacken the space that contains the number you wrote at the top of the column. This is not difficult, but there are some special rules concerning grid-in questions; so let's go over them before you practice gridding-in some numbers.

1. The only symbols that appear in the grid are the digits 0 to 9, a decimal point, and a slash (/), used to write fractions. Keep in mind that, since there is no negative sign, *the answer to every grid-in question must be a positive number or 0.*

2. You will receive credit for a correct answer no matter where you grid it. For example, the answer 17 could be gridded in any of three positions:

Nevertheless, we suggest that you consistently *write all your answers* the way numbers are usually displayed—*to the right, with blank spaces at the left.*

3. *Never round off your answers.* If a decimal answer will fit in the grid and you round it off, your answer will be marked wrong. For example, if the answer is .148 and you rounded it to the nearest hundredth and entered .15, you would receive *no credit.* If a decimal answer will not fit in the grid, enter a decimal point in the first column, followed by the first three digits. For example, if your answer is 0.373737 . . . , enter it as .373. You would receive credit if you rounded it to .374, but don't. You might occasionally make a mistake in rounding, whereas you'll *never* make a mistake if you just copy the first three digits. **Note:** If the correct answer has more than two decimal digits, *you must use all four columns of the grid.*

4. *Never write a 0 before the decimal point.* The first column of the grid doesn't even have a 0 in it. If the correct answer is 0.3333 . . . , you must grid it as .333. You can't grid 0.33, and 0.3 is not accurate enough.

5. *Never simplify fractions.*
   - If your answer is a fraction that will fit in the grid, such as $\frac{2}{3}$ or $\frac{4}{18}$ or $\frac{6}{34}$, *just enter it.* Don't waste time reducing it or converting it to a decimal.
   - If your answer is a fraction that won't fit in the grid, do not attempt to reduce it; use your calculator to *convert it to a decimal.* For example, $\frac{24}{65}$ won't fit in a grid; it would require five spaces: 2 4 / 6 5. Do not waste even a few seconds trying to reduce it; just divide on your calculator, and enter .369. Unlike $\frac{24}{65}$, the fraction $\frac{24}{64}$ *can be reduced*—to $\frac{12}{32}$, which doesn't help, or to $\frac{6}{16}$ or $\frac{3}{8}$, both of which could be entered. *Don't do it!* It takes time, and you might make a mistake. You won't make a mistake if you just use your calculator: 24 ÷ 64 = .375.

6. *Be aware that you can never enter a mixed number.* If your answer is $2\frac{1}{2}$, you *cannot* leave a space and enter it as 2 1/2. Also if you enter 2 1 / 2 , the machine will read it as $\frac{21}{2}$ and mark it wrong. You must enter $2\frac{1}{2}$ as the improper fraction $\frac{5}{2}$ or as the decimal 2.5.

7. Sometimes grid-in questions have more than one correct answer. On these questions you are to *grid-in only one of the acceptable answers.* For example, if a question asked for a positive number less than 100 which was divisible by both 5 and 7, you could enter *either* 35 *or* 70, but not both.

8. There is no penalty for a wrong answer to a grid-in question. Therefore, you might as well guess.

9. Be sure to *grid every answer carefully.* The computer does not read what you have written in the boxes; it reads only the answer in the grid. If the correct answer to a question is 100 and you write 100 in the boxes but accidentally grid-in 200, you get *no* credit.

10. If you know that the answer to a question is 100, can you just grid it in and not bother writing it on top? Yes, you will get full credit, and so some books recommend that you don't waste time writing the answer. This is terrible advice. Instead, *write each answer in the boxes.* It takes less than two seconds per answer to do

this, and it definitely cuts down on careless errors in gridding. More important, if you go back to check your work, it is much easier to read what's in the boxes than what's in the grid.

Now, check your understanding of these guidelines. Use the empty grids below to enter each of the following numbers.

1. 123

2. $\frac{7}{11}$

3. $2\frac{3}{4}$

4. $\frac{8}{30}$

5. 0

6. $\frac{48}{80}$

7. 1.1111 . . .

8. $\frac{19}{15}$

Solutions. Each grid contains the answer we recommend. Other acceptable answers, if any, are written below each grid.

1. **1 2 3**

   or _1 2 3_

2. **7 / 1 1**

   or _. 6 3 6_

3. **2 . 7 5**

   or _1 1 / 4_

4. **8 / 3 0**

   or _4 / 1 5_
   or _. 2 6 6_
   or _. 2 6 7_

5. **0**

6. **. 6**

   or _6 / 1 0_
   or _3 / 5_

7. **1 . 1 1**

   or _1 0 / 9_

8. **1 . 2 6**

   or _1 . 2 7_

If you missed even one of these, go back and reread the rules on gridding. *You never want to have a correct answer and get no credit because you didn't grid it properly.* When you do the grid-in problems on the practice PSATs in this book, actually grid in the answers. Make sure you understand all of these rules *now*. When you actually take the PSAT, don't even look at the gridding instructions.

► CHAPTER 8
Tactics and Strategies

In this chapter you will learn important strategies to help you answer both the multiple-choice and grid-in questions on the PSAT. However, as invaluable as these tactics are, use them only when you need them. *If you know how to solve a problem and are confident that you can do so accurately and reasonably quickly, JUST DO IT!*

TACTIC 8-1 / Test the choices, starting with C

TACTIC 8-1, often called *backsolving*, is useful when you are asked to solve for an unknown and you understand what needs to be done to answer the question but you want to avoid doing the algebra. The idea is simple: Test the various choices to see which one is correct.

NOTE: On the PSAT the answers to virtually all numerical multiple-choice questions are listed in either increasing or decreasing order. Consequently, Choice C is the middle value, and in applying **TACTIC 8-1**, *you should always start with Choice C*. For example, assume that Choices A, B, C, D, and E are given in increasing order. Try Choice C. If it works, you've found the answer. If Choice C doesn't work, you should know whether you need to test a larger number or a smaller one, and that information permits you to eliminate two more choices. If Choice C is too small, you need a larger number, and so Choices A and B are out; if Choice C is too big, eliminate Choices D and E, which are even larger.

Examples 1 and 2 illustrate the proper use of **TACTIC 8-1**.

EXAMPLE 1

If the average (arithmetic mean) of 5, 6, 7, and x is 10, what is the value of x?

(A) 8   (B) 13   (C) 18   (D) 22   (E) 28

Solution. Use **TACTIC 8-1**. Test Choice C: $x = 18$.

- Is the average of 5, 6, 7, and 18 equal to 10?
- No: $\frac{5 + 6 + 7 + 18}{4} = \frac{36}{4} = 9$, which is *too small*.
- Eliminate Choice C, and, since for the average to be 10, x must be *greater* than 18, eliminate Choices A and B, as well.
- Try Choice D: $x = 22$. Is the average of 5, 6, 7, and 22, equal to 10?
- Yes: $\frac{5 + 6 + 7 + 22}{4} = \frac{40}{4} = 10$. The answer is Choice D.

Remember that every problem that can be solved using **TACTIC 8-1** can be solved directly, usually in less time. Therefore, we again stress: *If you are confident that you can solve a problem quickly and accurately, just do so.*

See Section 9-E on averages for two direct methods for solving Example 1, each of which is *faster* than backsolving. If you know either method, you should use it, and save **TACTIC 8-1** for those problems that you can't easily solve directly.

EXAMPLE 2

Judy is now twice as old as Adam, but six years ago, she was five times as old as he was. How old is Judy now?

(A) 8   (B) 16   (C) 20   (D) 24   (E) 32

Solution. Use **TACTIC 8-1** and backsolve starting with Choice C. If Judy is now 20, Adam is 10, and six years ago, they would have been 14 and 4. Since Judy would have been less than five times as old as Adam, eliminate Choices C, D, and E, and try a smaller value. If Judy is now 16, Adam is 8; six years ago, they would have been 10 and 2. That's it; 10 *is* five times 2. The answer is Choice B. (See Example 4 in Section 9-H on word problems for the correct algebraic solution.)

Some tactics allow you to eliminate a few choices so that you can make an educated guess. On those problems where it can be used, **TACTIC 8-1** *always* gets you the right answer. The only reason not to use it on a particular problem is that you can *easily* solve the problem directly.

TACTIC **8-2 / Replace variables with numbers**

Mastery of **TACTIC 8-2** is critical for anyone developing good test-taking skills. This tactic can be used whenever the five choices involve the variables in the question. There are three steps:

1. Replace each letter with an easy-to-use number.
2. Solve the problem using those numbers.
3. Evaluate each of the five choices with the numbers you chose to see which choice is equal to the answer you obtained.

Examples 3 and 4 illustrate the proper use of **TACTIC 8-2**.

EXAMPLE 3

If a is equal to the sum of b and c, which of the following is equal to the difference of b and c?

(A) $a - b - c$ (B) $a - b + c$ (C) $a - c$ (D) $a - 2c$ (E) $a - b - 2c$

Solution.

- Choose three easy-to-use numbers that satisfy $a = b + c$: for example, $a = 5$, $b = 3$, $c = 2$.
- Then, solve the problem with these numbers: the difference of b and c is $3 - 2 = 1$.
- Finally, check each of the five choices to see which one is equal to 1:
  (A) Does $a - b - c = 1$? No. $5 - 3 - 2 = 0$
  (B) Does $a - b + c = 1$? No. $5 - 3 + 2 = 4$
  (C) Does $a - c = 1$? No. $5 - 2 = 3$
  (D) Does $a - 2c = 1$? Yes! $5 - 2(2) = 5 - 4 = 1$
  (E) Does $a - b - 2c = 1$? No. $5 - 3 - 2(2) = 2 - 4 = -2$
- The answer is Choice D.

EXAMPLE 4

If the sum of five consecutive even integers is t, then, in terms of t, what is the greatest of these integers?

(A) $\frac{t - 20}{5}$ (B) $\frac{t - 10}{5}$ (C) $\frac{t}{5}$ (D) $\frac{t + 10}{5}$ (E) $\frac{t + 20}{5}$

Solution.

- Choose five easy-to-use consecutive even integers: 2, 4, 6, 8, 10. Then their sum, t, is 30.
- Solve the problem with these numbers: the greatest of these integers is 10.
- When $t = 30$, the five choices are $\frac{10}{5}, \frac{20}{5}, \frac{30}{5}, \frac{40}{5}, \frac{50}{5}$.
- Only $\frac{50}{5}$, Choice E, is equal to 10.

Of course, if your algebra skills are good, Examples 3 and 4 can be solved without using **TACTIC 8-2**. The important point is that if you are uncomfortable with the correct algebraic solution, you don't have to omit these questions. You can use **TACTIC 8-2** and *always* get the correct answer.

Example 5 is somewhat different. You are asked to reason through a word problem involving only variables. Most students find problems like this one mind-boggling. Here, the use of **TACTIC 8-2** is essential. Without it, most students would find Example 5 very difficult, if not impossible.

> **HELPFUL HINT** *Replace the letters with numbers that are easy to use, not necessarily ones that make sense. It is perfectly OK to ignore reality. A school can have 2 students, apples can cost 10 dollars each, trains can go 5 miles per hour or 1000 miles per hour—it doesn't matter.*

EXAMPLE 5

A vendor sells h hot dogs and s sodas. If a hot dog costs twice as much as a soda, and if the vendor takes in a total of d dollars, how many *cents* does a soda cost?

(A) $\dfrac{100d}{s + 2h}$　(B) $\dfrac{s + 2h}{100d}$　(C) $\dfrac{100}{d(s + 2h)}$　(D) $100d(s + 2h)$　(E) $\dfrac{d}{100(s + 2h)}$

Solution.

- Replace h, s, and d with three easy-to-use numbers. Suppose a soda costs 50¢ and a hot dog $1.00. Then if he sold 2 sodas and 3 hot dogs, he took in $4.00.
- Which of the choices equals 50 when $s = 2$, $h = 3$, and $d = 4$?
- Only Choice A: $\dfrac{100(4)}{2 + 2(3)} = \dfrac{400}{8} = 50$.

> **HELPFUL HINT** *Of course, when you check the choices, you should use your calculator whenever necessary. However, you do not need to determine the value of each choice; you only need to know if it is the correct choice. In Example 5, Choices B and E are small fractions and could not possibly equal 50, and Choice D is clearly greater than 50; so don't waste your time evaluating them. Only Choices A and C are even possible.*

TACTIC 8-3 / Choose an appropriate number

TACTIC 8-3 is similar to **TACTIC 8-2**, in that we pick convenient numbers. However, no variable is given in the problem. **TACTIC 8-3** is especially useful in problems involving fractions, ratios, and percents.

> **HELPFUL HINT** *In problems involving fractions, the best number to use is the least common denominator of all the fractions. In problems involving percents, the easiest number to use is 100.*

EXAMPLE 6

On a certain college committee, $\frac{2}{3}$ of the members are female and $\frac{3}{8}$ of the females are varsity athletes. If $\frac{3}{5}$ of the committee members are not varsity athletes, what fraction of the members of the committee are male varsity athletes?

(A) $\frac{3}{20}$　(B) $\frac{11}{60}$　(C) $\frac{1}{4}$　(D) $\frac{2}{5}$　(E) $\frac{5}{12}$

Solution. Since the lowest common denominator (LCD) of the three fractions is 120, assume that the committee has 120 members. Then there are $\frac{2}{3} \times 120 = 80$ females. Of the 80 females, $\frac{3}{8} \times 80 = 30$ are varsity athletes. Since $\frac{3}{5} \times 120 = 72$ committee members are not varsity athletes, then $120 - 72 = 48$ are varsity athletes; of these, 30 are female and the other 18 are male. Finally, the fraction of the members of the committee who are male varsity athletes is $\frac{18}{120} = \frac{3}{20}$ (Choice A).

EXAMPLE 7

From 1995 to 2000 the sales of a book decreased by 80%. If the sales in 2005 were the same as in 1995, by what percent did they increase from 2000 to 2005?

(A) 80%   (B) 100%   (C) 120%   (D) 400%   (E) 500%

Solution. Since this problem involves percents, assume that 100 copies of the book were sold in 1995 (and 2005). Sales dropped by 80 (80% of 100) to 20 in 2000 and then increased by 80, from 20 back to 100, in 2005. By **KEY FACT C5**, the percent increase was

$$\frac{\text{the actual increase}}{\text{the original amount}} \times 100\% = \frac{80}{20} \times 100\% = 400\% \text{ (Choice D).}$$

TACTIC
8-4 / Eliminate absurd choices and guess

When you have no idea how to solve a problem, eliminate all the absurd choices and guess from among the remaining ones.

During the course of a PSAT, you will probably find at least a few multiple-choice questions that you read but have no idea how to solve. *Do not automatically omit these questions!* Often two or three of the answers are absurd. Eliminate them and *guess*. Occasionally, four of the choices are absurd. When this occurs, your answer is no longer a guess.

What makes a choice absurd? Here are a few things to note. Even if you don't know how to solve a problem, you may realize that

- the answer must be positive, but some of the choices are negative.
- the answer must be even, but some of the choices are odd.
- a ratio must be less than 1, but some choices are greater than or equal to 1.

Let's look at five examples. In some of them the information given is intentionally insufficient to solve the problem, but you will still be able to determine that some of the answers are absurd. Even when there is enough information to solve the problem, don't. Rather, see if you can determine which choices are absurd and should therefore be eliminated.

EXAMPLE 8

A region inside a semicircle of radius r is shaded. What is its area?

(A) $\frac{1}{4}\pi r^2$ (B) $\frac{1}{3}\pi r^2$ (C) $\frac{1}{2}\pi r^2$ (D) $\frac{2}{3}\pi r^2$ (E) $\frac{3}{4}\pi r^2$

Solution. Even if you have no idea how to find the area of the shaded region, you should know that since the area of a circle is πr^2, the area of a semicircle is $\frac{1}{2}\pi r^2$. So the area of the shaded region must be *less than* $\frac{1}{2}\pi r^2$. Eliminate Choices C, D, and E. On an actual problem, if the diagram is drawn to scale, you may be able to make an educated guess between Choices A and B. If not, just choose one or the other.

EXAMPLE 9

The average of 5, 10, 15, and x is 20. What is x?

(A) 0   (B) 20   (C) 25   (D) 45   (E) 50

Solution. If the average of four numbers is 20, and three of them are less than 20, the other one must be greater than 20. Eliminate Choices A and B and guess. If you further realize that since 5 and 10 are *a lot* less than 20, x will be *a lot* more than 20, then eliminate Choice C, as well.

EXAMPLE 10

A prize of $27,000 is to be divided in some ratio among three people. What is the largest share?

(A) $18,900   (B) $13,500   (C) $8100   (D) $5400   (E) $2700

Solution. If the prize were divided equally, each share would be worth $9000. If it is divided unequally, the largest share must be *more than* $9000; so eliminate Choices C, D, and E. In an actual question, you would be told what the ratio is, and that information might enable you to eliminate Choice A or Choice B. If not, you would just guess.

EXAMPLE 11

A jar contains only red and blue marbles. The ratio of the number of red marbles to the number of blue marbles is 5:3. What percent of the marbles are blue?

(A) 37.5%　(B) 50%　(C) 60%　(D) 62.5%　(E) 80%

Solution. Since there are 5 red marbles for every 3 blue ones, there are fewer blue ones than red ones. Therefore, *fewer than half* (50%) of the marbles are blue. Eliminate Choices B, C, D, and E. The answer is Choice A.

EXAMPLE 12

Square $WXYZ$ is divided into two unequal regions. If $WX = 4$, which of the following could be the area of the larger region?

(A) 8π　(B) $8\pi - 32$　(C) $16 - 8\pi$　(D) $32 - 8\pi$　(E) $8\pi - 16$

Solution. Since the area of the square is 16, the area of the larger region must be more than 8. Since π is slightly more than 3, 8π (which appears in each choice) is somewhat more than 24, approximately 25. Check the choices:

- (A) $8\pi \approx 25$, which is more than the area of the whole square.
- (B) $8\pi - 32$ is negative. Clearly impossible!
- (C) $16 - 8\pi$ is also negative.
- (D) $32 - 8\pi \approx 7$, which is too small.
- (E) $8\pi - 16 \approx 9$. The answer is E.

TACTIC

8-5 / Draw a diagram

On any geometry question for which a figure is not provided, draw one (as accurately as possible) in your test booklet. Often looking at the diagram will lead you to the correct method. Sometimes, as in Example 13 below, a careful examination of the diagram is sufficient to actually determine the correct answer.

EXAMPLE 13

A rectangle is 7 times as long as it is wide. If the width is w, what is the length of a diagonal?

(A) $2w\sqrt{5}$　(B) $5w\sqrt{2}$　(C) $7w$　(D) $8w$　(E) $50w$

Solution. First draw a rectangle that is 7 times as large as it is wide. (By marking off 7 widths, you should be able to do this quite accurately.) Then draw in a diagonal.

You probably realize that you can use the Pythagorean theorem to find the length of the diagonal, but by looking at the diagram, you should see that the diagonal is just slightly larger than the length, $7w$. Now check each answer choice using your calculator when necessary. Clearly, the answer is not $7w$, and $50w$ is way too big. Eliminate choices C and E. Even Choice D, $8w$, is probably too big, but don't eliminate it until you use your calculator to test choices A and B. $2\sqrt{5} \approx 4.5$, which is clearly too small; $5\sqrt{2} \approx 7.07$, which looks just right. Choose B.

8-6 / Use diagrams wisely. If a diagram is drawn to scale, trust it.

Remember that every diagram that appears on the PSAT has been drawn as accurately as possible, *unless* you see "<u>Note:</u> Figure not drawn to scale."

In figures that are drawn to scale, the following are true: Line segments that appear to be the same length, *are* the same length; if an angle clearly looks obtuse, it *is* obtuse; and if one angle appears larger than another, you may assume that it *is* larger.

HELPFUL HINT *On the PSAT, if you know how to solve a geometry problem, just do it directly. However, if you don't and if there is a diagram that has been drawn to scale, do not leave it out. Trusting the diagram to be accurate, you can always eliminate some of the choices and make an educated guess.*

Examples 14, 15, and 16 below all contain diagrams that have been drawn to scale. Of course, each of these relatively easy examples has a correct mathematical solution, but try to answer them by eliminating as many choices as possible by simply looking at the given diagram.

EXAMPLE 14

If in the figure at the right $AB = AC$, what is the value of x?

(A) 135 (B) 125 (C) 115 (D) 65 (E) 50

Solution. Clearly, the angle is obtuse; so x is greater than 90, and so you can immediately eliminate Choices D and E. If you attempt to "measure" x more accurately, by drawing a few lines in the diagram, you can eliminate Choice A and probably Choice B. Choose Choice C.

EXAMPLE 15

In the figure at the right, what is the sum of the measures of all the marked angles?

(A) 360° (B) 540° (C) 720° (D) 900°
(E) 1080°

Solution. Make your best estimate of each angle and add them up. The five choices are so far apart that even if you're off by 15° or more on some of the angles, you'll get the right answer. The sum of the estimates shown is 690°; so the correct answer *must* be 720° (Choice C).

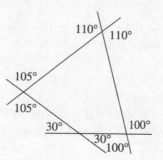

EXAMPLE 16

In the figure at the right, what is the value of x?

(A) 120 (B) 130 (C) 145 (D) 160 (E) 175

Solution. Since the diagram is drawn to scale, trust it. Look at x: it appears to be *about* $90 + 50 = 140$; it is *definitely* less than 160. Also, y is clearly less than 45; so x is greater than 135. The answer must be 145 (Choice C).

TACTIC 8-7 / **Use diagrams wisely. If a diagram is not drawn to scale, redraw it to scale.**

In figures that are not drawn to scale, make *no* assumptions. Lines that look parallel might not be; an angle that appears to be obtuse, might, in fact, be acute; two line segments might have the same length even though one looks twice as long as the other.

In the examples illustrating **TACTIC 8-6**, all of the diagrams were drawn to scale, and we were able to use the diagrams to our advantage. When diagrams have not been drawn to scale, you must be more careful.

> **HELPFUL HINT** *In order to redraw a diagram to scale, ask yourself, "What is wrong with the original diagram?" If an angle is marked 45°, but in the figure it looks like a 75° angle, redraw it. If two line segments appear to be parallel, but you have not been told that they are, redraw them so that they are clearly not parallel. If two segments appear to have the same length, but one is marked 5 and the other 10, redraw them so that the second segment is twice as long as the first.*

EXAMPLE 17

In $\triangle ABC$, what is the value of x?

(A) 15 (B) 30 (C) 45 (D) 60
(E) 75

Note: Figure not drawn to scale

Solution. In what way is this figure not drawn to scale? $AB = 8$ and $BC = 4$, but in the figure, AB is not nearly twice as long as BC. Although the figure is not drawn to scale, the square symbol at angle C indicates that angle C is a right angle. So draw a right triangle in which AB *is* twice as long as BC. Now you can see that x is about 60 (Choice D).

In fact, x is exactly 60. If the hypotenuse of a right triangle is twice the length of one of the legs, then it's a 30-60-90 triangle, and the angle formed by the hypotenuse and that leg is 60° (See Section 9-J).

EXAMPLE 18

In the figure at the right, which of the following statements *could* be true?

I. $AB < AC$
II. $AB > AC$
III. Area of $\triangle ABC = 50$

(A) None (B) I only (C) II only
(D) I and III only (E) II and III only

Note: Figure not drawn to scale

Solution. In the given diagram, AB is longer than AC, which is 10. But, we know that we *cannot trust the diagram*. Actually, there are two things wrong: angle C is labeled 40° but looks much more like 60° or 70°, and AC and BC are each labeled 10, but BC is much longer. Redraw the triangle with a smaller angle and two sides of the same length (see diagram at right).

Now just look: $\overline{AB}$ is clearly shorter than $\overline{AC}$. So I is true and II is false. If you draw in altitude $\overline{AD}$, it is also clear that h is less than 10.

$$A = \tfrac{1}{2}bh = \tfrac{1}{2}(10)h = 5h < 5 \times 10 = 50$$

The area must be less than 50. III is false. Only I is true (Choice B).

TACTIC 8-8 / **Subtract to find shaded regions**

Whenever part of a figure is shaded and part is unshaded, the straightforward way to find the area of the shaded portion is to find the area of the entire figure and subtract from it the area of the unshaded region. Occasionally, you may see an easy way to calculate the shaded area directly, but usually you should subtract.

EXAMPLE 19

In the figure at the right, the shaded region is bounded by two semicircles and two sides of square $ABCD$. If $AB = 2$, what is the area of the shaded region?

(A) $4 - 2\pi$ (B) $4 - \pi$ (C) $4 + 2\pi$
(D) $16 - 4\pi$ (E) $4\pi - 16$

Solution. The entire region is a square whose area is 4. Since each semicircle has a diameter of 2 (hence a radius of 1), together they form a circle of radius 1. The area of such a circle is $\pi(1)^2 = \pi$. So, the area of the shaded region is $4 - \pi$ (Choice B).

TACTIC 8-9 / **Add equations**

When a question involves two equations, almost always the best strategy is to either add them or subtract. If there are three or more equations, just add them.

> *Usually, answering a question that involves two or more equations does not require you to solve them.*

EXAMPLE 20

If $4x + y = 23$ and $x - 2y = 8$, what is the average of x and y?

(A) 0 (B) 2.5 (C) 3 (D) 3.5 (E) 5

Solution. Add the two equations:

$$\begin{array}{r} 4x + y = 23 \\ + x - 2y = 8 \\ \hline 5x - y = 31 \end{array}$$

This does not appear to help, so try subtracting the two equations:

$$\begin{array}{r} 4x + y = 23 \\ - x - 2y = 8 \\ \hline 3x + 3y = 15 \end{array}$$

Divide each side by 3:

$$x + y = 5$$

The average of x and y is their sum divided by 2:

$$\frac{x+y}{2} = \frac{5}{2} = 2.5$$

The answer is Choice B.

NOTE: You *could have* actually solved for x and y [$x = 6, y = -1$] and then taken their average. However, that method would have been more time-consuming and unnecessary.

EXAMPLE 21

If $a - b = 1$, $b - c = 2$, and $c - a = d$, what is the value of d?

(A) -3 (B) -1 (C) 1 (D) 3
(E) It cannot be determined from the information given.

Solution. Since there are more than two equations, add them:

$$
\begin{array}{r}
a - b = 1 \\
b - c = 2 \\
+\ c - a = d \\
\hline
0 = 3 + d \Rightarrow d = -3
\end{array}
$$

The answer is Choice A.

TACTIC ## 8-10 / Systematically make lists

When a question asks "how many," often the best strategy is to make a list. If you do this it is important that you make the list in a *systematic* fashion so that you don't inadvertently leave something out. Often, shortly after starting the list, you can see a pattern developing and can figure out how many more entries there will be without writing them all down.

Listing things systematically means writing them in numerical order (if the entries are numbers) or in alphabetical order (if the entries are letters). If the answer to "how many" is a small number (as in Example 22), just list all possibilities. If the answer is a large number (as in Example 23), start the list and write enough entries until you see a pattern.

EXAMPLE 22

The sum of three positive integers is 20. If one of them is 5, what is the greatest possible value of the product of the other two?

Solution. Since one of the integers is 5, the sum of the other two is 15. Systematically, list all possible pairs, (a, b), of positive integers whose sum is 15, and check their products. First let $a = 1$, then 2, and so on.

a	b	ab
1	14	14
2	13	26
3	12	36
4	11	44
5	10	50
6	9	54
7	8	56

The answer is 56.

EXAMPLE 23

A palindrome is a number, such as 74,947, that reads the same forwards and backwards. How many palindromes are there between 200 and 800?

Solution. First, write down the numbers in the 200s that end in 2:

202, 212, 222, 232, 242, 252, 262, 272, 282, 292

Now write the numbers beginning and ending in 3:

303, 313, 323, 333, 343, 353, 363, 373, 383, 393

By now you should see the pattern: there are ten numbers beginning with a 2, ten beginning with 3, and there will be ten beginning with 4, 5, 6, and 7 for a total of $6 \times 10 = 60$ palindromes.

TACTIC 8-11 / Handle strange symbols properly

On almost all PSATs, there are a few questions that use symbols, such as: , □, ☺, ✠, or ✤, that you have never before seen in a mathematics problem. How can you answer such a question? Don't panic! It's easy—you are always told exactly what the symbol means! All you have to do is follow the directions carefully.

When there are two questions using the same symbol, the first question is usually easy and involves only numbers; the second is more difficult and usually contains variables.

<u>Examples 24 and 25</u> refer to the following definition.

If a and b are unequal positive numbers, let the operation ☺ be defined by

$$a \, ☺ \, b = \frac{a+b}{a-b}$$

EXAMPLE 24

What is the value of 6 ☺ 2?

(A) 2   (B) 3   (C) 4   (D) 8   (E) 12

Solution. The definition of ☺ tells us that whenever two numbers surround a "happy face," we are to form a fraction in which the numerator is their sum and the denominator is their difference. So, 6 ☺ 2 is the fraction whose numerator is $6 + 2 = 8$ and whose denominator is $6 - 2 = 4$: $\frac{8}{4} = 2$ (Choice A).

EXAMPLE 25

If $c \, ☺ \, d = 3$, which of the following is true?

(A) $c = 3d$ (B) $c = 2d$ (C) $c = d$ (D) $d = 2c$ (E) $d = 3c$

Solution. $c \, ☺ \, d - 3 \Rightarrow \frac{c+d}{c-d} = 3 \Rightarrow c + d = 3c \quad 3d \to 4d = 2c \Rightarrow c = 2d$ (Choice B).

EXERCISES

None of these exercises *requires* the use of the tactics that you just learned. However, as you try each one, even if you know the correct mathematical solution, before solving it, think about which of the tactics could be used. An answer key follows the questions.

MULTIPLE-CHOICE QUESTIONS

1. If the average (arithmetic mean) of 10, 20, 30, 40, and a is 50, what is the value of a?

   (A) 50   (B) 60   (C) 100   (D) 150   (E) 250

2. Larry has 250 marbles, all red, white, and blue, in the ratio of $1:3:6$, respectively. How many blue marbles does he have?

   (A) 25   (B) 75   (C) 100   (D) 125   (E) 150

3. If w whistles cost c cents, how many whistles can you get for d dollars?

   (A) $\frac{100dw}{c}$ (B) $\frac{dw}{100c}$ (C) $100cdw$

   (D) $\frac{dw}{c}$ (E) cdw

4. If $x\%$ of w is 10, what is w?

   (A) $\frac{10}{x}$ (B) $\frac{100}{x}$ (C) $\frac{1000}{x}$ (D) $\frac{x}{100}$ (E) $\frac{x}{10}$

5. If 8% of c is equal to 12% of d, which of the following is equal to $c + d$?

   (A) $1.5d$ (B) $2d$ (C) $2.5d$ (D) $3d$ (E) $5d$

6. On a certain legislative committee, $\frac{3}{8}$ of the committee members are Republicans. If $\frac{2}{3}$ of the members are men and $\frac{3}{5}$ of the men are Democrats, what fraction of the members are Democratic women?

   (A) $\frac{3}{20}$ (B) $\frac{9}{40}$ (C) $\frac{1}{4}$ (D) $\frac{2}{5}$ (E) $\frac{5}{12}$

7. Kim receives a commission of $25 for every $2,000 worth of merchandise she sells. What percent is her commission?

(A) $1\frac{1}{4}$%   (B) $2\frac{1}{2}$%   (C) 5%   (D) 25%
(E) 125%

8. From 1990 to 1995, the value of one share of stock of *XYZ* corporation increased by 25%. If the value was *D* dollars in 1995, what was the value in 1990?

(A) 1.75*D*   (B) 1.25*D*   (C) 1.20*D*   (D) .80*D*
(E) .75*D*

9. What is the value of *p* if *p* is positive and $p \times p \times p = p + p + p$?

(A) $\frac{1}{3}$ (B) $\sqrt{3}$ (C) 3   (D) $3\sqrt{3}$ (E) 9

10. What is 4% of 5%?

(A) .09%   (B) .20%   (C) 2.0%
(D) 9%   (E) 20%

11. In the figure below, *TUVW* is a square and *TUX* is an equilateral triangle. If *VW* = 2, what is the area of the shaded region?

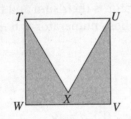

(A) $\sqrt{3}$ (B) 2   (C) 3   (D) $4 - 2\sqrt{3}$
(E) $4 - \sqrt{3}$

12. If $12a + 3b = 1$ and $7b - 2a = 9$, what is the average (arithmetic mean) of *a* and *b*?

(A) 0.1   (B) 0.5   (C) 1   (D) 2.5   (E) 5

13. The map below shows all the roads connecting five towns. How many different ways are there to go from *A* to *E* if you may not return to a town after you leave it and you may not go through both *C* and *D*?

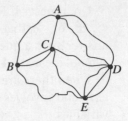

(A) 8   (B) 12   (C) 16   (D) 24   (E) 32

Questions 14–15 refer to the following definition.

For any numbers a, b, c $a ⭐ b ⭐ c = abc - (a + b + c)$.

14. What is the value of $3 ⭐ 5 ⭐ 2$?

(A) 0   (B) 5   (C) 10   (D) 20   (E) 30

15. For what positive number *x* is it true that $x ⭐ 2x ⭐ 3x = 0$?

(A) 0   (B) 1   (C) 2   (D) 3   (E) 6

16. In the figure below, if the radius of circle *O* is 10, what is the length of diagonal *AC* of rectangle *OABC*?

(A) $\sqrt{2}$ (B) $\sqrt{10}$ (C) $5\sqrt{2}$
(D) 10   (E) $10\sqrt{2}$

GRID-IN QUESTIONS

17. What is the area of a rectangle whose length is twice its width and whose perimeter is equal to the perimeter of a square whose area is 1? _____

18. For how many integers between 1 and 1000 is at least one of the digits a 9? _____

Answer Key

Next to the answer for each question is the number of the tactic that would be most helpful in answering the question, in the event that you do not see the direct solution.

1. *D* (TACTIC 8-1)

2. *E* (TACTIC 8-1)

3. *A* (TACTIC 8-2)

4. *C* (TACTIC 8-2)

5. *C* (TACTIC 8-3)

6. *B* (TACTIC 8-3)

7. *A* (TACTIC 8-4)

8. *D* (TACTIC 8-4)

9. *B* (TACTIC 8-1)

10. *B* (TACTIC 8-4)

11. *E* (TACTIC 8-8)

12. *B* (TACTIC 8-9)

13. *B* (TACTIC 8-10)

14. *D* (TACTIC 8-11)

15. *B* (TACTIC 8-11)

16. *D* (TACTIC 8-6)

17. $\frac{8}{9}$ (TACTIC 8-5)

18. 271 (TACTIC 8-10)

► CHAPTER 9
Review of PSAT Mathematics
Arithmetic

To do well on the PSAT, you need to feel comfortable with most topics of basic arithmetic. The first five sections of Chapter 9 provide you with a review of the basic arithmetic operations, signed numbers, fractions and decimals, ratios, percents, and averages. Because you will have a calculator with you at the test, you will not have to do long division, multiply three-digit numbers, or perform any other tedious calculations using paper and pencil. If you use a calculator with fraction capabilities, you can even avoid finding least common denominators and reducing fractions.

The solutions to more than one-third of the math questions on the PSAT depend on your knowing the **KEY FACTS** in these sections. Be sure to review them all.

9-A BASIC ARITHMETIC CONCEPTS

A *set* is a collection of "things" that have been grouped together in some way. Those "things" are called the *elements* or *members*. For example:

If A is the set of states in the United States, then California is an element of A.
If B is the set of letters in the English alphabet, then z is a member of B.
If C is the set of even integers, then 46 is in C.

The *union* of two sets, A and B, is the set consisting of all the elements that are in A or B or both. Note that this includes those elements that are in A and B. The union is represented as $A \cup B$.

The *intersection* of two sets, A and B, is the set consisting only of those elements that are in both A and B. The intersection is represented as $A \cap B$.

In describing a set of numbers, we usually list the elements inside a pair of braces. For example, let A be the set of prime numbers less than 10, and let B be the set of even positive integers less than 10.

$$A = \{2, 3, 5, 7\} \qquad B = \{2, 4, 6, 8\}$$
$$A \cup B = \{2, 3, 4, 5, 6, 7, 8\}$$
$$A \cap B = \{2\}$$

The *solution set* of an equation is the set of all numbers that satisfy the equation.

EXAMPLE 1

If $C = \{-2, -1, 0, 1, 2\}$ and D is the set that consists of the squares of each of the elements of C, how many numbers are elements of D?

Solution. 0 is in D (since $0^2 = 0$); 1 is in D (since $1^2 = 1$); and 4 is in D (since $2^2 = 4$). These are the only elements of D; so D has 3 elements. Note that $(-1)^2 = 1$ and $(-2)^2 = 4$, but we have already listed 1 and 4. $D = \{0, 1, 4\}$.

Let's start our review of arithmetic by reviewing the most important sets of numbers and their properties. On the PSAT the word *number* always means *real number*, a number that can be represented by a point on the number line.

Signed Numbers

The numbers to the right of 0 on the number line are called **positive** and those to the left of 0 are called **negative**. Note that 0 is neither positive nor negative. Negative numbers must be written with a *negative sign* (−3); positive numbers can be written with a *plus sign* (+3) but are usually written without a sign (3). All numbers can be called *signed numbers*.

The **absolute value** of a number a, denoted $|a|$, is the distance between a and 0 on the number line. Since 5 is 5 units to the right of 0 on the number line and −5 is 5 units to the left of 0, both have an absolute value of 5:

- $|5| = 5$ - $|-5| = 5$

EXAMPLE 2

How many integers are solutions of the inequality $|x| < 5$?

(A) 0 (B) 4 (C) 8 (D) 9 (E) infinitely many

Solution. There are 9 integers whose absolute values are less than 5:

$$-4, -3, -2, -1, 0, 1, 2, 3, 4 \text{ (Choice D).}$$

In arithmetic we are basically concerned with the addition, subtraction, multiplication, and division of numbers. The table below gives the terms for the results of these operations.

Operation	Symbol	Result	Example	
Addition	+	**Sum**	16 is the sum of 12 and 4	$12 + 4 = 16$
Subtraction	−	**Difference**	8 is the difference of 12 and 4	$12 - 4 = 8$
Multiplication*	×	**Product**	48 is the product of 12 and 4	$12 \times 4 = 48$
Division	÷	**Quotient**	3 is the quotient of 12 and 4	$12 \div 4 = 3$

*In certain situations, multiplication can also be indicated by a dot, parentheses, or the juxtaposition of symbols without any sign: $2^2 \cdot 2^4$, $3(4)$, $3(x + 2)$, $3a$, $4abc$.

Given any two numbers a and b, you can *always* find their sum, difference, product, and quotient (with a calculator, if necessary), but you can *never divide by zero*.

- $0 \div 7 = 0$, but $7 \div 0$ is meaningless

EXAMPLE 3

What is the sum of the product and quotient of 8 and 8?

Solution. Product: $8 \times 8 = 64$. Quotient: $8 \div 8 = 1$. Sum: $64 + 1 = 65$.

 KEY FACT A1 For any number a: $a \times 0 = 0$. Conversely, if the product of two or more numbers is 0, *at least one* of them must be 0.

If $ab = 0$, then $a = 0$ or $b = 0$.

If $rst = 0$, then $r = 0$ or $s = 0$ or $t = 0$.

EXAMPLE 4

What is the product of all the integers from −5 to 5, inclusive?

Solution. Before reaching for your calculator, look and think. You are asked for the product of eleven numbers, one of which is 0. So, by **KEY FACT A1**, the product is 0.

KEY FACT   **KEY FACT A2**   The product and quotient of two positive numbers or two negative numbers is positive; the product and quotient of a positive number and a negative number is negative.

$12 \times 2 = 24$	$12 \times (-2) = -24$	$(-12) \times 2 = -24$	$(-12) \times (-2) = 24$
$12 \div 2 = 6$	$12 \div (-2) = -6$	$(-12) \div 2 = -6$	$(-12) \div (-2) = 6$

To determine whether a product of more than two numbers is positive or negative, count the number of negative factors.

KEY FACT   **KEY FACT A3**
- The product of an *even* number of negative factors is positive.
- The product of an *odd* number of negative factors is negative.

EXAMPLE 5

Which of the following are equal to $(-1)^{25}$?
  I. $(-1)^{100}$
  II. $-(1)^{100}$
  III. $-(-1)^{100}$

(A) I only   (B) II only   (C) III only   (D) II and III only   (E) I, II, and III

Solution. Since 25 is odd and 100 is even, $(-1)^{25} = -1$, whereas $(-1)^{100} = 1$. (I is false.) Since $1^{100} = 1$, $-(1)^{100} = -1$. II is true. Since $(-1)^{100} = 1$, $-(-1)^{100} = -1$. III is true. Only II and III are true (Choice D).

KEY FACT   **KEY FACT A4**
- The sum of two positive numbers is positive.
- The sum of two negative numbers is negative.

$$6 + 2 = 8 \quad (-6) + (-2) = -8$$

- To find the sum of a positive and a negative number, find the difference of their absolute values and use the sign of the number with the larger absolute value.

To calculate $6 + (-2)$ or $(-6) + 2$, take the *difference*, $6 - 2 = 4$, and use the sign of the number whose absolute value is 6:

$$6 + (-2) = 4 \quad (-6) + 2 = -4$$

KEY FACT   **KEY FACT A5**   To subtract signed numbers, change the problem to an addition problem, by changing the sign of what is being subtracted, and use **KEY FACT A4**.

$$2 - 6 = 2 + (-6) = -4 \qquad 2 - (-6) = 2 + (6) = 8$$

$$(-2) - (-6) = (-2) + (6) = 4 \qquad (-2) - 6 = (-2) + (-6) = -8$$

In each case, the minus sign was changed to a plus sign, and either the 6 was changed to −6 or the −6 was changed to 6.

All arithmetic involving signed numbers can be accomplished on *any* calculator, but not all calculators handle negative numbers the same way. Be sure you know how to enter negative numbers and how to use them on *your* calculator.

Integers

The *integers* are $\{\ldots, -4, -3, -2, -1, 0, 1, 2, 3, 4, \ldots\}$
The *positive integers* are $\{1, 2, 3, 4, 5, \ldots\}$
The *negative integers* are $\{\ldots, -5, -4, -3, -2, -1\}$
Consecutive integers are two or more integers written in sequence in which each integer is 1 more than the preceding one. For example:

22, 23   6, 7, 8, 9   −2, −1, 0, 1 $n, n + 1, n + 2, n + 3, \ldots$

CAUTION: Never assume that *number* means *integer*: 3 is not the only number between 2 and 4—there are infinitely many, including 2.5, 3.99, $\frac{10}{3}$, π, and $\sqrt{10}$.

EXAMPLE 6

If $0 < x < 3$ and $2 < y < 8$, what is the largest integer value of $x + y$?

Solution. If x and y are integers, the largest value of $x + y$ is $2 + 7 = 9$. However, even though $x + y$ is to be an integer, neither x nor y must be. If $x = 2.5$ and $y = 7.5$, then $x + y = 10$.

The sum, difference, and product of two integers is *always* an integer; the quotient of two integers may be an integer, but not necessarily. The quotient $37 \div 10$ can be expressed as $\frac{37}{10}$ or $3\frac{7}{10}$ or 3.7. If the quotient is to be an integer, you can also say that the quotient is 3 and there is a *remainder* of 7. It depends upon your point of view. For example, if 37 pounds of rice is to be divided into 10 bags, each bag will hold 3.7 pounds; but if 37 books are to be divided among 10 people, each one will get 3 books and there will be 7 left over (the remainder).

The standard way to find quotients and remainders is to use long division. But on the PSAT, you should *never* do long division; you should use your calculators. To find the remainder when 100 is divided by 7, divide on your calculator: $100 \div 7 = 14.285714\ldots$ This tells you that the quotient is 14. Ignore everything to the right of the decimal point. To find the remainder, multiply: $14 \times 7 = 98$, and then subtract: $100 - 98 = 2$.

EXAMPLE 7

If the remainder when a is divided by 7 is 2 and the remainder when b is divided by 7 is 4, what is the remainder when ab is divided by 7?

(A) 0   (B) 1   (C) 3   (D) 6   (E) 8

Solution. a can be any number that is 2 more than a multiple of 7: 9, 16, 23, ... b can be any number that is 4 more than a multiple of 7: 11, 18, 25, ...

For simplicity, let $a = 9$ and $b = 11$. Then $ab = 99$, and when 99 is divided by 7, the quotient is 14 and the remainder is 1 (Choice B).

If a and b are integers, the following four terms are synonymous:

a is a **divisor** of b	a is a **factor** of b
b is **divisible** by a	b is a **multiple** of a

All these statements mean that, when b is divided by a, there is no remainder (or, more precisely, the remainder is 0). For example:

3 is a divisor of 12.	3 is a factor of 12.
12 is divisible by 3.	12 is a multiple of 3.

The only positive divisor of 1 is 1. All other positive integers have at least two positive divisors: 1 and itself, and possibly many more. For example, 6 is divisible by 1 and 6, as well as 2 and 3, whereas 7 is divisible only by 1 and 7. Positive integers, such as 7, which have *exactly two* positive divisors are called **prime numbers** or **primes**. Here are the first few primes:

$$2, 3, 5, 7, 11, 13, 17, 19, 23.$$

Memorize this list—it will come in handy. Note that 1 is *not* a prime.

EXAMPLE 8

What is the sum of the largest prime factor of 26 and the largest prime factor of 28?

Solution.
The factors of 26 are 1, 2, 13, and 26. The largest *prime* factor is 13.
The factors of 28 are 1, 2, 4, 7, 14, and 28. The largest *prime* factor is 7.
The sum of 13 and 7 is 20.

The **even numbers** are all the integer multiples of 2: $\{\ldots, -4, -2, 0, 2, 4, 6, \ldots\}$
The **odd numbers** are the integers not divisible by 2: $\{\ldots, -5, -3, -1, 1, 3, 5, \ldots\}$

 KEY FACT A6
1. If two integers are both even or both odd, their sum and difference are even.
2. If one integer is even and the other odd, their sum and difference are both odd.
3. The product of two integers is even unless both of them are odd.

Exponents and Roots

Repeated addition of the same number is indicated by multiplication:

$$11 + 11 + 11 + 11 + 11 + 11 + 11 = 7 \times 11$$

Repeated multiplication of the same number is indicated by an exponent:

$$11 \times 11 \times 11 \times 11 \times 11 \times 11 \times 11 = 11^7$$

In the expression 11^7, 11 is called the **base** and 7 is the **exponent**.

Although most of the exponents you will encounter on the PSAT are positive integers, you may occasionally see 0, negative integers, and rational numbers used as exponents. All of these are defined in the next **KEY FACT**.

 KEY FACT A7 For any number b and positive integer n:

- $b^0 = 1$
- $b^1 = b$
- $b^n = b \times b \times \ldots \times b$, where b is used as a factor n times
- $b^{-n} = \dfrac{1}{b^n}$
- $b^{\frac{1}{n}} = \sqrt[n]{b}$

For example,

$$2^0 = 1 \qquad 2^1 = 2 \qquad 2^4 = 2 \times 2 \times 2 \times 2 = 16$$
$$2^{-4} = \frac{1}{2^4} = \frac{1}{16} \qquad 16^{\frac{1}{4}} = \sqrt[4]{16} = 2$$

Now consider the following four calculations.

(i) $5^4 \times 5^3 = (5 \times 5 \times 5 \times 5) \times (5 \times 5 \times 5) = 5^7 = 5^{4+3}$

(ii) $\dfrac{5^6}{5^4} = \dfrac{5 \times 5 \times 5 \times 5 \times 5 \times 5}{5 \times 5 \times 5 \times 5} = 5 \times 5 = 5^2 = 5^{6-4}$

(iii) $(5^2)^3 = (5 \times 5)^3 = (5 \times 5) \times (5 \times 5) \times (5 \times 5) = 5^6 = 5^{2 \times 3}$

(iv) $5^3 \times 6^3 = (5 \times 5 \times 5) \times (6 \times 6 \times 6) = (5 \times 6)(5 \times 6)(5 \times 6) = (5 \times 6)^3$

These four examples illustrate the following important laws of exponents.

KEY FACT A8 For any numbers $b, c, m,$ and n:

(i) $b^m b^n = b^{m+n}$ (ii) $\dfrac{b^m}{b^n} = b^{m-n}$ (iii) $(b^m)^n = b^{mn}$ (iv) $b^m c^m = (bc)^m$

EXAMPLE 9

If $5^a \times 5^b = 5^{50}$, what is the average (arithmetic mean) of a and b?

Solution. Since $5^a \times 5^b = 5^{a+b}$, we see that $a + b = 50 \Rightarrow \dfrac{a+b}{2} = 25$.

EXAMPLE 10

What is the value of $16^{\frac{3}{4}}$?

Solution. By **KEY FACT A8** (iii), $16^{\frac{3}{4}} = (16^{\frac{1}{4}})^3 = (\sqrt[4]{16})^3 = 2^3 = 8$.

Squares and Square Roots

The exponent that appears most often on the PSAT is 2. It is used to form the square of a number, as in πr^2 (the area of a circle), $a^2 + b^2 = c^2$ (Pythagorean theorem), or $x^2 - y^2$ (the difference of two squares). Therefore, it is helpful to recognize the **perfect squares**, numbers that are the squares of integers. The squares of the integers from 0 to 15 are as follows:

x	0	1	2	3	4	5	6	7	8	9	10	11	12	13	14	15
x^2	0	1	4	9	16	25	36	49	64	81	100	121	144	169	196	225

There are two numbers that satisfy the equation $x^2 = 4$: $x = 2$ and $x = -2$. The positive number, 2, is called the **principal square root** of 4 and is denoted by the symbol $\sqrt{4}$. Clearly, each perfect square has a square root: $\sqrt{0} = 0$, $\sqrt{16} = 4$, $\sqrt{49} = 7$, and $\sqrt{121} = 11$. It is an important fact, however, that *every* positive number has a square root.

KEY FACT A9 For any positive number a, there is a positive number b that satisfies the equation $b^2 = a$. That number is called the principal square root of a and is written $b = \sqrt{a}$. Therefore, for any positive number a: $\sqrt{a} \times \sqrt{a} = (\sqrt{a})^2 = a$.

The only difference between $\sqrt{4}$ and $\sqrt{5}$ is that $\sqrt{4}$ is an integer, whereas $\sqrt{5}$ is not. Since 5 is greater than 4, we know that $\sqrt{5}$ is greater than $\sqrt{4} = 2$. In fact, $(2.2)^2 = 4.84$, which is close to 5, and $(2.23)^2 = 4.9729$, which is very close to 5. So, $\sqrt{5} \approx 2.23$. Using the square root key on your calculator, you can find the value of any square root to several decimal places of accuracy, much more than you need for the PSAT.

EXAMPLE 11

What is the circumference of a circle whose area is 10π?

(A) 5π (B) 10π (C) $\pi\sqrt{10}$ (D) $2\pi\sqrt{10}$ (E) $\pi\sqrt{20}$

Solution. Since the area of a circle is given by the formula $A = \pi r^2$, we have

$$\pi r^2 = 10\pi \Rightarrow r^2 = 10 \Rightarrow r = \sqrt{10}.$$

The circumference is given by the formula $C = 2\pi r$, so $C = 2\pi\sqrt{10}$ (Choice D). (See Section 9-L on circles.)

PEMDAS

When a calculation requires performing more than one operation, it is important to carry out the operations in the correct order. For decades students have memorized the sentence, "Please Excuse My Dear Aunt Sally," or just the first letters, PEMDAS, to remember the proper order of operations. The letters stand for:

- Parentheses: First do whatever appears in parentheses, following PEMDAS within the parentheses also, if necessary.
- Exponents: Next evaluate all terms with exponents.
- Multiplication and Division: Do all multiplications and divisions *in order from left to right*—do not multiply first and then divide.
- Addition and Subtraction: Finally, do all additions and subtractions *in order from left to right*—do not add first and then subtract.

Here are some worked-out examples.

1. $10 + 4 \times 2 = 10 + 8 = 18$ [Multiply before you add.]
   $(10 + 4) \times 2 = 14 \times 2 = 28$ [First add in the parentheses.]

2. $16 \div 2 \times 4 = 8 \times 4 = 32$ [Just go from left to right.]
   $16 \div (2 \times 4) = 16 \div 8 = 2$ [Multiply first.]

3. $5 \times 2^3 = 5 \times 8 = 40$ [Do exponents first.]
   $(5 \times 2)^3 = 10^3 = 1000$ [Multiply first.]

4. $10 + 15 \div (2 + 3) = 10 + 15 \div 5 = 10 + 3 = 13$ [Do parentheses first, then divide.]

5. $100 - 2^2(3 + 4 \times 5) = 100 - 2^2(23) = 100 - 4(23) = 100 - 92 = 8$
   [Do parentheses first (using PEMDAS), then the exponent, then multiplication.]

Almost every *scientific* calculator automatically follows PEMDAS—four-function calculators do not. Test each of the above calculations on *your* calculator. Be sure you know whether or not you need to use parentheses or to put anything in memory as you proceed.

KEY FACT   **KEY FACT A10**   **(The distributive law)** For any real numbers a, b, and c:

$$a(b + c) = ab + ac \qquad a(b - c) = ab - ac$$

and if $a \neq 0$

$$\frac{b + c}{a} = \frac{b}{a} + \frac{c}{a} \qquad \frac{b - c}{a} = \frac{b}{a} - \frac{c}{a}$$

HELPFUL HINT   *Be sure you use the distributive law with both multiplication and division whenever you can.*

EXAMPLE 12

Which of the following is equivalent to $\dfrac{x^5 + x^4}{x^4}$ for all nonzero numbers x?

(A) $x + 1$ (B) x^5 (C) $x^5 + 1$ (D) $x + x^4$ (E) x^{16}

Solution. $\dfrac{x^5 + x^4}{x^4} = \dfrac{x^5}{x^4} + \dfrac{x^4}{x^4} = x + 1$ (Choice A).

EXERCISES

MULTIPLE-CHOICE QUESTIONS

1. For how many integers n, is it true that $n^2 = n^3$?

   (A) None (B) 1 (C) 2
   (D) 4 (E) More than 4

2. If $x \blacklozenge y$ represents the number of integers greater than x and less than y, what is the value of $-\pi \blacklozenge \pi$?

   (A) 0 (B) 3 (C) 4 (D) 6 (E) 7

3. Which of the following is equal to $(5^8 \times 5^9)^{10}$?

   (A) 5^{27} (B) 5^{82} (C) 5^{170} (D) 5^{720} (E) 25^{720}

4. If p and q are primes greater than 100, which of the following must be true?

   I. $p + q$ is even
   II. pq is odd
   III. $p^2 - q^2$ is even

   (A) I only (B) II only (C) I and II only
   (D) I and III only (E) I, II, and III

5. If $(5^a)(5^b) = \dfrac{5^c}{5^d}$, what is d in terms of a, b, and c?

   (A) $\dfrac{c}{ab}$ (B) $c - a - b$ (C) $a + b - c$
   (D) $c - ab$ (E) $\dfrac{c}{a + b}$

GRID-IN QUESTIONS

6. A number is "nifty" if it is a multiple of 2 or 3. How many nifty numbers are there between -11 and 11?

7. If for any positive integer n, $\tau(n)$ represents the number of positive divisors of n, what is the value of $\tau(\tau(\tau(12)))$?

8. If the product of four consecutive integers is equal to one of the integers, what is the largest possible value of one of the integers?

9. At Ben's Butcher Shop, 199 pounds of chopped meat is being divided into packages, each weighing 2.5 pounds. How many pounds of meat are left when there isn't enough to make another whole package?

10. What is the largest number, x, that can be entered in the grid such that $\sqrt{x}$ is an integer?

6.

7.

8.

9.

10.

Answer Key

1. *C*   2. *E*   3. *C*   4. *E*   5. *B*

6. **1 5**

7. **3**

8. **3**

9. **1 . 5**

10. **9 8 0 1**

9-B FRACTIONS AND DECIMALS

Several questions on the PSAT involve fractions or decimals. In this section we will present all of the important facts you need to know for the PSAT. Even if you are using a calculator that has fraction capabilities, it is essential that you review all of this material thoroughly.

Comparing Fractions and Decimals

 KEY FACT B1 To compare two decimals, follow these rules:

- Whichever number has the greater number to the left of the decimal point is greater: since $10 > 9$, $10.001 > 9.896$ and since $1 > 0$, $1.234 > 0.8$.
- If the numbers to the left of the decimal point are equal (or if there are no numbers to the left of the decimal point), proceed as follows:
  1. If the numbers do not have the same number of digits to the right of the decimal point, add zeros to make the number of digits equal.
  2. Now, compare the numbers to the right of the decimal point (*ignoring* the decimal point itself).

For example, to compare 1.83 and 1.823, add a zero to the end of 1.83, forming 1.830. Now, thinking of them as whole numbers, compare the numbers to the right of the decimal point: $830 > 823 \Rightarrow 1.830 > 1.823$.

 KEY FACT B2 To compare two fractions, use your calculator to convert them to decimals. Then apply **KEY FACT B1**. This *always* works.

On the PSAT, *never* do long division to convert a fraction to a decimal (or for any other reason). Use your calculator.

For example, to compare $\frac{1}{3}$ and $\frac{3}{8}$, write $\frac{1}{3} = .333\ldots$ and $\frac{3}{8} = .375$. Since $.375 > .333$, $\frac{3}{8} > \frac{1}{3}$.

KEY FACT B3 **KEY FACTS B1** and **B2** apply to *positive* decimals and fractions. Clearly, any positive number is greater than any negative number. For negative decimals and fractions, note that if $a > b$, then $-a < -b$.

$$\frac{3}{8} > \frac{1}{3} \Rightarrow -\frac{1}{3} > -\frac{3}{8} \quad \text{and} \quad .83 > .829 \Rightarrow -.83 < -.829$$

Arithmetic Operations with Decimals and Fractions

On the PSAT, *all* decimal arithmetic (including whole numbers) that you can't easily do mentally should be done on your calculator.

This shortcut saves time and avoids careless errors. If you know that $12 \times 12 = 144$ and that $1.2 \times 1.2 = 1.44$, fine, but if you're not sure, use your calculator rather than paper and pencil. You should even use your calculator to multiply $.2 \times .2$ if there's any chance that you would write 0.4 instead of 0.04 as the answer.

If your calculator can perform operations on fractions (see Chapter 1), then you should use it on any problem that you can't solve mentally.

HELPFUL HINT *If your calculator can't do fractional arithmetic, you can still use it to solve any problem involving fractions by converting fractions to decimals and then checking the answers. However, it is usually faster to work with the fractions directly; so do this only if you are stuck.*

 KEY FACT B4 To multiply two fractions, multiply their numerators and multiply their denominators:

$$\frac{3}{5} \times \frac{4}{7} = \frac{3 \times 4}{5 \times 7} = \frac{12}{35}.$$

KEY FACT B5 To multiply a fraction by any other number, write that number as a fraction whose denominator is 1:

$$\frac{3}{5} \times 7 = \frac{3}{5} \times \frac{7}{1} = \frac{21}{5} \qquad \frac{3}{4} \times \pi = \frac{3}{4} \times \frac{\pi}{1} = \frac{3\pi}{4}$$

TACTIC B1

Reduce fractions before multiplying (divide the numerator and the denominator by a common factor).

EXAMPLE 1

Express the product, $\frac{3}{4} \times \frac{8}{9} \times \frac{15}{16}$, in lowest terms.

Solution. If you just multiply the numerators and denominators (with a calculator, of course), you get $\frac{360}{576}$, which is a nuisance to reduce. Also, dividing on your calculator won't help, since your answer is supposed to be a fraction in lowest terms. It is better to use **TACTIC B1** and reduce first:

$$\frac{{}^{1}\cancel{3}}{4} \times \frac{{}^{1}\cancel{8}}{\cancel{9}_{3}} \times \frac{{}^{5}\cancel{15}}{\cancel{16}_{2}} = \frac{1 \times 1 \times 5}{4 \times 1 \times 2} = \frac{5}{8}.$$

HELPFUL HINT *If your calculator does fractional arithmetic and it reduces all fractions automatically, then do not bother reducing; just multiply the fractions.*

TACTIC B2

When a problem requires you to find a fraction *of* a number, multiply.

EXAMPLE 2

If $\frac{5}{8}$ of the 320 seniors at Central High School are girls, and $\frac{4}{5}$ of the senior girls are taking a science course, how many senior girls are NOT taking a science course?

(A) 40   (B) 70   (C) 160   (D) 200
(E) It cannot be determined from the information given.

Solution. There are $\frac{5}{{}_{1}\cancel{8}} \times \cancel{320}^{40} = 200$ senior girls. Of these, $\frac{4}{{}_{1}\cancel{5}} \times \cancel{200}^{40} = 160$ are taking science. Then, $200 - 160 = 40$ are not taking science (Choice A).

 If you are going to use your calculator, enter the numbers without reducing. Given the choice of multiplying $\frac{48}{128} \times 80$ or $\frac{3}{8} \times 80$, *you* would prefer the second option, but with *your calculator*, the first one is just as easy.

The **reciprocal** of any nonzero number x, is the number $\frac{1}{x}$. The reciprocal of the fraction $\frac{a}{b}$ is the fraction $\frac{b}{a}$.

KEY FACT B6 To divide any number by a fraction, multiply that number by the reciprocal of the fraction:

$$20 \div \frac{2}{3} = \frac{20}{1} \times \frac{3}{2} = 30 \qquad \frac{3}{5} \div \frac{2}{3} = \frac{3}{5} \times \frac{3}{2} = \frac{9}{10}$$

EXAMPLE 3

A certain real estate course takes 36 hours to complete. If the course is divided into 40-minute classes, how many times does the class meet?

Solution. First, note that 40 minutes = $\frac{40}{60}$ hour = $\frac{2}{3}$ hour. Then, $36 \div \frac{2}{3} = \frac{36}{1} \times \frac{3}{2} = 54$.

 NOTE: In this problem, you could have avoided fractions by changing 36 hours to $36 \times 60 = 2{,}160$ minutes and then dividing: $2{,}160 \div 40 = 54$.

KEY FACT B7 To add or subtract fractions with the same denominator, add or subtract the numerators and keep the denominator:

$$\frac{4}{9} + \frac{1}{9} = \frac{5}{9} \quad \text{and} \quad \frac{4}{9} - \frac{1}{9} = \frac{3}{9} = \frac{1}{3}$$

To add or subtract fractions with different denominators, first rewrite the fractions as equivalent fractions with the same denominators:

$$\frac{1}{6} + \frac{3}{4} = \frac{2}{12} + \frac{9}{12} = \frac{11}{12}$$

NOTE: The *easiest* denominator to get is the product of the denominators ($6 \times 4 = 24$, in this example), but the *best* denominator to use is the *least common denominator*, which is the *least common multiple* (LCM) of the denominators (12 in this case). Using the least common denominator minimizes the amount of reducing that is necessary to express the answer in lowest terms.

EXAMPLE 4

Michael had a baseball card collection. Sally took $\frac{1}{3}$ of his cards and Heidi took $\frac{1}{4}$ of them. What fraction of his cards did Michael have left?

EXAMPLE 5

Michael had a baseball card collection. Sally took $\frac{1}{3}$ of his cards and Heidi took $\frac{1}{4}$ of what was left. What fraction of his cards did Michael have left?

CAUTION: Be sure to read questions carefully. In Example 4, Heidi took $\frac{1}{4}$ of the cards. In Example 5, however, she took only $\frac{1}{4}$ of the $\frac{2}{3}$ that were left after Sally took her cards: she took $\frac{1}{4} \times \frac{2}{3} = \frac{1}{6}$ of the cards.

Solution 4. $\frac{1}{3} + \frac{1}{4} = \frac{4}{12} + \frac{3}{12} = \frac{7}{12}$ of the cards were taken; so Michael had $\frac{5}{12}$ of them left.

Solution 5. $\frac{1}{3} + \frac{1}{6} = \frac{2}{6} + \frac{1}{6} = \frac{3}{6} = \frac{1}{2}$ of the cards were taken; so Michael had $\frac{1}{2}$ of them left.

Arithmetic Operations with Mixed Numbers

A *mixed number* is a number such as $3\frac{1}{2}$, which consists of an integer followed by a fraction. It is an abbreviation for the *sum* of the number and the fraction; so, $3\frac{1}{2}$ is an abbreviation for $3 + \frac{1}{2}$. Every mixed number can be written as an improper fraction, and every improper fraction can be written as a mixed number:

$$3\frac{1}{2} = 3 + \frac{1}{2} = \frac{3}{1} + \frac{1}{2} = \frac{7}{2} + \frac{1}{2} = \frac{6}{2} \quad \text{and} \quad \frac{7}{2} = \frac{6}{2} + \frac{1}{2} = 3 + \frac{1}{2} = 3\frac{1}{2}$$

 KEY FACT B8 To write a mixed number as an improper fraction or an improper fraction as a mixed number, follow these rules:

1. To write a mixed number ($3\frac{1}{2}$) as an improper fraction, multiply the whole number (3) by the denominator (2), add the numerator (1), and write the sum over the denominator (2): $\frac{3 \times 2 + 1}{2} = \frac{7}{2}$.

2. To write an improper fraction ($\frac{7}{2}$) as a mixed number, divide the numerator by the denominator; the quotient (3) is the whole number. Place the remainder (1) over the denominator to form the fractional part $\left(\frac{1}{2}\right)$: $3\frac{1}{2}$.

CAUTION: You can *never* grid-in a mixed number. You must change it to an improper fraction or a decimal. (See Chapter 11.)

KEY FACT B9 To add mixed numbers, add the integers and add the fractions:

- $5\frac{1}{4} + 3\frac{2}{3} = (5+3) + \left(\frac{1}{4} + \frac{2}{3}\right) = 8 + \left(\frac{3}{12} + \frac{8}{12}\right) = 8 + \frac{11}{12} = 8\frac{11}{12}$

- $5\frac{3}{4} + 3\frac{2}{3} = (5+3) + \left(\frac{3}{4} + \frac{2}{3}\right) = 8 + \left(\frac{9}{12} + \frac{8}{12}\right) = 8 + \frac{17}{12} = 8 + 1\frac{5}{12} =$

  $8 + 1 + \frac{5}{12} = 9\frac{5}{12}$

KEY FACT B10 To subtract mixed numbers, subtract the integers and also subtract the fractions. If, however, the fraction in the second number is greater than the fraction in the first number, you first have to borrow 1 from the integer part. For example, since $\frac{2}{3} > \frac{1}{4}$, you can't subtract $5\frac{1}{4} - 3\frac{2}{3}$ until you borrow 1 from the 5:

$$5\frac{1}{4} = 5 + \frac{1}{4} = (4+1) + \frac{1}{4} = 4 + \left(1 + \frac{1}{4}\right) = 4 + \frac{5}{4}.$$

Now, you have

$$5\frac{1}{4} - 3\frac{2}{3} = 4\frac{5}{4} - 3\frac{2}{3} = (4-3) + \left(\frac{5}{4} - \frac{2}{3}\right) = 1 + \left(\frac{15}{12} - \frac{8}{12}\right) = 1\frac{7}{12}.$$

KEY FACT B11 To multiply or divide mixed numbers, change them to improper fractions:

$$1\frac{2}{3} \times 3\frac{1}{4} = \frac{5}{3} \times \frac{13}{4} = \frac{65}{12} = 5\frac{5}{12}$$

HELPFUL HINT *All arithmetic operations on mixed numbers can be done directly on calculators with fraction capabilities—there is no need to change the mixed numbers to improper fractions or to borrow.*

HELPFUL HINT *Remember that on the PSAT, if you ever get stuck on a fraction problem, you can always convert the fractions to decimals and do all the work on your calculator.*

EXERCISES

MULTIPLE-CHOICE QUESTIONS

1. The school band has 24 boys and 16 girls. What fraction of the band members are girls?

   (A) $\frac{2}{5}$ (B) $\frac{3}{5}$ (C) $\frac{2}{3}$ (D) $\frac{3}{4}$ (E) $\frac{3}{2}$

2. Adam had a baseball card collection. One day he gave Noah $\frac{1}{5}$ of cards; the following day he gave Pete $\frac{3}{8}$ of the cards he had left. What fraction of his original collection did Adam still have?

   (A) $\frac{3}{10}$ (B) $\frac{17}{40}$ (C) $\frac{1}{2}$ (D) $\frac{23}{40}$ (E) $\frac{7}{10}$

3. For how many integers n between 20 and 30 is it true that $\frac{3}{n}$, $\frac{5}{n}$, and $\frac{7}{n}$ are all in lowest terms?

   (A) 2 (B) 3 (C) 4 (D) 5 (E) 6

4. What fractional part of a week is 63 hours?

   (A) $\frac{7}{24}$ (B) $\frac{3}{8}$ (C) $\frac{24}{63}$ (D) $\frac{4}{7}$ (E) $\frac{7}{9}$

5. If $\frac{3}{7}$ of a number is 35, what is $\frac{6}{7}$ of that number?

   (A) 6 (B) 15 (C) 17.5 (D) 30 (E) 70

GRID-IN QUESTIONS

6. $\frac{5}{8}$ of 24 is equal to $\frac{15}{7}$ of what number?

7. If $5a = 3$ and $3b = 5$, what is the value of $\frac{a}{b}$?

8. What is a possible value of x if $\frac{2}{3} < \frac{1}{x} < \frac{7}{9}$?

9. Michael gave $\frac{1}{12}$ of his money to Sally and $\frac{1}{5}$ of his remaining money to Heidi. If he still had $704, how much money did he have originally?

10. Let $A = \{1, 2, 3\}$ and $B = \{2, 3, 4\}$, and let C be the set consisting of the 9 fractions whose numerators are in A and whose denominators are in B. What is the product of all of the numbers in C?

Answer Key

1. *A*   2. *C*   3. *C*   4. *B*   5. *E*

Grid 6: 7
Grid 7: 9/25
Grid 8: 10/7
Grid 9: 960
Grid 10: 1/64

9-C PERCENTS

The word *percent* means hundredth. We use the symbol % to express the word "percent." For example, "15 percent" means "15 hundredths" and can be written with a % symbol, as a fraction, or as a decimal: $15\% = \frac{15}{100} = .15$.

 KEY FACT C1 To convert a percent to a decimal or a percent to a fraction, follow these rules:

1. To convert a percent to a decimal, drop the % symbol and move the decimal point two places to the left, adding zeros if necessary. (Remember that we assume that there is a decimal point to the right of any whole number.)
2. To convert a percent to a fraction, drop the % symbol, write the number over 100, and reduce.

$$25\% = 25 = \frac{25}{100} = \frac{1}{4} \qquad 100\% = 1.00 = \frac{100}{100}$$

$$12.5\% = 125 = \frac{12.5}{100} = \frac{125}{1000} = \frac{1}{8}$$

$$1\% = .01 = \frac{1}{100} \qquad \frac{1}{2}\% = .5\% = .005 = \frac{.5}{100} = \frac{1}{200}$$

$$250\% = 2.50 = \frac{250}{100} = \frac{5}{2}$$

 KEY FACT C2 To convert a decimal to a percent or a fraction to a percent, follow these rules:

1. To convert a decimal to a percent, move the decimal point two places to the right, adding zeros if necessary, and add the % symbol.
2. To convert a fraction to a percent, first convert the fraction to a decimal, and then complete step 1.

$$.375 = 37.5\% \quad .3 = 30\% \qquad 1.25 = 125\% \quad 10 = 1000\%$$

$$\frac{3}{4} = .75 = 75\% \qquad \frac{1}{3} = .33333... = 33.333...\% = 33\frac{1}{3}\%$$

You should be familiar with the following basic conversions.

$$\frac{1}{4} = 25\% \qquad \frac{1}{3} = 33\frac{1}{3}\% \qquad \frac{1}{2} = 50\% \qquad \frac{2}{3} = 66\frac{2}{3}\% \qquad \frac{3}{4} = 75\%$$

 Any problem involving percents can be done on your calculator (even if your calculator doesn't have a % key): to find 25% of 32, write 25% as a decimal and multiply: $32 \times .25 = 8$. Consider these three questions:

   (i) What is 35% of 200?
   (ii) 70 is 35% of what number?
   (iii) 70 is what percent of 200?

Each question can be answered easily by using your calculator, but you must first set up the question properly so that you know what to multiply or divide. In each case, there is one unknown; call it x. Now, just translate each sentence, replacing "is" with "=" and the unknown by x.

   (i) $x = 35\%$ of $200 \Rightarrow x = .35 \times 200 = 70$.
   (ii) $70 = 35\%$ of $x \Rightarrow 70 = .35x \Rightarrow x = 70 \div .35 = 200$.
   (iii) $70 = x\%$ of $200 \Rightarrow 70 = \frac{x}{100}(200) \Rightarrow x = 35$.

Another way to handle questions such as these is to set up the proportion $\frac{is}{of} = \frac{\%}{100}$. To use this method, think of "is," "of," and "%" as variables.

In each percent problem you are given two of them and need to find the third, which you label x. Of course, you then solve such equations by cross-multiplying. For example, the three problems we just solved could be handled as follows:

(i) <u>What</u> <u>is</u> 35% of 200? (Let x = the "is" number.)

$$\frac{x}{200} = \frac{35}{100} \Rightarrow 100x = 35(200) = 7000 \Rightarrow x = 70$$

(ii) 70 is 35% <u>of</u> <u>what number</u>? (Let x = the "of" number.)

$$\frac{70}{x} = \frac{35}{100} \Rightarrow 7000 = 35x \Rightarrow x = 200$$

(iii) 70 is <u>what</u> <u>%</u> of 200? (Let x = the %.)

$$\frac{70}{200} = \frac{x}{100} \Rightarrow 200x = 7000 \Rightarrow x = 35$$

EXAMPLE 1

Justin gave 30% of his baseball cards to Judy and 25% to Lior. If he still had 540 cards, how many did he have originally?

Solution. Originally, Justin had 100% of the cards (all of them). Since he gave away 55% of them, he had 100% − 55% = 45% of them left. So, 540 is 45% of what number? $540 = .45x \Rightarrow x = 540 \div .45 = 1200$.

EXAMPLE 2

After Sharon gave 157 baseball cards to Zach and 95 to Samir, she still had 348 left. What percent of her cards did Sharon give away?

Solution. Sharon gave away a total of 252 cards and had 348 left. Therefore, she started with 252 + 348 = 600 cards. So, 252 is what percent of 600?

$$252 = \frac{x}{100}(600) \Rightarrow 6x = 252 \Rightarrow x = 252 \div 6 = 42.$$

Sharon gave away 42% of her cards.

KEY FACT **KEY FACT C3** For any positive number a: a% of 100 is a. For example: 17.2% of 100 is 17.2; 600% of 100 is 600; and $\frac{1}{5}$% of 100 = $\frac{1}{5}$.

In any problem involving percents, try to use the number 100.

EXAMPLE 3

In 1980 the populations of Madison and Monroe were the same. From 1980 to 1990, however, the population of Madison increased by 25% while the population of Monroe decreased by 25%. In 1990, the population of Monroe was what percent of the population of Madison?

(A) 25% (B) 50% (C) 60% (D) $66\frac{2}{3}$% (E) $166\frac{2}{3}$%

Solution. Assume that in 1980 the population of each town was 100. Then, since 25% of 100 is 25, in 1990, the populations were 100 + 25 = 125 (Madison) and 100 − 25 = 75 (Monroe). Then, in 1990, Monroe's population was $\frac{75}{125} = \frac{3}{5} = 60\%$ of Madison's.

KEY FACT **KEY FACT C4** For any positive numbers a and b: a% of b = b% of a.

Percent Increase and Percent Decrease

KEY FACT C5 The *percent increase* of a quantity is

$$\frac{\text{the actual increase}}{\text{the original amount}} \times 100\%.$$

The *percent decrease* of a quantity is

$$\frac{\text{the actual decrease}}{\text{the original amount}} \times 100\%.$$

For example:

- If the price of a radio goes from \$60 to \$75, the actual increase is \$15, and the percent increase is $\frac{15}{60} \leftrightarrow 100\% = \frac{1}{4} \times 100\% = 25\%$.
- If a \$75 radio is on sale for \$60, the actual decrease in price is \$15, and the percent decrease is $5\frac{\cancel{15}^1}{\cancel{75}_5} \times 100\% = \frac{1}{5} \times 100\% = 20\%$.

Notice that the percent increase in going from 60 to 75 is *not* the same as the percent decrease in going from 75 to 60.

CAUTION: Percents over 100%, which come up most often on questions involving percent increases, are often confusing for many students. Be sure you understand that 100% of a particular number is that number, 200% of a number is 2 times the number, and 1000% of a number is 10 times the number. For example, if the value of an investment rises from \$1000 to \$5000, the investment is now worth 5 times, or 500%, as much as it was originally, but there has been only a 400% increase in value:

$$\frac{\text{the actual increase}}{\text{the original amount}} \times 100\% = \frac{4000}{1000} \times 100\% = 4 \times 100\% = 400\%.$$

EXAMPLE 4

The value of an investment doubled every 5 years from 1980 to 1995. What was the percent increase in the value during this time?

Solution. The value doubled 3 times from, say, \$100 in 1980 to \$200 in 1985, to \$400 in 1990, and to \$800 in 1995. So the value in 1995 was 8 times the value in 1980, but this was an increase of \$700 or 700%.

EXERCISES

MULTIPLE-CHOICE QUESTIONS

1. Ron bought a \$60 sweater on sale at 10% off. How much did he pay, including 5% sales tax?

   (A) \$51.00 (B) \$53.50 (C) \$55.00
   (D) \$56.70 (E) \$57.00

2. What is 5% of 10% of 40%?

   (A) 0.002% (B) 0.2% (C) 2%
   (D) 20% (E) 2,000%

3. What percent of 25 is b?

   (A) $\frac{b}{25}$ (B) $\frac{b}{4}$ (C) $\frac{25}{b}$ (D) $\frac{4}{b}$ (E) $4b$

4. 10 is $\frac{1}{10}$% of what number?

   (A) .01 (B) 1 (C) 100
   (D) 1,000 (E) 10,000

5. On a test consisting of 80 questions, Susan answered 75% of the first 60 questions correctly. What percent of the other 20 questions does she need to answer correctly for her grade on the entire exam to be 80%?

   (A) 85% (B) 87.5% (C) 90%
   (D) 95% (E) 100%

GRID-IN QUESTIONS

6. A supermarket reduced the price per pound of whole chickens by 20%. How many pounds of chicken can now be purchased for the amount of money that used to buy 20 pounds of chicken?

7. If c is a positive number, 300% of c is what percent of $300c$?

8. If 25 students took an exam and 7 of them failed, what percent of them passed?

9. A college has 3000 students. If 23.5% of them are freshmen, 29.2% of them are sophomores, and 27% of them are juniors, how many are seniors?

10. There are twice as many girls as boys in a science class. If 30% of the girls and 45% of the boys have already completed their lab reports, what percent of the students have not yet finished their reports?

6.   **7.**   **8.**   **9.**   **10.**

Answer Key

1. *D*　　**2.** *B*　　**3.** *E*　　**4.** *E*　　**5.** *D*

6. 25   **7.** 1   **8.** 72   **9.** 609   **10.** 65

9-D RATIOS AND PROPORTIONS

A *ratio* is a fraction that compares two quantities that are measured in the *same* units. One quantity is the numerator of the fraction, and the other quantity is the denominator.

For example, if there are 6 boys and 16 girls in the chess club, we say that the ratio of the number of boys to the number of girls in the club is 6 to 16, or $\frac{6}{16}$, often written as 6:16. Since a ratio is just a fraction, it can be reduced or converted to a decimal or a percent. The following are all different ways to express the same ratio:

$$6 \text{ to } 16 \qquad 6{:}16 \qquad \frac{6}{16} \qquad 3 \text{ to } 8 \qquad 3{:}8 \qquad \frac{3}{8} \qquad .375 \qquad 37.5\%$$

KEY FACT **KEY FACT D1** If a set of objects is divided into two groups in the ratio of $a{:}b$, then the first group contains $\frac{a}{a+b}$ of the objects and the second group contains $\frac{b}{a+b}$ of the objects.

EXAMPLE 1

A jar contains only red and blue marbles. If the ratio of the number of blue marbles to the number of red marbles in the jar is 2:3, what percent of the marbles are red?

Solution. The red marbles constitute $\frac{3}{2+3} = \frac{3}{5} = 60\%$ of the total number.

EXAMPLE 2

If 35% of the students in the honor society are male, what is the ratio of male students to female students in the society?

(Reminder: In problems involving percents, the best number to use is 100.)

Solution. Assume that there are 100 students in the society; then 35 of them are male, and $100 - 35 = 65$ of them are female. So, the ratio of males to females is $\frac{35}{65} = \frac{7}{13}$.

If we know a ratio, we *cannot* determine from that fact alone how many objects there are. In Example 1 above, since the ratio of blue marbles to red marbles is 2:3, there *might be* 2 blue marbles and 3 red ones, but *not necessarily*—there might be 200 blue marbles and 300 red ones, since the ratio 200:300 clearly reduces to 2:3. In the same way, all of the following are possibilities for the distribution of marbles.

Blue	4	6	8	20	400	8,000	**2x**
Red	6	9	12	30	600	12,000	**3x**

The important thing to observe is that the number of red marbles can be *any* multiple of 3, as long as the number of blue marbles is the *same* multiple of 2.

KEY FACT **KEY FACT D2** If two numbers are in the ratio of $a{:}b$, then for some number x, the first number is ax and the second number is bx.

 D1

In any ratio problem, write the letter x after each number and use some given information to solve for x.

EXAMPLE 3

If the ratio of boys to girls at a pep rally is 4:5, which of the following CANNOT be the number of children at the pep rally?

(A) 27   (B) 45   (C) 108   (D) 120   (E) 360

Solution. If $4x$ and $5x$ are the number of boys and girls at the pep rally, respectively, then the number of children present is $4x + 5x = 9x$. Therefore, the number of children must be a multiple of 9. Only 120 (Choice D), is not divisible by 9.

Ratios can be extended to three or four or more terms. For example, we can say that the ratio of freshmen to sophomores to juniors to seniors in the school play is 2:3:5:3, which means that for every 2 freshmen in the play, there are 3 sophomores, 5 juniors, and 2 seniors.

EXAMPLE 4

If the measures of the three angles in a triangle are in the ratio of 5:6:7, what is the measure of the largest angle?

Solution. Let the measures of the three angles be $5x$, $6x$, and $7x$. Since in any triangle the sum of the measures of the three angles is 180° (**KEY FACT J1**):

$$5x + 6x + 7x = 180 \Rightarrow 18x = 180 \Rightarrow x = 10.$$

Therefore, the measure of the largest angle is $7 \times 10 = 70°$.

A **_proportion_** is an equation that states that two ratios are equivalent. Since ratios are just fractions, any equation such as $\frac{4}{6} = \frac{10}{15}$, in which each side is a single fraction, is a proportion. Usually, the proportions you encounter on the PSAT involve one or more variables.

TACTIC **D2**

Solve proportions by cross-multiplying: if $\frac{a}{b} = \frac{c}{d}$, then $ad = bc$.

EXAMPLE 5

If $\frac{2}{7} = \frac{x}{91}$, what is the value of x?

Solution. Cross-multiply: $2(91) = 7x \Rightarrow 182 = 7x \Rightarrow x = 26$.

A **_rate_** is a fraction that compares two quantities measured in *different* units. The word *per* often appears in rate problems: miles per hour, dollars per week, cents per ounce, children per classroom, and so on.

TACTIC **D3**

Set up rate problems just like ratio problems. Solve the proportions by cross-multiplying.

EXAMPLE 6

Susan completed 25 math exercises in 35 minutes. At this rate, how many exercises can she do in 42 minutes?

Solution. Handle this rate problem exactly like a ratio problem. Set up a proportion and cross-multiply:

$$\frac{\text{exercises}}{\text{minutes}} = \frac{25}{35} = \frac{x}{42} \Rightarrow 35x = 25 \times 42 = 1050 \Rightarrow x = 30.$$

On the PSAT, many rate problems involve only variables. These problems are handled in exactly the same way.

EXAMPLE 7

If a apples cost c cents, how many apples can be bought for d dollars?

(A) $100acd$ (B) $\frac{100d}{ac}$ (C) $\frac{ad}{100c}$ (D) $\frac{c}{100ad}$ (E) $\frac{100ad}{c}$

Solution. First change d dollars to $100d$ cents, and set up a proportion: $\frac{\text{apples}}{\text{cents}} = \frac{a}{c} = \frac{x}{100d}$. Now cross-multiply:

$$100ad = cx \Rightarrow x = \frac{100ad}{c} \text{ (Choice E).}$$

Rate problems are examples of **direct variation**. We say that one variable **varies directly** with a second variable or that the two variables are **directly proportional** if their quotient is a constant. So if y varies directly with x, there is a constant k, such that $\frac{y}{x} = k$. The constant is the rate of increase or decrease. In Example 6, the number of math exercises Susan does varies directly with the number of minutes she spends on them. Susan's rate of solving is $\frac{5}{7}$ exercises per minute.

$$\text{The quotient } \frac{\text{exercises}}{\text{minutes}} \text{ is constant: } \frac{25}{35} = \frac{5}{7} \text{ and } \frac{30}{42} = \frac{5}{7}.$$

Notice that when two quantities vary directly, as the first quantity increases or decreases, so does the other. In Example 6 as the number of exercises increases, the number of minutes it takes Susan to do them also increases.

EXAMPLE 8

If x and y are directly proportional and $x = 12$ when $y = 3$, what is x when $y = 12$?

Solution. Since x and y are directly proportional, their quotient is a constant. So $\frac{12}{3} = 4 = \frac{x}{12} \Rightarrow x = 48$.

Occasionally on the PSAT you will encounter problems in which as one quantity increases, the other decreases. Problems such as these are examples of **inverse variation**. We say that one variable **varies inversely** with a second variable or that the two variables are **inversely proportional** if their product is a constant. So if y varies inversely with x there is a constant k such that $xy = k$.

EXAMPLE 9

If x and y are inversely proportional and $x = 12$ when $y = 3$, what is x when $y = 12$?

Solution. Since x and y are inversely proportional, their product is a constant. So $12 \times 3 = 36 = x(12) \Rightarrow x = 3$.

EXAMPLE 10

A landscaper has enough money on hand to hire six workers for ten days. Assuming each worker earns the same amount of money per day, for how many days could the landscaper meet his payroll if he hires fifteen workers?

(A) 4   (B) 6   (C) 12   (D) 15   (E) 25

Solution. As the number of workers increases, the number of days the money will last decreases. So this is an example of inverse variation. The product (workers) × (days) remains constant.

$$(6 \text{ workers}) \times (10 \text{ days}) = 60 \text{ worker-days} = (15 \text{ workers}) \times (d \text{ days}) \Rightarrow d = 4.$$

EXERCISES

MULTIPLE-CHOICE QUESTIONS

1. If the ratio of boys to girls in the French Club is 2:3, what percent of the club members are girls?

(A) $33\frac{1}{3}$% (B) 40%   (C) 60%   (D) $66\frac{2}{3}$%
(E) It cannot be determined from the information given.

2. In the diagram below, $c:d = 5:7$. What is $d - c$?

Note: Figure not drawn to scale.

(A) 15   (B) 30   (C) 75   (D) 105   (E) 165

3. The measures of the three angles in a triangle are in the ratio of 1:1:2. Which of the following must be true?

    I. The triangle is isosceles.
   II. The triangle is a right triangle.
  III. The triangle is equilateral.

  (A) None (B) I only (C) II only
  (D) I and II only (E) I and III only

4. Gilda can grade t tests in $\frac{1}{x}$ hours. At this rate, how many tests can she grade in x hours?

  (A) tx (B) tx^2 (C) $\frac{1}{t}$ (D) $\frac{x}{t}$ (E) $\frac{1}{tx}$

5. Kerry can polish i inches of a railing in m minutes. At this rate, how many feet can he polish in h hours?

  (A) $\frac{5hi}{m}$ (B) $\frac{60hi}{m}$ (C) $\frac{hi}{12m}$
  (D) $\frac{5m}{hi}$ (E) $5him$

GRID-IN QUESTIONS

6. If $\frac{a}{9} = \frac{9}{2a}$, what is the value of a^2?

7. Roselle can read 36 pages per hour. At this rate, how many pages can she read in 36 minutes?

8. If $3a = 2b$ and $3b = 5c$, what is the ratio of a to c?

9. In a quadrilateral, the ratio of the measures of the four angles is 5:6:6:7. What is the degree measure of the largest angle?

10. A club had 3 boys and 5 girls. During a membership drive the same number of boys and girls joined the club. How many members does the club have now if the ratio of boys to girls is 3:4?

6.
7.
8.
9.
10.

Answer Key

1. *C*   2. *B*   3. *D*   4. *B*   5. *A*

6. 40.5
7. 21.6
8. 10/9
9. 105
10. 14

9-E AVERAGES

The *average* of a set of n numbers is the sum of those numbers divided by n.

$$\text{Average} = \frac{\text{the sum of the } n \text{ numbers}}{n} \quad \text{or simply} \quad A = \frac{\text{sum}}{n}.$$

If you took three math tests so far this year and your grades were 81, 93, and 78, to calculate your average, you would add the three grades and divide by 3:

$$\frac{81 + 93 + 78}{3} = \frac{252}{3} = 84.$$

The technical name for this is *arithmetic mean*, and on the PSAT those words always appear in parentheses—for example, "What is the average (arithmetic mean) of 81, 93, and 78?"

Very often on the PSAT, you are *not* asked to find an average; rather, you are given the average of a set of numbers and asked to provide some other information. The key to solving all of these problems is to first find the sum of the numbers. Since $A = \frac{\text{sum}}{n}$, multiplying both sides by n yields this equation: sum $= nA$.

KEY FACT   **KEY FACT E1** If the average of a set of n numbers is A, the sum of those numbers is nA.

EXAMPLE 1

The average (arithmetic mean) of Carol's grades on the 6 French tests that she has taken this year is 86. If her average after the first 4 tests was 83, what was the average of her fifth and sixth tests?

(A) 84.5   (B) 87.5   (C) 89   (D) 90   (E) 92

Solution.

- Carol has earned a total of $6 \times 86 = 516$ points.
- On her first 4 tests she earned $4 \times 83 = 332$ points.
- On her last 2 tests Carol earned $516 - 332 = 184$ points.
- Carol's average on her last 2 tests is $\frac{184}{2} = 92$ (Choice E)

The difference between each number in a set and the average of those numbers is called a *deviation*.

KEY FACT   **KEY FACT E2** For any set of numbers, the sum of the deviations below the average is equal to the sum of the deviations above the average.

Here is a second solution of Example 1, using **KEY FACT E2**.

Solution. Assume that each of Carol's first 4 grades was 83. Then each of them has a deviation of 3 points below the average of 86, for a total deviation of 12 points below the average. Therefore, the total deviation above the average must be 12. This is easily achieved if each of the last 2 tests is 6 points above the average of 86, that is, if each one is 92.

EXAMPLE 2

In Mr. Walsh's biology class, the average (arithmetic mean) of the grades earned by the 15 girls was 90, and the average grade earned by the 10 boys was 80. What was the class average?

The answer to this question is *not* 85. When we combine two or more averages to form a single average, we cannot take the average of the averages. We must assign each average its proper *weight*. In this case, more students earned 90 then 80, so the class average must be closer to 90 than to 80—surely greater than 85. Here is the solution.

- The 15 girls earned a total of $15 \times 90 = 1350$ points.
- The 10 boys earned a total of $10 \times 80 = 800$ points.
- Together the 25 students earned a total of $1350 + 800 = 2150$ points.
- The class average was $2150 \div 25 = 86$.

The solution to Example 2 can be expressed as a single fraction:

$$\frac{15(90) + 10(80)}{25} = \frac{1350 + 800}{25} = \frac{2150}{25} = 86.$$

Two other terms that are associated with averages are **median** and **mode**. In a set of n numbers that are arranged in increasing order, the **median** is the middle number (if n is odd) or the average of the two middle numbers (if n is even). The **mode** is the number in the set that occurs most often.

EXAMPLE 3

In 1998, Judith sold 9 paintings. The selling prices were: $500, $1100, $2000, $500, $1200, $5000, $700, $500, $4000. What is the average (arithmetic mean) of the median and mode of this set of data?

Solution. The first step is to write the data in increasing order:

500, 500, 500, 700, <u>1100</u>, 1200, 2000, 4000, 5000.

The median is 1100, the middle number. The mode is 500, the number that appears more times than any other. The average of the median and the mode is

$$\frac{1100 + 500}{2} = \frac{1600}{2} = 800.$$

EXERCISES

MULTIPLE-CHOICE QUESTIONS

1. If the average (arithmetic mean) of 15, 16, 17, and w is 18, what is the value of w?

    (A) 16.5   (B) 18   (C) 24   (D) 48   (E) 72

2. Linda's average (arithmetic mean) on 4 tests is 80. What does she need on her fifth test to raise her average to 84?

    (A) 82   (B) 84   (C) 92   (D) 96   (E) 100

3. If $x + y = 5$, $y + z = 8$ and $z + x = 9$, what is the average (arithmetic mean) of x, y, and z?

    (A) $\frac{11}{3}$ (B) $\frac{11}{2}$ (C) $\frac{22}{3}$ (D) 11   (E) 22

4. If $a + b = 3(c + d)$, which of the following is the average (arithmetic mean) of a, b, c, and d?

    (A) $\frac{c + d}{4}$ (B) $\frac{3(c + d)}{8}$ (C) $\frac{c + d}{2}$

    (D) $\frac{3(c + d)}{4}$ (E) $c + d$

5. Which of the following is the average (arithmetic mean) of $x^2 - 10$, $30 - x^2$, and $6x + 10$?

    (A) $2x + 10$ (B) $2x + 30$ (C) $3x + 15$
    (D) $2x^2 + 6x + 30$ (E) $6x + 10$

GRID-IN QUESTIONS

6. What is the average (arithmetic mean) of the positive integers from 1 to 50, inclusive?

7. If $20a + 20b = 70$, what is the average (arithmetic mean) of a and b?

8. What is the average (arithmetic mean), in degrees, of the measures of the five angles in a pentagon?

9. Jason's average (arithmetic mean) on 4 tests is 80. Assuming he can earn no more than 100 on any test, what is the least he can earn on his fifth test and still have a chance for an 85 average after 7 tests?

10. Let M be the median and m the mode of the following set of numbers: 20, 80, 30, 50, 80, 100. What is the average (arithmetic mean) of M and m?

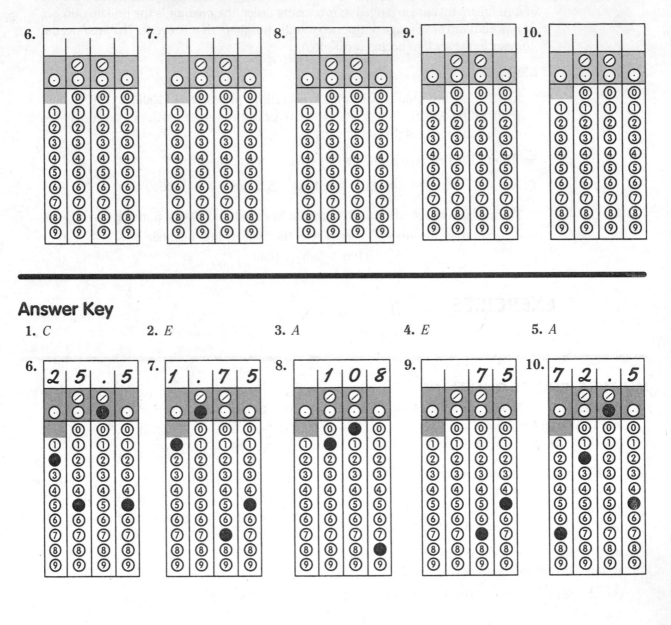

Answer Key

1. *C*   **2.** *E*   **3.** *A*   **4.** *E*   **5.** *A*

6. 25.5   **7.** 1.75   **8.** 108   **9.** 75   **10.** 72.5

Algebra

For the PSAT you need to know only a small part of the algebra normally taught in a high school elementary algebra course and none of the material taught in an intermediate or advanced algebra course. In Sections 9-F, 9-G, and 9-H, we will review only those topics that you absolutely need for the PSAT.

9-F POLYNOMIALS

Even though the terms *monomial*, *binomial*, *trinomial*, and *polynomial* are not used on the PSAT, you need to be able to work with simple polynomials, and these terms will make it easy to discuss the important concepts.

- A **monomial** is any number or variable or product of numbers and variables. Each of the following are monomials:

$$3 \quad -4 \quad x \quad y \quad 3x \quad -4xyz \quad 5x^3 \quad 1.5xy^2 \quad a^3b^4$$

The number that appears in front of the variables in a monomial is called the **coefficient**. The coefficient of $5x^3$ is 5. If there is no number, the coefficient is 1 or -1, because x means $1x$ and $-ab^2$ means $-1ab^2$.

- A **polynomial** is a monomial or the sum of two or more monomials. Each monomial that makes up the polynomial is called a **term** of the polynomial.

Polynomials that have two terms are called **binomials**, and polynomials that have three terms are called **trinomials**. The table below gives examples of each type.

Monomials	Binomials	Trinomials
x^2	$2x^2 + 3$	$x^2 + 5x - 1$
$3abc$	$3x^2 - 7$	$w^2 - 2w + 1$
$-a^2b^3$	$a^2b + b^2a$	$a^2 + 2ab + b^2$

Two terms are called *like terms* if they have exactly the same variables and exponents; they can differ only in their coefficients: $5a^2b$ and $-3a^2b$ are like terms, whereas a^2b and b^2a are not.

On the PSAT, you are often asked to evaluate a polynomial for specific values of the variables.

EXAMPLE 1

What is the value of $-2a^2b + ab$ when $a = -6$ and $b = 0.5$?

Solution. Rewrite the expression, replacing the letters a and b by the numbers -6 and 0.5, respectively. First, write each number in parentheses and then evaluate:

$$-2(-6)^2(0.5) + (-6)(0.5) = -2(36)(0.5) + (-3) = -36 - 3 = -39.$$

CAUTION: Be sure you follow PEMDAS: Handle exponents before the other operations. For example, in Example 1, you cannot multiply -2 by -6, get 12, and then square 12. You must first square -6, and then multiply by -2.

 KEY FACT F1 The only terms of a polynomial that can be combined are like terms.

 To add, subtract, multiply, and divide polynomials, use the usual laws of arithmetic. To avoid careless errors, write each polynomial in parentheses before performing any arithmetic operations.

KEY FACT F2 To add two polynomials, put a plus sign between them, erase the parentheses, and combine like terms.

EXAMPLE 2

What is the sum of $5x^2 + 10x - 7$ and $3x^2 - 4x + 2$?

Solution.

$$(5x^2 + 10x - 7) + (3x^2 - 4x + 2)$$
$$= 5x^2 + 10x - 7 + 3x^2 - 4x + 2$$
$$= (5x^2 + 3x^2) + (10x - 4x) + (-7 + 2)$$
$$= 8x^2 + 6x - 5.$$

KEY FACT F3 To subtract two polynomials, change the minus sign between them to a plus sign and change the sign of every term in the second parentheses. Then use **KEY FACT F2** to add them: erase the parentheses and combine like terms.

CAUTION: Make sure you get the order right in a subtraction problem.

EXAMPLE 3

Subtract $3x^2 - 4x + 2$ from $5x^2 + 10x - 7$.

Solution. Be careful. Start with the second polynomial and subtract the first:

$$(5x^2 + 10x - 7) - (3x^2 - 4x + 2)$$
$$= (5x^2 + 10x - 7) + (-3x^2 + 4x - 2)$$
$$= 2x^2 + 14x - 9$$

KEY FACT F4 To multiply monomials, first multiply their coefficients and then multiply their variables, by adding the exponents (see Section 12-A).

EXAMPLE 4

What is the product of $5xy^3z^5$ and $-2x^3y$?

Solution. $(5xy^3z^5)(-2x^2y) = 5(-2)(x)(x^3)(y^3)(y)(z^5) = -10x^4y^4z^5$.

All other polynomials are multiplied by using the distributive property.

KEY FACT F5 To multiply a monomial by any polynomial, just multiply each term of the polynomial by the monomial.

EXAMPLE 5

What is the product of $2a$ and $3a^2 - 6ab + b^2$?

Solution. $2a(3a^2 - 6ab + b^2) = 6a^3 - 12a^2b + 2ab^2$.

On the PSAT, the only other polynomials that you could be asked to multiply are two binomials.

KEY FACT F6 To multiply two binomials, use the so-called FOIL method, which is really nothing more than the distributive law. Multiply each term in the first parentheses by each term in the second parentheses and simplify by combining terms, if possible.

$(2x - 7)(3x + 2) = (2x)(3x) + (2x)(2) + (-7)(3x) + (-7)(2) = 6x^2 + 4x - 21x - 14 = 6x^2 - 17x - 14$

<u>F</u>irst terms   <u>O</u>uter terms   <u>I</u>nner terms   <u>L</u>ast terms

EXAMPLE 6

What is the value of $(x - 3)(x + 4) - (x - 5)(x + 6)$?

Solution. First, multiply both pairs of binomials:

$(x - 3)(x + 4) = x^2 + 4x - 3x - 12 = x^2 + x - 12$
$(x - 5)(x + 6) = x^2 + 6x - 5x - 30 = x^2 + x - 30$

Now, subtract: $(x^2 + x - 12) - (x^2 + x - 30) = x^2 + x - 12 - x^2 - x + 30 = 18$.

KEY FACT **KEY FACT F7** The three most important binomial products on the PSAT are

- $(x - y)(x + y) = x^2 - y^2$
- $(x - y)^2 = x^2 - 2xy + y^2$
- $(x + y)^2 = x^2 + 2xy + y^2$

HELPFUL HINT *If you memorize these products, you won't have to multiply the binomials out each time you need them.*

EXAMPLE 7

If $a - b = 9.2$ and $a + b = 5$, what is the value of $a^2 - b^2$?

Solution. The moment you see $a^2 - b^2$, you should think $(a - b)(a + b)$. So, $a^2 - b^2 = (a - b)(a + b) = (9.2)(5) = 46$.

On the PSAT, the only division of polynomials you will have to do is to divide a polynomial by a monomial. You will *not* have to do long division of polynomials.

KEY FACT **KEY FACT F8** To divide a polynomial by a monomial, use the distributive property.

EXAMPLE 8

What is the quotient when $24a^2b + 9ab^3c$ is divided by $6ab$?

Solution. By the distributive property, $\frac{24a^2b + 9ab^3c}{6ab} = \frac{24a^2b}{6ab} + \frac{9ab^3c}{6ab}$.
Now simplify each fraction: $4a + \frac{3}{2}b^2c$.

Occasionally on the PSAT you will be asked to simplify an algebraic expression. To do so, you will probably have to do some simple factoring.

KEY FACT **KEY FACT F9** To factor a polynomial, the first step is *always* to use the distributive property to remove the greatest common factor of all the terms.

For example:

$$6xy + 8yz = 2y(3x + 4z)$$
$$x^3 + x^2 + x = x(x^2 + x + 1)$$

KEY FACT **KEY FACT F10** To factor a trinomial, use trial and error to find the binomials whose product is that trinomial.

For example:

$$x^2 - 4x + 4 = (x - 2)(x - 2)$$
$$x^2 - 2x - 15 = (x - 5)(x + 3)$$
$$2x^2 + 12x + 16 = 2(x^2 + 6x + 8) = 2(x + 4)(x + 2)$$

EXAMPLE 9

Which of the following is equivalent to $\frac{2x^2 - 8}{x^2 - 4x + 4}$?

(A) 2 (B) $\frac{2(x+2)}{x-2}$ (C) $\frac{2(x+4)}{x-4}$ (D) $\frac{2x+2}{x-2}$ (E) $\frac{6}{4x-4}$

Solution.

$$\frac{2x^2 - 8}{x^2 - 4x + 4} = \frac{2(x^2 - 4)}{(x-2)(x-2)} = \frac{2(x-2)(x+2)}{(x-2)(x-2)} = \frac{2(x+2)}{x-2} \text{ (Choice B).}$$

 If you ever get stuck trying to simplify an algebraic expression, just plug in a number and test the answers. In Example 9, when $x = 3$, the value of

$$\frac{2x^2 - 8}{x^2 - 4x + 4} \text{ is } \frac{2(3)^2 - 8}{3^2 - 4(3) + 4} = \frac{18 - 8}{9 - 12 + 4} = \frac{10}{1} = 10.$$

Only Choice B is 10 when $x = 3$: $\frac{2(3+2)}{3-2} = \frac{2(5)}{1} = 10.$

Note that this does not depend on the choice of x. You can verify, for example, that if $x = 6$, the original expression and the correct answer choice are both equal to 4.

EXERCISES

MULTIPLE-CHOICE QUESTIONS

1. If $x^2 + y^2 = 36$ and $(x + y)^2 = 64$, what is the value of xy?

(A) 7 (B) 14 (C) 28 (D) 100
(E) It cannot be determined from the information given.

2. What is the value of $(500,001)^2 - (499,999)^2$?

(A) 2 (B) 4 (C) 1,000,000 (D) 2,000,000
(E) 1,000,000,000,000

3. If $\frac{1}{x} + \frac{1}{y} = \frac{1}{z}$ and $xy = z$, what is the average of x and y?

(A) 0 (B) $\frac{1}{2}$ (C) 1 (D) $\frac{z}{2}$ (E) $\frac{x+y}{2z}$

4. What is the average (arithmetic mean) of $x^2 + 2x - 3$, $3x^2 - 2x - 3$, and $30 - 4x^2$?

(A) $\frac{8x^2 + 4x + 24}{3}$ (B) $\frac{8x^2 + 24}{3}$ (C) $\frac{24 - 4x}{3}$
(D) -12 (E) 8

5. What is the value of $x^2 - 10x + 25$ when $x = 95$?

(A) 90 (B) 100 (C) 950
(D) 8,100 (E) 10,000

GRID-IN QUESTIONS

6. If $a^2 + b^2 = 4$ and $(a - b)^2 = 2$, what is the value of ab?

7. What is the value of $\frac{c^2 - d^2}{c - d}$ when $c = 23.4$ and $d = 34.5$?

8. If $x^2 - y^2 = 80$ and $x - y = 16$, what is the average of x and y?

9. What is the value of
$(2x + 3)(x + 6) - (2x - 5)(x + 10)$?

10. If $\left(\frac{1}{a} + a\right)^2 = 144$, what is the value of $\frac{1}{a^2} + a^2$?

Answer Key

1. *B*   **2.** *D*   **3.** *B*   **4.** *E*   **5.** *D*

6. 1   **7.** 57.9   **8.** 2.5   **9.** 68   **10.** 142

9-G SOLVING EQUATIONS AND INEQUALITIES

Most of the equations and inequalities that you will have to solve on the PSAT have only one variable and no exponents. A simple six-step method, illustrated below, can be used on all of them.

EXAMPLE 1

If $\frac{1}{2}x + 3(x - 2) = 2(x + 1) + 1$, what is the value of x?

Solution. Follow the steps outlined in the following table.

Step	What to Do	Example
1	Remove fractions and decimals by multiplying both sides by the Lowest Common Denominator (LCD).	Multiply each term by 2: $x + 6(x - 2) = 4(x + 1) + 2$
2	Remove all parentheses by using the distributive property.	$x + 6x - 12 = 4x + 4 + 2$
3	Combine like terms on each side.	$7x - 12 = 4x + 6$
4	By adding or subtracting, get all the variables on one side.	Subtract $4x$ from each side: $3x - 12 = 6$
5	By adding or subtracting, get all the plain numbers on the other side.	Add 12 to each side: $3x = 18$
6	Divide both sides by the coefficient of the variable.	Divide both sides by 3: $x = 6$

Note: If you start with an inequality and in Step 6 you divide by a negative number, remember to reverse the inequality.

Example 1 *is actually much more difficult than any equation on the PSAT,* because it requires all six steps. This never happens on the PSAT. Think of the six steps as a list of questions that must be answered. Ask whether each step is necessary. If it isn't, move on to the next one; if it is, do it.

Let's look at Example 2, which does not require all six steps.

EXAMPLE 2

For what real number x is it true that $4(2x - 7) = x$?

(A) −4   (B) −1   (C) 0   (D) 1   (E) 4

Solution. Do whichever of the six steps are necessary.

Step	Question	Yes/No	What to Do
1	Are there any fractions or decimals?	No	
2	Are there any parentheses?	Yes	Get rid of them: $8x - 28 = x$.
3	Are there any like terms to combine?	No	
4	Are there variables on both sides?	Yes	Subtract x from each side: $7x - 28 = 0$
5	Is there a plain number on the same side as the variable?	Yes	Add 28 to each side: $7x = 28$
6	Does the variable have a coefficient?	Yes	Divide both sides by 7: $x = 4$

 G1

Memorize these six steps *in order*, and use this method whenever you have to solve this type of equation or inequality.

Sometimes on the PSAT, you are given an equation with several variables and asked to solve for one of them in terms of the others.

TACTIC **G2**

When you have to solve for one variable in terms of the others, treat all of the others as if they were numbers, and apply the six-step method.

EXAMPLE 4

If $r = 5s - 2t$, what is the value of s in terms of r and t?

Solution. To solve for s, treat r and t as numbers, and use the six-step method with s as the only variable.

Step	Question	Yes/No	What to Do
1	Are there any fractions or decimals?	No	
2	Are there any parentheses?	No	
3	Are there any like terms to combine?	No	
4	Are there variables on both sides?	No	Remember: The only variable is s.
5	Is there a plain number on the same side as the variable?	Yes	Remember: We're considering t as a number, and it is on the same side as s, the variable. Add $2t$ to both sides: $r + 2t = 5s$
6	Does the variable have a coefficient?	Yes	Divide both sides by 5: $s = \frac{r + 2t}{5}$

The six-step method can also be used if a variable is in a denominator. Just be sure to start with Step 1 and get rid of the fraction.

EXAMPLE 5

If $\frac{1}{2x} + \frac{2}{3} = \frac{4}{3x}$, then $x =$

Solution. Multiply each term by $6x$, the LCD,

$$6x\left(\frac{1}{2x}\right) + 6x\left(\frac{2}{3}\right) = 6x\left(\frac{4}{3x}\right) \Rightarrow 3 + 4x = 8 \Rightarrow 4x = 5 \Rightarrow x = \frac{5}{4} \text{ (or 1.25)}$$

Occasionally, on the PSAT you will have to solve an equation, such as $2\sqrt{x} - 7 = 5$, that involves a square root. Proceed normally, treating the square root as your variable, using whichever of the six steps are necessary until you have that square root equal to a number. Then square both sides.

EXAMPLE 6

If $2\sqrt{x} - 7 = 5$, then $x =$

Solution.

Add 7 to each side: $2\sqrt{x} = 12$
Divide each side by 2: $\sqrt{x} = 6$
Now square each side: $(\sqrt{x})^2 = 6^2 \Rightarrow x = 36$

Systems of Linear Equations

The equations $x + y = 10$ and $x - y = 2$ each have infinitely many solutions. However, there is only one pair of numbers, $x = 6$ and $y = 4$, which satisfy both equations simultaneously: $6 + 4 = 10$ and $6 - 4 = 2$. These numbers are the only solution of the *system of equations*: $x + y = 10$ and $x - y = 2$.

A system of equations is a set of two or more equations involving two or more variables. To solve such a system, you must find values for each of the variables that will make each equation true. On the PSAT, the most useful method is to add or subtract the equations (usually add).

TACTIC **G3**

To solve a system of equations, add or subtract them. If there are more than two equations, add them.

EXAMPLE 7

If $2x + y = 10$ and $x - y = 2$, then what is the value of xy?

Solution. Add the two equations:

$$\begin{array}{r} 2x + y = 10 \\ + \quad x - y = 2 \\ \hline 3x \quad\quad = 12 \end{array} \qquad \text{so, } x = 4$$

Replacing x by 4 in $x - y = 2$, yields $y = 2$. So, $xy = (4)(2) = 8$.

EXAMPLE 8

If $3a + 5b = 10$ and $5a + 3b = 30$, what is the average (arithmetic mean) of a and b ?

(A) 2.5   (B) 4   (C) 5   (D) 20

(E) It cannot be determined from the information given.

Solution. Add the two equations:

$$\begin{array}{r} 3a + 5b = 10 \\ + \ 5a + 3b = 30 \\ \hline 8a + 8b = 40 \end{array}$$

Divide both sides by 8:

$$a + b = 5$$

The average of a and b is:

$$\frac{a + b}{2} = \frac{5}{2} = 2.5 \ \text{(Choice A)}$$

NOTE: It is not only unnecessary to first solve for a and b ($a = 7.5$ and $b = -2.5$), but because it is so much more time consuming, it would be foolish to do so.

EXERCISES

MULTIPLE-CHOICE QUESTIONS

1. If $5x + 12 = 5 - 2x$, what is the value of x ?

(A) $-\frac{17}{7}$ (B) -3 (C) -1 (D) 1 (E) $\frac{17}{7}$

2. If $\frac{1}{a - b} = 6$, then $a =$

(A) $b + 6$ (B) $b - 6$ (C) $b + \frac{1}{6}$

(D) $b - \frac{1}{6}$ (E) $\frac{1 - 6b}{6}$

3. If $\frac{1}{3}x + \frac{1}{6}x + \frac{1}{9}x = 33$, what is the value of x ?

(A) 3   (B) 18   (C) 27   (D) 54   (E) 72

4. If $ax - b = c - dx$, what is the value of x in terms of a, b, c, and d?

(A) $\frac{b + c}{a + d}$ (B) $\frac{c - b}{a - d}$ (C) $\frac{b + c - d}{a}$

(D) $\frac{c - b}{a + d}$ (E) $\frac{c}{b} - \frac{d}{a}$

5. If $\frac{a + 2b + 3c}{3} = \frac{a + 2b}{2}$, then $c =$

(A) $\frac{a + 2b}{6}$ (B) $\frac{a + 2b}{3}$ (C) $\frac{a + 2b}{2}$

(D) $a + 2b$ (E) $\frac{1}{2}$

GRID-IN QUESTIONS

6. If $9x + 10 = 32$, what is the value of $9x - 10$?

7. If $7x - 3 = 11$, what is the value of $(7x - 3)^2$?

8. If $a = 2b$, $3b = 4c$, and $5c = 6a - 7$, what is the value of c?

9. If $7y - 5x = 3$, what is the smallest integer value of x for which $y > 75$?

10. If $x^2 + 5 < 6$ and $2x^2 + 7 > 8$, what is one possible value of x?

Answer Key

1. *C* **2.** *C* **3.** *D* **4.** *A* **5.** *A*

or any number
satisfying *.71 < x < 1*

9-H WORD PROBLEMS

A typical PSAT has several word problems. In this chapter you have already seen word problems on consecutive integers in Section 12-A, fractions in Section 12-B, percents in Section 12-C, ratios and proportions in Section 12-D, and averages in Section 12-E. Later in this chapter you will see word problems involving probability, circles, triangles, and other geometric figures. A few of these problems can be solved with just arithmetic, but most of them require basic algebra.

Age Problems

HELPFUL HINT *In problems involving ages, remember that "years ago" means you need to subtract, and "years from now" means you need to add.*

Example 1 below is the same as Example 2 in Chapter 8. In Chapter 8 you were shown how to solve it by backsolving; now we will show you the correct algebraic solution.

EXAMPLE 1

Judy is now twice as old as Adam, but six years ago, she was five times as old as he was. How old is Judy now?

(A) 8   (B) 16   (C) 20   (D) 24   (E) 32

HELPFUL HINT *It is often very useful to organize the data from a word problem in a table.*

Solution. Let x = Adam's age now, and fill in the table below.

	Judy	Adam
Now	$2x$	x
6 years ago	$2x - 6$	$x - 6$

Now translate: Judy's age six years ago was five times Adam's age:

$$2x - 6 = 5(x - 6)$$
$$2x - 6 = 5x - 30 \Rightarrow 24 = 3x \Rightarrow x = 8.$$

Adam is now 8. However, 8 is *not* the answer. The question could have asked for Adam's age now or six years ago or at any time. It could have asked for Judy's age at any time or for their combined ages. What it did ask for is Judy's age now, which is 16, twice Adam's age (Choice B).

HELPFUL HINT *In all word problems on the PSAT, circle what you're looking for in your exam booklet. Don't answer the wrong question!*

Distance Problems

All distance problems involve one of three variations of the same formula:

$$\text{distance} = \text{rate} \times \text{time} \quad \text{rate} = \frac{\text{distance}}{\text{time}}$$
$$\text{time} = \frac{\text{distance}}{\text{rate}}$$

These are usually abbreviated, $d = rt$, $r = \frac{d}{t}$, and $t = \frac{d}{r}$.

EXAMPLE 2

Justin drove 1 mile, from Exit 10 to Exit 11 on the thruway, at 50 miles per hour. Adam drove the same distance at 60 miles per hour. How many *seconds* longer did it take Justin than Adam to drive that mile?

Solution. The time to drive 1 mile at 50 miles per hour is given by

$$t = \frac{1 \text{ mile}}{50 \text{ miles per hour}} = \frac{1}{50} \text{ hour} = \frac{1}{50} \times 60 \text{ minutes} =$$

$$\frac{6}{5} \text{ minutes} = 1\frac{1}{5} \text{ minutes}$$

The time to drive 1 mile at 60 miles per hour is given by

$$t = \frac{1 \text{ mile}}{60 \text{ miles per hour}} = \frac{1}{60} \text{ hour} = 1 \text{ minute.}$$

The difference is $\frac{1}{5}$ minute $= \frac{1}{5}$ (60 seconds) $= 12$ seconds.

Note that the solution to Example 2 used the time formula but required only arithmetic, not algebra. Example 3 requires an algebraic solution.

EXAMPLE 3

Eve drove from her home to college at an average speed of 60 miles per hour. Returning over the same route, due to construction delays, she was able to average only 45 miles per hour. If the return trip took 30 minutes longer, how many miles did she drive each way?

(A) 1.5   (B) 2   (C) 2.5   (D) 90   (E) 180

Solution. Let $x =$ the number of hours it took to go. Then to return, it took $x + 0.5$ hours (*not* $x + 30$). Now make a table.

	Rate	Time	Distance
going	60	x	$60x$
returning	45	$x + 0.5$	$45(x + 0.5)$

Since she drove the same distance going and returning:

$$60x = 45(x + 0.5) \Rightarrow 60x = 45x + 22.5 \Rightarrow 15x = 22.5 \Rightarrow x = 1.5.$$

Now be sure to answer the correct question. Choices A, B, and C are the time, in hours, for going, returning, and the round-trip; Choices D and E are the distances each way and round-trip. You could have been asked for any of the five. If you circled what you're looking for, you won't make a careless mistake. Eve drove $60(1.5) = 90$ miles each way, and so the correct answer is Choice D.

The d in $d = rt$ stands for "distance," but it could represent any type of work that is performed at a certain rate r for a certain amount of time t. Example 3 did not have to be about distance. Instead of driving 90 miles at 45 miles per hour for 2 hours, Eve could have read 90 pages at a rate of 45 pages per hour for 2 hours or planted 90 flowers at the rate of 45 flowers per hour for 2 hours or typed 90 words at a rate of 45 words per minute for 2 minutes.

Most algebraic word problems on the PSAT are not too difficult. If you get stuck on one, however, don't despair. Use one or more of the tactics that you learned in Chapter 9, especially backsolving, to eliminate choices and, if necessary, guess.

EXERCISES

MULTIPLE-CHOICE QUESTIONS

1. In 7 years Danielle will be twice as old as she was 8 years ago. How old is Danielle now?

   (A) 7　(B) 15　(C) 23　(D) 30　(E) 37

2. In the morning, Alan drove 100 miles at the rate of 60 miles per hour; in the afternoon, he drove another 100 miles at the rate of 40 miles per hour. What was his average rate of speed, in miles per hour, for the day?

   (A) 45　(B) 48　(C) 50　(D) 52　(E) 55

3. In a family of three, the father weighed 5 times as much as the child, and the mother weighed $\frac{3}{4}$ as much as the father. If the three of them weighed a total of 390 pounds, how much did the mother weigh?

   (A) 40　(B) 100　(C) 125　(D) 150　(E) 200

4. At 7:00 P.M., the hostess of the party remarked that only $\frac{1}{4}$ of her guests had arrived so far but that as soon as 10 more showed up, $\frac{1}{3}$ of the guests would be there. How many people were invited?

   (A) 20　(B) 32　(C) 80　(D) 120　(E) 144

5. If the sum of 5 consecutive integers is S, what is the largest of those integers in terms of S?

   (A) $\frac{S-10}{5}$　(B) $\frac{S+4}{4}$　(C) $\frac{S+5}{4}$

   (D) $\frac{S-5}{2}$　(E) $\frac{S+10}{5}$

GRID-IN QUESTIONS

6. A box contains only red, yellow, and green jelly beans. The number of red jelly beans is $\frac{4}{5}$ the number of green ones, and the number of green ones is $\frac{3}{4}$ the number of yellow ones. If there are 470 jelly beans in all, how many of them are yellow?

7. On a certain project the only grades awarded were 75 and 100. If 85 students completed the project and the average of their grades was 85, how many earned 100?

8. Since 1953, when Frank graduated from high school, he has gained two pounds every year. In 1983 he was 40% heavier than in 1953. What percent of his 1998 weight was his 1983 weight?

9. The number of baseball cards in Neil's collection is 80% of the number in Larry's collection. If Neil has 80 fewer baseball cards than Larry, how many do they have altogether?

10. What is the greater of two numbers whose product is 700, if the sum of the two numbers exceeds their difference by 20?

Answer Key

1. *C*   **2.** *B*   **3.** *D*   **4.** *D*   **5.** *E*

6. 200

7. 34

8. 87.5

9. 720

10. 70

Geometry

Although about 30% of the math questions on the PSAT involve geometry, you need to know only a relatively small number of facts—far fewer than you would learn in a geometry course—and, of course, you don't need to provide proofs. In the next six sections we will review all of the geometry that you need to know to do well on the PSAT. Also, we will present the material exactly as it appears on the PSAT, using the same vocabulary and notation, which may be slightly different from the terminology you have used in your math classes.

9-1 LINES AND ANGLES

An **angle** is formed by the intersection of two line segments, rays, or lines. The point of intersection is called the **vertex**. On the PSAT, angles are always measured in degrees.

 KEY FACT I1 Angles are classified according to their degree measures.

- An **acute** angle measures less than 90° (Figure 1).
- A **right** angle measures 90° (Figure 2).
- An **obtuse** angle measures more than 90° but less than 180° (Figure 3).
- A **straight** angle measures 180° (Figure 4).

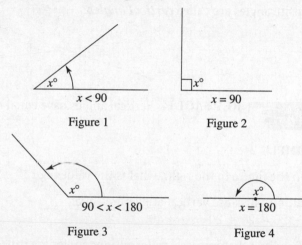

$x < 90$	$x = 90$
Figure 1	Figure 2
$90 < x < 180$	$x = 180$
Figure 3	Figure 4

NOTE: A small square like the one in Figure 2 above *always* means that the angle is a right angle. On the PSAT, if an angle has a square in it, it must be a 90° angle, *even if the figure has not been drawn to scale.*

 KEY FACT I2 If two or more angles form a straight angle, the sum of their measures is 180°.

$a + b = 180$ $w + x + y + z = 180$

KEY FACT I2 is one of the facts included in the Reference Information box on the first page of each math section of the PSAT.

EXAMPLE 1

In the figure at the right, R, S, and T are all on line ℓ. What is the average of a, b, c, and d?

Solution. Since $\angle RST$ is a straight angle, by **KEY FACT I2**, $a + b + c + d = 180$, and so their average is $\frac{180}{4} = 45$.

 KEY FACT I3 The sum of the measures of all the angles around a point is 360°.

NOTE: This fact is particularly important when the point is the center of a circle, as we shall see in Section 9-L.

$$a + b + c + d = 360$$

When two lines intersect, four angles are formed. The two angles in each pair of opposite angles are called **vertical angles**.

 KEY FACT I4 Vertical angles have equal measures.

EXAMPLE 2

In the figure to the right, what is the value of a?

Solution. Because vertical angles are equal, $3a - 20 = 2a + 20 \Rightarrow a = 40$.

$(3a - 20)°$
$(2a + 20)°$

Two lines that intersect to form right angles are called **perpendicular**.

Two lines that never intersect are said to be **parallel**. Consequently, parallel lines form no angles. However, if a third line, called a **transversal**, intersects a pair of parallel lines, eight angles are formed, and the relationships among these angles are very important.

 KEY FACT I5 If a pair of parallel lines is cut by a transversal that is not perpendicular to the parallel lines,

- Four of the angles are acute, and four are obtuse.
- All four acute angles are equal: $a = c = e = g$.
- All four obtuse angles are equal: $b = d = f = h$.
- The sum of any acute angle and any obtuse angle is 180°; for example, $d + e = 180$, $c + f = 180$, $b + g = 180$, . . .

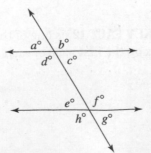

You must know **KEY FACT I5**—virtually every PSAT has questions based on it. However, you do *not* need to know the special terms you learned in your geometry class for these pairs of angles; those terms are not used on the PSAT.

EXAMPLE 3

In the figure at the right, $\overleftrightarrow{AB}$ is parallel to $\overleftrightarrow{CD}$. What is the value of x?

Solution. Let y be the measure of $\angle BED$. Then, by **KEY FACT I2**,

$$35 + 90 + y = 180 \Rightarrow 125 + y = 180 \Rightarrow y = 55.$$

Since $\overleftrightarrow{AB}$ and $\overleftrightarrow{CD}$ are parallel, by **KEY FACT I5**, $x = y \Rightarrow x = 55$.

EXERCISES

MULTIPLE-CHOICE QUESTIONS

1. In the figure shown, what is the value of $\frac{b+a}{b-a}$?

(A) 6 (B) 11 (C) 30 (D) 36 (E) 66

2. In the figure below, $x{:}y = 3{:}5$ and $z{:}y = 2{:}1$. What is the measure of the largest angle?

Note: Figure not drawn to scale

(A) 60 (B) 90 (C) 100 (D) 120 (E) 150

3. What is the measure of the angle formed by the minute and hour hands of a clock at 1:40?

(A) 120° (B) 135° (C) 150°
(D) 170° (E) 180°

4. In the figure below, lines k and l are parallel, and line k passes through D, one of the vertices of square $ABCD$. What is the value of w?

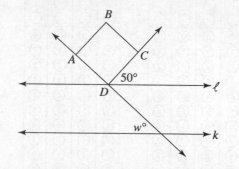

(A) 30 (B) 40 (C) 45 (D) 50 (E) 60

5. In the figure below, $\ell \parallel m$. Which of the following statements about $a + b$ is true?

Note: Figure not drawn to scale

(A) $a + b < 180$ (B) $a + b = 180$
(C) $180 < a + b \le 270$ (D) $270 < a + b \le 360$
(E) It cannot be determined from the information given.

GRID-IN QUESTIONS

6. In the figure below, what is the value of *b*?

7. In the figure below, if *a*:*b*:*c* = 3:4:1, what is the value of *a*?

8. In the figure below, what is the value of *c* if *d*:*c* = 3:2?

9. *A*, *B*, and *C* are points on a line with *B* between *A* and *C*. Let *M* and *N* be the midpoints of $\overline{AB}$ and $\overline{BC}$, respectively. If *AB* = 3*BC*, what is $\frac{AB}{MN}$?

10. In the figure below, lines *k* and *l* are parallel. What is the value of *y* − *x*?

6. **7.** **8.** **9.** **10.**

Answer Key

9-J TRIANGLES

More geometry questions on the PSAT pertain to triangles than to any other topic. To answer these questions correctly, you need to know several important facts about the angles and sides of triangles. The **KEY FACTS** in this section are extremely useful. *Be sure you learn them all.*

 KEY FACT J1 In any triangle, the sum of the measures of the three angles is 180°.

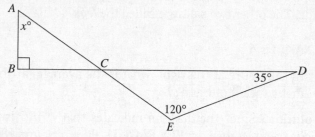

$$x + y + z = 180.$$

Reference FACT **KEY FACT J1** is one of the facts included in the Reference information box on the first page of each math section of the PSAT.

EXAMPLE 1

In the figure below, what is the value of x?

Solution. Use **KEY FACT J1** twice: first, in $\triangle CDE$ and then in $\triangle ABC$.

- m$\angle DCE + 115 + 30 = 180 \Rightarrow$ m$\angle DCE + 145 = 180 \Rightarrow$ m$\angle DCE = 35$
- Since vertical angles are equal, m$\angle ACB = 35$ [**KEY FACT I4**]
- $x + 90 + 35 = 180 \Rightarrow x + 125 = 180 \Rightarrow x = 55$

An ***exterior angle*** of a triangle is an angle formed by one side of the triangle and the extension of another side.

 KEY FACT J2 The measure of an exterior angle of a triangle is equal to the sum of the measures of the two opposite interior angles.

$$d = a + b$$

EXAMPLE 2

In the figure at the right, what is the value of w?

Solution. By **KEY FACT J2**: $w = 45 + 70 = 115$.

KEY FACT J3 In any triangle

- the longest side is opposite the largest angle.
- the shortest side is opposite the smallest angle.
- sides with the same length are opposite angles with the same measure.

A triangle with two equal sides is called ***isosceles***; it has two equal angles. A triangle with three equal sides is called ***equilateral***; it has three equal angles, each of which measures 60°.

EXAMPLE 3

Which of the following statements about △ABC in the figure at the right must be true?

Note: Figure not drawn to scale

I.   m∠A = 70°
II. BC = 10
III. Perimeter of △ABC = 30

(A) I only   (B) II only   (C) I and II only
(D) I and III only   (E) I, II, and III

Solution.

*   By **KEY FACT J1**, m∠A + 70 + 40 = 180 ⇒ m∠A = 70. (I is true.)
*   Therefore, m∠A = m∠C, and by **KEY FACT J3**, BC = 10. (II is true.)
*   Since ∠B is the smallest angle, AC is the smallest side. In particular, it is less than 10.
*   Therefore, the perimeter is less than 30. (III is false.)
*   Only I and II are true (Choice C).

Right triangles are triangles that have one right angle and two acute ones. The side opposite the 90° angle is called the **hypotenuse**, and by **KEY FACT J3**, it is the longest side. The other two sides are called the *legs*.

EXAMPLE 4

In the figure at the right, what is the average (arithmetic mean) of x and y?

Solution. Since the diagram indicates that △ABC is a right triangle, then, by **KEY FACT J1**, $90 + x + y = 180$ ⇒ $x + y = 90$. The average of x and y is $\frac{x+y}{2} = \frac{90}{2} = 45$.

The most important facts concerning right triangles are the **Pythagorean theorem** and its converse, which are given in **KEY FACT J4**.

 KEY FACT J4 If a, b, and c are the lengths of the sides of a triangle, with $a \le b \le c$, then the triangle is a right triangle if and only if $a^2 + b^2 = c^2$.

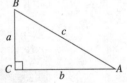

Reference FACT **KEY FACT J4** is one of the facts included in the Reference Information box on the first page of each math section of the PSAT.

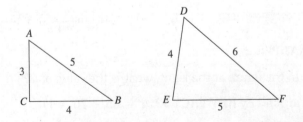

Since $3^2 + 4^2 = 5^2$, △ABC is a right triangle, whereas △DEF is not a right triangle, as $4^2 + 5^2 \ne 6^2$.

EXAMPLE 5

Which of the following are *not* the sides of a right triangle?

(A) 6, 8, 10   (B) 1, 1, $\sqrt{2}$ (C) 1, $\sqrt{3}$, 2   (D) $\sqrt{3}$, $\sqrt{4}$, $\sqrt{5}$ (E) 5, 12, 13

Solution. Just check each of the choices.

A: $6^2 + 8^2 = 36 + 64 = 100 = 10^2$ These *are* the sides of a right triangle.
B: $1^2 + 1^2 = 1 + 1 = 2 = (\sqrt{2})^2$ These *are* the sides of a right triangle.
C: $1^2 + (\sqrt{3})^2 = 1 + 3 = 4 = 2^2$ These *are* the sides of a right triangle.
D: $(\sqrt{3})^2 + (\sqrt{4})^2 = 3 + 4 = 7 \neq (\sqrt{5})^2$ These *are not* the sides of a right triangle.
E: $5^2 + 12^2 = 25 + 144 = 169 = 13^2$ These *are* the sides of a right triangle.
The answer is Choice D.

On the PSAT, the most common right triangles whose sides are *integers* are the 3-4-5 triangle and its multiples, such as 6-8-10 and 30-40-50.

Let x = length of each leg, and h = length of the hypotenuse, of an isosceles right triangle. By the Pythagorean theorem (**KEY FACT J4**), $x^2 + x^2 = h^2$. Then, $2x^2 = h^2$, and $h = \sqrt{2x^2} = x\sqrt{2}$.

KEY FACT J5 In a 45-45-90 right triangle, the sides are x, x, and $x\sqrt{2}$.

KEY FACT J5 is one of the facts included in the Reference information box on the first page of each math section of the PSAT.

- By multiplying the length of a leg by $\sqrt{2}$, you get the hypotenuse.
- By dividing the hypotenuse by $\sqrt{2}$, you get the length of each leg.

KEY FACT J6 A diagonal of a square divides the square into two isosceles right triangles.

An **altitude** of a triangle is a line segment drawn from a vertex, perpendicular to the opposite side.

KEY FACT J7 An altitude divides an equilateral triangle into two 30-60-90 right triangles.

Let $2x$ be the length of each side of equilateral triangle ABC, in which altitude AD is drawn. Then $\triangle ABD$ is a 30-60-90 right triangle, and its sides are x, $2x$, and h. By the Pythagorean theorem,

$x^2 + h^2 = (2x)^2 = 4x^2$, so $h^2 = 3x^2$, and $h = \sqrt{3x^2} = x\sqrt{3}$.

KEY FACT J8 In a 30-60-90 right triangle the sides are x, $x\sqrt{3}$, and $2x$.

KEY FACT J8 is one of the facts included in the Reference information box on the first page of each math section of the PSAT.

If you know the length of the shorter leg (x),

- multiply it by $\sqrt{3}$ to get the longer leg, and
- multiply it by 2 to get the hypotenuse.

If you know the length of the longer leg (a),

- divide it by $\sqrt{3}$ to get the shorter leg, and
- multiply the shorter leg by 2 to get the hypotenuse.

If you know the length of the hypotenuse (h),

- divide it by 2 to get the shorter leg, and
- multiply the shorter leg by $\sqrt{3}$ to get the longer leg.

EXAMPLE 6

What is the area of a square whose diagonal is 4?

(A) 4   (B) 8   (C) 16   (D) $4\sqrt{3}$ (E) $16\sqrt{3}$

Solution. Draw a diagonal in a square of side s, creating a 45-45-90 right triangle. By **KEY FACT J6**,

$s = \dfrac{4}{\sqrt{2}}$ and $A = s^2 = \left(\dfrac{4}{\sqrt{2}}\right)^2 = \dfrac{16}{2} = 8$. The answer is Choice B.

EXAMPLE 7

In equilateral triangle ABC, the length of altitude AD is 6. What is the perimeter of $\triangle ABC$?

(A) 18   (B) $6\sqrt{3}$ (C) $12\sqrt{3}$ (D) $18\sqrt{3}$ (E) 36

Solution. Use **KEY FACT J8**.

- Divide the longer leg, AD, of right triangle ADB by $\sqrt{3}$ to get the shorter leg, BD:
  $$\frac{6}{\sqrt{3}} = \frac{6}{\sqrt{3}} \times \frac{\sqrt{3}}{\sqrt{3}} = \frac{6\sqrt{3}}{3} = 2\sqrt{3}.$$
- Multiply BD by 2 to get side BC. Then $BC = 2(2\sqrt{3}) = 4\sqrt{3}$.
- Finally, multiply BC by 3 to get the perimeter: $3(4\sqrt{3}) = 12\sqrt{3}$.
- The answer is Choice C.

KEY FACT J9 (Triangle Inequality)

- The sum of the lengths of any two sides of a triangle is greater than the length of the third side.
- The difference of the lengths of any two sides of a triangle is less than the length of the third side.

EXAMPLE 8

If the lengths of two of the sides of a triangle are 7 and 8, which of the following could be the length of the third side?

I. 1
II. 2
III. 15

(A) None   (B) I only   (C) II only   (D) I and II only   (E) I, II, and III

Solution. Use **KEY FACT J9**.

- The third side must be *less* than $7 + 8 = 15$. So III is false.
- The third side must be *greater* than $8 - 7 = 1$. So I is false.
- *Any* number between 1 and 15 could be the length of the third side. So II is true.
- The answer is Choice C.

 KEY FACT J10 The area of a triangle is given by $A = \frac{1}{2}bh$, where b is the base and h is the height.

Reference FACT **KEY FACT J10** is one of the facts included in the Reference information box on the first page of each math section of the PSAT.

Note:
1. *Any* side of the triangle can be taken as the base.
2. The height is the altitude drawn to the base from the opposite vertex.
3. In a right triangle, either leg can be the base and the other the height.
4. The height may be outside the triangle. [See the figure below.]

In the figure below:
If AC is the base, BD is the height. If AB is the base, CE is the height. If BC is the base, AF is the height.

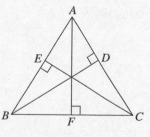

EXAMPLE 10

What is the area of an equilateral triangle whose sides are 10?
(A) 30   (B) $25\sqrt{3}$ (C) 50   (D) $50\sqrt{3}$ (E) 100

Solution. Draw an equilateral triangle and one of its altitudes.

- By **KEY FACT J7**, △ABD is a 30-60-90 right triangle.
- By **KEY FACT J8**, $BD = 5$ and $AD = 5\sqrt{3}$.
- The area of $\triangle ABC = \frac{1}{2}(10)(5\sqrt{3}) = 25\sqrt{3}$ (Choice B).

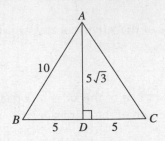

Replacing 10 by s in Example 10 yields a very useful result.

KEY FACT J11 If A represents the area of an equilateral triangle with side s, then $A = \frac{s^2\sqrt{3}}{4}$.

EXERCISES

MULTIPLE-CHOICE QUESTIONS

1. In the figure above, what is the value of w?

    (A) 90   (B) 100   (C) 110   (D) 120   (E) 130

2. Two sides of a right triangle are 5 and 7. Which of the following could be the length of the third side?

    I. $\sqrt{24}$
    II. $\sqrt{54}$
    III. $\sqrt{74}$

    (A) I only   (B) II only   (C) I and II
    (D) I and III   (E) I, II, and III

Questions 3 and 4 refer to the following figure.

3. What is the perimeter of △ABC?
    (A) 48   (B) $48 + 12\sqrt{2}$
    (C) $48 + 12\sqrt{3}$ (D) 72
    (E) It cannot be determined from the information given.

4. What is the area of △ABC?
    (A) 108   (B) $54 + 72\sqrt{2}$
    (C) $54 + 72\sqrt{3}$ (D) 198
    (E) It cannot be determined from the information given.

5. Which of the following expresses a true relationship between x and y in the figure above?

    (A) $y = 60 - x$ (B) $y = x$ (C) $x + y = 90$
    (D) $y = 180 - 3x$ (E) $x = 90 - 3y$

GRID-IN QUESTIONS

6. If the difference between the measures of the two smaller angles of a right triangle is 6°, what is the measure, in degrees, of the smallest angle?

7. What is the smallest integer x for which x, $x + 5$, and $2x - 15$ could be the lengths of the sides of a triangle?

8. If the measures of the angles of a triangle are in the ratio of $1:2:3$ and if the length of the smallest side is 10, what is the length of the longest side?

10. In the figure above, what is the value of x?

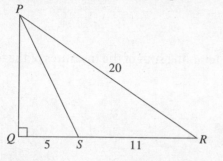

9. In the figure above, what is the value of PS?

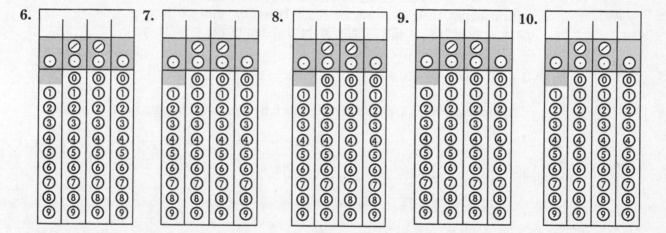

Answer Key

1. *C*   2. *D*   3. *C*   4. *C*   5. *A*

6. **42**   7. **11**   8. **20**   9. **13**   10. **115**

9-K QUADRILATERALS

A *quadrilateral* is a polygon with four sides. In this section we will present the key facts you need to know about three special quadrilaterals.

Every quadrilateral has two diagonals. If you draw in either one, you will divide the quadrilateral into two triangles. Since the sum of the measures of the three angles in each of the triangles is 180°, the sum of the measures of the angles in the quadrilateral is 360°.

KEY FACT K1 In any quadrilateral, the sum of the measures of the four angles is 360°.

EXAMPLE 1

In the figure at the right, what is the value of x?

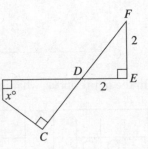

Solution. Since $\triangle DEF$ is an isosceles right triangle, $m\angle EDF = 45°$; also, since the two angles at vertex D are vertical angles, their measures are equal. Therefore, the measure of $\angle ADC$ is 45°. Finally, since the sum of the measures of all four angles of $ABCD$ is 360°:

$$45 + 90 + 90 + x = 360 \Rightarrow 225 + x = 360 \Rightarrow x = 135.$$

A *parallelogram* is a quadrilateral in which both pairs of opposite sides are parallel.

KEY FACT K2 Parallelograms have the following properties:

- Opposite sides are equal: $AB = CD$ and $AD = BC$.
- Opposite angles are equal: $a = c$ and $b = d$.
- Adjacent angles add up to 180°: $a + b = b + c = c + d = a + d = 180$.
- The diagonals bisect each other: $AE = EC$ and $DE = EB$.

EXAMPLE 2

In the figure at the right, $ABCD$ is a parallelogram. Which of the following statements must be true?

(A) $x < y$ (B) $x = y$ (C) $x > y$
(D) $x + y < 90$ (E) $x + y > 90$

Solution. Since $\overline{AB}$ and $\overline{CD}$ are parallel line segments cut by transversal $\overline{BD}$, m$\angle ABD$ = $y°$. In $\triangle ABD$ $AB > AD$, so by **KEY FACT J3**, the measure of the angle opposite $\overline{AB}$ is greater than the measure of the angle opposite $\overline{AD}$. Therefore, $x > y$ (Choice C).

A *rectangle* is a parallelogram in which all four angles are right angles. Two adjacent sides of a rectangle are usually called the **length** (l) and the **width** (w).

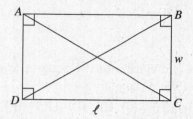

KEY FACT K3 Since a rectangle is a parallelogram, all of the properties listed in **KEY FACT K2** hold for rectangles. In addition,

- The measure of each angle in a rectangle is 90°.
- The diagonals of a rectangle have the same length: $AC = BD$.

A *square* is a rectangle in which all four sides have the same length.

KEY FACT K4 Since a square is a rectangle, all of the properties listed in **KEY FACTS K2** and **K3** hold for squares. In addition,

- All four sides have the same length.
- Each diagonal divides the square into two 45-45-90 right triangles.
- The diagonals are perpendicular to each other: $AC \perp BD$.

EXAMPLE 3

What is the length of each side of a square if its diagonals are 8?

Solution. Draw a diagram. In square *ABCD*, diagonal *AC* is the hypotenuse of a 45-45-90 right triangle, and side *AB* is a leg of that triangle. By **KEY FACT J5**,

$$AB = \frac{AC}{\sqrt{2}} = \frac{8}{\sqrt{2}} \times \frac{\sqrt{2}}{\sqrt{2}} = \frac{8\sqrt{2}}{2} = 4\sqrt{2}.$$

NOTE: On the PSAT, you don't have to rationalize denominators. On your calculator, just divide 8 by $\sqrt{2}$.

The **perimeter** (P) of any polygon is the sum of the lengths of all its sides.

KEY FACT **KEY FACT K5** In a rectangle, $P = 2(\ell + w)$, and in a square, $P = 4s$.

$$P = \ell + w + \ell + w = 2(\ell + w) \qquad P = s + s + s + s = 4s$$

EXAMPLE 4

A rectangle is divided into two squares, each with a perimeter of 10. What is the perimeter of the rectangle?

(A) 10   (B) 12.5   (C) 15   (D) 17.5   (E) 20

Solution. Don't do anything until you have drawn a diagram.

Since the perimeter of each square is 10, the length of each side is $10 \div 4 = 2.5$. Therefore, the perimeter of the rectangle is $6 \times 2.5 = 15$ (Choice C).

In Section 9-J we reviewed the formula for the **area** of a triangle. You also need to know the area formulas for a parallelogram, rectangle, and square.

 KEY FACT **KEY FACT K6** Here are the area formulas you need to know:

- For a parallelogram: $A = bh$
- For a rectangle: $A = \ell w$
- For a square: $A = s^2$ or $A = \frac{1}{2}d^2$

 Reference FACT The formula for the area of a rectangle, given in **KEY FACT K6** is one of the facts included in the Reference box on the first page of each math section of the PSAT.

EXAMPLE 5

In the figure at the right, the area of parallelogram ABCD is 40. What is the area of rectangle AFCE?

(A) 20   (B) 24   (C) 28   (D) 32   (E) 36

Solution. Since the base CD, is 10 and the area of ABCD is 40, the height AE must be 4. Then △AED must be a 3-4-5 right triangle with DE = 3, which implies that EC = 7. The area of the rectangle is 7 × 4 = 28 (Choice C).

EXERCISES

MULTIPLE-CHOICE QUESTIONS

1. In the figure below, ABCD is a parallelogram. What is the value of $a - b$?

(A) 25   (B) 55   (C) 70   (D) 90   (E) 125

2. What is the perimeter of a rectangle whose area is 21?

(A) 10   (B) 20   (C) 21   (D) 44
(E) It cannot be determined from the information given.

3. The length of a rectangle is 10 more than the side of a square, and the width of the rectangle is 10 less than the side of the square. If the area of the square is 125, what is the area of the rectangle?

(A) 25   (B) 115   (C) 125   (D) 135   (E) 225

4. What is the area of a square whose diagonals are 12?

(A) $5\sqrt{2}$ (B) $50\sqrt{2}$ (C) 72
(D) 144   (E) $144\sqrt{2}$

5. If the length of a rectangle is 4 times its width, and if its area is 144, what is its perimeter?

(A) 6   (B) 24   (C) 30   (D) 60   (E) 96

GRID-IN QUESTIONS

<u>Questions 6 and 7</u> refer to the following figure, in which *M*, *N*, *O*, and *P* are the midpoints of the sides of rectangle *ABCD*.

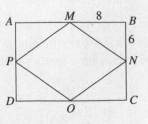

6. What is the perimeter of quadrilateral *MNOP*?

7. What is the area of quadrilateral *MNOP*?

8. If in the figures below, the area of rectangle *ABCD* is 100, what is the area of rectangle *EFGH*?

9. In quadrilateral *PQRS*, the measure of angle *S* is 20 more than the average of the measures of the other three. What is the measure of angle *S*?

10. If in the figure below, *M* and *N* are the midpoints of two of the sides of square *ABCD*, what is the area of the shaded region?

6.

7.

8.

9.

10.

Answer Key

1. *C*   2. *E*   3. *A*   4. *C*   5. *D*

6. **4 0**

7. **9 6**

8. **1 0 2**

9. **1 0 5**

10. **1 . 5**

9-L CIRCLES

A *circle* consists of all the points that are the same distance from one fixed point called the *center*. That distance is called the *radius* of the circle. The figure below is a circle of radius 1 unit whose center is at the point O. Since A, B, C, D, and E are all points on circle O, they are each 1 unit from O. The word *radius* is also used to represent any of the line segments joining the center and a point on the circle. The plural of *radius* is *radii*. In circle O, $\overline{OA}$, $\overline{OB}$, $\overline{OC}$, $\overline{OD}$, and $\overline{OE}$ are all radii. If a circle has radius r, each of the radii is r units long.

 KEY FACT L1 Any triangle, such as $\triangle COD$ in the figure above, formed by connecting the endpoints of two radii, is isosceles.

EXAMPLE 1

If A and B are points on circle O, what is the value of x?

Solution. Since $\triangle AOB$ is isosceles, angles A and B have the same measure. So $85 + x + x = 180 \Rightarrow 2x = 95 \Rightarrow x = 47.5$.

A line segment, such as $\overline{CD}$ in circle O at the beginning of this section, whose endpoints are on a circle, is called a *chord*. A chord such as $\overline{BE}$ in circle O that passes through the center is called a *diameter*. Since $\overline{BE}$ is made up of two radii, $\overline{OB}$ and $\overline{OE}$, a diameter is twice as long as a radius.

 KEY FACT L2 If d is the diameter and r the radius of a circle, then $d = 2r$.

 KEY FACT L3 A diameter is the longest chord that can be drawn in a circle.

EXAMPLE 2

A, B, and C, the three vertices of right triangle ABC, all lie on a circle whose radius is 4. Which of the following statements *could* be true?

   I. The hypotenuse of $\triangle ABC$ is 10
   II. The perimeter of $\triangle ABC$ is 25
   III. The area of $\triangle ABC$ is 35

(A) None   (B) I only   (C) II only   (D) III only   (E) I, II, and III

Solution. Since the radius is 4, the diameter is 8. Since each side of $\triangle ABC$ is a chord, none of the sides can be greater than 8; so AC cannot be 10 (I is false), and the perimeter can surely not exceed 24 (II is false). Since the area of a right triangle can be calculated using one of the legs as the base and the other as the height, the area cannot exceed $\frac{1}{2}(8)(8) = 32$ and so cannot equal 35 (III is false). None of the statements is true (Choice A).

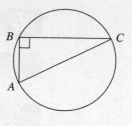

The total length around a circle, from A to B to C to D to E and back to A, is called the **circumference** of the circle. In every circle the ratio of the circumference to the diameter is exactly the same and is denoted by the symbol π (the Greek letter pi).

 KEY FACT L4 For every circle,

$$\pi = \frac{\text{circumference}}{\text{diameter}} = \frac{C}{d} \quad \text{or} \quad C = \pi d \quad \text{or} \quad C = 2\pi r$$

Reference FACT $C = 2\pi r$ is one of the facts included in the Reference Information box on the first page of each math section of the PSAT.

 KEY FACT L5 The value of π is *approximately* 3.14.

HELPFUL HINT On almost every question on the PSAT that involve circles, you are expected to leave your answer in terms of π; so don't multiply by 3.14 unless you need to. If you need an approximation—to test a choice, for example—then use your calculator. If you have a scientific calculator, use the π-key. This is not only faster than keying in 3.14 but also avoids careless mistakes in entering.

EXAMPLE 3

If the circumference of a circle is equal to the perimeter of a square whose sides are π, what is the radius of the circle?

Solution. If each side of the square is π, then its perimeter is 4π. Since the circumference of the circle is equal to the perimeter of the square, $C = 4\pi$. But $C = 2\pi r$, and so $2\pi r = 4\pi \Rightarrow r = 2$.

An **arc** consists of two points on a circle and all the points between them. If two points, such as P and Q in circle O, are the endpoints of a diameter, they divide the circle into two arcs called **semicircles**. On the PSAT, *arc AB* always refers to the small arc joining A and B.

An angle whose vertex is at the center of a circle is called a **central angle**.

KEY FACT L6 The degree measure of a complete circle is 360°.

 KEY FACT L6 is one of the facts included in the Reference box on the first page of each math section of the PSAT.

 KEY FACT L7 The degree measure of an arc equals the degree measure of the central angle that intercepts it.

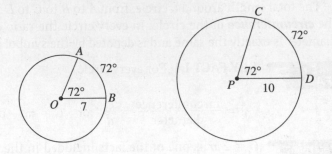

CAUTION: Degree measure is *not* a measure of length. In the circles above, arcs *AB* and *CD* each measure 72°, even though arc *CD* is much longer.

How long *is* arc *CD*? Since the radius of circle *P* is 10, its diameter is 20, and its circumference is 20π. Since there are 360° in a circle, arc *CD* is $\frac{72}{360}$, or $\frac{1}{5}$, of the circumference: $\frac{1}{5}(20\pi) = 4\pi$.

 KEY FACT L8 The formula for the area of a circle of radius r is $A = \pi r^2$.

 KEY FACT L8 is one of the facts included in the Reference box on the first page of each math section of the PSAT.

The area of circle *P*, above, is $\pi(10)^2 = 100\pi$ square units. The area of sector *CPD* is $\frac{1}{5}$ of the area of the circle: $\frac{1}{5}(100\pi) = 20\pi$.

 KEY FACT L9 If an arc measures $x°$, the length of the arc is $\frac{x}{360}(2\pi r)$, and the area of the sector formed by the arc and two radii is $\frac{x}{360}(\pi r^2)$.

Examples 4 and 5 refer to the figure below, in which the radius of the inner circle is 4 and the radius of the outer circle is 6.

EXAMPLE 4

What is the area of the shaded region, *ABCD*?

(A) 4π (B) 5π (C) 9π (D) 16π (E) 20π

Solution. To find the area of $ABCD$, subtract the area of sector DOC from the area of sector AOB. Each sector is a quarter-circle.

The area of $AOB = \frac{1}{4}\pi(6)^2 = \frac{1}{4}(36\pi) = 9\pi$.

The area of $COD = \frac{1}{4}\pi(4)^2 = \frac{1}{4}(16\pi) = 4\pi$.

So the area of $ABCD = 9\pi - 4\pi = 5\pi$ (Choice B).

EXAMPLE 5

What is the perimeter of the shaded region, $ABCD$?

(A) 5π (B) $2 + 5\pi$ (C) $4 + 5\pi$ (D) $4 + 20\pi$ (E) $4 + 24\pi$

Solution. Arcs AB and CD are each quarter-circles, and so their lengths are $\frac{1}{4}$ of the circumferences of circles whose diameters are 8 and 12.

$$AB = \frac{1}{4}(12\pi) = 3\pi \qquad CD = \frac{1}{4}(8\pi) = 2\pi$$

The lengths of line segments AD and BC are each $6 - 4 = 2$. So the perimeter $= 2 + 2 + 3\pi + 2\pi = 4 + 5\pi$ (Choice C).

A line that touches a circle at exactly one point is called a **tangent**. In the figure below, line l is **tangent** to circle O at point P.

KEY FACT **KEY FACT L10** A line tangent to a circle is perpendicular to the radius drawn to the point of contact.

EXAMPLE 6

If line l is tangent to Circle O at point P and if B is a point on l such that $PB = 8$ and $OB = 10$, what is the radius of the circle?

Solution. Draw a diagram and label it. Since radius $\overline{OP}$ is perpendicular to l, $\triangle OPB$ is a right triangle.
By the Pythagorean theorem,

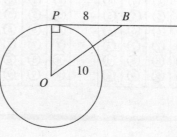

$$OP^2 + 8^2 = 10^2 \Rightarrow OP^2 + 64 = 100 \Rightarrow$$
$$OP^2 = 36 \Rightarrow OP = 6.$$

EXERCISES

MULTIPLE-CHOICE QUESTIONS

Questions 1 and 2 refer to the following figure.

1. What is the length of arc AB?

(A) 3π (B) 6π (C) 12π (D) 18π (E) 30π

2. What is the area of the shaded sector?

(A) 3π (B) 6π (C) 12π (D) 18π (E) 30π

3. What is the circumference of a circle whose area is 100π?

(A) 10 (B) 20 (C) 10π (D) 20π (E) 25π

4. What is the area of a circle whose circumference is π?

(A) $\frac{\pi}{4}$ (B) $\frac{\pi}{2}$ (C) π (D) 2π (E) 4π

5. What is the area of a circle whose radius is the diagonal of a square whose area is 4?

(A) 2π (B) $2\pi\sqrt{2}$ (C) 4π (D) 8π (E) 16π

GRID-IN QUESTIONS

6. The circumferences of two circles are in the ratio of 3:5. What is the ratio of the area of the smaller circle to the area of the larger circle?

7. In the figure below, the ratio of the length of arc CD to the circumference of the circle is 2:9. What is the value of w?

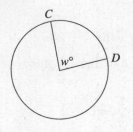

8. The circumference of a circle is aπ units, and the area of the circle is bπ square units. If a = b, what is the radius of the circle?

9. In the figure below, the radius of circle O is 3, and the area of the shaded region is kπ. What is the value of k?

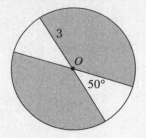

10. If the area of a circle whose diameter is π, is written as $a\pi^b$, what is the value of ab?

Answer Key

1. B   **2.** E   **3.** D   **4.** A   **5.** D

6. 9/25   7. 80   8. 2   9. 13/2   10. 3/4

9-M SOLID GEOMETRY

There is very little solid geometry on the PSAT. Basically, all you need to know are the formulas for the volume and surface areas of rectangular solids (including cubes) and cylinders.

A *rectangular solid* or *box* is a solid formed by six rectangles, called *faces*. The sides of the rectangles are called *edges*. As shown in the diagram below, the edges are called the *length*, *width*, and *height*. A *cube* is a rectangular solid in which the length, width, and height are equal, so all the edges are the same length.

edges

base

h = height

ℓ = length

w = width

RECTANGULAR SOLID

edge = e

e

e

e

CUBE

  KEY FACT M1 The formula for the volume of a rectangular solid is $V = \ell wh$.

  KEY FACT M1 is one of the facts included in the Reference box on the first page of each math section of the PSAT.

In a cube, all the edges are equal. Therefore, if e is the edge, the formula for the volume is $V = e^3$.

EXAMPLE 1

The base of a rectangular tank is 3 feet wide and 4 feet long; the height of the tank is 10 inches. If water is pouring into the tank at the rate of 3 cubic feet per hour, how many *minutes* will be required to fill the tank?

Solution. Draw a picture. Change all units to feet. Then the volume of the tank is $3 \times 4 \times \frac{5}{6} = 10$ cubic feet. At 3 cubic feet per hour, the required time is $\frac{10}{3}$ hours = $\frac{10}{3}(60) = 200$ minutes.

$\frac{5}{6}$ ft

4 ft

3 ft

To find the **surface area** of a rectangular solid, add the area of the six rectangular faces. Since the top and bottom faces are equal, the front and back faces are equal, and the left and right faces are equal, we can calculate the area of one face from each pair and then double the sum. In a cube, each of the six faces has the same area.

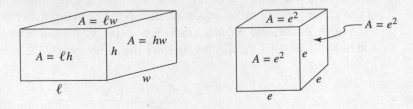

KEY FACT M2 The surface area of a rectangular solid is $A = 2(lw + lh + wh)$. The surface area of a cube is $A = 6e^2$.

EXAMPLE 2

The volume of a cube is v cubic yards, and its surface area is a square feet. If $v = a$, what is the length in inches of each edge?

Solution. Draw a diagram. If e is the length of the edge in yards, then $3e$ is the length in feet, and $36e$ is the length in inches. Therefore, $v = e^3$ and $a = 6(3e)^2 = 6(9e^2) = 54e^2$.

36e in.

3e ft.

e yd

Since $v = a$, $e^3 = 54e^2 \Rightarrow e = 54$; the length of each edge is $36(54) = 1944$ inches.

A **diagonal** of a box is a line segment joining a vertex on the top of the box to the opposite vertex on the bottom.

EXAMPLE 3

What is the length of a diagonal of a cube whose sides are 1?

Solution. Draw a diagram and label it. Since the base is a 1×1 square, its diagonal is $\sqrt{2}$. Then the diagonal of the cube is the hypotenuse of a right triangle whose legs are 1 and $\sqrt{2}$; so

$$d^2 = 1^2 + (\sqrt{2})^2 = 1 + 2 = 3, \text{ and } d = \sqrt{3}.$$

A **cylinder** is similar to a rectangular solid except that the base is a circle instead of a rectangle. The volume of a cylinder is the area of its circular base (πr^2) times its height (h).

KEY FACT M5 The formula for the volume, V, of a cylinder whose circular base has radius r and whose height is h is $V = \pi r^2 h$.

KEY FACT M5 is one of the facts included in the Reference box on the first page of each math section of the PSAT.

EXAMPLE 4

What is the height of a cylinder whose diameter is 10 and whose volume is 100π?

Solution. Since the diameter is 10, the radius is 5.

$$V = 100\pi = \pi r^2 h = \pi(5^2)h = 25\pi h \Rightarrow h = 4.$$

EXERCISES

MULTIPLE-CHOICE QUESTIONS

1. What is the volume, in cubic feet, of a rectangular solid whose length, width, and height are 1 foot 3 inches, 1 foot 4 inches, and 1 foot 6 inches?

   (A) 2.5   (B) 2.912   (C) 3.375
   (D) 49   (E) 4320

2. The volume of a cube is a cubic feet and its surface area is b square feet. If $a = b$, what is the length, in feet, of each edge?

   (A) 1   (B) 2   (C) 6   (D) 12   (E) 36

3. What is the volume of a cube whose surface area is 150?

   (A) 25   (B) 100   (C) 125
   (D) 1000   (E) 15,625

4. What is the surface area of a cube whose volume is 64?

   (A) 16   (B) 64   (C) 96   (D) 128   (E) 384

5. The height and radius of a cylinder are each equal to the edge of a cube. What is the ratio of the volume of the cube to the volume of the cylinder?

   (A) $\frac{1}{\pi}$ (B) π (C) π^2 (D) π^3
   (E) It cannot be determined from the information given.

GRID-IN QUESTIONS

6. What is the number of cubic inches in one cubic foot?

7. What is the volume, in cubic centimeters, of a cube in which the sum of the lengths of all the edges is 6 centimeters?

8. A solid metal cube with sides of 3 inches is placed in a rectangular tank whose length, width, and height are 3, 4, and 5 inches, respectively. What is the volume, in cubic inches, of water that the tank can now hold?

9. A rectangular tank has a base that is 16 inches by 5 inches and a height of 18 inches. If the tank is half full of water, by how many inches will the water level rise if 260 cubic inches of water are poured into it?

10. The base of a rectangular tank is 2 feet wide and 4 feet long; the height of the tank is 20 inches. If water is pouring into the tank at the rate of 2 cubic inches per second, how many *hours* will be required to fill the tank?

Answer Key

1. *A* 2. *C* 3. *C* 4. *C* 5. *A*

6. 1728   7. 1/8   8. 33   9. 13/4   10. 3.2

9-N COORDINATE GEOMETRY

The PSAT has very few questions on coordinate geometry, and they are always considered easy or medium, never hard. Most often they deal with the coordinates of points and occasionally with the slope of a line. You are *never* required to draw a graph.

In coordinate geometry, each point in the plane is assigned two numbers, an ***x-coordinate*** and a ***y-coordinate***, which are written as an ordered pair, **(x, y)**.

- Points to the right of the *y*-axis have positive *x*-coordinates, and those to the left have negative *x*-coordinates.
- Points above the *x*-axis have positive *y*-coordinates, and those below it have negative *y*-coordinates.
- If a point is on the *x*-axis, its *y*-coordinate is 0.
- If a point is on the *y*-axis, its *x*-coordinate is 0.

For example, point *A* in the figure below is labeled (2, 3) since it is 2 units to the right of the *y*-axis and 3 units above the *x*-axis. Similarly, $B(-3, -5)$ is 3 units to the left of the *y*-axis and 5 units below the *x*-axis.

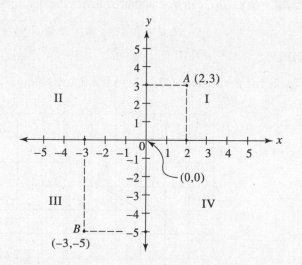

EXAMPLE 1

In the diagram at the right, which of the following must be true?

I. $a + b < ab$

II. $c + d < cd$

III. $a + b < c + d$

(A) I only (B) II only (C) III only (D) I and III only (E) I, II, and III

Solution. Since (a, b) is on the *x*-axis, $b = 0$. Therefore, $ab = 0$ and $a + b = a$, which is negative, since (a, b) is to the left of the *y*-axis. Since any negative number is less than 0, $a + b < ab$ (I is true). Since (c, d) is on the *y*-axis, $c = 0$. Therefore, $cd = 0$ and $c + d = d$, which is positive since (c, d) is above the *x*-axis. So $cd < c + d$ (II is false). Since $a + b$ is negative and $c + d$ is positive, $a + b < c + d$ (III is true). Only statements I and III are true (Choice D).

Often a question requires you to calculate the distance between two points. This is easiest when the points lie on the same horizontal or vertical line.

- All the points on a horizontal line have the same y-coordinate. To find the distance between any two of them, subtract the smaller x-coordinate from the larger x-coordinate.
- All the points on a vertical line have the same x-coordinate. To find the distance between any two of them, subtract the smaller y-coordinate from the larger y-coordinate.

HELPFUL HINT *If two points have been plotted on a graph and if they have the same x-coordinates or y-coordinates, you can find the distance between them by counting boxes.*

CAUTION: To find the distance between two points that do *not* lie on the same horizontal or vertical line, you cannot count boxes and you cannot subtract; you *must* use the distance formula.

KEY FACT N2 The distance d, between two points, $A(x_1, y_1)$ and $B(x_2, y_2)$, can be calculated using the distance formula:

$$d = \sqrt{(x_2 - x_1)^2 + (y_2 - y_1)^2}.$$

EXAMPLE 2

What is the perimeter of $\triangle ABC$, in the figure below?

    (A) 13 (B) 16 (C) $8 + \sqrt{34}$ (D) $10 + \sqrt{34}$ (E) $8 + \sqrt{74}$

Solution. By counting boxes or subtracting, you find that the distance from A to C is $6 - 1 = 5$, and the distance from B to C is $4 - 1 = 3$. To find the distance from A to B, use the distance formula:

$$AB = \sqrt{(6 - 1)^2 + (4 - 1)^2} = \sqrt{(5)^2 + (3)^2} = \sqrt{25 + 9} = \sqrt{34}$$

So the perimeter is $5 + 3 + \sqrt{34} = 8 + \sqrt{34}$ (Choice C).

KEY FACT N3 If $P(x_1, y_1)$ and $Q(x_2, y_2)$ are any two points, then the midpoint, M, of segment $\overline{PQ}$ is the point whose coordinates are $\left(\frac{x_1 + x_2}{2}, \frac{y_1 + y_2}{2}\right)$.

EXAMPLE 3

$ABCD$ is a rectangle whose vertices are at $A(2, 0)$, $B(0, 3)$, $C(8, 4)$, and $D(6, 7)$. If the diagonals intersect at E, what are the coordinates of E?

    (A) $(2, 3.5)$ (B) $(3, 5)$ (C) $(4, 0.5)$ (D) $(4, 3.5)$ (E) $(8, 7)$

Solution. Since, by **KEY FACT K2**, the diagonals of a parallelogram (and, hence, a rectangle) bisect each other, E is the midpoint of diagonal AC:

$$E = \left(\frac{2 + 6}{2}, \frac{7 + 0}{2}\right) = \left(\frac{8}{2}, \frac{7}{2}\right) = (4, 3.5) \text{ (Choice D)}.$$

Of course, you should make a quick sketch. This often allows you to see the correct answer and always allows you to eliminate choices that are clearly wrong.

The **slope** of a line is a number that indicates how steep the line is.

 KEY FACT N4

- Vertical lines do not have slopes.
- To find the slope of any nonvertical line, proceed as follows:
   1. Choose any 2 points $A(x_1, y_1)$ and $B(x_2, y_2)$ on the line.
   2. Take the differences of the y-coordinates, $y_2 - y_1$, and the x-coordinates, $x_2 - x_1$.
   3. Divide. Slope $= \frac{y_2 - y_1}{x_2 - x_1}$.

EXAMPLE 4

What is the slope of the line that passes through $(0, 3)$ and $(4, 0)$?

Solution. Use the slope formula: $\frac{0 - 3}{4 - 0} = \frac{-3}{4} = -\frac{3}{4}$.

 KEY FACT N5

- The slope of any horizontal line is 0.
- The slope of any line that goes up as you move from left to right is positive.
- The slope of any line that goes down as you move from left to right is negative.

EXAMPLE 5

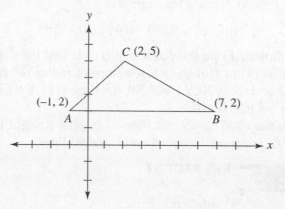

In the figure above, let r, s, and t represent the slopes of line segments $\overline{AB}$, $\overline{BC}$, and $\overline{AC}$, respectively. Which of the following is true?

(A) $r < s < t$
(B) $r < t < s$
(C) $s < r < t$
(D) $s < t < r$
(E) $t < r < s$

Solution. Since $\overline{AB}$ is horizontal, its slope is 0: $r = 0$; since $\overline{BC}$ goes down as you move from left to right, its slope is negative: $s < 0$; and since $\overline{AC}$ goes up as you move from left to right, its slope is positive: $t > 0$. Therefore,

$$s < r < t \text{ (Choice C)}.$$

Note that you *could have* calculated the slopes of $\overline{AC}$ and $\overline{BC}$, but it was unnecessary to do so.

KEY FACT N6

- If two nonvertical lines are parallel, their slopes are equal.
- If two nonvertical lines are perpendicular, the product of their slopes is -1.

If the product of two numbers, a and b, is -1, then $ab = -1 \Rightarrow a = -\frac{1}{b}$. So another way to express the second part of **KEY FACT N6** is to say that if two nonvertical lines are perpendicular, then the slope of one is the negative reciprocal of the slope of the other.

EXAMPLE 6

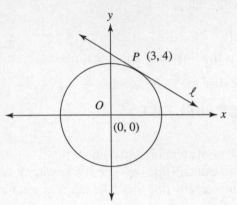

In the figure above, the center of the circle is at $(0, 0)$, and line l is tangent to the circle at P (3, 4). What is the slope of l?

(A) $-\frac{4}{3}$ (B) $-\frac{3}{4}$ (C) 0 (D) $\frac{3}{4}$ (E) $\frac{4}{3}$

Solution. From the diagram, it is clear that the slope of l is negative; so the answer must be (A) or (B). In fact, the slope of radius $\overline{OP}$ is $\frac{4 - 0}{3 - 0} = \frac{4}{3}$. By **KEY FACT L10**, $\overline{OP} \perp l$, and so, by **KEY FACT N6**, the slope of l is the negative reciprocal of $\frac{4}{3}$. The slope of l is $-\frac{3}{4}$ (Choice B).

On the PSAT you won't have to graph a straight line (or anything else), but you should recognize the equations of straight lines.

KEY FACT N7

For any real numbers a, b, m:

- The equation of a vertical line can be written as $x = a$.
- The equation of any nonvertical line can be written as $y = mx + b$.
- In the equation $y = mx + b$, m is the slope of the line, and b is the y-intercept.
- If $m = 0$, the line is horizontal, and its equation is $y = b$.

EXAMPLE 7

Which of the following is an equation of a line that is parallel to the line whose equation is $y = 2x - 3$?

(A) $y = 2x + 3$ (B) $y = -2x - 3$ (C) $y = \frac{1}{2}x + 3$ (D) $y = -\frac{1}{2}x + 3$
(E) $y = -\frac{1}{2}x - 3$

Solution. By **KEY FACT N7**, the slope of the line $y = 2x - 3$ is 2. By **KEY FACT N6**, parallel lines have equal slopes. Only Choice A, $y = 2x + 3$, also has a slope equal to 2.

EXERCISES

MULTIPLE-CHOICE QUESTIONS

1. What is the area of the rectangle, three of whose vertices are the points $A(2, 2)$, $B(6, 4)$, and $C(7, 2)$?

   (A) 10   (B) 25   (C) 40   (D) 50   (E) 100

2. A circle whose center is at $(2, -3)$ passes through the point $(4, 4)$. What is the area of the circle?

   (A) 5π (B) 37π (C) 53π (D) 85π
   (E) It cannot be determined from the information given.

3. $B(7, -7)$ is a point on a circle whose center is at $(3, 5)$. If AB is a diameter of the circle, what is the slope of AB?

   (A) -3 (B) $-\frac{1}{3}$ (C) $\frac{1}{3}$ (D) 3
   (E) It cannot be determined from the information given.

4. What is the slope of the line that passes through $(0, a)$ and $(b, 0)$, where $b \neq 0$?

   (A) $\frac{a}{b}$ (B) $-\frac{a}{b}$ (C) $\frac{b}{a}$ (D) $-\frac{b}{a}$
   (E) It cannot be determined from the information given.

5. A circle whose center is at $(6, 8)$ passes through the origin. Which of the following points is NOT on the circle?

   (A) $(12, 0)$ (B) $(6, -2)$ (C) $(16, 8)$
   (D) $(-2, 12)$ (E) $(-4, 8)$

GRID-IN QUESTIONS

<u>Questions 6 and 7</u> concern parallelogram ABCD, whose coordinates are $A(-6, 2)$, $B(-3, 6)$, $C(4, 6)$, $D(1, 2)$.

6. What is the area of parallelogram *ABCD*?

7. What is the perimeter of parallelogram *ABCD*?

8. If the coordinates of $\triangle JKL$ are $J(0, 0)$, $K(8, 0)$, and $L(2, 6)$, what is the sum of the slopes of the three sides of the triangle?

9. If $P(-3, 3)$ and $Q(1, -2)$ are the endpoints of one side of square *PQRS*, what is the area of the square?

10. What is the area of pentagon *ABCDE*?

Answer Key

6. 28

7. 24

8. 2

9. 41

10. 35

9-O BASIC PROBABILITY

The **probability** that an **event** will occur is a number between 0 and 1, usually written as a fraction, which indicates how likely it is that the event will happen. For example, if you spin the spinner at the right, there are four possible outcomes: it is equally likely that the spinner will stop in any of the four regions. There is one chance in four that it will stop in the region marked 2. So we say that the probability of spinning a 2 is one-fourth and write $P(2) = \frac{1}{4}$. Since 2 is the only even number on the spinner we could also say $P(\text{even}) = \frac{1}{4}$. There are three chances in four that the spinner will land in a region with an odd number in it, so $P(\text{odd}) = \frac{3}{4}$.

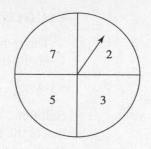

KEY FACT O1 If E is any event, the probability that E will occur is given by

$$P(E) = \frac{\text{the number of favorable outcomes}}{\text{the total number of possible outcomes}}$$

assuming that all of the possible outcomes are equally likely.

In the preceding example, each of the four regions is the same size; so it is equally likely that the spinner will land on the 2, 3, 5, or 7. Therefore,

$$P(\text{odd}) = \frac{\text{the number of ways of getting an odd number}}{\text{the total number of possible outcomes}} = \frac{3}{4}.$$

Let's look at some other probabilities associated with spinning this spinner once:

$$P(\text{number} > 8) = \frac{\text{the number of ways of getting a number} > 8}{\text{the total number of possible outcomes}} = \frac{0}{4} = 0$$

$$P(\text{prime number}) = \frac{\text{the number of ways of getting a prime number}}{\text{the total number of possible outcomes}} = \frac{4}{4} = 1$$

$$P(\text{number} < 5) = \frac{\text{the number of ways of getting a number} < 5}{\text{the total number of possible outcomes}} = \frac{2}{4} = \frac{1}{2}$$

KEY FACT O2 Let E be an event and $P(E)$ the probability it will occur.

Then with reference to the example above:

- If E is *impossible* (such as getting a number greater than 8), $P(E) = 0$.
- If it is *certain* that E will occur (such as getting a prime number), $P(E) = 1$.
- In all cases $0 \le P(E) \le 1$.
- The probability that event E will *not* occur is $1 - P(E)$.
- If 2 or more events constitute all the outcomes, the sum of their probabilities is 1.
  [For example, $P(\text{even}) + P(\text{odd}) = \frac{1}{4} + \frac{3}{4} = 1$].
- The more likely it is that an event will occur, the higher its probability (the closer to 1 it is); the less likely it is that an event will occur, the lower its probability (the closer to 0 it is).

EXAMPLE 1

A two-digit number is chosen at random. What is the probability that the number chosen is a multiple of 9?

Solution. There are 90 two-digit numbers (all of the integers between 10 and 99, inclusive). Of these 90 numbers, 10 of them (18, 27, 36, . . . , 99) are multiples of 9. Therefore,

$$\text{probability} = \frac{\text{the number of favorable outcomes}}{\text{the total number of possible outcomes}} = \frac{10}{90} = \frac{1}{9}.$$

KEY FACT O3 If an experiment is done two (or more) times, the probability that first one event will occur and then a second event will occur is the product of the probabilities.

EXAMPLE 2

The spinner at the beginning of this section is spun three times. What is the probability that it never lands on the 2?

(A) $\frac{1}{64}$ (B) $\frac{1}{4}$ (C) $\frac{27}{64}$ (D) $\frac{3}{4}$ (E) $\frac{9}{4}$

Solution. We want the probability that on each of the three spins the spinner lands on one of the three odd numbers. Since $P(\text{odd}) = \frac{3}{4}$, by **KEY FACT O3**, the probability of three consecutive odd numbers is

$$P(\text{odd 1st time}) \times P(\text{odd 2nd time}) \times P(\text{odd 3rd time}) = \frac{3}{4} \times \frac{3}{4} \times \frac{3}{4} = \frac{27}{64}.$$

Occasionally, on a PSAT there will be a question that relates to probability and geometry. The next **KEY FACT** will help you deal with that type of question.

 KEY FACT O4 If a point is chosen at random inside a geometrical figure, the probability that the chosen point lies in a particular region is

$$\frac{\text{the area of that region}}{\text{the area of the whole figure}}$$

EXAMPLE 3

If a point is chosen at random inside rectangle *ABCD*, what is the probability that the point lies in the shaded region?

Solution. The area of rectangle *ABCD* is $4 \times 10 = 40$. The area of right triangle *ABC* = $\frac{1}{2}(4 \times 10) = 20$, and the area of right triangle *EDF* = $\frac{1}{2}(2 \times 5) = 5$. So the area of the shaded region is $40 - 20 - 5 = 15$. The probability that the chosen point lies inside the shaded region is $\frac{15}{40} = \frac{3}{8}$.

EXERCISES

MULTIPLE-CHOICE QUESTIONS

Questions 1–3 refer to a jar that contains 5 marbles, 1 of each of the colors red, white, blue, green, and yellow.

1. If four marbles are removed from the jar, what is the probability that the yellow one was removed?

(A) $\frac{1}{20}$ (B) $\frac{1}{5}$ (C) $\frac{1}{4}$ (D) $\frac{4}{5}$ (E) $\frac{5}{4}$

2. If one marble is removed from the jar, what is the probability that it is red, white, or blue?

(A) $\frac{1}{15}$ (B) $\frac{1}{5}$ (C) $\frac{2}{5}$ (D) $\frac{3}{5}$ (E) $\frac{5}{3}$

3. If two marbles are removed from the jar, what is the probability that each of them is red, white, or blue?

(A) $\frac{6}{25}$ (B) $\frac{3}{10}$ (C) $\frac{9}{25}$ (D) $\frac{2}{3}$ (E) $\frac{6}{5}$

4. The Smiths have two children. If their older child is a boy, what is the probability that their younger child is also a boy?

(A) $\frac{1}{4}$ (B) $\frac{1}{3}$ (C) $\frac{1}{2}$ (D) $\frac{2}{3}$ (E) $\frac{3}{4}$

5. The Kleins have two children. What is the probability that both of their children are boys?

(A) $\frac{1}{4}$ (B) $\frac{1}{3}$ (C) $\frac{1}{2}$ (D) $\frac{2}{3}$ (E) $\frac{3}{4}$

GRID-IN QUESTIONS

6. If three coins are flipped, what is the probability that there are more heads than tails?

7. A box contains 10 slips of paper, each with a different number from 1 to 10 written on it. If one slip is removed at random, what is the probability that the number selected is a multiple of 2 or 3?

8. If two people are chosen at random, what is the probability that they were born on different days of the week?

9. A number is a *palindrome* if it reads exactly the same from right to left as it does from left to right. For example, 66, 818, and 2552 are all palindromes. If a three-digit number is chosen at random, what is the probability that it is a palindrome?

10. In the diagram above, the radius of the large circle is 5 and the radius of the small circle is 3. If a point is chosen at random inside the large circle, what is the probability that the point lies inside the small white circle?

6.   7.   8.   9.   10.

Answer Key

6. | 1 | / | 2 | or **.5**

7. | 7 | / | 1 | 0 | or **.7**

8. | 6 | / | 7 |

9. | 1 | / | 1 | 0 |

10. | 9 | / | 2 | 5 | or **.36**

9-P SEQUENCES

There are three types of sequences that occasionally appear on the PSAT: *arithmetic sequences*, *geometric sequences*, and *repeating sequences*.

An **arithmetic sequence** is a sequence in which the *difference* between any two consecutive terms is the same. For example, the sequence 8, 11, 14, 17, 20, . . . is an arithmetic sequence in which the common difference is 3. An easy way to find the nth term of such a sequence is to start with the first term and add the common difference $n-1$ times. In this example, the fifth term is 20, which can be obtained by taking the first term, 8, and adding the common difference, 3, four times: $8 + 4(3) = 8 + 12 = 20$.

KEY FACT P1 gives the formula for finding the nth term of any arithmetic sequence.

> **KEY FACT P1** If $a_1, a_2, a_3, \ldots$ is an arithmetic sequence whose common difference is d, then $a_n = a_1 + (n-1)\,d$.

EXAMPLE 1

What is the 100th term of the sequence 8, 11, 14, 17, 20, . . . ?

Solution. By **KEY FACT P1**, $a_{100} = a_1 + 99d = 8 + 99(3) = 8 + 297 = 305$.

A **geometric sequence** is a sequence in which the *ratio* between any two consecutive terms is the same. For example, the sequence 2, 8, 32, 128, 512, . . . is a geometric sequence: the ratios $\frac{8}{2}, \frac{32}{8}, \frac{128}{32}$ are all equal to 4.

An easy way to find the nth term of a geometric sequence is to start with the first term and multiply it by the common ratio $n-1$ times. For example, in the sequence 2, 8, 32, 128, 512, . . . the fourth term is 128, which can be obtained by taking the first term, 2, and multiplying it by the common ratio, 4, three times: $2 \times 4 \times 4 \times 4 = 2 \times 4^3 = 2 \times 64 = 128$. The next **KEY FACT** gives the formula for finding the nth term of a geometric sequence.

> **KEY FACT P2** If $a_1, a_2, a_3, \ldots$ is a geometric sequence whose common ratio is r, then $a_n = a_1\,(r)^{n-1}$.

EXAMPLE 2

What is the 100th term of the sequence 2, 8, 32, 128, 512, . . . ?

(A) 2^{99} (B) 2^{100} (C) 2×4^{99} (D) 2×4^{100} (E) 2×4^{101}

Solution. By **KEY FACT P2**, since this is a geometric sequence whose first term is 2 and whose common ratio is 4, $a_{100} = a_1(r)^{99} = 2 \times 4^{99}$ (Choice C).

A **repeating sequence** is a sequence in which a certain number of terms repeat indefinitely. Each of the following is a repeating sequence

   (i) $-1, 0, 1, -1, 0, 1, -1, 0, 1, \ldots$
   (ii) $1, 4, 2, 8, 5, 7, 1, 4, 2, 8, 5, 7, \ldots$
   (iii) red, white, blue, green, red, white, blue, green, . . .

On the PSAT, questions concerning repeating sequences usually ask you to find a particular term of the sequence, such as the 100th term or 1000th term. So you need to have a procedure for finding the term you want. For example, let's find the 500th term of the sequence 1, 4, 2, 8, 5, 7, 1, 4, 2, 8, 5, 7, . . . Think of this as a sequence in which the set {1, 4, 2, 8, 5, 7} of 6 numbers keeps repeating. Since the last number in the set is 7, if we write down 1 set or 2 sets or 3 sets or 10 sets, the last number will be 7. So the 6th, 12th, 18th, and 60th terms are all 7. In general, if n is a multiple of 6, the nth term is 7. So the 30th term, the 666th term, and the 6,000,000th terms are all 7. To answer the question, "What is the 500th term?" the first thing you should do is divide 500 by

6. If 500 is a multiple of 6, the answer will be 7. Using your calculator, you find that 500 ÷ 6 = 83.333. So 500 is not a multiple of 6. When 500 is divided by 6, the *integer* quotient is 83 (ignore the decimal portion). This means that in the first 500 terms of the sequence, the set {1, 4, 2, 8, 5, 7} repeats 83 times. Since 83 × 6 = 498, the 498th term is 7. The 499th term starts the next set; it is 1 and the 500th term is 4.

TACTIC P1

To find the *n*th term of a repeating sequence, divide *n* by the number of terms that repeat. If *r* is the integer remainder, then the *n*th term is the same as the *r*th term.

In the worked-out example preceding **TACTIC P1**, we found the 500th term of the sequence 1, 4, 2, 8, 7, 1, 4, 2, 8, 7, . . . Using **TACTIC P1**, we would proceed as follows:

500 ÷ 6 = 83.333 ⇒ the quotient is 83. Then 83 × 6 = 498 and 500 − 498 = 2 ⇒ the remainder is 2. So the 500th term is the same as the 2nd term, namely 4.

EXERCISES

MULTIPLE-CHOICE QUESTIONS

1. What is the 100th term of the sequence 4, 9, 14, 19, 24, . . . ?

   (A) 494   (B) 499   (C) 504   (D) 509   (E) 514

2. Consider the sequence 2, 6, 18, 54, 162, . . . What is the 25th term?

   (A) 3^{24} (B) 3^{25} (C) 2×3^{24} (D) 2×3^{25}
   (E) 6^{24}

3. If today is Saturday, what day will it be 500 days from today?

   (A) Saturday   (B) Sunday   (C) Tuesday
   (D) Wednesday   (E) Friday

4. If it is now September, what month will it be 555 months from now?

   (A) April   (B) June   (C) September
   (D) November   (E) December

5. The first term of sequence I is 2 and each subsequent term is 2 more than the preceding term. The first term of sequence II is 2 and each subsequent term is 2 times the preceding term. What is the ratio of the 32nd term of sequence II to the 32nd term of sequence I?

   (A) 1   (B) 2   (C) 2^{26} (D) 2^{27} (E) 2^{32}

GRID-IN QUESTIONS

6. The first term of a sequence is 1 and every term after the first one is 1 more than the square of the preceding term. What is the fifth term?

7. The first two terms of a sequence are 5 and 7. Each term after the second one is found by taking the average (arithmetic mean) of all the preceding terms. What is the 50th term of this sequence?

8. Consider the sequence 2, 6, 18, 54, 162, . . . If the 77th term is a and the 80th term is b, what is the value of $\frac{b}{a}$?

9. Consider the sequence 1, 2, 3, 1, 2, 3, 1, 2, 3, . . . What is the sum of the first 100 terms?

10. In a certain sequence the difference between any two consecutive terms is 4. If the 20th term is 100, what is the 2nd term?

Answer Key

1. B 2. C 3. C 4. E 5. C

9-Q INTERPRETATION OF DATA

On the PSAT it is likely that there will be one or two questions that will require you to interpret the data that appear in some type of table or graph. Occasionally you will be asked two questions based on the same set of data. In this case, the first question is usually quite easy, requiring only that you *read* the information in the table or graph. The second question is usually a little more challenging and may ask you to *interpret* the data or *manipulate* them or *make a prediction* based on them.

The data can be presented in the columns of a table or displayed graphically. The graphs that appear most often are circle graphs, bar graphs, line graphs, and scatter-plot graphs. In this section, we will illustrate each of these and give examples of the types of questions that may be asked.

A **line graph** indicates how one or more quantities change over time. The horizontal axis is usually marked off in units of time; the units on the vertical axis can represent almost any type of numerical data: dollars, weights, exam grades, number of people, and so on.

Here is a typical line graph:

PRICE PER SHARE OF STOCKS *A* AND *B* ON JANUARY 1 OF 6 YEARS

Before reading even one of the questions based on the above graph, you should have acquired *at least* the following information: (i) the graph gives the values of two different stocks; (ii) the graph covers the period from January 1, 1990, to January 1, 1995; (iii) during that time, both stocks rose in value. There are several questions that could be asked about the data in this graph. Here are two examples.

EXAMPLE 1

On January 1 of what year was the ratio of the value of a share of stock *A* to the value of a share of stock *B* the greatest?

(A) 1990   (B) 1991   (C) 1992   (D) 1993   (E) 1995

Solution. From 1993 to 1995, the values of the two stocks were fairly close; so those years are not candidates. In 1992, when the difference was greatest ($25), the ratio was 40:15 or 8:3 or 2.66. In 1990, the difference was less (only $20), but the ratio was 30:10 or 3:1 or 3. The ratio was greatest in 1990 (Choice A).

EXAMPLE 2

What was the average yearly increase in the value of a share of stock *A* from 1990 to 1995?

Solution. Over the five-year period from January 1, 1990, to January 1, 1995, the value of a share of stock *A* rose from $30 to $45, an increase of $15. The average yearly increase was $15 ÷ 5 years, or $3 per year.

The same information that was given in the preceding line graph could have been presented in a **table** or in a **bar graph**.

PRICE PER SHARE OF STOCKS *A* AND *B*
ON JANUARY 1 OF 6 YEARS

Stock	Prices (dollars)					
	1990	1991	1992	1993	1994	1995
Stock *A*	30	35	40	25	40	45
Stock *B*	10	20	15	35	40	40

**PRICE PER SHARE OF STOCKS *A* AND *B* ON
JANUARY 1 OF 6 YEARS**

In a bar graph, the taller the bar, the greater the value of the quantity. Bar graphs can also be drawn horizontally; in this case the longer the bar, the greater the quantity.

In a slight variation of the horizontal bar graph, the bars are replaced by a string of icons, or symbols. For example, the graph below, in which each picture of a person represents 100 students, conveys information about the languages studied by the students at State College in 2000.

**NUMBERS OF STUDENTS ENROLLED IN
LANGUAGE COURSES AT STATE COLLEGE IN 2000**

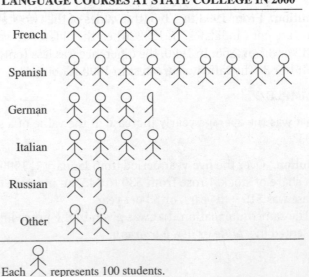

EXAMPLE 3

If the "Other" category includes five languages, what is the average (arithmetic mean) number of students studying each language offered at the college?

Solution. First determine the total number of students taking a language course. Either get the number for each language and add or just count the number of icons: there are 24 full icons and 2 half icons for a total of 25 icons, representing 2500 students. The 2500 students are divided among 10 languages (the 5 languages listed plus the 5 in the "Other" category): $2500 \div 10 = 250$.

EXAMPLE 4

If the number of students studying Italian next year is the same as the number taking Spanish this year, by what percent will the number of students taking Italian increase?

Solution. The number of students taking Italian would increase by 500 from 400 to 900. This represents a $\frac{500}{400} \times 100\% = 125\%$ increase.

A **_circle graph_** is another way to present data. In a circle graph, which is sometimes called a **_pie chart_**, the circle is divided into sectors, with the size of each sector exactly proportional to the quantity it represents. For example, the information included in the previous graph is presented in the circle graph below.

**NUMBERS OF STUDENTS ENROLLED IN
LANGUAGE COURSES AT STATE COLLEGE IN 2000**

Usually on the PSAT, in each sector of the circle is noted the number of degrees of its central angle or the percent of the total data it contains. For example, in the circle graph above, since 500 of the 2500 language students at State College are studying French, the sector representing French is exactly $\frac{1}{5}$ of the circle. On the PSAT this sector could be marked either 72° ($\frac{1}{5}$ of 360°) or 20% ($\frac{1}{5}$ of 100%), as in the graphs below.

**DISTRIBUTION OF THE 2500 STUDENTS
ENROLLED IN LANGUAGE COURSES**

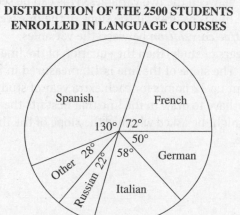

**DISTRIBUTION OF THE 2500 STUDENTS
ENROLLED IN LANGUAGE COURSES**

Yet another way to display data is in a **scatter-plot diagram**. Suppose that a group of 12 students took a college placement test in French. It is reasonable to expect that those students who had studied more French in high school would have higher scores. It is highly unlikely, however, that everyone who had studied French for three years, say, would have exactly the same score on the placement test. It is much more likely that the distribution of scores would be somewhat *scattered*, as in the following graph.

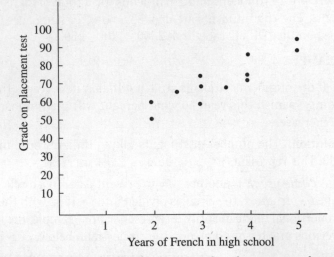

Notice that there can be no formula that exactly relates years of study and grade on the placement test: students who had studied French for three years had scores that ranged from 60 to 75. But there is a clear trend, and we can draw a line that approximates the relationship in the graph.

Because, on average, higher test scores correspond to more years of study, we say there is a **positive correlation** between the two variables. This can be seen in the graph by noting that the slope of the line is positive. If the slope of the line were negative, we would say that there is a **negative correlation** between the variables.

If y = test grade and x = years of study, then the equation of the line we drew in the graph above is $y = 12x + 30$. The slope of the line is 12, measured in points per year. That is, on average, scores went up 12 points for each extra year of study.

On the PSAT, you will *never* have to draw in the line that best fits the data or find the equation of the line, but you might be asked whether the slope of the line that best fits the data is positive or negative.

EXAMPLE 5

Score on the Math part of the SAT

The scatter-plot graph above shows the grades that a group of 12 college students earned on the final exam in Physics 101 and the scores they had on the Mathematics part of the SAT in high school. The line that best fits this data has been drawn in.

Which of the following statements is true?

   I. There is a positive correlation between scores on the Mathematics part of the SAT and grades on the physics final exam.

   II. If Adam and Bob are two of the students in the survey and Adam's math score on the SAT was higher than Bob's, then Adam had a higher grade on the physics final exam.

   III. The slope of the line in the graph, measured in points on the final exam per points on the Math SAT, is less than 0.5.

(A) I only   (B) II only   (C) III only   (D) I and III only   (E) I, II, and III

Solution. Since the line of best fit goes up from left to right, the slope is positive, and there is a positive correlation between the two variables (I is true). You don't need to measure the slope exactly. Clearly an increase of 50 points on the SAT corresponds to an increase of at most 5 or 10 points on the physics exam; so the slope is at most $\frac{5}{50} = 0.1$ or $\frac{10}{50} = 0.2$, clearly less than 0.5 (III is true). Since (750, 80) and (600, 95) are both points in the scatter plot, a higher SAT score does not necessarily correspond to a higher physics grade (II is false). I and III only are true (D).

EXERCISES

MULTIPLE-CHOICE QUESTIONS

Questions 1 and 2 refer to the following graph.

BAKER FAMILY HOUSEHOLD BUDGET IN 2000

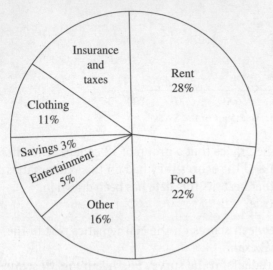

1. If the Baker's income in 2000 was $40,000, how much more did they spend on insurance and taxes than they did on clothing?

   (A) $1600   (B) $2000   (C) $3200   (D) $4400
   (E) $6000

2. What is the degree measure of the central angle of the sector representing insurance and taxes?

   (A) 45   (B) 54   (C) 60   (D) 72   (E) 90

Questions 3–5 refer to the following graph.

MATH SAT SCORES OF JUNIORS AT WESTSIDE HIGH SCHOOL

3. How many juniors at Westside High School took the SAT I?

   (A) 1000   (B) 1100   (C) 1200   (D) 1250
   (E) 1300

4. To the nearest 5%, what percent of the juniors had Math SAT scores of less than 600?

   (A) 70   (B) 75   (C) 80   (D) 85
   (E) It cannot be determined from the information given.

5. How many juniors had Verbal SAT I scores between 450 and 550?

   (A) 360   (B) 375   (C) 525   (D) 750
   (E) It cannot be determined from the information given.

Questions 6 and 7 refer to the following graph.

SPEEDS AT WHICH TOM DROVE ON SUNDAY MORNING

6. For what percent of the time was Tom driving at 40 miles per hour or faster?

   (A) 20   (B) 25   (C) $33\frac{1}{3}$ (D) 40   (E) 50

7. How far, in miles, did Tom drive between 8:30 and 9:00?

   (A) 0   (B) 20   (C) 30   (D) 40
   (E) It cannot be determined from the information given.

8. Ten houses were being built in a new development. The following scatter-plot graph shows the number of carpenters assigned to each house and the number of hours it took to finish the carpentry in the kitchen of each house.

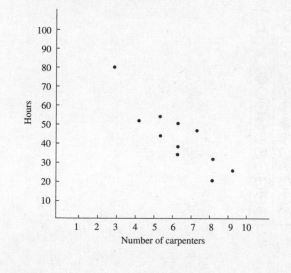

Which of the following statements must be true?

I. There is a positive correlation between the number of carpenters working on a house and the time it took to complete the work in the kitchen.

II. Whenever there were more than 7 carpenters working in a house, the job took less time than if there were fewer than 7 carpenters working.

III. The slope of the line that best fits the data is less than 0.5.

(A) I only (B) II only (C) III only
(D) II and III only (E) I, II, and III

GRID-IN QUESTIONS

9. On the basis of the data in the graph below, if 300 students took the physics exam, how many earned a grade of D?

DISTRIBUTION OF GRADES ON
THE FINAL EXAM IN PHYSICS

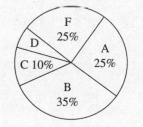

10. The following bar graph shows the number of men and women who earned Ph.D.'s in French at Southwestern University in 2001 and 2002.

From 2001 to 2002 the number of women earning Ph.D.'s increased by $x\%$, and the number of men earning Ph.D.'s decreased by $y\%$. What is the value of $x - y$?

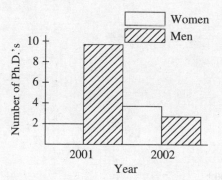

9. | 10.

Answer Key

1. A	3. A	5. E	7. B
2. B	4. C	6. E	8. D

9.

10.

9-R FUNCTIONS

Very little of what is taught about functions in high school math classes is tested on the PSAT. In this section we will review only those basic facts about functions and their graphs that you need to know for the PSAT.

As used on the PSAT, a *function* is a rule that assigns to each number in one set a number in another set. The function is usually designated by the letter f, although other letters, such as g and h, are sometimes used. The numbers in the first set are labeled x, and the number in the second set to which x is assigned by the function is designated by the letter y or by $f(x)$.

For example, we can write $y = f(x) = 2x + 3$. This function assigns to each real number x, the number $2x + 3$.

The number assigned to 5 is $2(5) + 3 = 10 + 3 = 13$, and
the number assigned to –5 is $2(–5) + 3 = –10 + 3 = –7$.

To express these facts, we write

$f(5) = 13$ and $f(–5) = –7$.

The proper way to think of the function $f(x) = 2x + 3$ is that f takes *anything* and assigns to it 2 times *that thing* plus 3:

$f(anything) = 2(that thing) + 3$

- $f(100) = 2(100) + 3 = 203$
- $f(a) = 2a + 3$
- $f(x^2) = 2x^2 + 3$
- $f(0) = 2(0) + 3 = 0 + 3 = 3$
- $f(a + b) = 2(a + b) + 3$
- $f(2x^2 + 3) = 2(2x^2 + 3) + 3 = 4x^2 + 9$

EXAMPLE 1

If $f(x) = x^2 + 2x$, what is $f(3) + f(–3)$?

Solution. $f(3) = 3^2 + 2(3) = 9 + 6 = 15$
                     $f(–3) = (–3)^2 + 2(–3) = 9 – 6 = 3$
Therefore, $f(3) + f(–3) = 15 + 3 = 18.$

EXAMPLE 2

If $f(x) = x^2 + 2x$, what is $f(x + 2)$?

(A) $x^2 + 2x + 4$ (B) $x^2 + 2x + 8$ (C) $x^2 + 6x + 4$ (D) $x^2 + 6x + 8$ (E) $x^3 + 4x^2 + 4x$

Solution. $f(x + 2) = (x + 2)^2 + 2(x + 2) = (x^2 + 4x + 4) + (2x + 4) = x^2 + 6x + 8$ (Choice D).

EXAMPLE 3

Let $f(x) = x^2 + 2x$ and $g(x) = x^2 – 2x$. If $g(4) = a$ and $f(a) = b$, what is the value of b?

Solution. $g(4) = 4^2 – 2(4) = 16 – 8 = 8$; so $a = 8$. Then $f(a) = f(8) = 8^2 + 2(8) = 64 + 16 = 80$. So $b = 80$.

The graph of a function, f, is a certain set of points in the coordinate plane. The point (x, y) is on the graph of f if and only if $y = f(x)$. So, for example, the graph of $f(x) = 2x + 3$ consists of all points (x, y) such that $y = 2x + 3$. Since $f(5) = 13$ and $f(–5) = –7$, then $(5, 13)$ and $(–5, –7)$ are both points on the graph of $f(x) = 2x + 3$. On the PSAT you may have to know whether a certain point is on the graph of a given function, but you won't have to actually graph the function.

EXAMPLE 4

Which of the following is NOT a point on the graph of $f(x) = x^2 + \dfrac{4}{x^2}$?

(A) $(1, 5)$ (B) $(–1, 5)$ (C) $(2, 5)$ (D) $(–2, –5)$ (E) $(4, 16.25)$

Solution.

$$f(1) = 1^2 + \frac{4}{1^2} = 1 + 4 = 5 \Rightarrow (1, 5) \text{ is a point on the graph.}$$

$$f(-1) = (-1)^2 + \frac{4}{(-1)^2} = 1 + 4 = 5 \Rightarrow (-1, 5) \text{ is a point on the graph.}$$

$$f(2) = 2^2 + \frac{4}{2^2} = 4 + 1 = 5 \Rightarrow (2, 5) \text{ is a point on the graph.}$$

$$f(-2) = (-2)^2 + \frac{4}{(-2)^2} = 4 + 1 = 5 \neq -5 \Rightarrow (-2, -5) \text{ is } NOT \text{ a point on the graph.}$$

The answer is Choice D.

EXERCISES

MULTIPLE-CHOICE QUESTIONS

1. If $f(x) = 2x - x^2$, what is the value of $f(-2)$?

   (A) –8 (B) –4 (C) 0 (D) 4 (E) 8

2. If $f(x) = 3x + 5$ and $f(2) = a$, what is $f(a)$?

   (A) 11 (B) 13 (C) 25 (D) 38 (E) 121

3. If $f(x) = 3x + 5$ and $g(x) = 5x + 3$, what is $g(6) - f(6)$?

   (A) 0 (B) 6 (C) 10 (D) 26 (E) 56

4. Let $f(x) = 3x + 5$ and $g(x) = 5x + 3$. If $f(2) = a$ and $g(a) = b$, what is b?

   (A) 11 (B) 24 (C) 44 (D) 58 (E) 143

5. If $f(x) = 3x - 5$ and $(2, b)$ is a point on the graph of $y = f(x)$, then $b =$

   (A) –1 (B) 1 (C) 3 (D) 5 (E) 11

GRID-IN QUESTIONS

6. If $f(x) = 3x + 5$ and $(a, 20)$ is a point on the graph of $y = f(x)$, then what is the value of a?

7. If $f(x) = 2^x + x^2$, what is $f(1)$?

8. Let $f(x) = x^2 + 1$ and $g(x) = 1 - x^2$. If $g(3) = a$ and $f(a) = b$, what is b?

9. If $f(x) = x^2 + 1$ and $f(3) = a$, what is $f(a)$?

10. If $f(x) = 4 - x^2$ and (a, b) is a point on the graph of $y = f(x)$, what is the greatest possible value of b?

6.

7.

8.

9.

10.

Answer Key

1. *A*   2. *D*   3. *C*   4. *D*   5. *B*

6.
```
      5
```

7.
```
      3
```

8.
```
    6 5
```

9.
```
  1 0 1
```

10.
```
      4
```

PART FIVE

Writing Skills

▶ **CHAPTER 10 : Improving Written Expression**

Improving Written Expression

You definitely want to study hard when you prepare for the Writing Skills section of the PSAT: a good score on this section of the test may make all the difference between your becoming a National Merit finalist and your coming out a runner-up.

There are three different kinds of questions on the Writing Skills section of the PSAT: improving sentences, identifying sentence errors, and improving paragraphs. More than half of them, twenty questions out of thirty-nine, involve choosing the best of five different versions of a sentence.

The Writing Skills questions test your ability to recognize clear, correct standard written English, the kind of writing your college professors will expect on the papers you turn in to them. You'll be expected to know basic grammar, such as subject-verb agreement, pronoun-antecedent agreement, correct verb tense, correct sentence structure, and correct diction. You'll need to know how to recognize a dangling participle and how to spot when two parts of a sentence are not clearly connected. You'll also need to know when a paragraph is (or isn't) properly developed and organized.

IMPROVING SENTENCES

The most numerous set of questions in the Writing Skills section involves spotting the form of a sentence that works best. In these improving sentence questions, you will be presented with five different versions of the same sentence; you must choose the best one. Here are the directions:

Improving Sentence Directions

Some or all parts of the following sentences are underlined. The first answer choice, (A), simply repeats the underlined part of the sentence. The other four choices present four alternative ways to phrase the underlined part. Select the answer that produces the most effective sentence, one that is clear and exact, and blacken the appropriate space on your answer sheet. In selecting your choice, be sure that it is standard written English and that it expresses the meaning of the original sentence.

EXAMPLE:

The first biography of author Eudora Welty came out in 1998, <u>and she was eighty-nine years old at the time.</u>

(A) and she was eighty-nine years old at the time
(B) at the time when she was eighty-nine
(C) upon becoming an eighty-nine year old
(D) when she was eighty-nine
(E) at the age of eighty-nine years old

SAMPLE ANSWER:

Ⓐ Ⓑ Ⓒ ● Ⓔ

TIPS FOR HANDLING IMPROVING SENTENCE QUESTIONS

1. **If you spot an error in the underlined section, eliminate any answer that repeats it.** If something in the underlined section of a sentence correction question strikes you as an obvious error, you can immediately ignore any answer choices that repeat it. Remember, you still don't have to be able to explain what is wrong. You just need to find a correct equivalent. If the error you found in the underlined section is absent from more than one of the answer choices, look over those choices again to see if they add any new errors.

2. **If you don't spot the error in the underlined section, look at the answer choices to see what is changed.** Sometimes it's hard to spot what's wrong with the underlined section in a sentence correction question. When that happens, turn to the answer choices. Find the changes in the answers. The changes will tell you what kind of error is being tested. When you substitute the answer choices in the original sentence, ask yourself which of these choices makes the sentence seem clearest to you. That may well be the correct answer choice.

3. **Make sure that all parts of the sentence are logically connected.** Not all parts of a sentence are created equal. Some parts should be subordinated to the rest, connected with subordinating conjunctions or relative pronouns, not just added on with *and*. Overuse of *and* frequently makes sentences sound babyish. Compare "We had dinner at the Hard Rock Cafe, and we went to a concert" with "After we had dinner at the Hard Rock Cafe, we went to a concert."

4. **Make sure that all parts of a sentence given in a series are similar in form.** If they are not, the sentence suffers from a lack of parallel structure. The sentence "I'm taking classes in algebra, history, and how to speak French" lacks parallel structure. *Algebra* and *history* are nouns, names of subjects. The third subject should also be a noun: *conversational French*.

5. **Pay particular attention to the shorter answer choices.** (This tactic also applies to certain paragraph correction questions.) Good prose is economical. Often the correct answer choice will be the shortest, most direct way of making a point. If you spot no grammatical errors or errors in logic in a concise answer choice, it may well be right.

EXAMPLE 1

Eliminate any answers with obvious errors.

<u>Being as I had studied for the test</u> with a tutor, I was confident.

(A) Being as I had studied for the test
(B) Being as I studied for the test
(C) Since I studied for the test
(D) Since I had studied for the test
(E) Because I studied for the test

Since you immediately recognize that *Being as* is not acceptable as a conjunction in standard written English, you can eliminate Choices A and B right away. But you also know that both *Since* and *Because* are perfectly acceptable conjunctions; so you have to look more closely at Choices C, D, and E. The only other changes these choices make are in the tense of the verb. Since the studying occurred before the taking of the test, the past perfect tense, *had studied*, is correct, so the answer is Choice D. Even if you hadn't known that, you could have figured it out. Since *because* and *since* are both acceptable conjunctions and since Choices C and E both use the same verb, *studied*, in the simple past tense, those two choices must be wrong. Otherwise, they would both be right, and the PSAT doesn't have questions with two right answers.

EXAMPLE 2

Look at the answer choices to see what has been changed.

Even the play's most minor characters work together with extraordinary skill, their interplay creates a moving theatrical experience.

(A) their interplay creates a moving theatrical experience
(B) a moving theatrical experience is created by their interplay
(C) and their interplay creates a moving theatrical experience
(D) and a moving theatrical experience being the creation of their interplay
(E) with their interplay they create a moving theatrical experience

Look at the underlined section of the sentence. Nothing seems wrong with it. It could stand on its own as an independent sentence: *Their interplay creates a moving theatrical experience*. Choices B and E are similar to it, for both could stand as independent sentences. Choices C and D, however, are not independent sentences; both begin with the linking word *and*. The error needing correction here is the common comma splice, in which two sentences are carelessly linked with only a comma. Choice C corrects this error in the simplest way possible, adding the word *and* to tie these sentences together.

EXAMPLE 3

Make sure that all parts of the sentence are logically connected.

The rock star always had enthusiastic fans and they loved him.

(A) and they loved him
(B) and they loving him
(C) what loved him
(D) who loved him
(E) which loved him

The original version of this sentence doesn't have any grammatical errors, but it is a poor sentence because it doesn't connect its two clauses logically. The second clause ("and they loved him") is merely adding information about the fans, so it should be turned into an adjective clause, introduced by a relative pronoun. Choices D and E both seem to fit, but you know that *which* should never be used to refer to people, so Choice D is obviously the correct answer.

EXAMPLE 4

Make sure that all parts of a sentence listed in a series are similar in form.

In this chapter we'll analyze both types of questions, suggest useful techniques for tackling them, providing some sample items for you to try.

(A) suggest useful techniques for tackling them, providing some sample items for you to try
(B) suggest useful techniques for tackling them, providing some sample items which you can try
(C) suggest useful tactics for tackling them, and provide some sample items for you to try
(D) and suggest useful techniques for tackling them by providing some sample items for you to try
(E) having suggested useful techniques for tackling them and provided some sample items for you to try

To answer questions like this correctly, you must pay particular attention to what the sentence means. You must first decide whether *analyzing, suggesting,* and *providing* are logically equal in importance here. Since they are—all are activities that "we" will do—they should be given equal emphasis. Only Choice C provides the proper parallel structure.

EXAMPLE 5

Pay particular attention to the shorter answer choices.

The turning point in the battle of Waterloo probably was <u>Blucher, who was arriving</u> in time to save the day.

(A) Blucher, who was arriving
(B) Blucher, in that he arrived
(C) Blucher's arrival
(D) when Blucher was arriving
(E) that Blucher had arrived

Which answer choice uses the fewest words? Choice C, *Blucher's arrival*. It also happens to be the right answer.

Choice C is both concise in style and correct in grammar. Look back at the original sentence. Strip it of its modifiers, and what is left? "The turning point . . . was Blucher." A turning point is not a person; it is a *thing*. The turning point in the battle was not Blucher, but Blucher's *action,* the thing he did. The correct answer is Choice C, *Blucher's arrival.* Pay particular attention to such concise answer choices. If a concise choice sounds natural when you substitute it for the original underlined phrase, it's a reasonable guess.

IDENTIFYING SENTENCE ERRORS

Almost one-third of the Writing Skills questions on the PSAT, fourteen of the thirty-nine, to be exact, are identifying sentence error questions in which you have to find an error in the underlined section of a sentence. You do not have to correct the sentence or explain what is wrong. Here are the directions.

Identifying Sentence Error Directions

The sentences in this section may contain errors in grammar, usage, choice of words, or idioms. There is either just one error per sentence, or the sentence is correct. Some words or phrases are underlined and lettered; everything else in the sentence is correct.

If an underlined word or phrase is incorrect, choose that letter; if the sentence is correct, select <u>No error</u>. Then blacken the appropriate space on your Answer Sheet.

EXAMPLE: **SAMPLE ANSWER:**

These fields have soil <u>so rich that</u> corn   Ⓐ Ⓑ ● Ⓓ Ⓔ
                        A
<u>growing here</u> commonly <u>had stood</u> more
    B   C
than six feet <u>tall</u>. <u>No error</u>.
              D   E

TIPS FOR HANDLING IDENTIFYING SENTENCE ERROR QUESTIONS

1. Remember that the error, if there is one, must be in the underlined part of the sentence. You don't have to worry about improvements that could be made in the rest of the sentence. For example, if you have a sentence in which the subject is plural and the verb is singular, you could call either one the error. But if only the verb is underlined, the error for that sentence is the verb.

2. Use your ear for the language. Remember, you don't have to name the error, or be able to explain why it is wrong. All you have to do is recognize that something *is* wrong. On the early, easy questions in the set, if a word or phrase sounds wrong to you, it probably is, even if you don't know why.

3. Look first for the most common errors. Be systematic: check the underlined sections one by one. Most of the sentences will have errors. If you are having trouble finding mistakes, check for some of the more common ones: subject-verb agreement, pronoun-antecedent problems, misuse of adjectives and adverbs, dangling modifiers. But look for errors only in the underlined parts of the sentence.

4. Remember that not every sentence contains an error. Ten to twenty percent of the time, the sentence is correct as it stands. Do not get so caught up in hunting for errors that you start seeing errors that aren't there. If no obvious errors strike your eye and the sentence sounds natural to your ear, go with Choice E: No error.

EXAMPLE 1

Only the underlined parts of the sentences may contain errors. Focus on what may need fixing in them.

Mr. Brown is one of the commuters who takes the 7:30 train from Brooktown
      A   B   C

every morning. No error
  D   E

Since *who* refers to *commuters*, it is plural, and needs a plural verb. Therefore, the error is Choice B. If you were writing this sentence yourself, you could correct it in any number of other ways. You could say, "Mr. Brown is a commuter who takes . . ." or "Mr. Brown, a commuter, takes . . ." or "Mr. Brown, who is one of the commuters, takes . . ." However, the actual question doesn't offer you any of these possibilities. You have to choose from the underlined choices. Don't waste your time considering other ways to fix the sentence.

EXAMPLE 2

See if your ear helps you with this question.

In my history class I learned why the American colonies opposed the British,
        A   B   C

how they organized the militia, and the work of the Continental Congress.
                                         D

No error
  E

The last part of this sentence probably sounds funny to you—awkward, strange, wooden. You may not know exactly what it is, but something sounds wrong here. If you followed your instincts and chose Choice D as the error, you would be right. The error is a lack of parallel structure. The sentence is listing three things you learned, and they should all be in the same form. Your ear expects the pattern to be the same. Since the first two items listed are clauses, the third should be too: "In my history class I learned why the American colonies opposed the British, how they organized the militia, and how the Continental Congress worked."

EXAMPLE 3

Go through the underlined sections systematically, checking them one by one.

Marilyn and <u>I</u> ran as <u>fast</u> as we could, but we missed our train, <u>which</u>
       A   B   C

made <u>us</u> late for work. <u>No error</u>
      D   E

Imagine that you have this sentence, and you can't see what is wrong with it. Start at the beginning and check each answer choice. *I* is part of the subject, so it is the right case: after all, you wouldn't say "Me ran fast." *Fast* can be an adverb, so it is being used correctly here. *Which* is a pronoun, and needs a noun for its antecedent. The only available noun is *train*, but that doesn't make sense (the train didn't make us late—*missing* the train made us late.) So there is your error, Choice C.

Once you have checked each answer choice, if you still can't find an error, choose Choice E, "No error." About twenty percent of the identifying sentence error questions have no errors!

IMPROVING PARAGRAPHS

In the improving paragraph questions, you will confront a flawed student essay followed by five questions. In some cases, you must select the answer choice that best rewrites and combines portions of two separate sentences. In others, you must decide where in the essay a sentence best fits. In still others, you must choose what sort of additional information would most strengthen the writer's argument. Here are the directions.

Improving Paragraph Directions

The passage below is the unedited draft of a student's essay. Some of the essay needs to be rewritten to make the meaning clearer and more precise. Read the essay carefully.

The essay is followed by five questions about changes that might improve all or part of its organization, development, sentence structure, use of language, appropriateness to the audience, or use of standard written English. Choose the answer that most clearly and effectively expresses the student's intended meaning. Indicate your choice by filling in the corresponding space on the answer sheet.

TIPS FOR HANDLING IMPROVING PARAGRAPH QUESTIONS

1. First read the passage; then read the questions. Whether you choose to skim the student essay quickly or to read it closely, you need to have a reasonable idea of what the student author is trying to say before you set out to correct this rough first draft.
2. First tackle the questions that ask you to improve individual sentences; then tackle the ones that ask you to strengthen the passage as a whole. In the sentence correction questions, you've just been weeding out ineffective sentences and selecting effective ones. Here you're doing more of the same. It generally takes less time to spot an effective sentence than it does to figure out a way to strengthen an argument or link up two paragraphs.
3. Consider whether the addition of signal words or phrases—transitions—would strengthen the passage or particular sentences within it. If the essay is trying to contrast two ideas, it might benefit from the addition of a contrast signal.

Contrast Signals: *although, despite, however, in contrast, nevertheless, on the contrary, on the other hand.*

If one portion of the essay is trying to support or continue a thought developed elsewhere in the passage, it might benefit from the addition of a support signal.

Support Signals: *additionally, furthermore, in addition, likewise, moreover.*

If the essay is trying to indicate that one thing causes another, it might benefit from the addition of a cause-and-effect signal.

Cause-and-Effect Signals: *accordingly, as a result of, because, consequently, hence, therefore, thus.*

Pay particular attention to answer choices that contain such signal words.

4. When you tackle the questions, *go back to the passage* to verify each answer choice. See whether your revised version of a particular sentence sounds right in its context. Ask yourself whether your choice follows naturally from the sentence before.

COMMON GRAMMAR AND USAGE ERRORS

Some errors are more common than others in this section. Here are a dozen that appear frequently on the examination. Watch out for them when you do the practice exercises and when you take the PSAT.

The Run-On Sentence

Mary's party was very exciting, it lasted until 2 A.M.
It is raining today, I need a raincoat.

You may also have heard this error called a comma splice. It can be corrected by making two sentences instead of one:

Mary's party was very exciting. It lasted until 2 A.M.

or by using a semicolon in place of the comma:

Mary's party was very exciting; it lasted until 2 A.M.

or by proper compounding:

Mary's party was very exciting and lasted until 2 A.M.

You can also correct this error with proper subordination. The second example above could be corrected:

Since it is raining today, I need a raincoat.
It is raining today, and so I need a raincoat.

The Sentence Fragment

Since John was talking during the entire class, making it impossible for anyone to concentrate.

This is the opposite of the first error. Instead of too much in one sentence, here you have too little. Do not be misled by the length of the fragment. It must have a main clause before it can be a complete sentence. All you have in this example is the cause. You still need a result. For example, the sentence could be corrected:

Since John's talking during the entire class made it impossible for anyone to concentrate, the teacher had him stay after school.

Error in the Case of a Noun or Pronoun

Between you and I, this test is not really very difficult.

Case problems usually involve personal pronouns, which are in the nominative case (*I, he, she, we, they, who*) when they are used as subjects or predicate nominatives and in the objective case (*me, him, her, us, them, whom*) when they are used as direct objects, indirect objects, and objects of prepositions. In this example, if you realize that *between* is a preposition, you know that *I* should be changed to the objective *me* because it is the object of a preposition.

Error in Subject-Verb Agreement

Harvard College, along with several other Ivy League schools, are sending students to the conference.

Phrases starting with *along with* or *as well as* or *in addition to* that are placed in between the subject and the verb do not affect the verb. The subject of this sentence is *Harvard College,* so the verb should be *is sending.*

There is three bears living in that house.

Sentences that begin with *there* have the subject after the verb. The subject of this sentence is *bears,* so the verb should be *are.*

Error in Pronoun-Number Agreement

Every one of the girls on the team is trying to do their best.

Every pronoun must have a specific noun or noun substitute for an antecedent, and it must agree with that antecedent in number (singular or plural). In this example, *their* refers to *one* and must be singular:

Every one of the girls on the team is trying to do her best.

Error in the Tense or Form of a Verb

After the sun set behind the mountain, a cool breeze sprang up and brought relief from the heat.

Make sure the verbs in a sentence appear in the proper sequence of tenses, so that it is clear what happened when. Since, according to the sentence, the breeze did not appear until after the sun had finished setting, the setting belongs in the past perfect tense:

After the sun had set behind the mountain, a cool breeze sprang up and brought relief from the heat.

Error in Logical Comparison

I can go to California or Florida. I wonder which is best.

When you are comparing only two things, you should use the comparative form of the adjective, not the superlative:

I wonder which is better.

Comparisons must also be complete and logical.

The rooms on the second floor are larger than the first floor.

It would be a strange building that had rooms larger than an entire floor. Logically, this sentence should be corrected to

The rooms on the second floor are larger than those on the first floor.

Adjective and Adverb Confusion

She did good on the test.

They felt badly about leaving their friends.

These are the two most common ways that adjectives and adverbs are misused. In the first example, when you are talking about how someone did, you want the adverb *well*, not the adjective *good:*

She did well on the test.

In the second example, after a linking verb like *feel*, you want a predicate adjective to describe the subject:

They felt bad about leaving their friends.

Error in Modification and Word Order

Reaching for the book, the ladder slipped out from under him.

A participial phrase at the beginning of the sentence should describe the subject of the sentence. Since it doesn't make sense to think of a ladder reaching for a book, this participle is left dangling with nothing to modify. The sentence needs some rewriting:

When he reached for the book, the ladder slipped out from under him.

Error in Parallelism

In his book on winter sports, the author discusses ice-skating, skiing, hockey, and how to fish in an ice-covered lake.

Logically, equal and similar ideas belong in similar form. This shows that they are equal. In this sentence, the author discusses four sports, and all four should be presented the same way:

In his book on winter sports, the author discusses ice skating, skiing, hockey, and fishing in an ice-covered lake.

Error in Diction or Idiom

The affects of the storm could be seen everywhere.

Your ear for the language will help you handle these errors, especially if you are accustomed to reading standard English. These questions test you on words that are frequently misused, on levels of usage (informal versus formal), and on standard English idioms. In this example, the verb *affect,* meaning "to influence," has been confused with the noun *effect,* meaning "result."

The effects of the storm could be seen everywhere.

The exercises that follow will give you practice in answering the three types of questions you'll find on the Identifying Sentence Errors questions, Improving Sentence questions, and Improving Paragraph questions. When you have completed each exercise, check your answers against the answer key. Then, read the answer explanations for any questions you either answered incorrectly or omitted.

PRACTICE EXERCISES

Identifying Sentence Error Directions

The sentences in this section may contain errors in grammar, usage, choice of words, or idioms. There is either just one error per sentence, or the sentence is correct. Some words or phrases are underlined and lettered; everything else in the sentence is correct.

If an underlined word or phrase is incorrect, choose that letter; if the sentence is correct, select <u>No error</u>. Then blacken the appropriate space on your Answer Sheet.

EXAMPLE:

These fields have soil <u>so rich that</u> corn
A

<u>growing here</u> commonly <u>had stood</u> more
B$$C

than six feet <u>tall</u>. <u>No error</u>.
DE

SAMPLE ANSWER:

Ⓐ Ⓑ ● Ⓓ Ⓔ

1. We were <u>already</u> <u>to leave for</u> the amusement park
AB
when John's car <u>broke down</u>; we <u>were forced to</u>
CD
postpone our outing. <u>No error</u>
E

2. <u>By order of</u> the Student Council, the <u>wearing of</u>
A$$B
slacks by <u>we</u> girls in school <u>has been permitted</u>.
C$$D
<u>No error</u>
E

3. <u>Each</u> one of the dogs in the show <u>require</u> a <u>special</u>
ABC
<u>kind of</u> diet. <u>No error</u>
D$$E

4. The major difficulty <u>confronting</u> the authorities
A
<u>was</u> the reluctance of the people <u>to talk</u>; they had
B$$C
been warned not <u>to say nothing</u> to the police.
D
<u>No error</u>
E

5. If I <u>were</u> you, I would never permit <u>him</u>
A$$B
<u>to take part</u> in such an <u>exhausting and painful</u>
C$$D
activity. <u>No error</u>
E

6. Stanford White, <u>who</u> is one of America's
A
<u>most notable</u> architects, <u>have designed</u> many
B$$C
famous buildings, <u>among them</u> the original
D
Madison Square Garden. <u>No error</u>
E

7. The notion <u>of allowing</u> the <u>institution of</u> slavery
AB
<u>to continue to</u> exist in a democratic society had no
C
appeal to either the violent followers of John
Brown <u>nor</u> the peaceful disciples of Sojourner
D
Truth. <u>No error</u>
E

8. Some students <u>prefer</u> watching filmstrips to
A
<u>textbooks</u> because they feel <u>uncomfortable with</u>
B$$C
the presentation <u>of</u> information in a non-oral
D
form. <u>No error</u>
E

9. There was so much conversation <u>in back of</u> me
A$$B
that I <u>couldn't</u> hear the actors <u>on</u> the stage.
C$$D
<u>No error</u>
E

10. This book is <u>too</u> elementary; <u>it can help</u> neither
　　　　　　　A　　　　　　　　　B

you <u>nor</u> <u>I</u>. <u>No error</u>
　　　C　　D　　　E

11. In a way <u>we</u> may say <u>that</u> we <u>have reached</u> the
　　　　　　　A　　　　　B　　　　C

<u>end of</u> the Industrial Revolution. <u>No error</u>
　D　　　　　　　　　　　　　　　　E

12. <u>Although</u> the books are <u>altogether</u> on the shelf,
　　　　A　　　　　　　　　　B

<u>they</u> are not arranged in <u>any kind of</u> order.
　C　　　　　　　　　　　D

<u>No error</u>
　E

13. The <u>reason for</u> my <u>prolonged absence</u> from class
　　　　　A　　　　B

<u>was</u> <u>because</u> I was ill for three weeks. <u>No error</u>
　C　　D　　　　　　　　　　　　　　E

14. <u>According to</u> researchers, the weapons and work
　　　　A

implements <u>used by</u> Cro-Magnon hunters appear
　　　　　　B

<u>being</u> <u>actually</u> quite "modern." <u>No error</u>
　C　　D　　　　　　　　　　E

15. Since we were caught <u>completely unawares</u>, the
　　　　　　　　　　　　A

<u>affect</u> of Ms. Rivera's remarks <u>was startling</u>; some
　B　　　　　　　　　　　　　C

were shocked, <u>but</u> others were angry. <u>No error</u>
　　　　　　D　　　　　　　　　E

16. The committee <u>had intended</u> both <u>you and I</u> to
　　　　　　　　A　　　　　B

speak at the assembly; <u>however</u>, <u>only</u> one of us
　　　　　　　　　C　　D

will be able to talk. <u>No error</u>
　　　　　　　　E

17. The existence of rundown "welfare hotels,"

<u>in which</u> homeless families <u>reside</u> at enormous
　A　　　　　　　　　　B

<u>cost to</u> the taxpayer, provides a shameful
　C

<u>commentary</u> of America's commitment to house
　D

the poor. <u>No error</u>
　　　　　E

18. We have heard that the <u>principal</u> has decided
　　　　　　　　　　A

<u>whom</u> the prizewinners <u>will be</u> <u>and</u> will announce
　B　　　　　　　　　C　　D

the names in the assembly today. <u>No error</u>
　　　　　　　　　　　　　　E

19. As soon as the sun <u>had rose</u> <u>over</u> the mountains,
　　A　　　　　　　B　　C

the valley became <u>unbearably hot</u> and stifling.
　　　　　　　　D

<u>No error</u>
　E

20. <u>They</u> are both <u>excellent books</u>, but this one <u>is</u> <u>best</u>.
　A　　　　　B　　　　　　　　C　D

<u>No error</u>
　E

21. Although the news <u>had come</u> as a surprise <u>to all</u> in
　　　　　　　A　　　　　　　　B

the room, both Jane and Oprah tried to do <u>her</u>
　　　　　　　　　　　　　　　　C

work <u>as though</u> nothing had happened.
　　D

<u>No error</u>
　E

22. <u>Even</u> well-known fashion designers have difficulty
　A

staying on top <u>from one season to another</u>
　　　　　　B

<u>because of</u> <u>changeable moods</u> and needs in the
　C　　　D

marketplace. <u>No error</u>
　　　　　E

23. Arms control has been <u>under discussion</u> for
　　　　　　　　　A

decades with the former Soviet Union, <u>but</u>
　　　　　　　　　　　　　B

solutions <u>are still</u> <u>alluding</u> the major powers.
　　　　C　　D

<u>No error</u>
　E

24. Perhaps sports enthusiasts are realizing <u>that</u>
　　　　　　　　　　　　　A

jogging is <u>not easy on</u> joints and tendons, for the
　　　　　B

<u>latest fad</u> is being <u>walking</u>. <u>No error</u>
　C　　　　　D　　　E

25. Technological advances <u>can cause</u> factual data to
                              A

become obsolete within a <u>short time</u>; <u>yet</u>, students
                            B   C

should concentrate on <u>reasoning skills</u>, not facts.
                         D

<u>No error</u>
  E

26. If <u>anyone</u> cares <u>to join</u> me in this campaign, <u>either</u>
  A   B   C

now or in the near future, <u>they</u> will be welcomed
                       D

gratefully. <u>No error</u>
           E

27. The poems <u>with which</u> he occasionally
               A

desired to <u>regale</u> the fashionable world were
           B

<u>invariably bad</u>—stereotyped, bombastic, and
     C

even ludicrous. <u>No error</u>
     D   E

28. <u>Ever since</u> the <u>quality of</u> teacher education came
     A   B

under public scrutiny, suggestions for <u>upgrading</u>
                            C

the profession <u>are abounding</u>. <u>No error</u>
             D   E

29. <u>Because</u> the door was locked and bolted, the police
   A

<u>were</u> forced <u>to break</u> into the apartment <u>through</u>
  B   C   D

the bedroom window. <u>No error</u>
             E

30. I <u>will</u> <u>always</u> remember <u>you</u> <u>standing by</u> me
   A   B   C   D

offering me encouragement. <u>No error</u>
                E

31. With special training, capuchin monkeys

<u>can enable</u> quadriplegics <u>as well as</u> other
    A   B

handicapped individuals <u>to become</u>
                C

<u>increasingly independent</u>. <u>No error</u>
     D   E

32. <u>Contrary to</u> what had previously been reported,
   A

the conditions <u>governing</u> the truce between Libya
             B

and Chad <u>arranged by</u> the United Nations <u>has</u> not
          C   D

yet been revealed. <u>No error</u>
          E

33. Avid readers generally either admire <u>or</u> dislike
                         A

Ernest Hemingway's journalistic <u>style of</u> writing;
                       B

<u>few have</u> no opinion <u>of him</u>. <u>No error</u>
  C   D   E

34. In 1986, the nuclear disaster at Chernobyl

<u>has aroused</u> intense speculation <u>about</u> the long-
   A   B

term <u>effects of</u> radiation that continued for
      C

<u>the better part of</u> a year. <u>No error</u>
     D   E

35. Howard Hughes, <u>who</u> <u>became</u> the subject of
              A   B

bizarre rumors <u>as a result of</u> his extreme
              C

reclusiveness, was well-known as an aviator,

industrialist, and <u>in producing motion pictures</u>.
                          D

<u>No error</u>
  E

36. The child is neither encouraged to be critical or to examine all the evidence before forming an opinion.

(A) neither encouraged to be critical or to examine
(B) neither encouraged to be critical nor to examine
(C) either encouraged to be critical or to examine
(D) encouraged either to be critical nor to examine
(E) not encouraged either to be critical or to examine

37. The process by which the community influence the actions of its members is known as social control.

(A) influence the actions of its members
(B) influences the actions of its members
(C) had influenced the actions of its members
(D) influences the actions of their members
(E) will influence the actions of its members

38. Play being recognized as an important factor improving mental and physical health and thereby reducing human misery and poverty.

(A) Play being recognized as
(B) By recognizing play as
(C) Their recognizing play as
(D) Recognition of it being
(E) Play is recognized as

39. To be sure, there would be scarcely any time left over for other things if school children would have been expected to have considered all sides of every matter on which they hold opinions.

(A) would have been expected to have considered
(B) should have been expected to have considered
(C) were expected to consider
(D) will be expected to have considered
(E) were expected to be considered

40. Using it wisely, leisure promotes health, efficiency and happiness.

(A) Using it wisely
(B) If it is used wisely
(C) Having used it wisely
(D) Because of its wise use
(E) Because of usefulness

41. In giving expression to the play instincts of the human race, new vigor and effectiveness are afforded by recreation to the body and to the mind.

(A) new vigor and effectiveness are afforded by recreation to the body and to the mind
(B) recreation affords new vigor and effectiveness to the body and to the mind
(C) there are afforded new vigor and effectiveness to the body and to the mind
(D) by recreation the body and the mind are afforded new vigor and effectiveness
(E) to the body and to the mind afford new vigor and effectiveness to themselves by recreation

42. Depending on skillful suggestion, argument is seldom used in advertising.

(A) Depending on skillful suggestion, argument is seldom used in advertising.
(B) Argument is seldom used in advertising, which depends instead on skillful suggestion.
(C) Skillful suggestion is depended on by advertisers instead of argument.
(D) Suggestion, which is more skillful, is used in place of argument by advertisers.
(E) Instead of suggestion, depending on argument is used by skillful advertisers.

43. When this war is over, no nation will <u>either be isolated in war or peace</u>.

(A) either be isolated in war or peace
(B) be either isolated in war or peace
(C) be isolated in neither war nor peace
(D) be isolated either in war or in peace
(E) be isolated neither in war or peace

44. Thanks to the prevailing westerly winds, dust <u>blowing east from the drought-stricken plains</u> travels halfway across the continent to fall on the cities of the East Coast.

(A) blowing east from the drought-stricken plains
(B) that, blowing east from the drought-stricken plains,
(C) from the drought-stricken plains and blows east
(D) that is from the drought-stricken plains blowing east
(E) blowing east that is from the plains that are drought-stricken

45. Americans are learning that their concept of a research worker <u>toiling alone in a laboratory and who discovers miraculous cures</u> has been highly idealized and glamorized.

(A) toiling alone in a laboratory and who discovers miraculous cures
(B) toiling alone in a laboratory and discovers miraculous cures
(C) toiling alone in a laboratory to discover miraculous cures
(D) who toil alone in the laboratory and discover miraculous cures
(E) has toiled alone hoping to discover miraculous cures

46. However many mistakes have been made in our past, the tradition of America, <u>not only the champion of freedom but also fair play</u>, still lives among millions who can see light and hope scarcely anywhere else.

(A) not only the champion of freedom but also fair play
(B) the champion of not only freedom but also of fair play
(C) the champion not only of freedom but also of fair play
(D) not only the champion but also freedom and fair play
(E) not the champion of freedom only, but also fair play

47. Examining the principal movements sweeping <u>through the world, it can be seen</u> that they are being accelerated by the war.

(A) Examining the principal movements sweeping through the world, it can be seen
(B) Having examined the principal movements sweeping through the world, it can be seen
(C) Examining the principal movements sweeping through the world can be seen
(D) Examining the principal movements sweeping through the world, we can see
(E) It can be seen examining the principal movements sweeping through the world

48. The FCC is broadening its view on what constitutes <u>indecent programming</u>, radio stations are taking a closer look at their broadcasters' materials.

(A) The FCC is broadening its view on what constitutes indecent programming
(B) The FCC, broadening its view on what constitutes indecent programming, has caused
(C) The FCC is broadening its view on what constitutes indecent programming, as a result
(D) Since the FCC is broadening its view on what constitutes indecent programming
(E) The FCC, having broadened its view on what constitutes indecent programming

49. As district attorney, Elizabeth Holtzman not only had the responsibility of supervising a staff of dedicated young lawyers <u>but she had the task of maintaining good relations with the police also</u>.

(A) but she had the task of maintaining good relations with the police also
(B) but she also had the task of maintaining good relations with the police
(C) but also had the task of maintaining good relations with the police
(D) but she had the task to maintain good relations with the police also
(E) but also she had the task to maintain good relations with the police

50. Many politicians are now trying to take uncontroversial positions on <u>issues; the purpose being to allow them to appeal</u> to as wide a segment of the voting population as possible.

(A) issues; the purpose being to allow them to appeal
(B) issues in order to appeal
(C) issues, the purpose is to allow them to appeal
(D) issues and the purpose is to allow them to appeal
(E) issues; that was allowing them to appeal

Improving Paragraph Directions

The passage below is the unedited draft of a student's essay. Some of the essay needs to be rewritten to make the meaning clearer and more precise. Read the essay carefully.

The essay is followed by six questions about changes that might improve all or part of its organization, development, sentence structure, use of language, appropriateness to the audience, or use of standard written English. Choose the answer that most clearly and effectively expresses the student's intended meaning. Indicate your choice by filling in the corresponding space on the answer sheet.

[1] Throughout history, people have speculated about the future. [2] Will it be a utopia? they wondered. [3] Will injustice and poverty be eliminated? [4] Will people accept ethnic diversity, learning to live in peace? [5] Will the world be clean and unpolluted? [6] Or will technology aid us in creating a trap for ourselves we cannot escape, for example such as the world in 1984? [7] With the turn of the millennium just around the corner these questions are in the back of our minds.

[8] Science fiction often portrays the future as a technological Garden of Eden. [9] With interactive computers, TVs and robots at our command, we barely need to lift a finger to go to school, to work, to go shopping, and education is also easy and convenient. [10] Yet, the problems of the real twentieth century seem to point in another direction. [11] The environment, far from improving, keeps deteriorating. [12] Wars and other civil conflicts breakout regularly. [13] The world's population is growing out of control. [14] The majority of people on earth live in poverty. [15] Many of them are starving. [16] Illiteracy is a problem in most poor countries. [17] Diseases and malnourishment is very common. [18] Rich countries like the U.S.A. don't have the resources to help the "have-not" countries.

[19] Instead, think instead of all the silly inventions such as tablets you put in your toilet tank to make the water blue, or electric toothbrushes. [20] More money is spent on space and defense than on education and health care. [21] Advancements in agriculture can produce enough food to feed the whole country, yet people in the U.S. are starving.

[22] Although the USSR is gone, the nuclear threat continues from small countries like Iran. [23] Until the world puts its priorities straight, we can't look for a bright future in the twenty-first century, despite the rosy picture painted for us by the science fiction writers.

51. Considering the context of paragraph 1, which of the following is the best revision of sentence 6?

(A) Or will technology create a trap for ourselves from which we cannot escape, for example the world in *1984*?

(B) Or will technology aid people in creating a trap for themselves that they cannot escape; for example, the world in *1984*?

(C) Or will technology create a trap from which there is no escape, as it did in the world in *1984*?

(D) Or will technology trap us in an inescapable world, for example, it did so in the world of *1984*?

(E) Perhaps technology will aid people in creating a trap for themselves from which they cannot escape, just as they did it in the world of *1984*.

52. With regard to the essay as a whole, which of the following best describes the writer's intention in paragraph 1?

(A) to announce the purpose of the essay

(B) to compare two ideas discussed later in the essay

(C) to take a position on the essay's main issue

(D) to reveal the organization of the essay

(E) to raise questions that will be answered in the essay

53. Which of the following is the best revision of the underlined segment of sentence 9 below?

[9] With interactive computers, TVs and robots at our command, we barely need to lift a finger to go to school, to work, to go shopping, and education is also easy and convenient.

(A) and to go shopping, while education is also easy and convenient

(B) to go shopping, and getting an education is also easy and convenient

(C) to go shopping as well as educating ourselves are all easy and convenient

(D) to shop, and an easy and convenient education

(E) to shop, and to get an easy and convenient education

54. Which of the following is the most effective way to combine sentences 14, 15, 16, and 17?

(A) The majority of people on earth are living in poverty and are starving, with illiteracy, and disease and being malnourished are also a common problems.

(B) Common problems for the majority of people on earth are poverty, illiteracy, diseases, malnourishment, and many are illiterate.

(C) The majority of people on earth are poor, starving, sick, malnourished, and illiterate.

(D) Common among the poor majority on earth is poverty, starvation, disease, malnourishment, and illiteracy.

(E) The majority of the earth's people living in poverty with starvation, disease, malnourishment and illiteracy a constant threat.

55. Considering the sentences that precede and follow sentence 19, which of the following is the most effective revision of sentence 19?

(A) Instead they are devoting resources on silly inventions such as tablets to make toilet tank water blue or electric toothbrushes.

(B) Instead, they waste their resources on producing silly inventions like electric toothbrushes and tablets for bluing toilet tank water.

(C) Think of all the silly inventions: tablets you put in your toilet tank to make the water blue and electric toothbrushes.

(D) Instead, tablets you put in your toilet tank to make the water blue or electric toothbrushes are examples of useless products on the market today.

(E) Instead of spending on useful things, think of all the silly inventions such as tablets you put in your toilet tank to make the water blue or electric toothbrushes.

56. Which of the following revisions would most improve the overall coherence of the essay?

(A) moving sentence 7 to paragraph 2
(B) moving sentence 10 to paragraph 1
(C) moving sentence 22 to paragraph 2
(D) deleting sentence 8
(E) deleting sentence 23

Answer Key

1. *A*	20. *D*	39. *C*
2. *C*	21. *C*	40. *B*
3. *B*	22. *E*	41. *B*
4. *D*	23. *D*	42. *B*
5. *E*	24. *D*	43. *D*
6. *C*	25. *C*	44. *A*
7. *D*	26. *D*	45. *C*
8. *B*	27. *E*	46. *C*
9. *B*	28. *D*	47. *D*
10. *D*	29. *E*	48. *D*
11. *E*	30. *C*	49. *C*
12. *B*	31. *E*	50. *B*
13. *D*	32. *D*	51. *C*
14. *C*	33. *D*	52. *E*
15. *B*	34. *A*	53. *E*
16. *B*	35. *D*	54. *C*
17. *D*	36. *E*	55. *B*
18. *B*	37. *B*	56. *C*
19. *B*	38. *E*	

Answer Explanations

1. *A* Error in diction. Should be *all ready*. *All ready* means the group is ready; *already* means prior to a given time, previously.

2. *C* Error in pronoun case. Should be *us*. The expression *us girls* is the object of the preposition *by*.

3. *B* Error in subject-verb agreement. Should be *requires*. Verb should agree with the subject (*each one*).

4. *D* Should be *to say anything*. *Not to say nothing* is a double negative.

5. *E* Sentence is correct.

6. *C* Error in subject-verb agreement. Since the subject is Stanford White (singular), change *have designed* to *has designed*.

7. *D* Error in use of correlatives. Change *nor* to *or*. The correct form of the correlative pairs *either* with *or*.

8. *B* Error in parallel structure. Change *textbooks* to *reading textbooks*. To have parallel structure, the linked sentence elements must share the same grammatical form.

9. *B* Error in diction. Change *in back of* to *behind*.

10. *D* Error in pronoun case. Should be *me*. Pronoun is the object of the verb *can help*.

11. *E* Sentence is correct.

12. *B* Error in diction. Should be *all together. All together* means in a group; *altogether* means entirely.

13. *D* Improper use of *because.* Change to *that* (*The reason . . . was that . . .*).

14. *C* Incorrect verbal. Change the participle *being* to the infinitive *to be.*

15. *B* Error in diction. Change *affect* (a verb meaning to influence or pretend) to *effect* (a noun meaning result).

16. *B* Error in pronoun case. Should be *me.* Subjects of infinitives are in the objective case.

17. *D* Error in idiom. Change *commentary of* to *commentary on.*

18. *B* Error in pronoun case. Should be *who.* The pronoun is the predicate complement of *will be* and is in the nominative case.

19. *B* Should be *had risen.* The past participle of the verb *to rise* is *risen.*

20. *D* Error in comparison of modifiers. Should be *better.* Do not use the superlative when comparing two things.

21. *C* Error in pronoun-number agreement. Should be *their* instead of *her.* The antecedent of the pronoun is *Jane and Oprah* (plural).

22. *E* Sentence is correct.

23. *D* Error in diction. Change *alluding* (meaning to refer indirectly) to *eluding* (meaning to evade).

24. *D* Confusion of verb and gerund (verbal noun). Change *is being walking* to *is walking.*

25. *C* Error in coordination and subordination. Change *yet* to *therefore* or another similar connector to clarify the connection between the clauses.

26. *D* Error in pronoun-number agreement. Should be *he* or *she.* The antecedent of the pronoun is *anyone* (singular).

27. *E* Sentence is correct.

28. *D* Error in sequence of tenses. Change *are abounding* to *have abounded.* The present perfect tense talks about an action that occurs at one time, but is seen in relation to another time.

29. *E* Sentence is correct.

30. *C* Error in pronoun case. Should be *your.* The pronoun modifying a gerund (verbal noun) should be in the possessive case.

31. *E* Sentence is correct.

32. *D* Error in subject-verb agreement. Since the subject is *conditions* (plural), change *has* to *have.*

33. *D* Error in pronoun. Since the sentence speaks about Hemingway's style rather than about Hemingway, the phrase should read *of it,* not *of him.*

34. *A* Error in sequence of tenses. Change *has aroused* to *aroused.* The present perfect tense (*has aroused*) is used for indefinite time. In this sentence, the time is defined as *the better part of a year.*

35. *D* Lack of parallel structure. Change *in producing motion pictures* to *motion picture producer.*

36. *E* This question involves two aspects of correct English. *Neither* should be followed by *nor; either* by *or.* Choices A and D are, therefore, incorrect. The words *neither . . . nor* and *either . . . or* should be placed before the two items being discussed—*to be critical* and *to examine.* Choice E meets both requirements.

37. *B* This question tests agreement. Errors in subject-verb agreement and pronoun-number agreement are both involved. *Community* (singular) needs a singular verb, *influences.* Also, the pronoun that refers to *community* should be singular (*its*).

38. *E* Error in following conventions. This is an incomplete sentence or fragment. The sentence needs a verb to establish a principal clause. Choice E provides the verb (*is recognized*) and presents the only complete sentence in the group.

39. *C* *Would have been expected* is incorrect as a verb in a clause introduced by the conjunction *if. Had been expected* or *were expected* is preferable. *To have considered* does not follow correct sequence of tense and should be changed to *to consider.*

40. *B* Error in modification and word order. One way of correcting a dangling participle is to change the participial phrase to a clause. Choices B and D substitute clauses for the phrase. However, Choice D changes the meaning of the sentence. Choice B is correct.

41. *B* Error in modification and word order. As it stands, the sentence contains a dangling modifier. This is corrected by making *recreation* the subject of the sentence, in the process switching from the passive to the active voice. Choice E also provides a subject for the sentence; however,

the meaning of the sentence is changed in Choice E.

42. B Error in modification and word order. As presented, the sentence contains a dangling participle, *depending*. Choice B corrects this error. The other choices change the emphasis presented by the author.

43. D Error in word order. *Either . . . or* should precede the two choices offered (*in war* and *in peace*).

44. A Sentence is correct.

45. C Error in parallelism. In the underlined phrase, you will find two modifiers of *worker-toiling* and *who discovers*. The first is a participial phrase, and the second a clause. This results in an error in parallel structure. Choice B also has an error in parallel structure. Choice C corrects this by eliminating one of the modifiers of *worker*. Choice D corrects the error in parallel structure but introduces an error in agreement between subject and verb—*who* (singular) and *toil* (plural). Choice E changes the tense and also the meaning of the original sentence.

46. C Error in parallelism. Parallel structure requires that *not only* and *but also* immediately precede the words they limit.

47. D Error in modification and word order. Choices A, B, and E are incorrect because of the dangling participle. Choice C is incoherent. Choice D correctly eliminates the dangling participle by introducing the subject *we*.

48. D Error in comma splice. The punctuation in Choices A and C creates a run-on sentence. Choices B and E are both ungrammatical. Choice D corrects the run-on sentence by changing the beginning clause into the adverb clause that starts with the subordinating conjunction *since*.

49. C Error in parallelism. Since the words *not only* immediately precede the verb in the first half of the sentence, the words *but also* should immediately precede the verb in the second half. This error in parallel structure is corrected in Choice C.

50. B Error in coordination and subordination. The punctuation in Choices A, C, D, and E creates an incomplete sentence or fragment. Choice B corrects the error by linking the elements with *in order to*.

51. C Choice A is awkward and shifts the pronoun usage in the paragraph from third to first person. Choice B is awkward and contains a semicolon error. A semicolon is used to separate two independent clauses. The material after the semicolon is a sentence fragment. Choice C is succinctly and accurately expressed. It is the best answer. Choice D contains a comma splice between *world* and *for*. A comma may not be used to join two independent clauses. Choice E is awkwardly expressed and contains the pronoun *it*, which lacks a clear referent.

52. E Choice A indirectly describes the purpose of paragraph 1 but does not identify the writer's main intention. Choices B, C, and D fail to describe the writer's main intention. Choice E accurately describes the writer's main intention. It is the best answer.

53. E Choice A is grammatically correct but cumbersome. Choice B contains an error in parallel construction. The clause that begins *and getting* is not grammatically parallel to the previous items on the list. Choice C contains a mixed construction. The first and last parts of the sentence are grammatically unrelated. Choice D contains faulty parallel structure. Choice E is correct and accurately expressed. It is the best answer.

54. C Choice A is wordy and awkwardly expressed. Choice B contains an error in parallel structure. The clause *and many are illiterate* is not grammatically parallel to the previous items on the list of problems. Choice C is concise and accurately expressed. It is the best answer. Choice D is concise, but it contains an error in subject-verb agreement. The subject is *poverty, starvation . . . etc.*, which requires a plural verb; the verb *is* is singular. Choice E is a sentence fragment; it has no main verb.

55. B Choice A contains an error in idiom. The standard phrase is *devoting to*, not *devoting on*. Choice B ties sentence 19 to the previous sentence and is accurately expressed. It is the best answer. Choice C fails to improve the coherence of the paragraph. Choice D is unrelated to the context of the paragraph. Choice E is insufficiently related to the context of the paragraph.

56. C Choice A should stay put because it provides a transition between the questions in paragraph 1 and the beginning of paragraph 2. Choice B is a pivotal sentence in paragraph 2 and should not be moved. Choice C fits the topics of paragraph 2; therefore, sentence 22 should be moved to paragraph 2. Choice C is the best answer. Choice D is needed as an introductory sentence in paragraph 2. It should not be deleted. Choice E provides the essay with a meaningful conclusion and should not be deleted.

PART SIX

Test Yourself

▶ **Chapter 11 : Six Model Tests**

► CHAPTER 11
Six Model Tests

Many students, after taking the PSAT/NMSQT, report that they found the experience very exhausting. More than two hours on difficult test material may prove to be very grueling.

To alleviate this situation, the authors wish to offer two suggestions:

1. Become acquainted with the time situation before taking the actual test. Taking the six model tests in this chapter under timed conditions will familiarize you with the situation before you take the actual test. This familiarity should enable you to find the actual test less rigorous.

2. Recognize that the two-hour test may be physically tiring; you will need to be well rested and physically fit. The best advice we can offer is that you stop preparation for the test a few days before the scheduled date. Rest and relaxation will enable you to avoid the fatigue of a long examination and will prove to be more profitable than last-minute cramming.

Answer Sheet
MODEL TEST A

Each mark should completely fill the appropriate space and should be as dark as all other marks. Make all erasures complete. Traces of an erasure may be read as an answer. See pages viii and 21 for explanations of timing and number of questions.

Section 1 — Critical Reading
25 minutes

1 Ⓐ Ⓑ Ⓒ Ⓓ Ⓔ
2 Ⓐ Ⓑ Ⓒ Ⓓ Ⓔ
3 Ⓐ Ⓑ Ⓒ Ⓓ Ⓔ
4 Ⓐ Ⓑ Ⓒ Ⓓ Ⓔ
5 Ⓐ Ⓑ Ⓒ Ⓓ Ⓔ
6 Ⓐ Ⓑ Ⓒ Ⓓ Ⓔ
7 Ⓐ Ⓑ Ⓒ Ⓓ Ⓔ
8 Ⓐ Ⓑ Ⓒ Ⓓ Ⓔ
9 Ⓐ Ⓑ Ⓒ Ⓓ Ⓔ
10 Ⓐ Ⓑ Ⓒ Ⓓ Ⓔ
11 Ⓐ Ⓑ Ⓒ Ⓓ Ⓔ
12 Ⓐ Ⓑ Ⓒ Ⓓ Ⓔ
13 Ⓐ Ⓑ Ⓒ Ⓓ Ⓔ
14 Ⓐ Ⓑ Ⓒ Ⓓ Ⓔ
15 Ⓐ Ⓑ Ⓒ Ⓓ Ⓔ
16 Ⓐ Ⓑ Ⓒ Ⓓ Ⓔ
17 Ⓐ Ⓑ Ⓒ Ⓓ Ⓔ
18 Ⓐ Ⓑ Ⓒ Ⓓ Ⓔ
19 Ⓐ Ⓑ Ⓒ Ⓓ Ⓔ
20 Ⓐ Ⓑ Ⓒ Ⓓ Ⓔ
21 Ⓐ Ⓑ Ⓒ Ⓓ Ⓔ
22 Ⓐ Ⓑ Ⓒ Ⓓ Ⓔ
23 Ⓐ Ⓑ Ⓒ Ⓓ Ⓔ
24 Ⓐ Ⓑ Ⓒ Ⓓ Ⓔ

Section 2 — Math
25 minutes

1 Ⓐ Ⓑ Ⓒ Ⓓ Ⓔ
2 Ⓐ Ⓑ Ⓒ Ⓓ Ⓔ
3 Ⓐ Ⓑ Ⓒ Ⓓ Ⓔ
4 Ⓐ Ⓑ Ⓒ Ⓓ Ⓔ
5 Ⓐ Ⓑ Ⓒ Ⓓ Ⓔ
6 Ⓐ Ⓑ Ⓒ Ⓓ Ⓔ
7 Ⓐ Ⓑ Ⓒ Ⓓ Ⓔ
8 Ⓐ Ⓑ Ⓒ Ⓓ Ⓔ
9 Ⓐ Ⓑ Ⓒ Ⓓ Ⓔ
10 Ⓐ Ⓑ Ⓒ Ⓓ Ⓔ
11 Ⓐ Ⓑ Ⓒ Ⓓ Ⓔ
12 Ⓐ Ⓑ Ⓒ Ⓓ Ⓔ
13 Ⓐ Ⓑ Ⓒ Ⓓ Ⓔ
14 Ⓐ Ⓑ Ⓒ Ⓓ Ⓔ
15 Ⓐ Ⓑ Ⓒ Ⓓ Ⓔ
16 Ⓐ Ⓑ Ⓒ Ⓓ Ⓔ
17 Ⓐ Ⓑ Ⓒ Ⓓ Ⓔ
18 Ⓐ Ⓑ Ⓒ Ⓓ Ⓔ
19 Ⓐ Ⓑ Ⓒ Ⓓ Ⓔ
20 Ⓐ Ⓑ Ⓒ Ⓓ Ⓔ

Section 3 — Critical Reading
25 minutes

25 Ⓐ Ⓑ Ⓒ Ⓓ Ⓔ
26 Ⓐ Ⓑ Ⓒ Ⓓ Ⓔ
27 Ⓐ Ⓑ Ⓒ Ⓓ Ⓔ
28 Ⓐ Ⓑ Ⓒ Ⓓ Ⓔ
29 Ⓐ Ⓑ Ⓒ Ⓓ Ⓔ
30 Ⓐ Ⓑ Ⓒ Ⓓ Ⓔ
31 Ⓐ Ⓑ Ⓒ Ⓓ Ⓔ
32 Ⓐ Ⓑ Ⓒ Ⓓ Ⓔ
33 Ⓐ Ⓑ Ⓒ Ⓓ Ⓔ
34 Ⓐ Ⓑ Ⓒ Ⓓ Ⓔ
35 Ⓐ Ⓑ Ⓒ Ⓓ Ⓔ
36 Ⓐ Ⓑ Ⓒ Ⓓ Ⓔ
37 Ⓐ Ⓑ Ⓒ Ⓓ Ⓔ
38 Ⓐ Ⓑ Ⓒ Ⓓ Ⓔ
39 Ⓐ Ⓑ Ⓒ Ⓓ Ⓔ
40 Ⓐ Ⓑ Ⓒ Ⓓ Ⓔ
41 Ⓐ Ⓑ Ⓒ Ⓓ Ⓔ
42 Ⓐ Ⓑ Ⓒ Ⓓ Ⓔ
43 Ⓐ Ⓑ Ⓒ Ⓓ Ⓔ
44 Ⓐ Ⓑ Ⓒ Ⓓ Ⓔ
45 Ⓐ Ⓑ Ⓒ Ⓓ Ⓔ
46 Ⓐ Ⓑ Ⓒ Ⓓ Ⓔ
47 Ⓐ Ⓑ Ⓒ Ⓓ Ⓔ
48 Ⓐ Ⓑ Ⓒ Ⓓ Ⓔ

For each question in this section, select the best answer from among the choices given, and fill in the corresponding circle on the answer sheet.

Directions

Each sentence below has one or two blanks, each blank indicating that something has been omitted. Beneath the sentence are five words or sets of words labeled A through E. Choose the word or set of words that, when inserted in the sentence, best fits the meaning of the sentence as a whole.

EXAMPLE:

Medieval kingdoms did not become constitutional republics overnight; on the contrary, the change was ----.

(A) unpopular   (B) unexpected
(C) advantageous   (D) sufficient   (E) gradual

---

1. Unhappily, the psychology experiment was ---- by the subjects' awareness of the presence of observers in their midst.

   (A) muted   (B) palliated   (C) marred
   (D) clarified   (E) concluded

2. Until James learned to be more ---- about writing down his homework assignments, he seldom knew when any assignment was due.

   (A) obstinate   (B) contrary   (C) opportunistic
   (D) methodical   (E) literate

3. Despite all the advertisements singing the ---- of the new product, she remained ---- its merits, wanting to see what *Consumer Reports* had to say about its claims.

   (A) virtues..an optimist about
   (B) praises..a skeptic about
   (C) joys..a convert to
   (D) defects..a cynic about
   (E) advantages..a believer in

4. After working on the project night and day for two full months, Sandy felt that she had earned a ----.

   (A) penalty   (B) scolding   (C) degree
   (D) chore   (E) respite

5. Even though the basic organization of the brain does not change after birth, details of its structure and function remain ---- for some time, particularly in the cerebral cortex.

   (A) plastic   (B) immutable   (C) essential
   (D) unknown   (E) static

Directions

Each of the passages below precedes two questions based on its content. Answer the questions following each passage on the basis of what is stated or implied in that passage.

Questions 6 and 7 are based on the following passage.

Spiders, and in particular hairy spiders, possess a highly developed sense of touch. Tarantulas, for example, perceive three distinct types of touch:
Line a light whisper that flutters the sensitive leg hairs;
5   a smooth rubbing of the body hair; a steady pressure against the body wall. Press a pencil against the tarantula's body wall and it will back away cautiously without reacting defensively. However, if the tarantula sees the pencil approaching from
10 above, the motion will excite a defensive reaction: it will rear up, lifting its front legs and baring its fangs, maintaining this attack stance until the pencil stops moving.

6. The author's attitude toward tarantulas can best be described as

   (A) apprehensive   (B) sentimental
   (C) approving   (D) objective   (E) defensive

7. The word "excite" in line 10 most nearly means

   (A) irritate   (B) delight   (C) stimulate
   (D) exhilarate   (E) discompose

Questions 8 and 9 are based on the following passage.

It is a relief to see people who can be interested in the arts without being "arty"—collectors who collect for their own delight rather than for show.
Line All too many so-called art lovers are in the
5   game for the prestige it brings them. They and the gallery owners who cater to them are doomed to be always on the look-out for the next hot artist, the next new thing.

GO ON TO NEXT PAGE ▶

8. The use of quotation marks around the word *arty* in line 2 primarily serves to

(A) offer an alternative description
(B) signify artistic expertise
(C) introduce a historical context
(D) emphasize the condescending tone
(E) refer to an authority

9. In context, the phrase "the next new thing" (line 8) refers to something that

(A) possesses inherent artistic worth
(B) costs more than most collectors can afford
(C) attracts attention primarily for its novelty
(D) is better than its predecessors
(E) offers little prestige to its owner

Directions

Each passage below is followed by questions based on its content. Answer the questions following each passage on the basis of what is stated or implied in that passage and in any introductory material that may be provided.

Questions 10–15 are based on the following passage.

The following passage is from a book written by the naturalist Konrad Lorenz and published in 1952.

In the chimney the autumn wind sings the song of the elements, and the old firs before my study window wave excitedly with their arms and
Line sing so loudly in chorus that I can hear their
5 sighing melody through the double panes. Suddenly, from above, a dozen black, streamlined projectiles shoot across the piece of clouded sky for which my window forms a frame. Heavily as stones they fall, fall to the tops of the firs where
10 they suddenly sprout wings, become birds and then light feather rags that the storm seizes and whirls out of my line of vision, more rapidly than they were borne into it.

I walk to the window to watch this extraordi-
15 nary game that the jackdaws are playing with the wind. A game? Yes, indeed, it is a game, in the most literal sense of the word: practiced movements, indulged in and enjoyed for their own sake and not for the achievement of a special object.
20 And rest assured, these are not merely inborn, purely instinctive actions, but movements that have been carefully learned. All these feats that the birds are performing, their wonderful exploitation of the wind, their amazingly exact assessment of
25 distances and, above all, their understanding of local wind conditions, their knowledge of all the up-currents, air pockets and eddies—all this proficiency is no inheritance, but, for each bird, an individually acquired accomplishment.
30 And look what they do with the wind! At first sight, you, poor human being, think that the storm is playing with the birds, like a cat with a mouse, but soon you see, with astonishment, that it is the fury of the elements that here plays the
35 role of the mouse and that the jackdaws are treating the storm exactly as the cat its unfortunate victim. Nearly, but only nearly, do they give the storm its head, let it throw them high, high into the heavens, till they seem to fall upwards, then,
40 with a casual flap of a wing, they turn themselves over, open their pinions for a fraction of a second from below against the wind, and dive—with an acceleration far greater than that of a falling stone—into the depths below. Another tiny jerk of
45 the wing and they return to their normal position and, on close-reefed sails, shoot away with breathless speed into the teeth of the gale, hundreds of yards to the west: this all playfully and without effort, just to spite the stupid wind that tries to
50 drive them towards the east. The sightless monster itself must perform the work of propelling the birds through the air at a rate of well over 80 miles an hour; the jackdaws do nothing to help beyond a few lazy adjustments of their black wings. Sover-
55 eign control over the power of the elements, intoxicating triumph of the living organism over the pitiless strength of the inorganic!

---

10. The "arms" mentioned in line 3 are

(A) wings (B) storm winds
(C) heraldic emblems (D) branches
(E) missiles

11. According to the passage, the bird's skill in adapting to wind conditions is

(A) genetically determined
(B) limited
(C) undependable
(D) dependent on the elements
(E) gained through practice

12. The phrase "rest assured" in line 20 most likely means

(A) sleep securely
(B) others are certain
(C) be confident
(D) remain poised
(E) in their sure leisure

13. The "sightless monster" mentioned in line 50 is

(A) an unobservant watcher
(B) a falling stone
(C) an airplane
(D) the powerful windstorm
(E) a blind predator

14. Throughout the passage, the author is most impressed by

(A) the direction-finding skills of the birds
(B) the jackdaws' superhuman strength
(C) his inability to join the jackdaws in their game
(D) the fleeting nature of his encounter with the birds
(E) the jackdaws' mastery of the forces of nature

15. The author does all of the following EXCEPT

(A) use a metaphor
(B) argue a cause
(C) clarify a term
(D) describe a behavior
(E) dismiss a notion

Questions 16–24 are based on the following passage.

The passage below, taken from a museum bulletin, discusses tapestry making as an art form.

Tapestries are made on looms. Their distinctive weave is basically simple: the colored weft threads interface regularly with the monochrome warps, as in darning or plain cloth, but as they do
Line
5 so, they form a design by reversing their direction when a change of color is needed. The wefts are beaten down to cover the warps completely. The result is a design or picture that is the fabric itself, not one laid upon a ground like an embroidery, a
10 print, or brocading. The back and front of a tapestry show the same design. The weaver always follows a preexisting model, generally a drawing or painting, known as the cartoon, which in most cases he reproduces as exactly as he can. Long
15 training is needed to become a professional tapestry weaver. It can take as much as a year to produce a yard of very finely woven tapestry.

Tapestry-woven fabrics have been made from China to Peru and from very early times to the
20 present day, but large wall hangings in this technique, mainly of wool, are typically Northern European. Few examples predating the late fourteenth century have survived, but from about 1400 tapestries were an essential part of aristo-
25 cratic life. The prince or great nobleman sent his plate and his tapestries ahead of him to furnish his castles before his arrival as he traveled through his domains; both had the same function, to display his wealth and social position. It has frequently
30 been suggested that tapestries helped to heat stone-walled rooms, but this is a modern idea; comfort was of minor importance in the Middle Ages. Tapestries were portable grandeur, instant splendor, taking the place, north of the Alps, of
35 painted frescoes further south. They were hung without gaps between them, covering entire walls

and often doors as well. Only very occasionally were they made as individual works of art such as altar frontals. They were usually commissioned or
40 bought as sets, or "chambers," and constituted the most important furnishings of any grand room, except for the display of plate, throughout the Middle Ages and the sixteenth century. Later, woven silks, ornamental wood carving, stucco
45 decoration, and painted leather gradually replaced tapestry as expensive wall coverings, until at last wallpaper was introduced in the late eighteenth century and eventually swept away almost everything else.

50 By the end of the eighteenth century, the "tapestry-room" [a room with every available wall surface covered with wall hangings] was no longer fashionable: paper had replaced wall coverings of wool and silk. Tapestries, of course, were still
55 made, but in the nineteenth century they often seem to have been produced mainly as individual works of art that astonish by their resemblance to oil paintings, tours de force woven with a remarkably large number of wefts per inch. In England
60 during the second half of the century, William Morris attempted to reverse this trend and to bring tapestry weaving back to its true principles, those he considered to have governed it in the Middle Ages. He imitated medieval tapestries in
65 both style and technique, using few warps to the inch, but he did not make sets; the original function for which tapestry is so admirably suited—completely covering the walls of a room and providing sumptuous surroundings for a life
70 of pomp and splendor—could not be revived. Morris's example has been followed, though with less imitation of medieval style, by many weavers of the present century, whose coarsely woven cloths hang like single pictures and can be
75 admired as examples of contemporary art.

GO ON TO NEXT PAGE ▶

16. Tapestry weaving may be characterized as which of the following?

    I. Time-consuming
    II. Spontaneous in concept
    III. Faithful to an original

    (A) I only
    (B) III only
    (C) I and II only
    (D) I and III only
    (E) II and III only

17. The word "distinctive" in line 1 means

    (A) characteristic   (B) stylish
    (C) discriminatory   (D) eminent
    (E) articulate

18. Renaissance nobles carried tapestries with them to demonstrate their

    (A) piety   (B) consequence
    (C) aesthetic judgment   (D) need for privacy
    (E) dislike for cold

19. The word "ground" in line 9 means

    (A) terrain   (B) dust   (C) thread   (D) base
    (E) pigment

20. The statement in line 31 ("but this . . . idea") is best described as an example of

    (A) a definition of a central concept
    (B) an acknowledgment of a principle
    (C) a dismissal of a common view
    (D) an emotional refutation
    (E) a moral proclamation

21. In line 40, the quotation marks around the word "chambers" serve to

    (A) emphasize the inadequacy of the particular choice of words
    (B) point out the triteness of the term
    (C) indicate the use of a colloquialism
    (D) illustrate the need for the word to be stressed when spoken aloud
    (E) indicate the word is being used in a special sense

22. The author regards William Morris (lines 59–64) as

    (A) a bold innovator
    (B) an uninspired hack
    (C) a medieval nobleman
    (D) a cartoonist
    (E) a traditionalist

23. In contrast to nineteenth-century tapestries, contemporary tapestries

    (A) are displayed in sets of panels
    (B) echo medieval themes
    (C) faithfully copy oil paintings
    (D) have a less fine weave
    (E) indicate the owner's social position

24. The primary purpose of the passage is to

    (A) explain the process of tapestry making
    (B) contrast Eastern and Western schools of tapestry
    (C) analyze the reasons for the decline in popularity of tapestries
    (D) provide a historical perspective on tapestry making
    (E) advocate a return to a more colorful way of life

IF YOU FINISH IN LESS THAN 25 MINUTES, YOU MAY CHECK YOUR WORK ON THIS SECTION ONLY. DO NOT TURN TO ANY OTHER SECTION IN THE TEST.

STOP

Reference

$A = \pi r^2$
$C = 2\pi r$

$A = \ell w$

$A = \frac{1}{2}bh$

$V = \ell w h$

$V = \pi r^2 h$

$c^2 = a^2 + b^2$

Special Right Triangles

Number of degrees in a circle: 360
Sum of the measures, in degrees, of the three angles of a triangle: 180

1. In the figure above, what is the value of y?

(A) 50   (B) 70   (C) 90   (D) 100   (E) 140

2. If $(a + 12) - 12 = 12$, then $a =$

(A) −12   (B) 0   (C) 12   (D) 24   (E) 36

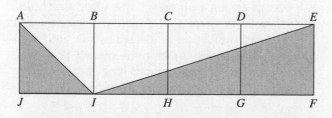

3. In the figure above, rectangle *AEFJ* is divided into four equal squares. What is the ratio of the area of the shaded region to the area of the white region?

(A) 1:2   (B) 3:5   (C) 5:8   (D) 1:1   (E) 5:3

4. The Albertville Little League raised some money. They used 72% of the money to buy uniforms, 19% for equipment, and the remaining $243 for a team party. How much money did the team raise?

(A) $2400   (B) $2450   (C) $2500
(D) $2600   (E) $2700

5. If it is now 1:30, what time will it be when the hour hand has moved through an angle of 20°?

(A) 1:45   (B) 1:50   (C) 2:00
(D) 2:10   (E) 2:15

6. In the figure above, lines *k* and *ℓ* are parallel, and line *k* passes through *C*, one of the vertices of equilateral triangle *ABC*. What is the value of *a*?

(A) 40   (B) 50   (C) 60   (D) 80   (E) 90

GO ON TO NEXT PAGE ▶

7. If the difference of two numbers is less than the sum of the numbers, which of the following must be true?

(A) Neither number is positive.
(B) At least one of the numbers is positive.
(C) Exactly one of the numbers is positive.
(D) Both numbers are positive.
(E) None of these statements must be true.

8. 20 is what percent of C?

(A) $20C\%$ (B) $\frac{1}{20C}\%$ (C) $\frac{20}{C}\%$

(D) $\frac{200}{C}\%$ (E) $\frac{2000}{C}\%$

9. Two sides of a right triangle are 5 and 9. Which of the following could be the length of the third side?

I. $\sqrt{56}$
II. $\sqrt{76}$
III. $\sqrt{106}$

(A) I only   (B) III only   (C) I and II only
(D) I and III only   (E) I, II, and III

10. Which of the following is an equation of a line that is parallel to the line whose equation is $y = 2x - 3$?

(A) $y = 2x + 3$ (B) $y = -2x - 3$
(C) $y = \frac{1}{2}x - 3$ (D) $y = -\frac{1}{2}x + 3$
(E) $y = -\frac{1}{2}x - 3$

11. If n is an integer and n, $n + 1$, and $n + 2$ are the lengths of the sides of a triangle, which of the following could be the value of n?

I. 1
II. 3
III. 13

(A) I only   (B) II only   (C) III only
(D) II and III only   (E) I, II, and III

12. A bank raised the minimum payment on its charge accounts from \$10 to \$20 per month. What was the percent increase in the minimum monthly payment?

(A) 10%   (B) 20%   (C) 50%
(D) 100%   (E) 200%

13. For the figure above, which of the following is an expression for y in terms of x?

(A) x (B) $60 - x$ (C) $x - 60$
(D) $180 - 3x$ (E) $90 - x$

Questions 14 and 15 refer to the following definition.

For any number x, $\|x\| = \frac{2}{3}x^2$.

14. What is the value of $\|6^2\|$?

(A) 16   (B) 24   (C) 144   (D) 576   (E) 864

15. If $y = \frac{2}{3}x$, which of the following is an expression for $\|y\|$ in terms of x?

(A) $\frac{2}{3}x^3$ (B) $\frac{4}{9}x^2$ (C) $\frac{4}{9}x^3$ (D) $\frac{8}{27}x^2$ (E) $\frac{8}{27}x^3$

16. If $f(x) = 9x + 9^x$, what is the value of $f\left(\frac{1}{2}\right)$?

(A) 3   (B) 6   (C) 7.5   (D) 9   (E) 9.9

17. The road from Jack's house to Jill's is exactly 10 kilometers. At different times, Jack and Jill each left home and walked toward the other's house. They walked at the same rate, and they met at noon, 4 kilometers from Jill's house. If Jack left at 10:00, at what time did Jill leave?

(A) 9:40   (B) 10:00   (C) 10:40
(D) 11:00   (E) 11:20

18. The Northport High School French Club has twice as many female members as male members. One day, the percentage of female members attending a meeting of the club was twice the percentage of male members. What percent of those attending the meeting were males?

(A) 20%   (B) 25%   (C) $33\frac{1}{3}\%$ (D) 50%

(E) It cannot be determined from the information given.

19. If a and b are the lengths of the legs of a right triangle whose hypotenuse is 10 and whose area is 20, what is the value of $(a + b)^2$?

(A) 100   (B) 120   (C) 140   (D) 180   (E) 200

20. A lottery prize worth d dollars was to be divided equally among 4 winners. It was subsequently discovered that there were 2 additional winners, and the prize would now be divided equally among all the winners. How much more money, in dollars, would each original winner have received if the additional winners were not discovered?

(A) $\frac{d}{12}$ (B) $\frac{d}{6}$ (C) $\frac{d}{4}$ (D) $\frac{12}{d}$ (E) $\frac{6}{d}$

IF YOU FINISH IN LESS THAN 25 MINUTES, YOU MAY CHECK YOUR WORK ON THIS SECTION ONLY. DO NOT TURN TO ANY OTHER SECTION IN THE TEST.

STOP

For each question in this section, select the best answer from among the choices given, and fill in the corresponding circle on the answer sheet.

Directions

Each sentence below has one or two blanks, each blank indicating that something has been omitted. Beneath the sentence are five words or sets of words labeled A through E. Choose the word or set of words that, when inserted in the sentence, best fits the meaning of the sentence as a whole.

EXAMPLE:

Medieval kingdoms did not become constitutional republics overnight; on the contrary, the change was ----.

(A) unpopular   (B) unexpected
(C) advantageous   (D) sufficient   (E) gradual

Ⓐ Ⓑ Ⓒ Ⓓ ●

---

25. Nothing anyone could say was able to alter North's ---- that his attempt to lie to Congress was justified.

(A) demand   (B) conviction   (C) maxim
(D) fear   (E) ambivalence

26. Excessive use of coal and oil eventually may ---- the earth's supply of fossil fuels, leaving us in need of a new source of energy.

(A) replenish   (B) magnify   (C) merge
(D) deplete   (E) redirect

27. Contemporary authorities have come to ---- the use of "healthy" in place of "healthful"; however, they still reject the use of "disinterested" in place of "uninterested."

(A) condone   (B) evaluate   (C) imitate
(D) disdain   (E) repudiate

28. Michael's severe bout of the flu ---- him so much that he was too tired to go to work for a week.

(A) recuperated   (B) diagnosed
(C) incarcerated   (D) captivated
(E) debilitated

29. Though Alec Guinness was determined to make a name for himself on the stage, when he considered the uncertainties of an actor's life, his ---- wavered.

(A) resolution   (B) reverence   (C) affectation
(D) theatricality   (E) skepticism

30. In *Gulliver's Travels*, Swift's intent is ----; he exposes the follies of English society by ridiculing the follies of the Lilliputians.

(A) elegiac   (B) prophetic   (C) satirical
(D) questionable   (E) derivative

31. Even the threat of sudden death could not ---- the intrepid pilot and explorer Beryl Markham; a true ----, she risked her life countless times to set records for flying small planes.

(A) intimidate..patrician
(B) divert..renegade
(C) interest..dilettante
(D) daunt..daredevil
(E) survive..firebrand

32. As an indefatigable consumer advocate, Ralph Nader is constantly engaged in ---- the claims of unscrupulous merchandisers and cautioning the public to exercise a healthy ----.

(A) asserting..autonomy
(B) deflating..prodigality
(C) debunking..skepticism
(D) affirming..indifference
(E) exaggerating..optimism

GO ON TO NEXT PAGE ▶

Each of the passages below precedes two questions based on its content. Answer the questions following each passage on the basis of what is stated or implied in that passsage.

Questions 33 and 34 are based on the following passage.

Can prison reform people, positively transforming their lives? Some who answer yes to this
question point to the example of Malcolm Little,
Line later known as Malcolm X. *The Autobiography of*
5 *Malcolm X* describes how Malcolm, a high school
dropout, in prison set himself the task of reading
straight through the dictionary; to him, reading
was purposeful, not aimless, and he plowed his
way through its hundreds of pages, from A for
10 *aardvark* to Z for *zymurgy.*

33. The author's attitude toward Malcolm's activities in
prison can best be described as

(A) nostalgic   (B) pessimistic
(C) condescending   (D) approving
(E) apologetic

34. In line 8, "plowed" most nearly means

(A) harrowed   (B) cultivated
(C) plunged recklessly   (D) prepared hastily
(E) proceeded steadily

Questions 35 and 36 are based on the following passage.

Many primates live together in an organized
troop or social group that includes members of all
ages and both sexes. Such troops always move
Line compactly together in a stable social unit. A
5 typical primate troop characteristically exhibits a
ranking hierarchy among the males in the troop.
This ranking hierarchy serves to alleviate conflict
within the troop. The highest-ranking male or
males defend, control, and lead the troop; the
10 strong social bond among members and their
safety is maintained.

35. According to the passage, primate societies are

(A) generally unstable
(B) hierarchically flexible
(C) extremely competitive
(D) dominated by adult males
(E) frequently in conflict with each other

36. According to the passage, the hierarchic structure
within a troop serves to

(A) protect the members of the troop
(B) facilitate food gathering
(C) establish friendships within the group
(D) keep members of other troops from joining
(E) teach the youngest members how to survive

The passages below are followed by questions on
their content; questions following a pair of related
passages may also be based on the relationship
between the paired passages. Answer the questions
on the basis of what is stated or implied in the
passages and in any introductory material that may
be provided.

Questions 37–48 are based on the following passages.

The following passages present two portraits of grand-
mothers. In Passage 1, Mary McCarthy shares her
memories of her Catholic grandmother, who raised
McCarthy and her brother after their parents' death.
In Passage 2, Caroline Heilbrun tells of her Jewish
grandmother, who died when Heilbrun was ten.

Passage 1

Luckily, I am writing a memoir and not a
work of fiction, and therefore I do not have to account for my grandmother's unpleasing character
Line and look for the Oedipal fixation or the traumatic
5 experience which would give her that clinical authenticity that is nowadays so desirable in portrai-
ture. I do not know how my grandmother got the
way she was; I assume, from family photographs
and from the inflexibility of her habits, that she
10 was always the same, and it seems as idle to in-
quire into her childhood as to ask what was ailing
Iago or look for the error in toilet-training that
was responsible for Lady Macbeth. My grandmother's sexual history, bristling with infant
15 mortality in the usual style of her period, was robust and decisive: three tall, handsome sons grew
up, and one attentive daughter. Her husband
treated her kindly. She had money, many grandchildren, and religion to sustain her. White hair,

GO ON TO NEXT PAGE ▶

20 glasses, soft skin, wrinkles, needlework—all the paraphernalia of motherliness were hers; yet it was a cold, grudging, disputatious old woman who sat all day in her sunroom making tapestries from a pattern, scanning religious periodicals, and setting
25 her iron jaw against any infraction of her ways.

Combativeness was, I suppose, the dominant trait in my grandmother's nature. An aggressive churchgoer, she was quite without Christian feeling; the mercy of the Lord Jesus had never entered
30 her heart. Her piety was an act of war against the Protestant ascendancy. The religious magazines on her table furnished her not with food for meditation but with fresh pretexts for anger; articles attacking birth control, divorce, mixed marriages,
35 Darwin, and secular education were her favorite reading. The teachings of the Church did not interest her, except as they were a rebuke to others; "Honor thy father and thy mother," a commandment she was no longer called upon to practice,
40 was the one most frequently on her lips. The extermination of Protestantism, rather than spiritual perfection, was the boon she prayed for. Her mind was preoccupied with conversion; the capture of a soul for God much diverted her fancy—it
45 made one less Protestant in the world. Foreign missions, with their overtones of good will and social service, appealed to her less strongly; it was not a *harvest* of souls that my grandmother had in mind.
50 This pugnacity of my grandmother's did not confine itself to sectarian enthusiasm. There was the defense of her furniture and her house against the imagined encroachments of visitors. With her, this was not the gentle and tremulous
55 protectiveness endemic in old ladies, who fear for the safety of their possessions with a truly touching anxiety, inferring the fragility of all things from the brittleness of their old bones and hearing the crash of mortality in the perilous tinkling of a
60 tea-cup. My grandmother's sentiment was more autocratic: she hated having her chairs sat in or her lawns stepped on or the water turned on in her basins, for no reason at all except pure officiousness; she even grudged the mailman his daily

65 promenade up her sidewalk. Her home was a center of power, and she would not allow it to be derogated by easy or democratic usage. Under her jealous eye, its social properties had atrophied, and it functioned in the family structure simply
70 as a political headquarters. The family had no friends, and entertaining was held to be a foolish and unnecessary courtesy as between blood relations. Holiday dinners fell, as a duty, on the lesser members of the organization: the daughters and
75 daughters-in-law (converts from the false religion) offered up Baked Alaska on a platter like the head of John the Baptist, while the old people sat enthroned at the table, and only their digestive processes acknowledged, with rumbling,
80 enigmatic salvos, the festal day.

Passage 2

My grandmother, one of Howe's sustaining women, not only ruled the household with an arm of iron, but kept a store to support them all, her blond, blue-eyed husband enjoying life rather than
85 struggling through it. My grandmother was one of those powerful women who know that they stand between their families and an outside world filled with temptations to failure and shame. I remember her as thoroughly loving. But there can be no
90 question that she impaired her six daughters for autonomy as thoroughly as if she had crippled them—more so. The way to security was marriage; the dread that stood in the way of this was sexual dalliance, above all pregnancy. The horror
95 of pregnancy in an unmarried girl is difficult, perhaps, to recapture now. For a Jewish girl not to be a virgin on marriage was failure. The male's rights were embodied in her lack of sexual experience, in the knowledge that he was the first, the owner.
100 All attempts at autonomy had to be frustrated. And of course, my grandmother's greatest weapon was her own vulnerability. She had worked hard, only her daughters knew how hard. She could not be comforted or repaid—as *my* mother would feel
105 repaid—by a daughter's accomplishments, only by her marriage.

---

37. McCarthy's attitude toward her grandmother is best described as

(A) tolerant   (B) appreciative   (C) indifferent
(D) nostalgic   (E) sardonic

38. The word "idle" in line 10 means

(A) slothful   (B) passive   (C) fallow
(D) useless   (E) unoccupied

39. According to McCarthy, a portrait of a character in a work of modern fiction must have

(A) photographic realism
(B) psychological validity
(C) sympathetic attitudes
(D) religious qualities
(E) historical accuracy

GO ON TO NEXT PAGE ▶

40. McCarthy's primary point in describing her grand-mother's physical appearance (lines 19–25) is best summarized by which of the following axioms?

(A) Familiarity breeds contempt.
(B) You can't judge a book by its cover.
(C) One picture is worth more than ten thousand words.
(D) There's no smoke without fire.
(E) Blood is thicker than water.

41. By describing the typical old woman's fear for the safety of her possessions (in lines 53–60), McCarthy emphasizes that

(A) her grandmother feared the approach of death
(B) old women have dangerously brittle bones
(C) her grandmother possessed considerable wealth
(D) her grandmother had different reasons for her actions
(E) visitors were unwelcome in her grandmother's home

42. The word "properties" in line 68 means

(A) belongings   (B) aspects   (C) holdings
(D) titles   (E) acreage

43. Heilbrun is critical of her grandmother primarily because

(A) she would not allow her husband to enjoy himself
(B) she could not accept her own vulnerability
(C) she fostered a sense of sexual inadequacy
(D) she discouraged her daughters' independence
(E) she physically injured her children

44. By describing the extent of the feeling against preg-nancy in unmarried girls (lines 94–99), Heilbrun helps the reader understand

(A) her fear of being scorned as an unwed mother
(B) why her grandmother strove to limit her daughters' autonomy
(C) her disapproval of contemporary sexual practices
(D) her awareness of her mother's desire for happiness
(E) how unforgiving her grandmother was

45. In stating that her grandmother's greatest weapon was her own vulnerability (lines 101–102), Heil-brun implies that her grandmother got her way by exploiting her children's

(A) sense of guilt
(B) innocence of evil
(C) feeling of indifference
(D) abdication of responsibility
(E) lack of experience

46. Both passages mention which of the following as being important to the writer's grandmother?

(A) governing the actions of others
(B) contributing to religious organizations
(C) protecting her children's virtue
(D) marrying off her daughters
(E) being surrounded by a circle of friends

47. Which technique is used in Passage 1 but not in Passage 2?

(A) relating the author's own experience
(B) stating an opinion
(C) making an assertion
(D) drawing a contrast
(E) making literary references

48. McCarthy would most likely react to the character-ization of her grandmother, like Heilbrun's grand-mother, as one of the "sustaining women" (lines 81–82) by pointing out that

(A) this characterization is not in good taste
(B) the characterization fails to account for her grandmother's piety
(C) the details of the family's social life support this characterization
(D) her grandmother's actual conduct is not in keeping with this characterization
(E) this characterization slightly exaggerates her grandmother's chief virtue

IF YOU FINISH IN LESS THAN 25 MINUTES, YOU MAY CHECK YOUR WORK ON THIS SECTION ONLY. DO NOT TURN TO ANY OTHER SECTION IN THE TEST.

STOP

Multiple-Choice Directions

For questions 21–28, determine which of the five choices is correct. You may use any blank space on the page for your work.

NOTES:

- You may use a calculator whenever you believe it will be helpful.
- Use the diagrams provided to help you solve the problems. Unless you see the phrase
  <u>Note</u>: Figure not drawn to scale

under a diagram, it has been drawn as accurately as possible. Unless it is stated that a figure is three-dimensional, you may assume that it lies in a plane.

Reference

$A = \pi r^2$
$C = 2\pi r$

$A = \ell w$

$A = \frac{1}{2}bh$

$V = \ell wh$

$V = \pi r^2 h$

$c^2 = a^2 + b^2$

Special Right Triangles

Number of degrees in a circle: 360
Sum of the measures, in degrees, of the three angles of a triangle: 180

---

21. If the ratio of the number of boys to girls in a club is 2:3, what percent of the club members are girls?

(A) $33\frac{1}{3}\%$ (B) 40%   (C) 50%
(D) 60%   (E) $66\frac{2}{3}\%$

22. The Salem Soccer League is divided into d divisions. Each division has t teams, and each team has p players. How many players are there in the entire league?

(A) $\frac{pt}{d}$ (B) $\frac{dt}{p}$ (C) $\frac{d}{pt}$ (D) $d + t + p$
(E) dtp

23. Which of the following is *NOT* a solution of $3x^2 + 2y = 5$?

(A) $x = 1$ and $y = 1$
(B) $x = -1$ and $y = 1$
(C) $x = 1$ and $y = -1$
(D) $x = 3$ and $y = -11$
(E) $x = -3$ and $y = -11$

24. Sally wrote the number 1 on 1 slip of paper, the number 2 on 2 slips of paper, the number 3 on 3 slips of paper, the number 4 on 4 slips of paper, the number 5 on 5 slips of paper, and the number 6 on 6 slips of paper. All the slips of paper were placed in a bag, and Lana drew one slip at random. What is the probability that the number on the slip Lana drew was odd?

(A) $\frac{1}{9}$ (B) $\frac{1}{7}$ (C) $\frac{3}{7}$ (D) $\frac{1}{2}$ (E) $\frac{4}{7}$

25. If $|x| = |y|$, which of the following must be true?

   I. $-x = -y$
  II. $x^2 = y^2$
 III. $x^3 = y^3$
(A) I only   (B) II only   (C) I and II only
(D) II and III only   (E) I, II, and III

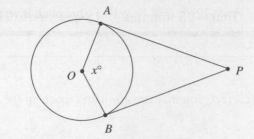

26. In the figure above, $\overline{PA}$ and $\overline{PB}$ are tangent to circle O. If $m\angle P = 50°$, what is the value of x?

(A) 50   (B) 90   (C) 120   (D) 130   (E) 150

27. Which of the following expressions is equal to $2^{3x} + 2^{3x} + 2^{3x} + 2^{3x}$?

(A) 2^{3x+2} (B) 2^{3x+4} (C) 2^{6x}

(D) 2^{12x} (E) 2^{9x^2}

28. The circumference of circle II is 4 feet longer than the circumference of circle I. How many feet longer is the radius of circle II than the radius of circle I?

(A) $\frac{1}{4\pi}$ (B) $\frac{2}{\pi}$ (C) $\frac{1}{\pi}$ (D) 2

(E) It cannot be determined from the information given.

Student-Produced Response Directions

In questions 29–38, first solve the problem, and then enter your answer on the grid provided on the answer sheet. The instructions for entering your answers follow.

- First, write your answer in the boxes at the top of the grid.
- Second, grid your answer in the columns below the boxes.
- Use the fraction bar in the first row or the decimal point in the second row to enter fractions and decimals.

Answer: $\frac{8}{15}$ Answer: 1.75   Answer: 100

Write your answer in the boxes

Grid-in your answer

Either position is acceptable

- Grid only one space in each column.
- Entering the answer in the boxes is recommended as an aid in gridding but is not required.
- The machine scoring your exam can read only what you grid; so you **must grid-in your answers correctly to get credit.**
- If a question has more than one correct answer, grid-in only one of them.
- The grid does not have a minus sign; so no answer can be negative.
- A mixed number *must* be converted to an improper fraction or a decimal before it is gridded. Enter $1\frac{1}{4}$ as $\frac{5}{4}$ or 1.25; the machine will interpret 11/4 as $\frac{11}{4}$ and mark it wrong.

- **All decimals must be entered as accurately as possible.** Here are three acceptable ways of gridding

$$\frac{3}{11} = 0.272727\ldots$$

- Note that rounding to .273 is acceptable because you are using the full grid, but you would receive **no credit** for .3 or .27, because they are less accurate.

GO ON TO NEXT PAGE ▶

Lines ℓ and k are parallel.

29. In the figure above, what is the value of $a + b + c + d$?

30. If $a = 6$ and $b = -6$, what is the value of $2a - 3b$?

31. If A is the median of $\{1, 2, 3, 4, 5, 6\}$ and B is the median of $\{1, 2, 3, 4, 5, 6, 7\}$, what is the average (arithmetic mean) of A and B?

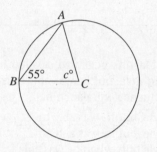

32. In the figure above, C is the center of the circle. What is the value of c?

33. If Elaine drove 190 kilometers between 12:00 noon and 3:20 P.M., what was her average speed, in kilometers per hour?

34. From 1990 until 1998 the value of an investment increased by 10% every year. The value of that investment on January 1, 1996, was how many times greater than the value on January 1, 1994?

35. How many two-digit numbers do not contain the digit 9?

36. If the average (arithmetic mean) of five numbers is 95 and the average of three of them is 100, what is the average of the other two?

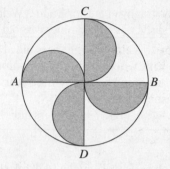

37. In the circle above, diameters AB and CD are perpendicular, and each of the four shaded regions is a semicircle. The shaded area is how many times the white area?

38. When a group of people were tested for a rare disease, 99.6% of them were found not to have the disease. If 10 people did have the disease, how many people were tested?

IF YOU FINISH IN LESS THAN 25 MINUTES, YOU MAY CHECK YOUR WORK ON THIS SECTION ONLY. DO NOT TURN TO ANY OTHER SECTION IN THE TEST.

STOP

Improving Sentence Directions

Some or all parts of the following sentences are underlined. The first answer choice, (A), simply repeats the underlined part of the sentence. The other four choices present four alternative ways to phrase the underlined part. Select the answer that produces the most effective sentence, one that is clear and exact, and blacken the appropriate space on your answer sheet. In selecting your choice, be sure that it is standard written English and that it expresses the meaning of the original sentence.

EXAMPLE: **SAMPLE ANSWER:**

The first biography of author Eudora Welty came out   Ⓐ Ⓑ Ⓒ ● Ⓔ
in 1998, <u>and she was eighty-nine years old at the time.</u>

(A) and she was eighty-nine years old at the time
(B) at the time when she was eighty-nine
(C) upon becoming an eighty-nine year old
(D) when she was eighty-nine
(E) at the age of eighty-nine years old

---

1. Although serfs were lucky to drink their ale from cracked wooden bowls, nobles customarily <u>drunk their wine from</u> elaborately chased drinking horns.

   (A) drunk their wine from
   (B) have drinked their wine from
   (C) drank their wine from
   (D) had drunken their wine from
   (E) drinking their wine from

2. Before the search party reached the scene of the accident, <u>the rain began to fall</u>, making rescue efforts more difficult.

   (A) the rain began to fall
   (B) the rain had began to fall
   (C) it began to rain
   (D) the rain had begun to fall
   (E) it started to rain

3. For many students, <u>keeping a journal during college seems satisfying their need</u> for self-expression.

   (A) keeping a journal during college seems satisfying their need
   (B) keeping a journal during college seems to satisfy their need
   (C) keeping a journal during college seeming satisfying their need
   (D) to keep a journal during college seems satisfying their need
   (E) the keeping of a journal during college seems to satisfy their need

4. Peter Martins began to develop his own choreographic <u>style, but he was able</u> to free himself from the influence of Balanchine.

   (A) style, but he was able to
   (B) style; but he was able to
   (C) style only when he was able to
   (D) style only when he is able to
   (E) style: only when he was able to

5. <u>Irregardless of the outcome</u> of this dispute, our two nations will remain staunch allies.

   (A) Irregardless of the outcome
   (B) Regardless of how the outcome
   (C) With regard to the outcome
   (D) Regardless of the outcome
   (E) Disregarding the outcome

6. With the onset of winter, <u>the snows began to fall, we were soon forced to remain indoors</u> most of the time.

   (A) the snows began to fall, we were soon forced to remain indoors
   (B) the snows began to fall; we were soon forced to remain indoors
   (C) the snows began to fall: we were soon forced to remain indoors
   (D) the snows began to fall, having forced us to remain indoors
   (E) the snows had begun to fall; we were soon forced to remain indoors

GO ON TO NEXT PAGE ▶

7. "Araby," along with several other stories from Joyce's *Dubliners*, are going to be read at Town Hall by the noted Irish actor Brendan Coyle.

   (A) are going to be read
   (B) were going to be read
   (C) are gone to be read
   (D) is going to be read
   (E) is gone to be read

8. In 1980 the Democrats lost not only the executive branch, but also their majority in the United States Senate.

   (A) lost not only the executive branch but also their majority
   (B) lost not only the executive branch but also its majority
   (C) not only lost the executive branch but also their majority
   (D) lost the executive branch but also their majority
   (E) lost not only the executive branch but their majority also

9. Before considering an applicant for this job, he must have a degree in electrical engineering as well as three years in the field.

   (A) Before considering an applicant for this job, he must have
   (B) Before considering an applicant for this job, he should have
   (C) We will not consider an applicant for this job without
   (D) To consider an applicant for this job, he must have
   (E) We will not consider an applicant for this job if he does not have

10. To invest intelligently for the future, mutual funds provide an excellent opportunity for the average investor.

    (A) To invest intelligently for the future, mutual funds
    (B) As an intelligent investment for the future, mutual funds
    (C) Investing intelligently for the future, mutual funds
    (D) To invest with intelligence, mutual funds
    (E) Having invested intelligently, you must determine that mutual funds

11. She was told to give the award to whomever she thought had contributed most to the welfare of the student body.

    (A) to whomever she thought
    (B) to whoever she thought
    (C) to the senior whom she thought
    (D) to whomever
    (E) to him whom she thought

12. Since he is lying the book on the table where it does not belong.

    (A) Since he is lying the book on the table where it does not belong.
    (B) He is lying the book on the table where it does not belong.
    (C) Because he is laying the book on the table where it does not belong.
    (D) Since he is laying the book on the table where it does not belong.
    (E) He is laying the book on the table where it does not belong.

13. Mary is as fast as, if not faster than, anyone in her class and should be on the team.

    (A) as fast as, if not faster than, anyone
    (B) as fast, if not faster than, anyone else
    (C) as fast as, if not more fast than, anyone
    (D) as fast as, if not faster than, anyone else
    (E) as swift as, if not faster than, anyone

14. Senator Schumer is one of the legislators who are going to discuss the budget with the president.

    (A) one of the legislators who are going
    (B) one of the legislators who is going
    (C) one of the legislators who has gone
    (D) the legislators who is going
    (E) the legislators who has gone

15. New research studies show that alcohol and tobacco are as harmful to elderly women as elderly men.

    (A) are as harmful to elderly women as elderly men
    (B) are so harmful to elderly women as elderly men
    (C) being as harmful to elderly women as elderly men
    (D) are as harmful to elderly women as to elderly men
    (E) are as harmful to elderly women as to men being elderly

16. Chronic fatigue syndrome is not a normal condition; rather, it is an abnormal response to stress factors such as anxiety or infection.

    (A) condition; rather, it is an abnormal response to stress factors such as
    (B) condition, it is a rather abnormal response to stress factors such as
    (C) condition; but it is an abnormal response to stress factors such as
    (D) condition rather, it is an abnormal response to stress factors like
    (E) condition, rather it is a way of responding abnormally to such stress factors as

GO ON TO NEXT PAGE ▶

17. A cynic is when someone has a tendency to disbe-lieve that any actions can have wholly unselfish motivations.

(A) A cynic is when someone has a tendency to disbelieve that any actions can have wholly unselfish motivations.

(B) Someone who has a tendency to disbelieve that any actions can have wholly unselfish motivations, and he is a cynic.

(C) A cynic is when someone tends not to believe that any actions might have had wholly unselfish motivations.

(D) A cynic is someone which has a tendency to disbelieve that any actions can be wholly unselfishly motivated.

(E) A cynic is someone who tends to disbelieve that any actions can have wholly unselfish motivations.

18. When NASA has been informed of the dangerous weather conditions, the head of the space agency decided to postpone the shuttle launch.

(A) When NASA has been informed of the danger-ous weather conditions

(B) Because NASA having been informed of the dangerous weather conditions

(C) Although NASA was informed with the dan-gerous weather conditions

(D) When NASA was informed of the dangerous weather conditions

(E) When NASA has been informed with the dan-gerous weather conditions

19. Henry James wrote the play *Guy Domville* primar-ily because he hoped revitalizing of his waning literary career.

(A) he hoped revitalizing of his waning literary career

(B) he hoped revitalizing of his literary career that was waning

(C) his hoping was the revitalizing of his waning literary career

(D) he hoped to revitalize his waning literary career

(E) he hoped revitalizing of his literary career that had waned

20. While strolling in Golden Gate Park one day, seeing the carousel with its elegantly carved horses delighted the young couple.

(A) seeing the carousel with its elegantly carved horses delighted the young couple

(B) the sight of the carousel with its elegantly carved horses delighted the young couple

(C) the young couple was delighted by the sight of the carousel with its elegantly carved horses

(D) the carousel delighted the young couple with its elegantly carved horses when they saw it

(E) to have seen the carousel's elegantly carved horses delighted the young couple

GO ON TO NEXT PAGE ▶

21. <u>Being that</u> my car is getting <u>its</u> annual tune-up, I
         A   B

<u>will not be able</u> <u>to pick you up</u> tomorrow
       C   D

morning. <u>No error</u>
             E

22. The average taxpayer <u>can't hardly</u> believe that
                                  A

income tax fraud is <u>so widespread as</u> <u>to justify</u>
                          B   C

such precautions as the authorities <u>have taken</u>.
                                          D

<u>No error</u>
   E

23. No one <u>but</u> <u>he</u> knew <u>which</u> questions
                A   B   C

<u>were going</u> to be asked on this test. <u>No error</u>
     D   E

24. You are being <u>quite</u> cynical when you say
                          A

<u>that the reason</u> we have <u>such a large</u> turnout
       B   C

<u>is because</u> we are serving refreshments.
       D

<u>No error</u>
   E

25. <u>Although</u> I <u>am playing</u> golf for more <u>than</u> three
         A   B   C

years, I cannot manage <u>to break</u> 90. <u>No error</u>
                            D   E

26. Studies <u>have found</u> that a mild salt solution is
                    A

more <u>affective</u> <u>than</u> the commercial preparations
       B   C

available in drug stores <u>in the treatment of</u> this
                              D

ailment. <u>No error</u>
             E

27. If I have to make a choice <u>between</u> John, Henry
         A   B

and <u>her</u>, I think I'll select Henry because of his
       C

self-control <u>during</u> moments of stress. <u>No error</u>
                D   E

28. <u>In order to raise public consciousness concerning</u>
         A

environmental problems, <u>you</u> should distribute
                              B

leaflets, write to <u>your representative</u> in Congress,
                        C

<u>as well as signing</u> the necessary petitions.
       D

<u>No error</u>
   E

29. Members of a scientific expedition discovered the

Titanic, <u>which</u> sank after <u>it</u> struck an iceberg,
              A   B

<u>furthermore</u> it was not possible for them to
     C

<u>raise it</u>. <u>No error</u>
     D   E

30. Scientists <u>show</u> that change, <u>whether</u> good or bad,
       A   B

leads to stress <u>and</u> that the <u>accumulation from</u>
                 C   D

stress-related changes can cause major illness.

<u>No error</u>
   E

31. We have spent <u>all together</u> <u>too much</u> money on
                       A   B

this project; we have <u>exceeded</u> our budget and
                        C

<u>can expect</u> no additional funds until the beginning
   D

of the new year. <u>No error</u>
                     E

32. Between thirty <u>and</u> forty students <u>seem willing</u> to
                       A   B

volunteer; <u>the rest</u> are not <u>planning to</u> participate
            C   D

in the program. <u>No error</u>
                    E

33. The horse <u>that</u> won the trophies <u>differed with</u> the
                  A   B

<u>other horses</u> in <u>overall appearance</u> as well as
   C   D

ability. <u>No error</u>
            E

34. The business executive, <u>planning</u> to attend the
                                A

conference in New Orleans, <u>could not decide</u>
                              B

whether to travel on or <u>remaining at</u> the hotel was
                          C

the <u>better</u> choice. <u>No error</u>
       D   E

Improving Paragraph Directions

The passage below is the unedited draft of a student's essay. Some of the essay needs to be rewritten to make the meaning clearer and more precise. Read the essay carefully.

The essay is followed by five questions about changes that might improve all or part of its organization, development, sentence structure, use of language, appropriateness to the audience, or use of standard written English. Choose the answer that most clearly and effectively expresses the student's intended meaning. Indicate your choice by filling in the corresponding space on the answer sheet.

[1] In the twentieth century, women have held a major part in influencing social change and social status. [2] In such developing countries as Saudi Arabia, restrictions on women are gradually being lifted, and they have gained the right to be in public without your head covered.

[3] In the area of social status, women have fought for better treatment and more respect. [4] An example of this is the fight for women in the workplace. [5] Not long ago most women stayed at home and took care of their families, while their husbands worked at white collar and blue collar jobs. [6] But now many women work as doctors, lawyers, and other established positions. [7] Women are finally out in the work force competing with men for the same jobs.

[8] In the area of politics and government, many women have attained high positions. [9] Hillary Rodham Clinton became a role model for many young women in this country. [10] Two women are now members of the U.S. Supreme Court. [11] Several women also are governors, senators and representatives. [12] There will never again be an all-male cabinet. [13] Ever since women's suffrage, women have won the rights reserved for men. [14] The result was that women now have a voice in the actions of our country.

[15] In the areas of health, medicine, sciences, and the military, women have also come into their own. [16] Although the world still has a long way to go before women achieve total equality with men, the twentieth century may long be remembered as the time when the first steps were taken.

GO ON TO NEXT PAGE ▶

35. Considering the essay as a whole, which revision of sentence 1 would serve best as the essay's opening sentence?

(A) The social status of women has undergone a major change during the twentieth century.

(B) Twentieth century women will have a major influence in changing their social status.

(C) As a major influence in the twentieth century, women have had their social status changed.

(D) Under the influence of twentieth century women, their status has changed.

(E) Being influenced by social change in the twentieth century, the status of women has changed.

36. Which is the most effective revision of the underlined segment of sentence 2 below?

In such developing countries as Saudi Arabia, restrictions on women are gradually being lifted, and they have gained the right to be in public without your head covered.

(A) for example, women are gaining rights like the one to be in public bareheaded

(B) which means that they have gained the right to be in public with their heads uncovered

(C) and they have the right, for example, for you to go bareheaded in public

(D) and women now have gained the right to be bareheaded in public

(E) to the extent that women can exercise the right of going into public with their head uncovered

37. Which revision of sentence 8 provides the best transition between the second and the third paragraphs?

(A) The competition has extended into politics and government, where many women have replaced men in high positions.

(B) Irregardless, in the field of politics and government many women have attained high positions.

(C) High positions in government and politics have been attained by women.

(D) Among the jobs that women have attained are in politics and government.

(E) The world of politics and government has changed because women have attained high positions.

38. Sentence 8 is the topic sentence of the third paragraph. Which of the following is the best revision of sentence 9?

(A) The wife of the president, Hillary Rodham Clinton, made herself a role model for many young American women.

(B) In the 1992 national election, Hillary Rodham Clinton helped her husband win the presidency of the United States.

(C) After seven years as prime minister of England, Margaret Thatcher was finally defeated by a male, John Major.

(D) While she was the leader of India, Indira Ghandi was assassinated.

(E) In recent years both Margaret Thatcher of England and Indira Ghandi of India, for example, served as leaders of their countries.

39. Which sentence in the third paragraph should be revised or deleted because it contributes least to the development of the main idea of the paragraph?

(A) Sentence 10 (B) Sentence 11
(C) Sentence 12 (D) Sentence 13
(E) Sentence 14

IF YOU FINISH IN LESS THAN 30 MINUTES, YOU MAY CHECK YOUR WORK ON THIS SECTION ONLY. DO NOT TURN TO ANY OTHER SECTION IN THE TEST.

STOP

Answer Key

Section 1 Critical Reading

1. C	10. D	19. D
2. D	11. E	20. C
3. B	12. C	21. E
4. E	13. D	22. E
5. A	14. E	23. D
6. D	15. B	24. D
7. C	16. D	
8. D	17. A	
9. C	18. B	

Section 2 Mathematics

1. D	8. E	15. D
2. C	9. D	16. C
3. D	10. A	17. C
4. E	11. D	18. A
5. D	12. D	19. D
6. D	13. B	20. A
7. B	14. E	

Section 3 Critical Reading

25. B	34. E	43. D
26. D	35. D	44. B
27. A	36. A	45. A
28. E	37. E	46. A
29. A	38. D	47. E
30. C	39. B	48. D
31. D	40. B	
32. C	41. D	
33. D	42. B	

Section 4 Mathematics

21. D	24. C	27. A
22. E	25. B	28. B
23. C	26. D	

29. 3 2 0

30. 3 0

31. 3 . 7 5

32. 7 0

or *1 5 / 4*

33. 5 7

34. 1 . 2 1

35. 7 2

36. 8 7 . 5

37. 1

38. 2 5 0 0

Section 5 Writing Skills

1. *C*	9. *E*	17. *E*	25. *B*	33. *B*
2. *D*	10. *B*	18. *D*	26. *B*	34. *C*
3. *B*	11. *B*	19. *D*	27. *B*	35. *A*
4. *C*	12. *E*	20. *C*	28. *D*	36. *D*
5. *D*	13. *D*	21. *A*	29. *C*	37. *A*
6. *B*	14. *A*	22. *A*	30. *D*	38. *E*
7. *D*	15. *D*	23. *B*	31. *A*	39. *E*
8. *A*	16. *A*	24. *D*	32. *E*	

Scoring Chart—Model Test A

Critical Reading Sections

Section 1: 24 Questions (1–24)

Number correct	_____	(A)
Number omitted	_____	(B)
Number incorrect	_____	(C)
$\frac{1}{4}$ (C)	_____	(D)
(A) − (D)	_____	Raw Score I

Section 3: 24 Questions (25–48)

Number correct	_____	(A)
Number omitted	_____	(B)
Number incorrect	_____	(C)
$\frac{1}{4}$ (C)	_____	(D)
(A) − (D)	_____	Raw Score II

Total Critical Reading Raw Score

Raw Scores I + II   _____

Mathematics Sections

Section 2: 20 Questions (1–20)

Number correct	_____	(A)
Number omitted	_____	(B)
Number incorrect	_____	(C)
$\frac{1}{4}$ (C)	_____	(D)
(A) − (D)	_____	Raw Score I

Section 4: First 8 Questions (21–28)

Number correct	_____	(A)
Number omitted	_____	(B)
Number incorrect	_____	(C)
$\frac{1}{4}$ (C)	_____	(D)
(A) − (D)	_____	Raw Score II

Section 4: Next 10 Questions (29–38)

Number correct   _____   Raw Score III

Total Mathematical Raw Score

Raw Scores I + II + III   _____

NOTE: In each section (A) + (B) + (C) should equal the number of questions in that section.

Writing Skills Section

Section 5: 39 Questions (1–39)

Number correct	_____	(A)
Number omitted	_____	(B)
Number incorrect	_____	(C)
$\frac{1}{4}$ (C)	_____	(D)

Writing Skills Raw Score

(A) − (D)   _____

Evaluation Chart

Study your score. Your raw score is an indication of your probable achievement on the PSAT/NMSQT. As a guide to the amount of work you need or want to do with this book, study the following.

Raw Score			Self-rating
Critical Reading	*Mathematics*	*Writing*	
42–48	35–38	33–39	Superior
37–46	30–34	28–32	Very good
32–36	25–29	23–27	Good
26–35	21–24	17–22	Above average
20–25	17–20	12–16	Average
12–19	10–16	7–11	Below average
less than 12	less than 10	less than 7	Inadequate

Answer Explanations

Section 1 Critical Reading

1. *C* The use of "unhappily" tells us that the experiment was somehow damaged or *marred* by the presence of observers.

2. *D* James didn't know when assignments were due because there was something wrong with the way he wrote them down. He was not orderly or *methodical* about it.

3. *B* The word "despite" signals a contrast. Despite the advertised *praises*, she had doubts—she remained *a skeptic* about the product. Note also that "singing the praises of" is a cliché, a customary phrase.

4. *E* Again, think of your own answer before looking at the choices. What would you need after two full months of solid work? A rest, or *respite*.

5. *A* The phrase "even though" tells us that there will be a contrast. This requires a word that is opposite in meaning to "does not change." *Plastic* can mean adaptable or pliable when used as an adjective, as it is here.

6. *D* The author's presentation of factual information about tarantulas is scientifically *objective* (impartial).

7. *C* To excite a defensive response is to *stimulate* or arouse that reaction.

8. *D* The word *arty* means aspiring to be artistic, generally unsuccessfully, as in the rich man's arty wife, who dabbles in watercolors. Here the author looks down on collectors who collect art because they want to be thought artistic. The use of quotation marks serves to underscore or *emphasize the* author's *condescending tone*.

9. *C* The collectors look for the next new thing just because it is new, and therefore desirable: it has novelty value, not necessarily intrinsic value. Thus, the next new thing *attracts attention primarily for its novelty*.

10. *D* Blown about by the storm, the *branches* of the fir trees move from side to side: "the old firs . . . wave excitedly with their arms."

11. *E* The author states that the jackdaw's proficiency is not inherited or innate, but "an individually acquired accomplishment." In other words, it has been *gained through practice*.

12. *C* The author is stressing that you can *be* sure or *confident* of the truth of what he says.

13. *D* The "sightless monster" is the "stupid wind" that tries to dive the jackdaws toward the east. Note how the author personifies the wind, writing as if the wind had some degree of human intelligence and responsiveness.

14. *E* The concluding sentence of the passage celebrates the birds' "Sovereign control over the power of the elements," in other words, their *mastery of the forces of nature*. Though Choice B may seem tempting, you can rule it out: Lorenz emphasizes the storm's strength ("the pitiless strength of the inorganic"), not the strength of the birds. Choices A, C, and D are unsupported by the passage.

15. *B* The author uses several metaphors ("close-reefed sails," "the teeth of the gale," etc.) and clarifies what he means by the term *game*. He describes the jackdaws' behavior in detail and dismisses the notion that their behavior is purely instinctive. However, he never *argues a cause*.

16. *D* Tapestry weaving is time-consuming, taking "as much as a year to produce a yard." In addition, it is faithful to the original ("The weaver always follows a preexisting model."). It is not, however, spontaneous in concept.

17. *A* The author mentions tapestry's distinctive or *characteristic* weave as something that distinguishes tapestry-woven materials from other fabrics (prints, brocades, etc.).

18. *B* By using tapestries "to display his wealth and social position," the nobleman is using them to demonstrate his *consequence* or importance.

19. *D* The "ground" upon which embroidery is laid is the cloth *base* upon which the embroiderer stitches a design.

20. *C* The author refers to the suggestion that tapestries served primarily as a source of warmth only to *dismiss* or reject the idea. To prove his point he asserts that comfort had little importance in medieval times.

21. *E* Here the word "chambers" *is being used in a special sense* to mean a set of wall hangings made to fit a specific room.

22. *E* In describing Morris as someone who attempted to bring back tapestry making to its true, medieval principles, the author depicts him as a *traditionalist*, someone who attempts to preserve or restore ancient cultural practices or beliefs.

23. *D* In comparison to the tightly-woven tapestries of the nineteenth-century, present-day wall hangings are described as "coarsely woven cloths." Thus, they *have a less fine weave* than their predecessors.

24. *D* Although the passage explains the process of tapestry making and mentions that large wall hangings are Western rather than Eastern in origin, Choices A and B do not reflect the passage's primary purpose. This purpose is to *provide a historical perspective on tapestry making.*

Section 2 Mathematics

For many problems, the explanation provides a reference to one or more **KEY FACTS** from Chapter 9. These are the mathematical facts that you need to solve that problem. If a solution refers to **KEY FACT J2**, for example, the solution depends on the second **KEY FACT** discussed in Section J of Chapter 9.

For some problems, an alternative solution, indicated by two asterisks (**), follows the first solution. When this occurs, usually one of the solutions is the direct mathematical one and the other is based on one of the tactics discussed in Chapters 8 and 9.

1. *D* Since $x + y + 30 = 180$ and $y = 2x$, we get

$$x + 2x + 30 = 180 \Rightarrow 3x = 150 \Rightarrow$$
$$x = 50 \Rightarrow y = 2x = 100.$$

2. *C* The left-hand side of $(a + 12) - 12 = 12$ is just a. So, $a = 12$.

Of course, you can use **TACTIC 8-1: back-solve, starting (and ending) with C.

3. *D* Let each side of the small squares be 1. Then each square has area 1, and the area of rectangle *AEFJ* is 4. The shaded area consists of $\triangle AJI$ and $\triangle EFI$. The white region is $\triangle AEI$, whose area is $\frac{1}{2}(4)(1) = 2$. The area of the shaded region is $4 - 2 = 2$, and so the ratio of the areas is $2:2 = 1:1$.

**Just look at the diagram. Exactly half of square *ABIJ* and exactly half of rectangle *BEFI* are shaded. The areas of the shaded and white regions are equal.

4. *E* Since $72\% + 19\% = 91\%$, the $243 spent on the party represents the other 9% of the money raised. Then $.09m = 243 \Rightarrow m = 243 \div .09 = 2700$.

5. *D* Every hour the hour hand moves through $30°$ ($\frac{1}{12}$ of $360°$). So it will move through $20°$ in $\frac{2}{3}$ of an hour or 40 minutes; 40 minutes after 1:30 is 2:10.

6. *D* Since *ABC* is an equilateral triangle, $x = 60$. So, $60 + 40 + y = 180 \Rightarrow y = 80$. Then by **KEY FACT I6** (when parallel lines are cut by a transversal, the four acute angles have the same measure), $y = a$. So, $a = 80$.

Use **TACTIC 8-6 (trust the diagram)—a appears to be slightly less than a 90° angle.

7. *B* Let x and y be the two numbers:

$$x < y < x + y \Rightarrow -y < y \Rightarrow 0 < 2y \Rightarrow y \text{ is}$$

positive. Therefore, at least one of the numbers is positive. (Note that there are no restrictions on x.)

8. *E* Solve the equation $20 = \frac{x}{100}C$:

$$2000 = xC \Rightarrow x = \frac{2000}{C}\%.$$

Use **TACTIC 8-3: substitute an easy-to-use number: 20 is 100% of 20. Which of the choices is equal to 100% when $C = 20$? Only $\frac{2000}{C}\%$.

9. *D* Whenever we know two of the three sides of a right triangle, we can find the third side by using the Pythagorean theorem. First, assume that the two given sides are both legs, and let x represent the hypotenuse. Then

$$x^2 = 5^2 + 9^2 = 25 + 81 = 106 \Rightarrow x = \sqrt{106}$$

and III is true. Now assume that one side is a leg and that the longer side is the hypotenuse; let y represent the other leg. Then

$$5^2 + y^2 = 9^2 \Rightarrow 25 + y^2 = 81 \Rightarrow$$
$$y^2 = 56 \Rightarrow y = \sqrt{56}$$

and I is true. Therefore, I and III only are true.

10. *A* By **KEY FACT N7**, the slope of the line $y = 2x - 3$ is 2. By **KEY FACT N6**, parallel lines have equal slopes. Only Choice A, $y = 2x + 3$, also has a slope equal to 2.

11. *D* Just check each choice. Is there a triangle whose sides are 1, 2, 3? No, the sum of any two sides of a triangle must be *greater* than the third side (**KEY FACT J12**). (I is false.) Are there triangles whose sides are 3, 4, 5 and 13, 14, 15. Yes. (II and III are true.) Statements II and III only are true.

12. *D* By **KEY FACT C5**, the percent increase in the bank's charge is $\frac{\text{the actual increase}}{\text{the original amount}} \times 100\%$. The charge was originally \$10 and the actual increase was \$10. So, the percent increase is $\frac{10}{10} \times 100 = 100\%$.

13. *B* Since the sum of the three measures is 180°:
$$180 = x + 2x + 3y = 3x + 3y = 3(x + y) \Rightarrow$$
$$x + y = 60 \Rightarrow y = 60 - x.$$

Use **TACTIC 8-3: pick an easy-to-use value for x. Note that in the diagram x appears to be about 50, but you can pick any value: say 10. Then $10 + 20 + 3y = 180 \Rightarrow 3y = 150 \Rightarrow y = 50$. Which of the choices equals 10 when y is 50? Only $60 - x$.

14. *E* $\|6^2\| = \frac{2}{3}(6^2)^2 = \frac{2}{3}(36)^2 = \frac{2}{3}(1296) = 864$.

15. *D* $\|y\| = \|\frac{2}{3}x\| = \frac{2}{3}(\frac{2}{3}x)^2 = \frac{2}{3}(\frac{4}{9}x^2) = \frac{8}{27}x^2$.

Use **TACTIC 8-2: replace the variables with numbers. Let $x = 3$. Then $y = \frac{2}{3}(3) = 2$, and $\|2\| = \frac{2}{3}(2)^2 = \frac{2}{3}(4) = \frac{8}{3}$. Which of the choices is equal to $\frac{8}{3}$ when $x = 3$? Only $\frac{8}{27}x^2$.

16. *C* $f(\frac{1}{2}) = 9(\frac{1}{2}) + 9^{\frac{1}{2}} = 4.5 + \sqrt{9} = 4.5 + 3 = 7.5$.

17. *C* Jill walked 4 kilometers and Jack walked 6 kilometers; so Jill walked $\frac{4}{6} = \frac{2}{3}$ the distance that Jack walked. Since their rates were the same, she did it in $\frac{2}{3}$ the time: $\frac{2}{3}$ of 2 hours is $\frac{4}{3}$ of an hour, or 1 hour and 20 minutes. She left at 10:40.

**Jack walked 6 kilometers in exactly 2 hours; so, he was walking at a rate of 3 kilometers per hour. Jill walked 4 kilometers, also at 3 kilometers per hour; so her walking time was $4 \div 3$ or $1\frac{1}{3}$ hours ($t = d \div r$: See Section 12-H). Therefore, Jill left $1\frac{1}{3}$ hours, or 1 hour and 20 minutes, before noon—at 10:40.

18. *A* Even if you can do the algebra, this type of problem is easier by using **TACTIC 8-3**: choose easy-to-use numbers. Assume that there are 100 females and 50 males in the club and that 20% of the females and 10% of the males attended the meeting. Then, 20 females and 5 males were there, and 5 is 20% of 25, the total number attending.

19. *D* $(a + b)^2 = a^2 + 2ab + b^2 = (a^2 + b^2) + 2ab$. By the Pythagorean Theorem, $a^2 + b^2 = 10^2 = 100$; and since the area is 20, $\frac{1}{2}ab = 20 \Rightarrow ab = 40$, and $2ab = 80$. Then
$$(a^2 + b^2) + 2ab = 100 + 80 = 180.$$

20. *A* Originally the fund of d dollars was to be divided among 4 winners, in which case each of them would have received $\frac{d}{4}$ dollars. Instead, the fund was divided among 6 winners, and each received $\frac{d}{6}$ dollars. This represents a loss to each of the original winners of $\frac{d}{4} - \frac{d}{6} = \frac{3d}{12} - \frac{2d}{12} = \frac{d}{12}$ dollars.

**Unless you are comfortable with the algebra, plug in a number for d; say $d = 24$. Then the 4 winners would have received $24 \div 4 = 6$ dollars each. Now the 6 winners will receive $24 \div 6 = 4$ dollars each, a difference of \$2. Which of the choices is equal to 2 when $d = 24$? Only $\frac{d}{12}$.

Section 3 Critical Reading

25. *B* Remember to think of your own answer before looking at the choices. North clearly had a strong belief; no one's words could convince him otherwise. This would guide you to choose *conviction*, one meaning of which is belief.

26. *D* If we are likely to be in need of a new source of energy, we must be about to run out of the old source of fuel. This would happen if we *deplete* or exhaust our supply. The phrase "excessive use" is also a clue that we may be running out, through using too much.

27. *A* The word "however" signals a contrast. The sentence says the authorities reject the use of "disinterested." Therefore, *in contrast*, they accept or *condone* the use of "healthy."

28. *E* The flu weakened or *debilitated* Michael, leaving him too tired to return to work.

29. *A* The word "though" also signals a contrast. Although Alec Guinness had his mind set on becoming an actor, his determination or *resolution* wavered. Note that *resolution* is not just a statement of intent; it can mean firmness of intent as well.

30. *C* The key word here is "ridiculing," meaning making fun of or mocking. It complements *satirical* or sarcastic and cutting.

31. *D* Someone who risks his or her life frequently is a *daredevil*. Since the threat of death does not keep Markham from such activities, the first missing word must be *daunt*, meaning to frighten or lessen one's courage.

32. *C* "Unscrupulous merchandisers" make false claims. *Debunking* means exposing falseness in something. Nader, who is an advocate or protector of the consumer, teaches people to be suspicious and to exercise *skepticism*. Note that "exercising skepticism" is a cliché, a very commonly used phrase.

33. *D* The author's attitude is clearly *approving*: she notes that some commentators cite Malcolm's change in prison as an example of positive transformation; she also uses words with positive connotations ("purposeful") to describe Malcolm's method of tackling his task.

34. *E* In plowing his way through the dictionary, Malcolm *proceeded steadily* and purposefully from the beginning to the end.

35. *D* Lines 8–9 of the passage say that in primate troops, males "defend, control and lead the troop." Therefore, the troops are *dominated by adult males*.

36. *A* The passage says that the ranking hierarchy lessens conflict within the troop. Therefore, it is meant to *protect the members of the troop* from internal strife.

37. *E* In candidly exposing her grandmother's flaws, the author exhibits a *sardonic* or scornful and sarcastic attitude.

38. *D* McCarthy sees as little point in speculating about her grandmother's childhood as she does in wondering about the toilet training of a fictional character like Lady Macbeth. Such speculations are, to McCarthy's mind, idle or *useless*.

39. *B* The author states (somewhat ironically) that modern fictional characters must have "clinical authenticity." In other words, they must appear to be genuine or *valid* in *psychological* terms.

40. *B* Although the grandmother's outward appearance was soft and motherly, her essential nature was hard as nails. Clearly, you cannot judge a book (person) by its cover (outward appearance).

41. *D* McCarthy is building up a portrait of her grandmother as a pugnacious, autocratic person. She describes the fear old ladies have for their belongings as a very human (and understandable) reaction: aware of their own increasing fragility (and eventual death), old ladies identify with their fragile possessions and are protective of them. McCarthy's grandmother was also protective of her belongings, but she was not the typical "gentle and tremulous" elderly woman. She was a petty tyrant and had decidedly *different reasons for her actions*.

42. *B* Because her grandmother was more interested in maintaining her power than in being hospitable, the social properties or *aspects* of the family home had withered and decayed till no real sociability existed.

43. *D* Heilbrun's central criticism is that her grandmother "impaired her six daughters for autonomy" or independence. In other words, *she discouraged her daughters' independence*.

44. *B* Heilbrun realizes that people nowadays may have difficulty understanding what motivated her grandmother to control her daughters' lives and restrict their autonomy so thoroughly. By describing how great the horror of pregnancy in an unmarried girl was, she helps the reader understand *why her grandmother* acted as she did.

45. *A* By dwelling on how hard she had worked to support her daughters and how much she would be hurt if they failed to pay her back by making good marriages, Heilbrun's grandmother exploited their *sense of guilt*.

46. *A* The common factor in both grandmothers' lives is their need to govern the *actions of others*. McCarthy's grandmother tyrannized everyone from the mailman to her daughters and daughters-in-law; Heilbrun's grandmother "ruled the household with an arm of iron," governing her daughters' lives.

47. *E* McCarthy refers casually to Iago and Lady Macbeth, key figures in Shakespeare's tragedies. Heilbrun makes no such *literary references*.

48. *D* While Heilbrun's grandmother was a "sustaining woman" who provided for her family, McCarthy's grandmother was a grudging woman, not a sustaining one. Thus, McCarthy would most likely point out that *her grandmother's actual conduct is not in keeping with this characterization*.

Section 4 Mathematics

For many problems, the explanation provides a reference to one or more **KEY FACTS** from Chapter 9. These are the mathematical facts that you need to solve that problem. If a solution refers to **KEY FACT J2**, for example, the solution depends on the second **KEY FACT** discussed in Section J of Chapter 9.

For some problems, an alternative solution, indicated by two asterisks (**), follows the first solution. When this occurs, usually one of the solutions is the direct mathematical one and the other is based on one of the tactics discussed in Chapters 8 and 9.

21. *D* Since the ratio of the number of boys to girls is 2:3, the number of boys is $2x$, the number of girls is $3x$, and the total number of members is $2x + 3x = 5x$. So the girls make up $\frac{3x}{5x} = \frac{3}{5} =$ 60% of the members.

22. *E* Since d divisions each have t teams, multiply to get dt teams, and since each team has p players, multiply the number of teams (dt) by p to get the total number of players: dtp.

Use TACTIC 8-2. Choose easy-to-use numbers for t, d, and p. For example, assume that there are 2 divisions, each with 4 teams So, there are $2 \times 4 = 8$ teams. Then assume that each of the teams has 10 players, for a total of $8 \times 10 = 80$ players. Now check the five choices. Which one is equal to 80 when $d = 2$, $t = 4$, and $p = 10$? Only dtp.

23. *C* Test each set of values to see which one does not work. Only Choice C, $x = 1$ and $y = -1$ does not work: $3(1)^2 + 2(-1) = 3 - 2 = 1$, not 5. The other choices all work.

24. *C* There is a total of $1 + 2 + 3 + 4 + 5 + 6 = 21$ slips of paper. Since odd numbers are written on $1 + 3 + 5 = 9$ of them, the probability of drawing an odd number is $\frac{9}{21} = \frac{3}{7}$.

25. *B* If $|x| = |y|$, then $x = y$ or $x = -y$. So $x^2 = y^2$ or $x^2 = (-y)^2 = y^2$. (II is true.) If $x = 1$ and $y = -1$, then both I and III are false. Only statement II is true.

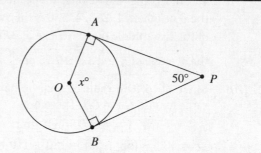

26. *D* Since $\overline{OA}$ and $\overline{OB}$ are radii drawn to the points of contact of two tangents, by **KEY FACT L10**, $\overline{OA} \perp \overline{PA}$ and $\overline{OB} \perp \overline{PB}$. So angles A and B are right angles. Finally, by **KEY FACT K1**, the sum of the measures of the four angles in any quadrilateral is 360; so

$90 + 90 + 50 + x = 360 \Rightarrow 230 + x = 360 \Rightarrow x = 130$.

27. *A* $2^{3x} + 2^{3x} + 2^{3x} + 2^{3x} = 4(2^{3x}) = 2^2(2^{3x}) = 2^{3x+2}$.

**Let $x = 1$; then $2^{3x} = 2^3 = 8$, and $2^{3x} + 2^{3x} + 2^{3x} + 2^{3x} = 8 + 8 + 8 + 8 = 32$. Which of the choices equals 32 when $x = 1$? Only $2^{3x+2}(2^5 = 32)$.

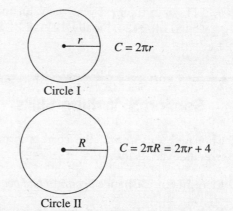

Circle I $C = 2\pi r$

Circle II $C = 2\pi R = 2\pi r + 4$

28. *B* Let r and R be the radii of circle I and circle II, respectively. Since the circumference of circle I is $2\pi r$, the circumference of circle II is $2\pi r + 4 = 2(\pi r + 2)$. But, of course, the circumference of circle II is also $2\pi R$. Therefore,

$$2\pi R = 2(\pi r + 2) \Rightarrow \pi R = \pi r + 2 \Rightarrow$$
$$R = r + \frac{2}{\pi}.$$

29. *(320)* Since $a + 100 = 180$, $a = 80$. But since ℓ and k are parallel, the four acute angles are all equal: $80 = a = b = c = d$, so their sum is $4 \times 80 = 320$.

30. *(30)* Evaluate: $2(6) - 3(-6) = 12 + 18 = 30$.

31. $\left(3.75 \text{ or } \frac{15}{4}\right)$ The median of the 7 numbers 1, 2, 3, 4, 5, 6, 7 is the middle one: 4. The median of the 6 numbers 1, 2, 3, 4, 5, 6 is the average of the two middle ones: $\frac{3+4}{2} = 3.5$. Finally, the average of 4 and 3.5 is 3.75 or $\frac{15}{4}$.

32. *(70)* Since all of the radii of a circle have the same length, $CA = CB$. Therefore,
$$\text{m}\angle A = \text{m}\angle B = 55°, \text{ and}$$
$$c = 180 - (55 + 55) = 180 - 110 = 70.$$

33. *(57)* To find Elaine's average speed in kilometers per hour, divide the distance she went, in kilometers (190), by the time it took, in hours. Elaine drove for 3 hours and 20 minutes, which is $3\frac{1}{3}$ hours (20 minutes = $\frac{20}{60}$ hour = $\frac{1}{3}$ hour). Elaine's average speed is $190 \div 3\frac{1}{3} = 190 \div \frac{10}{3} = 190 \times \frac{3}{10} = 57$.

34. *(1.21)* Since this is a percent problem, assume the value of the investment on January 1, 1994 was $100. Since 10% of 100 is 10, one year later the value of the investment had increased by $10 to $110. Now, 10% of 110 is 11, so in the next year the value increased by $11 to $121. Finally, 121 is 1.21×100.

35. *(72)* There are 90 two-digit numbers (the integers from 10 to 99 inclusive). To find out how many of them do not contain the digit 9, calculate how many of them *do* contain the digit 9, and subtract that number from 90. There are a total of 18 two-digit numbers that contain the digit 9—the 10 numbers from 90 to 99 plus the 8 other numbers that end in 9: 19, 29, . . . , 89. Finally, there are $90 - 18 = 72$ two-digit numbers that do not contain the digit 9.

36. *(87.5)* If the average of 5 numbers is 95, the sum of those numbers is $5 \times 95 = 475$. Similarly, the sum of the 3 numbers whose average is 100 is 300, leaving 175 ($475 - 300$) as the sum of the 2 remaining numbers. The average of these 2 numbers is their sum divided by 2: $175 \div 2 = 87.5$.

37. *(1)* Assume that the radius of the large circle is 2. Then the area of the circle is 4π. The radius of each semicircle is 1, and since the area of a circle of radius 1 is π, the area of each semicircle is $\frac{1}{2}\pi$, and the total shaded area is $4\left(\frac{1}{2}\pi\right) = 2\pi$. Since the shaded area is exactly one-half of the circle, the white area is also one-half of the circle. The areas are equal, and so the shaded area is 1 times the white area.

38. *(2500)* If 99.6% of the people tested did not have the disease, then 0.4% of them did have the disease. If $x =$ the number of people tested, then $10 = 0.004x \Rightarrow x = 10 \div .004 = 2500$.

Section 5 Writing Skills

1. *C* Choice C uses *drank*, the correct form of the irregular verb *drink*.

2. *D* Error in tense. Change *began* to *had begun*.

3. *B* Error in idiom. *Seems satisfying their need* is unidiomatic. *Seems to satisfy their need* is correct.

4. *C* Error in coordination and subordination. Choice C corrects the error in conjunction use.

5. *D* Error in following conventions. *Irregardless* is a nonstandard use of *regardless*.

6. *B* Comma splice. The run-on sentence is corrected in Choice B.

7. *D* Errors in subject-verb agreement. The phrase *along with several other stories* is not part of the subject of the sentence. The subject is *"Araby"* (singular); the verb should be *is going to be read* (singular).

8. *A* Sentence is correct. Choice B introduces an error in agreement. Choices C, D, and E misuse the *not only . . . but also* construction.

9. *E* Error in modification and word order. The dangling modifier is corrected in Choice E.

10. *B* Error in modification and word order. The dangling construction is corrected in Choices B and E. However, only Choice B retains the meaning of the original sentence.

11. *B* The error in case is corrected in Choice B. *Whoever* is the subject of the verb *had contributed*.

12. *E* In this question we find two errors. Both the sentence fragment and the misuse of the intransitive verb *lie* are corrected in Choice E.

13. *D* Error in logical comparison. The faulty comparison is corrected in Choice D.

14. *A* The original sentence is correct. The subject of *are going* is *legislators* (plural). Therefore, Choices B and C are incorrect. Choices D and E change the meaning of the original sentence.

15. *D* Incomplete comparison. They are as harmful *to* women as they are *to* men.

16. *A* Sentence is correct.

17. *E* Error in usage. Do not use *when* or *where* after *is* in making a definition.

18. *D* Error in sequence of tenses. The present perfect tense ("has been informed") indicates some vague time before now, or a time that lasts up to the present. NASA, however, was told about the dangerous weather conditions at a definite time in the past. Therefore, you should use either the simple past tense ("was informed") or the past perfect tense ("had been informed") here.

19. *D* Error in idiom. Either James hoped *for* the revitalization of his career, or he hoped *to* revitalize it. In this case, the verbal *to revitalize* is correct.

20. *C* Dangling modifier. Ask yourself who are strolling in the park. Choice C rearranges the words in the sentence to make "While strolling in Golden Gate Park one day" clearly refer to "the young couple."

21. *A* Error in diction. Change *Being that* to *Since*.

22. *A* Error in following conventions. Double negative. Change *can't* to *can*.

23. *B* Error in pronoun case. *But*, as used in this sentence, is a preposition meaning *except*. Change *he* to *him*.

24. *D* Error in following conventions. Change *reason . . . is because* to *reason . . . is that*.

25. *B* Error in tense. Change *am playing* to *have been playing*.

26. *B* Error in diction. Change *affective* to *effective*.

27. *B* Error in diction. *Among* should be used when three or more items are being considered.

28. *D* Error in parallelism. Change *as well as signing* to *and sign* in order to match the other items in the list.

29. *C* Error in coordination and subordination. Incorrect sentence connector. Change *furthermore* to the coordinating conjunction *but* to clarify the relationship between the clauses.

30. *D* Error in idiom. Change *accumulation from* to *accumulation of*.

31. *A* Error in diction. *Altogether* is correct.

32. *E* Sentence is correct.

33. *B* Error in idiom. Change *differ with* (which relates to difference of opinion) to *differ from* (which relates to difference in appearance).

34. *C* Error in parallelism. Change *remaining at* to the infinitive *to remain at* in order to match *to travel on*.

35. *A* Choice A accurately describes the content of the essay. The original introductory sentence is misleading. The essay is about changes in the status of women, not about the role women played in causing the changes. It is the best answer.

Choice B is a variation of the original introductory sentence but the use of the future verb tense fails to convey the actual content of the essay.

Choice C is a confusing sentence consisting of two illogically unrelated clauses.

Choice D fails to convey the contents of the essay. It also contains the pronoun *their*, which does not have a clear antecedent.

Choice E is virtually meaningless. It also contains a dangling participle. The phrase that begins *Being influenced . . .* should modify *women*, not *status*.

36. *D* Choice A inserts a comma splice between *lifted* and *for example*. Two independent clauses should be separated by a period or semicolon.

Choice B contains the pronoun *they*, which lacks a specific reference.

Choice C improperly shifts pronouns from third person to second person.

Choice D is effectively expressed. It is the best answer.

Choice E is cumbersome and awkwardly worded.

The phrase *the right of going into public* contains an idiom error. The correct phrase is *right to go into public*.

37. *A* Choice A provides a smooth transition by alluding to the discussion of competition in the second paragraph and introducing the main topic of the third. A is the best answer.

Choice B uses a nonstandard transitional word *irregardless*, which in the context makes no sense.

Choice C contains no specifically transitional material.

Choice D would be a decent transition were it not for its mixed construction. The first half of the sentence doesn't fit grammatically with the second half.

Choice E introduces a new idea that is unrelated to the content of the third paragraph.

38. *E* Choice A is illogical; becoming role model is not an example of attaining a high position in politics and government.

Choice B is not a good example of attaining a high position in politics.

Choice C is irrelevant. Margaret Thatcher's defeat is not an example of an achievement in politics and government.

Choice D is slightly off the mark. The sentence emphasizes Indira Ghandi's assassination instead of her leadership.

Choice E gives two examples of women who have attained a high position in politics and government. It is the best answer.

39. *E* All the sentences except sentence 14 support the idea stated in the topic sentence, that women have made gains in politics and government. Threfore, Choice E is the best answer.

Answer Sheet
MODEL TEST B

Each mark should completely fill the appropriate space and should be as dark as all other marks. Make all erasures complete. Traces of an erasure may be read as an answer. See pages viii and 21 for explanations of timing and number of questions.

Section 1 — Critical Reading
25 minutes

1 (A) (B) (C) (D) (E)
2 (A) (B) (C) (D) (E)
3 (A) (B) (C) (D) (E)
4 (A) (B) (C) (D) (E)
5 (A) (B) (C) (D) (E)
6 (A) (B) (C) (D) (E)
7 (A) (B) (C) (D) (E)
8 (A) (B) (C) (D) (E)
9 (A) (B) (C) (D) (E)
10 (A) (B) (C) (D) (E)
11 (A) (B) (C) (D) (E)
12 (A) (B) (C) (D) (E)
13 (A) (B) (C) (D) (E)
14 (A) (B) (C) (D) (E)
15 (A) (B) (C) (D) (E)
16 (A) (B) (C) (D) (E)
17 (A) (B) (C) (D) (E)
18 (A) (B) (C) (D) (E)
19 (A) (B) (C) (D) (E)
20 (A) (B) (C) (D) (E)
21 (A) (B) (C) (D) (E)
22 (A) (B) (C) (D) (E)
23 (A) (B) (C) (D) (E)
24 (A) (B) (C) (D) (E)

Section 2 — Math
25 minutes

1 (A) (B) (C) (D) (E)
2 (A) (B) (C) (D) (E)
3 (A) (B) (C) (D) (E)
4 (A) (B) (C) (D) (E)
5 (A) (B) (C) (D) (E)
6 (A) (B) (C) (D) (E)
7 (A) (B) (C) (D) (E)
8 (A) (B) (C) (D) (E)
9 (A) (B) (C) (D) (E)
10 (A) (B) (C) (D) (E)
11 (A) (B) (C) (D) (E)
12 (A) (B) (C) (D) (E)
13 (A) (B) (C) (D) (E)
14 (A) (B) (C) (D) (E)
15 (A) (B) (C) (D) (E)
16 (A) (B) (C) (D) (E)
17 (A) (B) (C) (D) (E)
18 (A) (B) (C) (D) (E)
19 (A) (B) (C) (D) (E)
20 (A) (B) (C) (D) (E)

Section 3 — Critical Reading
25 minutes

25 (A) (B) (C) (D) (E)
26 (A) (B) (C) (D) (E)
27 (A) (B) (C) (D) (E)
28 (A) (B) (C) (D) (E)
29 (A) (B) (C) (D) (E)
30 (A) (B) (C) (D) (E)
31 (A) (B) (C) (D) (E)
32 (A) (B) (C) (D) (E)
33 (A) (B) (C) (D) (E)
34 (A) (B) (C) (D) (E)
35 (A) (B) (C) (D) (E)
36 (A) (B) (C) (D) (E)
37 (A) (B) (C) (D) (E)
38 (A) (B) (C) (D) (E)
39 (A) (B) (C) (D) (E)
40 (A) (B) (C) (D) (E)
41 (A) (B) (C) (D) (E)
42 (A) (B) (C) (D) (E)
43 (A) (B) (C) (D) (E)
44 (A) (B) (C) (D) (E)
45 (A) (B) (C) (D) (E)
46 (A) (B) (C) (D) (E)
47 (A) (B) (C) (D) (E)
48 (A) (B) (C) (D) (E)

For each question in this section, select the best answer from among the choices given, and fill in the corresponding circle on the answer sheet.

Directions

Each sentence below has one or two blanks, each blank indicating that something has been omitted. Beneath the sentence are five words or sets of words labeled A through E. Choose the word or set of words that, when inserted in the sentence, best fits the meaning of the sentence as a whole.

EXAMPLE:

Medieval kingdoms did not become constitutional republics overnight; on the contrary, the change was ----.

(A) unpopular　(B) unexpected
(C) advantageous　(D) sufficient　(E) gradual

Ⓐ Ⓑ Ⓒ Ⓓ ●

---

1. Criticism that tears down without suggesting areas of improvement is not ---- and should be avoided if possible.

    (A) representative　(B) constructive
    (C) mandatory　(D) pertinent　(E) sagacious

2. Although weeks remain for concessions to be made and for new approaches to be attempted, negotiations have reached such a state that management and union leaders are ---- that their differences can no longer be reconciled.

    (A) encouraged　(B) bewildered
    (C) apprehensive　(D) relieved　(E) skeptical

3. Although her early poetry was clearly ---- in nature, the critics thought she had promise and eventually would find her own voice.

    (A) conservative　(B) narrative　(C) melodious
    (D) derivative　(E) individual

4. The columnist was very gentle when she mentioned her friends, but she was bitter and even ---- when she discussed people who ---- her.

    (A) laconic..infuriated
    (B) acerbic..irritated
    (C) remorseful..encouraged
    (D) militant..distressed
    (E) stoical..alienated

5. A ---- cannot recognize any faults in his country, no matter how flagrant they may be.

    (A) zealot　(B) patriarch　(C) chauvinist
    (D) renegade　(E) vigilante

Directions

Each of the passages below precedes two questions based on its content. Answer the questions following each passage on the basis of what is stated or implied in that passage.

Questions 6 and 7 are based on the following passage.

Though the life story of the human species goes back a million years, there is no doubt that human beings came only recently to the Western
Line Hemisphere. None of the sites of aboriginal habi-
5　tation uncovered in North and South America compares in antiquity to Old World sites. Human occupation of the New World may date back several tens of thousands of years, but no one rationally argues that human life has been here
10　even 100,000 years.

6. The passage primarily functions to

    (A) challenge a prevailing hypothesis
    (B) present accepted scientific thinking
    (C) introduce a controversial theory
    (D) acknowledge a discovery
    (E) define a problem

7. The word "occupation" in line 7 most nearly means

    (A) inhabiting　(B) vocation　(C) subjugation
    (D) career　(E) exploitation

A man stood upon a railroad bridge in Northern Alabama, looking down into the swift waters
twenty feet below. The man's hands were behind
Line his back, the wrists bound with a cord. A rope
5 loosely encircled his neck. It was attached to a
stout cross-timber above his head, and the slack
fell to the level of his knees. Some loose boards
laid upon the sleepers supporting the metals of
the railway supplied a footing for him and his
10 executioners—two private soldiers of the Federal
army, directed by a sergeant, who in civil life may
have been a deputy sheriff.

8. This opening paragraph of a short story serves
primarily to

(A) reveal a character's personality
(B) describe a contemporary problem
(C) present two conflicting viewpoints
(D) establish a physical setting
(E) introduce an antiwar argument

9. The word "civil" in line 11 means

(A) polite   (B) individual   (C) legal
(D) collective   (E) nonmilitary

Directions

Each passage below is followed by questions based on
its content. Answer the questions following each passage on the basis of what is stated or implied in that
passage and in any introductory material that may be
provided.

Questions 10–15 are based on the following passage.

*In this excerpt from a book published in 1990, author
Mary Catherine Bateson introduces the concept of life
as a work in progress.*

This is a study of five artists engaged in that
act of creation that engages us all—the composition of our lives. Each of us has worked by impro-
Line visation, discovering the shape of our creation
5 along the way, rather than pursuing a vision
already defined.

In a stable society, composing a life is somewhat like throwing a pot or building a house in a
traditional form: the materials are known, the
10 hands move skillfully in tasks familiar from thousands of performances, the fit of the completed
whole in the common life is understood. Traditional styles of pottery or building are not usually
rigid; they respond to chance and allow a certain
15 scope for individual talent and innovation. But
the traditional craftsperson does not face the task
of solving every problem for the first time. In a
society like our own, we make a sharp contrast
between creativity and standardization, yet even
20 those who work on factory production lines must
craft their own lives, whether graceful and assured
or stunted and askew.

Today the materials and skills from which a
life is composed are no longer clear. It is no longer
25 possible to follow the paths of previous generations. This is true for both men and women, but it
is especially true for women, whose whole lives no
longer need to be dominated by the rhythms of
procreation and the dependencies that these
30 created, but who still must live with the disconti-
nuities of female biology and still must balance
conflicting demands. Our lives not only take new
directions; they are subject to repeated redirec-
tion, partly because of the extension of our years
35 of health and vitality. Just as the design of a building or of a vase must be rethought when the scale
is changed, so must the design of lives. Many of
the most basic concepts we use to construct a
sense of self or the design of a life have changed
40 their meanings: Work. Home. Love. Commitment.

When the choices and rhythms of lives
change, as they have in our time, the study of lives
becomes an increasing preoccupation. This is especially true now for women. Women today read
45 and write biographies to gain perspective on their
own lives. Each reading provokes a dialogue of
comparison and recognition, a process of memory
and articulation that makes one's own experience
available as a lens of empathy. We gain even more
50 from comparing notes and trying to understand
the choices of our friends. When one has matured
surrounded by implicit disparagement, the undis-
covered self is an unexpected resource. Self-
knowledge is empowering.

55 Nevertheless, there is a pattern deeply rooted
in myth and folklore that recurs in biography and
may create inappropriate expectations and blur
our ability to see the actual shape of lives. Much

GO ON TO NEXT PAGE ▶

biography of exceptional people is built around the image of a quest, a journey through a timeless landscape toward an end that is specific, even though it is not fully known. The pursuit of a quest is a pilgrim's progress in which it is essential to resist the transitory contentment of attractive way stations and side roads, in which obstacles are overcome because the goal is visible on the horizon, onward and upward. The end is already apparent in the beginning. The model of an ordinary successful life that is held up for young people is one of early decision and commitment, often to an educational preparation that launches a single rising trajectory. Ambition, we imply, should be focused, and young people worry about whether they are defining their goals and making the right decisions early enough to get on track. You go to medical school and this determines later alternatives, whether you choose prosperity in the suburbs or the more dramatic and exceptional life of discovery and dedication. Graduation is supposed to be followed by the first real job, representing a step on an ascending ladder. We don't expect long answers when we ask children what they want to be when they grow up, any more than we expect a list of names in response to questions about marriage; the real success stories are supposed to be permanent and monogamous.

These assumptions have not been valid for many of history's most creative people, and they are increasingly inappropriate today. The landscape through which we move is in constant flux. Children cannot even know the names of the jobs and careers that will be open to them; they must build their fantasies around temporary surrogates. Goals too clearly defined can become blinkers. Just as it is less and less possible to replicate the career of a parent, so it will become less and less possible to go on doing the same thing through a lifetime. In the same way, we will have to change our sense of the transitory and learn to see success in marriages that flourish for a time and then end. Increasingly, we will recognize the value in lifetimes of continual redefinition, following the Biblical injunction, "Whatsoever thy hand findeth to do, do it with thy might" (Ecclesiastes 9:10).

---

10. The primary function of the first paragraph (lines 1–6) is to

(A) point out the smallness of the author's chosen sample

(B) illustrate the complexity of the topic under discussion

(C) establish a context for the discussion to follow

(D) introduce the theme of artistic vision

(E) indicate the author's bias against stability

11. The word "throwing" in line 7 most nearly means

(A) tossing (B) warping (C) fashioning
(D) shattering (E) juggling

12. Which activity most resembles the task of crafting a life today as the author has come to view it?

(A) dissecting a laboratory specimen

(B) improvising a jazz piece

(C) writing a Shakespearean sonnet

(D) sculpting a bust from a block of marble

(E) baking a cake following a recipe

13. The word "scale" in line 36 most nearly means

(A) ascent (B) tone (C) decorative trim
(D) surface roughness (E) relative size

14. To those who envision life as a pilgrim's progress, "attractive way stations and side roads" (lines 64–65) are

(A) unattainable goals

(B) appropriate destinations

(C) harmful distractions

(D) unavoidable necessities

(E) ordinary variations

15. The author discusses the value in "lifetimes of continual redefinition" in terms that suggest that she

(A) regrets the necessity of such redefinition

(B) is unaware of the reluctance with which many people confront change

(C) would have preferred to live in a more settled time

(D) is eager to embrace new possibilities

(E) views herself as a conservative thinker

GO ON TO NEXT PAGE ▶

Questions 16–24 are based on the following passage.

The following excerpt is from "Eyes on the Prize," the companion guide to the public television series on America's civil rights struggle.

During the 1930's National Association for the Advancement of Colored People (NAACP) attorneys Charles H. Houston, William Hastie, James
Line M. Nabrit, Leon Ransom, and Thurgood Marshall
5 charted a legal strategy designed to end segregation in education. They developed a series of legal cases challenging segregation in graduate and professional schools. Houston believed that the battle against segregation had to begin at the highest
10 academic level in order to mitigate fear of race mixing that could create even greater hostility and reluctance on the part of white judges. After establishing a series of favorable legal precedents in higher education, NAACP attorneys planned to
15 launch an all-out attack on the separate-but-equal doctrine in primary and secondary schools. The strategy proved successful. In four major United States Supreme Court decisions precedents were established that would enable the NAACP to con-
20 struct a solid legal foundation upon which the Brown case could rest: *Missouri ex rel. Gaines* v. *Canada*, Registrar of the University of Missouri (1938); *Sipuel* v. *Board of Regents of the University of Oklahoma* (1948); *McLaurin* v. *Oklahoma*
25 *State Regents for Higher Education* (1950); and *Sweatt* v. *Painter* (1950).

In the Oklahoma case, the Supreme Court held that the plaintiff was entitled to enroll in the University. The Oklahoma Regents responded by
30 separating black and white students in cafeterias and classrooms. The 1950 McLaurin decision ruled that such internal separation was unconstitutional. In the Sweatt ruling, delivered on the same day, the Supreme Court held that the main-
35 tenance of separate law schools for whites and blacks was unconstitutional. A year after Herman Sweatt entered the University of Texas law school, desegregation cases were filed in the states of Kansas, South Carolina, Virginia, and Delaware,
40 and in the District of Columbia asking the courts to apply the qualitative test of the Sweatt case to the elementary and secondary schools and to declare the separate-but-equal doctrine invalid in the area of public education.
45 The 1954 *Brown* v. *Board of Education* decision declared that a classification based solely on race violated the 14th Amendment to the United States Constitution. The decision reversed the 1896 *Plessy* v. *Ferguson* ruling which had estab-
50 lished the separate-but-equal doctrine. The *Brown* decision more than any other case launched the

"equalitarian revolution" in American jurisprudence and signalled the emerging primacy of equality as a guide to constitutional decisions;
55 nevertheless, the decision did not end state sanctioned segregation. Indeed, the second *Brown* decision, known as *Brown II* and delivered a year later, played a decisive role in limiting the effectiveness and impact of the 1954 case by providing
60 southern states with the opportunity to delay the implementation of desegregation.

The intervention of the federal government and the deployment of the National Guard in the 1954 Little Rock crisis, and again in 1963 when
65 the enrollment of James Meredith desegregated the University of Mississippi, highlights the role of federal power in promoting social change during this era. While black local and national leaders organized and orchestrated the legal struggles, and
70 students joined in freedom rides and staged sit-ins, another equally important dimension of the rights quest took shape: the battle between federal and state authority and the evolution of the doctrine of federalism. The fact remains that the
75 United States Supreme Court lacked the power to enforce its decisions. President Dwight D. Eisenhower's use of federal troops in Little Rock was a major departure from the reluctance of past presidents to display federal power in the South,
80 especially to protect the lives and rights of black citizens.

Black Americans had joyfully applauded the *Brown* decision, equating it with the Emancipation Proclamation. White southerners, on the
85 other hand, almost universally denounced the ruling and even questioned the right of the Supreme Court to deliver such a blow to their way of life. It is possible to decipher two interlocking, mutually reinforcing strands in the southern reaction to
90 Brown: massive resistance and interposition.

Massive resistance assumed many forms. In hundreds of communities local businessmen and social and political leaders organized White Citizens' Councils to undermine black pressure for
95 desegregation of schools and civil rights. Council leaders employed economic sanctions, held rallies, and used intimidating rhetoric to instill fear in local blacks. Prominent southern politicians also demonstrated their displeasure.
100 An array of southern governors acquired national notoriety in their public displays of defiance to court-ordered desegregation of secondary schools and state universities. It was their obstinate adherence to the doctrine of interposition
105 which provoked the confrontation between state and federal authority. This doctrine holds that a state may reject a federal mandate it considers to

be an encroachment upon a state's rights. But this is only half of the explanation of how the confron-
110 tations originated, especially in the Meredith episode. The other half involves the protracted delays, futile negotiations, and considerable vacillation of the Kennedy administration before it finally began to act decisively to protect Meredith's
115 life and right to attend 'Ole Miss.'

---

16. According to the passage, Houston aimed his legislative challenge at the graduate and professional school level on the basis of the assumption that

(A) the greatest inequities existed at the highest academic and professional levels

(B) the separate-but-equal doctrine applied solely to the highest academic levels

(C) there were clear precedents for reform in existence at the graduate school level

(D) the judiciary would feel less apprehensive about desegregation on the graduate level

(E) the consequences of desegregation would become immediately apparent at the graduate school level

17. The word "decision" in line 31 means

(A) firmness   (B) settlement   (C) ruling
(D) perseverance   (E) litigation

18. The passage suggests that the reaction of the Oklahoma Regents to the 1948 *Sipuel* decision was one of

(A) resigned tolerance

(B) avowed uncertainty

(C) moderate amusement

(D) distinct displeasure

(E) unquestioning approbation

19. The word "maintenance" in line 34 means

(A) repair   (B) livelihood   (C) firm assertion
(D) ongoing support   (E) continuity

20. Which of the following best describes the relationship between the *McLaurin* decision and the 1954 *Brown* v. *Board of Education* decision?

(A) The *McLaurin* decision superseded the *Brown* decision.

(B) The *Brown* decision provided a precedent for the *McLaurin* decision.

(C) The *Brown* decision reversed the *McLaurin* decision.

(D) The *McLaurin* decision limited the application of the *Brown* decision.

(E) The *McLaurin* decision provided legal authority for the *Brown* decision.

21. In line 91, the word "assumed" most nearly means

(A) took for granted

(B) adopted

(C) feigned

(D) seized

(E) broke down

22. Which of the following titles best describes the content of the passage?

(A) Executive Intervention in the Fight Against Segregated Education

(B) The *Brown* Decision and the Equalitarian Revolution

(C) A Long War: The Struggle to Desegregate American Education

(D) The Emergence of Federalism and the Civil Rights Movement

(E) Education Reform and the Role of the NAACP

23. The aspect of Houston's work most clearly brought out in the passage is its

(A) psychological canniness

(B) judicial complexity

(C) fundamental efficiency

(D) radical intellectualism

(E) exaggerated idealism

24. The passage's attitude toward the Kennedy administration's initial handling of the Meredith case is one of

(A) grudging respect

(B) unmitigated disdain

(C) qualified forbearance

(D) marked ambivalence

(E) futile regret

IF YOU FINISH IN LESS THAN 25 MINUTES, YOU MAY CHECK YOUR WORK ON THIS SECTION ONLY. DO NOT TURN TO ANY OTHER SECTION IN THE TEST.

STOP

Multiple-Choice Directions

For each question in this section, determine which of the five choices is correct, and blacken that choice on your answer sheet. You may use any blank space on the page for your work.

NOTES:
- You may use a calculator whenever you believe it will be helpful.
- Use the diagrams provided to help you solve the problems. Unless you see the phrase
  <u>Note:</u> Figure not drawn to scale

under a diagram, it has been drawn as accurately as possible. Unless it is stated that a figure is three dimensional, you may assume that it lies in a plane.

Reference

$A = \pi r^2$
$C = 2\pi r$ $A = \ell w$ $A = \frac{1}{2}bh$ $V = \ell wh$ $V = \pi r^2 h$ $c^2 = a^2 + b^2$ **Special Right Triangles**

Number of degrees in a circle: 360
Sum of the measures, in degrees, of the three angles of a triangle: 180

1. If $4x + 8x + 12x = -24$, then $x =$
   (A) -1 (B) $-\frac{1}{2}$ (C) 0 (D) $\frac{1}{2}$ (E) 1

2. What is 20% of 20% of 20?
   (A) .08   (B) .2   (C) .8   (D) 2.0   (E) 8.0

3. If $7 - (7 - m) = 7$, then $m =$
   (A) -14 (B) -7 (C) 0 (D) 7 (E) 14

4. In the figure above, what is the average of a, b, c, and d?
   (A) 60   (B) 70   (C) 80   (D) 90
   (E) It cannot be determined from the information given.

5. For all positive numbers c and d, the operation * is defined by $c * d = \sqrt{cd}$. If $n > 1$, what does $n * \frac{1}{n}$ equal?
   (A) n (B) n^2 (C) $\frac{1}{n}$ (D) $\frac{1}{n^2}$ (E) 1

6. What is the area of a square whose diagonal is d?
   (A) $d\sqrt{2}$ (B) $2d$ (C) $\frac{d^2}{2}$ (D) d^2 (E) $2d^2$

7. Maryline was a years old b years ago. How old will she be in c years?
   (A) $a + b + c$ (B) $a - b + c$ (C) $c - a - b$
   (D) $b - a + c$ (E) $a - b - c$

Year	1994	1995	1996	1997	1998	1999
Number	4	5	10	6	9	12

8. The table above shows the number of races that Nicholas entered each year from 1994 to 1999. In what year did he enter 50% more races than the year before?
   (A) 1995   (B) 1996   (C) 1997
   (D) 1998   (E) 1999

9. If the average (arithmetic mean) of the measures of two angles of a quadrilateral is 90°, what is the average of the measures of the other two angles?
   (A) 45°   (B) 90°   (C) 120°
   (D) 180°   (E) 240°

10. Twenty workers were sharing equally the cost of a present for their supervisor. When 4 of the workers decided not to contribute, each of the others had to pay $1.50 more. How much, in dollars, did the present cost?
   (A) 50   (B) 80   (C) 100   (D) 120   (E) 150

GO ON TO NEXT PAGE ▶

11. Camille planted $\frac{3}{5}$ of the flowers she bought in 3.2 hours. At this rate, how many more <u>minutes</u> will she need to finish planting the flowers?

(A) $2\frac{2}{15}$　(B) $76\frac{4}{5}$　(C) 128

(D) 192　(E) 320

12. If n is an even integer, what is the sum of the smallest even integer greater than $n + 6$ and the largest even integer less than $n + 9$?

(A) $2n + 13$　(B) $2n + 14$　(C) $2n + 15$
(D) $2n + 16$　(E) $2n + 17$

13. If it is now September, what month will it be 710 months from now?

(A) April　(B) June　(C) September
(D) November　(E) December

14. What is the value of a if a is positive and $(a)(a)(a) = a + a + a$?

(A) $\frac{1}{3}$　(B) $\sqrt{3}$　(C) 3　(D) $3\sqrt{3}$　(E) 9

15. In the figure above, $w + x + y + z =$

(A) 130　(B) 180　(C) 260　(D) 360
(E) It cannot be determined from the information given.

16. If p pretzels cost c cents, how many pretzels can be bought for d dollars?

(A) cdp　(B) $100cdp$　(C) $\frac{dp}{100c}$
(D) $\frac{100cd}{p}$　(E) $\frac{100dp}{c}$

17. Eddie's Electronics sells three models of cellular phones, priced at $100, $125, and $225. In January 1999, the store sold exactly the same number of each model. What percent of the total income from the sales of cellular phones was attributable to sales of the cheapest model?

(A) $22\frac{2}{9}\%$　(B) $28\frac{4}{7}\%$　(C) $33\frac{1}{3}\%$　(D) $44\frac{4}{9}\%$
(E) It cannot be determined from the information given.

18. If $f(x) = x^{\frac{1}{2}} + x^{\frac{1}{4}}$, what is the value of $f(16)$?

(A) 6　(B) 8　(C) 12　(D) 32　(E) 64

19. A school has 100 varsity athletes: 40 boys and 60 girls, of whom 30 are juniors and 70 are seniors. If 15 junior girls are varsity athletes, how many senior boys are varsity athletes?

(A) 5　(B) 10　(C) 15　(D) 20　(E) 25

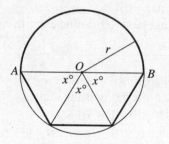

20. In the figure above, if AB is a diameter, what is the perimeter of the region outlined in black?

(A) $r(\pi + 3)$　(B) $r(2\pi + 3)$
(C) $r(\pi + 3\sqrt{2})$　(D) $r(\pi + 3\sqrt{3})$
(E) It cannot be determined from the information given.

IF YOU FINISH IN LESS THAN 25 MINUTES, YOU MAY CHECK YOUR WORK ON THIS SECTION ONLY. DO NOT TURN TO ANY OTHER SECTION IN THE TEST.

STOP

For each question in this section, select the best answer from among the choices given and fill in the corresponding circle on the answer sheet.

Directions

Each sentence below has one or two blanks, each blank indicating that something has been omitted. Beneath the sentence are five words or sets of words labeled A through E. Choose the word or set of words that, when inserted in the sentence, best fits the meaning of the sentence as a whole.

EXAMPLE:

Medieval kingdoms did not become constitutional republics overnight; on the contrary, the change was ----.

(A) unpopular   (B) unexpected
(C) advantageous   (D) sufficient   (E) gradual

Ⓐ Ⓑ Ⓒ Ⓓ ●

---

25. The wicked queen was filled with ---- delight when she gazed on the poisoned apple with which she planned to kill Snow White.

(A) malicious   (B) innocent   (C) muted
(D) ravenous   (E) heartwarming

26. Though editors often recommend major alterations in first novels, Hemingway's editors suggested he make only ---- changes in his manuscript.

(A) naturalistic   (B) minute   (C) ambiguous
(D) ineffective   (E) unexpected

27. Later movie choreographers, finding Busby Berkeley's musical spectacles ----, sought ---- ways to bring music and dance to film.

(A) outdated..fresh
(B) enjoyable..different
(C) dazzling..tiresome
(D) hackneyed..trite
(E) contrived..affected

28. Many educators believe that, far from being a temporary stopgap, useful only as a transitional measure, bilingual education has proved to have definite ---- education in any one tongue.

(A) correlations with
(B) advantages over
(C) connotations for
(D) limitations on
(E) influence on

29. In a time of general architectural simplicity and minimalism, the ornate new civic center was ---- for its flamboyance.

(A) representative   (B) contemptible
(C) conspicuous   (D) definitive
(E) conventional

30. Like the theory of evolution, the big-bang model of the universe's formation has undergone modification and ---- but it has ---- all serious challenges.

(A) alteration..confirmed
(B) refinement..resisted
(C) transformation..ignored
(D) evaluation..acknowledged
(E) refutation..misdirected

31. Unable to ---- her wholehearted distaste for media events and unnecessary publicity, Dean Brower continued to make ---- comments throughout the entire ceremony.

(A) control..garbled
(B) maintain..copious
(C) conceal..effusive
(D) disguise..caustic
(E) express..vitriolic

32. The term "rare earths" is in fact a ----, for, paradoxically, the rare-earth elements are in actuality ----, being present in low concentration in virtually all minerals.

(A) truism..essential
(B) misnomer..ubiquitous
(C) disclaimer..ephemeral
(D) metaphor..figurative
(E) mnemonic..unmemorable

GO ON TO NEXT PAGE ▶

Each of the passages below precedes two questions based on its content. Answer the questions following each passage on the basis of what is stated or implied in that passage.

Questions 33 and 34 are based on the following passage.

The curtain rises; the Cardinal and Daniel de Bosola enter from the right. In appearance, the Cardinal is something between an El Greco
Line cardinal and a Van Dyke noble lord. He has the
5 tall, spare form—the elongated hands and features—of the former; the trim pointed beard, the imperial repose, the commanding authority of the latter. But the El Greco features are not really those of asceticism or inner mystic spirituality.
10 They are the index to a cold, refined but ruthless cruelty in a highly civilized controlled form. Neither is the imperial repose an aloof mood of proud detachment. It is a refined expression of satanic pride of place and talent.

33. The word "spare" in line 5 most nearly means

(A) excessive (B) superfluous (C) pardonable
(D) lean (E) inadequate

34. The "satanic pride of place" referred to in lines 13–14 most directly represents

(A) the cardinal's love for his cathedral
(B) the splendor of the ecclesiastic residence
(C) an urge to seek sanctuary from the forces of evil
(D) the cardinal's pact with the devil
(E) the cardinal's delight in his worldly rank

Questions 35 and 36 are based on the following passage.

Among the Plains Indians, two separate strains of decorative art evolved: the figurative, representational art created by the men of the
Line tribe, and the geometric, abstract art crafted by
5 the women. According to Dunn and Highwater, the artist's sex governed both the kind of article to be decorated and the style to be followed in its ornamentation. Thus, the decorative works created by tribesmen consistently depict living
10 creatures (men, horses, buffaloes) or magical beings (ghosts and other supernatural lifeforms). Those created by women, however, are clearly nonrepresentational: no figures of men or animals appear in this classically geometric art.

35. The word "strains" (line 2) most nearly means

(A) tunes (B) pressures (C) varieties
(D) injuries (E) pressures

36. Which of the following titles best summarizes the content of the passage?

(A) The Ongoing Influence of Plains Indian Art
(B) Male and Female in Tribal Life
(C) Indian Art and Abstract Expressionism
(D) Design Specialization in Plains Art
(E) The History of Indian Representational Art

The passages below are followed by questions on their content; questions following a pair of related passages may also be based on the relationship between the paired passages. Answer the questions on the basis of what is stated or implied in the passages and in any introductory material that may be provided.

Questions 37–48 are based on the following passages.

The following passages are excerpted from popular studies of dolphins.

Passage 1

Most of the intelligent land animals have prehensile, grasping organs for exploring their environment—hands in human beings and their
Line anthropoid relatives, the sensitive inquiring trunk
5 in the elephant. One of the surprising things about the dolphin is that his superior brain is unaccompanied by any type of manipulative organ. He has, however, a remarkable range-finding ability involving some sort of echo-sounding. Perhaps
10 this acute sense—far more accurate than any that human ingenuity has been able to devise artificially—brings him greater knowledge of his watery surroundings than might at first seem possible. Human beings think of intelligence as
15 geared to things. The hand and the tool are to us the unconscious symbols of our intellectual attainment. It is difficult for us to visualize another kind of lonely, almost disembodied intelligence floating in the wavering green fairyland of the
20 sea—an intelligence possibly near or comparable

GO ON TO NEXT PAGE ▶

to our own but without hands to build, to transmit knowledge by writing, or to alter by one hairsbreadth the planet's surface. Yet at the same time there are indications that this is a warm, friendly,
25 and eager intelligence quite capable of coming to the assistance of injured companions and striving to rescue them from drowning. Dolphins left the land when mammalian brains were still small and primitive. Without the stimulus provided by agile
30 exploring fingers, these great sea mammals have yet taken a divergent road toward intelligence of a high order. Hidden in their sleek bodies is an impressively elaborated instrument, the reason for whose appearance is a complete enigma. It is as
35 though both the human being and the dolphin were each part of some great eye which yearned to look both outward on eternity and inward to the sea's heart—that fertile entity like the mind in its swarming and grotesque life.

Passage 2

40   Nothing about dolphins has been more widely or passionately discussed over the centuries than their supposed intelligence and communicative abilities. In fact, a persistent dogma holds that dolphins are among the most intelligent of animals
45 and that they communicate with one another in complex ways. Implicit in this argument is the belief that dolphin cultures are at least as ancient and rich as our own.

To support the claim of high intelligence
50 amongst dolphins, proponents note that they have large brains, live in societies marked as much by co-operative as by competitive interactions and rapidly learn the artificial tasks given to them in captivity. Indeed, dolphins are clearly capable of
55 learning through observation and have good memories. People who spend time with captive dolphins are invariably impressed by their sense of humor, playfulness, quick comprehension of body language, command of situations, mental agility,
60 and emotional resilience. Individual dolphins have distinctive personalities and trainers often speak of being trained by their subjects, rather than the other way round.

The extremely varied repertoires of sounds
65 made by dolphins are often invoked as *prima facie* evidence of advanced communication abilities. In addition, some "scientific" experiments done by John Lilly and his associates during the 1950s and

1960s were claimed to show that dolphins
70 communicate not only with one another but also with humans, mimicking human speech and reaching out across the boundaries that divide us.

These conclusions about dolphin intelligence and communication have not withstood critical
75 scrutiny. While they have fueled romantic speculation, their net impact has been to mislead. Rather than allowing dolphins to be discovered and appreciated for what they are, Lilly's vision has forced us to measure these animals' value accord-
80 ing to how close they come to equalling or exceeding our own intelligence, virtue, and spiritual development.

The issues of dolphin intelligence and communication have been inseparable in most
85 people's minds, and the presumed existence of one has been taken as proof of the other, a classic case of begging the question. Not surprisingly then, most experiments to evaluate dolphin intelligence have measured the animals' capacity for cognitive
90 processing as exhibited in their understanding of the rudiments of language.

From the early work of researchers like Dwight Batteau and Jarvis Bastian through the more recent work of Louis Herman and associates,
95 dolphins have been asked to accept simple information, in the form of acoustic or visual symbols representing verbs and nouns, and then to act on the information following a set of commands from the experimenter.

100   The widely publicized results have been somewhat disappointing. Although they have demonstrated that dolphins do have the primary skills necessary to support understanding and use of a language, they have not distinguished the
105 dolphins from other animals in this respect. For example, some seals, animals we do not normally cite as members of the intellectual or communicative elite, have been found to have the same basic capabilities.

110   What, then, do the results of experiments to date mean? Either we have not devised adequate tests to permit us to detect, measure, and rank intelligence as a measure of a given species' ability to communicate, or we must acknowledge that the
115 characteristics which we regard as rudimentary evidence of intelligence are held more commonly by many "lower" animals than we previously thought.

GO ON TO NEXT PAGE ▶

37. According to Passage 1, which of the following statements about dolphins is true?

    (A) They have always been water-dwelling creatures.
    (B) They at one time possessed prehensile organs.
    (C) They lived on land in prehistoric times.
    (D) Their brains are no longer mammalian in nature.
    (E) They developed brains to compensate for the lack of a prehensile organ.

38. The author of Passage 1 suggests that human failure to understand the intelligence of the dolphin is due to

    (A) the inadequacy of human range-finding equipment
    (B) a lack of knowledge about the sea
    (C) the want of a common language
    (D) the primitive origins of the human brain
    (E) the human inclination to judge other life by our own

39. In Passage 1, the author's primary purpose is apparently to

    (A) examine the dolphin's potential for surpassing humankind
    (B) question the need for prehensile organs in human development
    (C) refute the theory that dolphins are unable to alter their physical environment
    (D) reassess the nature and extent of dolphin intelligence
    (E) indicate the superiority of human intelligence over that of the dolphin

40. The word "acute" in line 10 means

    (A) excruciating (B) severe (C) keen
    (D) sudden and intense (E) brief in duration

41. The "impressively elaborated instrument" referred to in lines 32–33 is best interpreted to mean which of the following?

    (A) a concealed manipulative organ
    (B) an artificial range-finding device
    (C) a complex, intelligent brain
    (D) the dolphin's hidden eye
    (E) an apparatus for producing musical sounds

42. According to the author's simile in lines 38–39, the human mind and the heart of the sea are alike in that both

    (A) teem with exotic forms of life
    (B) argue in support of intelligence
    (C) are necessary to the evolution of dolphins
    (D) are directed outward
    (E) share a penchant for the grotesque

43. Which of the following best characterizes the tone of Passage 1?

    (A) restrained skepticism
    (B) pedantic assertion
    (C) wondering admiration
    (D) amused condescension
    (E) ironic speculation

44. The author of Passage 2 puts quotation marks around the word *scientific* in line 67 to indicate he

    (A) is faithfully reproducing Lilly's own words
    (B) intends to define the word later in the passage
    (C) believes the reader is unfamiliar with the word as used by Lilly
    (D) advocates adhering to the scientific method in all experiments
    (E) has some doubts as to how scientific those experiments were

45. The author of Passage 2 maintains that the writings of Lilly and his associates have

    (A) overstated the extent of dolphin intelligence
    (B) been inadequately scrutinized by critics
    (C) measured the worth of the dolphin family
    (D) underrated dolphins as intelligent beings
    (E) established criteria for evaluating dolphin intelligence

46. By calling the argument summarized in lines 83–87 a classic case of begging the question, the author of Passage 2 indicates he views it with

    (A) trepidation (B) optimism (C) detachment
    (D) skepticism (E) credulity

47. Which of the following would most undercut the studies on which the author bases his conclusion in lines 110–118?

    (A) evidence proving dolphin linguistic abilities to be far superior to those of other mammals
    (B) an article recording attempts by seals and walruses to communicate with human beings
    (C) the reorganization of current intelligence tests by species and level of difficulty
    (D) a reassessment of the definition of the term "lower animals"
    (E) the establishment of a project to develop new tests to detect intelligence in animals

48. The author of Passage 2 would find Passage 1

    (A) typical of the attitudes of Lilly and his associates
    (B) remarkable for the perspective it offers
    (C) indicative of the richness of dolphin culture
    (D) supportive of his fundamental point of view
    (E) intriguing for its far-reaching conclusions

IF YOU FINISH IN LESS THAN 25 MINUTES, YOU MAY CHECK YOUR WORK ON THIS SECTION ONLY. DO NOT TURN TO ANY OTHER SECTION IN THE TEST.

STOP

Multiple-Choice Directions

For questions 21–28, determine which of the five choices is correct. You may use any blank space on the page for your work.

NOTES:
- You may use a calculator whenever you believe it will be helpful.
- Use the diagrams provided to help you solve the problems. Unless you see the phrase

<u>Note:</u> Figure not drawn to scale

under a diagram, it has been drawn as accurately as possible. Unless it is stated that a figure is three dimensional, you may assume that it lies in a plane.

Reference

$A = \pi r^2$
$C = 2\pi r$ $A = \ell w$ $A = \frac{1}{2}bh$ $V = \ell wh$ $V = \pi r^2 h$ $c^2 = a^2 + b^2$ **Special Right Triangles**

Number of degrees in a circle: 360
Sum of the measures, in degrees, of the three angles of a triangle: 180

---

21. If $a = -2$, what is the value of $a^4 + a^3 + a^2 + a$?

(A) -30 (B) -10 (C) 0   (D) 10   (E) 30

<u>Questions 22 and 23</u> refer to the information in the following table, which shows the number of members in each of five clubs at James Madison High School and, for each club, the number of members who are seniors.

Club	Number of Members	Number of Seniors
A	20	5
B	30	7
C	23	5
D	27	6
E	25	6

22. What is the average (arithmetic mean) number of members per club?

(A) 23   (B) 24   (C) 24.5   (D) 25   (E) 26

23. Which club has the highest percent of members who are seniors?

(A) A   (B) B   (C) C   (D) D   (E) E

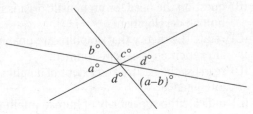

<u>Note:</u> Figure not drawn to scale

24 In the figure above, what is the value of b?

(A) 30   (B) 36   (C) 45   (D) 60   (E) 72

25. A rectangle is three times as long as it is wide. If the width is a, what is the length of a diagonal?

(A) $a\sqrt{3}$ (B) $a\sqrt{5}$ (C) $a\sqrt{10}$
(D) $5a$ (E) $10a$

Note: Figure not drawn to scale

26. In the figure above, O is the center of a circle whose radius is 12. If the length of arc PQR is 3π, what is the measure of $\angle POR$?

(A) 30° (B) 45° (C) 60° (D) 75° (E) 90°

27. If $\sqrt{x+1} + 3 = 5$, what is the value of x?

(A) 2 (B) 3 (C) 5 (D) 63 (E) There is no value of x that satisfies the given equation.

28. In the figure above, a small circle is drawn inside a larger circle. If the shaded area and unshaded area are equal, what is the ratio of the radius of the large circle to the radius of the small circle?

(A) $\frac{\sqrt{2}}{1}$ (B) $\frac{2}{1}$ (C) $\frac{2\sqrt{2}}{1}$ (D) $\frac{2}{\sqrt{2}-1}$

(E) It cannot be determined from the information given.

In questions 29–38, first solve the problem, and then enter your answer on the grid provided on the answer sheet. The instructions for entering your answers follow.

- First, write your answer in the boxes at the top of the grid.
- Second, grid your answer in the columns below the boxes.
- Use the fraction bar in the first row or the decimal point in the second row to enter fractions and decimals.

Answer: $\frac{8}{15}$ Answer: 1.75   Answer: 100

Write your answer in the boxes

Grid-in your answer

Either position is acceptable

- Grid only one space in each column.
- Entering the answer in the boxes is recommended as an aid in gridding but is not required.
- The machine scoring your exam can read only what you grid, so you **must grid-in your answers correctly to get credit.**
- If a question has more than one correct answer, grid-in only one of them.
- The grid does not have a minus sign; so no answer can be negative.
- A mixed number *must* be converted to an improper fraction or a decimal before it is gridded. Enter $1\frac{1}{4}$ as $\frac{5}{4}$ or 1.25; the machine will interpret 11/4 as $\frac{11}{4}$ and mark it wrong.

- **All decimals must be entered as accurately as possible.** Here are three acceptable ways of gridding

$$\frac{3}{11} = 0.272727\ldots$$

- Note that rounding to .273 is acceptable because you are using the full grid, but you would receive **no credit** for .3 or .27, because they are less accurate.

29. What is the area, in square inches, of a rectangle whose perimeter is 80 inches and whose width is 8 inches?

30. If $3^n = 81$, what is the value of 4^n?

31. If the average (arithmetic mean) of x, y, and 10 is 50, what is the average of x and y?

32. What is the area of a right triangle if the lengths of its two longest sides are 24 and 30?

33. What number when divided by 13 has a quotient of 11 and a remainder of 11?

34. Line k passes through the origin and the point $(2, y)$, where $3 < y < 4$. What is one possible value for the slope of line k?

35. If y varies inversely with x, and $y = 8$ when $x = 4$, what is the value of y when $x = 5$?

36. Each integer from 1 to 50 whose units digit is a 3 is written on a separate slip of paper. If the slips are placed in a box and one is chosen at random, what is the probability that the number chosen is prime?

37. Justin was 28 years old in 1997, when his son, Lior, was born. In what year will Justin be exactly three times as old as Lior?

38. What is the units digit of 7^{30}?

IF YOU FINISH IN LESS THAN 25 MINUTES, YOU MAY CHECK YOUR WORK ON THIS SECTION ONLY. DO NOT TURN TO ANY OTHER SECTION IN THE TEST.

STOP

Improving Sentence Directions

Some or all parts of the following sentences are underlined. The first answer choice, (A), simply repeats the underlined part of the sentence. The other four choices present four alternative ways to phrase the underlined part. Select the answer that produces the most effective sentence, one that is clear and exact, and blacken the appropriate space on your answer sheet. In selecting your choice, be sure that it is standard written English and that it expresses the meaning of the original sentence.

EXAMPLE:

The first biography of author Eudora Welty came out in 1998, <u>and she was eighty-nine years old at the time.</u>

(A) and she was eighty-nine years old at the time
(B) at the time when she was eighty-nine
(C) upon becoming an eighty-nine year old
(D) when she was eighty-nine
(E) at the age of eighty-nine years old

SAMPLE ANSWER:

Ⓐ Ⓑ Ⓒ ● Ⓔ

---

1. We are more concerned that the best possible candidate be hired <u>than that bureaucratic affirmative action rules be followed</u> to the letter.

    (A) than that bureaucratic affirmative action rules be followed
    (B) and not about following bureaucratic affirmative action rules
    (C) than that one should follow bureaucratic affirmative action rules
    (D) than your following bureaucratic affirmative action rules
    (E) and not in any bureaucratic affirmative action rules being followed

2. <u>By the government failing to keep its pledges</u> will earn the distrust of all other nations in the alliance.

    (A) By the government failing to keep its pledges
    (B) Because the government failed to keep its pledges
    (C) Since the government has failed to keep its pledges
    (D) Failing to keep its government pledges
    (E) If the government fails to keep its pledges, it

3. <u>Although I calculate that he will be here</u> any minute, I cannot wait much longer for him to arrive.

    (A) Although I calculate that he will be here
    (B) Although I reckon that he will be here
    (C) Because I calculate that he will be here
    (D) Although I am confident that he will be here
    (E) Because I am confident that he will be here

4. Bernard Malamud was a forty-year-old college professor in <u>Oregon and his short story "The Magic Barrel"</u> was published in *The Partisan Review*.

    (A) Oregon and his short story "The Magic Barrel"
    (B) Oregon, his short story "The Magic Barrel"
    (C) Oregon; his short story "The Magic Barrel"
    (D) Oregon when his short story "The Magic Barrel"
    (E) Oregon, furthermore, his short story "The Magic Barrel"

5. <u>Being as how a dangerous cloud of radiation was released</u> at the Chernobyl nuclear plant, that accident can be considered the most serious in the history of nuclear energy.

    (A) Being as how a dangerous cloud of radiation was released
    (B) Because a dangerous cloud of radiation was released
    (C) Due to the release of a dangerous cloud of radiation
    (D) In addition to a dangerous cloud of radiation being released
    (E) Releasing a dangerous cloud of radiation

6. In keeping with the hallowed Cuban tradition of putting on a show to impress the visitors, <u>the capital being painted and festooned</u> with banners and portraits of Castro, Marx, and Lenin.

    (A) the capital being painted and festooned
    (B) the capital been painted and festooned
    (C) the capital painted and being festooned
    (D) the capital's painting and festooning
    (E) the capital has been painted and festooned

GO ON TO NEXT PAGE ▶

7. Employers have begun to provide health club facilities for their employees because exercise builds stamina, <u>decreases tension, and absenteeism is reduced.</u>

   (A) decreases tension, and absenteeism is reduced
   (B) tension is decreased, and absenteeism is reduced
   (C) decreases tension, and reducing absenteeism
   (D) decreases tension, and reduces absenteeism
   (E) decreasing tension, and absenteeism is reduced

8. <u>She not only was competent but also friendly</u> in nature.

   (A) She not only was competent but also friendly
   (B) She not was only competent but friendly also
   (C) She not only was competent but friendly also
   (D) She was not only competent but also friendly
   (E) She was not only was competent but friendly also

9. The dean informed us that the <u>applicant had not and never will be accepted by the college because of his high school record.</u>

   (A) applicant had not and never will be accepted by the college because of his high school record
   (B) applicant had not and never would be accepted by the college because of his high school record
   (C) applicant had not been and never will be accepted by the college because of his high school record
   (D) applicant had not and never could be accepted by the college because of his high school record
   (E) applicant had not been and never would be accepted by the college because of his high school record

10. Numerous American industries have lost sales to foreign <u>imports, in addition to which, to regain profits</u>, some companies have merged with foreign plants.

    (A) imports, in addition to which, to regain profits
    (B) imports; to regain profits
    (C) imports; as a result, to regain profits
    (D) imports, to regain profits
    (E) imports, yet to regain profits

11. New York City hosted a four-day extravaganza for the Statue of Liberty during the July 4, 1986 <u>weekend; the purpose being to celebrate</u> Miss Liberty's one hundredth birthday.

    (A) weekend; the purpose being to celebrate
    (B) weekend because of celebrating
    (C) weekend, the purpose being to celebrate
    (D) weekend to celebrate
    (E) weekend; for the purpose of celebrating

12. For scientist Barbara McClintock, <u>being free to pursue her own research was more important</u> than being widely acclaimed.

    (A) being free to pursue her own research was more important
    (B) the importance of being free to pursue her own research was greater
    (C) having freedom in pursuing research was more important
    (D) to have the freedom to pursue her own research was more important
    (E) freedom to pursue her own research had greater importance

13. The scouts were told <u>to take an overnight hike, pitch camp, prepare dinner, and that they should be in bed by 9 P.M.</u>

    (A) to take an overnight hike, pitch camp, prepare dinner, and that they should be in bed by 9 P.M.
    (B) to take an overnight hike, pitch camp, prepare dinner, and that they should go to bed by 9 P.M.
    (C) to take an overnight hike, pitch camp, prepare dinner, and be in bed by 9 P.M.
    (D) to take an overnight hike, pitch camp, prepare dinner, and going to bed by 9 P.M.
    (E) to engage in an overnight hike, pitch camp, prepare dinner, and that they should be in bed by 9 P.M.

14. <u>We want the teacher to be the one</u> who has the best rapport with the students.

    (A) We want the teacher to be the one
    (B) We want the teacher to be he
    (C) We want him to be the teacher
    (D) We desire that the teacher to be him
    (E) We anticipate that the teacher will be him

GO ON TO NEXT PAGE ▶

15. The layer of ozone in the earth's upper atmosphere, which protects life from harmful ultraviolet radiation but which has been damaged by artificial chemicals, may take a decade or two longer to recover than previously thought.

(A) radiation but which has been damaged by artificial chemicals, may take a decade or two longer to recover than previously thought

(B) radiation, which however has been damaged by artificial chemicals, it may take a decade or two longer to recover than previously thought

(C) radiation but which has been damaged by artificial chemicals, may take a decade or two longer to recover than they have been previously thought

(D) radiation but which have been damaged by artificial chemicals, they may take a decade or two longer for recovery than previously thought

(E) radiation, may take a decade or two longer to recover than previously thought because of the artificial chemicals having been damaging to it

16. Analysts expect the economy of Japan to grow faster than Europe during the coming year.

(A) Japan to grow faster than Europe during the coming year

(B) Japan will have grown faster than Europe during the year to come

(C) Japan to be growing faster than Europe during the coming year

(D) Japan to grow faster than Europe's during the coming year

(E) Japan to grow more fast than Europe's during the coming year

17. A pariah is when someone is being avoided by others and then he is cast out by society.

(A) A pariah is when someone is being avoided by others and then he is cast out by society.

(B) A pariah is a person avoided by others, someone cast out by society.

(C) A pariah is being avoided by others and then he is cast out by society.

(D) A pariah is where someone avoided by others then is cast out by society.

(E) A pariah is when someone has been avoided by others and then he is cast out by society.

18. Insofar as so many California condors were killed by hunters, the survival of the species was threatened.

(A) Insofar as so many California condors were killed by hunters, the survival of

(B) Insofar as so many California condors had been killed by hunters, the survival of

(C) Insofar as hunters killed so many California condors, the survival as

(D) Because so many California condors were killed by hunters, the survival of

(E) Insofar as so many California condors were killed by hunters, their survival as

19. Publishing, it is said, is one of the few businesses where a company makes bigger headlines for how much money it spends than for how much money it takes in.

(A) businesses where a company makes bigger headlines for how much money it spends than for how much money it takes in

(B) businesses where a company's spending makes bigger headlines than however much of money it can take in

(C) businesses where companies make bigger headlines for how much money they spending than they do for how much money they taking in

(D) businesses at which a company makes bigger headlines for how much money it spends than for how much its intake is

(E) businesses where a company makes even bigger headlines for how much money it spends than how much money it takes in

20. In spite of their robber baron reputations, John D. Rockefeller and Henry Ford deserving of acclaim for having endowed major philanthropic organizations.

(A) Ford deserving of acclaim for having endowed

(B) Ford deserving acclaim for having endowed

(C) Ford deserve acclaim for having endowed

(D) Ford deserve of acclaim because endowing

(E) Ford deserving acclaim, both endowed

21. Please help <u>me</u> decide <u>which</u> of the two activities
          A   B

    to choose—going to the theater with John <u>or</u>
                                 C

    <u>to attend</u> tonight's dinner-dance at the hotel.
      D

    <u>No error</u>
      E

22. When I <u>have to decide</u> <u>which</u> of two applicants for
          A   B

    a job to hire, I find <u>myself</u> giving the position to
                   C

    the one who uses the <u>best</u> English. <u>No error</u>
                 D   E

23. <u>Because</u> I was seated on the dais <u>just</u> <u>in back of</u>
    A   B   C

    the speaker, I could see the audience's

    <u>reaction to</u> his vituperative remarks. <u>No error</u>
      D   E

24. A complete system <u>of</u> checks and balances
                A

    <u>have been incorporated</u> in <u>our</u> Constitution
          B   C

    to protect the <u>principle</u> of equality. <u>No error</u>
             D   E

25. Dr. Martin Luther King, <u>who</u> <u>led</u> a bus boycott
                    A   B

    to eliminate bus segregation, will be

    <u>forever remembered</u> for <u>his</u> speech "I Have a
          C   D

    Dream." <u>No error</u>
          E

26. <u>As a result of</u> the bad weather, she is the <u>only</u> one
    A   B

    of my friends <u>who</u> <u>plan</u> to attend the graduation
             C   D

    exercises. <u>No error</u>
          E

27. During the recent gasoline shortage, the
    A

    <u>amount of</u> accidents on our highways <u>decreased</u>
      B   C

    <u>markedly</u>. <u>No error</u>
      D   E

28. <u>Having secured</u> the ball on a fumble, <u>we</u> <u>took</u>
    A   B   C

    <u>advantage of</u> our opponent's error and scored a
        D

    field goal. <u>No error</u>
          E

29. <u>Although</u> Mr. Jimenez <u>is</u> in this country <u>for only</u>
    A   B   C

    two years, he talks <u>like</u> a native. <u>No error</u>
              D   E

GO ON TO NEXT PAGE ▶

30. Because Charles received a <u>number of</u> free tickets
    <u>A</u>   <u>B</u>

for the World Series, he asked whether I <u>will go</u> to
                                      <u>C</u>

the game with <u>him</u>. <u>No error</u>
              <u>D</u>   <u>E</u>

31. Your argument is no <u>different from</u>
                    <u>A</u>

<u>the last speaker</u> who also <u>opposes</u> this <u>timely</u>
   <u>B</u>   <u>C</u>   <u>D</u>

legislation. <u>No error</u>
            <u>E</u>

32. Every woman in the ward <u>fervently</u> hopes that
                       <u>A</u>

<u>their</u> child <u>will be</u> a normal and <u>healthy baby</u>.
 <u>B</u>   <u>C</u>   <u>D</u>

<u>No error</u>
  <u>E</u>

33. <u>Due to</u> the <u>excessively high</u> interest rate on
   <u>A</u>   <u>B</u>

installment buying, <u>it</u> is <u>advisable</u> to purchase
                <u>C</u>   <u>D</u>

goods on a cash basis. <u>No error</u>
                  <u>E</u>

34. <u>Bear in mind</u> that <u>since</u> words are tools, <u>only</u>
    <u>A</u>   <u>B</u>   <u>C</u>

experienced writers <u>are permitted in taking</u>
                <u>D</u>

liberties in writing style. <u>No error</u>
                     <u>E</u>

Improving Paragraph Directions

The passage below is the unedited draft of a student's essay. Some of the essay needs to be rewritten to make the meaning clearer and more precise. Read the essay carefully.

The essay is followed by five questions about changes that might improve all or part of its organization, development, sentence structure, use of language, appropriateness to the audience, or use of standard written English. Choose the answer that most clearly and effectively expresses the student's intended meaning. Indicate your choice by filling in the corresponding space on the answer sheet.

[1] *Much of Russia lies under a cover of snow and ice for most of the year.* [2] *Permafrost covers the tundra.* [3] *Ports in northern Russia are not navigable for most of the year simply because they are frozen in.* [4] *In the south, the Black Sea gives Russia access to warm water ports.* [5] *The reason that the Black Sea is important is because it gives them the ability to export timber, furs, coal, oil, and other raw materials that are traded for food and manufactured goods.* [6] *The Black Sea will continue to help their economic growth.*

[7] *The English Channel has served as a barrier between Great Britain and the rest of Europe.* [8] *It has prevented attacks on Great Britain for hundreds of years.* [9] *Except for the Norman invasion over 900 years ago.* [10] *This allowed the nation to develop economically and remain politically stable.* [11] *The isolation of Great Britain allowed the industrial revolution to begin in England.*

[12] *Much of Egypt is covered by desert.* [13] *The desert is irrigated by the Nile River.* [14] *It is longer than any river in the world.* [15] *The land along the river has historically been the site of farms and other settlements.* [16] *For centuries, the river has deposited rich particles of soil for growing crops along its banks.* [17] *Since building the Aswian High Dam in 1968, the farmers downstream from the dam have been using artificial fertilizer.* [18] *The banks of the Nile and the river's delta are among the most productive farming areas in the world.* [19] *Therefore, Egypt's people depend on the Nile.*

[20] *Russia, Great Britain, and Egypt are only three countries that have been shaped and developed by bodies of water.*

35. Which is the best revision of the underlined seg-ment of sentence 5 below?

The reason that the Black Sea is important is <u>*because it gives them the ability to export*</u> *timber, furs, coal, oil, and other raw materials that are traded for food and manufactured goods.*

(A) that it enables Russia to export
(B) its ability to allow exports of
(C) the ability of Russia to export
(D) because of exporting opportunities of
(E) for Russian exports of

36. In the context of the second paragraph, which is the best revision of sentences 8 and 9?

(A) The English Channel has prevented Great Britain's being attacked for hundreds of years; except for the Norman invasion in 1066.
(B) It has prevented attacks, except for the Norman invasion of 1066, on Great Britain for hundreds of years
(C) Except for not preventing the Norman invasion over 900 years ago, the English Channel has prevented attacks on Great Britain for hundreds of years
(D) It has prevented attacking Great Britain for 900 years, except the Normans
(E) For hundreds of years it has prevented attacks on Great Britain, except for the Norman invasion in 1066.

37. Which is the best way to combine sentences 12, 13, and 14?

(A) The Nile, the longest river in the world, irri-gates the desert that covers much of Egypt.
(B) Egypt, which is covered by desert, is irrigated by the Nile, which is longer than any river in the world.
(C) The desert, which covers much of Egypt, is irrigated by the Nile, which is longer than any river in the world.
(D) The longest river in the world, the Nile River, irrigates the Egyptian desert, which means that the river irrigates most of the country.
(E) Much of the desert covering much of Egypt lies alongside the Nile, the longest river in the world, and much of it is irrigated by it.

38. Which of the following sentences is most in need of further support and development?

(A) sentence 1   (B) sentence 2   (C) sentence 5
(D) sentence 11   (E) sentence 14

39. Considering the essay as a whole, which one of the following least accurately describes the function of paragraph 4?

(A) It summarizes the essay's main idea.
(B) It serves to unify the essay.
(C) It proves the validity of the essay's main idea.
(D) It defines the purpose of the essay.
(E) It gives a sense of completion to the essay.

IF YOU FINISH IN LESS THAN 30 MINUTES, YOU MAY CHECK YOUR WORK ON THIS SECTION ONLY. DO NOT TURN TO ANY OTHER SECTION IN THE TEST.

STOP

360 ▶ **CHAPTER 11 / Model Test B**

Answer Key

Section 1 Critical Reading

1. *B*	10. *C*	19. *D*
2. *C*	11. *C*	20. *E*
3. *D*	12. *B*	21. *B*
4. *B*	13. *E*	22. *C*
5. *C*	14. *C*	23. *A*
6. *B*	15. *D*	24. *B*
7. *A*	16. *D*	
8. *D*	17. *C*	
9. *E*	18. *D*	

Section 2 Mathematics

1. *A*	8. *D*	15. *C*
2. *C*	9. *B*	16. *E*
3. *D*	10. *D*	17. *A*
4. *B*	11. *C*	18. *A*
5. *E*	12. *D*	19. *E*
6. *C*	13. *D*	20. *A*
7. *A*	14. *B*	

Section 3 Critical Reading

25. *A*	33. *D*	41. *C*
26. *B*	34. *E*	42. *A*
27. *A*	35. *C*	43. *C*
28. *B*	36. *D*	44. *E*
29. *C*	37. *C*	45. *A*
30. *B*	38. *E*	46. *D*
31. *D*	39. *D*	47. *A*
32. *B*	40. *C*	48. *A*

Section 4 Mathematics

21. *D*	24. *B*	27. *B*
22. *D*	25. *C*	28. *A*
23. *A*	26. *B*	

29.

30.

31.

32.

33.

34.

or any number
between 1.5 and 2

35.

or *6.4*

36.

or *.8*

37.

38.

Section 5 Writing Skills

1. *A*	9. *E*	17. *B*	25. *E*	33. *A*
2. *E*	10. *B*	18. *D*	26. *D*	34. *D*
3. *D*	11. *D*	19. *A*	27. *B*	35. *A*
4. *D*	12. *A*	20. *C*	28. *E*	36. *E*
5. *B*	13. *C*	21. *D*	29. *B*	37. *A*
6. *E*	14. *A*	22. *D*	30. *C*	38. *D*
7. *D*	15. *A*	23. *C*	31. *B*	39. *C*
8. *D*	16. *D*	24. *B*	32. *B*	

Scoring Chart—Model Test B

Critical Reading Sections

Section 1: 24 Questions (1–24)
Number correct   _____ (A)
Number omitted   _____ (B)
Number incorrect   _____ (C)
$\frac{1}{4}$ (C)   _____ (D)
(A) − (D)   _____ Raw Score I

Section 3: 24 Questions (25–48)
Number correct   _____ (A)
Number omitted   _____ (B)
Number incorrect   _____ (C)
$\frac{1}{4}$ (C)   _____ (D)
(A) − (D)   _____ Raw Score II

Total Critical Reading Raw Score
Raw Scores I + II   _____

Mathematics Sections

Section 2: 20 Questions (1–20)
Number correct   _____ (A)
Number omitted   _____ (B)
Number incorrect   _____ (C)
$\frac{1}{4}$ (C)   _____ (D)
(A) − (D)   _____ Raw Score I

Section 4: First 8 Questions (21–28)
Number correct   _____ (A)
Number omitted   _____ (B)
Number incorrect   _____ (C)
$\frac{1}{4}$ (C)   _____ (D)
(A) − (D)   _____ Raw Score II

Section 4: Next 10 Questions (29–38)
Number correct   _____ Raw Score III

Total Mathematical Raw Score
Raw Scores I + II + III   _____

NOTE: In each section (A) + (B) + (C) should equal the number of questions in that section.

Writing Skills Section

Section 5: 39 Questions (1–39)
Number correct   _____ (A)
Number omitted   _____ (B)
Number incorrect   _____ (C)
$\frac{1}{4}$ (C)   _____ (D)

Writing Skills Raw Score
(A) − (D)   _____

Evaluation Chart

Study your score. Your raw score is an indication of your probable achievement on the PSAT/NMSQT. As a guide to the amount of work you need or want to do with this book, study the following.

Raw Score			Self-rating
Critical Reading	*Mathematics*	*Writing*	
42–48	35–38	33–39	Superior
37–46	30–34	28–32	Very good
32–36	25–29	23–27	Good
26–35	21–24	17–22	Above average
20–25	17–20	12–16	Average
12–19	10–16	7–11	Below average
less than 12	less than 10	less than 7	Inadequate

Answer Explanations

Section 1 Critical Reading

1. *B* Criticism that suggests areas of improvement is said to be *constructive*. Remember, before you look at the answer choices, to read the sentence and try to think of a word that makes sense.

2. *C* The leaders would be *apprehensive* (worried) in such circumstances that they could not achieve their goal of reconciliation. Note that the phrase "negotiations have reached such a state" generally implies that they have reached a sorry state.

3. *D* "Although" signals a contrast. The critics believe the poet will find her own voice in time; in other words, she will sound like herself, not like other poets whose works she may have read. Now, however, she sounds like other poets; her work is *derivative*, lacking originality.

4. *B* The columnist was *acerbic* (bitingly sarcastic) in writing of those who provoked or *irritated* her. Note the use of *but* to establish the contrast between the two clauses and the use of *even* to indicate that the missing word is stronger than *bitter*.

5. *C* According to the dictionary, if you're a *chauvinist*, you love your country to excess. Such excessive patriotism would prevent you from seeing your country's flaws.

6. *B* Phrases like "there is no doubt that" and "no one rationally argues that" clearly indicated that the author is *presenting accepted scientific thinking*.

7. *A* Human occupation of the New World is a synonym for human habitation or *inhabiting* of the Americas.

8. *D* While the central character, the bound man awaiting execution, appears in this paragraph, the paragraph reveals little if anything of his personality. Therefore, Choice A is incorrect. The mention of the Federal or Union army and of northern Alabama suggest that the story takes place during the Civil War; it is not a contemporary story. Therefore, Choice B is incorrect. The paragraph does not present conflicting viewpoints. Therefore, Choice C is incorrect. Likewise, the paragraph is descriptive, not argumentative; it does not introduce an antiwar argument. Therefore, Choice E is incorrect. Depicting the railroad bridge above the water, with its cross-timbers above and its metal tracks, the paragraph *establishes the story's physical setting* and sets the stage for the action to come. Choice D is correct.

9. *E* Substitute the answer choices in the original sentence. The sergeant is a person who might have been a deputy sheriff before he joined the army—that is, in his civil or *nonmilitary* life.

10. *C* In describing her book as a study of five artists creating their lives as an improvised work in progress, Bateson *establishes a context for the discussion to follow*.

11. *C* To throw a pot is to *fashion* or shape it on a potter's wheel.

12. *B* In its nonlinear, constantly changing, improvisatory manner, the act of crafting a life in our time most resembles the act of *improvising a jazz piece*.

13. *E* Changes in the scale of a design are changes in its *relative size*.

14. *C* While the way stations (stopping places along one's route) and side roads are attractive, they are temptations set in the pilgrim's path, luring the pilgrim away from his or her quest. Thus, they are *harmful distractions* that stand in the way of reaching one's goal in life.

15. *D* In encouraging us to follow the biblical injunction, "Whatsoever thy hand findeth to do, do it with thy might," the author is inviting us to face the challenges of change with enthusiasm and, like her, to *embrace the new possibilities* that await us.

16. *D* Houston believed that the battle had to begin at the graduate level "to mitigate fear" (relieve *apprehension*) of race mixing or miscegenation. Otherwise, the judges might have ruled against the NAACP-sponsored complaints.

17. *C* Note the immediate context of the quoted word. "The 1950 McLaurin decision *ruled* that ..." In this legal context, *decision* and *ruling* are synonymous.

18. *D* The Regents responded to their defeat in *Sipuel v. Board of Regents of the University of Oklahoma* by separating black and white students in cafeterias and classrooms (thus undermining the effect of the decision). Hence, it seems likely that their reaction to the decision was one of *distinct displeasure*.

19. *D* Maintenance for a law school involves providing *ongoing support* to ensure the school's continued existence.

20. *E* The 1950 *McLaurin* decision was one of the decisions that provided legal precedents for the 1954 *Brown* decision.

Choice A is incorrect. *McLaurin* preceded *Brown* (1954). Therefore, it could not have superseded a decision that had yet to be made. Choice B is incorrect. *Brown I* followed *McLaurin*. Therefore, it could not have set a precedent for *McLaurin*. Choice C is incorrect. *Brown I* reversed *Plessy* v. *Ferguson*. It built on *McLaurin*. Choice D is incorrect. *McLaurin* preceded *Brown I*. Therefore, it could not have limited the application of a decision that had yet to be made.

21. *B* White resistance to the *Brown* decision took on or *adopted* many different forms.

22. *C* Taken as a whole, the passage deals with the entire struggle to desegregate U.S. education, from the NAACP's legal maneuvers of the 1930's to the executive actions of the 1950's and 1960's. Only this title is broad enough to cover the passage as a whole.

Choice A is incorrect. The passage deals with the long legal maneuvers far more than it deals with executive intervention. Choice B is incorrect. The passage deals with much more than *Brown* v. *Board of Education*. Choices D and E are incorrect. They ignore the central subject of desegregation.

23. *A* In assessing the judges' possible reaction to race mixing in the lower grades, Houston displayed *psychological canniness*. He was shrewd in seeing potential dangers and in figuring out strategies to avoid these dangers.

24. *B* In the final paragraph, the author assigns a share of the blame for the confrontation between state and federal authorities to the actions of the Kennedy administration, who engaged in "protracted delays, futile negotiations, and considerable vacillation" before acting to protect Meredith. Clearly, his attitude is one of *unmitigated disdain* (unrelieved scorn).

Section 2 Mathematics

For many problems, the explanation provides a reference to one or more **KEY FACTS** from Chapter 9. These are the mathematical facts that you need to solve that problem. If a solution refers to **KEY FACT J2**, for example, the solution depends on the second **KEY FACT** discussed in Section J of Chapter 9.

For some problems, an alternative solution, indicated by two asterisks (**), follows the first solution. When this occurs, usually one of the solutions is the direct mathematical one and the other is based on one of the tactics discussed in Chapters 8 and 9.

1. *A* If $4x + 8x + 12x = -24$, then $24x = -24$ and $x = -1$.

**Note that x *must* be negative; so only A and B are possible. Test these choices.

2. *C* Note that $20\% = \frac{1}{5}$
$$\frac{1}{5} \text{ of } 20 = 4, \text{ and } \frac{1}{5} \text{ of } 4 = \frac{4}{5} = 0.8.$$

**Use your calculator: 20% of 20% of 20 = $0.2 \times 0.2 \times 20 = 0.8$.

3. *D* Since $7 = 7 - (7 - m) = 7 - 7 + m = m$, then $m = 7$.

4. *B* By **KEY FACT I4**, vertical angles are equal; so the measure of the unmarked angle is 40. Then
$$a + b + c + d + 40 + 40 = 360 \Rightarrow$$
$$a + b + c + d = 280 \Rightarrow$$
$$\frac{a + b + c + d}{4} = \frac{280}{4} = 70.$$

5. *E* $n * \frac{1}{n} = \sqrt{n(\frac{1}{n})} = \sqrt{1} = 1$.

**Choose an easy-to-use number—say, 2. (Note that 1 would *not* be a good choice because then each of the 5 choices would be 1.) Then,

$$2 * \frac{1}{2} = \sqrt{2(\frac{1}{2})} = \sqrt{1} = 1.$$

Only 1 equals 1 when $n = 2$.

6. *C* By **KEY FACT K6**, the area of a square is $\frac{d^2}{2}$. If you don't know that fact, draw a square, and let the sides be 1. Then by **KEY FACTS J5** and **J6**, the diagonal, d, is $\sqrt{2}$, and $d^2 = 2$. Since the area of the square is 1, the area is equal to $\frac{d^2}{2}$.

7. *A* If b years ago Maryline was a years old, she is now $a + b$, and in c years she will be $a + b + c$.

Use **TACTIC 8-2: substitute numbers. If 2 years ago Maryline was 10, how old will she be in 3 years? She is now 12, and in 3 years will be 15. Only $a + b + c$ equals 15 when $a = 10$, $b = 2$, and $c = 3$.

8. *D* Check the answers, starting with Choice E.

E: In 1999 he entered 3 more races than in 1998, an increase of $\frac{3}{9} = \frac{1}{3} < 50\%$.

D: In 1998 he entered 3 more races than in 1997, an increase of $\frac{3}{6} = \frac{1}{2} = 50\%$. (From 1994 to 1995 the increase was 25%, from 1995 to 1996 it was 100%, and from 1996 to 1997 there was a decrease.)

9. *B* The sum of the measures of the four angles in any quadrilateral is 360° (**KEY FACT K1**). If the average of the measures of two of them is 90°, then they total 180° (**TACTIC E1**), which leaves 180° for the other two angles, so their average is 90°.

**Draw a quadrilateral, two of whose angles measure 90°. If you draw a rectangle, it is clear that the average of the measures of the other two angles is also 90°; if your quadrilateral is not a rectangle, estimate the measures of the other angles.

10. *D* Let x be the amount in dollars that each of the 20 workers was going to contribute; then $20x$ represents the cost of the present. When 4 workers dropped out, the remaining 16 each had to pay $(x + 1.50)$ dollars, so

$$16(x + 1.5) = 20x \Rightarrow 16x + 24 = 20x \Rightarrow$$
$$24 = 4x \Rightarrow x = 6$$

and so the cost of the present was $20 \times 6 = \$120$.

Use **TACTIC 8-1 and backsolve. Try Choice C, 100. If the present cost $100, then each of the 20 workers would have had to pay $5. When 4 dropped out, the remaining 16 would have had to pay $100 ÷ 16 = \$6.25$, an increase of $1.25. Since the actual increase was $1.50, the gift was more expensive. Eliminate Choices A, B, and C. Try Choice D, 120; it works.

11. *C* First convert 3.2 hours to minutes by multiplying by 60: $3.2 \times 60 = 192$. Since planting $\frac{3}{5}$ of the flowers took 192 minutes, divide by 3 to find how long it took to plant $\frac{1}{5}$ of the flowers: $192 \div 3 = 64$. Then $\frac{2}{5}$ of the planting will take twice as long: $2 \times 64 = 128$ minutes.

**By dividing 192 by $\frac{3}{5}$, you can find that planting all the flowers would take 320 minutes; then take $\frac{2}{5}$ of that.

**Note that since more than half of the flowers have been planted, the answer is less than 192. Eliminate Choices D and E. Also eliminate Choice A, which is ridiculously small. At worst, guess between Choices B and C, but note that even $76\frac{4}{5}$ seems too small.

12. *D* Since the sum of two even numbers is even, $n + 6$ is even; add 2 to get the next even integer: $n + 8$. Since the sum of an even and an odd number is odd, $n + 9$ is odd; subtract 1 to get the next lower even number: $n + 8$. Finally, take the sum: $n + 8 + n + 8 = 2n + 16$.

This is a perfect situation for **TACTIC 8-2. Let $n = 2$. Then $n + 6 = 8$, and the next even number is 10; $n + 9 = 11$ and the even number just less than 11 is 10: $10 + 10 = 20$. Only $2n + 16$ is 20 when $n = 2$.

13. *D* The months of the year form a repeating sequence with 12 terms in the set that repeats. The nth term is the same as the rth term where r is the remainder when n is divided by 12.

$710 \div 12 = 59.166 \Rightarrow$ the quotient is 59.
$59 \times 12 = 708$ and $710 - 708 = 2 \Rightarrow$
the remainder is 2.

So 710 months from September will be the same month as 2 months from September, namely November.

14. *B* Write the given equation as: $a^3 = 3a$.
Since a is positive, divide both sides by a: $a^2 = 3$. Take the square root of each side: $a = \sqrt{3}$.

Use **TACTIC 8-1: test the choices, starting with Choice C.

15. *C* In $\triangle ABC$ below,
$$w + x + 50 = 180 \Rightarrow w + x = 130.$$
Similarly, in $\triangle ADE$,
$$y + z + 50 = 180 \Rightarrow y + z = 130.$$
So $w + x + y + z = 130 + 130 = 260.$

Use **TACTIC 8-6: trust the diagram. w, x, y, and z appear to be *about* 100, 45, 70, and 50, respectively, for a total of 265. Your estimate may be slightly more or less but should surely be between 230 and 290. Only 260, Choice C, is even close.

16. *E* Since p pretzels cost c cents, each pretzel costs $\frac{c}{p}$ cents. By dividing the number of cents we have by $\frac{c}{p}$, we find out how many pretzels we can buy. Since d dollars equals $100d$ cents, we divide $100d$ by $\frac{c}{p}$, which is equivalent to multiplying $100d$ by $\frac{p}{c}$: $100d\left(\frac{p}{c}\right) = \frac{100dp}{c}$.

Use **TACTIC 8-2. Assume 2 pretzels cost 10 cents; then pretzels cost 5 cents each, or 20 for a dollar. For 3 dollars, we can buy 60 pretzels. Which of the choices equals 60 when $p = 2$, $c = 10$, and $d = 3$? Only $\frac{100dp}{c}$.

17. *A* Assume Eddie sold only one phone of each model. Then his total sales were
$\$100 + \$125 + \$225 = \$450$; so $\frac{100}{450} = \frac{2}{9}$ of the total sales were attributable to the cheapest phone: $\frac{2}{9} = \frac{2}{9}(100)\% = 22\frac{2}{9}\%$.

18. *A* $f(16) = (16)^{\frac{1}{2}} + (16)^{\frac{1}{4}} = \sqrt{16} + \sqrt[4]{16} = 4 + 2 = 6.$
**If you use your calculator, you don't need to change $16^{\frac{1}{2}}$ to $\sqrt{16}$. Just enter $(16)^{\frac{1}{2}} + (16)^{\frac{1}{4}}$. If you prefer, you can enter the exponents as .5 and .25.

19. *E* Draw a Venn diagram and label each region. Since there are 15 junior girls, there are $30 - 15 = 15$ junior boys and $60 - 15 = 45$ senior girls. Therefore, the number of senior boys is $100 - (15 + 15 + 45) = 100 - 75 = 25$.

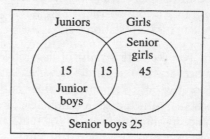

20. *A* Since $3x = 180$, then $x = 60$, and each triangle is equilateral with sides of r. The curved portion of the region is a semicircle of radius r, and its length is one-half the circumference:
$$\frac{1}{2}(2\pi r) = \pi r.$$
The total perimeter of the outlined region is $\pi r + 3r = r(\pi + 3)$.

Section 3 Critical Reading

25. *A* The delight a wicked queen feels about poisoning someone is clearly *malicious* (spiteful, delighting in others' ills).

26. *B* "Though" signals a contrast, in this case a contrast between the huge changes most editors suggest and the *minute* (tiny) changes Hemingway's editors wanted.

27. *A* Finding Berkeley's spectacles *outmoded* or old-fashioned, the choreographers who come after him look for *fresh* ways to stage musical numbers in films.

28. *B* If bilingual education is more than a mere stop-gap (a somewhat negative description), it must possess certain positive qualities. Thus, it has *advantages over* education in a single tongue. Note the use of *far from* to signal the contrast between the negative and positive views on bilingual education.

29. *C Ornate* means highly decorated. An ornate building would stand out from simple, unadorned neighbors: it would be *conspicuous* for its flamboyance.

30. *B* The writer concedes that the big-bang theory has been changed somewhat: it has undergone *refinement* or polishing. However, he denies that its validity has been threatened seriously by any rival theories: it has *resisted* or defied all challenges.

The use of the support signal *and* indicates that the first missing word is similar to "modification." The use of the contrast signal *but* indicates that the second missing word is contrary in meaning to "undergone modification."

31. *D* Because the dean was not able to *disguise* her distaste for the media barrage, she failed to stifle her *caustic* or sarcastically biting remarks about the event. Note the implicit cause-and-effect relationship between the opening phrase and the central clause of the sentence.

32. *B* If the rare earths are actually present to some degree in essentially all minerals, then they are not rare after all. Thus, the term "rare earths" is a *misnomer* (incorrect designation), for the rare earths are actually *ubiquitous* (omnipresent; found everywhere). Watch out for words that signal the unexpected. Note the use of "paradoxically" here.

33. *D* "Spare" is being used to describe the Cardinal's physical appearance. He is tall and *lean*, like one of the extremely long, thin figures in an El Greco portrait.

34. *E* The word "place" here refers to the cardinal's *rank* or worldly position. Like Satan, he takes pride in his high station in life.

35. *C* The two separate strains of decorative art discussed are two separate *varieties* or kinds of decorative art. Remember, when answering a vocabulary-in-context question, test each answer choice by substituting it in the sentence for the word in quotes.

36. *D* The second sentence states that "the artist's sex governed both the kind of article to be decorated and the style to be followed in its ornamentation." Male and female Plains artists specialize or limit themselves to certain traditional designs. The title that best summarizes this content is *Design Specialization in Plains Arts*.

Choice A is incorrect. The passage does not discuss the continuing or ongoing effect of Plains art. Choice B is too broad to be correct. The passage deals specifically with male and female *artistic roles* in the tribe, not with male and female roles in general. Choice C is incorrect. While the passage describes female Indian art as being geometrical and abstract, it never relates it to the school of modern art known as abstract expressionism. Choice E is too narrow to be correct. The passage deals with Indian abstract or geometrical art as well as Indian representational art.

Remember, when asked to choose a title, watch out for choices that are too specific or too broad.

37. *C* Passage 1 states: "Dolphins left the land when mammalian brains were still small and primitive." This indicates that dolphins were once land animals, mammals like ourselves, whose evolutionary development took them back into the sea.

38. *E* The passage indicates that human beings think of intelligence in terms of our own ability to manipulate our environment—our ability to build and do all sorts of things with our hands. Since dolphins have no hands, we have trouble appreciating their high level of intelligence.

39. *D* Passage 1 attempts to *reassess the nature and extent of dolphin intelligence*, first giving reasons why human beings may have trouble appreciating how intelligent dolphins really are and then, in the concluding sentence, reflecting how dolphin intelligence (that looks "inward to the sea's heart") may complement human intelligence (that looks "outward on eternity").

40. *C* The dolphin's acute echo-sounding sense is a sharp, *keen* sense that enables the dolphin to sound or measure the ocean depths by using echoes.

41. *C* The entire passage has concentrated on the dolphin's brain; so it is safe to assume that this is what is meant by the "impressively elaborated instrument." The items listed in the other answer choices have not been mentioned at all. Note that Choice B, an artificial range-finding device, is incorrect because the dolphin's range-finding ability is entirely natural, not artificial.

42. *A* The sea's heart is like the human mind in that it swarms or *teems* (abounds) with grotesque or *exotic forms of life*.

43. *C* The author's tone is distinctly admiring. The passage speaks of the dolphins' "remarkable range-finding ability," mentions their care for each other, and repeatedly praises dolphin intelligence.

44. *E* The quotation marks here indicate that the word in quotes is being used in a special sense (often an ironic one). In this case, as the next paragraph makes abundantly clear, the author is critical of both the results and the influence of Lilly's experiments. He *has some doubts as to how scientific those experiments were*.

45. *A* In claiming that "dolphins communicate not only with one another but also with humans, mimicking human speech and reaching out across the boundaries that divide us," Lilly and his associates have *overstated* their case, misrepresenting *the extent of dolphin intelligence*.

Choice B is incorrect. In stating that Lilly's conclusions have not withstood (stood up against) critical scrutiny, the author indicates that they *have* been critically scrutinized to an appropriate degree.

46. *D* "Begging the question" refers to assuming the truth of the very point whose truth or falsehood you're trying to establish. The author of Passage 2 considers the reasoning in this argument flawed; he views it with doubt or *skepticism*.

47. *A* If dolphins were proven far superior in linguistic capability to seals and other lower animals, that clearly would contradict the results of the studies the author cites and would thus *undercut* or weaken their impact.

48. *A* In its glorification of dolphin intelligence as something that equals or possibly exceeds human intelligence, Passage 1 seems *typical of the attitudes of Lilly and his associates.*

Section 4 Mathematics

For many problems, the explanation provides a reference to one or more **KEY FACTS** from Chapter 9. These are the mathematical facts that you need to solve that problem. If a solution refers to **KEY FACT J2**, for example, the solution depends on the second **KEY FACT** discussed in Section J of Chapter 9.

For some problems, an alternative solution, indicated by two asterisks (**), follows the first solution. When this occurs, usually one of the solutions is the direct mathematical one and the other is based on one of the tactics discussed in Chapters 8 and 9.

21. *D* Be careful with the minus signs and the negatives:
$$(-2)^4 + (-2)^3 + (-2)^2 + (-2) =$$
$$16 + (-8) + 4 + (-2) = 16 - 8 + 4 - 2 = 10.$$

22. *D* The average is just the sum of the number of members in the five clubs divided by 5.
$$20 + 30 + 23 + 27 + 25 = 125$$
and $125 \div 5 = 25.$

23. *A* In club A, one-fourth or 25% (5 of 20) of the members are seniors. In each of the other clubs the number of seniors is *less than* one-fourth of the membership of the club.

24. *B* Since vertical angles have the same measure (**KEY FACT I4**), $c = d$, $d = a$, and $b = a - b \Rightarrow a = 2b$. Therefore, $c = d = a = 2b$. Also, the sum of the measures of all 6 angles is 360° (**KEY FACT I3**), so
$$a + b + c + d + a - b + d =$$
$$2a + c + 2d = 360.$$

Replacing c, d, and a by $2b$ yields $10b = 360 \Rightarrow b = 36.$

25. *C* Use **TACTIC 8-5**: Draw a diagram and label it.

Use the Pythagorean theorem to find d, the length of the diagonal:
$$a^2 + (3a)^2 = d^2 \Rightarrow a^2 + 9a^2 = d^2 \Rightarrow$$
$$10a^2 = d^2 \Rightarrow d = a\sqrt{10}.$$

Use **TACTIC 8-2 and let $a = 1$. Then use **TACTIC 8-5**, and draw the rectangle (to scale), that is, let the width be 1 and the length be 3.

Now use **TACTIC 8-6**: trust your eyes. Clearly, the diagonal is longer than 3 and shorter than 4 (the width plus the length is 4). The answer *must* be $a\sqrt{10}$, the *only* choice between 3 and 4, when $a = 1$.

26. *B* Since the radius of circle O is 12, the diameter is 24, and the circumference is 24π. Therefore, arc PQR is $\frac{1}{8}$ of the circumference, and m$\angle POR$ is $\frac{1}{8}(360°) = 45°.$

27. *B* $\sqrt{x+1} + 3 = 5 \Rightarrow \sqrt{x+1} = 2 \Rightarrow x + 1 = 4 \Rightarrow x = 3.$

Use **TACTIC 8-1: backsolve starting with 5, Choice C. Is $\sqrt{5+1} + 3 = 5$? Since $\sqrt{6}$ is not an integer, you can tell immediately that the answer is "No." But use your calculator to evaluate it: $\sqrt{6} + 3 \approx 5.45$, which is a little too big. Eliminate Choices C and D, and try 3, Choice B. It works: $\sqrt{3+1} = 3 = \sqrt{4} + 3 = 2 + 3 = 5.$

28. *A* Let R be the radius of the large circle, and r the radius of the small circle. The area of the white region is πr^2, whereas the area of the shaded region is $\pi R^2 - \pi r^2$. Therefore,

$$\pi R^2 - \pi r^2 = \pi r^2 \Rightarrow R^2 = 2r^2 \Rightarrow$$
$$\frac{R^2}{r^2} = 2 \Rightarrow \frac{R}{r} = \sqrt{2}.$$

The ratio of the radius of the large circle to the radius of the small circle is $\frac{\sqrt{2}}{1}$.

29. *(256)* Draw a rectangle and label it.

The perimeter is
$$2w + 2l = 16 + 2l = 80.$$
So $2l = 64$, and $l = 32$. Finally, the area is
$$lw = 8 \times 32 = 256.$$

30. *(256)* Mentally, or with your calculator, multiply $3 \times 3 \times 3 \times \ldots$ until the product is 81. In fact, $3^4 = 81$. Now just multiply to get that $4^4 = 256$.

31. *(70)* Since the average of x, y, and 10 is 50, their sum is 150 (**KEY FACT E1**). Then,

$$x + y + 10 = 150 \Rightarrow x + y = 140 \Rightarrow$$
$$\frac{x + y}{2} = \frac{140}{2} = 70.$$

Since 10 is 40 less than 50, x and y together must be 40 more than 50 (KEY FACT E2). Assume each is 20 more than 50; that is, x and y are both 70. Then their average is 70.

32. *(216)* Draw a right triangle and label one leg 24 and the hypotenuse 30. Find the length of the other leg and then calculate the area by taking $\frac{1}{2}$ the product of the legs. Before using the Pythagorean theorem, ask yourself whether this is a multiple of one of the basic right triangles you know: 3-4-5 or 5-12-13. It is: $24 = 6 \times 4$ and $30 = 6 \times 5$, and so the other leg is $6 \times 3 = 18$. The area is $\frac{1}{2}(18)(24) = 216$.

****If you don't recognize the triangle, use the Pythagorean theorem and a calculator:

$$24^2 + x^2 = 30^2 \Rightarrow$$
$$x^2 = 900 - 576 = 324 \Rightarrow x = 18.$$

33. *(154)* If n divided by 13 has a quotient of 11 and a remainder of 11, then

$$n = 13(11) + 11 = 143 + 11 = 154.$$

**

$$13\overline{)\,n}^{\;11\,r.11} \Rightarrow n = 143 + 11 = 154.$$
$$\underline{-143}$$
$$11$$

34. *(Any number between 1.5 and 2)* Choose a value for y: 3.5 say, and use the slope formula. The slope of the line through $(0, 0)$ and $(2, 3.5)$ is $\frac{3.5 - 0}{2 - 0} = \frac{3.5}{2} = 1.75$.

****Draw a quick sketch.

The line through the origin and $(2,3)$ has slope $\frac{3}{2} = 1.5$. Likewise the slope of the line through the origin and $(2,4)$ is $\frac{4}{2} = 2$. So, the slope could be any number greater than 1.5 and less than 2 (expressed as a fraction or a decimal).

35. $\left(\frac{32}{5} \text{ or } 6.4\right)$ If y varies inversely with x, there is a constant k such that $xy = k$; so $k = (8)(4) = 32$. Thus, $32 = 5y$, and $y = \frac{32}{5}$ or 6.4.

36. $\left(\frac{4}{5} \text{ or } .8\right)$ There are five integers less that 50 whose units digit is a 3: 3, 13, 23, 33, and 43. Of these, four of them (all but 33) are prime. Then, the probability of drawing a prime is $\frac{4}{5}$.

37. (2011)

Year	Justin's Age	Lior's Age
1997	28	0
$1997 + x$	$28 + x$	x

The equation is

$$28 + x = 3x \Rightarrow 28 = 2x \Rightarrow x = 14.$$

So, Justin will be three times as old as Lior 14 years after 1997, in 2011 (when they will be 42 and 14, respectively).

38. (9) Since 7^{30} has over 20 digits, most calculators cannot give you the exact value. You can, however, use your calculator to see a pattern emerge. The first few powers of 7 are: 7; 49; 343; 2,401; 16,807; 117,649; . . . The units digits form a repeating sequence:

$$7, 9, 3, 1, 7, 9, 3, 1, \ldots$$

Since every fourth number, 7^4, 7^8, . . . , ends in 1, 7^{28} ends in 1. Then 7^{29} ends in 7, and 7^{30} ends in 9.

Section 5 Writing Skills

1. *A* The sentence's use of parallel structure is effective and correct.

2. *E* This choice corrects the sentence fragment.

3. *D* Error in diction. Do not use *calculate* when you mean *think*.

4. *D* Error in coordination and subordination. The addition of *when* makes the sentence more effective by tightening up the relationship between the clauses.

5. *B* Wordiness. Choice B expresses the author's meaning directly and concisely. All other choices are either indirect or ungrammatical.

6. *E* This choice corrects the sentence fragment.

7. *D* Error in parallelism. Changing *absenteeism is reduced* to *reduces absenteeism* maintains parallel structure.

8. *D* This choice eliminates the error in parallelism.

9. *E* Omission of important word and error in verb tense are corrected in Choice E.

10. *B* Comma splice. Choices A, D, and E are run-on sentences. Choice C is verbose.

11. *D* Choice A contains a sentence fragment. Choices B, C, and E are verbose.

12. *A* Sentence is correct.

13. *C* Error in parallelism. This choice does not violate parallel structure.

14. *A* Sentence is correct.

15. *A* Sentence is correct.

16. *D* Illogical comparison. Compare Japan's economy with Europe's economy, not Japan's economy with Europe.

17. *B* Error in usage. Do not use *when* or *where* after *is* in making a definition.

18. *D* Incorrect subordinating conjunction. The species was threatened *because* so many condors had been killed.

19. *A* Sentence is correct.

20. *C* Sentence fragment. Choice C supplies the missing main verb.

21. *D* Error in parallelism. Change *to attend* to *attending*.

22. *D* Faulty comparison. When comparing two persons or things, use the comparative form (*better*) instead of the superlative (*best*).

23. *C* Error in diction. Use *behind* instead of *in back of*.

24. *B* Error in subject-verb agreement. A system *has been incorporated* is correct.

25. *E* Sentence is correct.

26. *D* Error in subject-verb agreement. The antecedent of *who* is *one*. Change *plan* to *plans*.

27. *B* Error in following conventions. Change *amount of* to *number of*.

28. *E* Sentence is correct.

29. *B* Wrong tense. Change *is* to *has been*.

30. *C* Error in sequence of tenses. Change *will go* to *would go*.

31. *B* Error in logical comparison. Do not compare a person with a thing. Correct form: *Your argument is no different from that of the last speaker.* . . .

32. *B* Error in pronoun-antecedent agreement. Woman (singular) requires a singular pronoun. Change *their* to *her*.

33. *A* Error in idiom. Do not use *due to* when you mean *because of*.

34. *D* Faulty verbal. Change *in taking* to the infinitive *to take*.

35. *A* Only Choice A is concisely expressed in standard English. All the other choices are awkward or nonstandard.

36. *E* Choice A has a sentence fragment after the semicolon.

Choice B divides the main clause awkwardly.

Choice C is wordy and repetitious. It unnecessarily repeats *the English Channel*, the subject of sentence 7.

Choice D is an unclear, awkwardly constructed sentence.

Choice E is an accurate and logical revision. It is the best answer.

37. *A* Choice A succinctly and effectively combines the three sentences. It is the best answer.

Choice B contains a faulty comparison. The Nile cannot be longer than itself.

Choice C is similar to B.

Choice D is accurate but wordy and repetitious.

Choice E is awkwardly expressed.

38. *D* Sentence 11 states a complex idea that needs further explanation. The other sentences are facts that stand on their own. Therefore D is the best answer.

39. C Choice C does not describe the function of the last paragraph. The essay's main idea is validated by the contents of the essay's three main paragraphs, not by the final paragraph.

Answer Sheet
MODEL TEST C

Each mark should completely fill the appropriate space and should be as dark as all other marks. Make all erasures complete. Traces of an erasure may be read as an answer. See pages viii and 21 for explanations of timing and number of questions.

Section 1 — Critical Reading
25 minutes

1 Ⓐ Ⓑ Ⓒ Ⓓ Ⓔ
2 Ⓐ Ⓑ Ⓒ Ⓓ Ⓔ
3 Ⓐ Ⓑ Ⓒ Ⓓ Ⓔ
4 Ⓐ Ⓑ Ⓒ Ⓓ Ⓔ
5 Ⓐ Ⓑ Ⓒ Ⓓ Ⓔ
6 Ⓐ Ⓑ Ⓒ Ⓓ Ⓔ
7 Ⓐ Ⓑ Ⓒ Ⓓ Ⓔ
8 Ⓐ Ⓑ Ⓒ Ⓓ Ⓔ
9 Ⓐ Ⓑ Ⓒ Ⓓ Ⓔ
10 Ⓐ Ⓑ Ⓒ Ⓓ Ⓔ
11 Ⓐ Ⓑ Ⓒ Ⓓ Ⓔ
12 Ⓐ Ⓑ Ⓒ Ⓓ Ⓔ
13 Ⓐ Ⓑ Ⓒ Ⓓ Ⓔ
14 Ⓐ Ⓑ Ⓒ Ⓓ Ⓔ
15 Ⓐ Ⓑ Ⓒ Ⓓ Ⓔ
16 Ⓐ Ⓑ Ⓒ Ⓓ Ⓔ
17 Ⓐ Ⓑ Ⓒ Ⓓ Ⓔ
18 Ⓐ Ⓑ Ⓒ Ⓓ Ⓔ
19 Ⓐ Ⓑ Ⓒ Ⓓ Ⓔ
20 Ⓐ Ⓑ Ⓒ Ⓓ Ⓔ
21 Ⓐ Ⓑ Ⓒ Ⓓ Ⓔ
22 Ⓐ Ⓑ Ⓒ Ⓓ Ⓔ
23 Ⓐ Ⓑ Ⓒ Ⓓ Ⓔ
24 Ⓐ Ⓑ Ⓒ Ⓓ Ⓔ

Section 2 — Math
25 minutes

1 Ⓐ Ⓑ Ⓒ Ⓓ Ⓔ
2 Ⓐ Ⓑ Ⓒ Ⓓ Ⓔ
3 Ⓐ Ⓑ Ⓒ Ⓓ Ⓔ
4 Ⓐ Ⓑ Ⓒ Ⓓ Ⓔ
5 Ⓐ Ⓑ Ⓒ Ⓓ Ⓔ
6 Ⓐ Ⓑ Ⓒ Ⓓ Ⓔ
7 Ⓐ Ⓑ Ⓒ Ⓓ Ⓔ
8 Ⓐ Ⓑ Ⓒ Ⓓ Ⓔ
9 Ⓐ Ⓑ Ⓒ Ⓓ Ⓔ
10 Ⓐ Ⓑ Ⓒ Ⓓ Ⓔ
11 Ⓐ Ⓑ Ⓒ Ⓓ Ⓔ
12 Ⓐ Ⓑ Ⓒ Ⓓ Ⓔ
13 Ⓐ Ⓑ Ⓒ Ⓓ Ⓔ
14 Ⓐ Ⓑ Ⓒ Ⓓ Ⓔ
15 Ⓐ Ⓑ Ⓒ Ⓓ Ⓔ
16 Ⓐ Ⓑ Ⓒ Ⓓ Ⓔ
17 Ⓐ Ⓑ Ⓒ Ⓓ Ⓔ
18 Ⓐ Ⓑ Ⓒ Ⓓ Ⓔ
19 Ⓐ Ⓑ Ⓒ Ⓓ Ⓔ
20 Ⓐ Ⓑ Ⓒ Ⓓ Ⓔ

Section 3 — Critical Reading
25 minutes

25 Ⓐ Ⓑ Ⓒ Ⓓ Ⓔ
26 Ⓐ Ⓑ Ⓒ Ⓓ Ⓔ
27 Ⓐ Ⓑ Ⓒ Ⓓ Ⓔ
28 Ⓐ Ⓑ Ⓒ Ⓓ Ⓔ
29 Ⓐ Ⓑ Ⓒ Ⓓ Ⓔ
30 Ⓐ Ⓑ Ⓒ Ⓓ Ⓔ
31 Ⓐ Ⓑ Ⓒ Ⓓ Ⓔ
32 Ⓐ Ⓑ Ⓒ Ⓓ Ⓔ
33 Ⓐ Ⓑ Ⓒ Ⓓ Ⓔ
34 Ⓐ Ⓑ Ⓒ Ⓓ Ⓔ
35 Ⓐ Ⓑ Ⓒ Ⓓ Ⓔ
36 Ⓐ Ⓑ Ⓒ Ⓓ Ⓔ
37 Ⓐ Ⓑ Ⓒ Ⓓ Ⓔ
38 Ⓐ Ⓑ Ⓒ Ⓓ Ⓔ
39 Ⓐ Ⓑ Ⓒ Ⓓ Ⓔ
40 Ⓐ Ⓑ Ⓒ Ⓓ Ⓔ
41 Ⓐ Ⓑ Ⓒ Ⓓ Ⓔ
42 Ⓐ Ⓑ Ⓒ Ⓓ Ⓔ
43 Ⓐ Ⓑ Ⓒ Ⓓ Ⓔ
44 Ⓐ Ⓑ Ⓒ Ⓓ Ⓔ
45 Ⓐ Ⓑ Ⓒ Ⓓ Ⓔ
46 Ⓐ Ⓑ Ⓒ Ⓓ Ⓔ
47 Ⓐ Ⓑ Ⓒ Ⓓ Ⓔ
48 Ⓐ Ⓑ Ⓒ Ⓓ Ⓔ

Section 4 — Math
25 minutes

21 (A) (B) (C) (D) (E)
22 (A) (B) (C) (D) (E)
23 (A) (B) (C) (D) (E)
24 (A) (B) (C) (D) (E)
25 (A) (B) (C) (D) (E)
26 (A) (B) (C) (D) (E)
27 (A) (B) (C) (D) (E)
28 (A) (B) (C) (D) (E)

Section 5 — Writing
30 minutes

1 (A) (B) (C) (D) (E)
2 (A) (B) (C) (D) (E)
3 (A) (B) (C) (D) (E)
4 (A) (B) (C) (D) (E)
5 (A) (B) (C) (D) (E)
6 (A) (B) (C) (D) (E)
7 (A) (B) (C) (D) (E)
8 (A) (B) (C) (D) (E)
9 (A) (B) (C) (D) (E)
10 (A) (B) (C) (D) (E)
11 (A) (B) (C) (D) (E)
12 (A) (B) (C) (D) (E)
13 (A) (B) (C) (D) (E)
14 (A) (B) (C) (D) (E)
15 (A) (B) (C) (D) (E)
16 (A) (B) (C) (D) (E)
17 (A) (B) (C) (D) (E)
18 (A) (B) (C) (D) (E)
19 (A) (B) (C) (D) (E)
20 (A) (B) (C) (D) (E)
21 (A) (B) (C) (D) (E)
22 (A) (B) (C) (D) (E)
23 (A) (B) (C) (D) (E)
24 (A) (B) (C) (D) (E)
25 (A) (B) (C) (D) (E)
26 (A) (B) (C) (D) (E)
27 (A) (B) (C) (D) (E)
28 (A) (B) (C) (D) (E)
29 (A) (B) (C) (D) (E)
30 (A) (B) (C) (D) (E)
31 (A) (B) (C) (D) (E)
32 (A) (B) (C) (D) (E)
33 (A) (B) (C) (D) (E)
34 (A) (B) (C) (D) (E)
35 (A) (B) (C) (D) (E)
36 (A) (B) (C) (D) (E)
37 (A) (B) (C) (D) (E)
38 (A) (B) (C) (D) (E)
39 (A) (B) (C) (D) (E)

For each question in this section, select the best answer from among the choices given, and fill in the corresponding circle on the answer sheet.

1. Impressed by the extraordinary potential of the new superconductor, scientists predict that its use will ---- the computer industry, creating new products overnight.

   (A) justify   (B) alienate   (C) nullify
   (D) revolutionize   (E) overestimate

2. No matter how ---- the revelations of the coming year may be, they will be hard put to match those of the past decade, which have ---- transformed our view of the emergence of Mayan civilization.

   (A) minor..dramatically
   (B) profound..negligibly
   (C) striking..radically
   (D) bizarre..nominally
   (E) questionable..possibly

3. Few other plants can grow beneath the canopy of the sycamore tree, whose leaves and pods produce a natural herbicide that leaches into the soil, ---- other plants that might compete for water and nutrients.

   (A) inhibiting   (B) distinguishing
   (C) nourishing   (D) encouraging
   (E) refreshing

4. Black women authors such as Zora Neale Hurston, originally ---- by both white and black literary establishments to obscurity as minor novelists, are being rediscovered by black feminist critics today.

   (A) inclined   (B) relegated   (C) subjected
   (D) diminished   (E) characterized

5. Critics of the movie version of *The Color Purple* ---- its saccharine, overoptimistic mood as out of keeping with the novel's more ---- tone.

   (A) applauded..somber
   (B) condemned..hopeful
   (C) acclaimed..positive
   (D) denounced..sanguine
   (E) decried..acerbic

Questions 6 and 7 are based on the following passage.

Little vegetation grows in the vast South African tableland known as the Nama Karroo. The open plateau, home to springboks and other
Line   members of the antelope family, seems a rocky,
5   inhospitable place. Yet the springboks find sustenance, searching among the rocks and pebbles, and coming up with mouthfuls of "stones" which they munch contentedly. These stones are in actuality plants, members of the genus Lithops, some
10   of the strangest succulents in the world. Nature has camouflaged these stone plants so well that even trained botanists have trouble telling them apart from the rocks surrounding them.

6. The quotation marks around the word "stones" (line 7) primarily serve to emphasize that the plants

   (A) are extraordinarily hard
   (B) are inedible by humans
   (C) are not literally stones
   (D) can be recognized by antelopes
   (E) survive in an arid environment

GO ON TO NEXT PAGE ▶

7. The context suggests that a succulent (line 10) is most likely

(A) a rock form
(B) an antelope
(C) a desert insect
(D) a type of camouflage
(E) a kind of plant

Questions 8 and 9 are based on the following passage.

Judging from the reactions of the general public, modern art's main characteristic is its obscurity. Everybody gripes about obscurity in
Line painting, in poetry, in music. However, any truly
5 original work of art is bound to seem obscure to John Q. Public. After all, no great work of art finds an appreciative public waiting for it. Works of art are born as intellectual foundlings. Oddly enough, even the art specialists themselves can be caught
10 unawares. Early in his career André Gide, working as a lowly publisher's reader, read the manuscript of Proust's magnificent *Remembrance of Things Past*. Gide turned it down. Cold.

8. The author of the passage does all of the following EXCEPT

(A) use a metaphor
(B) offer an example
(C) make an assertion
(D) pose a question
(E) deny a possibility

9. The statement "Cold" in line 13 primarily serves to emphasize the

(A) stubborn character of authors
(B) poor quality of training given publishers' readers
(C) lack of hesitation about rejecting the manuscript
(D) surprising popularity of Proust's novel
(E) commercial nature of the publishing industry

Directions

Each passage below is followed by questions based on its content. Answer the questions following each passage on the basis of what is stated or implied in that passage and in any introductory material that may be provided.

Questions 10–15 are based upon the following passage.

In the following passage from Jane Austen's novel Pride and Prejudice, *the heroine Elizabeth Bennet faces an unexpected encounter with her father's cousin (and prospective heir), the clergyman Mr. Collins.*

It was absolutely necessary to interrupt him now.

"You are too hasty, Sir," she cried. "You forget
Line that I have made no answer. Let me do it without
5 further loss of time. Accept my thanks for the compliment you are paying me. I am very sensible of the honour of your proposals, but it is impossible for me to do otherwise than decline them."

"I am not now to learn," replied Mr. Collins
10 with a formal wave of the hand, "that it is usual with young ladies to reject the addresses of the man whom they secretly mean to accept, when he first applies for their favour; and that sometimes the refusal is repeated a second or even a third
15 time. I am therefore by no means discouraged by what you have just said, and shall hope to lead you to the altar ere long."

"Upon my word, Sir," cried Elizabeth, "your hope is rather an extraordinary one after my
20 declaration. I do assure you that I am not one of those young ladies (if such young ladies there are) who are so daring as to risk their happiness on the chance of being asked a second time. I am perfectly serious in my refusal. You could not make
25 *me* happy, and I am convinced that I am the last woman in the world who would make *you* so. Nay, were your friend Lady Catherine to know me, I am persuaded she would find me in every respect ill qualified for the situation."

30 "Were it certain that Lady Catherine would think so," said Mr. Collins very gravely—"but I cannot imagine that her ladyship would at all dis-

GO ON TO NEXT PAGE ▶

approve of you. And you may be certain that when I have the honour of seeing her again I shall speak

35 in the highest terms of your modesty, economy, and other amiable qualifications."

"Indeed, Mr. Collins, all praise of me will be unnecessary. You must give me leave to judge for myself, and pay me the compliment of believing

40 what I say. I wish you very happy and very rich, and by refusing your hand, do all in my power to prevent your being otherwise. In making me the offer, you must have satisfied the delicacy of your feelings with regard to my family, and may take

45 possession of Longbourn estate whenever it falls, without any self-reproach. This matter may be considered, therefore, as finally settled." And rising as she thus spoke, she would have quitted the room, had not Mr. Collins thus addressed her.

50 "When I do myself the honour of speaking to you next on this subject I shall hope to receive a more favourable answer than you have now given me; though I am far from accusing you of cruelty at present, because I know it to be the established

55 custom of your sex to reject a man on the first application, and perhaps you have even now said as much to encourage my suit as would be consistent with the true delicacy of the female character."

"Really, Mr. Collins," cried Elizabeth

60 with some warmth, "you puzzle me exceedingly. If what I have hitherto said can appear to you in the form of encouragement, I know not how to express my refusal in such a way as may convince you of its being one."

---

10. It can be inferred that in the paragraphs immediately preceding this passage

(A) Elizabeth and Mr. Collins quarreled
(B) Elizabeth met Mr. Collins for the first time
(C) Mr. Collins asked Elizabeth to marry him
(D) Mr. Collins gravely insulted Elizabeth
(E) Elizabeth discovered that Mr. Collins was a fraud

11. The word "sensible" in line 6 means

(A) logical   (B) perceptible
(C) sound in judgment   (D) keenly aware
(E) appreciable

12. Instead of having the intended effect, Elizabeth's initial refusal of Mr. Collins (lines 3–8)

(A) causes her to rethink rejecting him
(B) makes him less inclined to wed
(C) gives her the opportunity to consider other options
(D) persuades him she dislikes him intensely
(E) fails to put an end to his suit

13. It can be inferred from lines 30–33 that Mr. Collins

(A) will take Elizabeth's words seriously
(B) admires Elizabeth's independence
(C) is very disappointed by her decision
(D) would accept Lady Catherine's opinion
(E) means his remarks as a joke

14. The reason Elizabeth insists all praise of her "will be unnecessary" (lines 37–38) is that she

(A) feels sure Lady Catherine will learn to admire her in time
(B) is too shy to accept compliments readily
(C) has no intention of marrying Mr. Collins
(D) believes a clergyman should be less effusive
(E) values her own worth excessively

15. On the basis of his behavior in this passage, Mr. Collins may best be described as

(A) malicious in intent
(B) both obtuse and obstinate
(C) unsure of his acceptance
(D) kindly and understanding
(E) sensitive to Elizabeth's wishes

Questions 16–24 are based on the following passage.

African elephants now are an endangered species. The following passage, taken from a newspaper article written in 1989, discusses the potential ecological disaster that might occur if the elephant were to become extinct.

The African elephant—mythic symbol of a continent, keystone of its ecology and the largest land animal remaining on earth—has become the

Line object of one of the biggest, broadest international
5 efforts yet mounted to turn a threatened species off the road to extinction. But it is not only the elephant's survival that is at stake, conservationists say. Unlike the endangered tiger, unlike even the great whales, the African elephant is in great
10 measure the architect of its environment. As a voracious eater of vegetation, it largely shapes the forest-and-savanna surroundings in which it lives, thereby setting the terms of existence for millions

of other storied animals—from zebras to gazelles to giraffes and wildebeests—that share its habitat. And as the elephant disappears, scientists and conservationists say, many other species will also disappear from vast stretches of forest and savanna, drastically altering and impoverishing whole ecosystems.

Just as the American buffalo was hunted almost to extinction a century ago, so the African elephant is now the victim of an onslaught of commercial killing, stimulated in this case by soaring global demand for ivory. Most of the killing is illegal, and conservationists say that although the pressure of human population and development contributes to the elephants' decline, poaching is by far the greatest threat. The elephant may or may not be on the way to becoming a mere zoological curiosity like the buffalo, but the trend is clear.

In an atmosphere of mounting alarm among conservationists, a new international coordinating group backed by 21 ivory-producing and ivory-consuming countries has met and adopted an ambitious plan of action. Against admittedly long odds, the multinational rescue effort is aimed both at stopping the slaughter of the elephants in the short term and at nurturing them as a vital "keystone species" in the long run.

It is the elephant's metabolism and appetite that make it a disturber of the environment and therefore an important creator of habitat. In a constant search for the 300 pounds of vegetation it must have every day, it kills small trees and underbrush and pulls branches off big trees as high as its trunk will reach. This creates innumerable open spaces in both deep tropical forests and in the woodlands that cover part of the African savannas. The resulting patchwork, a mosaic of vegetation in various stages of regeneration, in turn creates a greater variety of forage that attracts a greater variety of other vegetation-eaters than would otherwise be the case.

In studies over the last 20 years in southern Kenya near Mount Kilimanjaro, Dr. David Western has found that when elephants are allowed to roam the savannas naturally and normally, they spread out at "intermediate densities." Their foraging creates a mixture of savanna woodlands (what the Africans call bush) and grassland. The result is a highly diverse array of other plant-eating species: those like the zebra, wildebeest and gazelle, that graze; those like the giraffe, bushbuck and lesser kudu, that browse on tender shoots, buds, twigs and leaves; and plant-eating primates like the baboon and vervet monkey. These herbivores attract carnivores like the lion and cheetah.

When the elephant population thins out, Dr. Western said, the woodlands become denser and the grazers are squeezed out. When pressure from poachers forces elephants to crowd more densely onto reservations, the woodlands there are knocked out and the browsers and primates disappear.

Something similar appears to happen in dense tropical rain forests. In their natural state, because the overhead forest canopy shuts out sunlight and prevents growth on the forest floor, rain forests provide slim pickings for large, hoofed plant-eaters. By pulling down trees and eating new growth, elephants enlarge natural openings in the canopy, allowing plants to regenerate on the forest floor and bringing down vegetation from the canopy so that smaller species can get at it.

In such situations, the rain forest becomes hospitable to large plant-eating mammals such as bongos, bush pigs, duikers, forest hogs, swamp antelopes, forest buffaloes, okapis, sometimes gorillas and always a host of smaller animals that thrive on secondary growth. When elephants disappear and the forest reverts, the larger animals give way to smaller, nimbler animals like monkeys, squirrels and rodents.

---

16. The passage is primarily concerned with

(A) explaining why elephants are facing the threat of extinction

(B) explaining difficulties in providing sufficient forage for plant eaters

(C) explaining how the elephant's impact on its surroundings affects other species

(D) distinguishing between savannas and rain forests as habitats for elephants

(E) contrasting elephants with members of other endangered species

17. The word "mounted" in line 5 means

(A) ascended   (B) increased   (C) launched
(D) attached   (E) exhibited

18. In the opening paragraph, the author mentions tigers and whales in order to emphasize which point about the elephant?

(A) Like them, it faces the threat of extinction.

(B) It is herbivorous rather than carnivorous.

(C) It moves more ponderously than either the tiger or the whale.

(D) Unlike them, it physically alters its environment.

(E) It is the largest extant land mammal.

GO ON TO NEXT PAGE ▶

19. A necessary component of the elephant's ability to transform the landscape is its

(A) massive intelligence
(B) fear of predators
(C) ravenous hunger
(D) lack of grace
(E) ability to regenerate

20. It can be inferred from the passage that

(A) the lion and the cheetah commonly prey upon elephants
(B) the elephant is dependent upon the existence of smaller plant-eating mammals for its survival
(C) elephants have an indirect effect on the hunting patterns of certain carnivores
(D) the floor of the tropical rain forest is too overgrown to accommodate larger plant-eating species
(E) the natural tendency of elephants is to crowd together in packs

21. In lines 40 and 41, the quotation marks around the phrase "keystone species" serve to

(A) emphasize the triteness of the phrase
(B) contradict the literal meaning of the term
(C) indicate the author's desire to write colloquially
(D) imply the phrase has ironic connotations
(E) indicate the phrase is being used in a special or technical sense

22. The passage contains information that would answer which of the following questions?

I. How does the elephant's foraging affect its surroundings?
II. How do the feeding patterns of gazelles and giraffes differ?
III. What occurs in the rain forest when the elephant population dwindles?

(A) I only
(B) II only
(C) I and II only
(D) II and III only
(E) I, II, and III

23. The word "host" in line 91 means

(A) food source for parasites
(B) very large number
(C) provider of hospitality
(D) military force
(E) angelic company

24. Which of the following statements best expresses the author's attitude toward the damage to vegetation caused by foraging elephants?

(A) It is a regrettable by-product of the feeding process.
(B) It is a necessary but undesirable aspect of elephant population growth.
(C) It fortuitously results in creating environments suited to diverse species.
(D) It has the unexpected advantage that it allows scientists access to the rain forest.
(E) It reinforces the impression that elephants are a disruptive force.

IF YOU FINISH IN LESS THAN 25 MINUTES, YOU MAY CHECK YOUR WORK ON THIS SECTION ONLY. DO NOT TURN TO ANY OTHER SECTION IN THE TEST.

STOP

Multiple-Choice Directions

For each question in this section, determine which of the five choices is correct, and blacken that choice on your answer sheet. You may use any blank space on the page for your work.

NOTES:
- You may use a calculator whenever you believe it will be helpful.
- Use the diagrams provided to help you solve the problems. Unless you see the phrase
                    <u>Note:</u> Figure not drawn to scale
under a diagram, it has been drawn as accurately as possible. Unless it is stated that a figure is three dimensional, you may assume that it lies in a plane.

Reference

$A = \pi r^2$
$C = 2\pi r$

$A = \frac{1}{2}bh$

$V = \ell wh$

$V = \pi r^2 h$

$c^2 = a^2 + b^2$

Special Right Triangles

Number of degrees in a circle: 360
Sum of the measures, in degrees, of the three angles of a triangle: 180

---

1. If $b - 8 = 0$, what is the value of $b + 8$?
   (A) -16 (B) -8 (C) 0 (D) 8 (E) 16

2. Isaac has twice as many toys as Sidney. If Isaac has t toys, how many does Sidney have?
   (A) $2t$ (B) t^2 (C) $\frac{t}{2}$ (D) $\frac{2}{t}$ (E) $t + 2$

3. In the figure above, what is the value of x?
   (A) 40 (B) 60 (C) 70 (D) 80 (E) 140

4. What is the value of n if $10^{2n+1} = 1,000,000$?
   (A) 2 (B) 2.5 (C) 3 (D) 5 (E) 6

5. What is the product of 1.5 and 1.7 rounded to the nearest tenth?
   (A) 2.2 (B) 2.5 (C) 2.6 (D) 3.0 (E) 3.2

6. A square has the same area as a circle of diameter 4. What is the length of each side of the square?
   (A) $2\sqrt{\pi}$ (B) $4\sqrt{\pi}$ (C) 2π (D) 4π (E) 8π

7. Aurelie is now 5 times as old as Maurice, but 7 years from now, she will be 3 times as old as he will be then. How old is Aurelie now?
   (A) 15 (B) 20 (C) 21 (D) 25 (E) 35

8. What is the length of each of the six equal sides of a regular hexagon, if the perimeter of the hexagon is equal to the perimeter of a square whose area is 36?
   (A) 4 (B) 6 (C) 12 (D) 24 (E) 36

9. If for any number b, the operations $\diamond$ and $\blacklozenge$ are defined by $b\diamond = b + 1$ and $\blacklozenge b = b - 1$, which of the following is NOT equal to $(3\diamond)(\blacklozenge 5)$?
   (A) $(1\diamond)(\blacklozenge 9)$ (B) $7\diamond + \blacklozenge 9$ (C) $(4\diamond)(\blacklozenge 4)$
   (D) $(7\diamond)(\blacklozenge 3)$ (E) $15\diamond \div \blacklozenge 2$

10. If $\frac{n + 2}{5}$ is an integer, what is the remainder when n is divided by 5?
    (A) 1 (B) 2 (C) 3 (D) 4
    (E) It cannot be determined from the information given.

11. The day of a quiz, only Michelle was absent. The average (arithmetic mean) grade of the other students was 85. When Michelle took a makeup quiz, her grade was 30, which lowered the class's average to 80. How many students are in the class?
    (A) 8 (B) 9 (C) 10 (D) 11 (E) 12

12. At Music Warehouse the regular price for a CD is d dollars. How many CDs can be purchased there for m dollars when the CDs are on sale at 20% off the regular price?
    (A) $\frac{4d}{5m}$ (B) $\frac{4m}{5d}$ (C) $\frac{5d}{4m}$ (D) $\frac{5m}{4d}$ (E) $\frac{md}{20}$

GO ON TO NEXT PAGE ▶

13. In a group of 40 people, 13 own dogs and 18 own cats. If 16 have neither a dog nor a cat, how many people have both?

(A) 0 (B) 3 (C) 6 (D) 7 (E) 11

14. How many integers are solutions of the inequality $3|x| + 1 < 16$?

(A) 0 (B) 4 (C) 8 (D) 9
(E) Infinitely many

15. Each of the 15 members of a club owns a certain number of teddy bears. The following chart shows the number of teddy bears owned.

Number of Teddy Bears	Number of Members
6	2
8	5
10	4
13	4

What is the average (arithmetic mean) of the median and the mode of this set of data?
(A) 4.5 (B) 8 (C) 8.5 (D) 9 (E) 9.5

16. What is the value of $3^{\frac{1}{2}} \times 3^{\frac{1}{3}} \times 3^{\frac{1}{6}}$?
(A) $3^{\frac{1}{36}}$ (B) $3^{\frac{1}{11}}$ (C) $27^{\frac{1}{36}}$ (D) $27^{\frac{1}{11}}$ (E) 3

17. In the figure above, the small square is inscribed in the circle, which is inscribed in the large square. What is the ratio of the area of the large square to the area of the small square?

(A) $\sqrt{2}$:1 (B) $\sqrt{3}$:1 (C) 2:1 (D) $2\sqrt{2}$:1
(E) It cannot be determined from the information given.

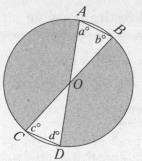

18. In the figure above, O is the center of the circle and $AD = 10$. If the area of the shaded region is 20π, what is the value of $a + b + c + d$?

(A) 144 (B) 216 (C) 240 (D) 270 (E) 288

19. If $r + 2s = a$ and $r - 2s = b$, which of the following is an expression for rs?

(A) ab (B) $\frac{a+b}{2}$ (C) $\frac{a-b}{2}$
(D) $\frac{a^2 - b^2}{4}$ (E) $\frac{a^2 - b^2}{8}$

20. If a is increased by 25% and b is decreased by 25%, the resulting numbers will be equal. What is the ratio of a to b?

(A) $\frac{3}{5}$ (B) $\frac{3}{4}$ (C) $\frac{1}{1}$ (D) $\frac{4}{3}$ (E) $\frac{5}{3}$

IF YOU FINISH BEFORE 25 MINUTES, YOU MAY CHECK YOUR WORK ON THIS SECTION ONLY. DO NOT TURN TO ANY OTHER SECTION IN THE TEST.

STOP

For each question in this section, select the best answer from among the choices given and fill in the corresponding circle on the answer sheet.

Directions

Each sentence below has one or two blanks, each blank indicating that something has been omitted. Beneath the sentence are five words or sets of words labeled A through E. Choose the word or set of words that, when inserted in the sentence, best fits the meaning of the sentence as a whole.

EXAMPLE:

Medieval kingdoms did not become constitutional republics overnight; on the contrary, the change was ----.

(A) unpopular   (B) unexpected
(C) advantageous   (D) sufficient   (E) gradual

Ⓐ Ⓑ Ⓒ Ⓓ ●

---

25. In order that they may be able to discriminate wisely among the many conflicting arguments put before them, legislators must be trained to ---- the truth.

    (A) confuse   (B) condemn   (C) ignore
    (D) condone   (E) discern

26. In their new collections of lighthearted, provocative dresses, French fashion designers are gambling that even ---- professional women are ready for a bit of ---- in style.

    (A) strict..reticence
    (B) serious..frivolity
    (C) elegant..tradition
    (D) modern..harmony
    (E) unsentimental..propriety

27. The airline customer service representative tried to ---- the ---- passenger by offering her a seat in first class.

    (A) pacify..placid
    (B) thwart..irate
    (C) divert..grateful
    (D) authorize..listless
    (E) mollify..angry

28. People who find themselves unusually ---- and ready to drowse off at unexpected moments may be suffering from a hormonal imbalance.

    (A) lethargic   (B) distracted   (C) obdurate
    (D) benign   (E) perfunctory

29. The expression "he passed away" is ---- for "he died."

    (A) a reminder   (B) a commiseration
    (C) a simile   (D) a euphemism
    (E) an exaggeration

30. Despite the enormous popularity and influence of his book, *Thunder Out of China*, White's career ----.

    (A) soared   (B) endured   (C) accelerated
    (D) revived   (E) foundered

31. Written just after Martin Luther King's assassination, Lomax's book has all the virtues of historical ---- but lacks the greater virtue of historical ----, which comes from long and mature reflection upon events.

    (A) precision..accuracy
    (B) criticism..distance
    (C) immediacy..perspective
    (D) outlook..realism
    (E) currency..testimony

32. Relishing his triumph, Kevin Costner especially ---- the chagrin of the critics who had predicted his ----.

    (A) regretted..success
    (B) acknowledged..comeback
    (C) understated..bankruptcy
    (D) distorted..mortification
    (E) savored..failure

GO ON TO NEXT PAGE ▶

Directions

Each of the passages below precedes two questions based on its content. Answer the questions following each passage on the basis of what is stated or implied in that passage

Questions 33 and 34 are based on the following passage.

There was a time when poetry mattered in America—a time when T. S. Eliot could fill a football stadium with poetry fans, when literature
Line enjoyed a central place in our culture, and young
5 men and women dreamed about becoming writers. That time is long gone. Today if young people dream of writing at all, they dream of writing rap songs or sitcom scripts, pop lit, not enduring works of art.

33. The reference to the football stadium in line 3 serves primarily to
(A) demonstrate the connection between sports and poetry
(B) show Eliot's deep appreciation of football
(C) emphasize the popularity of poetry in the period
(D) suggest a potential site for poetry readings today
(E) point out Eliot's adventurousness

34. The word "enjoyed" in line 4 most nearly means
(A) fancied   (B) relished   (C) possessed
(D) appreciated   (E) flourished

Questions 35 and 36 are based on the following passage.

Echoing leaders in the field such as Noam Chomsky, many linguists argue that the capacity for language is a uniquely human property. They
Line contend that chimpanzees and related primates
5 are incapable of using language because their brains lack the human brain structures that make language. Other researchers, however, disagree, citing experiments in which apes have been taught to use symbolic communication systems, such as
10 American Sign Language. In one study, for example, Georgia State professor E. Sue Savage-Rambaugh has worked with a "keyboard" consisting of 400 symbols to communicate with bonobos (also known as pygmy chimpanzees).

35. The word "property" in line 3 most nearly means
(A) trait   (B) wealth   (C) ownership
(D) oddity   (E) affliction

36. Savage-Rambaugh and Chomsky disagree in their evaluations of
(A) primates' value in experimental research
(B) primates' abilities in language acquisition
(C) primates' abilities to manipulate artifacts
(D) researchers' knowledge of American Sign Language
(E) researchers' impartiality in primate studies

Directions

The passages below are followed by questions on their content; questions following a pair of related passages may also be based on the relationship between the paired passages. Answer the questions on the basis of what is stated or implied in the passages and in any introductory material that may be provided.

Questions 37–48 are based on the following passages.

The following passages are excerpted from two recent essays that relate writing to sports. The author of Passage 1 deals with having had a novel rejected by his publisher. The author of Passage 2 explores how his involvement in sports affected his writing career.

Passage 1

In consigning this manuscript to a desk drawer, I am comforted by the behavior of baseball players. There are *no* pitchers who do not give up home runs, there are *no* batters who do not strike
Line
5 out. There are *no* major league pitchers or batters who have not somehow learned to survive giving up home runs and striking out. That much is obvious.

What seems to me less obvious is how
10 these "failures" must be digested, or put to use, in the overall experience of the player. A jogger once explained to me that the nerves of the ankle are so sensitive and complex that each time a runner sets his foot down, hundreds of messages are conveyed
15 to the runner's brain about the nature of the terrain and the requirements for weight distribution, balance, and muscle-strength. I'm certain that the

GO ON TO NEXT PAGE ▶

ninth-inning home run that Dave Henderson hit off Donny Moore registered complexly and
20 permanently in Moore's mind and body and that the next time Moore faced Henderson, his pitching was informed by his awful experience of October 1986. Moore's continuing baseball career depended to some extent on his converting that
25 encounter with Henderson into something useful for his pitching. I can also imagine such an experience destroying an athlete, registering in his mind and body in such a negative way as to produce a debilitating fear.

30 Of the many ways in which athletes and artists are similar, one is that, unlike accountants or plumbers or insurance salesmen, to succeed at all they must perform at an extraordinary level of excellence. Another is that they must be willing to
35 extend themselves irrationally in order to achieve that level of performance. A writer doesn't have to write all-out all the time, but he or she must be ready to write all-out any time the story requires it. Hold back and you produce what just about any
40 literate citizen can produce, a "pretty good" piece of work. Like the cautious pitcher, the timid writer can spend a lifetime in the minor leagues.

And what more than failure—the strike out, the crucial home run given up, the manuscript
45 criticized and rejected—is more likely to produce caution or timidity? An instinctive response to painful experience is to avoid the behavior that produced the pain. To function at the level of excellence required for survival, writers like
50 athletes must go against instinct, must absorb their failures and become stronger, must endlessly repeat the behavior that produced the pain.

Passage 2

The athletic advantages of this concentration, particularly for an athlete who was making up for
55 the absence of great natural skill, were considerable. Concentration gave you an edge over many of

your opponents, even your betters, who could not isolate themselves to that degree. For example, in football if they were ahead (or behind) by several
60 touchdowns, if the game itself seemed to have been settled, they tended to slack off, to ease off a little, certainly to relax their own concentration. It was then that your own unwavering concentration and your own indifference to the larger point of
65 view paid off. At the very least you could deal out surprise and discomfort to your opponents.

But it was more than that. Do you see? The ritual of physical concentration, of acute engagement in a small space while disregarding all the
70 clamor and demands of the larger world, was the best possible lesson in precisely the kind of selfish intensity needed to create and to finish a poem, a story, or a novel. This alone mattered while all the world going on, with and without you, did not.

75 I was learning first in muscle, blood, and bone, not from literature and not from teachers of literature or the arts or the natural sciences, but from coaches, in particular this one coach who paid me enough attention to influence me to teach
80 some things to myself. I was learning about art and life through the abstraction of athletics in much the same way that a soldier is, to an extent, prepared for war by endless parade ground drill. His body must learn to be a soldier before heart,
85 mind, and spirit can.

Ironically, I tend to dismiss most comparisons of athletics to art and to "the creative process." But only because, I think, so much that is claimed for both is untrue. But I have come to believe—indeed I have to believe it insofar as I believe in the
90 validity and efficacy of art—that what comes to us first and foremost through the body, as a sensuous affective experience, is taken and transformed by mind and self into a thing of the spirit. Which is
95 only to say that what the body learns and is taught is of enormous significance—at least until the last light of the body fails.

---

37. Why does the author of Passage 1 consign his manuscript to a desk drawer?

(A) to protect it from the inquisitive eyes of his family
(B) to prevent its getting lost or disordered
(C) because his publisher wishes to take another look at it
(D) because he chooses to watch a televised baseball game
(E) to set it aside as unmarketable in its current state

38. Why is the author of Passage 1 "comforted by the behavior of baseball players" (lines 1–8)?

(A) He treasures the timeless rituals of America's national pastime.
(B) He sees he is not alone in having to confront failure and move on.
(C) He enjoys watching the frustration of the batters who strike out.
(D) He looks at baseball from the viewpoint of a behavioral psychologist.
(E) He welcomes any distraction from the task of revising his novel.

GO ON TO NEXT PAGE ▶

39. What function in the passage is served by the discussion of the nerves in the ankle in lines 11–17?

  (A) It provides a momentary digression from the overall narrative flow.
  (B) It emphasizes how strong a mental impact Henderson's home run must have had on Moore.
  (C) It provides scientific confirmation of the neuromuscular abilities of athletes.
  (D) It illustrates that the author's interest in sports is not limited to baseball alone.
  (E) It conveys a sense of how confusing it is for the mind to deal with so many simultaneous messages.

40. The word "registered" in line 19 means

  (A) enrolled formally
  (B) expressed without words
  (C) corresponded exactly
  (D) made an impression
  (E) qualified officially

41. The attitude of the author of Passage 1 to accountants, plumbers, and insurance salesmen (lines 30–36) can best be described as

  (A) respectful   (B) cautious   (C) superior
  (D) cynical   (E) hypocritical

42. In the concluding paragraphs of Passage 1, the author appears to

  (A) romanticize the writer as someone heroic in his or her accomplishments
  (B) deprecate athletes for their inability to react to experience instinctively
  (C) minimize the travail that artists and athletes endure to do their work
  (D) advocate the importance of literacy to the common citizen
  (E) suggest a cautious approach would reduce the likelihood of future failure

43. The author of Passage 2 prizes

  (A) his innate athletic talent
  (B) the respect of his peers
  (C) his ability to focus
  (D) the gift of relaxation
  (E) winning at any cost

44. The word "settled" in line 61 means

  (A) judged   (B) decided   (C) reconciled
  (D) pacified   (E) inhabited

45. What does the author mean by "indifference to the larger point of view" (lines 64–65)?

  (A) inability to see the greater implications of the activity in which you were involved
  (B) hostility to opponents coming from larger, better trained teams
  (C) reluctance to look beyond your own immediate concerns
  (D) refusing to care how greatly you might be hurt by your opponents
  (E) being more concerned with the task at hand than with whether you win or lose

46. What is the function of the phrase "to an extent" in line 82?

  (A) It denies a situation.
  (B) It conveys a paradox.
  (C) It qualifies a statement.
  (D) It represents a metaphor.
  (E) It minimizes a liability.

47. The author finds it ironic that he tends to "dismiss most comparisons of athletics to art" (lines 86–87) because

  (A) athletics is the basis for great art
  (B) he finds comparisons generally unhelpful
  (C) he is making such a comparison
  (D) he typically is less cynical
  (E) he rejects the so-called creative process

48. The authors of both passages would agree that

  (A) the lot of the professional writer is more trying than that of the professional athlete
  (B) athletics has little to do with the actual workings of the creative process
  (C) both artists and athletes learn hard lessons in the course of mastering their art
  (D) it is important to concentrate on the things that hurt us in life
  (E) participating in sports provides a distraction from the isolation of a writer's life

IF YOU FINISH IN LESS THAN 25 MINUTES, YOU MAY CHECK YOUR WORK ON THIS SECTION ONLY. DO NOT TURN TO ANY OTHER SECTION IN THE TEST.

STOP

Multiple-Choice Directions

For questions 21–28, determine which of the five choices is correct. You may use any blank space on the page for your work.

NOTES:

- You may use a calculator whenever you believe it will be helpful.
- Use the diagrams provided to help you solve the problems. Unless you see the phrase

Note: Figure not drawn to scale

under a diagram, it has been drawn as accurately as possible. Unless it is stated that a figure is three dimensional, you may assume that it lies in a plane.

Reference

$A = \pi r^2$
$C = 2\pi r$

$A = \frac{1}{2}bh$

$V = \ell wh$

$V = \pi r^2 h$

$c^2 = a^2 + b^2$

Special Right Triangles

Number of degrees in a circle: 360
Sum of the measures, in degrees, of the three angles of a triangle: 180

---

21. If a basket of fruit contains 5 pounds of apples, 3 pounds of oranges, and 1 pound of pears, by weight, what fraction of the fruit is oranges?

    (A) $\frac{1}{9}$ (B) $\frac{1}{5}$ (C) $\frac{1}{3}$ (D) $\frac{3}{8}$ (E) $\frac{1}{2}$

22. In the figure above, what is the value of a?

    (A) 30 (B) 35 (C) 36 (D) 45 (E) 80

23. If $\frac{5}{8}$ of the members of the chess club are boys, what is the ratio of girls to boys in the club?

    (A) $\frac{4}{8}$ (B) $\frac{3}{5}$ (C) $\frac{5}{3}$ (D) $\frac{8}{5}$
    (E) It cannot be determined from the information given.

24. A rectangle has a perimeter equal to the circumference of a circle of radius 3. If the width of the rectangle is 3, what is its length?

    (A) $3\pi - 3$ (B) $4.5\pi - 3$ (C) $6\pi - 3$
    (D) $9\pi - 3$ (E) $3\pi + 3$

25. If p, q, and r are prime numbers greater than 5, which of the following could be true?

    I. $p - q$ is prime
    II. $p + q$ is prime
    III. $p + q + r$ is prime

    (A) I only (B) II only (C) I and II only
    (D) I and III only (E) I, II, and III

26. If A (3, −2) and B (7, 2) are the endpoints of a diameter of a circle, what is the area of the circle?

    (A) $2\sqrt{2}\,\pi$ (B) $4\sqrt{2}\,\pi$ (C) 8π (D) 16π
    (E) 32π

27. If $13 - 2\sqrt{x} = 7$, then what is the value of x?

    (A) −9 (B) 6 (C) 9 (D) 16 (E) There is no value of x that satisfies the equation.

28. The estate of a wealthy man was distributed as follows: 10% to his wife, 5% divided equally among his 3 children, 5% divided equally among his 5 grandchildren, and the balance to a charitable trust. If the trust received $1,000,000, how much did each grandchild inherit?

    (A) $10,000 (B) $12,500 (C) $20,000
    (D) $62,500 (E) $100,000

GO ON TO NEXT PAGE ▶

Student-Produced Response Directions

In questions 29–38, first solve the problem, and then enter your answer on the grid provided on the answer sheet. The instructions for entering your answers follow.

- First, write your answer in the boxes at the top of the grid.
- Second, grid your answer in the columns below the boxes.
- Use the fraction bar in the first row or the decimal point in the second row to enter fractions and decimals.

Write your answer in the boxes

Grid-in your answer

Answer: $\frac{8}{15}$ Answer: 1.75   Answer: 100

Either position is acceptable

- Grid only one space in each column.
- Entering the answer in the boxes is recommended as an aid in gridding but is not required.
- The machine scoring your exam can read only what you grid, so you **must grid-in your answers correctly to get credit.**
- If a question has more than one correct answer, grid-in only one of them.
- The grid does not have a minus sign; so no answer can be negative.
- A mixed number *must* be converted to an improper fraction or a decimal before it is gridded. Enter $1\frac{1}{4}$ as $\frac{5}{4}$ or 1.25; the machine will interpret 11/4 as $\frac{11}{4}$ and mark it wrong.

- **All decimals must be entered as accurately as possible.** Here are three acceptable ways of gridding

$$\frac{3}{11} = 0.272727\ldots$$

- Note that rounding to .273 is acceptable because you are using the full grid, but you would receive **no credit** for .3 or .27, because they are less accurate.

29. In the figure above, if *PS* bisects ∠*RST*, what is the value of *w*?

30. There are 150 people in line outside a ballpark. If Peter is the 10th person from the front and Wendy is the 110th person from the front, how many people are there between Peter and Wendy?

31. In the figure below, what is the value of *x*?

Note: Figure not drawn to scale

GO ON TO NEXT PAGE ▶

32. If r, s, and t are prime numbers less than 15, what is the greatest possible value of $\frac{r-s}{t}$?

33. If $\frac{2}{x} + \frac{3}{4} = \frac{4}{5}$, then $x =$

34. In the figure below, the radius of the large circle is 3 and the radius of each of the small white circles is 1. If a point, P, is chosen at random inside the big circle, what is the probability that P lies in the shaded region?

Note: Figure not drawn to scale

35. Two circles have diameters of 12 inches and 10 inches, respectively. The area of the larger circle is what percent *more* than the area of the smaller circle? (Grid-in your answer without a percent sign.)

36. One hundred dollars has been divided among five people. Each one received a whole number of dollars, and no two people received the same amount. If the largest share was $35 and the smallest share was $10, what is the most money that the person with the third largest share could have received?

37. Twenty-five students took a quiz, and the grades they earned ranged from 2 to 10. If exactly 22 of them passed by earning a grade of 7 or higher, what is the highest possible average (arithmetic mean) the class could have earned on the quiz?

38. Let $[x] =$ the largest integer that is less than or equal to x. For example, $[2.66] = 2$ and $[5] = 5$. What is the value of $[2\pi] - [-2\pi]$?

IF YOU FINISH IN LESS THAN 25 MINUTES, YOU MAY CHECK YOUR WORK ON THIS SECTION ONLY. DO NOT TURN TO ANY OTHER SECTION IN THE TEST.

STOP

388 ▶ CHAPTER 11 / Model Test C

Improving Sentence Directions

Some or all parts of the following sentences are underlined. The first answer choice, (A), simply repeats the underlined part of the sentence. The other four choices present four alternative ways to phrase the underlined part. Select the answer that produces the most effective sentence, one that is clear and exact, and blacken the appropriate space on your answer sheet. In selecting your choice, be sure that it is standard written English and that it expresses the meaning of the original sentence.

EXAMPLE: **SAMPLE ANSWER:**

The first biography of author Eudora Welty came out   Ⓐ Ⓑ Ⓒ ● Ⓔ
in 1998, <u>and she was eighty-nine years old at the time.</u>

(A) and she was eighty-nine years old at the time
(B) at the time when she was eighty-nine
(C) upon becoming an eighty-nine year old
(D) when she was eighty-nine
(E) at the age of eighty-nine years old

---

1. Fifty-three thousand shouting <u>enthusiasts filled the stadium, they had come</u> to watch the first game of the season and to cheer the home team.

    (A) enthusiasts filled the stadium, they had come
    (B) enthusiasts filled the stadium to come
    (C) enthusiasts, filling the stadium, had come
    (D) enthusiasts filled the stadium; and had come
    (E) enthusiasts filling the stadium, who had come

2. During the judging of the animals at the show, the judges could not decide <u>whether Brown's collie or Jones's terrier was the best</u> dog.

    (A) whether Brown's collie or Jones's terrier was the best
    (B) if Brown's collie or Jones's terrier was the better
    (C) whether Brown's collie or Jones's terrier was the better
    (D) if Brown's collie or Jones's terrier was the best
    (E) whether Brown's collie or Jones's terrier had been the best

3. <u>Finally reviewing the extensive evidence against the defendant</u>, he was found guilty.

    (A) Finally reviewing the extensive evidence against the defendant,
    (B) Reviewing the extensive evidence against the defendant,
    (C) The jury finally reviewed the extensive evidence against the defendant,
    (D) When the jury finally reviewed the extensive evidence against the defendant,
    (E) The jury finally reviewed the evidence against the defendant,

4. <u>Paul Gauguin was married and had family responsibilities and he</u> ran away to the South Seas to paint.

    (A) Paul Gauguin was married and had family responsibilities and he
    (B) Although being married and having family responsibilities, Paul Gauguin
    (C) Although Paul Gauguin was married and had family responsibilities, he
    (D) Being married, and therefore having family responsibilities, Paul Gauguin
    (E) Despite the fact that Paul Gauguin was married and had family responsibilities, he

5. A key difference between mice and voles is tail <u>length, a mouse's tail is</u> twice as long as the tail of a vole.

    (A) length, a mouse's tail is
    (B) length; a mouse's tail is
    (C) length, the tail of a mouse is
    (D) length; a mouse's tail, it is
    (E) length, mice's tails are

GO ON TO NEXT PAGE ▶

6. As a retired executive, he is now busier than ever; he makes his living by speaking before business and philanthropic groups, writing books and articles, and he is a director of three major corporations.

(A) by speaking before business and philanthropic groups, writing books and articles, and he is a director of
(B) by speaking before business and philanthropic groups, and he writes books and articles as well as being a director of
(C) by speaking before business and philanthropic groups, and he writes books and articles, and directs
(D) by speaking before business and philanthropic groups, writing books and articles, and directing
(E) by speaking before business and philanthropic groups, in addition to writing books and articles, and he is a director of

7. The president established a special commission for the space program; the purpose being to investigate the causes of the *Challenger* disaster.

(A) program; the purpose being to
(B) program; whose purpose being to
(C) program, the purpose was to
(D) program to
(E) program; in order to

8. When Harriet Tubman decided to help runaway slaves escape to the North, she knew that her mission would bring her into danger in both South and North.

(A) When Harriet Tubman decided to help runaway slaves escape
(B) When Harriet Tubman decides to help runaway slaves escape
(C) When Harriet Tubman decided about helping runaway slaves escape
(D) After the decision by Harriet Tubman to help runaway slaves escape
(E) After Harriet Tubman's making of the decision to help runaway slaves escape

9. The growing impoverishment of women and children in American society distresses Senator Moynihan, and he is also infuriated.

(A) distresses Senator Moynihan, and he is also infuriated
(B) distresses Senator Moynihan, infuriating him
(C) distresses and infuriates Senator Moynihan
(D) is distressing Senator Moynihan, making him infuriated
(E) is a cause of distress to Senator Moynihan, and of a fury

10. Being a successful reporter demands powers of observation, fluency, and persistence.

(A) Being a successful reporter demands
(B) Being a successful reporter who demands
(C) To be a successful reporter who demands
(D) Being a successful reporter demanding
(E) To be a successful reporter demanding

11. Had I been at the scene of the accident, I could have administered first aid to the victims.

(A) Had I been at the scene of the accident
(B) If I were at the scene of the accident
(C) If I was at the scene of the accident
(D) I should have been at the scene of the accident
(E) I should have been at the scene of the accident, and

12. The Northern Lights, or Aurora Borealis, is so named because it is a light display that takes place in the northern skies.

(A) because it is a light display that takes place
(B) as a light display taking place
(C) because of taking place
(D) due to the fact that it is a light display
(E) contrary to the fact of taking place

13. It is not for you to assume responsibility; it is rather me who is the guilty person in this matter.

(A) me who is   (B) me who am   (C) I who is
(D) I who are   (E) I who am

14. Brightly colored birds soared to and fro, indifferent with the ships that ploughed the blue Caribbean waters.

(A) Brightly colored birds soared to and fro, indifferent with the ships that ploughed
(B) Brightly colored birds soared to and from, indifferent with the ships which ploughed
(C) Brightly colored birds soared to and fro, indifferent to the ships that ploughed
(D) Bright colored birds soared to and fro, indifferently with the ships, they ploughed
(E) Brighly colored birds soaring to and fro, indifferent with the ships that ploughed

GO ON TO NEXT PAGE ▶

15. The Metropolitan Museum of Art's collection of medieval sculptures, like so many other aspects of the museum, have benefited significantly from the generosity of J. Pierpont Morgan, the financier.

(A) sculptures, like so many other aspects of the museum, have benefited significantly from

(B) sculptures, like so many other aspects of the museum, have significant benefits from

(C) sculptures, like so many other aspects of the museum, has benefited significantly from

(D) sculptures, similar to many other aspects of the museum, have benefited significantly from

(E) sculptures, like so many other aspects of the museum, have benefited significantly through

16. Native Americans did not fare well in the mission system, perishing in vast numbers from measles and other diseases introduced by the Spanish.

(A) fare well in the mission system, perishing

(B) fare good in the mission system, perishing

(C) fare well in the mission system, they perished

(D) fare well from the mission system, perishing

(E) fare well in the mission system, despite perishing

17. Standoffish and reserved, Charles Lindbergh was uncomfortable with the applause he received from the crowds which have cheered his historic flight.

(A) received from the crowds which have cheered his historic flight

(B) receives from the crowds which cheer his historic flight

(C) received from the cheering crowds about his historic flight

(D) received from the crowds when they cheer his historic flight

(E) received from the crowds that cheered his historic flight

18. Study-abroad programs can enhance students' acquisition of a foreign language, improve their knowledge of the host culture, and even their world views can be transformed.

(A) culture, and even their world views can be transformed

(B) culture, and even can transform their world views

(C) culture, and their world views can even be transformed

(D) culture, and even transform their world views

(E) culture, and even transforming their world views

19. Once dried and pinned as specimens, dragonflies lose most of their color and become increasing fragile.

(A) Once dried and pinned as specimens, dragonflies lose most of their color and become increasing fragile.

(B) Once dried and pinned as a specimen, dragonflies lose most of their color and become increasing fragile.

(C) Once they have been dried and pinned as specimens, dragonflies lose most of their color, becoming increasing fragile.

(D) They were once dried and pinned as specimens, and then dragonflies lose most of their color and become increasingly fragile.

(E) Once dried and pinned as specimens, dragonflies lose most of their color and become increasingly fragile.

20. By the time Jews began to arrive in the United States in significant numbers in the early twentieth century, they already have established an affinity with political liberalism in Europe.

(A) they already have established an affinity with

(B) they all ready have established an affinity with

(C) they already have established an affinity for

(D) an affinity had already been established by them toward

(E) they already had established an affinity with

21. <u>After</u> his heart attack, he <u>was ordered</u> <u>to lay</u> in bed
    A   B   C

    and rest <u>for</u> two weeks. <u>No error</u>
              D   E

22. While <u>my</u> aunt and I <u>were traveling</u> <u>through</u> our
          A   B   C

    national parks, my aunt was <u>frightened</u> by a bear.
                                      D

    <u>No error</u>
        E

23. <u>Only</u> recently, the <u>newly</u> organized football
    A   B

    association <u>added</u> two new teams to <u>their</u> league.
                    C   D

    <u>No error</u>
        E

24. <u>In view of</u> the controversy with the school board,
    A

    neither the teachers <u>nor</u> the principal <u>are being</u>
                          B   C

    considered for salary increases <u>at this time</u>.
                                          D

    <u>No error</u>
        E

25. While we <u>have rummaged</u> <u>through</u> the attic, we
                    A   B

    found <u>not only</u> an album of our trip to Europe
              C

    but also a <u>multitude of</u> old news clippings.
                    D

    <u>No error</u>
        E

26. Of <u>all</u> the <u>members of</u> the United States team,
        A   B

    Greg Lemond <u>became</u> the first <u>to win</u> the
                    C   D

    prestigious Tour de France bike race. <u>No error</u>
                                                E

27. Before we <u>adopt</u> this legislation, we <u>ought to</u>
                  A   B

    consider the <u>affect</u> the new law will have on <u>our</u>
                      C   D

    retired and disabled citizens. <u>No error</u>
                                        E

28. The legendary Mark McGwire <u>has established</u>
                                      A

    an <u>enviable</u> <u>record, and it</u> probably will not
           B   C

    <u>be broken</u> during the next fifty years. <u>No error</u>
        D   E

29. Toni Cade Bambara, <u>who</u> is a black American
                          A

    writer, <u>has been active</u> in civil rights and women's
                  B

    issues, <u>nor is she</u> <u>attuned to</u> Afro-American
                C   D

    relationships. <u>No error</u>
                        E

30. The boom in sales of video cassette records <u>can be</u>
                                                    A

    <u>attributed to</u> <u>numerous</u> things, <u>including being</u>
          B   C   D

    price reduction and the growth of rental stores.

    <u>No error</u>
        E

GO ON TO NEXT PAGE ▶

31. After a six-month study semester abroad, she was
A   B

happy to get home to comfortable familiar
C   D

surroundings and appetizing food. No error
                                         E

32. Much more experimental data are required before
  A   B   C

we can accept this theory. No error
                   D   E

33. Because he has been warned only about the
                     A   B

danger of walking on the railroad trestle, he dared
            C

several of his friends to walk on the tracks.
       D

No error
   E

34. Where is it possible to find if it was James Russell
                                 A   B

Lowell or Henry Wadsworth Longfellow who
     C   D

wrote "Hiawatha" ? No error
               E

Improving Paragraph Directions

The passage below is the unedited draft of a student's essay. Some of the essay needs to be rewritten to make the meaning clearer and more precise. Read the essay carefully.

The essay is followed by five questions about changes that might improve all or part of its organization, development, sentence structure, use of language, appropriateness to the audience, or its use of standard written English. Choose the answer that most clearly and effectively expresses the student's intended meaning. Indicate your choice by filling in the corresponding space on the answer sheet.

[1] Although some people believe that certain celebrations have no point, celebrations are one of the few things that all people have in common. [2] They take place everywhere. [3] Listing all of them would be an impossible task. [4] People of all kinds look forward to celebrations for keeping traditions alive for generation after generation. [5] Those who criticize celebrations do not understand the human need to preserve tradition and culture.

[6] In the Muslim religion, the Ead is a celebration. [7] It begins as soon as Ramadan (the fasting month) is over. [8] During the Ead, families gather together. [9] New clothes are bought for children, and they receive money from both family and friends. [10] Also, each family, if they can afford it, slaughters a sheep or a cow. [11] They keep a small fraction of the meat, and the rest they must give to the poor. [12] They also donate money to a mosque.

[14] Many celebrations involve eating meals. [15] In the United States, people gather together on Thanksgiving to say thank you for their blessings by having a huge feast with turkey, sweet potatoes, and cranberry sauce. [16] Christmas and Easter holiday dinners are a custom in the Christian religion. [17] They have a roast at Christmas. [18] At Easter they serve ham. [19] The Jewish people celebrate Passover with a big meal called

a seder. [20] They say prayers, drink wine, and sing songs to remember how Jews suffered centuries ago when they escaped from slavery in Egypt.

[21] A celebration is held each year to honor great people like Dr. Martin Luther King. [22] His birthday is celebrated because of this man's noble belief in equality of all races. [23] People wish to remember not only his famous speeches, including "I Have A Dream," but also about him being assassinated in Memphis in 1968. [24] He died while fighting for the equality of minorities. [25] Unlike religious celebrations, celebrations for great heroes like Martin Luther King are for all people everywhere in the world. [26] He is a world-class hero and he deserved the Nobel Prize for Peace that he won.

35. To improve the unity of the first paragraph, which of the following is the best sentence to delete?

(A) sentence 1
(B) sentence 2
(C) sentence 3
(D) sentence 4
(E) sentence 5

GO ON TO NEXT PAGE ▶

36. In the context of the third paragraph, which is the best way to combine sentences 16, 17, and 18?

  (A) A roast at Christmas, ham at Easter—that's what Christians eat.
  (B) Christians customarily serve a roast for Christmas dinner, at Easter ham is eaten.
  (C) At customary holiday dinners, Christians eat a roast at Christmas and ham is for Easter dinner.
  (D) Christians often celebrate the Christmas holiday with a roast for dinner and Easter with a traditional ham.
  (E) Christmas and Easter dinners are the custom in the Christian religion, where they have a roast at Christmas and ham at Easter.

37. In an effort to provide a more effective transition between paragraphs 3 and 4, which of the following would be the best revision of sentence 21 below?

A celebration is held each year to honor great people like Dr. Martin Luther King.

  (A) There are also some celebrations to honor great people like Dr. Martin Luther King.
  (B) Martin Luther King is also celebrated in the United States.
  (C) In the United States, celebrating to honor great people like Dr. Martin Luther King has become a tradition.
  (D) In addition to observing religious holidays, people hold celebrations to honor great leaders like Dr. Martin Luther King.
  (E) Besides holding religion-type celebrations, celebrations to honor great people like Dr. Martin Luther King are also held.

38. Which is the best revision of the underlined segment of sentence 23 below?

People wish to remember not only his famous speeches, including "I Have A Dream," but <u>also about him being assassinated</u> in Memphis in 1968.

  (A) that his assassination occurred
  (B) about his being assassination
  (C) the fact that he was assassinated
  (D) about the assassination, too,
  (E) his assassination

39. Considering the essay as a whole, which one of the following best explains the main function of the last paragraph?

  (A) to summarize the main idea of the essay
  (B) to refute a previous argument stated in the essay
  (C) to give an example
  (D) to provide a solution to a problem
  (E) to evaluate the validity of the essay's main idea

IF YOU FINISH IN LESS THAN 30 MINUTES, YOU MAY CHECK YOUR WORK ON THIS SECTION ONLY. DO NOT TURN TO ANY OTHER SECTION IN THE TEST.

STOP

394 ▶ CHAPTER 11 / Model Test C

Answer Key

Section 1 Critical Reading

1. D	10. C	19. C
2. C	11. D	20. C
3. A	12. E	21. E
4. B	13. D	22. E
5. E	14. C	23. B
6. C	15. B	24. C
7. E	16. C	
8. D	17. C	
9. C	18. D	

Section 2 Mathematics

1. E	8. A	15. D
2. C	9. C	16. E
3. C	10. C	17. C
4. B	11. D	18. E
5. C	12. D	19. E
6. A	13. D	20. A
7. E	14. D	

Section 3 Critical Reading

25. E	33. C	41. C
26. B	34. C	42. A
27. E	35. A	43. C
28. A	36. B	44. B
29. D	37. E	45. E
30. E	38. B	46. C
31. C	39. B	47. C
32. E	40. D	48. C

Section 4 Mathematics

21. C	24. A	27. C
22. B	25. D	28. B
23. B	26. C	

29. 1 1 5

30. 9 9

31. 8 8 . 5

32. 1 1 / 2

or **5.5**

33. 4 0

34. 7 / 9

or **.777** or **.778**

35. 4 4

36. 2 1

37. 9 . 3 6

38. 1 3

Section 5 Writing Skills

1. *C*	9. *C*	17. *B*	25. *A*	33. *A*
2. *C*	10. *A*	18. *D*	26. *E*	34. *A*
3. *D*	11. *A*	19. *E*	27. *C*	35. *C*
4. *C*	12. *A*	20. *E*	28. *C*	36. *D*
5. *B*	13. *E*	21. *C*	29. *C*	37. *D*
6. *D*	14. *C*	22. *E*	30. *D*	38. *E*
7. *D*	15. *C*	23. *D*	31. *D*	39. *C*
8. *A*	16. *A*	24. *C*	32. *E*	

Scoring Chart—Model Test C

Critical Reading Sections

Section 1: 24 Questions (1–24)
Number correct	_____	(A)
Number omitted	_____	(B)
Number incorrect	_____	(C)
$\frac{1}{4}$ (C)	_____	(D)
(A) − (D)	_____	Raw Score I

Section 3: 24 Questions (25–48)
Number correct	_____	(A)
Number omitted	_____	(B)
Number incorrect	_____	(C)
$\frac{1}{4}$ (C)	_____	(D)
(A) − (D)	_____	Raw Score II

Total Critical Reading Raw Score
Raw Scores I + II _____

Mathematics Sections

Section 2: 20 Questions (1–20)
Number correct	_____	(A)
Number omitted	_____	(B)
Number incorrect	_____	(C)
$\frac{1}{4}$ (C)	_____	(D)
(A) − (D)	_____	Raw Score I

Section 4: First 8 Questions (21–28)
Number correct	_____	(A)
Number omitted	_____	(B)
Number incorrect	_____	(C)
$\frac{1}{4}$ (C)	_____	(D)
(A) − (D)	_____	Raw Score II

Section 4: Next 10 Questions (29–38)
Number correct _____ Raw Score III

Total Mathematical Raw Score
Raw Scores I + II + III _____

NOTE: In each section (A) + (B) + (C) should equal the number of questions in that section.

Writing Skills Section

Section 5: 39 Questions (1–39)
Number correct	_____	(A)
Number omitted	_____	(B)
Number incorrect	_____	(C)
$\frac{1}{4}$ (C)	_____	(D)

Writing Skills Raw Score
(A) − (D) _____

Evaluation Chart

Study your score. Your raw score is an indication of your probable achievement on the PSAT/NMSQT. As a guide to the amount of work you need or want to do with this book, study the following.

Raw Score			Self-rating
Critical Reading	*Mathematics*	*Writing*	
42–48	35–38	33–39	Superior
37–46	30–34	28–32	Very good
32–36	25–29	23–27	Good
26–35	21–24	17–22	Above average
20–25	17–20	12–16	Average
12–19	10–16	7–11	Below average
less than 12	less than 10	less than 7	Inadequate

Answer Explanations

Section 1 Critical Reading

1. *D* Such an extraordinarily useful material would *revolutionize* or make radical changes in an industry.

2. *C* A contrast is set up here by the expression "no matter how." It tells us that, although future "revelations" (surprising news) may be *striking*, they will not equal past ones. These past revelations *radically* transformed or thoroughly changed our view.

3. *A* Since "few other plants can grow beneath the canopy of the sycamore," it must be *inhibiting* or restraining the other plants.

4. *B* Certain authors have been *relegated* or sent off to "obscurity," a state of being hidden or forgotten. There they must be "rediscovered."

5. *E* Critics sometimes praise but more often *decry* or condemn things. Here the critics see the "saccharine" (too sweet) mood of the movie as inconsistent with the *acerbic* (sour, bitter) tone of the book.

6. *C* The next sentence says that these stones in actuality are plants. Thus, the quotation marks around the word "stones" serve to underscore that these stonelike objects *are not literally stones*.

7. *E* Examine the context: "These stones are in actuality *plants*, members of the genus Lithops, some of the strangest succulents in the world." A succulent is clearly *a kind of plant*.

8. *D* The author uses a metaphor: she likens original artworks that no one is quite ready to appreciate to "intellectual foundlings," or deserted children that no family is willing to claim. The author offers an example of an art specialist's rejection of a work of art that eventually is seen as a masterpiece (Gide's rejection of Proust's novel). The author makes several assertions: "modern art's main characteristic is its obscurity"; "any truly original work of art is bound to seem obscure to John Q. Public." The author denies a possibility: "no great work of art finds an appreciative public waiting for it." However, she never *poses* or asks *a question*. The correct answer is Choice D.

9. *C* Choice C is correct because the word "cold" gives emphasis to the immediately preceding description of Gide's rejection of Proust's manu-

script. As an adverb, *cold* means *totally* or *with complete finality*. Clearly, Gide had no *hesitation about rejecting the manuscript*.

10. *C* Among other clues, Mr. Collins states that he hopes to lead Elizabeth "to the altar ere long."

11. *D* Elizabeth is "sensible of the honour" Mr. Collins is paying her by proposing. She is all too *keenly aware* of his intentions and wants nothing to do with them.

12. *E* Elizabeth expects that by refusing Mr. Collins's proposal, she will *put an end to his suit*; that is the result she desires. However, her rejection *fails* to have this intended effect. Instead, Mr. Collins in his stubbornness and conceit continues to pursue her and even takes her refusal as an encouraging sign.

13. *D* Mr. Collins breaks off in the middle of a sentence that begins, "Were it certain that Lady Catherine would think so—." He then finishes it awkwardly by saying, "but I cannot imagine that her ladyship would at all disapprove of you." By implication, his unspoken thought was that, if Lady Catherine *didn't* approve of Elizabeth, then Mr. Collins wouldn't want to marry her after all.

14. *C* Mr. Collins plans to praise Elizabeth to Lady Catherine in order to ensure Lady Catherine's approval of his bride. Elizabeth insists all such praise will be unnecessary because she *has no intention of marrying Mr. Collins* and thus has no need of Lady Catherine's approval.

15. *B* *Obtuse* means thickheaded, and *obstinate* means stubborn. Both apply to Mr. Collins, who can't seem to understand that Elizabeth is telling him "no."

16. *C* The author's emphasis is on the elephant as an important "creator of habitat" for other creatures.

17. *C* To mount an effort to rescue an endangered species is to *launch* or initiate a campaign.

18. *D* The elephant is the architect of its environment in that it *physically alters its environment*, transforming the landscape around it.

19. *C* The author states that it is the elephant's metabolism and appetite—in other words, its voracity or *ravenous hunger*—that leads to its creating open spaces in the woodland and transforming the landscape.

20. *C* Since the foraging of elephants creates a varied landscape that attracts a diverse group of plant-eating animals and since the presence of these plant eaters in turn attracts carnivores, it follows that elephants *have an indirect effect on the hunting patterns of carnivores.*

21. *E* Here the phrase "keystone species" *is being used in a special or technical sense* to mean a species whose very presence contributes to a diversity of life and whose extinction would consequently lead to the extinction of other forms of life.

22. *E* You can arrive at the correct answer choice through the process of elimination.

Question I is answerable on the basis of the passage. The elephant's foraging opens up its surroundings by knocking down trees and stripping off branches. Therefore, you can eliminate Choices B and D.

Question II is answerable on the basis of the passage. Gazelles are grazers; giraffes are browsers. Therefore, you can eliminate Choice A.

Question III is answerable on the basis of the passage. The concluding sentence states that when elephants disappear, the forest reverts. Therefore, you can eliminate Choice C.

Only Choice E is left. It is the correct answer.

23. *B* The author is listing the many species that depend on the elephant as a creator of habitat. Thus, the host of smaller animals is the *very large number* of these creatures that thrive in the elephant's wake.

24. *C* The author is in favor of the effect of elephants on the environment; he feels an accidental or *fortuitous result* of their foraging is that it allows a greater variety of creatures to exist in mixed-growth environments.

Section 2 Mathematics

For many problems, the explanation provides a reference to one or more **KEY FACTS** from Chapter 9. These are the mathematical facts that you need to solve that problem. If a solution refers to **KEY FACT J2**, for example, the solution depends on the second **KEY FACT** discussed in Section J of Chapter 9.

For some problems, an alternative solution, indicated by two asterisks (**), follows the first solution. When this occurs, usually one of the solutions is the direct mathematical one and the other is based on one of the tactics discussed in Chapters 8 and 9.

1. *E* $b - 8 = 0 \Rightarrow b = 8 \Rightarrow b + 8 = 16.$

2. *C* If Isaac has twice as many toys as Sydney, then Sydney has half as many as Isaac: $\frac{t}{2}$. This is so easy that you shouldn't have to plug in a number, but you could: If Isaac has 10 toys, then Sydney has 5, and only Choice C equals 5 when *t* is 10.

3. *C* By **KEY FACT J2**, the measure of an exterior angle of a triangle is equal to the sum of the measures of the two opposite interior angles; so $140 = x + x = 2x \Rightarrow x = 70.$
**Let the third angle in the triangle be *y*. Then $140 + y = 180 \Rightarrow y = 40$; and $40 + x + x = 180 \Rightarrow x = 70.$

4. *B* Since $1{,}000{,}000 = 10^6$, then
$$2n + 1 = 6 \Rightarrow 2n = 5 \Rightarrow n = 2.5.$$

5. *C* Use your calculator: $1.5 \times 1.7 = 2.55$, which, to the nearest tenth, is 2.6.

6. *A* Since **KEY FACT L8** circle's diameter is 4, its radius is 2, and its area is $\pi(2)^2 = 4\pi$. Since the area of the square is also 4π, the length of each side is $\sqrt{4\pi} = 2\sqrt{\pi}$.

7. *E* Set up a table.

	Maurice	Aurelie
Now	x	$5x$
In 7 years	$x + 7$	$5x + 7$

Then
$5x + 7 = 3(x + 7) \Rightarrow 5x + 7 = 3x + 21 \Rightarrow 2x = 14 \Rightarrow x = 7$. Aurelie, therefore, is 35.

Use **TACTIC 8-1, but since Aurelie is 5 times as old as Maurice, avoid Choice C, the only answer that is not a multiple of 5. Try B, 20. Then Maurice is 4. In 7 years, he'll be 11 and Aurelie will be 27, which is less than 3 times as old. Try a larger number: 25 or 35.

8. **A** Since the area of the square is 36, its sides are 6, and its perimeter is 24. Since the perimeter of the hexagon is also 24, each of its six sides is 4.

$$P = 24$$

$$24 = 6s$$
$$s = 4$$

9. **C** The first step is to calculate $(3\diamond)(\blacklozenge 5)$:
$$(3\diamond)(\blacklozenge 5) = (3 + 1)(5 - 1) = 4 \times 4 = 16.$$
Now check each answer until you find one that is NOT equal to 16.
A: $(1\diamond)(\blacklozenge 9) = (1 + 1)(9 - 1) = (2)(8) = 16.$
B: $(7\diamond)(\blacklozenge 9) = (7 + 1) + (9 - 1) = 8 + 8 = 16.$
C: $(4\diamond)(\blacklozenge 4) = (4 + 1)(4 - 1) = 5 \times 3 \neq 16.$

10. **C** Pick an integer for $\frac{n+2}{5}$, say 2. Then
$$\frac{n+2}{5} = 2 \Rightarrow n + 2 = 10 \Rightarrow n = 8,$$
and 5 goes into 8 once with a remainder of 3.

11. **D** Let n represent the number of students in the class other than Michelle. These n students earned a total of $85n$ points (**TACTIC E1**). When Michelle was included, there were $n + 1$ students who earned a total of $85n + 30$ points. Since the class average was then 80:
$$80 = \frac{85n + 30}{n + 1} \Rightarrow$$
$$85n + 30 = 80(n + 1) = 80n + 80 \Rightarrow$$
$$5n = 50 \Rightarrow n = 10, \text{ and so } n + 1 = 11.$$

Assume that everyone in the class (except Michelle) had a grade of 85. Then the only one who scored less than the average of 80 was Michelle, who earned 30 points. Therefore, the total deviation below the average was 50. That means that the total deviation above the average was also 50 (KEY FACT E3**). Since the deviation of each of the other students was 5, there must have been $50 \div 5 = 10$ of them.

12. **D** At the regular price, a CD costs d dollars; at 20% off, each one costs 80% of d dollars:
$$\frac{80}{100}(d) = \frac{80d}{100} = \frac{4d}{5} \text{ dollars.}$$
To find out how many you can buy, divide the amount of money, m, by the price per CD, $\frac{4d}{5}$:
$$m \div \frac{4d}{5} = m\left(\frac{5}{4d}\right) = \frac{5m}{4d}.$$

Use **TACTIC 8-3 and plug in easy-to-use numbers. If CDs regularly cost $10, then on sale at 20% off, they cost $8 each. How many can be purchased on sale for $40? The answer is 5.

Which of the choices equals 5 when $d = 10$ and $m = 40$? Only $\frac{5m}{4d}$.

13. **D** Since 16 of the 40 people have neither a dog nor a cat, 24 people have at least one, possibly both. Since 18 of those 24 have cats, 6 of them have dogs, but no cat. But since 13 have dogs, it must be that 7 dog owners also have cats.

**A Venn diagram may make this easier.

Let $x =$ the number of people who have both a cat and a dog.

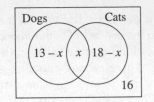

$$(13 - x) + x + (18 - x) = 24 \Rightarrow$$
$$31 - x = 24 \Rightarrow x = 7.$$

14. **D** $3|x| + 1 < 16 \Rightarrow 3|x| < 15 \Rightarrow |x| < 5$. There are 9 integers whose absolute value is less than 5: $-4, -3, -2, -1, 0, 1, 2, 3, 4$.

15. **D** The mode is 8, since more people have 8 teddy bears than any other number. Since there are 15 members, the median is the eighth piece of data when arranged in increasing order; so the median is 10. Finally, the average of 8 and 10 is 9.

16. **E** By **KEY FACT A21**,
$$3^{\frac{1}{2}} \times 3^{\frac{1}{3}} \times 3^{\frac{1}{6}} = 3^{\left(\frac{1}{2} + \frac{1}{3} + \frac{1}{6}\right)} = 3^1 = 3$$

**Just enter the given expression into your calculator.

17. **C** Let s and S be the sides of the small and large squares, respectively.

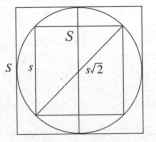

Then S and $s\sqrt{2}$ are each equal to the diameter of the circle; so
$$S = s\sqrt{2} \Rightarrow \frac{S}{s} = \sqrt{2} \Rightarrow \frac{S^2}{s^2} = 2.$$
Since s^2 and S^2 are the areas of the squares, the desired ratio is $2:1$.

18. *E* Since the diameter of the circle is 10, the radius is 5 and the area is 25π. Also, since the area of the shaded region is 20π, it is $\frac{20}{25} = \frac{4}{5}$ of the circle, and the white area is $\frac{1}{5}$ of the circle. Then the sum of the measures of the two white central angles is $\frac{1}{5}$ of 360°, or 72°. The sum of the measures of all six angles in the two triangles is 360°; so $a + b + c + d = 360 - 72 = 288$.

19. *E* An easy way to solve this is to use **TACTIC 8-3**. Let $r = 2$ and $s = 1$. So $rs = 2$, $a = 4$ and $b = 0$. Now, plug in 4 for a and 0 for b and see which of the five choices is equal to 2. Only E works: $\frac{a^2 - b^2}{8} = \frac{4^2 - 0^2}{8} = \frac{16}{8} = 2$.

**Here is the correct algebraic solution.

Add the two equations:

$$r + 2s = a$$
$$+\ r - 2s = b$$
$$\overline{2r = a + b}$$

Divide by 2: $r = \dfrac{a + b}{2}$

Now, multiply the second equation by -1 and add it to the first:

$$r + 2s = a$$
$$+\ {-r + 2s = -b}$$
$$\overline{4s = a - b}$$

Divide by 4: $s = \dfrac{a - b}{4}$

So, $rs = \dfrac{a + b}{2} \cdot \dfrac{a - b}{4} = \dfrac{a^2 - b^2}{8}$.

This is the type of algebra you want to avoid.

20. *A* $a + 25\%(a) = 1.25a$, and $b - 25\%(b) = 0.75b$. So, $1.25a = .75b$, and $\dfrac{a}{b} = \dfrac{.75}{1.25} = \dfrac{3}{5}$

**If after increasing a and decreasing b, the results are equal, a must be smaller than b. So, *the ratio of a to b must be less than 1*. Eliminate Choices C, D, and E. Now, either test Choices A and B, or just guess. To test Choice B, pick two numbers in the ratio of 3 to 4—30 and 40, for example. Then, 30 increased by 25% is 37.5, and 40 decreased by 25% is 30. The results are not equal; so eliminate Choice B. The answer is $\frac{3}{5}$. (50 decreased by 25% *is* 37.5.)

Section 3 Critical Reading

25. *E* To make the correct decisions, the lawmakers must be able to *discern* or recognize the truth.

26. *B* There is a chance that *serious* women may not be attracted by an inappropriate *frivolity* or lightheartedness in style—hence the gamble.

27. *E* A customer service agent would try to *mollify* or soothe an *angry* passenger by giving her an upgrade to a better class of service.

28. *A* If falling asleep at times you wouldn't normally wish to, you clearly would strike yourself as unusually *lethargic* (drowsily slow to respond; sluggish; listless).

29. *D* A *euphemism* is by definition a mild expression used in place of a more unpleasant or distressing one. The blunt expression "he died" is unpleasantly direct for some people, who substitute the vague euphemism "he passed away."

30. *E* *Despite* signals a contrast. If someone writes an enormously popular book, you would expect his career to prosper. Instead, White's career *foundered* or came to grief.

31. *C* Because it was written immediately after the assassination, the book has *immediacy*, but it lacks *perspective*; the author had not had enough time to distance himself from his immediate reactions to the event and think about it.

32. *E* The key word here is "chagrin." Because Costner has triumphed, the critics who predicted his *failure* feel chagrin (great annoyance mixed with disappointment or humiliation). Costner, for his part, greatly enjoys his success and especially enjoys or *savors* their embarrassment and vexation.

33. *C* If poetry fans can fill an entire football stadium, there must be a lot of them. Thus, the reference to the football stadium suggests the size of the audience for poetry and thus *emphasizes the popularity of poetry in the period*.

34. *C* To say that literature enjoyed a central place in the culture is to say that literature *possessed* or occupied such a place.

35. *A* Chomsky and others contend that the capacity for language is a uniquely human property or *trait*.

36. *B* Where Chomsky and Savage-Rambaugh differ has to do with the primates' capacity to use language, in other words, their *abilities in language acquisition*.

37. *E* The italicized introduction states that the author has had his manuscript rejected by his publisher. He is consigning or committing it to a desk drawer *to set it aside as unmarketable*.

38. *B* The rejected author identifies with these baseball players, who constantly must face "failure." *He sees he is not alone in having to confront failure and move on.*

39. *B* The author uses the jogger's comment to make a point about the *mental impact Henderson's home run must have had on Moore*. He reasons that, if each step a runner takes sends so many complex messages to the brain, then Henderson's ninth-inning home run must have flooded Moore's brain with messages, impressing its image indelibly in Moore's mind.

40. *D* The author is talking of the impact of Henderson's home run on Moore's mind. Registering in Moore's mind, the home run *made an impression* on him.

41. *C* The author looks on himself as someone who "to succeed at all . . . must perform at an extraordinary level of excellence." This level of excellence, he maintains, is not demanded of accountants, plumbers, and insurance salesmen, and he seems to pride himself on belonging to such a demanding profession. Thus, his attitude to members of less demanding professions can best be described as *superior*.

42. *A* The description of the writer defying his pain and extending himself irrationally to create a "masterpiece" despite the rejections of critics and publishers is a highly romantic one that elevates *the writer as someone heroic in his or her accomplishments.*

43. *C* The author of Passage 2 discusses the advantages of his ability to concentrate. Clearly, he prizes *his ability to focus* on the task at hand.

44. *B* When one football team is ahead of another by several touchdowns and there seems to be no way for the second team to catch up, the outcome of the game appears *decided* or settled.

45. *E* The "larger point of view" focuses on what to most people is the big question: the outcome of the game. The author is indifferent to this larger point of view. Concentrating on his own performance, he is *more concerned with the task at hand than with* winning or losing the game.

46. *C* Parade ground drill clearly does not entirely prepare a soldier for the reality of war. It only does so "to an extent." By using this phrase, the author is *qualifying his statement*, making it less absolute.

47. *C* One would expect someone who dismisses or rejects most comparisons of athletics to art to avoid making such comparisons. The author, however, *is making such a comparison*. This reversal of what would have been expected is an instance of irony.

48. *C* To learn to overcome failure, to learn to give one's all in performance, to learn to focus on the work of the moment, to learn "the selfish intensity needed to create and to finish a poem, a story, or a novel"—these are hard lessons that *both athletes and artists learn.*

Section 4 Mathematics

For many problems, the explanation provides a reference to one or more **KEY FACTS** from Chapter 9. These are the mathematical facts that you need to solve that problem. If a solution refers to **KEY FACT J2**, for example, the solution depends on the second **KEY FACT** discussed in Section J of Chapter 9.

For some problems, an alternative solution, indicated by two asterisks (**), follows the first solution. When this occurs, usually one of the solutions is the direct mathematical one and the other is based on one of the tactics discussed in Chapters 8 and 9.

21. *C* The weight of the fruit is $5 + 3 + 1 = 9$ pounds, of which 3 pounds are oranges. Hence, the desired fraction is $\frac{3}{9} = \frac{1}{3}$.

22. *B* Since the sum of the five angles is 180°:
$$4a + 40 = 180 \Rightarrow 4a = 140 \Rightarrow a = 35.$$

23. *B* Use **TACTIC 8-3** and choose an easy-to-use number. Since $\frac{5}{8}$ of the members are boys, assume there are 8 members, 5 of whom are boys. Then the other 3 are girls, and the ratio of girls to boys is 3 to 5, or $\frac{3}{5}$.

24. *A* Refer to the figures below.

The circumference of a circle of radius 3 is 6π (**KEY FACT L4**). By **KEY FACT K5**, the perimeter of a rectangle is $2(\ell + w)$, so $6\pi = 2(\ell + 3) \Rightarrow$
$$\ell + 3 = 3\pi \Rightarrow \ell = 3\pi - 3.$$

25. *D* $13 - 11 = 2$, so I could be true. Since $5 + 7 + 11 = 23$, III could be true. Since all primes greater than 5 are odd, $p + q$ must be even and so cannot be a prime. (Statement II is false.) Statements I and III only are true.

26. *C* Use the distance formula, **KEY FACT N2**, to calculate the length of diameter $\overline{AB}$:

$$AB = \sqrt{(7-3)^2 + (2-(-2))^2} = \sqrt{4^2 + 4^2} = \sqrt{32}.$$

So the diameter is $\sqrt{32}$ and the radius is $\frac{\sqrt{32}}{2}$. Then, by **KEY FACT L8**, the area is

$$A = \pi r^2 = \pi\left(\frac{\sqrt{32}}{2}\right)^2 = \pi\left(\frac{32}{4}\right) = 8\pi.$$

Note: You do not need to simplify $\sqrt{32}$. You also don't need to use your calculator to evaluate $\sqrt{32}$, but if you do, don't round off. Take whatever appears in your calculator's window, divide it by 2 and then square it—you will get exactly 8. Of course, *do not* multiply by 3.14.

27. *C* $13 - 2\sqrt{x} = 7 \Rightarrow -2\sqrt{x} = -6 \Rightarrow \sqrt{x} = 3 \Rightarrow x = 9.$

You can use **TACTIC 8-1 and backsolve. Choice C, 9, works.

28. *B* The trust received 80% of the estate (10% went to the man's wife, 5% to his children, and 5% to his grandchildren). If E represents the value of the estate, then

$$0.80E = 1,000,000 \Rightarrow$$
$$E = 1,000,000 \div .80 = 1,250,000.$$

Each grandchild received 1% (one fifth of 5%) of the estate, or \$12,500.

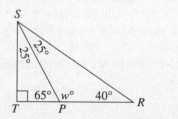

29. (*115*) We can find any or all of the angles in the figure. The easiest way to get w is to note that the measure of $\angle PST = 25$ and so, by **KEY FACT J2**, $w = 25 + 90 = 115.$

30. (*99*) From the 109 people in front of Wendy, remove Peter plus the 9 people in front of Peter: $109 - 10 = 99.$

31. (*88.5*) $(x + 1) + (x + 2) = 180 \Rightarrow$
$2x + 3 = 180 \Rightarrow 2x = 177 \Rightarrow x = 88.5.$

32. ($\frac{11}{2}$ *or 5.5*) To make the fraction $\frac{r-s}{t}$ as large as possible, make the numerator, $r - s$, as large as you can, and the denominator t, as small as you can. So let t be 2, the smallest prime. In order for the difference $r - s$ to be as large as possible, let r be large, and subtract as little as possible. Therefore, let r be 13, the largest prime less than 15, and let s be 2, the smallest prime. (Note that the question did not say that s and t had to be different, only that they had to be primes.) Finally, $\frac{r-s}{t} = \frac{13-2}{2} = \frac{11}{2}$ or 5.5.

33. (*40*) To solve the equation $\frac{2}{x} + \frac{3}{4} = \frac{4}{5}$, subtract $\frac{3}{4}$ from each side:

$$\frac{2}{x} + \frac{3}{4} = \frac{4}{5} \Rightarrow \frac{2}{x} = \frac{1}{20} \Rightarrow x = 40$$

Note: Do not waste time getting a common denominator; just use your calculator.

34. ($\frac{7}{9}$ *or .777 or .778*) Since the radius of the large circle is 3 by **KEY FACT L8**, its area is 9π. Each of the small circles has a radius of 1 and an area of π. So the total area of the white region is 2π, leaving 7π for the area of the shaded region. Therefore, the probability that P lies in the shaded region is $\frac{7\pi}{9\pi} = \frac{7}{9}$.

35. (*44*) Since the diameters of the circles are in the ratio of 12:10 or 6:5, the ratio of their areas is $6^2:5^2 = 36:25$. Convert the ratio to a percent: $36:25 = \frac{36}{25} = \frac{144}{100} = 144\%$. So, the area of the large circle is 144% of the area of the small one, or is 44% *more* than the area of the small one.

**With your calculator, actually calculate the areas. The radius of the large circle is 6, so its area is $\pi(6)^2 = 36\pi$. Similarly, the radius of the small circle is 5 and its area is $\pi(5)^2 = 25\pi$. The difference in the areas is $36\pi - 25\pi = 11\pi$, and 11π is 44% of 25π $\left(\frac{11\pi}{25\pi} = \frac{11}{25} = \frac{44}{100}\right)$.

36. *(21)* Draw a diagram. For the third place share to be as large as possible, the fourth place share must be as small as possible. However, it must be more than 10, so let it be 11. Then the amount, in dollars, left for second and third place is $100 - (35 + 11 + 10) = 100 - 56 = 44$. So, the second place share could be $23 and the third place share $21.

37. *(9.36)* For the average to be as high as possible, each student needs to have scored the maximum number of points. Therefore, assume that each of the 22 students who passed earned a grade of 10, that only one student earned a 2, and that the other two students who failed each earned a 6, the highest possible failing grade. Then the average is $\frac{10(22) + 2 + 2(6)}{25} = \frac{234}{25} = 9.36$.

38. *(13)* Since π is approximately 3.14, 2π is approximately 6.28, and $[2\pi] = 6$. Now, be careful: -2π is approximately -6.28, and the largest integer less than -6.28 is -7. Finally, $[2\pi] - [-2\pi] = 6 - (-7) = 6 + 7 = 13$.

Section 5 Writing Skills

1. *C* Comma splice. Choices A, D, and E are run-on sentences. Choice B is constructed awkwardly.

2. *C* Comparison of modifiers. When comparing two things, you should use the comparative degree (*better*) rather than the superlative degree (*best*).

3. *D* This choice corrects the sentence fragment.

4. *C* Error in coordination and subordination. The subordinating conjunction *Although* best connects the sentence's two clauses.

5. *B* Comma splice. Choices A, C, and E are run-on sentences; Choice D is unidiomatic.

6. *D* Error in parallelism. Parallel structure is maintained in Choice D.

7. *D* Choices A, B, and E contain sentence fragments; Choice C creates a comma splice.

8. *A* Error in coordination and subordination. The past tense and the subordinating conjunction *when* are correctly used in Choice A.

9. *C* Choice C expresses the author's meaning directly and concisely. All other choices are either indirect or ungrammatical.

10. *A* Choices B, C, D, and E are sentence fragments.

11. *A* Sentence is correct.

12. *A* Sentence is correct.

13. *E* The errors in pronoun case and subject-verb agreement are corrected in Choice E. *I* should be used instead of *me* because it is the predicate nominative of the verb *is*. *Who*, having as its antecedent the pronoun *I*, is a first-person singular pronoun. The first-person singular verb *am* should be used.

14. *C* Error in idiomatic usage. The birds are indifferent *to* the ships.

15. *C* Error in subject-verb agreement. The subject of the sentence, *collection*, is singular; the verb should be singular as well.

16. *A* Sentence is correct.

17. *B* Error in sequence of tenses. *Was* and *received* are in the simple past tense. Both indicate a definite time in the past. *Have cheered* is in the present perfect tense. It indicates sometime before now but not a definite time. The sequence is illogical.

18. *D* Error in parallelism. Choice D corrects the lack of parallel structure.

19. *E* Adjective-adverb confusion. The dragonflies become *increasingly* fragile.

20. *E* Error in sequence of tenses. The *had* before *established* indicates a time prior to *began to arrive*.

21. *C* Error in diction. Use *lie* instead of *lay*.

22. *E* Sentence is correct.

23. *D* Error in pronoun number agreement. Since antecedent is *association*, change *their* to *its*.

24. *C* Error in subject-verb agreement. In a neither-nor construction the verb agrees with the noun or pronoun that comes immediately before the verb. *Principal is being considered* is correct.

25. *A* Error in tense. Change *have rummaged* to *were rummaging*.

26. *E* Sentence is correct.

27. *C* Error in diction. Use *effect* instead of *affect*.

28. *C* Error in coordination and subordination. Delete the comma and substitute *that* for *and it*. The second clause describes McGwire's record.

29. *C* Error in coordination and subordination. Change conjunction and word for *nor is she* to *and she is* to clarify the relationship between the clauses.

30. *D* Error in diction. The word *being* is unnecessary. Change *including being* to *including*.

31. *D* Adjective and adverb confusion. Change *comfortable* to *comfortably*.

32. *E* Sentence is correct.

33. *A* Error in tense. Change *has been warned* to *had been warned*.

34. *A* Error in diction. Use *if* to indicate a condition. Substitute *whether*.

35. *C* All sentences except sentence 3 contribute to the paragraph's main point, that celebrations help to unite people and keep traditions alive. Therefore, Choice C is the best answer.

36. *D* Choice A is fresh, but its tone is not consistent with the rest of the essay.

Choice B contains a comma splice between *dinner* and *at*.

Choice C emphasizes the idea properly but contains an error in parallel construction.

Choice D places the emphasis where it belongs and expresses the idea effectively. It is the best answer.

Choice E is repetitious, and it contains an error in pronoun reference. The pronoun *they* has no specific referent.

37. *D* Choice A does not provide a significantly better transition.

Choice B does nothing to improve the relationship between paragraphs 3 and 4.

Choice C is awkwardly worded and does not include transitional material.

Choice D provides an effective transition between paragraphs. It is the best answer.

Choice E tries to provide a transition, but it is wordy and it contains a dangling participle.

38. *E* Choice A places emphasis on the location of the assassination instead of on the event itself, an emphasis that the writer did not intend.

Choice B contains a nonstandard usage. The phrase *to remember about* is not standard.

Choice C is grammatically correct but wordy.

Choice D is the same as B.

Choice E is a succinct and proper revision. It is the best answer.

39. *C* The main purpose of the last paragraph is to provide an example of a celebration that unites people and preserves tradition. Therefore, Choice C is the best answer.

Answer Sheet
MODEL TEST D

Each mark should completely fill the appropriate space and should be as dark as all other marks. Make all erasures complete. Traces of an erasure may be read as an answer. See pages viii and 21 for explanations of timing and number of questions.

Section 1 — Critical Reading
25 minutes

1 Ⓐ Ⓑ Ⓒ Ⓓ Ⓔ
2 Ⓐ Ⓑ Ⓒ Ⓓ Ⓔ
3 Ⓐ Ⓑ Ⓒ Ⓓ Ⓔ
4 Ⓐ Ⓑ Ⓒ Ⓓ Ⓔ
5 Ⓐ Ⓑ Ⓒ Ⓓ Ⓔ
6 Ⓐ Ⓑ Ⓒ Ⓓ Ⓔ
7 Ⓐ Ⓑ Ⓒ Ⓓ Ⓔ
8 Ⓐ Ⓑ Ⓒ Ⓓ Ⓔ
9 Ⓐ Ⓑ Ⓒ Ⓓ Ⓔ
10 Ⓐ Ⓑ Ⓒ Ⓓ Ⓔ
11 Ⓐ Ⓑ Ⓒ Ⓓ Ⓔ
12 Ⓐ Ⓑ Ⓒ Ⓓ Ⓔ
13 Ⓐ Ⓑ Ⓒ Ⓓ Ⓔ
14 Ⓐ Ⓑ Ⓒ Ⓓ Ⓔ
15 Ⓐ Ⓑ Ⓒ Ⓓ Ⓔ
16 Ⓐ Ⓑ Ⓒ Ⓓ Ⓔ
17 Ⓐ Ⓑ Ⓒ Ⓓ Ⓔ
18 Ⓐ Ⓑ Ⓒ Ⓓ Ⓔ
19 Ⓐ Ⓑ Ⓒ Ⓓ Ⓔ
20 Ⓐ Ⓑ Ⓒ Ⓓ Ⓔ
21 Ⓐ Ⓑ Ⓒ Ⓓ Ⓔ
22 Ⓐ Ⓑ Ⓒ Ⓓ Ⓔ
23 Ⓐ Ⓑ Ⓒ Ⓓ Ⓔ
24 Ⓐ Ⓑ Ⓒ Ⓓ Ⓔ

Section 2 — Math
25 minutes

1 Ⓐ Ⓑ Ⓒ Ⓓ Ⓔ
2 Ⓐ Ⓑ Ⓒ Ⓓ Ⓔ
3 Ⓐ Ⓑ Ⓒ Ⓓ Ⓔ
4 Ⓐ Ⓑ Ⓒ Ⓓ Ⓔ
5 Ⓐ Ⓑ Ⓒ Ⓓ Ⓔ
6 Ⓐ Ⓑ Ⓒ Ⓓ Ⓔ
7 Ⓐ Ⓑ Ⓒ Ⓓ Ⓔ
8 Ⓐ Ⓑ Ⓒ Ⓓ Ⓔ
9 Ⓐ Ⓑ Ⓒ Ⓓ Ⓔ
10 Ⓐ Ⓑ Ⓒ Ⓓ Ⓔ
11 Ⓐ Ⓑ Ⓒ Ⓓ Ⓔ
12 Ⓐ Ⓑ Ⓒ Ⓓ Ⓔ
13 Ⓐ Ⓑ Ⓒ Ⓓ Ⓔ
14 Ⓐ Ⓑ Ⓒ Ⓓ Ⓔ
15 Ⓐ Ⓑ Ⓒ Ⓓ Ⓔ
16 Ⓐ Ⓑ Ⓒ Ⓓ Ⓔ
17 Ⓐ Ⓑ Ⓒ Ⓓ Ⓔ
18 Ⓐ Ⓑ Ⓒ Ⓓ Ⓔ
19 Ⓐ Ⓑ Ⓒ Ⓓ Ⓔ
20 Ⓐ Ⓑ Ⓒ Ⓓ Ⓔ

Section 3 — Critical Reading
25 minutes

25 Ⓐ Ⓑ Ⓒ Ⓓ Ⓔ
26 Ⓐ Ⓑ Ⓒ Ⓓ Ⓔ
27 Ⓐ Ⓑ Ⓒ Ⓓ Ⓔ
28 Ⓐ Ⓑ Ⓒ Ⓓ Ⓔ
29 Ⓐ Ⓑ Ⓒ Ⓓ Ⓔ
30 Ⓐ Ⓑ Ⓒ Ⓓ Ⓔ
31 Ⓐ Ⓑ Ⓒ Ⓓ Ⓔ
32 Ⓐ Ⓑ Ⓒ Ⓓ Ⓔ
33 Ⓐ Ⓑ Ⓒ Ⓓ Ⓔ
34 Ⓐ Ⓑ Ⓒ Ⓓ Ⓔ
35 Ⓐ Ⓑ Ⓒ Ⓓ Ⓔ
36 Ⓐ Ⓑ Ⓒ Ⓓ Ⓔ
37 Ⓐ Ⓑ Ⓒ Ⓓ Ⓔ
38 Ⓐ Ⓑ Ⓒ Ⓓ Ⓔ
39 Ⓐ Ⓑ Ⓒ Ⓓ Ⓔ
40 Ⓐ Ⓑ Ⓒ Ⓓ Ⓔ
41 Ⓐ Ⓑ Ⓒ Ⓓ Ⓔ
42 Ⓐ Ⓑ Ⓒ Ⓓ Ⓔ
43 Ⓐ Ⓑ Ⓒ Ⓓ Ⓔ
44 Ⓐ Ⓑ Ⓒ Ⓓ Ⓔ
45 Ⓐ Ⓑ Ⓒ Ⓓ Ⓔ
46 Ⓐ Ⓑ Ⓒ Ⓓ Ⓔ
47 Ⓐ Ⓑ Ⓒ Ⓓ Ⓔ
48 Ⓐ Ⓑ Ⓒ Ⓓ Ⓔ

For each question in this section, select the best answer from among the choices given, and fill in the corresponding circle on the answer sheet.

Directions

Each sentence below has one or two blanks, each blank indicating that something has been omitted. Beneath the sentence are five words or sets of words labeled A through E. Choose the word or set of words that, when inserted in the sentence, best fits the meaning of the sentence as a whole.

EXAMPLE:

Medieval kingdoms did not become constitutional republics overnight; on the contrary, the change was ----.

(A) unpopular (B) unexpected
(C) advantageous (D) sufficient (E) gradual

Ⓐ Ⓑ Ⓒ Ⓓ ●

---

1. Among naturalists, the statistics of elephant population decline have prompted a cry of ----, with newspaper articles and even a television special ---- the species' slow extinction.

   (A) warning..celebrating
   (B) alarm..deploring
   (C) jubilation..hastening
   (D) desperation..boycotting
   (E) anxiety..refuting

2. Advances in health care have lengthened life spans, lowered infant mortality rates, and thus ---- the overpopulation problem.

   (A) eliminated (B) aggravated (C) minimized
   (D) distorted (E) discouraged

3. Even Republican members of the committee, who normally would have defended the administration's actions, found themselves forced to ---- the secret plans to raise money for the contras.

   (A) deprecate (B) conceal (C) explicate
   (D) implement (E) validate

4. The renovation of historic Union Station is salutary not just as an example of ---- restoration but also as a reminder that in this age of retrenchment and diminished dreams, ambitious federal public works programs can still ----.

   (A) impeccable..succeed
   (B) inadequate..inspire
   (C) flawless..terminate
   (D) archaic..flourish
   (E) partial..impede

5. Among contemporary writers of fiction, Mrs. Woolf is ---- figure, in some ways as radical as James Joyce, in others no more modern than Jane Austen.

   (A) a doctrinaire
   (B) an introspective
   (C) a peripheral
   (D) a disinterested
   (E) an anomalous

Directions

Each of the passages below precedes two questions based on its content. Answer the questions following each passage on the basis of what is stated or implied in that passage

Questions 6 and 7 are based on the following passage.

In 1908 Canada celebrated its 300th anniversary—the tercentenary of Champlain's founding of Quebec City. To commemorate the event, the
Line Canadian government decided to strike a special
5 medallion to be awarded to families that had held their farms in an unbroken line for at least two hundred years. Engraved on each medallion was a motto summing up the history of French Canada: "With Sword, With Cross, With Plow."

6. The word "strike" (line 4) most nearly means

   (A) delete (B) discover (C) boycott
   (D) produce (E) beat

7. According to the passage, the medallions were intended to be given to

   (A) lineal descendants of early settlers
   (B) the founders of Quebec City
   (C) members of the Canadian government
   (D) survivors of the Battle of Quebec
   (E) heirs of Samuel Champlain

GO ON TO NEXT PAGE ▶

A star's explosion is an awesome event. The most violent of these cataclysms, which produce supernovae, probably destroys a star completely.
Line Much smaller explosions, however, occur fre-
5 quently, producing what astronomers call novae and dwarf novae. Approximately twenty-five novae occur in our galaxy every year, only two or three near enough to be observed. If the exploding star is in a nearby part of the galaxy, it may create a
10 "new star," one not previously visible to the naked eye. In these smaller explosions the star loses only a minute fraction of its mass and survives to explode again.

8. According to the passage, our observations of novae are hampered by their

(A) extreme brightness
(B) loss of mass
(C) total destruction
(D) distance from earth
(E) tremendous violence

9. By the term "new star" (line 10) the author most likely means one that has

(A) recently gained in mass
(B) moved from a distant galaxy
(C) become bright enough to strike the eye
(D) not previously risen above the horizon
(E) become visible by rotating in its orbit

Directions

Each passage below is followed by questions based on its content. Answer the questions following each passage on the basis of what is stated or implied in that passage and in any introductory material that may be provided.

Questions 10–15 are based on the following passage.

In this autobiographical excerpt, the author, the daughter of migrant workers, describes a childhood incident whose significance she came to understand only with the passage of time.

When school was out, I hurried to find my sister and get out of the schoolyard before seeing anybody in my class. But Barbara and her friends
Line had beaten us to the playground entrance and they
5 seemed to be waiting for us. Barbara said, "So now you're in the A class." She sounded impressed.
"What's the A class?" I asked.
Everybody made superior yet faintly envious giggling sounds. "Well, why did you think the
10 teacher moved you to the front of the room, dopey? Didn't you know you were in the C class before, way in the back of the room?"
Of course I hadn't known. The Wenatchee fifth grade was bigger than my whole school had
15 been in North Dakota, and the idea of subdivisions

within a grade had never occurred to me. The sub-dividing for the first marking period had been done before I came to the school, and I had never, in the six weeks I'd been there, talked to anyone
20 long enough to find out about the A, B, and C classes.
I still could not understand why that had made such a difference to Barbara and her friends. I didn't yet know that it was disgraceful and dirty
25 to be a transient laborer and ridiculous to be from North Dakota. I thought living in a tent was more fun than living in a house. I didn't know that we were gypsies, really (how that thought would have thrilled me then!), and that we were regarded with
30 the suspicion felt by those who plant toward those who do not plant. It didn't occur to me that we were all looked upon as one more of the untrust-worthy natural phenomena, drifting here and there like mists or winds, that farmers of certain
35 crops are resentfully forced to rely on. I didn't know that I was the only child who had camped on the Baumanns' land ever to get out of the C class. I did not know that school administrators and civic leaders held conferences to talk about the
40 problem of transient laborers.
I only knew that for two happy days I walked to school with Barbara and her friends, played hopscotch and jump rope with them at recess, and was even invited into the house for some ginger
45 ale—an exotic drink I had never tasted before.

GO ON TO NEXT PAGE ▶

10. The tone of this passage as a whole is

(A) reflective (B) joyful (C) impersonal
(D) pessimistic (E) suspicious

11. This passage is presented from the point of view of

(A) an understanding teacher
(B) a younger sister
(C) a mature adult
(D) a helpful parent
(E) an envious pupil

12. The narrator had most probably been placed in the C class because

(A) she was a poor reader
(B) she had come from a small school
(C) the marking system confused her
(D) all migrant children were placed in the C class
(E) all migrant children lived in tents

13. The author's tone in listing all the items she "didn't yet know" (lines 24–40) is

(A) embarrassed (B) arrogant (C) objective
(D) gloomy (E) ironic

14. In lines 44–45, the author refers to her first taste of ginger ale to emphasize

(A) her eventual dependence on soft drinks
(B) the rarity of ginger ale in the town of Wenatchee
(C) how exceptionally refreshing a soft drink can be
(D) Barbara's generosity in giving the author a treat
(E) her lack of everyday experiences we take for granted

15. After the narrator was moved to the A class, what was the attitude of Barbara and Barbara's friends toward her?

(A) dislike (B) acceptance (C) dismay
(D) apology (E) jealousy

Questions 16–24 are based on the following passage.

Students of the modern civil rights movement regularly contrast the figures of Malcolm X and Martin Luther King. The black protest movement in America has always had strong, controversial leaders. Two of the strongest, Booker T. Washington and W. E. B. Du Bois, who shaped the course of the movement in the early part of the century, are discussed in this excerpt from a black studies text published in 1982.

During the nineteenth century and the early decades of the twentieth, when blacks were virtually powerless, propagandists like Frederick
Line Douglass, Booker T. Washington, and W. E. B. Du
5 Bois naturally loomed large in the pantheon of black leaders. The term propagandist—used here in its neutral meaning as denoting one who employs symbols to influence the feelings and behavior of an audience—is a particularly apt
10 description of the role played by Du Bois, the leading black intellectual and the most important black protest spokesman in the first half of the twentieth century. As platform lecturer and particularly as editor of several publications, Du Bois
15 was a caustic and prophetic voice, telling whites that racist social institutions oppressed blacks and telling blacks that change in their subordinate status was impossible unless they demanded it insistently and continuously. Du Bois himself, in his
20 noted autobiographical work, *Dusk of Dawn*, aptly evaluated his principal contribution when he

wrote of "my role as a master of propaganda."

Central to Du Bois's role as a propagandist were the ideologies that he articulated. And Du
25 Bois's ideas reflected most of the diverse themes in black thinking about how to assault the bastions of prejudice and discrimination. Most important, he articulated the blacks' desire for full participation in the larger American society and demanded
30 "the abolition of all caste distinctions based simply on race and color." On the other hand, he also exhibited a nationalist side—a strong sense of group pride, advocacy of racial unity, and a profound identification with blacks in other parts of
35 the world. As he said in one of his oft-quoted statements,

One ever feels his twoness—an American, a Negro: two souls, two thoughts, two unreconciled strivings; two warring ideals in one dark
40 body, whose dogged strength alone keeps it from being torn asunder. The history of the American Negro is the history of this strife—this longing to attain self-conscious manhood, to merge his double self into a better
45 and truer self. In this merging he wishes neither of the older selves to be lost. . . . He simply wishes to make it possible for a man to be both a Negro and an American without being cursed and spit upon by his fellows, with-
50 out having the doors of opportunity closed roughly in his face.

In addition, Du Bois was both a pioneering advocate of black capitalism, and later was one of the country's most prominent black Marxists.
55 Essentially a protest leader he was also criticized at times for enunciating tactics of accommodation. An elitist who stressed the leadership role of a college-educated Talented Tenth, he articulated a fervent commitment to the welfare of the black
60 masses.

Given the persistent and intransigent nature of the American race system, which proved quite impervious to black attacks, Du Bois in his speeches and writings moved from one proposed
65 solution to another, and the salience of various parts of his philosophy changed as his perceptions of the needs and strategies of black America shifted over time. Aloof and autonomous in his personality, Du Bois did not hesitate to depart
70 markedly from whatever was the current mainstream of black thinking when he perceived that the conventional wisdom being enunciated by black spokesmen was proving inadequate to the task of advancing the race. His willingness to seek
75 different solutions often placed him well in

advance of his contemporaries, and this, combined with a strong-willed, even arrogant personality made his career as a black leader essentially a series of stormy conflicts.
80 Thus Du Bois first achieved his role as a major black leader in the controversy that arose over the program of Booker T. Washington, the most prominent and influential black leader at the opening of the twentieth century. Amidst the wave
85 of lynchings, disfranchisement, and segregation laws, Washington, seeking the good will of powerful whites, taught blacks not to protest against discrimination, but to elevate themselves through industrial education, hard work, and property
90 accumulation; then, they would ultimately obtain recognition of their citizenship rights. At first Du Bois agreed with this gradualist strategy, but in 1903 with the publication of his most influential book, *Souls of Black Folk*, he became the chief
95 leader of the onslaught against Washington that polarized the black community into two wings— the "conservative" supporters of Washington and his "radical" critics.

---

16. Judging from lines 19–22, Du Bois regarded his work as a propagandist as

    (A) a necessary evil
    (B) a temporary distraction
    (C) an academic failure
    (D) a particular achievement
    (E) an inappropriate occupation

17. In lines 37–41, Du Bois emphasizes the American Negro's

    (A) origins
    (B) duality
    (C) opportunity
    (D) manliness
    (E) idealism

18. The word "dogged" in line 40 means

    (A) brutal and ruthless
    (B) tenacious and unyielding
    (C) loyal and domesticated
    (D) hunted down
    (E) canine

19. The word "accommodation" in lines 56 and 57 means

    (A) lodging
    (B) spaciousness
    (C) open resistance
    (D) automatic adjustment
    (E) reconciliation of differences

20. The author's attitude toward Du Bois's departure from conventional black policies can best be described as

    (A) skeptical (B) derisive (C) shocked
    (D) approving (E) resigned

21. The author uses all of the following techniques in the passage EXCEPT

    (A) extended quotation
    (B) rhetorical question
    (C) establishment of a time frame
    (D) listing of examples
    (E) comparison and contrast

22. The author's primary purpose in the closing paragraph is to

    (A) explain how Du Bois was influenced by Washington
    (B) compare the personalities of Du Bois and Washington
    (C) explain why Du Bois gained power in the black community
    (D) describe Du Bois's role in early-twentieth-century black leadership
    (E) correct the misconception that Du Bois shunned polarization

GO ON TO NEXT PAGE ▶

23. Which of the following statements about Du Bois does the passage best support?

- (A) He sacrificed the proven strategies of earlier black leaders to his craving for political novelty.
- (B) Preferring conflict to harmony, he followed a disruptive course that alienated him from the bulk of his followers.
- (C) He proved unable to change with the times in mounting fresh attacks against white racism.
- (D) He relied on the fundamental benevolence of the white population for the eventual success of his movement.
- (E) Once an adherent of Washington's policies, he ultimately lost patience with them for their ineffectiveness.

24. It can be inferred that Booker T. Washington in comparison with Du Bois could be described as all of the following EXCEPT

- (A) submissive to the majority
- (B) concerned with financial success
- (C) versatile in adopting strategies
- (D) traditional in preaching industry
- (E) respectful of authority

IF YOU FINISH IN LESS THAN 25 MINUTES, YOU MAY CHECK YOUR WORK ON THIS SECTION ONLY. DO NOT TURN TO ANY OTHER SECTION IN THE TEST.

STOP

Multiple-Choice Directions

For each question in this section, determine which of the five choices is correct, and blacken that choice on your answer sheet. You may use any blank space on the page for your work.

NOTES:
- You may use a calculator whenever you believe it will be helpful.
- Use the diagrams provided to help you solve the problems. Unless you see the phrase
                    Note: Figure not drawn to scale
under a diagram, it has been drawn as accurately as possible. Unless it is stated that a figure is three dimensional, you may assume that it lies in a plane.

Reference

$A = \pi r^2$
$C = 2\pi r$

$A = \ell w$

$A = \frac{1}{2}bh$

$V = \ell wh$

$V = \pi r^2 h$

$c^2 = a^2 + b^2$

Special Right Triangles

Number of degrees in a circle: 360
Sum of the measures, in degrees, of the three angles of a triangle: 180

1. If today is Saturday, what day will it be 100 days from now?

   (A) Saturday   (B) Sunday   (C) Monday
   (D) Tuesday   (E) Thursday

2. Michelle types 60 words per minute, and Paul types 20 words per minute. How many minutes did Paul take to type the same number of words that it took Michelle 30 minutes to type?

   (A) 10 (B) 30 (C) 60 (D) 90 (E) 180

3. In the figure above, $x =$
   (A) 43 (B) 47 (C) 57 (D) 133 (E) 137

4. Which of the following is equal to $\frac{1}{2}$%?
   I. $\frac{1}{2} \div 100$
   II. $\frac{1}{100} \div 2$
   III. 0.005
   (A) I only   (B) II only   (C) III only
   (D) I and II only   (E) I, II, and III

5. In the figure above, what is the value of a?
   (A) 10 (B) 50 (C) 60 (D) 75 (E) 90

6. $(3a^2b^3)^3 =$
   (A) $9a^5b^6$ (B) $9a^6b^9$ (C) $27a^5b^6$
   (D) $27a^6b^9$ (E) $27a^8b^{27}$

7. What is the area of the circle whose center is at the origin and that passes through the point $(-3, 3)$?
   (A) $3\sqrt{2}\pi$ (B) 3π (C) 9π
   (D) 18π (E) 36π

8. Mustapha rode his bicycle 6 miles north, 5 miles east, and then 6 miles north again. How far is he, in miles, from his starting point?
   (A) 13 (B) 16 (C) 17 (D) 20 (E) 30

9. Justin read exactly half of his book on Monday. On Tuesday, after reading 100 pages more, he determined that he still had 10% of the book to read. How many pages are in the book?
   (A) 200 (B) 250 (C) 400 (D) 500 (E) 600

GO ON TO NEXT PAGE ▶

10. In the figure above, what is the perimeter of pentagon *ABCDE*, formed by right triangle *ABE* and square *BCDE*?

(A) 20   (B) $12 + 4\sqrt{2}$ (C) $12 + 8\sqrt{2}$
(D) $16 + 4\sqrt{3}$ (E) $12 + 8\sqrt{3}$

11. Liz counted from 1 to 50 saying "buzz" instead of a number whenever that number was divisible by 3 or had a 3 in it. How many times did she say "buzz"?

(A) 25   (B) 27   (C) 29   (D) 30   (E) 31

12. Sharon was 24 when her son Samir was born. If she is now 4 times as old as he is, how many years ago was she 5 times as old as he was?

(A) 2   (B) 4   (C) 6   (D) 12   (E) 18

13. If $f(x) = x^2 - x$, what is the value of $f(3) - f(-3)$?

(A) -6 (B) 0   (C) 6   (D) 12   (E) 18

14. If *a*, *b*, and *c* are even integers with $a < b < c$, and $b = 50$, what is the greatest possible value of $a + b - c$?

(A) 2   (B) 46   (C) 48   (D) 52   (E) 54

15. At James Buchanan High School 100 seniors are taking Spanish and 80 seniors are taking French. If 20 seniors are taking both Spanish and French, what is the ratio of the number of seniors taking only Spanish to the number taking only French?

(A) $\frac{3}{4}$ (B) $\frac{1}{1}$ (C) $\frac{5}{4}$ (D) $\frac{4}{3}$
(E) It cannot be determined from the information given.

16. For any numbers *x* and *y*, the operation ✚ is defined by $x ✚ y = x^2 - y^2$. Which of the following expressions is equal to $(a + b) ✚ (a - b)$?

(A) $2a^2$ (B) $2a^2 + 2b^2$ (C) $2a^2 - 2b^2$
(D) $-4ab$ (E) $4ab$

17. What is the circumference of the circle whose center is the point (3, 5) and that passes through $(-3, 5)$?

(A) 3π (B) 6π (C) 9π (D) 12π (E) 36π

18. In the figure above, what is the ratio of *b* to *a*?

(A) $\frac{1}{5}$ (B) $\frac{1}{4}$ (C) $\frac{1}{3}$ (D) $\frac{1}{2}$
(E) It cannot be determined from the information given.

19. If the average of *a*, *b*, *c*, and *d* is equal to the average of *a*, *b*, and *c*, what is *d* in terms of *a*, *b*, and *c*?

(A) $a + b + c$ (B) $\frac{a + b + c}{3}$ (C) $\frac{4(a + b + c)}{3}$
(D) $\frac{3(a + b + c)}{4}$ (E) $\frac{(a + b + c)}{4}$

20. What is the average (arithmetic mean) of 2^{50} and 2^{60}?

(A) 55   (B) 110   (C) 2^{55} (D) $2^{25} + 2^{30}$
(E) $2^{49} + 2^{59}$

IF YOU FINISH IN LESS THAN 25 MINUTES, YOU MAY CHECK YOUR WORK ON THIS SECTION ONLY. DO NOT TURN TO ANY OTHER SECTION IN THE TEST.

STOP

For each question in this section, select the best answer from among the choices given, and fill in the corresponding circle on the answer sheet.

Directions

Each sentence below has one or two blanks, each blank indicating that something has been omitted. Beneath the sentence are five words or sets of words labeled A through E. Choose the word or set of words that, when inserted in the sentence, best fits the meaning of the sentence as a whole.

EXAMPLE:

Medieval kingdoms did not become constitutional republics overnight; on the contrary, the change was ----.

(A) unpopular   (B) unexpected
(C) advantageous   (D) sufficient   (E) gradual

Ⓐ Ⓑ Ⓒ Ⓓ ●

---

25. Because of the recent flood of counterfeit twenty dollar bills, the teller carefully ---- each bill handed him by a customer.

    (A) rescinded   (B) squandered   (C) repudiated
    (D) returned   (E) scrutinized

26. Edison's remark that genius is "one percent inspiration and ninety-nine percent perspiration" implies the value of ----.

    (A) eagerness   (B) thoughtfulness
    (C) eccentricity   (D) diligence   (E) intuition

27. They greeted his proposal with ---- and refused to give it serious study.

    (A) acclaim   (B) detachment   (C) fervor
    (D) derision   (E) approbation

28. The epiphyte plants of the rain forest use trees for physical support but do not, like ----, sap nutrients from their hosts.

    (A) fauna   (B) predators   (C) parasites
    (D) insectivores   (E) stumps

29. Holroyd manages to make each successive phase of George Bernard Shaw's life seem significant of itself, rather than simply as ---- of what was to come or as raw material for Shaw's plays.

    (A) an application   (B) a foretoken
    (C) a predilection   (D) a plagiarism
    (E) a recollection

30. Unlike the archetypal reclusive scientist-scholar, lost in a fog of abstruse speculations, Feynman was ---- soul much given to convivial company.

    (A) a gregarious   (B) a recondite
    (C) a dispassionate   (D) a pragmatic
    (E) an introverted

31. For centuries, physicists have had good reason to believe in the principle of equivalence propounded by Galileo: it has ---- many rigorous tests that ---- its accuracy to extraordinary precision.

    (A) endured..compromised
    (B) passed..presupposed
    (C) borne..postulated
    (D) survived..proved
    (E) inspired..equated

32. ---- stereotypes that depict Latinos as cut off from the American mainstream, the Latino National Political Survey found a high degree of ---- the mainstream among people of Hispanic descent.

    (A) Supporting..familiarity with
    (B) Debunking..assimilation into
    (C) Creating..commitment to
    (D) Dismantling..indifference to
    (E) Subverting..hostility toward

GO ON TO NEXT PAGE ▶

Questions 33 and 34 are based on the following passage.

In 1660 Robert Boyle investigated the properties of vacuums in a series of pioneering experiments. Using an improved suction pump,
Line Boyle pumped the air out of a glass jar,
5   successfully producing a vacuum. He then explored what happened to various objects in a vacuum; for example, when he put a burning candle into the jar and pumped out the air, the flame died. Boyle's experiments seem obvious today, but
10 they represent a radical departure from the scientific conventions of his day, when the established method of "discovering" something was to debate it logically, following rules laid down by Aristotle 2000 years before.

33. The author's attitude towards Boyle's experiments can best be described as

(A) condescension   (B) ambivalence
(C) admiration   (D) resentment
(E) disenchantment

34. The word "conventions" in line 11 most nearly means

(A) scholarly gatherings
(B) legal contracts
(C) direct observations
(D) academic institutions
(E) accepted practices

Questions 35 and 36 are based on the following passage.

With the opening of Japan to the West 150 years ago, Europeans and Americans became fascinated by all things Japanese. Even the humble
Line utensils of Japanese daily life—rice bowls, chop-
5   sticks, bamboo ladles, paper lanterns—struck Westerners as exotic. Western artists were quick to exploit the rage for Japanese themes. In England, W. S. Gilbert revived his fortunes, writing the libretto for the operetta *The Mikado*, set in Japan.
10 Indeed, Japanese themes inspired artists to some of their best work: Debussy is said to have composed *La Mer* (The Sea) while staring at a copy of Hokusai's woodcut *The Great Wave*.

35. The word "rage" (line 7) most nearly means

(A) temper   (B) wrath   (C) craze
(D) oddness   (E) rejection

36. The reference to W. S. Gilbert (lines 7–10) suggests which of the following?

(A) His libretto for *The Mikado* was not very good.
(B) He had recently made his first visit to Japan.
(C) His career had been in need of a boost.
(D) He left England to take up residence in Japan.
(E) His previous librettos had touched on Japanese themes.

Questions 37–48 are based on the following passages.

The following passages deal with the exotic world of subatomic physics. Passage 1, written by a popularizer of contemporary physics, was published in 1985. Passage 2 appeared in a general magazine in 1993.

Passage 1

The classical idea of matter was something with solidity and mass, like wet stone dust pressed in a fist. If matter was composed of atoms, then
Line the atoms too must have solidity and mass. At the
5   beginning of the twentieth century the atom was imagined as a tiny granite pebble. Then, in the physics of Niels Bohr, the miniature billiard ball became something akin to a musical instrument, a finely tuned Stradivarius 10 billion times smaller
10 than the real thing. With the advent of quantum mechanics, the musical instrument gave way to pure music. On the atomic scale, the solidity and mass of matter dissolved into something light and airy. Suddenly physicists were describing atoms in
15 the vocabulary of the composer—"resonance," "frequency," "harmony," "scale." Atomic electrons

GO ON TO NEXT PAGE ▶

sang in choirs like seraphim, cherubim, thrones, and dominions. Classical distinctions between matter and light became muddled. In the new physics, light bounced about like particles, and matter undulated in waves like light.

In recent decades, physicists have uncovered elegant subatomic structures in the music of matter. They use a strange new language to describe the subatomic world: *quark, squark, gluon, gauge, technicolor, flavor, strangeness, charm*. There are *up* quarks and *down* quarks, *top* quarks and *bottom* quarks. There are particles with *truth* and *antitruth*, and there are particles with *naked beauty*. The simplest of the constituents of ordinary matter—the proton, for instance—has taken on the character of a Bach fugue, a four-part counterpoint of matter, energy, space, and time. At matter's heart there are arpeggios, chromatics, syncopation. On the lowest rung of the chain of being, Creation dances.

Already, the astronomers and the particle physicists are engaged in a vigorous dialogue. The astronomers are prepared to recognize that the large-scale structure of the universe may have been determined by subtle interactions of particles in the first moments of the Big Bang. And the particle physicists are hoping to find confirmation of their theories of subatomic structure in the astronomers' observations of deep space and time. The snake has bitten its tail and won't let go.

Passage 2

Imagine an infinitesimal particle that is as heavy as a large atom and less tangible than a shadow. For 15 years, hundreds of physicists have been chasing such an improbable phantom. Their quarry is the top quark, the sole missing member of a family of subatomic particles that form the basic building blocks of matter. Of six types of quarks that are believed to exist, five have already been discovered. "The top," says Harvard University theorist Sheldon Glashow, "is not just another quark. It's the last blessed one, and the sooner we find it, the better everyone will feel."

Physicists will celebrate because the top is the absent jewel in the crown of the so-called Standard Model, a powerful theoretical synthesis that has reduced a once-bewildering zoo of particles to just a few fundamental constituents, including three whimsically named couplets of quarks. Up and down quarks combine to create everyday protons and neutrons, while charm and strange quarks make up more esoteric particles, the kind produced by accelerators and high-energy cosmic rays. In 1977 physicists discovered a fifth quark they dubbed bottom, and they have been looking for its partner, top, ever since. Not finding it would amaze and befuddle particle physicists. Without the top, a large chunk of the theoretical edifice, like an arch without a keystone, would come crashing down.

Theorists have already deduced that the top quark is heavier than any known particle. "A single top quark," exclaims Fermilab physicist Alvin Tollestrup, "probably weighs at least as much as a whole silver atom does." (With an atomic weight of 108, a silver atom is made up of hundreds of up and down quarks.) Exactly how much top quarks weigh is a question scientists are anxious to answer, but first they must find some to measure—a task considerably complicated by the fact that in nature these massive but ethereal entities made only a cameo appearance, just after the Big Bang.

Top quarks emerged from the primordial radiation "around a thousandth of a billionth of a second after the Big Bang," estimates University of Michigan theorist Gordon Kane. But as the early universe expanded and cooled, they vanished. Their fleeting existence left behind a fundamental puzzle that physicists are struggling to solve: What makes some particles so massive while others—photons, for example—have no mass at all? Because of its boggling heft, the top quark should help illuminate what mysterious mechanisms—including perhaps other, still weightier particles—are responsible for imparting mass, and hence solidity, to the physical world.

---

37. Which of the following would be the most appropriate title for Passage 1?

    (A) Linguistic Implications of Particle Physics
    (B) The Influence of Music on Particle Interactions
    (C) Matter's Transformation: The Music of Subatomic Physics
    (D) Trends in Physics Research: Eliminating the Quark
    (E) The Impossible Dream: Obstacles to Proving the Existence of Matter

38. The author of Passage 1 refers to quarks, squarks, and charms (paragraph 2) primarily in order to

    (A) demonstrate the similarity between these particles and earlier images of the atom
    (B) make a distinction between appropriate and inappropriate terms
    (C) object to suggestions of similar frivolous names
    (D) provide examples of idiosyncratic nomenclature in contemporary physics
    (E) cite preliminary experimental evidence supporting the existence of subatomic matter

GO ON TO NEXT PAGE ▶

39. The author's tone in the second paragraph of Passage 1 can best be described as one of

(A) scientific detachment
(B) moderate indignation
(C) marked derision
(D) admiring wonder
(E) qualified skepticism

40. "Matter's heart" mentioned in line 34 is

(A) outer space
(B) the subatomic world
(C) the language of particle physics
(D) harmonic theory
(E) flesh and blood

41. In line 46, the image of the snake biting its tail is used to emphasize

(A) the dangers of circular reasoning
(B) the vigor inherent in modern scientific dialogue
(C) the eventual triumph of the classical idea of matter
(D) the unity underlying the astronomers' and particle physicists' theories
(E) the ability of contemporary scientific doctrine to swallow earlier theories

42. The author of Passage 2 describes the top quark as "an improbable phantom" because it is

(A) nonexistent   (B) discoverable   (C) lively
(D) visionary   (E) elusive

43. Glashow's comment in lines 55–58 reflects his

(A) apprehension   (B) impatience
(C) imagination   (D) jubilation
(E) spirituality

44. From the term's use, we can infer that a "cameo appearance" (line 87) is most likely

(A) noisy   (B) colorful   (C) explosive
(D) brief   (E) massive

45. The author of Passage 2 does all of the following EXCEPT

(A) cite an authority   (B) use a simile
(C) define a term   (D) pose a question
(E) deny a possibility

46. The author of Passage 2 mentions the silver atom (lines 77–82) primarily to

(A) clarify the monetary value of the top quark
(B) explain what is meant by atomic weight
(C) illustrate how hefty a top quark is compared with other particles
(D) suggest the sorts of elements studied under cosmic ray bombardment
(E) demonstrate the malleability of silver as an element

47. Compared to Passage 1, Passage 2 can best be described as

(A) more emotional   (B) more reportorial
(C) less factual   (D) less technical
(E) more figurative

48. As Passage 2 suggests, since the time Passage 1 was written, the Standard Model has

(A) determined even more whimsical names for the subatomic particles under discussion
(B) taken into account the confusion of the particle physicists
(C) ruled out some of the particles whose existence had been previously hypothesized
(D) refuted significant aspects of the Big Bang theory of the formation of the universe
(E) collapsed for lack of proof of the existence of top quarks

IF YOU FINISH IN LESS THAN 25 MINUTES, YOU MAY CHECK YOUR WORK ON THIS SECTION ONLY. DO NOT TURN TO ANY OTHER SECTION IN THE TEST.

STOP

Multiple-Choice Directions

For questions 21–28, determine which of the five choices is correct. You may use any blank space on the page for your work.

NOTES:
- You may use a calculator whenever you believe it will be helpful.
- Use the diagrams provided to help you solve the problems. Unless you see the phrase
  <u>Note:</u> Figure not drawn to scale

under a diagram, it has been drawn as accurately as possible. Unless it is stated that a figure is three dimensional, you may assume that it lies in a plane.

Reference

$A = \pi r^2$
$C = 2\pi r$

$A = \frac{1}{2}bh$

$V = \ell wh$

$V = \pi r^2 h$

$c^2 = a^2 + b^2$

Special Right Triangles

Number of degrees in a circle: 360
Sum of the measures, in degrees, of the three angles of a triangle: 180

---

21. Neil paid $357 including 5% sales tax for a suit. What was the cost of the suit, not counting the tax?

    (A) $339.15   (B) $340.00   (C) $342.00
    (D) $352.00   (E) $374.85

22. When a digital clock reads 1:35, the sum of the digits is 9. What is the largest possible sum that can be obtained in this way?

    (A) 17   (B) 19   (C) 21   (D) 23   (E) 27

23. If 12 of the 20 members of a club are female, what is the ratio of males to females in the club?

    (A) 2:5   (B) 3:5   (C) 2:3   (D) 3:2   (E) 5:2

24. A number n is chosen at random from the set of positive integers less than 10. What is the probability that $\frac{8}{n} > n$?

    (A) $\frac{1}{8}$ (B) $\frac{2}{9}$ (C) $\frac{1}{3}$ (D) $\frac{2}{3}$ (E) $\frac{7}{9}$

25. If $5^x = a$ and $5^y = b$, then $ab =$

    (A) 5^{xy} (B) 5^{x+y} (C) 10^{x+y}
    (D) 25^{xy} (E) 9^{x+y}

26. The equation $|10 - \sqrt{x}| = 7$ has two solutions. What is their sum?

    (A) 0   (B) 9   (C) 18   (D) 20   (E) 298

27. x varies inversely with y and y varies directly with z. If when $x = 12$, $y = 10$, and $z = 20$, what is the value of $y + z$ when $x = 6$?

    (A) 15   (B) 30   (C) 45   (D) 60   (E) 120

28. Which of the following could be the number of points of intersection between two triangles?

    I. 3
    II. 4
    III. 6

    (A) I only   (B) III only   (C) I and II only
    (D) I and III only   (E) I, II, and III

GO ON TO NEXT PAGE ▶

Student-Produced Response Directions

In questions 29–38, first solve the problem, and then enter your answer on the grid provided on the answer sheet. The instructions for entering your answers follow.

- First, write your answer in the boxes at the top of the grid.
- Second, grid your answer in the columns below the boxes.
- Use the fraction bar in the first row or the decimal point in the second row to enter fractions and decimals.

Answer: $\frac{8}{15}$ Answer: 1.75   Answer: 100

Write your answer in the boxes

Grid-in your answer

Either position is acceptable

- Grid only one space in each column.
- Entering the answer in the boxes is recommended as an aid in gridding but is not required.
- The machine scoring your exam can read only what you grid, so you **must grid-in your answers correctly to get credit.**
- If a question has more than one correct answer, grid-in only one of them.
- The grid does not have a minus sign; so no answer can be negative.
- A mixed number *must* be converted to an improper fraction or a decimal before it is gridded. Enter $1\frac{1}{4}$ as $\frac{5}{4}$ or 1.25; the machine will interpret 11/4 as $\frac{11}{4}$ and mark it wrong.

- **All decimals must be entered as accurately as possible.** Here are three acceptable ways of gridding
$$\frac{3}{11} = 0.272727\ldots$$

- Note that rounding to .273 is acceptable because you are using the full grid, but you would receive **no credit** for .3 or .27, because they are less accurate.

---

29. If Noah drives at an average speed of 60 miles per hour, how many *minutes* will it take him to drive 330 miles?

30. Twelve more than the product of 4 and 9 is equal to the sum of 13 and what number?

31. What is the value of *x* in the figure above?

32. Bobbi spent $125 for a tape recorder and some cassettes. The tape recorder cost $100 more than the cassettes. What percent of the cost of the two items was for the tape recorder?

33. The area of a square is equal to the area of a right triangle whose legs are 8 and 16. What is the length of each side of the square?

34. Each integer from 1 to 60 whose units digit is a 5 is written on a separate slip of paper. If the slips are placed in a box and one is chosen at random, what is the probability that the number chosen is prime?

35. If $\frac{c+d}{c-d} = \frac{13}{3}$, what is the value of $\frac{d}{c}$?

36. In the figure above, all of the line segments meet to form right angles. What is the perimeter of the region?

37. In △ABC, $AB = \sqrt{10}$ and $AC = \sqrt{50}$. What is the largest integer that could be the length of side BC?

38. In the figure below, a square is inscribed in a circle. If the radius of the circle is 5 and the area of the shaded region is expressed as $25(\pi - b)$, what is the value of b?

1. With the exception of <u>Frank and I, everyone in the class finished</u> the assignment before the bell rang.

   (A) Frank and I, everyone in the class finished
   (B) Frank and me, everyone in the class finished
   (C) Frank and me, everyone in the class had finished
   (D) Frank and I, everyone in the class had finished
   (E) Frank and me everyone in the class finished

2. The players' representatives agreed <u>to return to their teams and they would discuss</u> the terms offered them by the management.

   (A) to return to their teams and they would discuss
   (B) to return to their teams to discuss
   (C) to returning to their teams, and therefore discussing
   (D) to return to their teams and to the discussion of
   (E) on the return to their teams to the discussing

3. The form of terrorism that makes diplomats its target reached Sweden in <u>1975, the West German embassy in Stockholm was seized</u> by Germans linked to the Baader-Meinhof gang.

   (A) 1975, the West German embassy in Stockholm was seized
   (B) 1975, and the West German embassy in Stockholm was seized
   (C) 1975, despite the West German embassy in Stockholm was seized
   (D) 1975, when the West German embassy in Stockholm was seized
   (E) 1975, the West German embassy in Stockholm's being seized

4. Arlington National Cemetery, <u>the site of the Tomb of the Unknowns, is located on</u> the former Custis estate in Virginia.

   (A) the site of the Tomb of the Unknowns, is located on
   (B) being the cite of the Tomb of the Unknowns, has been located at
   (C) where is located the Tomb of the Unknowns, is at
   (D) being the site of the Tomb of the Unknowns, is at
   (E) which includes the site of the Tomb of the Unknowns, is located by

5. In the normal course of events, <u>Juan will graduate high school, he will enter</u> college in two years.

   (A) Juan will graduate high school, he will enter
   (B) Juan will graduate high school and enter
   (C) Juan will be graduated from high school and enter
   (D) Juan will have graduated from high school and enter
   (E) Juan will graduate high school; he will enter

6. <u>Unlike 20 years ago, baseball players in today's world</u> may declare themselves free agents and encourage bids from teams in both leagues.

   (A) Unlike 20 years ago, baseball players in today's world
   (B) Unlike 20 years ago, people playing baseball today
   (C) Baseball players today, opposed to 20 years ago,
   (D) Unlike their counterparts 20 years ago, baseball players today
   (E) Opposed to their counterparts 20 years ago, today's baseball players

GO ON TO NEXT PAGE ▶

7. The number of California condors, decimated by increasing human intrusions into traditional condor breeding grounds, are currently given as fewer than three hundred.

   (A) are currently given as fewer than three hundred
   (B) currently are given as fewer than three hundred
   (C) is currently given as fewer than three hundred
   (D) were given currently as fewer than three hundred
   (E) are currently going to be given as fewer than three hundred

8. Many economists maintain that the current low interest rates not only promote investment in the stock market but also made it more profitable.

   (A) but also made it more profitable
   (B) but also makes it more profitable
   (C) but also made it more able to profit
   (D) but made it also more profitable
   (E) but also make it more profitable

9. Ever since the massacres in Bosnia, there has been much opposition from they who maintain that it was an act of genocide.

   (A) from they who maintain that it was an act of genocide
   (B) from they who maintain that it had been an act of genocide
   (C) from those who maintain that it was an act of genocide
   (D) from they maintaining that it was an act of genocide
   (E) from they maintaining that it had been an act of genocide

10. During the winter of 2005, Americans discovered the need to conserve energy, and attempts were made to meet the crisis.

    (A) discovered the need to conserve energy, and attempts were made to meet the crisis
    (B) discovered the need to conserve energy and that the crisis had to be met
    (C) discovered the need to conserve energy and made attempts to meet the crisis
    (D) needed to conserve energy and to meet the crisis
    (E) needed to conserve energy, and attempts were made to meet the crisis

11. When one eats in this restaurant, you often find that the prices are high and that the food is poorly prepared.

    (A) When one eats in this restaurant, you often find
    (B) When you eat in this restaurant, one often find
    (C) When you eat in this restaurant, you often find
    (D) If you eat in this restaurant, you often find
    (E) When one ate in this restaurant, he often found

12. The giving of foreign aid is a tool of national policy, the hoped-for return is often indirect and long term.

    (A) policy, the hoped-for return is often indirect and long term
    (B) policy, however the hoped-for return is often indirect and long term
    (C) policy, though the hoped-for return is often indirect and long term
    (D) policy, albeit the hoped-for return is often indirect and long term
    (E) policy, despite the hoped-for return is often indirect and long term

13. Strict economic sanctions that have been imposed against Cuba ban investments in that country and numerous goods may not be imported.

    (A) ban investments in that country and numerous goods may not be imported
    (B) ban investments there and the importation of numerous goods
    (C) ban investing there and numerous goods may not be imported
    (D) ban investments in that country, also, numerous goods may not be imported
    (E) ban investing there and numerous goods have not imported

14. Feeding natural wildlife during fall migration not advocated being that it entices them to stay and possibly starve during the winter.

    (A) not advocated being that it entices them to stay and possibly starve
    (B) is not advocated since it entices them to stay and possibly starve
    (C) is not advocated being that it entices them to stay, perhaps starving
    (D) has not been advisable because of eating patterns
    (E) is not advocated; they can starve

GO ON TO NEXT PAGE ▶

15. One need not subscribe for Freud's ideas to recognize the importance of helping individuals to shape lives under their own control.

   (A) One need not subscribe for Freud's ideas to recognize the importance of helping
   (B) You need not subscribe for Freud's ideas to recognize the importance to help
   (C) One needs not subscribe for Freud's ideas to recognize the importance of helping
   (D) One need not subscribe to Freud's ideas to recognize the importance of helping
   (E) No one need subscribe to Freud's ideas to recognize the importance for helping

16. Housed in the former Bankside Power Station, the Tate Gallery is the only one of London's museums that specialize in modern art.

   (A) that specialize in modern art
   (B) which specialize in modern art
   (C) that specialize about modern art
   (D) that have been specializing in modern art
   (E) that specializes in modern art

17. The violin teacher criticized her pupils for not having practiced as regular as they should have over the summer break.

   (A) pupils for not having practiced as regular as they should have
   (B) pupils for not having practiced so regular as they had ought to
   (C) pupils for not having practiced as regularly as they should have
   (D) pupils because they had not practiced as regular as they should of
   (E) pupils for them not having practiced as regularly as they should have

18. Among our grandest and longest-lived illusions is the concept of the noble savage.

   (A) Among our grandest and longest-lived illusions is the concept of the noble savage.
   (B) Among our grandest and longest-lived illusions are the concept of the noble savage.
   (C) The concept for the noble savage has been our grandest and longest-lived illusions.
   (D) Among our grandest and mostly long-lived allusions is the noble savage concept.
   (E) The concept of the noble savage is amongst our most grand and long-lived illusions.

19. Used since the seventeenth century to demonstrate variations in atmospheric pressure, the storm glass is still a reliable way to predict the weather.

   (A) Used since the seventeenth century to demonstrate variations in atmospheric pressure
   (B) It has been used to demonstrate variations in atmospheric pressure since the seventeenth century
   (C) Being that it was used since the seventeenth century to demonstrate how atmospheric pressure varies
   (D) They have used it since the seventeenth century to demonstrate variations in atmospheric pressure
   (E) Since the seventeenth century having been used to demonstrate variations in atmospheric pressure

20. The war between the British and the French did not end until they defeated them decisively at the Battle of Waterloo.

   (A) did not end until they defeated them decisively
   (B) had not ended until they defeated them decisively
   (C) did not end until the British defeated the French so decisive
   (D) was not ended after the British defeated the French decisively
   (E) did not end until the British defeated the French decisively

The sentences in this section may contain errors in grammar, usage, choice of words, or idioms. There is either just one error per sentence, or the sentence is correct. Some words or phrases are underlined and lettered; everything else in the sentence is correct.

If an underlined word or phrase is incorrect, choose that letter; if the sentence is correct, select <u>No error</u>. Then blacken the appropriate space on your Answer Sheet.

EXAMPLE:

The region has a climate <u>so severe that</u> plants
                           A

<u>growing there</u> rarely <u>had been</u> more than twelve
     B   C

inches <u>high</u>. <u>No error</u>
        D   E

SAMPLE ANSWER:

Ⓐ Ⓑ ● Ⓓ Ⓔ

---

21. I <u>only</u> <u>bought</u> <u>what</u> was necessary; I was not
       A   B   C

    <u>extravagant</u>. <u>No error</u>
         D   E

22. Bailing <u>vigorously</u>, we managed <u>to remain</u> afloat
               A   C

    until we <u>were rescued</u> by the Coast Guard.
                  D

    <u>No error</u>
        E

23. We <u>had ought to</u> finish our trip before dark
          A

    <u>because</u> <u>it</u> gets very cold after the sun
        B   C

    <u>goes down</u>. <u>No error</u>
        D   E

24. <u>Because of</u> its efficacy in treating many ailments
        A

    and because <u>it has brought about</u> remarkable
                      B

    cures, cortisone <u>has become</u> an important
                          C

    <u>addition</u> to the druggist's stock. <u>No error</u>
        D   E

25. After the rain <u>had fallen</u> <u>steadily</u> for five days, <u>then</u>
                       A   B   C

    the football field was a <u>massive sea</u> of mud.
                                 D

    <u>No error</u>
        E

26. The ship had <u>almost completely</u> <u>sank</u> <u>by the time</u>
                      A   B   C

    the rescuers <u>arrived on</u> the scene. <u>No error</u>
                      D   E

27. Marc Chagall, <u>Russian-born</u> painter and
                       A

    printmaker, <u>who</u> died in 1985, painted many
                    B

    <u>beautiful executed</u> fantasies <u>both</u> in the United
         C   D

    States and France. <u>No error</u>
                            E

28. <u>Although</u> many television viewers complain about
        A

    Donald Trump's attitude, <u>it</u> <u>seems</u> perfectly all
                                  B   C

    right to <u>myself</u>. <u>No error</u>
                 D   E

29. The America's Cup, <u>which</u> was first won by the
                            A

    United States yacht *America*, <u>grew out of</u> the
                                        B

    London Exposition of 1951 and <u>now becoming</u> a
                                        C

    world <u>yachting</u> championship. <u>No error</u>
              D   E

GO ON TO NEXT PAGE ▶

30. The Salem witchcraft trials in 1692 inspired

Arthur Miller to write *The Crucible*, to serve for a
$\overline{\qquad A \qquad}$ $\overline{\qquad B \qquad}$

parable for America during the era of
     $\overline{\text{C}}$ $\overline{\text{D}}$

McCarthyism. No error
     $\overline{\qquad E \qquad}$

31. As soon as the captains heard that a school of
$\overline{\text{A}}$

bluefish were near the wreck, the fishing fleet
     $\overline{\qquad B \qquad}$ $\overline{\qquad C \qquad}$

set out from the harbor. No error
$\overline{\qquad D \qquad}$ $\overline{\qquad E \qquad}$

32. After five years of booming markets and
     $\overline{\text{A}}$

unparalleled expansion, Wall Street's major

securities firms planning to slow their growth
     $\overline{\qquad B \qquad}$ $\overline{\text{C}}$

that has transformed them into sprawling global
     $\overline{\qquad D \qquad}$

behemoths. No error
     $\overline{\qquad E \qquad}$

33. Neither the reporters nor the editor were
$\overline{\text{A}}$ $\overline{\text{B}}$

satisfied with the salary offer made by the
$\overline{\qquad C \qquad}$ $\overline{\text{D}}$

publisher. No error
     $\overline{\qquad E \qquad}$

34. Although winter conditions in northern Idaho and

Montana are like some parts of Alaska, in spite of
     $\overline{\text{A}}$ $\overline{\qquad B \qquad}$

this superficial resemblance the regions differ
     $\overline{\qquad C \qquad}$

markedly. No error
$\overline{\text{D}}$ $\overline{\text{E}}$

Improving Paragraph Directions

The passage below is the unedited draft of a student's essay. Some of the essay needs to be rewritten to make the meaning clearer and more precise. Read the essay carefully.

The essay is followed by five questions about changes that might improve all or part of its organization, development, sentence structure, use of language, appropriateness to the audience, or use of standard written English. Choose the answer that most clearly and effectively expresses the student's intended meaning. Indicate your choice by filling in the corresponding space on the answer sheet.

[1] At the beginning of the twentieth century, no one knew the technological developments that would be made by the 1990s. [2] The area of communication media is one of the significant developments in the twentieth century. [3] Also nuclear energy and great advancements in medicine and the treatment of disease.

[4] One important development was the invention of communication satellites which allow images and messages to be sent wirelessly around the world. [5] One advantage is that current events can be sent worldwide in seconds. [6] News used to travel by boat and take weeks or months to get overseas. [7] When a disaster struck the World Trade Center, the world saw it immediately and condemned the terrorists' actions. [8] One weak aspect of communication satellites is that they are launched from a space shuttle, and that is an extremely costly operation. [9] They also cost millions of dollars to build and operate. [10] Therefore, many poor countries are left out of the so-called "Global Village."

[11] The invention and use of nuclear energy is another important technological development. [12] One positive feature of nuclear energy is that energy is cheaper, and can be made easy. [13] This is important in countries like France where almost all of the electricity is nuclear. [14] A negative consequence of nuclear energy is the probability of major nuclear accidents. [15] Watch out for human error and careless workmanship. [16] They were the cause of the meltdown in Chernobyl, which killed hundreds or maybe even thousands, and radiated half the Earth.

GO ON TO NEXT PAGE ▶

[17] There have been many significant technological advances in medicine in the twentieth century. [18] One development was the invention of the CAT scan. [19] The CAT scan allows doctors to make a picture of your brain to see if there is a growth on it. [20] One positive effect of the CAT scan is that doctors can diagnose brain tumors and brain cancer at an early stage. [21] One negative effect is that CAT scans are costly, so they are not used in third world countries.

---

35. Considering the main idea of the whole essay, which of the following is the best revision of sentence 1?

(A) In 1900 no one could anticipate the technological developments in the 1990s.
(B) Recent technological achievements would blow the minds of people at the beginning of the twentieth century.
(C) The twentieth century has seen remarkable technological achievements, but there has also been a price to pay for progress.
(D) No one knows if the twenty-first century will produce as much technological progress as the twentieth century did.
(E) Technological progress in communications, nuclear energy, and medicine is wonderful, but in the process we are destroying ourselves and our environment.

36. Which is the best revision of the underlined segment of sentence 12 below?

One positive feature of nuclear energy is that energy is cheaper, and can be made easy.

(A) energy is cheaper and can be made easily
(B) energy is made cheaper and more easily made
(C) it is cheap and easy to make
(D) it is both cheap as well as made easily
(E) it's more cheaper and easier to make

37. To improve the coherence of paragraph 2, which of the following is the best sentence to delete from the essay?

(A) sentence 5 (B) sentence 6
(C) sentence 7 (D) sentence 8
(E) sentence 9

38. With regard to the entire essay, which of the following best explains the writer's intention in paragraphs 2, 3, and 4?

(A) to compare and contrast three technological achievements
(B) to provide examples of the pros and cons of technological progress
(C) to analyze the steps needed for achievement in three areas
(D) to convince the reader to be open to technological change
(E) to advocate more funds for technological research and development

39. Assume that sentences 17 and 18 were combined as follows: *A significant advance in medicine has been the invention of the CAT scan.* Which of the following is the best way to continue the paragraph?

(A) The CAT scan allows your doctors to make pictures of a brain to see if it has a growth on it, a cancer is growing, or tumors at an early stage.
(B) The CAT scan permits your doctors to make a picture and see if your brain has a growth on it, or whether or not you have brain tumors or brain cancer at an early stage.
(C) Taking pictures with a CAT scan, your brain is studied by doctors for growths, brain tumors, and cancer at an early stage.
(D) Doctors may make pictures of your brain to see if there is a growth, a tumor, or cancer at an early stage on it.
(E) With this device a doctor may look into a patient's brain to check for growths and to detect cancerous tumors at an early stage.

IF YOU FINISH IN LESS THAN 30 MINUTES, YOU MAY CHECK YOUR WORK ON THIS SECTION ONLY. DO NOT TURN TO ANY OTHER SECTION IN THE TEST.

STOP

428 ▶ CHAPTER 11 / Model Test D

Answer Key

Section 1 Critical Reading

1. *B*
2. *B*
3. *A*
4. *A*
5. *E*
6. *D*
7. *A*
8. *D*
9. *C*
10. *A*
11. *C*
12. *D*
13. *E*
14. *E*
15. *B*
16. *D*
17. *B*
18. *B*
19. *E*
20. *D*
21. *B*
22. *D*
23. *E*
24. *C*

Section 2 Mathematics

1. *C*
2. *D*
3. *B*
4. *E*
5. *C*
6. *D*
7. *D*
8. *A*
9. *B*
10. *B*
11. *A*
12. *A*
13. *A*
14. *B*
15. *D*
16. *E*
17. *D*
18. *D*
19. *B*
20. *E*

Section 3 Critical Reading

25. *E*
26. *D*
27. *D*
28. *C*
29. *B*
30. *A*
31. *D*
32. *B*
33. *C*
34. *E*
35. *C*
36. *C*
37. *C*
38. *D*
39. *D*
40. *B*
41. *D*
42. *E*
43. *B*
44. *D*
45. *E*
46. *C*
47. *B*
48. *C*

Section 4 Mathematics

21. *B*
22. *D*
23. *C*
24. *B*
25. *B*
26. *E*
27. *D*
28. *E*

29. 330
30. 35
31. 65
32. 90
33. 8
34. 1/6
35. 5/8
36. 52
37. 10
38. 2

Section 5 Writing Skills

1. *C*	9. *C*	17. *C*	25. *C*	33. *B*
2. *B*	10. *C*	18. *A*	26. *B*	34. *B*
3. *D*	11. *C*	19. *A*	27. *C*	35. *C*
4. *A*	12. *C*	20. *E*	28. *D*	36. *C*
5. *C*	13. *B*	21. *A*	29. *C*	37. *B*
6. *D*	14. *B*	22. *E*	30. *B*	38. *B*
7. *C*	15. *D*	23. *A*	31. *D*	39. *E*
8. *E*	16. *E*	24. *B*	32. *B*	

Scoring Chart—Model Test D

Critical Reading Sections

Section 1: 24 Questions (1–24)
Number correct   _____ (A)
Number omitted   _____ (B)
Number incorrect   _____ (C)
$\frac{1}{4}$ (C)   _____ (D)
(A) − (D)   _____ Raw Score I

Section 3: 24 Questions (25–48)
Number correct   _____ (A)
Number omitted   _____ (B)
Number incorrect   _____ (C)
$\frac{1}{4}$ (C)   _____ (D)
(A) − (D)   _____ Raw Score II

Total Critical Reading Raw Score
Raw Scores I + II   _____

Mathematics Sections

Section 2: 20 Questions (1–20)
Number correct   _____ (A)
Number omitted   _____ (B)
Number incorrect   _____ (C)
$\frac{1}{4}$ (C)   _____ (D)
(A) − (D)   _____ Raw Score I

Section 4: First 8 Questions (21–28)
Number correct   _____ (A)
Number omitted   _____ (B)
Number incorrect   _____ (C)
$\frac{1}{4}$ (C)   _____ (D)
(A) − (D)   _____ Raw Score II

Section 4: Next 10 Questions (29–38)
Number correct   _____ Raw Score III

Total Mathematical Raw Score
Raw Scores I + II + III   _____

NOTE: In each section (A) + (B) + (C) should equal the number of questions in that section.

Writing Skills Section

Section 5: 39 Questions (1–39)
Number correct   _____ (A)
Number omitted   _____ (B)
Number incorrect   _____ (C)
$\frac{1}{4}$ (C)   _____ (D)

Writing Skills Raw Score
(A) − (D)   _____

Evaluation Chart

Study your score. Your raw score is an indication of your probable achievement on the PSAT/NMSQT. As a guide to the amount of work you need or want to do with this book, study the following.

Raw Score			Self-rating
Critical Reading	*Mathematics*	*Writing*	
42–48	35–38	33–39	Superior
37–46	30–34	28–32	Very good
32–36	25–29	23–27	Good
26–35	21–24	17–22	Above average
20–25	17–20	12–16	Average
12–19	10–16	7–11	Below average
less than 12	less than 10	less than 7	Inadequate

Answer Explanations

Section 1 Critical Reading

1. *B* Naturalists would be *alarmed* by the idea that the elephant population might be decreasing. They would *deplore* (disapprove of, lament) the notion that the species was slowly dying out.

2. *B* To *aggravate* a problem is to make it worse. When people live longer and fewer babies die, overpopulation is made worse.

3. *A* The structure of the sentence ("Even . . . who normally would") signals a contrast. The Republican committee members did *not* defend the administration's actions. Instead, they *deprecated* (condemned; disapproved) them.

4. *A* Both missing words must be positive. The speaker is praising the installation as *impeccable* (without fault) and saying that, despite recent drawbacks, such programs can still *succeed*.

5. *E* If Mrs. Woolf combines both modern radical and old-fashioned nonradical elements in her fiction, then she presents *an anomalous* or contradictory image.

6. *D* To strike a medallion is to make or *produce* it by impressing or stamping it.

7. *A* The recipients of the Tercentenary medallion were to be members of "families that had held their farms in an unbroken line for at least two hundred years," in other words *lineal descendants of the early settlers* or farm owners.

8. *D* The passage states that "25 novae occur in our galaxy every year, but only two or three are *near enough* to be observed." Thus, our observations of novae are hampered by their *distance*.

9. *C* The star is new in the sense that it previously has not been visible to the casual observer, the "naked eye." By exploding, it has increased in visibility: it has *become bright enough to strike the eye*.

10. *A* The author is *reflecting on* or considering her childhood. She is remembering and analyzing past events.

11. *C* The speaker is an *adult*, looking back in time. Her description implies that she did not understand the prejudice of the other children because she was young and innocent. As an adult, she is clear about the attitude of the other pupils; as a child, it made no sense to her.

12. *D* Paragraph 5 states: "I was the only child who had camped on the Baumanns' land ever to get out of the C class." This suggests that the school administrators dealt with the "problem of transient laborers" by *placing all migrant children in the C class*.

13. *E* The author does not personally believe that being a migrant worker is disgraceful. That is what the townsfolk believed. She uses the townsfolk's own words ("disgraceful and dirty," "gypsies," "untrustworthy") to imply exactly the opposite beliefs. In doing so, her tone is clearly *ironic*.

14. *E* Most people would agree that ginger ale is a common beverage, not "an exotic drink." By referring to it as exotic, the author underscores how unfamiliar she was as the child of migrant workers with *everyday experiences we take for granted*.

15. *B* Barbara and her friends began to play with the narrator and to invite her to their homes because of her transfer to the A class. This upward change in her academic status led to a similar change in her social status: the other children began to treat her with *acceptance*.

16. *D* Given that Du Bois chose to describe himself as "a master of propaganda," he most probably regarded his work as a propagandist as *a particular achievement* on his part.

17. *B* Du Bois describes at length the sense of "twoness" he feels as a black American. In other words, he emphasizes the American Negro's *duality*.

18. *B* The body's *dogged* strength enables it to resist being pulled apart. In stubbornly resisting the forces that threaten to tear him in two, the black American is *tenacious* (persistent) and *unyielding* (resolute).

19. *E* As you can tell from the lines immediately preceding and following this sentence, the author is giving examples of Du Bois's own "twoness" by showing that at various times he advocated contradictory courses. Thus, at times he advocated black capitalism; at other times, black Marxism. At times, he focused on the black educated elite; at other times, on the black masses. Most times, he counseled uncompromising protest; at some times, however, he counseled the *reconciliation of differences,* or accommodation.

20. *D* Although the author points out that Du Bois's methods led him into conflicts, he describes Du Bois as "often . . . well in advance of his contemporaries" and stresses that his motives for departing from the mainstream were admirable. Thus, his attitude can best be described as *approving*.

21. *B* The author extensively quotes from Du Bois's writings (lines 37–51). He establishes the time frame during which Du Bois was active. He lists examples of propagandists (Douglass, Washington, Du Bois). He contrasts Du Bois's increasingly radical stance with Washington's conservative, gradualist strategy. However, he never asks a rhetorical question. In fact, he never poses any sort of question.

22. *D* The final two paragraphs discuss Du Bois in relationship to black leaders in general and then provide the specific example of his relationship to Booker T. Washington.

Choice A is incorrect. The author mentions Du Bois's early support of Washington's gradualist approach in order to contrast it with his later departure from Washington's conservatism. Choice B is incorrect. The author discusses Du Bois's personality only in passing; he discusses Washington's personality not at all. Choice C is incorrect. The author's chief concern is to describe Du Bois's position, not analyze what lay behind his achieving this position. He spends more time showing why Du Bois angered his fel-low blacks than he does showing why Du Bois attracted his fellow blacks. Choice E is incorrect. It is unsupported by the passage.

23. *E* The last sentence points out that Du Bois originally agreed with Washington's program.

Choice A is incorrect. Nothing in the passage suggests that Du Bois sacrificed effective strategies out of a desire to try something new. Choice B is incorrect. Du Bois gained in influence, effectively winning away large numbers of blacks from Washington's policies. Choice C is incorrect. Du Bois's quickness to depart from conventional black wisdom when it proved inadequate to the task of advancing the race shows him to be well able to change with the times. Choice D is incorrect. Washington, not Du Bois, is described as seeking the goodwill of powerful whites.

24. *C* The author does *not* portray Washington as versatile. Instead, he portrays Du Bois as versatile.

Choice A is incorrect. The author portrays Washington as submissive to the majority; he shows him teaching blacks not to protest. Choice B is incorrect. The author portrays Washington as concerned with financial success; he shows him advocating property accumulation. Choice D is incorrect. The author portrays Washington as traditional in preaching industry; he shows him advocating hard work. Choice E is incorrect. The author portrays Washington as respectful of authority; he shows him deferring to powerful whites.

Section 2 Mathematics

For many problems, the explanation provides a reference to one or more **KEY FACTS** from Chapter 9. These are the mathematical facts that you need to solve that problem. If a solution refers to **KEY FACT J2**, for example, the solution depends on the second **KEY FACT** discussed in Section J of Chapter 9.

For some problems, an alternative solution, indicated by two asterisks (**), follows the first solution. When this occurs, usually one of the solutions is the direct mathematical one and the other is based on one of the tactics discussed in Chapters 8 and 9.

1. *C* Divide 100 by 7: $100 = 7 \times 14 + 2$; so, 100 days is 2 days more than 14 weeks. Since 14 weeks (or 98 days) from today it will again be Saturday, 100 days from today it will be Monday.

**Look for a pattern. Since there are 7 days in a week, after every 7 days it will again be Saturday; that is, it will be Saturday after 7, 14, 21, 28, . . . days. Since the largest multiple of 7 less than 100 is 98, then 98 days from now, it will again be Saturday. Count two more days to Monday.

2. *D* Typing at $\frac{1}{3}$ the speed, it took Paul 3 times as long: $3 \times 30 = 90$.

3. *B* The sum of the measures of the three angles in any triangle is 180°. (**KEY FACT J1**) So $90 + 43 + x = 180 \Rightarrow 133 + x = 180 \Rightarrow x = 47$.

4. *E* $\frac{1}{2}\%$ *means* $\frac{1}{2}$ divided by 100, so I is true. Since $\frac{1}{2}$ = 0.5 and 0.5 divided by 100 = 0.005, III is also true. Finally, with your calculator verify that $\frac{1}{100}$ divided by 2 is equal to 0.005; so II is true, as well. I, II, and III are all true.

5. *C* Since the sum of the measures of the two acute angles in a right triangle is 90°, *x* = 65 and *y* = 55. Then 65 + *a* + 55 = 180 ⇒ *a* = 60.

6. *D* By the laws of exponents [**KEY FACT A16**], $(3a^2b^3)^3 = 3^3(a^2)^3(b^3)^3 = 27a^6b^9$.

Use TACTIC 8-3: substitute numbers. If *a* and *b* are 1, $(3a^2b^3)^3 = 3^3 = 27$. Eliminate Choices A and B. If *a* = 1 and *b* = 2, $(3a^2b^3)^3 = (3·1·8)^3 = 24^3$. Use your calculator to evaluate $24^3 = 13,824$; test Choices C, D, and E. Only Choice D works.

7. *D* Draw a picture. By the Pythagorean theorem, $r^2 = 3^2 + 3^2 = 9 + 9 = 18$. The formula for the area of the circle is $A = \pi r^2$, so $A = 18\pi$.

8. *A* Draw a picture and label all the line segments. Now add two segments to create a right triangle. Since the legs are 5 and 12, the hypotenuse is 13. If you don't recognize a 5-12-13 right triangle, just use the Pythagorean theorem.

Use TACTIC 8-4 and eliminate the absurd choices. He rode 17 miles. Clearly, the direct path is shorter. Eliminate Choices C, D, and E. Since it's probably *much* shorter, eliminate Choice B, as well.

9. *B* Since Justin read 50% of his book on Monday and still had 10% left after Tuesday, the 100 pages he read on Tuesday represents 40% of the book. Therefore, if *x* = number of pages in the book, .40*x* = 100, and *x* = 100 ÷ .40 = 250.

10. *B* Since *BCDE* is a square, each of its sides is equal to 4. Triangle *ABE* is a 45-45-90 triangle, whose hypotenuse *EB* = 4. Then by **KEY FACT J5**, $AE = AB = \frac{4}{\sqrt{2}} = 2\sqrt{2}$. So the perimeter is $4 + 4 + 4 + 2\sqrt{2} + 2\sqrt{2} = 12 + 4\sqrt{2}$.

Use TACTIC 8-6: trust the diagram. *AE* and *AB* are clearly shorter than *BE*, which is 4, but more than half as long. A good guess would be about 3. Then the perimeter is approximately 18 (4 + 4 + 4 + 3 + 3). Now, use your calculator on the 5 choices; to the nearest whole number, they are: 20, 18, 23, 22, 26. Obviously, the right one is Choice B.

11. *A* Between 1 and 50 there are 16 multiples of 3: 3, 6, 9, . . ., 45, 48. Then there are 5 numbers that end in 3: 3, 13, 23, 33, 43, but 2 of them, 3 and 33, were already counted; so we have 3 more. Finally, there are the 10 numbers from 30 to 39, but 4 of them, 30, 33, 36, and 39, were already counted as multiples of 3; that's 6 more. The total is 16 + 3 + 6 = 25.

12. *A* Organize the data in a table. Assume Sharon was 5 times as old as Samir after *x* years and 4 times as old after *y* years.

	Sharon	**Samir**
When Samir was born	24	0
x years later	24 + *x*	*x*
y years later	24 + *y*	*y*

24 + *x* = 5*x* ⇒ 4*x* = 24 ⇒ *x* = 6.
24 + *y* = 4*y* ⇒ 3*y* = 24 ⇒ *y* = 8.

Sharon was 5 times as old as Samir 2 years ago. (They are now 32 and 8; 2 years ago they were 30 and 6.)

**To avoid the algebra, you can just use trial and error. In less time than it takes to explain it, you could make a little table:

Sharon	24	27	30	32
Samir	0	3	6	8

So when Samir is 3, Sharon is 9 times as old; when he's 6, she's 5 times as old, and when he's 8, she's 4 times as old.

13. *A* $f(3) = 3^2 - 3 = 9 - 3 = 6$, and
$f(-3) = (-3)^2 - (-3) = 9 + 3 = 12$.
So $f(3) - f(-3) = 6 - 12 = -6$.

14. *B* To make $a + b - c$ as large as possible, let a and b be as large as they can and then subtract the smallest number possible. Since it is given that b is 50 and that $a < b < c$, the greatest possible value of $a + b - c$ is $48 + 50 - 52 = 46$.

15. *D* Draw a Venn diagram.

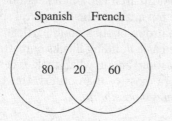

Of the 100 students taking Spanish, 20 take French, and 80 don't; they take *only* Spanish. Similarly, of the 80 students taking French, 20 also take Spanish, and 60 take *only* French. The desired ratio is $80{:}60 = 4{:}3 = \frac{4}{3}$.

16. *E* $(a + b) \clubsuit (a - b) =$
$(a^2 + 2ab + b^2) - (a^2 - 2ab + b^2) = 4ab$.

Use TACTIC 8-2. Let $a = 3$ and $b = 2$. Then
$(3 + 2) \clubsuit (3 - 2) = 5^2 - 1^2 = 25 - 1 = 24$.
Which of the choices is equal to 24 when $a = 3$ and $b = 2$? Only $4ab$.

17. *D* Since the distance between (3, 5) and (−3, 5) is 6, the radius is 6, the diameter is 12, and the circumference is 12π.

18. *D*

Since $6a = 360$ (**KEY FACT I3**), $a = 60$ and m∠$AOB = 2a = 120$. Since $OA = OB$ (they are both radii), △AOB is isosceles:

$$2b + 120 = 180 \Rightarrow 2b = 60 \Rightarrow b = 30.$$
So, $\frac{b}{a} = \frac{30}{60} = \frac{1}{2}$.

19. *B* The easiest observation is that, if adding a fourth number, d, to a set doesn't change the average, then d is equal to the existing average. If you don't realize that, solve for d:

$$\frac{a + b + c + d}{4} = \frac{a + b + c}{3} \Rightarrow$$
$$3a + 3b + 3c + 3d = 4a + 4b + 4c \Rightarrow$$
$$3d = a + b + c \Rightarrow d = \frac{a + b + c}{3}.$$

20. *E* To find the average of two numbers, divide their sum by 2: $\frac{2^{50} + 2^{60}}{2}$. Now use the distributive property and divide each term in the numerator by 2:
$\frac{2^{50}}{2} + \frac{2^{60}}{2} = 2^{49} + 2^{59}$.

Section 3 Critical Reading

25. *E* A marked increase in counterfeiting would motivate banks to order their tellers to take a close look at or *scrutinize* any bills that might be fake.

26. *D Diligence* is steady effort or energy: when you work with diligence you tend to produce perspiration.

27. *D Derision* is making fun of something. Since they did not take his proposal seriously, they treated it with derision. Choice B is a less appropriate answer because *detachment* or indifference is not so nearly opposite to "serious study."

28. *C* By definition, *parasites* sap or drain nutrients from their hosts.

29. *B* A *foretoken* is an advance indication. Earlier phases of one's life may be foretokens of later stages.

30. *A* *Unlike* signals a contrast. Feynman was not reclusive or solitary. Instead, he was *gregarious* or sociable.

31. *D* The physicists have had good reason to believe in the principle because it has *survived* rigorous or strict tests. These tests have *proved* that the principle is accurate. Note how the second clause supports the first, explaining why the physicists have had reason to be confident in the principle.

32. *B* If Latinos have been *assimilated* or absorbed into the American mainstream, then that *debunks* (exposes as false; reveals the foolishness of) the idea that Latinos are cut off from the mainstream.

33. *C* Viewing Boyle's experiments as "pioneering" (line 2) or trailblazing, the author clearly regards them with *admiration*.

34. *E* The scientific conventions from which Boyle radically departed were the *accepted practices* of his day. With his emphasis on experiment and direct observation rather than on logic alone, he helped create the modern empirical approach to science.

35. *C* A rage for Japanese themes is a *craze* or sudden fashion for anything related to Japan.

36. *C* Since Gilbert's fortunes needed to be revived by a hit new show, it's clear that his *career had been in need of a boost*.

37. *C* The opening paragraph discusses changes in the idea of matter, emphasizing the use of musical terminology to describe the concepts of physics. The second paragraph then goes on to develop the theme of the music of matter.

   Choice B is incorrect. Music does not directly influence the interactions of particles; physicists merely use musical terms to describe these interactions.

38. *D* The author mentions these terms as examples of what he means by the strange new language or *idiosyncratic nomenclature* of modern particle physics.

39. *D* In his references to the elegance of the newly discovered subatomic structures and to the dance of Creation, the author conveys his *admiration* and *wonder*.

40. *B* "Matter's heart," where the physicist can observe the dance of Creation, is *the subatomic world*, the world of quarks and charms.

41. *D* The image of the snake swallowing its tail suggests that the astronomers' and physicists' theories are, at bottom, one and the same. In other words, there is an *underlying unity* connecting them.

42. *E* Like a ghost, the top quark evades its pursuers. It is *elusive*.

43. *B* Glashow is eager for the end of the hunt. His words ("last blessed one," "the sooner . . . the better") reflect his *impatience*.

44. *D* The fact that top quarks appeared just after the Big Bang and shortly thereafter vanished suggests that a cameo appearance must be *brief*.

45. *E* The author of Passage 2 cites authorities (Glashow, Tollestrup, Kane) and use similes ("like an arch without a keystone"). She defines the top quark as the theoretical sixth member of the group of subatomic particles that make up the basic building blocks of matter. She poses a question about what makes certain particles more massive than others. However, she never *denies a possibility*.

46. *C* Physicists are familiar with the weight of a silver atom. In citing Tollestrup's statement that the top quark probably weighs as much as a silver atom, the author is illustrating just *how hefty* or massive a top quark is.

47. *B* With its citing of dates, giving of atomic weights, and quotations from prominent scientific figures, Passage 2 is far *more reportorial* than Passage 1. It attempts to answer the journalist's six basic questions: who, what, when, where, why, and how.

48. *C* Passage 2 states that the new theoretical model of the subatomic world "has reduced a once-bewildering zoo of particles to just a few fundamental constituents." Passage 1, for its part, lists all sorts of colorful terms—squark, gauge, technicolor, flavor—whose names fail to appear in Passage 2. This suggests that some of these specific particles whose existence had been previously hypothesized have been *ruled out* by the new theoretical synthesis.

Section 4 Mathematics

For many problems, the explanation provides a reference to one or more **KEY FACTS** from Chapter 9. These are the mathematical facts that you need to solve that problem. If a solution refers to **KEY FACT J2**, for example, the solution depends on the second **KEY FACT** discussed in Section J of Chapter 9.

For some problems, an alternative solution, indicated by two asterisks (**), follows the first solution. When this occurs, usually one of the solutions is the direct mathematical one and the other is based on one of the tactics discussed in Chapters 8 and 9.

21. *B* Since $357 was the cost including 5% tax, *divide* 357 by 1.05: $357 \div 1.05 = 340$.
(If c is the cost, $357 = c + .05c = 1.05c$.)

22. *D* The largest sum is 23, which occurs at 9:59.

23. *C* If 12 of the members are female, then $20 - 12 = 8$ of them are male. Then the ratio of males to females is 8:12, which reduces to 2:3.

**Even if you can't do the above, there are clearly fewer males than females, and so the ratio must be less than 1:1. Eliminate D and E, and guess.

24. *B* There are 9 positive integers less than 10: 1, 2, ..., 9. For which of them is $\frac{8}{x} > x$? Only 1 and 2: $\frac{8}{1} > 1$ and $\frac{8}{2} > 2$. For all the others $\frac{8}{x} < x$. The probability is $\frac{2}{9}$.

25. *B* $ab = (5^x)(5^y) = 5^{x+y}$. **(KEY FACT A16)**.

Use **TACTIC 8-2. Choose easy-to-use numbers for x and y; $x = 1$ and $y = 2$, for example. Then, $a = 5^1 = 5$ and $b = 5^2 = 25$. So $ab = 125$. Check the choices. Only 5^{x+y} works.

26. *E* If $|10 - \sqrt{x}| = 7$, then either

$$
\begin{array}{lll}
10 - \sqrt{x} = 7 & \text{or} & 10 - \sqrt{x} = -7 \\
-\sqrt{x} = -3 & \text{or} & -\sqrt{x} = -17 \\
\sqrt{x} = 3 & \text{or} & \sqrt{x} = 17 \\
x = 9 & \text{or} & x = 289
\end{array}
$$

So the sum of the two solutions is $9 + 289 = 298$.

27. *D* Since x varies inversely with y, there is a constant k such that $xy = k$. So $k = 10 \times 12 = 120$. Then when $x = 6$, $6y = 120 \Rightarrow y = 20$. Since y varies directly with z, there is a constant j such that $\frac{y}{z} = j$. So $j = \frac{10}{20} = \frac{1}{2}$. Then when $x = 6$, $y = 20$ and $\frac{1}{2} = \frac{20}{z} \Rightarrow z = 40$.
So $y + z = 20 + 40 = 60$.

28. *E* Each of the three choices is possible as shown in the figures below. I, II, and III are true.

29. *(330)* A speed of 60 miles per hour is equivalent to a speed of 1 mile per minute.

$$\frac{60 \text{ miles}}{1 \text{ hour}} = \frac{60 \text{ miles}}{60 \text{ minutes}} = \frac{1 \text{ mile}}{1 \text{ minute}} .$$

So 330 miles will take 330 minutes.

**Divide: 330 miles $\div$ 60 miles per hour = 5.5 hours.
Convert: 5.5 hours $\times$ 60 minutes per hour = 330 minutes.

30. *(35)* $12 + (4)(9) = 12 + 36 = 48$, and $48 - 13 = 35$.

31. *(65)* Since the sum of the six angles is 360° **(KEY FACT I3)**,

$$5x + 35 = 360 \Rightarrow 5x = 325 \Rightarrow x = 65.$$

32. *(90)* If x is the cost of the cassettes, then the price of the tape recorder is $100 + x$, and
$$125 = x + (100 + x) = 2x + 100 \Rightarrow$$
$2x = 25 \Rightarrow x = 12.5$, which is 10% of the total cost of 125. So the tape recorder cost 90% of the total.

33. *(8)* Since the area of the triangle is $\frac{1}{2}(8)(16) = 64$, the area of the square is also 64. Each side of the square, therefore, is 8.

34. $\left(\frac{1}{6}\right)$ The box contains 6 slips of paper numbered 5, 15, 25, 35, 45, and 55. Of these 6 numbers, only 5 is a prime; so the probability of picking a prime is $\frac{1}{6}$.

35. $\left(\frac{5}{8}\right)$ Cross-multiply: $3c + 3d = 13c + 13d \Rightarrow 16d = 10c$.
Divide each side by $16c$: $\frac{16d}{16c} = \frac{10c}{16c} \Rightarrow \frac{d}{c} = \frac{10}{16} = \frac{5}{8}$.

36. *(52)* Ignore the x's and the y's. In any "staircase," the perimeter is just twice the sum of the height and the length; so the perimeter is $2(12 + 14) = 2(26) = 52$.

37. (10) In any triangle, the length of the longest side must be less than the sum of the other two sides **(KEY FACT J12)**. Therefore, BC must be less than $\sqrt{10} + \sqrt{50}$. Since $\sqrt{10}$ is slightly more than 3 and $\sqrt{50}$ is slightly more than 7, their sum is slightly more than 10 (but less than 11). So the largest integer BC could be is 10.

38. (2) The area of the shaded region is the area of the circle minus the area of the square. The diagonal of the square is a diameter of the circle and so is equal to 10. By **KEY FACT K8**, the area of the square is given by the formula $A = \frac{d^2}{2}$. So the area of the square is 50 and the area of the circle is 25π. Therefore, the area of the shaded region is $25\pi - 50 = 25(\pi - 2)$.

Section 5 Writing Skills

1. *C* This corrects the two errors in this sentence— the error in case (*me* for *I*) and the error in tense (*had finished* for *finished*).

2. *B* Error in coordination and subordination. This change corrects the wordiness and weakness of the original sentence.

3. *D* Comma splice. The addition of the conjunction *when* corrects the run-on sentence and shows the relationship between the two clauses.

4. *A* Sentence is correct.

5. *C* This corrects the two errors in the sentence— the idiom error *graduate high school* and the comma splice.

6. *D* Error in logical comparison. You cannot compare *players* to *years*; you must compare them to other players, their *counterparts*.

7. *C* Error in subject-verb agreement. As the subject of a sentence *The number* generally is considered a singular noun and therefore requires a singular verb (*is given*).

8. *E* Changing *made* to *make* corrects the error in the sequence of tenses.

9. *C* Error in pronoun case. *From* is a preposition and requires a pronoun in the objective case—*from those* (*people*).

10. *C* This corrects the lack of parallel structure.

11. *C* Shift of pronoun person. Do not shift from *you* to *one*.

12. *C* Comma splice. The addition of the conjunction *though* corrects the run-on sentence.

13. *B* Error in parallelism. This corrects the lack of parallel structure.

14. *B* Choice B expresses the author's meaning directly and concisely. All other choices are either indirect or ungrammatical.

15. *D* Error in idiomatic usage. The proper preposition to use with *subscribe* is *to*, not *for*.

16. *E* Error in subject-verb agreement. The subject of the clause, the relative pronoun *that*, is singular: *only one* museum specializes in modern art. The verb should be singular as well.

17. *C* Adjective-adverb confusion. Change *regular* to *regularly*.

18. *A* Sentence is correct.

19. *A* Sentence is correct.

20. *E* Ambiguous pronoun reference. The original sentence fails to make clear who defeated whom at Waterloo. Choice E eliminates the ambiguity without introducing new errors.

21. *A* Misplaced modifier. *I bought only* is preferable.

22. *E* Sentence is correct.

23. *A* Error in diction. Change *had ought* to *ought*.

24. *B* Lack of parallel structure. Change clause to a phrase in order to parallel the preceding phrase. Change *it has brought about* to *of its*.

25. *C* Error in sentence connector. Both *after* and *then* are sentence connectors, but only one should be used to avoid redundancy. Delete *then*.

26. *B* Error in tense. The past perfect tense of *sink* is *had sunk*.

27. *C* Misuse of adjective instead of adverb. Change *beautiful* to *beautifully*.

28. *D* Misuse of pronoun. *Myself* (reflexive pronoun) must be preceded in the same sentence by either the pronoun *I* or *me*. It should not be used in place of *me* (personal pronoun).

29. *C* Error in tense. Change *now becoming* to *became*.

30. *B* Error in idiom. Change *to serve for* to *to serve as*.

31. *D* Lack of subject-verb agreement. *School* is singular and should be followed by *was* (singular).

32. *B* Sentence fragment. By changing *planning* to *plan*, we correct the error.

33. *B* Lack of subject-verb agreement. In a neither-nor construction the verb agrees with the noun or pronoun that comes immediately before the verb. The verb should agree with *editor* (singular). Change *were* to *was*.

34. *B* Incomplete comparison. Do not omit words necessary to complete comparisons. Compare weather conditions with weather conditions, not with regions. Change "like some parts of Alaska" to "like *those in* some parts of Alaska."

35. *C* Choice A implies that the essay's purpose is to admire the technological achievements of the twentieth century. The essay, however, has another purpose. Choice B is similar to A and also contains an inappropriate colloquialism. Choice C accurately captures the essay's theme—that technological progress is neither all good nor all bad. It is the best answer. Choice D suggests that the essay will discuss the prospects for continued technological progress, but the essay has a different purpose. Choice E names the three areas

discussed in the essay but, contrary to the point of the essay, suggests that we would be better off without technological progress.

36. *C* Choice A unnecessarily repeats *energy* and contains an incomplete comparison. Energy is cheaper than what? Choice B contains an incomplete comparison. Energy is cheaper than what? It also contains an error in parallel construction. Choice C is succinct and accurately expressed. It is the best answer. Choice D contains an error in parallel construction. Choice E also contains a faulty comparison. Cheaper and easier than what?

37. *B* Although related to communications, the information contained in sentence 6 is not germane to the discussion of communication satellites. Therefore, B is the best answer.

38. *B* Choice A does not accurately describe either the paragraph structure or the point of the essay. Choice B precisely describes the structure of each paragraph. It is the best answer. Choices C and D describe neither the paragraph structure nor the point of the essay. Choice E is an inference that might be drawn from the essay, but the writer never says so.

39. *E* Choice A unnecessarily repeats *CAT scan* and contains faulty parallelism. Choice B unnecessarily repeats *CAT scan* and is needlessly wordy. Choice C contains a dangling participle. The phrase that begins *Taking pictures* should modify *doctors,* not *brain.* Choice D has no discernible connection with the previous sentence. Choice E is a succinct and error-free follow-up to the previous sentence. It is the best answer.

Answer Sheet
MODEL TEST E

Each mark should completely fill the appropriate space and should be as dark as all other marks. Make all erasures complete. Traces of an erasure may be read as an answer. See pages viii and 21 for explanations of timing and number of questions.

Section 1 — Critical Reading
25 minutes

1. Ⓐ Ⓑ Ⓒ Ⓓ Ⓔ
2. Ⓐ Ⓑ Ⓒ Ⓓ Ⓔ
3. Ⓐ Ⓑ Ⓒ Ⓓ Ⓔ
4. Ⓐ Ⓑ Ⓒ Ⓓ Ⓔ
5. Ⓐ Ⓑ Ⓒ Ⓓ Ⓔ
6. Ⓐ Ⓑ Ⓒ Ⓓ Ⓔ
7. Ⓐ Ⓑ Ⓒ Ⓓ Ⓔ
8. Ⓐ Ⓑ Ⓒ Ⓓ Ⓔ
9. Ⓐ Ⓑ Ⓒ Ⓓ Ⓔ
10. Ⓐ Ⓑ Ⓒ Ⓓ Ⓔ
11. Ⓐ Ⓑ Ⓒ Ⓓ Ⓔ
12. Ⓐ Ⓑ Ⓒ Ⓓ Ⓔ
13. Ⓐ Ⓑ Ⓒ Ⓓ Ⓔ
14. Ⓐ Ⓑ Ⓒ Ⓓ Ⓔ
15. Ⓐ Ⓑ Ⓒ Ⓓ Ⓔ
16. Ⓐ Ⓑ Ⓒ Ⓓ Ⓔ
17. Ⓐ Ⓑ Ⓒ Ⓓ Ⓔ
18. Ⓐ Ⓑ Ⓒ Ⓓ Ⓔ
19. Ⓐ Ⓑ Ⓒ Ⓓ Ⓔ
20. Ⓐ Ⓑ Ⓒ Ⓓ Ⓔ
21. Ⓐ Ⓑ Ⓒ Ⓓ Ⓔ
22. Ⓐ Ⓑ Ⓒ Ⓓ Ⓔ
23. Ⓐ Ⓑ Ⓒ Ⓓ Ⓔ
24. Ⓐ Ⓑ Ⓒ Ⓓ Ⓔ

Section 2 — Math
25 minutes

1. Ⓐ Ⓑ Ⓒ Ⓓ Ⓔ
2. Ⓐ Ⓑ Ⓒ Ⓓ Ⓔ
3. Ⓐ Ⓑ Ⓒ Ⓓ Ⓔ
4. Ⓐ Ⓑ Ⓒ Ⓓ Ⓔ
5. Ⓐ Ⓑ Ⓒ Ⓓ Ⓔ
6. Ⓐ Ⓑ Ⓒ Ⓓ Ⓔ
7. Ⓐ Ⓑ Ⓒ Ⓓ Ⓔ
8. Ⓐ Ⓑ Ⓒ Ⓓ Ⓔ
9. Ⓐ Ⓑ Ⓒ Ⓓ Ⓔ
10. Ⓐ Ⓑ Ⓒ Ⓓ Ⓔ
11. Ⓐ Ⓑ Ⓒ Ⓓ Ⓔ
12. Ⓐ Ⓑ Ⓒ Ⓓ Ⓔ
13. Ⓐ Ⓑ Ⓒ Ⓓ Ⓔ
14. Ⓐ Ⓑ Ⓒ Ⓓ Ⓔ
15. Ⓐ Ⓑ Ⓒ Ⓓ Ⓔ
16. Ⓐ Ⓑ Ⓒ Ⓓ Ⓔ
17. Ⓐ Ⓑ Ⓒ Ⓓ Ⓔ
18. Ⓐ Ⓑ Ⓒ Ⓓ Ⓔ
19. Ⓐ Ⓑ Ⓒ Ⓓ Ⓔ
20. Ⓐ Ⓑ Ⓒ Ⓓ Ⓔ

Section 3 — Critical Reading
25 minutes

25. Ⓐ Ⓑ Ⓒ Ⓓ Ⓔ
26. Ⓐ Ⓑ Ⓒ Ⓓ Ⓔ
27. Ⓐ Ⓑ Ⓒ Ⓓ Ⓔ
28. Ⓐ Ⓑ Ⓒ Ⓓ Ⓔ
29. Ⓐ Ⓑ Ⓒ Ⓓ Ⓔ
30. Ⓐ Ⓑ Ⓒ Ⓓ Ⓔ
31. Ⓐ Ⓑ Ⓒ Ⓓ Ⓔ
32. Ⓐ Ⓑ Ⓒ Ⓓ Ⓔ
33. Ⓐ Ⓑ Ⓒ Ⓓ Ⓔ
34. Ⓐ Ⓑ Ⓒ Ⓓ Ⓔ
35. Ⓐ Ⓑ Ⓒ Ⓓ Ⓔ
36. Ⓐ Ⓑ Ⓒ Ⓓ Ⓔ
37. Ⓐ Ⓑ Ⓒ Ⓓ Ⓔ
38. Ⓐ Ⓑ Ⓒ Ⓓ Ⓔ
39. Ⓐ Ⓑ Ⓒ Ⓓ Ⓔ
40. Ⓐ Ⓑ Ⓒ Ⓓ Ⓔ
41. Ⓐ Ⓑ Ⓒ Ⓓ Ⓔ
42. Ⓐ Ⓑ Ⓒ Ⓓ Ⓔ
43. Ⓐ Ⓑ Ⓒ Ⓓ Ⓔ
44. Ⓐ Ⓑ Ⓒ Ⓓ Ⓔ
45. Ⓐ Ⓑ Ⓒ Ⓓ Ⓔ
46. Ⓐ Ⓑ Ⓒ Ⓓ Ⓔ
47. Ⓐ Ⓑ Ⓒ Ⓓ Ⓔ
48. Ⓐ Ⓑ Ⓒ Ⓓ Ⓔ

Section 4 — Math
25 minutes

21 Ⓐ Ⓑ Ⓒ Ⓓ Ⓔ
22 Ⓐ Ⓑ Ⓒ Ⓓ Ⓔ
23 Ⓐ Ⓑ Ⓒ Ⓓ Ⓔ
24 Ⓐ Ⓑ Ⓒ Ⓓ Ⓔ
25 Ⓐ Ⓑ Ⓒ Ⓓ Ⓔ
26 Ⓐ Ⓑ Ⓒ Ⓓ Ⓔ
27 Ⓐ Ⓑ Ⓒ Ⓓ Ⓔ
28 Ⓐ Ⓑ Ⓒ Ⓓ Ⓔ

29 30

31 32 33

34 35 36

37 38

Section 5 — Writing
30 minutes

1 Ⓐ Ⓑ Ⓒ Ⓓ Ⓔ
2 Ⓐ Ⓑ Ⓒ Ⓓ Ⓔ
3 Ⓐ Ⓑ Ⓒ Ⓓ Ⓔ
4 Ⓐ Ⓑ Ⓒ Ⓓ Ⓔ
5 Ⓐ Ⓑ Ⓒ Ⓓ Ⓔ
6 Ⓐ Ⓑ Ⓒ Ⓓ Ⓔ
7 Ⓐ Ⓑ Ⓒ Ⓓ Ⓔ
8 Ⓐ Ⓑ Ⓒ Ⓓ Ⓔ
9 Ⓐ Ⓑ Ⓒ Ⓓ Ⓔ
10 Ⓐ Ⓑ Ⓒ Ⓓ Ⓔ
11 Ⓐ Ⓑ Ⓒ Ⓓ Ⓔ
12 Ⓐ Ⓑ Ⓒ Ⓓ Ⓔ
13 Ⓐ Ⓑ Ⓒ Ⓓ Ⓔ
14 Ⓐ Ⓑ Ⓒ Ⓓ Ⓔ
15 Ⓐ Ⓑ Ⓒ Ⓓ Ⓔ
16 Ⓐ Ⓑ Ⓒ Ⓓ Ⓔ
17 Ⓐ Ⓑ Ⓒ Ⓓ Ⓔ
18 Ⓐ Ⓑ Ⓒ Ⓓ Ⓔ
19 Ⓐ Ⓑ Ⓒ Ⓓ Ⓔ
20 Ⓐ Ⓑ Ⓒ Ⓓ Ⓔ
21 Ⓐ Ⓑ Ⓒ Ⓓ Ⓔ
22 Ⓐ Ⓑ Ⓒ Ⓓ Ⓔ
23 Ⓐ Ⓑ Ⓒ Ⓓ Ⓔ
24 Ⓐ Ⓑ Ⓒ Ⓓ Ⓔ
25 Ⓐ Ⓑ Ⓒ Ⓓ Ⓔ
26 Ⓐ Ⓑ Ⓒ Ⓓ Ⓔ
27 Ⓐ Ⓑ Ⓒ Ⓓ Ⓔ
28 Ⓐ Ⓑ Ⓒ Ⓓ Ⓔ
29 Ⓐ Ⓑ Ⓒ Ⓓ Ⓔ
30 Ⓐ Ⓑ Ⓒ Ⓓ Ⓔ
31 Ⓐ Ⓑ Ⓒ Ⓓ Ⓔ
32 Ⓐ Ⓑ Ⓒ Ⓓ Ⓔ
33 Ⓐ Ⓑ Ⓒ Ⓓ Ⓔ
34 Ⓐ Ⓑ Ⓒ Ⓓ Ⓔ
35 Ⓐ Ⓑ Ⓒ Ⓓ Ⓔ
36 Ⓐ Ⓑ Ⓒ Ⓓ Ⓔ
37 Ⓐ Ⓑ Ⓒ Ⓓ Ⓔ
38 Ⓐ Ⓑ Ⓒ Ⓓ Ⓔ
39 Ⓐ Ⓑ Ⓒ Ⓓ Ⓔ

For each question in this section, select the best answer from among the choices given, and fill in the corresponding circle on the answer sheet.

Directions

Each sentence below has one or two blanks, each blank indicating that something has been omitted. Beneath the sentence are five words or sets of words labeled A through E. Choose the word or set of words that, when inserted in the sentence, best fits the meaning of the sentence as a whole.

EXAMPLE:

Medieval kingdoms did not become constitutional republics overnight; on the contrary, the change was -----.

(A) unpopular   (B) unexpected
(C) advantageous   (D) sufficient   (E) gradual

Ⓐ Ⓑ Ⓒ Ⓓ ●

---

1. Though he was reputedly a skilled craftsman, the judging committee found his work ---- and lacking in polish.

    (A) crude   (B) accomplished
    (C) distinguished   (D) adequate
    (E) conceptual

2. Taxonomy—the branch of biology that describes and classifies living creatures—has ---- for approximately 1.4 million creatures.

    (A) need   (B) names   (C) sanctions
    (D) relevance   (E) scope

3. During the height of the mating season, disputes often erupt in the small rookery where space is ---- and male egrets must ---- a patch on which to build their nests.

    (A) inadequate..mull over
    (B) circumscribed..rule out
    (C) unavailable..pick through
    (D) unconditional..seek out
    (E) limited..vie for

4. Because he could not support the cures he obtained with scientific data, he was accused by some skeptics of being ----.

    (A) a zealot   (B) an artist   (C) a mendicant
    (D) a charlatan   (E) a dilettante

5. Critics have been misled by Tennessee Williams's obvious ---- exaggerated theatrical gestures into ---- his plays as mere melodramas, "full of sound and fury, signifying nothing."

    (A) disinclination for..disparaging
    (B) repudiation of..misrepresenting
    (C) indulgence in..acclaiming
    (D) propensity for..denigrating
    (E) indifference to..lauding

Directions

Each of the passages below precedes two questions based on its content. Answer the questions following each passage on the basis of what is <u>stated</u> or <u>implied</u> in that passage.

Questions 6 and 7 are based on the following passage.

There came a day when all the teachers left the Institute and began the hunt for schools. I learn from hearsay (for my mother was mortally
Line afraid of firearms) that the hunting of ducks and
5 bears and men is wonderfully interesting, but I am sure that the man who has never hunted a country school has something to learn of the pleasures of the chase. I see now the white, hot roads lazily rise and fall and wind before me under the burning
10 July sun; I feel the deep weariness of heart and

limb as ten, eight, six miles stretch relentlessly ahead; I feel my heart sink heavily as I hear again and again, "Got a teacher? Yes?"

6. Lines 2–5 suggest that the author had no firsthand knowledge of hunting living creatures because

    (A) he had too much sympathy for the hunter's prey to become a hunter himself
    (B) his studies had left him no time for recreational activities
    (C) small-arms weapons had been forbidden in his home
    (D) hunting was an inappropriate activity for prospective teachers
    (E) his mother had once been wounded by a gunshot

7. To the author, his job-hunting journey through the countryside seemed to be all of the following EXCEPT

(A) tortuous   (B) interminable   (C) tiring
(D) carefree   (E) discouraging

Questions 8 and 9 are based on the following passage.

     True scientists are no strangers to hard work. To prove a hypothesis or confirm a discovery, they conduct test after test, examining their subject
Line from every possible angle that might cast fresh
5 light upon it. They never jump to conclusions, but inch by methodical inch creep up upon them, slowly, unerringly, surely. This is the essence of modern scientific method, the method championed by Boyle and Hooke and other seventeenth
10 century experimental scientists.

8. The author characterizes true scientists as all of the following EXCEPT

(A) systematic   (B) deliberate   (C) accurate
(D) diligent   (E) intuitive

9. As used in line 8, the word "championed" most nearly means

(A) challenged   (B) triumphed   (C) espoused
(D) overpowered   (E) defeated

Directions

Each passage below is followed by questions based on its content. Answer the questions following each passage on the basis of what is <u>stated</u> or <u>implied</u> in that passage and in any introductory material that may be provided.

Questions 10–15 are based on the following passage.

Noted for their destructiveness, tornadoes have long fascinated both scientists and the public at large. The following passage is from a magazine article on tornadoes written in 1984.

     A tornado is the product of a thunderstorm, specifically of the interaction of a strong thunderstorm with winds in the troposphere (the active
Line layer of the atmosphere that extends nine to 17
5 kilometers up from the ground). The process by which a tornado is formed is one in which a small fraction of the tremendous energy of the thunderstorm, whose towering cumulonimbus cloud can be 10 to 20 kilometers across and more than 17
10 kilometers high, is concentrated in an area no more than several hundred meters in diameter. Before going into the process in detail let me first describe the phenomenon itself.
     A tornado is a vortex; air rotates around the
15 tornado's axis about as fast as it moves toward and along the axis. Drawn by greatly reduced atmospheric pressure in the central core, air streams into the base of the vortex from all directions through a shallow layer a few tens of meters deep
20 near the ground. In the base the air turns abruptly to spiral upward around the core and finally merges, at the hidden upper end of the tornado, with the airflow in the parent cloud. The pressure within the core may be as much as 10 percent less
25 than that of the surrounding atmosphere; about the same difference as that between sea level and an altitude of one kilometer. Winds in a tornado are almost always cyclonic, which in the Northern Hemisphere means counterclockwise.
30   The vortex frequently—not always—becomes visible as a funnel cloud hanging part or all of the way to the ground from the generating storm. A funnel cloud forms only if the pressure drop in the core exceeds a critical value that depends on the
35 temperature and the humidity of the inflowing air. As air flows into the area of lower pressure, it expands and cools; if it cools enough, the water vapor in it condenses and forms droplets. The warmer and drier the inflowing air is, the greater
40 the pressure drop must be for condensation to occur and a cloud to form. Sometimes no condensation funnel forms, in which case the tornado reveals itself only through the dust and debris it carries aloft.
45   A funnel can be anywhere from tens of meters to several kilometers long, and where it meets the parent cloud its diameter ranges from a few meters to hundreds of meters. Usually it is cone-

GO ON TO NEXT PAGE ▶

shaped, but short, broad, cylindrical pillars are
50 formed by very strong tornadoes, and long, rope-
like tubes that trail off horizontally are also common. Over a tornado's brief lifetime (never more
than a few hours) the size and shape of the funnel
may change markedly, reflecting changes in the
55 intensity of the winds or in the properties of the
inflowing air. Its color varies from a dirty white to
gray to dark blue gray when it consists mostly of
water droplets, but if the core fills with dust, the
funnel may take on a more exotic hue, such as the
60 red of west Oklahoma clay. Tornadoes can also be
noisy, often roaring like a freight train or a jet engine. This may result from the interaction of the
concentrated high winds with the ground.

10. Tornadoes are characterized by which of the
following?

   I. Brevity of duration
  II. Intense concentration of energy
 III. Uniformity of shape

(A) I only
(B) II only
(C) I and II only
(D) II and III only
(E) I, II, and III

11. Which of the following titles best summarizes the
content of this passage?

(A) The Composition and Nature of Tornadoes
(B) Predicting the Tornado's Path
(C) The Destructive Impact of Tornadoes
(D) Harnessing the Tornado's Energy
(E) Facts and Fictions About Tornadoes

12. As used in line 16, the word "drawn" most nearly
means

(A) elongated (B) sketched (C) drained
(D) inferred (E) pulled

13. The passage suggests that which of the following is
true of a tornado?

(A) Its winds are invariably counterclockwise.
(B) It can last for days at a time.
(C) Its funnel cloud will not form if the air is cool
and dry.
(D) It exceeds its parent cloud in size.
(E) It responds to changes in temperature and
humidity.

14. According to the author, a direct relation may
exist between the color a tornado takes on and

(A) the composition of the terrain it passes over
(B) the intensity of the winds it concentrates
(C) the particular shape of funnel it forms
(D) the direction in which its winds rotate
(E) the degree of noise involved

15. In the final paragraph the author does all of the following EXCEPT

(A) suggest a hypothesis
(B) provide a concrete example
(C) indicate a time span
(D) argue a viewpoint
(E) use a simile

Questions 16–24 are based on the following passage.

*The following passage is an excerpt from "An American
Childhood," the autobiography of the writer Annie Dil-
lard published in 1987.*

    Outside in the neighborhoods, learning our
way around the streets, we played among the enormous stone monuments of the millionaires—both
Line those tireless Pittsburgh founders of the heavy
5 industries from which the nation's wealth derived
(they told us at school) and the industrialists'
couldn't-lose bankers and backers, all of whom
began as canny boys, the stories of whose rises
to riches adults still considered inspirational to
10 children.
    We were unthinkingly familiar with the
moguls' immense rough works as so much weird
scenery on long drives. We saw the long, low-
slung stripes of steel factories by the rivers; we saw
15 pyramidal heaps of yellow sand at glassworks by
the shining railroad tracks; we saw rusty slag
heaps on the outlying hilltops, and coal barges
tied up at the docks. We recognized, on infrequent
trips downtown, the industries' smooth corporate
20 headquarters, each to its own soaring building—
Gulf Oil, Alcoa, U.S. Steel, Koppers Company,
Pittsburgh Plate Glass, Mellon Bank. Our classmates' fathers worked in these buildings, or at
nearby corporate headquarters for Westinghouse
25 Electric, Jones & Laughlin Steel, Allegheny
Ludlum, Westinghouse Air Brake, and H. J. Heinz.
    The nineteenth-century industrialists' institu-
tions—galleries, universities, hospitals, churches,
Carnegie libraries, the Carnegie Museum, Frick
30 Park, Mellon Park—were, many of them, my
stomping grounds. These absolute artifacts of

GO ON TO NEXT PAGE ▶

philanthropy littered the neighborhoods with
marble. Millionaires' encrusted mansions, now obsolete and turned into parks or art centers,
35 weighed on every block. They lent their expansive,
hushed moods to the Point Breeze neighborhoods
where we children lived and where those fabulous
men had lived also, or rather had visited at night
in order to sleep. Everywhere I looked, it was the
40 Valley of the Kings, their dynasty just ended, and
their monuments intact but already out of fashion.

All these immensities wholly dominated the
life of the city. So did their several peculiar social
legacies: their powerful Calvinist mix of piety and
45 acquisitiveness, which characterized the old and
new Scotch-Irish families and the nation they
helped found; the wall-up hush of what was, by my
day, old money—amazing how fast it ages if you
let it alone—and the clang and roar of making
50 that money; the owners' Presbyterian churches,
their anti-Catholicism, anti-Semitism, Republi-
canism, and love of continuous work; their dogmatic practicality; their easy friendliness; their
Pittsburgh-centered innocence, and, paradoxically,
55 their egalitarianism.

For all the insularity of the old guard,
Pittsburgh was always an open and democratic
town. "Best-natured people I ever went among," a
Boston visitor noted two centuries earlier. In colo-
60 nial days, everybody went to balls, regardless of
rank. No one had any truck with aristocratic pretensions—hadn't they hated the British lords in
Ulster? People who cared to rave about their
bloodlines, Mother told us, had stayed in Europe,
65 which deserved them. We were vaguely proud of
living in a city so full of distinctive immigrant
groups, among which we never thought to number ourselves. We had no occasion to visit the
steep hillside neighborhoods—Polish, Hungarian,
70 Rumanian, Italian, Slav—of the turn-of-the-
century immigrants who poured the steel and
stirred the glass and shoveled the coal.

We children played around the moguls' enormous pale stone houses, restful as tombs, set back
75 just so on their shaded grounds. Henry Clay
Frick's daughter, unthinkably old, lived alone in
her proud, sinking mansion; she had lived alone
all her life. No one saw her. Men mowed the wide
lawns and seeded them, and pushed rollers over
80 them, over the new grass seed and musket balls
and arrowheads, over the big trees' roots, bones,
shale, coal.

We knew bits of this story, and we knew none
of it. We knew that before big industry there had
85 been small industry here—H. J. Heinz setting up a
roadside stand to sell horseradish roots from his
garden. There were the makers of cannonballs for
the Civil War. There were the braggart and rowdy
flatboat men and keelboat men, and the honored

90 steamboat builders and pilots. There were local
men getting rich in iron and glass manufacturing
and trade downriver. There was a whole continent-
ful of people passing through, native-born and immigrant men and women who funneled down
95 Pittsburgh, where two rivers converged to make a
third river. It was the gateway to the West; they
piled onto flatboats and launched out into the
Ohio River singing, to head for new country. There
had been a Revolutionary War, and before that the
100 French and Indian War. And before that, and first
of all, had been those first settlers come walking
bright-eyed in, into nowhere from out of nowhere,
the people who, as they said, "broke wilderness,"
the pioneers. This was the history.

16. The opening paragraph suggests the author regards the inspirational tales of the lives of the industrialists with a sense of

(A) optimism   (B) reverence   (C) discomfort
(D) irony   (E) envy

17. The author and her fellow children regarded the
enormous buildings as

(A) unnatural phenomena to observe
(B) a backdrop to their lives
(C) a challenge to the imagination
(D) signs of excessive consumption
(E) intimations of immortality

18. The author calls the moguls fabulous (line 37)
because they were

(A) fictitious   (B) celebrated   (C) wonderful
(D) startling   (E) affluent

19. The author's remark in lines 48 and 49 ("amazing
how fast . . . alone") can best be described as

(A) an extended metaphor
(B) an ironic aside
(C) a faulty hypothesis
(D) a concrete example
(E) a personal reminiscence

20. By "People who cared to rave about their bloodlines
. . . had stayed in Europe, which deserved them"
(lines 63–65), the author's mother means

(A) only Europe was worthy enough to have citizens descended from noble blood
(B) aristocrats tended to be disinclined to travel
(C) Americans were ashamed of their lack of
noble birth, and therefore avoided Europe
(D) it served Europe right if all those snobs who
boasted about their lineage stayed right there
(E) it was madness for an American to try to trace
his bloodlines; only a European could succeed

GO ON TO NEXT PAGE ▶

21. The author uses the description of the Frick lawns in lines 78–82 chiefly to help

(A) indicate the opulence of the moguls' lifestyle
(B) counteract the isolation of Henry Clay Frick's daughter
(C) convey a sense of Pittsburgh's buried past
(D) highlight the distinction between the moguls and their employees
(E) argue in favor of preserving open spaces in cities

22. The opening sentence of the last paragraph (lines 83–84) presents the reader with

(A) a euphemism   (B) an epitaph   (C) a simile
(D) a paradox   (E) a reminiscence

23. In the phrase "broke wilderness" (line 103), "broke" most likely means

(A) shattered   (B) bankrupted   (C) unraveled
(D) interrupted   (E) penetrated

24. The passage's closing paragraph is organized according to

(A) geographical principles
(B) reverse chronological order
(C) cause and effect
(D) personal recollections
(E) extensive quotations

IF YOU FINISH IN LESS THAN 25 MINUTES, YOU MAY CHECK YOUR WORK ON THIS SECTION ONLY. DO NOT TURN TO ANY OTHER SECTION IN THE TEST.

STOP

Multiple-Choice Directions

For each question in this section, determine which of the five choices is correct, and blacken that choice on your answer sheet. You may use any blank space on the page for your work.

NOTES:
- You may use a calculator whenever you believe it will be helpful.
- Use the diagrams provided to help you solve the problems. Unless you see the phrase
    <u>Note:</u> Figure not drawn to scale
  under a diagram, it has been drawn as accurately as possible. Unless it is stated that a figure is three dimensional, you may assume that it lies in a plane.

Reference

$A = \pi r^2$
$C = 2\pi r$

$A = \ell w$

$A = \frac{1}{2}bh$

$V = \ell wh$

$V = \pi r^2 h$

$c^2 = a^2 + b^2$

Special Right Triangles

Number of degrees in a circle: 360
Sum of the measures, in degrees, of the three angles of a triangle: 180

1. If Mr. Beck earns \$16 per hour, how many hours will he have to work in order to earn \$88?
   (A) 5   (B) 5.5   (C) 6.5   (D) 23.5   (E) 1408

2. Sarah saves \$8 every day. If 11 days ago she had \$324, how many dollars will she have 11 days from now?
   (A) 148   (B) 236   (C) 412   (D) 500   (E) 566

3. Which of the following is an expression for "the product of 7 and the average (arithmetic mean) of a and b?"
   (A) $\frac{7a+b}{2}$ (B) $\frac{7a+7b}{2}$ (C) $\frac{7+a+b}{3}$
   (D) $7 + \frac{a+b}{2}$ (E) $\frac{7+7a+7b}{3}$

4. If $\frac{3}{4}$ of a number is 7 more than $\frac{1}{6}$ of the number, what is $\frac{5}{3}$ of the number?
   (A) 12   (B) 15   (C) 18   (D) 20   (E) 24

5. In parallelogram $ABCD$ above, what is the value of x?
   (A) 2   (B) 4   (C) 6   (D) 20   (E) 60

6. An operation, ∗, is defined as follows: for any positive numbers a and b, $a \ast b = \sqrt{a + \sqrt{b}}$. Which of the following is an integer?
   (A) 11∗5   (B) 4∗9   (C) 4∗16
   (D) 7∗4   (E) 9∗9

7. A factory that is open exactly 25 days each month produces 64 engines each day it is open. How many years will it take to produce 96,000 engines?
   (A) fewer than 5
   (B) 5
   (C) more than 5 but less than 10
   (D) 10
   (E) more than 10

8. In the figure above, what is the value of x?
   (A) 20   (B) 70   (C) 60   (D) 110
   (E) It cannot be determined from the information given.

GO ON TO NEXT PAGE ▶

9. If $x - y = 5$, and $x^2 - y^2 = 75$, what is the value of y?

(A) −10 (B) −5 (C) 5 (D) 10

(E) It cannot be determined from the information given.

10. Julie inherited 40% of her father's estate. After paying a tax equal to 30% of her inheritance, what percent of her father's estate did she own?

(A) 10% (B) 12% (C) 18%
(D) 28% (E) 30%

11. For any positive integer $n > 1$: $n!$ represents the product of the first n positive integers. For example, $3! = 1 \times 2 \times 3 = 6$. Which of the following is (are) equal to $(3!)(4!)$?

I. 7!
II. 12!
III. 4! + 5!

(A) I only (B) II only (C) III only

(D) I and III (E) I, II, and III

12. In the figure above, $BC = BE$. If R represents the perimeter of rectangle $ABCD$ and T represents the perimeter of triangle CBE, what is the value of $R - T$?

(A) 3 (B) 12 (C) 30 (D) $18 - 6\sqrt{2}$

(E) It cannot be determined from the information given.

13. There are 12 men on a basketball team, and in a game 5 of them play at any one time. If the game is one hour long and if each man plays exactly the same amount of time, how many minutes does each man play?

(A) 10 (B) 12 (C) 24 (D) 25 (E) 30

14. Which of the following expresses the circumference of a circle in terms of A, its area?

(A) $2A$ (B) $2A\sqrt{\pi}$ (C) $2\pi\sqrt{A}$
(D) $2\sqrt{\pi A}$ (E) $2\pi A$

15. What is the value of k if the line that passes through $(3, -3)$ and $(k, 5)$ has a slope of $\frac{2}{3}$?

(A) 0 (B) 6 (C) $8\frac{1}{3}$ (D) 15

(E) It cannot be determined from the information given.

16. If x is an odd number, what is the difference between the smallest odd number greater than $5x + 4$ and the largest odd number less than $3x + 7$?

(A) $2x$ (B) $2x - 3$ (C) $8x + 7$ (D) $8x + 8$
(E) It cannot be determined from the information given.

17. The measures of the angles of a triangle are in the ratio of $1:2:3$. What is the ratio of the length of the smallest side to the length of the longest side?

(A) $1:\sqrt{2}$ (B) $1:\sqrt{3}$ (C) $1:2$ (D) $1:3$
(E) It cannot be determined from the information given.

18. A car going 50 miles per hour set out on a 200-mile trip at 12:00 P.M. Exactly 20 minutes later, a second car left from the same place and followed the same route. How fast, in miles per hour, was the second car going if it caught up with the first car at 2:00 P.M.?

(A) 55 (B) 60 (C) 65 (D) 70 (E) 75

19. If a varies inversely with b and $b = 5$ when $a = 3$, what is the value of b when $a = 10$?

(A) $\frac{1}{2}$ (B) $\frac{3}{2}$ (C) 2 (D) $\frac{50}{3}$ (E) 30

20. If in 1965 Yann was four times as old as Isabel and in 1970 he was three times as old as she was, how old was Yann when Isabel was born?

(A) 25 (B) 30 (C) 35
(D) 40 (E) 45

IF YOU FINISH IN LESS THAN 25 MINUTES, YOU MAY CHECK YOUR WORK ON THIS SECTION ONLY. DO NOT TURN TO ANY OTHER SECTION IN THE TEST.

STOP

For each question in this section, select the best answer from among the choices given, and fill in the corresponding circle on the answer sheet.

| Directions |

Each sentence below has one or two blanks, each blank indicating that something has been omitted. Beneath the sentence are five words or sets of words labeled A through E. Choose the word or set of words that, when inserted in the sentence, best fits the meaning of the sentence as a whole.

EXAMPLE:

Medieval kingdoms did not become constitutional republics overnight; on the contrary, the change was ----.

(A) unpopular   (B) unexpected
(C) advantageous   (D) sufficient   (E) gradual

Ⓐ Ⓑ Ⓒ Ⓓ ●

---

25. The dean tried to retain control of the situation on campus, but her attempt was ---- by the board of trustees.

(A) endorsed   (B) frustrated   (C) disclosed
(D) witnessed   (E) justified

26. The extended heat wave left many people ----, lacking their usual energy and interest in life.

(A) isolated   (B) fervid   (C) intemperate
(D) listless   (E) nomadic

27. Disliking sudden changes in plans when she traveled abroad, Ethel refused to make any alterations to her ----.

(A) manuscript   (B) itinerary   (C) residence
(D) detour   (E) wardrobe

28. Though Mark had reservations about many of the fraternity's policies, he diplomatically kept them to himself and allowed his fellow members to interpret his ---- as a sign of ---- on his part.

(A) complaints..reluctance
(B) silence..acquiescence
(C) arguments..pugnacity
(D) comments..inarticulateness
(E) selfishness..wisdom

29. Just as avarice is the mark of the miser, indulgence is the mark of the ----.

(A) pauper   (B) philanthropist   (C) coward
(D) martinet   (E) glutton

30. Given the many areas of conflict still awaiting ----, the outcome of the peace talks remains ----.

(A) justification..pragmatic
(B) settlement..permanent
(C) resolution..problematic
(D) compromise..plausible
(E) arbitration..pacific

31. While some people take satisfaction from a religious or mystical explanation of human intelligence, for Bonner, the more ---- and ---- the explanation, the better she likes it.

(A) rational..materialistic
(B) logical..spiritual
(C) pragmatic..dubious
(D) theoretical..rudimentary
(E) occult..viable

32. Unfortunately, the book comes down so firmly on the nature side of the nature-nurture debate that it tends to ---- many of the subtleties of the argument, leaving the reader with a highly ---- view of the issue.

(A) carry through..lucid
(B) skim over..simplistic
(C) go beyond..dogmatic
(D) sidestep..cerebral
(E) highlight..arbitrary

GO ON TO NEXT PAGE ▶

Questions 33 and 34 are based on the following passage.

To students today, continental drift is a commonplace. They cheerfully talk about supercontinents that break apart or about shifts in the
Line earth's crust as if everyone has always known that
5 this solid earth beneath our feet is seated on large, rigid plates that float on a soft, partly molten layer of the earth's mantle. Not so. It was not quite a century ago that Alfred Wegener first proposed the theory that the components making up the super-
10 continent Pangaea had slowly moved thousands of miles apart over lengthy periods of geologic time.

33. The term "a commonplace" (line 1) most nearly means

   (A) a customary location
   (B) a traditional rank
   (C) an accepted concept
   (D) a vulgar saying
   (E) an inexpensive property

34. The passage's final sentence (lines 7–11) primarily serves to emphasize the

   (A) definitive nature of an experiment
   (B) recent origin of a theory
   (C) sudden end to a controversy
   (D) limited possibilities for research
   (E) stubborn character of a scientist

Questions 35 and 36 are based on the following passage.

The morning after the battle of Fredericksburg, the ground before the stone wall was covered with wounded, dead, and dying Northerners. Hours
Line passed by as soldiers from both sides listened to
5 the cries for water and pleas for help. Finally, Richard Kirkland, a young Confederate sergeant, could bear it no more. Receiving permission from his general to help the wounded, he ventured over the wall. Under Northern fire, he reached the
10 nearest sufferer and gave him water. As soon as they understood his intent, the enemy ceased fire, and for an hour and a half Kirkland tended the wounded unharmed.

35. The primary function of the passage is to

   (A) establish that Kirkland sought his commander's approval before taking action
   (B) indicate the young sergeant's eagerness to be seen as a hero
   (C) dramatize the degree of suffering experienced during the Civil War
   (D) depict an instance of heroism under fire
   (E) analyze the military importance of the battle of Fredericksburg

36. The word "bear" (line 7) most nearly means

   (A) carry   (B) endure   (C) produce
   (D) conduct   (E) warrant

Questions 37–48 are based on the following passages.

In the following passages, the novelist Virginia Woolf and a contemporary literary critic separately discuss the relationship between women and fiction.

Passage 1

The most superficial inquiry into women's writing instantly raises a host of questions. Why, we ask at once, was there no continuous writing
Line done by women before the eighteenth century?
5 Why did they then write almost habitually as men, and in the course of that writing produce, one after another, some of the classics of English fiction? And why did their art then, and why to some extent does their art still, take the form of fiction?
10   A little thought will show us that we are asking questions to which we shall get, as answer, only further fiction. The answer lies at present locked in old diaries, stuffed away in old drawers, half obliterated in the memories of the aged. It is
15 to be found in the lives of the obscure—in those almost unlit corridors of history where the figures

of generations of women are so dimly, so fitfully perceived. For very little is known about women. The history of England is the history of the male
20 line, not of the female. Of our fathers we know always some fact, some distinction. They were soldiers or they were sailors; they filled that office or they made that law. But of our mothers, our grandmothers, our great-grandmothers, what
25 remains? Nothing but a tradition. One was beautiful; one was red-haired; one was kissed by a Queen. We know nothing of them except their names and the dates of their marriages and the number of children they bore.
30   Thus, if we wish to know why at any particular time women did this or that, why they wrote nothing, why on the other hand they wrote masterpieces, it is extremely difficult to tell. Anyone who should seek among those old papers, who should
35 turn history wrong side out and so construct a faithful picture of the daily life of the ordinary woman in Shakespeare's time, in Milton's time, in Johnson's time, would not only write a book of astonishing interest, but would furnish the critic
40 with a weapon which he now lacks. The extraordinary woman depends on the ordinary woman. It is only when we know what were the conditions of the average woman's life—the number of her children, whether she had money of her own, if she
45 had a room to herself, whether she had help in bringing up her family, if she had servants, whether part of the housework was her task—it is only when we can measure the way of life and the experience of life made possible to the ordinary
50 woman that we can account for the success or failure of the extraordinary woman as writer.

Passage 2

As the works of dozens of women writers have been rescued from what E. P. Thompson calls "the enormous condescension of posterity," and consid-
55 ered in relation to each other, the lost continent of the female tradition has risen like Atlantis from the sea of English literature. It is now becoming clear that, contrary to Mill's theory, women have had a literature of their own all along. The woman
60 novelist, according to Vineta Colby, was "really neither single nor anomalous," but she was also

more than a "register and spokesman for her age." She was part of a tradition that had its origins before her age, and has carried on through our own.

65   Many literary historians have begun to reinterpret and revise the study of women writers. Ellen Moers sees women's literature as an international movement, "apart from, but hardly subordinate to the mainstream: an undercurrent, rapid
70 and powerful. This 'movement' began in the late eighteenth century, was multinational, and produced some of the greatest literary works of two centuries, as well as most of the lucrative potboilers." Other critics are beginning to agree that
75 when we look at women writers collectively we can see an imaginative continuum, the recurrence of certain patterns, themes, problems, and images from generation to generation.

    This book is an effort to describe the female
80 literary tradition in the English novel from the generation of the Brontes to the present day, and to show how the development of this tradition is similar to the development of any literary subculture. It is important to see the female literary tra-
85 dition in these broad terms, in relation to the wider evolution of women's self-awareness and to the ways any minority group finds its direction of self-expression relative to a dominant society, because we cannot show a pattern of deliberate
90 progress and accumulation. It is true, as Ellen Moers writes, that "women studied with a special closeness the works written by their own sex"; in terms of influences, borrowings, and affinities, the tradition is strongly marked. But it is also full of
95 holes and hiatuses, because of what Germaine Greer calls the "phenomenon of the transience of female literary fame"; "almost uninterruptedly since the Interregnum, a small group of women have enjoyed dazzling literary prestige during
100 their own lifetimes, only to vanish without trace from the records of posterity." Thus each generation of women writers has found itself, in a sense, without a history, forced to rediscover the past anew, forging again and again the consciousness
105 of their sex. Given this perpetual disruption, and also the self-hatred that has alienated women writers from a sense of collective identity, it does not seem possible to speak of a movement.

GO ON TO NEXT PAGE ▶

37. The questions in lines 2–9 chiefly serve to

(A) suggest how the author defines women's writing
(B) outline the direction of the author's research
(C) underscore how little is known about the subject
(D) divert the reader's attention from the central issue
(E) express the author's reluctance to appear dogmatic

38. The word "filled" in line 22 means

(A) inflated   (B) blocked   (C) furnished
(D) held   (E) pervaded

39. Woolf's point in lines 23–29 about how little is known about women is made primarily through

(A) case histories   (B) examples   (C) statistics
(D) metaphors   (E) repeated quotations

40. The individual women mentioned in lines 25–29 are presented primarily as instances of people who

(A) encountered royalty
(B) gave birth to children
(C) observed family traditions
(D) sought to become writers
(E) lived largely unrecorded lives

41. Which of the following would be the most appropriate title for Passage 2?

(A) A Unique Phenomenon: Nineteenth- and Twentieth-Century Feminine Literary Movements
(B) A Literature of Their Own: The Female Literary Tradition
(C) The Role of the Ordinary Woman in Modern Literature
(D) The Emergence of the Contemporary Women's Novel
(E) Fame Versus Fortune: The Dilemma of the Woman Writer

42. In the first paragraph of Passage 2, the author makes use of all the following techniques EXCEPT

(A) extended metaphor
(B) enumeration and classification
(C) classical allusion
(D) direct quotation
(E) comparison and contrast

43. The metaphor of the newly arisen "lost continent" (lines 55–57) is used primarily to convey

(A) the vast degree of effort involved in reinterpreting women's literature
(B) the number of works of literature that have been created by women
(C) the way forgotten literary works have resurfaced after many years
(D) the extent to which books written by women appeared unrelated
(E) the overwhelming size of the problem confronting the author

44. In the second paragraph of Passage 2, the author's attitude toward the literary critics cited can best be described as one of

(A) irony   (B) ambivalence   (C) disparagement
(D) receptiveness   (E) awe

45. The word "closeness" in line 92 means

(A) proximity in space
(B) narrow margin of victory
(C) disposition to secrecy
(D) cautiousness about expenditures
(E) minute attention to details

46. Which of the following words could best be substituted for "forging" (line 104) without substantially changing the author's meaning?

(A) counterfeiting   (B) creating   (C) exploring
(D) diverting   (E) straining

47. It can be inferred from Passage 2 that the author considers Moers's work to be

(A) fallacious and misleading
(B) scholarly and definitive
(C) admirable but inaccurate in certain of its conclusions
(D) popular but irrelevant to mainstream female literary criticism
(E) idiosyncratic but of importance historically

48. Compared with the author of Passage 2, the author of Passage 1 is

(A) more academic and less colloquial
(B) less effusive and more detached
(C) less didactic and more dogmatic
(D) less scholarly and more descriptive
(E) more radical and less entertaining

IF YOU FINISH IN LESS THAN 25 MINUTES, YOU MAY CHECK YOUR WORK ON THIS SECTION ONLY. DO NOT TURN TO ANY OTHER SECTION IN THE TEST.

STOP

Multiple-Choice Directions

For questions 21–38, determine which of the five choices is correct. You may use any blank space on the page for your work.

NOTES:
- You may use a calculator whenever you believe it will be helpful.
- Use the diagrams provided to help you solve the problems. Unless you see the phrase
  <u>Note:</u> Figure not drawn to scale
  under a diagram, it has been drawn as accurately as possible. Unless it is stated that a figure is three dimensional, you may assume that it lies in a plane.

Reference

$A = \pi r^2$
$C = 2\pi r$

$A = \frac{1}{2}bh$

$V = \ell wh$

$V = \pi r^2 h$

$c^2 = a^2 + b^2$

Special Right Triangles

Number of degrees in a circle: 360
Sum of the measures, in degrees, of the three angles of a triangle: 180

---

21. What is the value of $2x^2 - 4x - 3$ when $x = -5$?

(A) 27   (B) 67   (C) 73   (D) 87   (E) 117

Note: Figure not drawn to scale

22. In the figure above, what is the value of y?

(A) 20   (B) 40   (C) 50   (D) 80
(E) It cannot be determined from the information given.

23. If $\frac{1}{b} + \frac{1}{b} + \frac{1}{b} + \frac{1}{b} = 12$, then $b =$

(A) $\frac{1}{12}$ (B) $\frac{1}{4}$ (C) $\frac{1}{3}$ (D) 3   (E) 4

24. Lucy had to unpack c cartons. After unpacking d of them, what percent of the cartons were not yet unpacked?

(A) $100(c - d)\%$ (B) $\frac{c-d}{100}\%$ (C) $\frac{c-d}{100c}\%$
(D) $\frac{100(c-d)}{d}\%$ (E) $\frac{100(c-d)}{c}\%$

25. In the figure above, $\triangle ABC$ is a right triangle. What is the value of $a + b + c + d$?

(A) 180   (B) 240   (C) 270   (D) 300   (E) 360

26. If $\frac{1}{x} + \frac{1}{3} + \frac{1}{4} = 1$, then $x =$

(A) $\frac{5}{12}$ (B) $\frac{7}{5}$ (C) 2   (D) $\frac{12}{5}$ (E) 5

27. In the figure at the right, $AB = AC$ and the sides of triangle ABC are tangent to circle O, at points D, E, and F. If m$\angle A = 30°$, what is m$\angle DOE$?

(A) 75   (B) 90
(C) 105   (D) 120   <u>Note:</u> Figure not drawn to scale
(E) 150

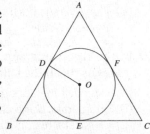

28. $A = \{1, 2\}$ $B = \{2, 3\}$ $C = \{3, 4\}$

In how many ways is it possible to choose one number from each set so that the three numbers could be the lengths of the three sides of a triangle?

(A) None   (B) 1   (C) 4   (D) 6   (E) 8

GO ON TO NEXT PAGE ▶

Student-Produced Response Directions

In questions 29–38, first solve the problem, and then enter your answer on the grid provided on the answer sheet. The instructions for entering your answers follow.

- First, write your answer in the boxes at the top of the grid.
- Second, grid your answer in the columns below the boxes.
- Use the fraction bar in the first row or the decimal point in the second row to enter fractions and decimals.

Answer: $\frac{8}{15}$ Answer: 1.75   Answer: 100

Write your answer in the boxes

Grid-in your answer

Either position is acceptable

- Grid only one space in each column.
- Entering the answer in the boxes is recommended as an aid in gridding but is not required.
- The machine scoring your exam can read only what you grid, so you **must grid-in your answers correctly to get credit.**
- If a question has more than one correct answer, grid-in only one of them.
- The grid does not have a minus sign; so no answer can be negative.
- A mixed number *must* be converted to an improper fraction or a decimal before it is gridded. Enter $1\frac{1}{4}$ as $\frac{5}{4}$ or 1.25; the machine will interpret 11/4 as $\frac{11}{4}$ and mark it wrong.

- **All decimals must be entered as accurately as possible.** Here are three acceptable ways of gridding

$$\frac{3}{11} = 0.272727\ldots$$

- Note that rounding to .273 is acceptable because you are using the full grid, but you would receive **no credit** for .3 or .27, because they are less accurate.

---

29. If $a * b = (a + b)^2 - (a - b)^2$, what is the value of $7 * 11$?

30. If $3x - 11 = 11 - 3x$, what is the value of x?

31. Jim, Kim, Ben, and Len divided $1000 as follows: Kim got twice as much as Jim, Ben got 3 times as much as Jim, and Len got $100. How much, in dollars, did Jim get?

32. If $x, y,$ and z are different positive integers less than 10, what is the greatest possible value of $\frac{x^2 - y}{z}$?

33. $A (-3, 2)$ and $B (5, -1)$ are the endpoints of a diameter of a circle whose center is at (x, y). What is the value of $x + y$?

34. $\frac{3}{7} = 0.428571428571\ldots$, with the digits 4, 2, 8, 5, 7, 1 repeating indefinitely in that order. What digit is in the 200th place to the right of the decimal point?

35. In the addition problem below, each letter represents a different digit.

$$\begin{array}{r} AB \\ +CD \\ \hline AAA \end{array}$$

What is the value of $A + B + C + D$?

36. The figure below consists of 4 circles with the same center. The radii of the 4 circles are 1, 2, 3, and 4.

If a and b are the areas in the figure above of the shaded region and white region, respectively, what is the value of $\frac{a}{b}$?

37. In a jar containing only red and blue marbles, 40% of the marbles are red. If the average weight of a red marble is 40 grams and the average weight of a blue marble is 60 grams, what is the average weight, in grams, of all the marbles in the jar?

38. How many sides does a polygon have if the measure of each interior angle is twice the measure of each exterior angle?

IF YOU FINISH IN LESS THAN 25 MINUTES, YOU MAY CHECK YOUR WORK ON THIS SECTION ONLY. DO NOT TURN TO ANY OTHER SECTION IN THE TEST.

STOP

456 ▶ CHAPTER 11 / Model Test E

Improving Sentence Directions

Some or all parts of the following sentences are underlined. The first answer choice, (A), simply repeats the underlined part of the sentence. The other four choices present four alternative ways to phrase the underlined part. Select the answer that produces the most effective sentence, one that is clear and exact, and blacken the appropriate space on your answer sheet. In selecting your choice, be sure that it is standard written English and that it expresses the meaning of the original sentence.

EXAMPLE:

The first biography of author Eudora Welty came out in 1998, and she was eighty-nine years old at the time.

(A) and she was eighty-nine years old at the time
(B) at the time when she was eighty-nine
(C) upon becoming an eighty-nine year old
(D) when she was eighty-nine
(E) at the age of eighty-nine years old

SAMPLE ANSWER:

Ⓐ Ⓑ Ⓒ ● Ⓔ

---

1. The police officer refused to permit us to enter the apartment, saying that he had orders to stop him going into the building.

   (A) stop him going   (B) prevent him going
   (C) stop his going   (D) stop us going
   (E) stop our going

2. After conducting the orchestra for six concerts, Beethoven's *Ninth Symphony* was scheduled.

   (A) After conducting
   (B) After his conducting
   (C) While conducting
   (D) Although he conducted
   (E) After he had conducted

3. Jackie Robinson became the first black player in major league baseball, he paved the way for black athletes to be accepted on the field.

   (A) Jackie Robinson became the first black player in major league baseball, he
   (B) Jackie Robinson, in becoming the first black player in major league baseball, he
   (C) Jackie Robinson became the first black player in major league baseball; he
   (D) Jackie Robinson, the first black player in major league baseball; he
   (E) Jackie Robinson had become the first black player in major league baseball and he

4. Sitting in the Coliseum, the music couldn't hardly be heard because of the cheering and yelling of the spectators.

   (A) the music couldn't hardly be heard because of
   (B) the music couldn't hardly be heard due to
   (C) the music could hardly be heard due to
   (D) we could hardly be heard because of
   (E) we could hardly hear the music because of

5. The contents of the examination came as a shock to the student, everything on it having no resemblance to what she had studied.

   (A) as a shock to the student, everything on it having
   (B) to the student as a shock, being that everything on it had
   (C) to the student as a shock, with everything on it having
   (D) as a shock to the student, everything on it has
   (E) as a shock to the student; everything on it had

6. Across the nation, curricular changes sweeping the universities as schools reassess the knowledge that educated people should have.

   (A) curricular changes sweeping the universities as schools
   (B) curricular changes are sweeping the universities as schools
   (C) changes are sweeping the curricular since schools
   (D) curricular changes sweeping the universities causing schools to
   (E) curricular changes sweep the universities, but schools

7. If you have enjoyed these kind of programs, write to your local public television station and ask for more.

   (A) these kind of programs
   (B) those kind of programs
   (C) these kinds of programs
   (D) these kind of a program
   (E) these kind of a program

8. In her critique of the newly opened restaurant, the reviewer discussed the elaborate menu, the impressive wine list, and how the waiters functioned.

    (A) list, and how the waiters functioned
    (B) list and how the waiters functioned
    (C) list, and the excellent service
    (D) list, and even the excellent service
    (E) list, and how the waiters usually function

9. Contemporary poets are not abandoning rhyme, but some avoiding it.

    (A) but some avoiding it
    (B) but it is avoided by some of them
    (C) but it is being avoided
    (D) but some are avoiding it
    (E) but it has been being avoided by some

10. Your complaint is no different from the last customer who expected a refund.

    (A) Your complaint is no different from the last customer
    (B) Your complaint is no different from that of the last customer
    (C) Your complaint is similar to the last customer
    (D) Your complaint is no different then that of the last customer
    (E) Your complaint is the same as the last customer

11. According to the review board, many laboratory tests were ordered by the staff of the hospital that had no medical justification.

    (A) many laboratory tests were ordered by the staff of the hospital that
    (B) many laboratory tests were ordered by the staff of the hospital who
    (C) the staff of the hospital ordered many laboratory tests that
    (D) the staff of the hospital, who ordered many laboratory tests that
    (E) the ordering of many laboratory tests by the staff of the hospital which

12. Confident about the outcome, President Clinton, along with his staff, are traveling to the conference.

    (A) Confident about the outcome, President Clinton, along with his staff, are traveling
    (B) Confident about the outcome, President Clinton's party are traveling
    (C) Confident about the outcome, President Clinton, along with his staff, is traveling
    (D) With confidence about the outcome, President Clinton, along with his staff, are traveling
    (E) President Clinton, along with his staff, is traveling confidently about the outcome

13. Helen Keller was blind and deaf from infancy and she learned to communicate using both sign language and speech.

    (A) Helen Keller was blind and deaf from infancy and she
    (B) Although blind and deaf from infancy, Helen Keller
    (C) Although being blind and deaf from the time she was an infant, Helen Keller
    (D) Being blind and deaf from infancy, Helen Keller
    (E) Helen Keller, being blind and deaf from infancy, she

14. Standing alone beside her husband's grave, grief overwhelmed the widow and she wept inconsolably.

    (A) grief overwhelmed the widow and she wept inconsolably
    (B) grief overwhelmed the widow, who wept inconsolably
    (C) grief overwhelmed the widow that wept inconsolably
    (D) the widow, overwhelmed by grief, wept inconsolably
    (E) the widow was overwhelmed by grief, she wept inconsolably

15. Survivors of a major catastrophe are likely to exhibit aberrations of behavior because of the trauma they have experienced.

    (A) likely to exhibit aberrations of behavior because of the trauma they have experienced
    (B) likely to exhibit aberrations of behavior because of them having experienced a trauma
    (C) liable to exhibit aberrations from behavior due to the trauma they experienced
    (D) liable to exhibit aberrations of behavior, the reason being that they have experienced a trauma
    (E) likely for exhibiting aberrations of behavior due to the trauma they had experienced

16. Because the warranty on the defective toaster has expired, the store manager cannot do nothing about the problem.

    (A) has expired, the store manager cannot do nothing about the problem
    (B) has expired, the store manager cannot do anything against the problem
    (C) has expired, the store manager can do nothing about the problem
    (D) had expired, the store manager cannot do nothing about the problem
    (E) has expired, the store manager cannot do nothing for the problem

GO ON TO NEXT PAGE ▶

17. In 1940, during the Battle of Britain, German bombs severely have damaged Holy Trinity Church in London, but the two bronze angels on the altar rail survived the bombardment unscathed.

(A) In 1940, during the Battle of Britain, German bombs severely have damaged Holy Trinity Church

(B) In 1940, during the Battle of Britain, German bombs severe have damaged Holy Trinity Church

(C) In 1940, during the Battle of Britain, German bombs severely damaging Holy Trinity Church

(D) During the Battle of Britain in 1940, German bombs severely have damaged Holy Trinity Church

(E) In 1940, during the Battle of Britain, German bombs severely damaged Holy Trinity Church

18. Not surprising, given the popularity of the spectacles in which they appeared, gladiators captured the public imagination.

(A) Not surprising, given the popularity of the spectacles in which they appeared

(B) Not surprising, because they were given the popularity of the spectacles in which they appeared

(C) Not surprisingly, given the popularity of the spectacles in which they appeared

(D) Not surprisingly, giving the popularity of the spectacles in which they appeared

(E) Not surprising, given the popularity of the spectacles where they appeared

19. Whether we admit it or not, biomedical research is currently supported on the backs of postdoctoral fellows, who make the industry possible by providing cheap labor.

(A) research is currently supported on the backs of postdoctoral fellows, who make the industry possible by providing

(B) research are currently supported on the backs of postdoctoral fellows, who make possible the industry for providing

(C) research is currently supported in back of postdoctoral fellows, who have made the industry possible by providing

(D) research is currently supported on the backs of postdoctoral fellows, with them making the industry possible by the provision of

(E) research is currently being supported on the backs of postdoctoral fellows, being that they make the industry possible by providing

20. Because the insect order Odonata, to which dragonflies belong, is not well studied, authoritative manuals on dragonflies that could be read and understood by the untrained observer were scarce until recently.

(A) belong, is not well studied, authoritative manuals on dragonflies that could be read and understood by the untrained observer were scarce until recently

(B) belong, are not well studied, authoritative manuals on dragonflies, which could be read and understood by the untrained observer were scarce until recently

(C) belong, is not well studied, until recently there were not scarcely any authoritative manuals on dragonflies that the untrained observer could read and understand

(D) belonged, was not well studied, authoritarian manuals on dragonflies that observers could have read and understood without being trained until recently were scarce

(E) belong, is not well studied, authoritative manuals on the dragonfly that could be read and understood by the untrained observer was scarcely until recently

21. Notice the <u>immediate</u> <u>affect</u> <u>this</u> drug has on the
          A   B   C

    <u>behavior of</u> the rats in the cage. <u>No error</u>
      D   E

22. <u>In spite of</u> official denials, news sources reported
     A

    <u>that</u> the bombs that hit Tripoli in 1986 were <u>really</u>
    B   C

    <u>intended to kill</u> Muammar al-Qaddafi. <u>No error</u>
        D   E

23. <u>Neither</u> the teacher nor her pupils <u>were</u> <u>enthused</u>
    A   B   C

    <u>about going on</u> the field trip. <u>No error</u>
      D   E

24. <u>While</u> the Egyptian president Anwar El-Sadat was
    A

    reviewing a military parade in 1981, <u>a band of</u>
                                B

    commandos <u>had shot</u> him and others
             C

    in the <u>vicinity.</u> <u>No error</u>
         D   E

25. Please do not be <u>aggravated</u> by his <u>bad manners</u>
              A   B

    <u>since</u> he is <u>merely</u> trying to attract attention.
     C   D

    <u>No error</u>
     E

26. Neither the opera singers <u>or</u> the general public
                        A

    <u>had seen</u> <u>as much glitter</u> in years as they did
      B   C

    during *Turandot*, the <u>finale of</u> the opera season.
                      D

    <u>No error</u>
     E

27. His story about having been abducted by

    <u>strange beings</u> in a spaceship was <u>so</u> <u>incredulous</u>
       A   B   C

    <u>that</u> no one believed him. <u>No error</u>
     D   E

28. The hot air balloon had burst as they

    <u>were preparing</u> <u>for</u> launch, and the platform
       A   B

    <u>had broke</u> <u>as a result.</u> <u>No error</u>
      C   D   E

29. Ann Landers, <u>whose</u> name is a household word
              A

    to millions <u>of</u> readers, <u>are</u> <u>well-known</u> for family
           B   C   D

    advice. <u>No error</u>
         E

30. Child custody in surrogate mother cases is just

one of the many controversial issues that are
‾‾‾‾‾‾‾‾‾‾‾‾‾‾‾‾   ‾‾‾‾ ‾‾‾
        A   B   C

currently being decided upon in the courts.
                   ‾‾‾‾‾‾‾‾‾‾‾
                        D

No error
‾‾‾‾‾‾‾‾
   E

31. If you continue to drive so recklessly, you
       ‾‾   ‾‾‾‾‾‾‾‾‾‾‾‾
        A   B

are likely to have a serious accident in the very
‾‾‾‾‾‾‾‾   ‾‾‾‾
   C   D

near future. No error
            ‾‾‾‾‾‾‾‾
               E

32. The general, along with the members of
                  ‾‾‾‾‾‾‾‾‾
                      A

his general staff, seem to favor
   ‾‾‾‾‾‾‾‾‾‾‾‾‾ ‾‾‾‾
         B   C

immediate retaliation . No error
‾‾‾‾‾‾‾‾‾‾‾‾‾‾‾‾‾‾‾‾   ‾‾‾‾‾‾‾‾
         D   E

33. The rescue workers resented him criticizing their
                               ‾‾‾ ‾‾‾‾‾‾‾‾‾‾
                                A   B

efforts because he had ignored their requests for
                     ‾‾‾‾‾‾‾‾‾‾
                          C

assistance up to that time. No error
          ‾‾‾‾‾‾‾‾‾‾‾‾‾‾   ‾‾‾‾‾‾‾‾
                 D   E

34. Casey Jones, who was killed in the line of duty,
                  ‾‾‾   ‾‾‾‾
                   A   B

became a hero to fellow railroad workers and
‾‾‾‾‾‾
   C

was to be immortalized by a ballad. No error
‾‾‾‾‾‾‾‾‾‾‾‾‾‾‾‾‾‾‾‾   ‾‾‾‾‾‾‾‾
         D   E

Improving Paragraph Directions

The passage below is the unedited draft of a student's essay. Some of the essay needs to be rewritten to make the meaning clearer and more precise. Read the essay carefully.

The essay is followed by five questions about changes that might improve all or part of its organization, development, sentence structure, use of language, appropriateness to the audience, or use of standard written English. Choose the answer that most clearly and effectively expresses the student's intended meaning. Indicate your choice by filling in the corresponding space on the answer sheet.

[1] Members of our community have objected to the inclusion of various pieces of art in the local art exhibit. [2] They say that these pieces offend community values. [3] The exhibit in its entirety should be presented.

[4] The reason for this is that people have varied tastes, and those who like this form of art have a right to see the complete exhibit. [5] An exhibit like this one gives the community a rare chance to see the latest modern art nearby, and many people have looked forward to it with great anticipation. [6] It would be an unfortunate blow to those people for it not to be shown.

[7] The exhibit may contain pieces of art that tend to be slightly erotic, but what is being shown that most people haven't already seen? [8] So, give it an R or an X rating and don't let small children in. [9] But how *many small children voluntarily go to see an art exhibit? [10] The exhibit includes examples of a new style of modern art. [11] The paintings show crowds of nude people. [12] The exhibit is at the library's new art gallery. [13] For centuries artists have been painting and sculpting people in the nude. [14] Why are these works of art different? [15] Perhaps they are more graphic in some respects, but we live in a entirely different society than from the past. [16] It is strange indeed for people in this day and age to be offended by the sight of the human anatomy.*

[17] If people don't agree with these pieces, they simply should just not go. [18] But they should not be allowed to prevent others from seeing it.

GO ON TO NEXT PAGE ▶

35. Taking into account the sentences that precede and follow sentence 3, which of the following is the best revision of sentence 3?

(A) On the other hand, the whole exhibit should be presented.

(B) The exhibit, however, should be presented in its entirety.

(C) The exhibit should be entirely presented regardless of what the critics say.

(D) But another point of view is that the exhibit should be presented in its entirety.

(E) Still other members also say the whole exhibit should be presented in its entirety.

36. In the context of paragraph 3, which of the following is the best revision of sentences 10, 11, and 12?

(A) Paintings on exhibit at the library showing crowds of nude people and done in a new style of modern art.

(B) The exhibit, on display at the library, includes paintings of crowds of nude people done in a new style of modern art.

(C) The exhibit includes paintings in a new style of modern art, which shows crowds of nude people at the library.

(D) The library is the site of the exhibit which shows a new style of modern art, with paintings showing crowds of nude people.

(E) The new style of modern art includes examples of paintings showing crowds of nude people on exhibit in the library.

37. To improve the clarity and coherence of the whole essay, where is the best place to relocate the ideas contained in sentences 10, 11, and 12?

(A) before sentence 1

(B) between sentences 1 and 2

(C) bbetween sentences 8 and 9

(D) between sentences 15 and 16

(E) after sentence 18

38. Which of the following is the best revision of the underlined segment of sentence 15 below?

Perhaps they are more graphic in some respects, but we live in a entirely different society than from the past.

(A) an entirely different society than of the past

(B) a completely different society than the past

(C) a society completely different than from past societies

(D) a society which is entirely different from the way societies have been in the past

(E) an entirely different society from that of the past

39. Which of the following revisions of sentence 17 provides the best transition between paragraphs 3 and 4?

(A) If anyone doesn't approve of these pieces, they simply should not go to the exhibit.

(B) Anyone disagreeing with the pieces in the exhibit shouldn't go to it.

(C) Anyone who disapproves of nudity in art simply shouldn't go to the exhibit.

(D) If anyone dislikes the sight of nudes in art, this show isn't for them.

(E) Don't go if you disapprove of nudity in art.

IF YOU FINISH IN LESS THAN 30 MINUTES, YOU MAY CHECK YOUR WORK ON THIS SECTION ONLY. DO NOT TURN TO ANY OTHER SECTION IN THE TEST.

STOP

462 ► CHAPTER 11 / Model Test E

Answer Key

Section 1 Critical Reading

1. *A*
2. *B*
3. *E*
4. *D*
5. *D*
6. *C*
7. *D*
8. *E*
9. *C*
10. *C*
11. *A*
12. *E*
13. *E*
14. *A*
15. *D*
16. *D*
17. *B*
18. *B*
19. *B*
20. *D*
21. *C*
22. *D*
23. *E*
24. *B*

Section 2 Mathematics

1. *B*
2. *D*
3. *B*
4. *D*
5. *C*
6. *D*
7. *B*
8. *E*
9. *C*
10. *D*
11. *C*
12. *B*
13. *D*
14. *D*
15. *D*
16. *A*
17. *C*
18. *B*
19. *B*
20. *B*

Section 3 Critical Reading

25. *B*
26. *D*
27. *B*
28. *B*
29. *E*
30. *C*
31. *A*
32. *D*
33. *C*
34. *B*
35. *D*
36. *B*
37. *C*
38. *D*
39. *B*
40. *E*
41. *B*
42. *B*
43. *C*
44. *D*
45. *E*
46. *B*
47. *C*
48. *D*

Section 4 Mathematics

21. *B*
22. *C*
23. *C*
24. *E*
25. *C*
26. *D*
27. *C*
28. *C*

29. 3 0 8

30. 2 2 / 6

or *11/3*
3.66

31. 1 5 0

32. 7 9

33. 3 / 2

or *1.5*

34. 8

35. 2 1

36. 1

37. 5 2

38. 6

Section 5 Writing Skills

1. *E*	9. *D*	17. *E*	25. *A*	33. *A*
2. *E*	10. *B*	18. *C*	26. *A*	34. *D*
3. *C*	11. *C*	19. *A*	27. *C*	35. *D*
4. *E*	12. *C*	20. *A*	28. *C*	36. *B*
5. *E*	13. *B*	21. *B*	29. *C*	37. *A*
6. *B*	14. *D*	22. *E*	30. *D*	38. *E*
7. *C*	15. *A*	23. *C*	31. *E*	39. *C*
8. *C*	16. *C*	24. *C*	32. *C*	

Scoring Chart—Model Test E

Critical Reading Sections	Mathematics Sections

Critical Reading Sections

Section 1: 24 Questions (1–24)

Number correct _____ (A)

Number omitted _____ (B)

Number incorrect _____ (C)

$\frac{1}{4}$ (C) _____ (D)

(A) − (D) _____ Raw Score I

Section 3: 24 Questions (25–48)

Number correct _____ (A)

Number omitted _____ (B)

Number incorrect _____ (C)

$\frac{1}{4}$ (C) _____ (D)

(A) − (D) _____ Raw Score II

Total Critical Reading Raw Score

Raw Scores I + II _____

Mathematics Sections

Section 2: 20 Questions (1–20)

Number correct _____ (A)

Number omitted _____ (B)

Number incorrect _____ (C)

$\frac{1}{4}$ (C) _____ (D)

(A) − (D) _____ Raw Score I

Section 4: First 8 Questions (21–28)

Number correct _____ (A)

Number omitted _____ (B)

Number incorrect _____ (C)

$\frac{1}{4}$ (C) _____ (D)

(A) − (D) _____ Raw Score II

Section 4: Next 10 Questions (29–38)

Number correct _____ Raw Score III

Total Mathematical Raw Score

Raw Scores I + II + III _____

NOTE: In each section (A) + (B) + (C) should equal the number of questions in that section.

Writing Skills Section

Section 5: 39 Questions (1–39)

Number correct _____ (A)

Number omitted _____ (B)

Number incorrect _____ (C)

$\frac{1}{4}$ (C) _____ (D)

Writing Skills Raw Score

(A) − (D) _____

Evaluation Chart

Study your score. Your raw score is an indication of your probable achievement on the PSAT/NMSQT. As a guide to the amount of work you need or want to do with this book, study the following.

	Raw Score		Self-rating
Critical Reading	*Mathematics*	*Writing*	
42–48	35–38	33–39	Superior
37–46	30–34	28–32	Very good
32–36	25–29	23–27	Good
26–35	21–24	17–22	Above average
20–25	17–20	12–16	Average
12–19	10–16	7–11	Below average
less than 12	less than 10	less than 7	Inadequate

Answer Explanations

Section 1 Critical Reading

1. *A* *Though* calls for a contrast. From someone with the reputation of a skilled craftsman, we expect fine work; instead, the work here is not polished but *crude.*

2. *B* According to the definition set off by dashes, the science of taxonomy is to classify or categorize living creatures, sorting them into groups with individual *names.*

3. *E* Why would fights break out in a small rookery? They would do so because there is not enough room to accommodate all the birds that need to build a nest. Because space is *limited*, each bird therefore must *vie for* (struggle or fight) its own patch of land.

4. *D* A person who could not support his claims for alleged cures with hard scientific data might as a consequence be called a *charlatan* (a faker or quack) by skeptics or disbelievers in his powers.

5. *D* It is Williams's *propensity* or liking for theatricality that causes critics to *denigrate* or belittle his plays as mere melodrama. Note how the use of *mere* and the sense of the Shakespearean quotation convey the idea that Williams's plays have been sullied or belittled.

6. *C* To "learn from hearsay" is to learn not from one's own personal experience but from the comments of others. Why did the author have to learn about the pleasures of hunting from hearsay and not from his own experience? The comment in parentheses suggests the reason. His mother was terrified of guns. Therefore, we can assume that he had no chance to learn about hunting because *small-arms weapons had been forbidden in his home.*

7. *D* Use the process of elimination to answer this question.

   Is the author's journey through the countryside a *tortuous* (twisting) one? Yes; the road he travels winds before him. Therefore, you can eliminate Choice A.

   Does his journey seem *interminable* to him? Yes; the "miles stretch relentlessly ahead," never letting up. Therefore, you can eliminate Choice B.

   Is his journey *tiring* to him? Yes; he feels "deep weariness of heart and limb." Therefore, you can eliminate Choice C.

   Does his hunt for a school feel *discouraging* to him? Yes; he feels "his heart sink heavily" as

he hears there is no job opening. Therefore, you can eliminate Choice E.

   Is his journey a *carefree* one? No; throughout his journey he has the ongoing anxiety about when and where he will find a job. The correct answer is Choice D.

8. *E* You can arrive at the correct answer by the process of elimination.

   True scientists do not jump to conclusions but methodically work their way toward them. Therefore, they are *systematic* and *deliberate.* You can eliminate Choices A and B.

   True scientists work toward their conclusions unerringly, that is, without making errors. Therefore, they are *accurate.* You can eliminate Choice C.

   True scientists are not strangers to hard work. Instead, they are *diligent* or hard-working. You can eliminate Choice D.

   Only Choice E is left. It is the correct answer. The author never characterizes true scientists as *intuitive* or instinctive in their approach to science.

9. *C* To champion a method or cause is to *espouse* (adopt or embrace) it.

10. *C* You can arrive at the correct answer by the process of elimination.

    Statement I is true. The passage states that the tornado's lifetime is never more than a few hours. Therefore, you can eliminate Choices B and D.

    Statement II is true. The first paragraph indicates that a fraction of the thunderstorm's tremendous energy "is concentrated into an area no more than several hundred meters in diameter." A later portion of the passage refers to the tornado's "concentrated high winds." Therefore, you can eliminate Choice A.

    Statement III is untrue. The passage indicates that tornadoes may vary markedly in size and shape. Therefore, you can eliminate Choice E.

    Only Choice C is left. It is the correct answer.

11. *A* The passage describes tornadoes as the product of thunderstorms and goes on to discuss various aspects of their nature (energy concentration, pressure drops, intense winds, funnel clouds, etc.).

12. *E* The reduced atmospheric pressure in the core region *pulls* or draws air to the base of the tornado.

13. *E* Paragraph three states that the "warmer and drier the inflowing air is, the greater the pressure drop must be for condensation to occur and a cloud to form." This suggests that temperature

and humidity affect the tornado and that it *responds to changes in temperature and humidity*.

Choice A is incorrect. The passage indicates that in the Northern Hemisphere a tornado's winds may be counterclockwise; it never suggests that a tornado's winds are *invariably* counterclockwise. Choice B is incorrect. Paragraph four states that a tornado's lifetime is never more than a few hours. Choice C is incorrect. The *warmer* and *drier* the air is, the greater the pressure drop has to be for the funnel cloud to form. This does not suggest that the cloud will not form if the air is cool and dry. Choice D is incorrect. A thunderstorm's cumulonimbus cloud can be more than 17 kilometers high. A tornado's funnel cloud is described as smaller than this.

14. *A* The author states that "if the core fills with dust, the funnel may take on a more exotic hue, such as the red of west Oklahoma clay." The hue or color of the funnel thus depends on what the soil in that region is made of.

15. *D* The author suggests a hypothesis (tornado noise "may result from the interaction of the concentrated high winds with the ground"). He provides a concrete example ("the red of west Oklahoma clay"). He indicates a time span ("never more than a few hours"). He uses similes ("roaring like a freight train"). He does not, however, argue a particular point of view.

16. *D* The author calls the industrialists and their "couldn't-lose" bankers and backers "canny boys" (shrewd fellows) and says the adults considered stories about these wheelers and dealers "inspirational to children." Clearly, she finds neither the stories nor the men inspirational: she looks on both with *irony*.

17. *B* In stating that she and the other children were "unthinkingly familiar" with the moguls' enormous buildings "as so much weird scenery on long drives," the author reveals that the children viewed these buildings as an accepted *backdrop to their lives*, something they saw in passing without giving it much thought.

18. *B* The moguls were fabulous men in being *celebrated* or famed for their wealth and philanthropy.

19. *B* The author's remark here can best be described as *an ironic aside*, a parenthetic comment that digresses from the theme or topic under discussion.

20. *D* The mother's tone in this comment is highly sardonic. Clearly, she is not someone who cares to rave or talk boastfully about her good birth and noble connections. Instead, she dismisses such people as snobs and dismisses Europe as a fit home for snobs.

21. *C* Beneath the lawns lie musket balls and arrowheads and bones, all relics of *Pittsburgh's buried past*. Note that in the paragraph that immediately follows this description the author cites details from Pittsburgh's history.

22. *D* To say that one knows something and does not know it is to state a *paradox*, an apparently self-contradictory declaration.

23. *E* In breaking the wilderness, the first white settlers *penetrated* the forest, bursting through the undergrowth into territory known only to the Native Americans.

24. *B* Summing up Pittsburgh's history, the author starts with modern big industry and works her way back in time till she concludes citing the pioneers who were the first white settlers in the region. Thus, she organizes the paragraph in *reverse chronological order*.

Section 2 Mathematics

For many problems, the explanation provides a reference to one or more **KEY FACTS** from Chapter 9. These are the mathematical facts that you need to solve that problem. If a solution refers to **KEY FACT J2**, for example, the solution depends on the second **KEY FACT** discussed in Section J of Chapter 9.

For some problems, an alternative solution, indicated by two asterisks (**), follows the first solution. When this occurs, usually one of the solutions is the direct mathematical one and the other is based on one of the tactics discussed in Chapters 8 and 9.

1. *B* $88 \div \$16$ per hour $= 5.5$ hours. If you prefer, set up a ratio and cross-multiply:

$$\frac{16\,\text{dollars}}{1\,\text{hour}} = \frac{88\,\text{dollars}}{x\,\text{hours}}.$$

2. *D* In 11 days Sarah saves $88. If 11 days ago she had $324, she now has $324 + \$88 = \$412$, and 11 days from now will have $412 + \$88 = \$500$.

3. *B* The average of a and b is $\frac{a+b}{2}$, and the product of that with 7 is $7\left(\frac{a+b}{2}\right) = \frac{7a+7b}{2}$.

**It is easier and quicker to do this directly. So substitute for a and b, only if you get stuck or confused. If $a = 2$ and $b = 4$, their average is 3, and the product of 7 and their average is 21. Only Choice B is equal to 21 when $a = 2$ and $b = 4$.

4. *D* Let the number be x, and write the equation
$$\frac{3}{4}x = 7 + \frac{1}{6}x.$$

Multiply both sides by 12: $\qquad 9x = 84 + 2x$

Subtract $2x$ from each side and divide by 7:
$$7x = 84 \Rightarrow x = 12$$

Be careful: 12 is *not* the answer. You were asked for $\frac{5}{3}$ of the number. $\frac{5}{3}(12) = 20$.

5. *C* By **KEY FACT K2**, the sum of the measures of two adjacent angles of a parallelogram is 180°. Therefore,
$$180 = 10x + 25x - 30 = 35x - 30,$$
which implies that $35x = 210$ and $x = 6$.

6. *D* There's nothing to do except check the choices, although it is often faster to start with E and work toward A.
   E: $9*9 = \sqrt{9} + \sqrt{9} = \sqrt{9} + 3 = \sqrt{12}$, which is not an integer.
   D: $7*4 = \sqrt{7} + \sqrt{4} = \sqrt{7} + 2 = \sqrt{9} = 3$, an integer. The answer is D. Once you find the answer, do not waste any time trying the other choices—they won't work.

7. *B* The factory produces 64 engines per day × 25 days per month × 12 months per year = 19,200 engines per year, and $96,000 \div 19,200 = 5$.

8. *E* Label each angle in the diagram.

Since vertical angles are equal, $a = 20$, and so $x + y = 160$. We can see that $b = 70$, but there are no other vertical angles, and it is impossible to determine x or y from the information given.

9. *C* Since $x^2 - y^2 = (x - y)(x + y)$, then
$$75 = x^2 - y^2 = (x - y)(x + y) = 5(x + y).$$
Therefore, $x + y = 15$. Adding the equations
$x + y = 15$ and $x - y = 5$, we get
$$2x = 20 \Rightarrow x = 10 \Rightarrow y = 5.$$
**Use TACTIC 8-1: backsolve. Choice C works.

10. *D* If Julie had to pay 30% of the value of her inheritance in taxes, she still owned 70% of her inheritance: 70% of 40% is 28% ($0.70 \times 0.40 = 0.28$).

****Assume the estate was worth \$100. Julie received 40% or \$40. Her tax was 30% of \$40, or \$12. She still had \$28, or 28% of the \$100 estate.

11. *C* The given expression $(3!)(4!) = 6(24) = 144$. Now, evaluate the three choices.

   I: $7! = 5040$, which is much too big (false).
   II: $12!$ is even bigger (false).
   III: $4! + 5! = 24 + 120 = 144$ (true).

   III only is true.

12. *B* It is given that $BE = BC$; also $BC = AD$, since they are opposite sides of a rectangle. Label each of them w, as shown in the diagram.

Then $R = 18 + 2w$ and $T = 6 + 2w$.
So $R - T = 18 - 6 = 12$.

13. *D* Since the game takes one hour, or 60 minutes, and there are always 5 men playing, there are a total of $5 \times 60 = 300$ minutes of playing time. If that is evenly divided among the 12 players, each one plays $300 \div 12 = 25$ minutes.

****Try the choices. If 5 men played the first 10 or 12 minutes and 5 other men played the next 10 or 12 minutes, there wouldn't be 5 men available to play the rest of the game. So 10 and 12 are much too small. Eliminate A and B. If 5 men played for 30 minutes and 5 other men played the next 30 minutes, the game would be over, and 2 men wouldn't have played at all. Eliminate E since 30 is too large. The answer must be 24 or 25.

14. *D* Since $A = \pi r^2$, $r^2 = \frac{A}{\pi}$ and $r = \sqrt{\frac{A}{\pi}} = \frac{\sqrt{A}}{\sqrt{\pi}}$.

The circumference =
$$2\pi r = 2\pi \frac{\sqrt{A}}{\sqrt{\pi}} = 2\sqrt{\pi}\sqrt{A} = 2\sqrt{\pi A}.$$

15. *D* By **KEY FACT N4**, the slope $= \frac{y_2 - y_1}{x_2 - x_1}$.

Then $\frac{2}{3} = \frac{5 - (-3)}{k - 3} = \frac{8}{k - 3}$. Cross-multiply:
$$24 = 2k - 6 \Rightarrow 2k = 30 \Rightarrow k = 15.$$

****If you don't remember the formula, make a quick sketch:

Since the slope is positive, k is greater than 3, and since the slope is less than 1, the line is going up too slowly for k to be 6 or 8. Guess 15.

16. *A* If x is odd, so are $5x$ and $5x + 4$. To get the smallest odd number greater than $5x + 4$, add 2: $5x + 6$. On the other hand, $3x + 7$ is even, and the largest odd number smaller than it is 1 less than $3x + 7$, namely $3x + 6$. The required difference is $(5x + 6) - (3x + 6) = 2x$.

Use **TACTIC 8-2 and let $x = 3$. The smallest odd number greater than 19 is 21 and the largest odd number less than 16 is 15: $21 - 15 = 6$. Which answer equals 6 when $x = 3$? Only A.

17. *C* It's worth remembering that when the three angles of a triangle are in the ratio of 1:2:3, the triangle is a 30-60-90 right triangle. (If you don't know that, solve the equation $x + 2x + 3x = 180$.) In a 30-60-90 right triangle the sides are a, $a\sqrt{3}$, and $2a$; so the desired ratio is a:$2a$ = 1:2.

18. *B* At 2:00, the first car had been going 50 miles per hour for 2 hours and so had gone 100 miles. The second car covered the same 100 miles in 1 hour and 40 minutes, or $1\frac{2}{3} = \frac{5}{3}$ hours. Therefore, its rate was $100 \div \frac{5}{3} = 100 \times \frac{3}{5} = 60$ miles per hour.

19. *B* Since a varies inversely with b, there is a constant k such that $ab = k$. So $k = (3)(5) = 15$. Therefore, $10b = 15 \Rightarrow b = \frac{15}{10} = \frac{3}{2}$.

20. *B* Make a table to determine Yann's and Isabel's ages.

Let x represent Isabel's age in 1965, and fill in the table as shown.

	1965	1970
Yann	$4x$	$4x + 5$
Isabel	x	$x + 5$

In 1970, Yann was 3 times as old as Isabel, so
$$4x + 5 = 3(x + 5) = 3x + 15 \Rightarrow x = 10.$$

So in 1965, Isabel was 10 and Yann was 40. Since he is 30 years older than she is, he was 30 when she was born.

Section 3 Critical Reading

25. *B* The use of *but* indicates that the dean's attempt to keep control failed. It did so because it was *frustrated* by the board of trustees. None of the other possible actions of the board of trustees would necessarily have caused the dean's attempt to fail.

26. *D* To lack one's usual energy and interest in life is by definition to be *listless* (languid, spiritless). Note how the phrase following the comma serves to define the missing word.

27. *B* A plan for a journey is by definition an *itinerary*.

28. *B* Mark keeps his reservations or reluctance to go along with his fraternity's policies to himself: he says nothing. By saying nothing, he lets his fraternity brothers assume his *silence* is a sign of *acquiescence* or agreement.

29. *E* A *glutton* is by definition a person who eats or drinks excessively, someone who indulges his or her appetites without restraint.

30. *C* The phrase "given the . . ." signals cause and effect. *Because* many areas of conflict are still in need of *resolution* or settlement, we do not know what the outcome of the peace talks will be. In other words, the end result of the talks remains *problematic* (unclear and unsettled; perplexing).

31. *A* *While* signals a contrast. Bonner does not like religious or mystical (spiritual; not apparent to the senses) explanations of intelligence. Instead she likes *rational* (logical) and *materialistic* ones that define reality as explainable only in terms of physical matter.

32. *D* It would be unfortunate for a book to come down very firmly on one side of a debate if, in the process, it *skimmed over* (examined superficially or missed entirely) tricky spots in the argument and gave the reader a *simplistic*, oversimplified picture of the subject.

33. *C* If students talk about continental drift as if everyone has always known about the concept, then it is an *accepted concept* or commonplace.

34. *B* The author is denying that everyone has always known about the theory of continental drift. ("Not so.") He states that it was "not quite" a century ago that the theory was proposed. Thus, he is emphasizing the relatively *recent origin* of the theory.

35. *D* The passage serves simply to portray or *depict an instance of heroism under fire*.

36. *B* Kirkland could no longer bear or *endure* the cries of the dying.

37. *C* Repetition often is used rhetorically for emphasis. By asking question after question about why women's writing has taken the shape it has, the author *underscores* or emphasizes *how little is known about* a significant subject.

38. *D* To fill an office is to work in or *hold* that job.

39. *B* To make her point, Woolf gives *examples* of three women about whom little is known.

40. *E* "One was beautiful; one was red-haired; one was kissed by a Queen." What did these women have in common? They all led *largely unrecorded lives*: their grandchildren know only stray fragments about the history of these women's lives.

41. *B* Both the author's use of the phrase "a literature of their own" in the opening paragraph and her ongoing exploration of what she means by the female literary tradition in the English novel support this choice.

Choice A is incorrect. It is not the uniqueness of the phenomenon but the traditional nature of the phenomenon that interests the author. Choice C is incorrect. The passage deals specifically with women's *literary* tradition. Choice D is incorrect. The passage is concerned with the roots of female writing, not with its present-day manifestations. Choice E is incorrect. The author presents no such choice.

42. *B* The writer neither lists (*enumerates*) nor sorts (*classifies*) anything in the opening paragraph.

Choice A is incorrect. The writer likens the female tradition to a lost continent and develops the metaphor by describing the continent "rising . . . from the sea of English literature." Choice C is incorrect. The author refers or *alludes* to the classical legend of Atlantis. Choice D is incorrect. The author quotes Colby and Thompson. Choice E is incorrect. The author contrasts the revised view of women's literature with Mill's view.

43. *C* The legend of Atlantis tells of a continent that sank beneath the sea, only to rise again. The author uses the metaphor of the newly arisen lost continent to give the reader a sense of how an enormous body of *literary works written by women* has once more come to public attention, *resurfacing after many years*.

44. *D* The author opens the paragraph by stating that many literary critics have begun reinterpreting the study of women's literature. She then goes on to cite individual comments that support her assertion. Clearly, she is *receptive* or open to the ideas of these writers, for they and she share a common sense of the need to reinterpret their common field.

Choices A and B are incorrect. The author cites the literary critics straightforwardly, presenting their statements as evidence supporting her thesis. Choice C is incorrect. The author does not *disparage* or belittle these critics. By quoting them respectfully she implicitly acknowledges their competence. Choice E is incorrect. The author quotes the critics as acknowledged experts in the field. However, she is quite ready to disagree with their conclusions (as she disagrees with Moers's view of women's literature as an international movement). Clearly, she does not look on these critics with *awe*.

45. *E* To study something with a special closeness is to pay *minute attention to details*.

46. *B* If women writers have no history, they have to rediscover the past. In the process, they *create* or forge their consciousness of what their sex has achieved. Here *forge* is used with its meaning of *fashion* or *make*, as blacksmiths forge metal by hammering it into shape. It is in this sense that James Joyce used *forge* in *A Portrait of the Artist as a Young Man*, whose hero goes forth to "forge in the smithy of (his) soul the uncreated conscience of (his) race."

47. *C* The author both cites Moers's work in support of her own assertions and argues against the validity of Moers's conclusion that women's literature is an international movement. Thus, while she finds Moers's work basically *admirable* and worthy of respect, she considers it *inaccurate* in some of the conclusions it draws.

Choice A is incorrect. The author would not cite Moers as she does in the second paragraph if she believed Moers to be wholly *misleading*. Choice B is incorrect. Since the author disagrees with at least one of Moers's conclusions, she obviously does not find Moers's work the *definitive* or final word. Choices D and E are incorrect. Neither is supported by the author's mentions of Moers.

48. *D* Woolf does not document her argument with extensive quotations from literary critics. Instead, she uses telling examples ("One was beautiful; one was red-haired; one was kissed by a Queen") to show how little we know about our grandmothers' actual lives. She is *less scholarly and more descriptive* in her approach to the subject.

Section 4 Mathematics

For many problems, the explanation provides a reference to one or more **KEY FACTS** from Chapter 9. These are the mathematical facts that you need to solve that problem. If a solution refers to **KEY FACT J2**, for example, the solution depends on the second **KEY FACT** discussed in Section J of Chapter 9.

For some problems, an alternative solution, indicated by two asterisks (**), follows the first solution. When this occurs, usually one of the solutions is the direct mathematical one and the other is based on one of the tactics discussed in Chapters 8 and 9.

21. *B* If $x = -5$, then
$$2x^2 - 4x - 3 = 2(-5)^2 - 4(-5) - 3 =$$
$$2(25) + 20 - 3 = 67.$$

22. *C* Since $x + 100 = 180$, $x = 80$; also,
$$y + y + x = 180 \Rightarrow$$
$$2y + 80 = 180 \Rightarrow$$
$$2y = 100 \Rightarrow y = 50.$$

23. *C* $12 = \frac{1}{b} + \frac{1}{b} + \frac{1}{b} + \frac{1}{b} = \frac{4}{b} \Rightarrow 12b = 4 \Rightarrow$
$b = \frac{4}{12} = \frac{1}{3}.$

24. *E* If *d* of the cartons were unpacked, $c - d$ were still full, so the fraction of the cartons that were not yet unpacked was $\frac{c-d}{c}$. To get the percent, multiply the fractional part by 100%: $\frac{100(c - d)}{c}$%.

Use **TACTIC 8-2. If Lucy had 10 cartons to unpack, then after unpacking 2 of them, 80% (8 of the 10) still had to be unpacked. Only $\frac{100(c-d)}{c}$% equals 80% when $c = 10$ and $d = 2$.

25. *C* Since the sum of the measures of the two acute angles of a right triangle is $90°$, $a + d = 90$. Also, $b + c = 180$. Therefore, $a + b + c + d = 90 + 180 = 270.$

26. *D* First add $\frac{1}{3} + \frac{1}{4}$ and then subtract that sum from both sides:
$$\frac{1}{x} + \left(\frac{1}{3} + \frac{1}{4}\right) = \frac{1}{x} + \frac{7}{12} = 1 \Rightarrow \frac{1}{x} = \frac{5}{12}.$$

Finally, take the reciprocal of each side (or cross-multiply): $x = \frac{12}{5}.$

27. *C* Since $AB = AC$, by **KEY FACT J2**, m$\angle B$ = m$\angle C$. So, by **KEY FACT J1**,
$$30 + \text{m} \angle B + \text{m} \angle C = 180 \Rightarrow$$
$$\text{m} \angle B + \text{m} \angle C = 150 \Rightarrow \text{m} \angle B = 75.$$

Also, since $\overline{AB}$ and $\overline{BC}$ are tangents, then, by **KEY FACT L10**, the radii $\overline{OD}$ and $\overline{OE}$ are perpendicular to $\overline{AB}$ and $\overline{BC}$, respectively, and hence form 90° angles. Finally, by **KEY FACT K1**, the sum of the four angles in quadrilateral *ODBE* is 360:

$$75 + 90 + 90 + \text{m} \angle DOE = 360 \Rightarrow$$
$$255 + \text{m} \angle DOE = 360 \Rightarrow \text{m} \angle DOE = 105.$$

28. *C* According to the triangle inequality (**KEY FACT J9**), the sum of the lengths of two sides of a triangle must be greater than the length of the third. Now use **TACTIC 8-10**: systematically test each possibility. Try choosing 1 from *A*: you can't choose 2 from *B*, because $1 + 2 = 3$, which is not greater than any number in *C*; you can, however, choose 3 from *B* and 3 from *C*. So one way is (1,3,3). The other ways are (2,2,3), (2,3,3), and (2,3,4), a total of 4 ways.

29. (*308*) Don't do any algebra. Just replace *a* and *b* by 7 and 11 in the original expression:
$$(7 + 11)^2 - (7 - 11)^2 =$$
$$18^2 - (-4)^2 = 324 - 16 = 308.$$

30. $\left(\frac{22}{6} \text{ or } \frac{11}{3} \text{ or } 3.66\right)$ Notice that the left-hand side of the equation is the negative of the right-hand side, meaning that each side is equal to 0. Therefore,
$$3x - 11 = 0 \Rightarrow 3x = 11 \Rightarrow x = \frac{11}{3}.$$

**Just solve the equation
$$3x - 11 = 11 - 3x \Rightarrow 6x = 22 \Rightarrow x = \frac{22}{6}.$$
Note that it is *not* necessary to reduce $\frac{22}{6}$. (It's not even advisable.)

31. *(150)* Since Len got $100, the other three shared the remaining $900. If x represents Jim's share, then Kim got $2x$ and Ben got $3x$. Then $900 = x + 2x + 3x = 6x \Rightarrow x = 150$.

32. *(79)* For a fraction to be large, the numerator should be as large as possible and the denominator as small as possible. The greatest value that $x^2 - y$ could have is 80, by letting $x = 9$ and $y = 1$. Since x, y, and z are different, the least that z could be is 2, and the value of the fraction would be $\frac{80}{2}$, or 40. However, if you interchange x and y, you get 79 for the numerator ($9^2 - 2$) and 1 for the denominator: $\frac{79}{1}$ or 79.

33. *($\frac{3}{2}$ or 1.5)* The center of a circle is the midpoint of any diameter. Therefore, by the midpoint formula (**KEY FACT N3**)

$$(x, y) = \left(\frac{-3+5}{2}, \frac{2+(-1)}{2}\right) = \left(\frac{2}{2}, \frac{1}{2}\right) = \left(1, \frac{1}{2}\right).$$

So $x + y = 1 + \frac{1}{2} = 1\frac{1}{2}$.

Note: Since you cannot grid-in a mixed number, you *must* enter $1\frac{1}{2}$ as $\frac{3}{2}$ or 1.5.

34. *(8)* Since the repeating portion of this decimal number is 6 digits long, divide 200 by 6 to determine how many times the sequence 4, 2, 8, 5, 7, 1 repeats in the first 200 digits. When 200 is divided by 6, the quotient is 33.333 . . . Ignore the decimal portion. There are 33 complete repetitions, and since $33 \times 6 = 198$, the 198th digit ends the 33rd group and so is a 1. Then the 199th digit is 4, and the 200th digit is 8.

35. *(21)* The sum of 2 two-digit numbers must be less than 200; so $A = 1$, and the sum is 111. Since B and D are positive, $B + D$ cannot be 1 and so must be 11, which means that 1 is carried into the tens column. In the tens column we must add 1 (for A), the 1 we carried, and C, and the sum is 11. Then $1 + 1 + C = 11$, and $C = 9$.

So, $A = 1$, $C = 9$, and $B + D = 11$. Therefore, $A + B + C + D = 1 + 9 + 11 = 21$.

36. *(1)* Since the entire region is a circle of radius 4, its area is $\pi(4)^2 = 16\pi$. The shaded region is a circle of radius 3 minus the small white circle of radius 1; so its area is $9\pi - \pi = 8\pi$ ($a = 8\pi$). The area of the white region can be found by subtracting the area of the shaded region (8π) from the total area (16π). So $b = 16\pi - 8\pi = 8\pi$. Finally, $\frac{a}{b} = \frac{8\pi}{8\pi} = 1$.

37. *(52)* This is a weighted average (**KEY FACT E6**): $\frac{40\%(40) + 60\%(60)}{100\%} = \frac{16 + 36}{1} = 52$.

**If you prefer, assume there are 100 marbles, 40 of which are red and 60 of which are blue: $\frac{40(40) + 60(60)}{100} = \frac{1600 + 3600}{100} = 52$.

38. *(6)* Let x = measure of each exterior angle, and $2x$ = measure of each interior angle. Since the sum of the measures of an interior and exterior angle is 180: $180 = x + 2x = 3x \Rightarrow x = 60$. Since the sum of the measures of all the exterior angles is 360°, there are $360 \div 60 = 6$ angles and, of course, 6 sides.

Section 5 Writing Skills

1. *E* Error in pronoun case. The noun or pronoun preceding a gerund (*going*) should be in the possessive case.

2. *E* Error in modification. The dangling modifier is best corrected in Choice E.

3. *C* Comma splice. Choices A and B are run-on sentences. Choices D and E are ungrammatical.

4. *E* Error in modification and double negative. Both are corrected in Choice E.

5. *E* Error in coordination and subordination. By changing *having* to *had* and connecting the two main clauses with a semicolon, you tighten the sentence and eliminate wordiness.

6. *B* Sentence fragment. Choice B expresses the author's meaning directly and concisely. All other choices are indirect, ungrammatical, or fail to retain the meaning of the original statement.

7. *C* Error in agreement. *Kind* should be modified by *this* or *that; kinds,* by *these* or *those.*

8. *C* Error in parallelism. *New, list,* and *service* are all nouns. Thus, parallel structure is retained in Choice C.

9. *D* This corrects the sentence fragment smoothly.

10. *B* Error in logical comparison. Compare *complaints* with *complaints*, not with *customers*. The faulty comparison is corrected in Choice B.

11. *C* Error in modification. Choice C corrects the misplaced modifier and eliminates the unnecessary use of the passive voice.

12. *C* Error in subject-verb agreement. The phrase *along with his staff* is not part of the subject of the sentence. The subject is *President Clinton* (singular); the verb should be *is traveling* (singular).

13. *B* Error in coordination and subordination. The use of the subordinating conjunction *Although* and the deletion of unnecessary words strengthen this sentence.

14. *D* Choices A, B, and C have dangling modifiers; Choice E creates a run-on sentence.

15. *A* Sentence is correct.

16. *C* Double negative. Change *cannot do nothing* to *can do nothing*.

17. *E* Error in sequence of tenses. The present perfect tense (*have damaged*) refers to some unspecified time in the past. Here, however, the author is telling about something that occurred at a definite time in the past: "In 1940, during the Battle of Britain." In this context, the simple past tense (*damaged*) is correct.

18. *C* Adjective-adverb confusion. The adverb phrase *Not surprisingly* modifies (describes or limits) the rest of the sentence.

19. *A* Sentence is correct.

20. *A* Sentence is correct.

21. *B* Error in diction. *Affect* is a verb and should not be used in place of *effect*.

22. *E* Sentence is correct.

23. *C* Error in diction. There is no such verb as *enthuse*. Change *enthused* to *enthusiastic*.

24. *C* Error in tense. Change *had shot* to *shot*.

25. *A* Error in diction. Use *irritated* instead of *aggravated*.

26. *A* Error in idiom. Change *neither . . . or* to *neither . . . nor*.

27. *C* Error in diction. Change *incredulous* to *incredible*.

28. *C* Error in tense. Change *had broke* to *had broken*.

29. *C* Error in subject-verb agreement. The subject, *Ann Landers*, is singular; the verb should be singular—*is*.

30. *D* Error in diction. Issues are *decided* or settled. The actual choice made is what is *decided upon*. Delete *upon*.

31. *E* Sentence is correct.

32. *C* Error in subject-verb agreement. The subject, *general*, is singular; the verb should be singular—*seems*.

33. *A* Error in pronoun case. The possessive pronoun precedes a gerund. Change *him* to *his*.

34. *D* Error in tense. Change *was to be immortalized* to *was immortalized*.

35. *D* Choices A, B, and C abruptly state the contrasting point of view without regard to the context.

Choice D takes the context into account and provides for a smooth progression of thought. It is the best answer.

Choice E is confusing. It is unclear until the end of the sentence whether the *other members* support or oppose the exhibit.

36. *B* Choice A lacks a main verb; therefore, it is a sentence fragment.

Choice B accurately combines the sentences. It is the best answer.

Choice C expresses the idea in a way that the writer could not have intended.

Choice D subordinates important ideas and emphasizes a lesser one.

Choice E restates the idea in a manner that changes the writer's intended meaning.

37. *A* Choice A is the best choice because the sentences contain basic information about the topic. Readers are left in the dark unless the information appears as early as possible in the essay.

38. *E* Choice A contains faulty idiom; the phrase *than of the past* is nonstandard usage. Choice B contains a faulty comparison; *society* and *the past* cannot be logically compared. Choice C contains an error in idiom; the phrase *than from* is redundant. Choice D is correct but excessively wordy. Choice E is the best answer.

39. *C* Choice A provides a reasonable transition, but it contains an error in pronoun-antecedent agreement. The pronoun *they* is plural; its antecedent *anyone* is singular.

Choice B contains an error in diction. One can *disapprove of* but not *disagree with* a piece of art.

Choice C alludes to the content of the previous paragraph and is clearly and succinctly expressed. It is the best answer.

Choice D contains an error in pronoun-antecedent agreement. The pronoun *them* is plural; the antecedent *anyone* is singular.

Choice E is inconsistent in tone and mood with the rest of the essay.

Answer Sheet
MODEL TEST F

Each mark should completely fill the appropriate space, and should be as dark as all other marks. Make all erasures complete. Traces of an erasure may be read as an answer. See pages viii and 21 for explanations of timing and number of questions.

Section 1 — Critical Reading
25 minutes

1 Ⓐ Ⓑ Ⓒ Ⓓ Ⓔ
2 Ⓐ Ⓑ Ⓒ Ⓓ Ⓔ
3 Ⓐ Ⓑ Ⓒ Ⓓ Ⓔ
4 Ⓐ Ⓑ Ⓒ Ⓓ Ⓔ
5 Ⓐ Ⓑ Ⓒ Ⓓ Ⓔ
6 Ⓐ Ⓑ Ⓒ Ⓓ Ⓔ
7 Ⓐ Ⓑ Ⓒ Ⓓ Ⓔ
8 Ⓐ Ⓑ Ⓒ Ⓓ Ⓔ
9 Ⓐ Ⓑ Ⓒ Ⓓ Ⓔ
10 Ⓐ Ⓑ Ⓒ Ⓓ Ⓔ
11 Ⓐ Ⓑ Ⓒ Ⓓ Ⓔ
12 Ⓐ Ⓑ Ⓒ Ⓓ Ⓔ
13 Ⓐ Ⓑ Ⓒ Ⓓ Ⓔ
14 Ⓐ Ⓑ Ⓒ Ⓓ Ⓔ
15 Ⓐ Ⓑ Ⓒ Ⓓ Ⓔ
16 Ⓐ Ⓑ Ⓒ Ⓓ Ⓔ
17 Ⓐ Ⓑ Ⓒ Ⓓ Ⓔ
18 Ⓐ Ⓑ Ⓒ Ⓓ Ⓔ
19 Ⓐ Ⓑ Ⓒ Ⓓ Ⓔ
20 Ⓐ Ⓑ Ⓒ Ⓓ Ⓔ
21 Ⓐ Ⓑ Ⓒ Ⓓ Ⓔ
22 Ⓐ Ⓑ Ⓒ Ⓓ Ⓔ
23 Ⓐ Ⓑ Ⓒ Ⓓ Ⓔ
24 Ⓐ Ⓑ Ⓒ Ⓓ Ⓔ

Section 2 — Math
25 minutes

1 Ⓐ Ⓑ Ⓒ Ⓓ Ⓔ
2 Ⓐ Ⓑ Ⓒ Ⓓ Ⓔ
3 Ⓐ Ⓑ Ⓒ Ⓓ Ⓔ
4 Ⓐ Ⓑ Ⓒ Ⓓ Ⓔ
5 Ⓐ Ⓑ Ⓒ Ⓓ Ⓔ
6 Ⓐ Ⓑ Ⓒ Ⓓ Ⓔ
7 Ⓐ Ⓑ Ⓒ Ⓓ Ⓔ
8 Ⓐ Ⓑ Ⓒ Ⓓ Ⓔ
9 Ⓐ Ⓑ Ⓒ Ⓓ Ⓔ
10 Ⓐ Ⓑ Ⓒ Ⓓ Ⓔ
11 Ⓐ Ⓑ Ⓒ Ⓓ Ⓔ
12 Ⓐ Ⓑ Ⓒ Ⓓ Ⓔ
13 Ⓐ Ⓑ Ⓒ Ⓓ Ⓔ
14 Ⓐ Ⓑ Ⓒ Ⓓ Ⓔ
15 Ⓐ Ⓑ Ⓒ Ⓓ Ⓔ
16 Ⓐ Ⓑ Ⓒ Ⓓ Ⓔ
17 Ⓐ Ⓑ Ⓒ Ⓓ Ⓔ
18 Ⓐ Ⓑ Ⓒ Ⓓ Ⓔ
19 Ⓐ Ⓑ Ⓒ Ⓓ Ⓔ
20 Ⓐ Ⓑ Ⓒ Ⓓ Ⓔ

Section 3 — Critical Reading
25 minutes

25 Ⓐ Ⓑ Ⓒ Ⓓ Ⓔ
26 Ⓐ Ⓑ Ⓒ Ⓓ Ⓔ
27 Ⓐ Ⓑ Ⓒ Ⓓ Ⓔ
28 Ⓐ Ⓑ Ⓒ Ⓓ Ⓔ
29 Ⓐ Ⓑ Ⓒ Ⓓ Ⓔ
30 Ⓐ Ⓑ Ⓒ Ⓓ Ⓔ
31 Ⓐ Ⓑ Ⓒ Ⓓ Ⓔ
32 Ⓐ Ⓑ Ⓒ Ⓓ Ⓔ
33 Ⓐ Ⓑ Ⓒ Ⓓ Ⓔ
34 Ⓐ Ⓑ Ⓒ Ⓓ Ⓔ
35 Ⓐ Ⓑ Ⓒ Ⓓ Ⓔ
36 Ⓐ Ⓑ Ⓒ Ⓓ Ⓔ
37 Ⓐ Ⓑ Ⓒ Ⓓ Ⓔ
38 Ⓐ Ⓑ Ⓒ Ⓓ Ⓔ
39 Ⓐ Ⓑ Ⓒ Ⓓ Ⓔ
40 Ⓐ Ⓑ Ⓒ Ⓓ Ⓔ
41 Ⓐ Ⓑ Ⓒ Ⓓ Ⓔ
42 Ⓐ Ⓑ Ⓒ Ⓓ Ⓔ
43 Ⓐ Ⓑ Ⓒ Ⓓ Ⓔ
44 Ⓐ Ⓑ Ⓒ Ⓓ Ⓔ
45 Ⓐ Ⓑ Ⓒ Ⓓ Ⓔ
46 Ⓐ Ⓑ Ⓒ Ⓓ Ⓔ
47 Ⓐ Ⓑ Ⓒ Ⓓ Ⓔ
48 Ⓐ Ⓑ Ⓒ Ⓓ Ⓔ

Section 4 — Math
25 minutes

21 Ⓐ Ⓑ Ⓒ Ⓓ Ⓔ
22 Ⓐ Ⓑ Ⓒ Ⓓ Ⓔ
23 Ⓐ Ⓑ Ⓒ Ⓓ Ⓔ
24 Ⓐ Ⓑ Ⓒ Ⓓ Ⓔ
25 Ⓐ Ⓑ Ⓒ Ⓓ Ⓔ
26 Ⓐ Ⓑ Ⓒ Ⓓ Ⓔ
27 Ⓐ Ⓑ Ⓒ Ⓓ Ⓔ
28 Ⓐ Ⓑ Ⓒ Ⓓ Ⓔ

29
30
31
32
33
34
35
36
37
38

Section 5 — Writing
30 minutes

1 Ⓐ Ⓑ Ⓒ Ⓓ Ⓔ
2 Ⓐ Ⓑ Ⓒ Ⓓ Ⓔ
3 Ⓐ Ⓑ Ⓒ Ⓓ Ⓔ
4 Ⓐ Ⓑ Ⓒ Ⓓ Ⓔ
5 Ⓐ Ⓑ Ⓒ Ⓓ Ⓔ
6 Ⓐ Ⓑ Ⓒ Ⓓ Ⓔ
7 Ⓐ Ⓑ Ⓒ Ⓓ Ⓔ
8 Ⓐ Ⓑ Ⓒ Ⓓ Ⓔ
9 Ⓐ Ⓑ Ⓒ Ⓓ Ⓔ
10 Ⓐ Ⓑ Ⓒ Ⓓ Ⓔ
11 Ⓐ Ⓑ Ⓒ Ⓓ Ⓔ
12 Ⓐ Ⓑ Ⓒ Ⓓ Ⓔ
13 Ⓐ Ⓑ Ⓒ Ⓓ Ⓔ
14 Ⓐ Ⓑ Ⓒ Ⓓ Ⓔ
15 Ⓐ Ⓑ Ⓒ Ⓓ Ⓔ
16 Ⓐ Ⓑ Ⓒ Ⓓ Ⓔ
17 Ⓐ Ⓑ Ⓒ Ⓓ Ⓔ
18 Ⓐ Ⓑ Ⓒ Ⓓ Ⓔ
19 Ⓐ Ⓑ Ⓒ Ⓓ Ⓔ
20 Ⓐ Ⓑ Ⓒ Ⓓ Ⓔ
21 Ⓐ Ⓑ Ⓒ Ⓓ Ⓔ
22 Ⓐ Ⓑ Ⓒ Ⓓ Ⓔ
23 Ⓐ Ⓑ Ⓒ Ⓓ Ⓔ
24 Ⓐ Ⓑ Ⓒ Ⓓ Ⓔ
25 Ⓐ Ⓑ Ⓒ Ⓓ Ⓔ
26 Ⓐ Ⓑ Ⓒ Ⓓ Ⓔ
27 Ⓐ Ⓑ Ⓒ Ⓓ Ⓔ
28 Ⓐ Ⓑ Ⓒ Ⓓ Ⓔ
29 Ⓐ Ⓑ Ⓒ Ⓓ Ⓔ
30 Ⓐ Ⓑ Ⓒ Ⓓ Ⓔ
31 Ⓐ Ⓑ Ⓒ Ⓓ Ⓔ
32 Ⓐ Ⓑ Ⓒ Ⓓ Ⓔ
33 Ⓐ Ⓑ Ⓒ Ⓓ Ⓔ
34 Ⓐ Ⓑ Ⓒ Ⓓ Ⓔ
35 Ⓐ Ⓑ Ⓒ Ⓓ Ⓔ
36 Ⓐ Ⓑ Ⓒ Ⓓ Ⓔ
37 Ⓐ Ⓑ Ⓒ Ⓓ Ⓔ
38 Ⓐ Ⓑ Ⓒ Ⓓ Ⓔ
39 Ⓐ Ⓑ Ⓒ Ⓓ Ⓔ

For each question in this section, select the best answer from among the choices given, and fill in the corresponding circle on the answer sheet.

Directions

Each sentence below has one or two blanks, each blank indicating that something has been omitted. Beneath the sentence are five words or sets of words labeled A through E. Choose the word or set of words that, when inserted in the sentence, best fits the meaning of the sentence as a whole.

EXAMPLE:

Medieval kingdoms did not become constitutional republics overnight; on the contrary, the change was ----.

(A) unpopular   (B) unexpected
(C) advantageous   (D) sufficient   (E) gradual

Ⓐ Ⓑ Ⓒ Ⓓ ●

---

1. The traditional French café is slowly becoming ----, a victim to the growing popularity of *le fast food*.

    (A) celebrated   (B) indispensable
    (C) prevalent   (D) extinct   (E) fashionable

2. Although we expected the women's basketball coach to be ---- over the recent victory of the team, we found her surprisingly ----.

    (A) ecstatic..gleeful
    (B) ambivalent..devious
    (C) triumphant..responsive
    (D) elated..naive
    (E) jubilant..disheartened

3. The debate coach suggested that he eliminate his ---- remarks in his otherwise serious speech because they were ----.

    (A) bantering..inappropriate
    (B) jesting..accurate
    (C) solemn..irrelevant
    (D) tacit..digressive
    (E) perfunctory..inconsiderate

4. Many young people and adults, uncomfortable with math, feel it is a subject best ---- engineers, scientists, and that small, elite group endowed at birth with a talent for the ---- world of numbers.

    (A) ignored by..abstract
    (B) suited to..accessible
    (C) studied by..interminable
    (D) left to..esoteric
    (E) avoided by..abstruse

5. Her novel published to universal acclaim, her literary gifts acknowledged by the chief figures of the Harlem Renaissance, her reputation as yet ---- by envious slights, Hurston clearly was at the ---- of her career.

    (A) undamaged..ebb
    (B) untarnished..zenith
    (C) untainted..end
    (D) blackened..mercy
    (E) unmarred..whim

Directions

Each passage below is followed by questions based on its content. Answer the questions following each passage on the basis of what is <u>stated</u> or <u>implied</u> in that passage and in any introductory material that may be provided.

Questions 6 and 7 are based on the following passage.

"The very first requirement in a hospital (is) that it should do the sick no harm." So wrote Florence Nightingale, nursing pioneer. Most peo-
Line ple picture Nightingale as the brave "Lady with the
5 Lamp" who journeyed to the Crimea to nurse British soldiers wounded in the war. It was after the war, however, that Nightingale came into her own as the world's most renowned authority on hospital reform. In *Notes on Hospitals*, Nightingale
10 addressed every aspect of hospital construction and management, from replacing wooden bedsteads with iron ones, to minimizing infection by dividing hospitals into airy, self-contained pavilions.

6. Which statement best expresses the author's central point about Florence Nightingale?

    (A) She deserved great praise for her work with wounded soldiers in the Crimea.
    (B) She worried about the effects of infection on mortality rates.
    (C) Her greatest accomplishments were in improving hospital planning and administration.
    (D) She preferred airy, separate hospital units to large wards.
    (E) Her change of focus to hospital administration represented a loss to the nursing profession.

GO ON TO NEXT PAGE ▶

7. In line 10, the word "addressed" most nearly means

(A) orated   (B) labeled   (C) set apart
(D) dealt with   (E) averted

Questions 8 and 9 are based on the following passage.

Critics call Edgar Allan Poe the father of detective fiction. Whom then should we call detective fiction's mother? Agatha Christie, say some
Line mystery readers. Dorothy Sayers, say others. Well
5 before Christie and Sayers wrote their classic British whodunits, however, an American named Anna Katharine Green wrote a best-seller about the murder of a Fifth Avenue millionaire. *The Leavenworth Case*, which sold over 150,000
10 copies, marked the initial appearance of Inspector Ebenezer Gryce, the first serial detective in genre history. Today, with two novels back in print after nearly a century, Gryce's long-neglected creator is finally beginning to receive the recognition she
15 deserves.

8. The author's purpose in writing this passage is most likely to

(A) relegate a writer to obscurity
(B) contrast the careers of Poe and Green
(C) introduce the concept of the serial detective
(D) dismiss the contributions of British authors
(E) reclaim a forgotten literary pioneer

9. The word "marked" (line 10) most nearly means

(A) graded   (B) noticed   (C) denoted
(D) branded   (E) disfigured

Questions 10–15 are based on the following passage.

The following passage is excerpted from a book on prominent black Americans during Franklin Delano Roosevelt's presidency.

Like her white friends Eleanor Roosevelt and Aubrey Williams, Mary Bethune believed in the fundamental commitment of the New Deal to as-
Line sist the black American's struggle and in the need
5 for blacks to assume responsibilities to help win that struggle. Unlike those of her white liberal associates, however, Bethune's ideas had evolved out of a long experience as a "race leader." Founder of a small black college in Florida, she
10 had become widely known by 1935 as an organizer of black women's groups and as a civil and political rights activist. Deeply religious, certain of her own capabilities, she held a relatively uncluttered view of what she felt were the New Deal's and her
15 own people's obligations to the cause of racial justice. Unafraid to speak her mind to powerful whites, including the President, or to differing black factions, she combined faith in the ultimate willingness of whites to discard their prejudice
20 and bigotry with a strong sense of racial pride and commitment to Negro self-help.

More than her liberal white friends, Bethune argued for a strong and direct black voice in initiating and shaping government policy. She pursued
25 this in her conversations with President Roosevelt, in numerous memoranda to Aubrey Williams, and in her administrative work as head of the National Youth Administration's Office of Negro Affairs. With the assistance of Williams, she was successful in
30 having blacks selected to NYA posts at the national, state, and local levels. But she also wanted a black presence throughout the federal government. At the beginning of the war she joined other black leaders in demanding appointments to the Selective
35 Service Board and to the Department of the Army; and she was instrumental in 1941 in securing Earl Dickerson's membership on the Fair Employment Practices Committee. By 1944, she was still making appeals for black representation in "all public pro-
40 grams, federal, state, and local," and "in policy-making posts as well as rank and file jobs."

GO ON TO NEXT PAGE ▶

Though recognizing the weakness in the Roosevelt administration's response to Negro needs, Mary Bethune remained in essence a black partisan champion of the New Deal during the 1930s and 1940s. Her strong advocacy of administration policies and programs was predicated on a number of factors: her assessment of the low status of black Americans during the Depression; her faith in the willingness of some liberal whites to work for the inclusion of blacks in the government's reform and recovery measures; her conviction that only massive federal aid could elevate the Negro economically; and her belief that the thirties and forties were producing a more self-aware and self-assured black population. Like a number of her white friends in government, Bethune assumed that the preservation of democracy and black people's "full integration into the benefits and the responsibilities" of American life were inextricably tied together. She was convinced that, with the help of a friendly government, a militant, aggressive "New Negro" would emerge out of the devastation of depression and war, a "New Negro" who would "save America from itself," who would lead America toward the full realization of its democratic ideas.

10. The author's primary goal in the passage is to do which of the following?
(A) criticize Mary Bethune for adhering too closely to New Deal policies
(B) argue that Mary Bethune was too optimistic in her assessment of race relations
(C) explore Mary Bethune's convictions and her influence on black progress in the Roosevelt years
(D) point out the weaknesses of the white liberal approach to black needs during Roosevelt's presidency
(E) summarize the attainments of blacks under the auspices of Roosevelt's New Deal

11. It can be inferred from the passage that Aubrey Williams was which of the following?
I. A man with influence in the National Youth Administration
II. A white liberal
III. A man of strong religious convictions
(A) I only
(B) II only
(C) I and II only
(D) II and III only
(E) I, II, and III

12. The author mentions Earl Dickerson (lines 36–37) primarily in order to
(A) cite an instance of Bethune's political impact
(B) contrast his career with that of Bethune
(C) introduce the subject of a subsequent paragraph
(D) provide an example of Bethune's "New Negro"
(E) show that Dickerson was a leader of his fellow blacks

13. The word "instrumental" in line 36 means
(A) subordinate (B) triumphant (C) musical
(D) gracious (E) helpful

14. It can be inferred from the passage that Bethune believed the "New Negro" would "save America from itself" (lines 61–67) by
(A) joining the Army and helping America overthrow its Fascist enemies
(B) helping America accomplish its egalitarian ideals
(C) voting for administration antipoverty programs
(D) electing other blacks to government office
(E) expressing a belief in racial pride

15. The author uses all the following techniques in the passage EXCEPT
(A) comparison and contrast
(B) development of an extended metaphor
(C) direct quotation
(D) general statement and concrete examples
(E) repetition of central ideas

In this excerpt from the novel Hard Times *by Charles Dickens, the reader is introduced to Thomas Gradgrind, headmaster of a so-called model school.*

Thomas Gradgrind, sir. A man of realities. A man of facts and calculations. A man who proceeds upon the principle that two and two are
Line four, and nothing over, and who is not to be talked
5 into allowing for anything over. Thomas Gradgrind, sir—peremptorily Thomas—Thomas Gradgrind. With a rule and a pair of scales, and the multiplication table always in his pocket, sir, ready to weigh and measure any parcel of human
10 nature, and tell you exactly what it comes to. It is a mere question of figures, a case of simple arithmetic. You might hope to get some other nonsensical belief into the head of George Gradgrind, or Augustus Gradgrind, or John Gradgrind, or Joseph
15 Gradgrind (all suppositions, non-existent persons), but into the head of Thomas Gradgrind—no, sir!

Mr. Gradgrind walked homeward from the school in a state of considerable satisfaction. It was
20 his school, and he intended it to be a model. He intended every child in it to be a model—just as the young Gradgrinds were all models.

There were five young Gradgrinds, and they were models every one. They had been lectured at
25 from their tenderest years; coursed, like little hares. Almost as soon as they could run alone, they had been made to run to the lecture-room. The first object with which they had an association, or of which they had a remembrance, was a
30 large blackboard with a dry Ogre chalking ghastly white figures on it.

Not that they knew, by name or nature, anything about an Ogre. Fact forbid! I only use the word to express a monster in a lecturing castle,
35 with Heaven knows how many heads manipulated into one, taking childhood captive, and dragging it into gloomy statistical dens by the hair.

No little Gradgrind had ever seen a face in the moon; it was up in the moon before it could speak
40 distinctly. No little Gradgrind had ever learnt the silly jingle, Twinkle, twinkle, little star; how I wonder what you are! No little Gradgrind had ever known wonder on the subject of the stars, each little Gradgrind having at five years old dissected
45 the Great Bear like a Professor Owen, and driven Charles's Wain like a locomotive engine-driver. No little Gradgrind had ever associated a cow in a field with that famous cow with the crumpled horn who tossed the dog who worried the cat who killed
50 the rat who ate the malt, or with that yet more famous cow who swallowed Tom Thumb: it had never heard of those celebrities, and had only been introduced to a cow as a graminivorous ruminating quadruped with several stomachs.

---

16. The phrase "peremptorily Thomas" in line 6 emphasizes Gradgrind's

(A) absolute insistence upon facts
(B) dislike of the name Augustus
(C) need to remind himself of the simplest details
(D) desire to be on a first-name basis with others
(E) inability to introduce himself properly

17. The word "rule" in line 7 means

(A) legal regulation
(B) academic custom
(C) scientific principle
(D) dominion over schoolchildren
(E) straight edge used in measuring

18. Gradgrind's mood as he marches homeward (lines 18–19) can best be characterized as one of

(A) uncertainty (B) complacency
(C) boredom (D) relief (E) cynicism

19. The author's tone in describing Thomas Gradgrind's educational methodology is

(A) openly admiring
(B) acutely concerned
(C) bitterly scornful
(D) broadly satirical
(E) warmly nostalgic

20. The passage suggests that Gradgrind rejects from his curriculum anything that is in the least

(A) analytical (B) mechanical (C) fanciful
(D) dogmatic (E) pragmatic

21. The passage is narrated from the point of view of

(A) Thomas Gradgrind
(B) an observer who does not know Gradgrind at first but who comes to know about him in the course of the passage
(C) an observer whose understanding of Gradgrind is necessarily incomplete
(D) an observer who knows all about Gradgrind's thoughts and feelings
(E) an instructor at Gradgrind's model school

GO ON TO NEXT PAGE ▶

22. It can be inferred from the passage that the Great Bear and Charles's Wain most likely are

(A) subjects of nursery rhymes
(B) groupings of stars
(C) zoological phenomena
(D) themes of popular songs
(E) popular toys for children

23. Which of the following axioms is closest to Gradgrind's view of education as presented in the passage?

(A) Experience keeps a dear school, but fools will learn in no other.
(B) Let early education be a sort of amusement, that you may be better able to find out the natural bent.
(C) Education is what you have left over after you have forgotten everything you have learned.
(D) A teacher who can arouse a feeling for one single good action accomplishes more than one who fills our memory with rows on rows of natural objects, classified with name and form.
(E) Modern science, as training the mind to an exact and impartial analysis of fact, is an education specially fitted to promote sound citizenship.

24. In line 52, the word "celebrities" refers to

(A) the little Gradgrinds
(B) famous professors
(C) heavenly bodies
(D) locomotive engine-drivers
(E) fictional characters

IF YOU FINISH IN LESS THAN 25 MINUTES, YOU MAY CHECK YOUR WORK ON THIS SECTION ONLY. DO NOT TURN TO ANY OTHER SECTION IN THE TEST.

STOP

Multiple-Choice Directions

For each question in this section, determine which of the five choices is correct, and blacken that choice on your answer sheet. You may use any blank space on the page for your work.

NOTES:
- You may use a calculator whenever you believe it will be helpful.
- Use the diagrams provided to help you solve the problems. Unless you see the phrase
                    Note: Figure not drawn to scale
under a diagram, it has been drawn as accurately as possible. Unless it is stated that a figure is three dimensional, you may assume that it lies in a plane.

Reference

$A = \pi r^2$
$C = 2\pi r$

$A = \frac{1}{2}bh$

$V = \ell wh$

$V = \pi r^2 h$

$c^2 = a^2 + b^2$

Special Right Triangles

Number of degrees in a circle: 360
Sum of the measures, in degrees, of the three angles of a triangle: 180

1. What is the value of m if $(7 - 2)(7 - m) = 35$?
   (A) -7 (B) -5 (C) 0   (D) 5   (E) 7

2. In the figure above, what is the value of a?
   (A) 10   (B) 20   (C) 28   (D) 36   (E) 45

3. Samir studied for exactly 225 minutes. If he began studying at 10:05 A.M., at what time did he stop studying?

   (A) 12:30 P.M.   (B) 1:00 P.M.   (C) 1:30 P.M.
   (D) 1:50 P.M.   (E) 2:00 P.M.

4. What positive number n satisfies the equation, $(9)(9)(9)n = \frac{(27)(27)}{n}$?
   (A) $\frac{1}{3}$ (B) 1   (C) 3   (D) 9   (E) 27

Note: Figure not drawn to scale

5. In the figure above, if x is 140 more than y, what is the value of y?
   (A) 10   (B) 15   (C) 20   (D) 30   (E) 40

6. If $x^2 = 10$, what is x^6?
   (A) $10\sqrt{10}$ (B) 100   (C) $100\sqrt{10}$
   (D) 1000   (E) $1000\sqrt{10}$

7. If $a, b, c,$ and d are four consecutive integers, which of the following could be their average (arithmetic mean)?

   I. 99
   II. 99.5
   III. 100

   (A) I only   (B) II only   (C) I and II only
   (D) II and III only   (E) I, II, and III

8. The following chart lists the monthly salaries in 1985 of five people and the percent change in their salaries from 1985 to 1995.

Name	1985 Salary	% change
Ann	$4200	+6%
Ben	$4000	+11%
Dan	$3500	+25%
Ken	$5000	−12%
Len	$3200	+35%

Who had the highest salary in 1995?

(A) Ann   (B) Ben   (C) Dan
(D) Ken   (E) Len

9. If the measures of the angles of a triangle are in the ratio of 1:2:3, what is the ratio of the lengths of the sides?

(A) 1:2:3   (B) 1:1:$\sqrt{2}$ (C) 1:$\sqrt{3}$:2   (D) 3:4:5
(E) It cannot be determined from the information given.

10. What is the diameter of a circle whose area is A?

(A) $2\sqrt{\frac{A}{\pi}}$ (B) $\sqrt{\frac{A}{\pi}}$ (C) $\frac{A}{2\pi}$

(D) $\frac{A}{\pi}$ (E) $\frac{2\sqrt{A}}{\pi}$

11. A, B, and C are points with $AC = 2AB$. Which of the following could be true?

 I. A, B, and C are the vertices of a right triangle.
 II. A, B, and C are three of the vertices of a square.
 III. A, B, and C all lie on the circumference of a circle.

(A) I only   (B) III only   (C) I and II only
(D) I and III only   (E) I, II, and III

12. Last year Ross bought two paintings. Last week he sold them for $1200 each. He had a 20% profit on one painting and a 20% loss on the other. What was his net loss or profit?

(A) He lost exactly $100.
(B) He lost less than $100.
(C) He lost more than $100.
(D) He earned less than $100.
(E) He earned more than $100.

13. What is the measure in degrees of the smaller angle formed by the hour hand and the minute hand of a clock at 3:30?

(A) 15   (B) 60   (C) 70   (D) 75   (E) 90

14. If m is an integer, which of the following could be true?

 I. $\frac{15}{m}$ is an even integer
 II. $\frac{m}{15}$ is an even integer
 III. $15m$ is a prime

(A) I only   (B) II only   (C) III only
(D) I and II only   (E) II and III only

Questions 15–16 refer to the following definition.

For any integers m and n: $m*n$ represents the remainder when m is divided by n.

15. What is the value of

$6*1 + 6*2 + 6*3 + 6*4 + 6*5 + 6*6$?

(A) 0   (B) 3   (C) 6   (D) 9   (E) 14

16. If $a < b$, what is the maximum possible value of $a*b + b*a$?

(A) $a + b$ (B) $ab - 1$ (C) $2a - 1$
(D) $2b - 1$ (E) $a + b - 1$

17. If $x + y = 10, y + z = 15$, and $x + z = 17$, what is the average (arithmetic mean) of x, y, and z?

(A) 7   (B) 14   (C) 15   (D) 21
(E) It cannot be determined from the information given.

18. If x is a positive integer, which of the following CANNOT be an integer?

(A) $\sqrt{x - 1}$ (B) $\sqrt{x^2 - 1}$ (C) $\frac{1}{x}$
(D) $\frac{x + 2}{x + 1}$ (E) $\frac{7}{x + 1}$

19. Which of the following CANNOT be expressed as the sum of two or more consecutive positive integers?

(A) 12   (B) 13   (C) 14   (D) 15   (E) 16

20. If p painters can complete a job in d days, how long will it take q painters, working at the same rate, to complete 25% of the job?

(A) $\frac{pd}{4q}$ (B) $\frac{q}{4pd}$ (C) $\frac{4pd}{q}$ (D) $\frac{pq}{4d}$ (E) $\frac{pqd}{4}$

IF YOU FINISH IN LESS THAN 25 MINUTES, YOU MAY CHECK YOUR WORK ON THIS SECTION ONLY. DO NOT TURN TO ANY OTHER SECTION IN THE TEST.

STOP

For each question in this section, select the best answer from among the choices given, and fill in the corresponding circle on the answer sheet.

Directions

Each sentence below has one or two blanks, each blank indicating that something has been omitted. Beneath the sentence are five words or sets of words labeled A through E. Choose the word or set of words that, when inserted in the sentence, best fits the meaning of the sentence as a whole.

EXAMPLE:

Medieval kingdoms did not become constitutional republics overnight; on the contrary, the change was ----.

(A) unpopular   (B) unexpected
(C) advantageous   (D) sufficient   (E) gradual

Ⓐ Ⓑ Ⓒ Ⓓ ●

---

25. Once known only to importers of exotic foreign delicacies, the kiwi fruit has been transplanted successfully to America and is now ---- a much wider market.

    (A) accessible to
    (B) unknown to
    (C) perplexing to
    (D) comparable to
    (E) uncultivated by

26. Continuously looking for new ways of presenting her material, for fresh methods of capturing her students' attention, she has been ---- in the classroom.

    (A) a pedant   (B) a misfit   (C) an innovator
    (D) a stoic   (E) a martinet

27. This coming trip to France should provide me with ---- test of the value of my conversational French class.

    (A) an intimate   (B) an uncertain
    (C) a pragmatic   (D) a pretentious
    (E) an arbitrary

28. Allowing women a voice in tribal government did not ---- Cherokee custom, for traditional Cherokee society was matrilineal, granting women the right to own property and to divorce their husbands.

    (A) violate   (B) emulate   (C) retrace
    (D) preclude   (E) fulfill

29. In a shocking instance of ---- research, one of the most influential researchers in the field of genetics reported on experiments that were never carried out and published deliberately ---- scientific papers on his nonexistent work.

    (A) comprehensive..abstract
    (B) theoretical..challenging
    (C) erroneous..impartial
    (D) derivative..authoritative
    (E) fraudulent..deceptive

30. Many of the characters portrayed by Clint Eastwood are strong but ---- types, rugged men of few words.

    (A) ruthless   (B) equivocal   (C) laconic
    (D) stingy   (E) vociferous

31. Like sauces, without a certain amount of spice, conversations grow ----.

    (A) eloquent   (B) heated   (C) elaborate
    (D) straightforward   (E) insipid

32. Both ---- and ----, Scrooge seldom smiled and never gave away a halfpenny.

    (A) sanguine..miserly
    (B) acerbic..magnanimous
    (C) morose..munificent
    (D) crabbed..parsimonious
    (E) sullen..philanthropic

GO ON TO NEXT PAGE ▶

Each of the passages below precedes two questions based on its content. Answer the questions following each passage on the basis of what is <u>stated</u> or <u>implied</u> in that passage

Questions 33 and 34 are based on the following passage.

Although commonly held up as a cornerstone of American democracy, the Mayflower Compact had little impact on the growth of freedom in
Line America. Indeed, the compact limited its signers'
5 liberty. That was its intent. Of the *Mayflower*'s 100 emigrants, less than half were Pilgrims. The rest were "strangers," non-Pilgrims who, finding themselves hundreds of miles north of their planned destination in Virginia, believed them-
10 selves outside the bounds of governmental authority. Rather than respect the rules of the Pilgrims, these strangers wanted to go their own way. By signing the compact, both Pilgrims and non-Pilgrims agreed to accept whatever form of
15 government was established after landing.

33. The phrase "held up" in line 1 most nearly means

(A) delayed   (B) cited   (C) accommodated
(D) carried   (E) waylaid

34. The author of the passage can best be described as

(A) a debunker   (B) an atheist
(C) a mythmaker   (D) an elitist
(E) an authoritarian

Questions 35 and 36 are based on the following passage.

He was good-looking, in a Southern, romantic poet sort of way. He needed those good looks, one of the aunts said; why else would my otherwise
Line sensible mother have married a man like him, an
5 actor-writer who lived on dreams and spent his evenings carrying a spear at the Opera House. But that was in later times, when he had moved out of the rundown communal house in the Berkeley Hills, leaving my mother and the ever-changing
10 body of honorary uncles and aunts to patch the ancient water heater and pump out the basement when the overpressured valve finally blew.

35. The tone of the aunt's comment about the narrator's father (line 2) can best be described as

(A) adulatory   (B) disparaging   (C) effusive
(D) nostalgic   (E) neutral

36. In line 10, "body" most nearly means

(A) rich flavor   (B) central core
(C) bulky mass   (D) physical structure
(E) collective group

The passages below are followed by questions on their content; questions following a pair of related passages may also be based on the relationship between the paired passages. Answer the questions on the basis of what is <u>stated</u> or <u>implied</u> in the passages and in any introductory material that may be provided.

Questions 37–48 are based on the following passages.

The following passages are excerpted from recent essays about flying.

Passage 1

Flying alone in an open plane is the purest experience of flight possible. That pure experience is felt at its most intense in acrobatic flying, when
Line you are upside down, or pointed at the sky or at
5 the earth, and moving in ways that you can only in the unsubstantial medium of the air. Acrobatic flying is a useless skill in its particulars—nobody *needs* to do a loop or a roll, not even a fighter pilot—but this skill extends your control of the
10 plane and yourself and makes extreme actions in the sky comfortable. When you reach the top of a loop, upside down and engine at full throttle, and tilt your head back to pick up the horizon line behind you, you are as far outside instinctive hu-
15 man behavior as you can go—hanging in space, the sky below you and the earth above, inscribing a circle on emptiness. And then the nose drops across the horizon; your speed increases and the plane scoops through into normal flight, and you
20 are back in the normal world, with the earth put back in its place. The going out and coming back are what makes a loop so satisfying.

After a while, that is. At first it was terrifying, like being invited to a suicide that you didn't want
25 to commit. "This is a loop," my instructor said casually. He lowered the plane's nose to gain airspeed, and then pulled sharply up. The earth, and my stomach, fell away from me; and we were upside down, and I could feel gravity clawing at
30 me, pulling me out into the mile of empty space between me and the ground. I grabbed at the sides of the cockpit and hung on until gravity was on my side again.

"You seemed a little nervous that time," the
35 instructor said when the plane was right side up again. "You've got to have confidence in that seat belt, or you'll never do a decent loop. So this time,

GO ON TO NEXT PAGE ▶

when we get on top, I want you to put both arms out of the cockpit." And I did it. It was like step-
40 ping off a bridge, but I did it, and the belt held, and the plane came round. And after that I could fly a loop. It was, as I said, satisfying.

Passage 2

The black plane dropped spinning, and flattened out spinning the other way; it began to
45 carve the air into forms that built wildly and musi-cally on each other and never ended. Reluctantly, I started paying attention. Rahm drew high above the world an inexhaustibly glorious line; it piled over our heads in loops and arabesques. The plane
50 moved every way a line can move, and it con-trolled three dimensions, so the line carved mas-sive and subtle slits in the air like sculptures. The plane looped the loop, seeming to arch its back like a gymnast; it stalled, dropped, and spun out of
55 it climbing; it spiraled and knifed west on one side's wings and back east on another; it turned cartwheels, which must be physically impossible; it played with its own line like a cat with yarn. How did the pilot know where in the air he was? If
60 he got lost, the ground would swat him.

His was pure energy and naked spirit. I have thought about it for years. Rahm's line unrolled in time. Like music, it split the bulging rim of the future along its seam. It pried out the present. We
65 watchers waited for the split-second curve of beauty in the present to reveal itself. The human pilot, Dave Rahm, worked in the cockpit right at the plane's nose; his very body tore into the future for us and reeled it down upon us like a curling peel.

70 Like any fine artist, he controlled the tension of the audience's longing. You desired, unwit-tingly, a certain kind of roll or climb, or a return to a certain portion of the air, and he fulfilled your hope slantingly, like a poet, or evaded it until you
75 thought you would burst, and then fulfilled it sur-prisingly, so you gasped and cried out.

The oddest, most exhilarating and exhausting thing was this: he never quit. The music had no periods, no rests or endings; the poetry's beautiful
80 sentence never ended; the line had no finish; the sculptured forms piled overhead, one into another without surcease. Who could breathe, in a world where rhythm itself had no periods?

I went home and thought about Rahm's per-
85 formance that night, and the next day, and the next.

I had thought I knew my way around beauty a little bit. I knew I had devoted a good part of my life to it, memorizing poetry and focusing my
90 attention on complexity of rhythm in particular, on force, movement, repetition, and surprise, in both poetry and prose. Now I had stood among dandelions between two asphalt runways in Bellingham, Washington, and begun learning
95 about beauty. Even the Boston Museum of Fine Arts was never more inspiring than this small northwestern airport on this time-killing Sunday afternoon in June. Nothing on earth is more glad-dening than knowing we must roll up our sleeves
100 and move back the boundaries of the humanly possible once more.

---

37. According to the author of Passage 1, training in acrobatic flying

(A) has only theoretical value
(B) expands a pilot's range of capabilities
(C) is an essential part of general pilot training
(D) comes naturally to most pilots
(E) should be required only of fighter pilots

38. The word "medium" in line 6 means

(A) midpoint
(B) appropriate occupation
(C) method of communication
(D) environment
(E) compromise

39. To "pick up the horizon line" (line 13) is to

(A) lift it higher
(B) spot it visually
(C) measure its distance
(D) choose it eagerly
(E) increase its visibility

40. Passage 1 suggests that the author's grabbing at the sides of the cockpit (lines 31–33) was

(A) instinctive   (B) terrifying   (C) essential
(D) habit forming   (E) life threatening

41. The word "held" (line 40) most nearly means

(A) carried   (B) detained   (C) accommodated
(D) remained valid   (E) maintained its grasp

42. By putting both arms out of the cockpit (lines 38–40), the author

(A) chooses the path of least resistance
(B) enables himself to steer the plane more freely
(C) relies totally on his seat belt to keep him safe
(D) allows himself to give full expression to his nervousness
(E) is better able to breathe deeply and relax

43. The author's use of the word "satisfying" (line 42) represents

(A) a simile   (B) an understatement
(C) a fallacy   (D) a euphemism
(E) a hypothesis

GO ON TO NEXT PAGE ▶

44. The author of Passage 2 mentions her initial reluctance to watch the stunt flying (lines 46–47) in order to

(A) demonstrate her hostility to commercial entertainment
(B) reveal her fear of such dangerous enterprises
(C) minimize her participation in aerial acrobatics
(D) indicate how captivating the demonstration was
(E) emphasize the acuteness of her perceptions

45. By fulfilling "your hope slantingly, like a poet" (lines 73–74), the author means that

(A) the pilot flew the plane on a diagonal
(B) Rahm was a writer of popular verse
(C) the pilot had a bias against executing certain kinds of rolls
(D) Rahm refused to satisfy your expectations directly
(E) the pilot's sense of aesthetic judgment was askew

46. At the end of Passage 2, the author is left feeling

(A) empty in the aftermath of the stunning performance she has seen
(B) jubilant at the prospect of moving from Boston to Washington
(C) exhilarated by her awareness of new potentials for humanity
(D) glad that she has not wasted any more time memorizing poetry
(E) surprised by her response to an art form she had not previously believed possible

47. Compared with Passage 2, Passage 1 is

(A) less informative
(B) more tentative
(C) more argumentative
(D) more speculative
(E) less lyrical

48. How would the author of Passage 2 most likely react to the assessment of acrobatic flying in lines 6–11?

(A) She would consider it too utilitarian an assessment of an aesthetic experience.
(B) She would reject it as an inaccurate description of the pilot's technique.
(C) She would admire it as a poetic evocation of the pilot's art.
(D) She would criticize it as a digression from the author's main point.
(E) She would regard it as too effusive to be appropriate to its subject.

IF YOU FINISH IN LESS THAN 25 MINUTES, YOU MAY CHECK YOUR WORK ON THIS SECTION ONLY. DO NOT TURN TO ANY OTHER SECTION IN THE TEST.

STOP

Reference

$A = \pi r^2$
$C = 2\pi r$

$A = \frac{1}{2}bh$

$V = \ell wh$

$V = \pi r^2 h$

$c^2 = a^2 + b^2$

Special Right Triangles

Number of degrees in a circle: 360
Sum of the measures, in degrees, of the three angles of a triangle: 180

21. If $2x - 1 = 9$, what is $20x - 1$?

(A) 19 (B) 80 (C) 90 (D) 99 (E) 100

22. If $8 - (8 + w) = 8$, then $w =$

(A) −16 (B) −8 (C) 0 (D) 8 (E) 16

23. One positive number is $\frac{1}{5}$ of another number. If the product of the numbers is 20, what is their sum?

(A) 4 (B) 8 (C) 10 (D) 12 (E) 20

24. Mr. Riccardo wrote a number on the chalkboard. When he added 3 to the number, he got the same result as when he multiplied the number by 3. What is the number he wrote?

(A) −3 (B) 0 (C) 1.5 (D) $\sqrt{3}$ (E) 3

25. If a team played g games and lost l of them, what fraction of the games played did the team win?

(A) $\frac{l-g}{l}$ (B) $\frac{l-g}{g}$ (C) $\frac{g-l}{g}$

(D) $\frac{g}{g-l}$ (E) $\frac{g-l}{l}$

26. If Steven was born on Friday, September 13, 1998, and Daniel was born exactly 200 days later, on what day of the week was Daniel born?

(A) Monday (B) Tuesday (C) Friday
(D) Saturday (E) Sunday

27. In the figure above, the shaded region is bounded by two semicircles and two sides of a square. If the area of the square is 20, what is the area of the shaded region?

(A) $20 - \pi$ (B) $5(4 - \pi)$ (C) 4π
(D) $\sqrt{20}(2 + \pi)$ (E) $2\sqrt{20} + 10\pi$

28. If $a - b = 10$, $b - c = 20$ and $c - d = 30$, what is the value of $a - d$?

(A) 40 (B) 50 (C) 60 (D) 80 (E) 100

GO ON TO NEXT PAGE ▶

Student-Produced Response Directions

In questions 29–38, first solve the problem, and then enter your answer on the grid provided on the answer sheet. The instructions for entering your answers follow.

- First, write your answer in the boxes at the top of the grid.
- Second, grid your answer in the columns below the boxes.
- Use the fraction bar in the first row or the decimal point in the second row to enter fractions and decimals.

Answer: $\frac{8}{15}$

Write your answer in the boxes

Grid-in your answer

Answer: 1.75

Answer: 100

Either position is acceptable

- Grid only one space in each column.
- Entering the answer in the boxes is recommended as an aid in gridding but is not required.
- The machine scoring your exam can read only what you grid, so you **must grid-in your answers correctly to get credit.**
- If a question has more than one correct answer, grid-in only one of them.
- The grid does not have a minus sign; so no answer can be negative.
- A mixed number *must* be converted to an improper fraction or a decimal before it is gridded. Enter $1\frac{1}{4}$ as $\frac{5}{4}$ or 1.25; the machine will interpret 11/4 as $\frac{11}{4}$ and mark it wrong.

- **All decimals must be entered as accurately as possible.** Here are three acceptable ways of gridding

$$\frac{3}{11} = 0.272727\ldots$$

- Note that rounding to .273 is acceptable because you are using the full grid, but you would receive **no credit** for .3 or .27, because they are less accurate.

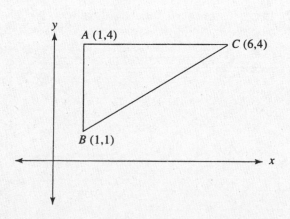

29. In the figure above, what is the area of △ABC?

30. In the figure above, what is the value of *a* if *b* = 60?

31. If the average (arithmetic mean) of 20, 30, 40, 50 and *y* is 100, what is the value of *y*?

32. At Central High School, 40% of the members of the Spanish club are boys. How many members does the club have if 30 of the members are girls?

33. Line l passes through the points (1, 3) and (4, 7). Line m passes through (7, 5) parallel to l, and line n passes through (7, 5) perpendicular to l. What is the sum of the slopes of lines m and n?

34. The first two terms of a sequence are 1 and 2. Every other term in the sequence is the sum of the two terms immediately preceding it. For example, the third term is $1 + 2 = 3$ and the fourth term is $2 + 3 = 5$. How many of the first 100 terms are odd?

35. If $5(\sqrt{x} - 3) = 3\sqrt{x} - 5$, then $x =$

36. If 3 bangs = 2 clangs and 4 bangs = 5 tangs, then 1 clang is equal to how many tangs?

37. There are 25 students in a class, 40% of whom are girls. If the average (arithmetic mean) weight of the girls is 120 pounds and the average weight of the boys in the class is 150 pounds, what is the average weight of the children in the class?

38. In the figure above, the diagonals of the three squares are 3, 4, and 5. What is the ratio of the shaded area to the striped area?

IF YOU FINISH IN LESS THAN 25 MINUTES, YOU MAY CHECK YOUR WORK ON THIS SECTION ONLY. DO NOT TURN TO ANY OTHER SECTION IN THE TEST.

STOP

490   ▶ **CHAPTER 11 / Model Test F**

Improving Sentence Directions

Some or all parts of the following sentences are underlined. The first answer choice, (A), simply repeats the underlined part of the sentence. The other four choices present four alternative ways to phrase the underlined part. Select the answer that produces the most effective sentence, one that is clear and exact, and blacken the appropriate space on your answer sheet. In selecting your choice, be sure that it is standard written English and that it expresses the meaning of the original sentence.

EXAMPLE:

The first biography of author Eudora Welty came out in 1998, <u>and she was eighty-nine years old at the time</u>.

(A) and she was eighty-nine years old at the time
(B) at the time when she was eighty-nine
(C) upon becoming an eighty-nine year old
(D) when she was eighty-nine
(E) at the age of eighty-nine years old

SAMPLE ANSWER:

Ⓐ Ⓑ Ⓒ ● Ⓔ

---

1. Maya Angelou is <u>almost as talented a performer as she is a poet</u>.

    (A) almost as talented a performer as she is a poet
    (B) almost equally talented, whether a performer or a poet
    (C) of the same talent as a performer and a poet, almost
    (D) a talented poet, and almost so talented in performing
    (E) talented as a poet, with almost as much talent in performing

2. The <u>imminent historian stood</u> in bed, recuperating from a viral infection, while his paper was being read at the convention.

    (A) imminent historian stood
    (B) imminent historian remained
    (C) eminent historian stayed
    (D) eminent historian stood
    (E) eminent historian had remained

3. At the zoo, the brightly plumaged <u>birds that fluttered</u> overhead like tropical flowers in a breeze.

    (A) birds that fluttered   (B) birds fluttering
    (C) birds which fluttered   (D) birds fluttered
    (E) birds aflutter

4. In India, Mahatma Gandhi was more than a <u>political leader he was</u> the enlightened one embodying the soul of the nation.

    (A) political leader he was
    (B) political leader; he was
    (C) political leader, he was
    (D) political leader which was
    (E) political leader, although he was

5. When the National Association for the Advancement of Colored People examined discrimination in the music business, <u>its report concentrating on offstage employment opportunities</u>.

    (A) its report concentrating on offstage employment opportunities
    (B) its report having concentrated on offstage employment opportunities
    (C) its report concentrated on offstage employment opportunities
    (D) its report concentrating in offstage employment opportunities
    (E) its report concentrated in offstage employment opportunities

6. <u>Some doctors volunteer to serve the poor in addition to their regular practices, they find</u> healing the poor provides different insights than healing the rich.

    (A) Some doctors volunteer to serve the poor in addition to their regular practices, they find
    (B) Besides their regular practices, some doctors serve the poor to find
    (C) In addition to running their regular practices, some doctors volunteer to serve the poor; they find that
    (D) Some doctors, in volunteering to serve the poor, find
    (E) Running their regular practices and serving the poor help some doctors realize that

7. Because of a teacher shortage in the math and science disciplines, educators are encouraging retired scientists and engineers to pursue a second career in teaching.

   (A) Because of a teacher shortage in the math and science disciplines, educators are encouraging
   (B) Educators, faced with a teacher shortage in technical disciplines have encouraged
   (C) In addition to a teacher shortage in the math and science areas, educators encourage
   (D) Teacher shortages in the math and science disciplines have forced educators to hire
   (E) Because there is a teacher shortage in the math and science disciplines, educators encourage

8. Neither the principal or the teachers had been satisfied with the addition of a crossing guard, and wanted a traffic light installed at the street crossing.

   (A) Neither the principal or the teachers had been satisfied with the addition of a crossing guard, and
   (B) Neither the principal nor the teachers were satisfied with the addition of a crossing guard; they
   (C) Because neither the principal or the teachers had been satisfied with the addition of a cross-ing guard, they
   (D) As the result of the addition of a crossing guard, the principal and the teachers
   (E) Neither the principal nor the teachers feels the crossing guard is sufficient; and they

9. Most of the students like to read these kind of detective stories as recreational reading.

   (A) these kind of detective stories
   (B) these kind of detective story
   (C) this kind of detective story
   (D) this kinds of detective story
   (E) those kind of detective story

10. Because of his now chronic throat ailment, the tenor recently has not and apparently never will sing again.

    (A) has not and apparently never will sing
    (B) had not sung and apparently never would sing
    (C) has not and apparently never would sing
    (D) has not sung and apparently never will sing
    (E) had not and apparently never will sing

11. Having the best record for attendance, the school awarded him a medal at graduation.

    (A) the school awarded him a medal
    (B) the school awarded a medal to him
    (C) he was awarded a medal by the school
    (D) a medal was awarded to him by the school
    (E) a school medal was awarded to him

12. Several regulations were proposed by the president of the university that had a sexist bias, according to women students.

    (A) Several regulations were proposed by the president of the university that
    (B) Several regulations were proposed by the president of the university who
    (C) The proposal of several regulations by the president of the university which
    (D) The president of the university, who proposed several regulations that
    (E) The president of the university proposed several regulations that

13. The difference between the candidates is that one is radical; the other, conservative.

    (A) one is radical; the other, conservative
    (B) one is radical; the other being conservative
    (C) while one is radical; the other, conservative
    (D) one is radical, the other, conservative
    (E) one is radical, although the other is more conservative

14. Police academies, on seeing as how new recruits lack basic driving skills, are teaching recruits the basics on test fields and neighborhood streets.

    (A) Police academies, on seeing as how new recruits lack basic driving skills, are teaching
    (B) Since new police recruits lack basic driving skills, police academies are teaching
    (C) Police academies, because new recruits are lacking basic driving skills, teach
    (D) As a result of new recruits lacking basic driving skills, police academies are teaching
    (E) Even though new recruits lack basic driving skills, police academies are teaching

GO ON TO NEXT PAGE ▶

15. Although the babysitter had expected the twins to protest being told to go to bed, they went to their room without scarcely a murmur.

(A) being told to go to bed, they went to their room without scarcely a murmur
(B) being told to go to bed, they had gone off to their room without scarcely a murmur
(C) being told that they should go to bed, they went to their room without scarcely a murmur
(D) being told to go to bed, however, they went to their room without scarcely a murmur
(E) being told to go to bed, they went to their room with scarcely a murmur

16. Although hydroponics is unsuitable for growing root vegetables and trees, which require soil and space, the system is ideal for cultivating a wide variety of plants such as tomatoes and beans.

(A) Although hydroponics is unsuitable for growing root vegetables and trees, which require
(B) Although hydroponics being unsuitable for growing root vegetables and trees, which require
(C) Although hydroponics is unsuitable for growing root vegetables and trees, being that they require
(D) Although hydroponics is unsuited to grow root vegetables and trees, these require
(E) Although hydroponics is unsuitable for growing root vegetables and trees, and they require

17. Acutely aware of how much he owed to the generosity of Mr. Fezziwig, young Ebenezer addressed his benefactor respectively.

(A) Acutely aware of how much he owed to the generosity of Mr. Fezziwig, young Ebenezer addressed his benefactor respectively.
(B) Being that he was acutely aware of how much he owed to the generosity of Mr. Fezziwig, young Ebenezer addressed his benefactor respectively.
(C) Young Ebenezer was acutely aware of how much he owed to the generosity of Mr. Fezziwig, so he addressed his benefactor respectively.
(D) Acutely aware of how much he owed to the generosity of Mr. Fezziwig, young Ebenezer addressed his benefactor respectfully.
(E) Acutely aware of how much he owed to the generosity of Mr. Fezziwig, young Ebenezer addressed his respective benefactor.

18. Although the suspect resolutely maintained his innocence, the jury found his story entirely incredulous.

(A) the jury found his story entirely incredulous
(B) the jury found his entire story incredulous
(C) his story was found by the jury to be entirely incredulous
(D) the jury found his story entirely incredible
(E) the jury had found his story entirely incredulous

19. Many studies of new drugs are funded by major pharmaceutical firms, which suggests the possibility of bias in their conclusions.

(A) which suggests the possibility of bias in their conclusions
(B) thus the possibility of bias to their conclusions is suggested
(C) a state of affairs that suggests the possibility of bias in their conclusions
(D) and the possibility of bias in their conclusions being suggested
(E) this fact suggests the possibility of bias in their conclusions

20. Intended to promote safety in the workplace, the regulation stipulates that protective goggles must be worn while welding.

(A) that protective goggles must be worn while welding
(B) that protective goggles while welding must be worn
(C) that, while welding, protective goggles must be worn
(D) that one must wear protective goggles while you weld
(E) that you must wear protective goggles when you are welding

GO ON TO NEXT PAGE ▶

21. <u>As</u> <u>some</u> of the conglomerates gain more power,
$\quad$ A $\quad$ B

the legal codes <u>regarding</u> bankruptcy and
$\qquad\qquad\qquad$ C

monopoly <u>will need</u> further consideration.
$\qquad\qquad$ D

<u>No error</u>
E

22. In 1777, the Second Continental Congress

<u>has adopted</u> a resolution <u>to designate</u> the design
$\quad$ A $\qquad\qquad\qquad$ B

for the American flag, <u>but</u> no flags were issued
$\qquad\qquad\qquad$ C

<u>until</u> 1783. <u>No error</u>
$\quad$ D $\qquad$ E

23. He <u>dashed into</u> the burning building, <u>irregardless</u>
$\qquad$ A $\qquad\qquad\qquad$ B

of the risk <u>involved</u>, to warn the
$\qquad\qquad$ C

<u>sleeping occupants.</u> <u>No error</u>
$\qquad$ D $\qquad$ E

24. <u>According to</u> Ms. Lynch's portfolio, <u>there</u> is
$\qquad$ A $\qquad\qquad\qquad$ B

little doubt that she and her staff <u>is</u>
$\qquad\qquad\qquad$ C

<u>eminently qualified</u> for the assignment.
$\qquad$ D

<u>No error</u>
E

25. Neither the Republican members of the

committee <u>who</u> supported the proposed
$\qquad$ A

legislation <u>or</u> the Democratic members who
$\qquad$ B

opposed it controlled a <u>clear majority</u>; the votes of
$\qquad\qquad\qquad$ C

the independents <u>were</u> crucial. <u>No error</u>
$\qquad\qquad$ D $\qquad$ E

26. <u>No one</u> can predict <u>what</u> the <u>affect</u> of the
$\quad$ A $\qquad\qquad$ B $\qquad$ C

government investigations <u>will be</u> on American
$\qquad\qquad\qquad$ D

politics in the near future. <u>No error</u>
$\qquad\qquad\qquad$ E

27. <u>In order to</u> give adequate attention to all students,
$\quad$ A

many teachers <u>prefer</u> team teaching, <u>which</u>
$\qquad\qquad$ B $\qquad\qquad$ C

divides students according to <u>his and her</u> abilities.
$\qquad\qquad\qquad$ D

<u>No error</u>
E

28. I was <u>irritated by</u> <u>you</u> coming into the room <u>as</u>
    　　　　A　　　　B　　　　　　　　　　　C
    you did—<u>shouting</u> and screaming. <u>No error</u>
    　　　　　　D　　　　　　　　　　　　　E

29. Just <u>like</u> prehistoric man, some <u>groups of</u>
    　　　A　　　　　　　　　　　　　　B
    southwestern Indians <u>have dwelled</u> in caves along
    　　　　　　　　　　　C
    <u>steep, rocky</u> ledges. <u>No error</u>
    　　D　　　　　　　　E

30. I <u>find</u> that sculpture <u>more unusual</u> <u>than</u> any of the
    　A　　　　　　　B　　　　　C
    other sculptures exhibited <u>during</u> this special
    　　　　　　　　　　　　　D
    exhibit. <u>No error</u>
    　　　　　E

31. <u>One</u> of the basic economic reactions is <u>that</u> as
    A　　　　　　　　　　　　　　　　　B
    bond prices fall, stock prices <u>rise</u>, and
    　　　　　　　　　　　　　C
    <u>an increase in interest rates</u>. <u>No error</u>
    　　　　　D　　　　　　　　　E

32. <u>Some</u> of the major networks <u>have created</u>
    　A　　　　　　　　　　　　　B
    <u>special prepared</u> news stories about life on city
    　　　C
    streets <u>to publicize</u> the plight of the homeless.
    　　　　　D
    <u>No error</u>
    　E

33. <u>Some women</u> have made a <u>clear-cut choice</u>
    　　A　　　　　　　　　　B
    between a career and motherhood; others have
    <u>been creating</u> a <u>balance between</u> the two.
    　　C　　　　　　D
    <u>No error</u>
    　E

34. The renter of the car <u>initialed</u> the clause in the
    　　　　　　　　　　A
    contract <u>to indicate</u> <u>his</u> awareness that he
    　　　　　B　　　　C
    <u>was liable</u> for any damage to the automobile.
    　D
    <u>No error</u>
    　E

[1] For two hundred years United States citizens have taken for granted their right to life, liberty, and the pursuit of happiness. [2] From the experiences in the former Yugoslavia to the repressive regime in the People's Republic of China, Americans should know, however, that human rights are always in danger.

[3] During the period of the conquistadores and Spanish colonial rule of Latin America, for example. [4] Latin American natives were often violated and repressed by European settlers, an example of this is the fact that the land formerly owned by the native Latin Americans was taken away from them so the people lost the right to own land. [5] Secondly, the Latin American people were forced to work this land as slaves on their own land. [6] These human rights violations were overcome by the independence movements led by such freedom fighters as Bolivar and San Martin in the late 1800s.

[7] In the Soviet Union, the extremely repressive Stalinist regime after WW II violated the rights of the Russian peasants, known as kulaks. [8] Collectivizing their farmlands by force, their rights were violated by Stalin. [9] Therefore, their private possessions were lost. [10] Another way by which they had their human rights violated was by forcing political opponents to remain silent, to work in labor camps, or to be killed. [11] After Stalin's death in 1953, one of his successors, Nikita Khrushchev, attempted to denounce the Stalinist regime. [12] However, it took another thirty years and the collapse of the Soviet Union to bring about basic human rights in Russia.

[13] About the history of human rights violations, the Serbs in the former Yugoslavia and the leaders of Communist China should know that they can't go on forever. [14] Eventually, their power will be usurped, or the people will rise up to claim their God-given human rights.

---

35. Taking into account the sentences that precede and follow sentence 3, which of the following is the best revision of sentence 3?

    (A) As an example, the time that the Spanish were expanding their empire and searching for gold.
    (B) Take, for example, during the era of the conquistadores and Spanish colonial rule in Latin America.
    (C) Consider, for example, the period of the conquistadores and Spanish colonial rule in Latin America.
    (D) The Spanish expanded their empire into Latin America in the 16th century.
    (E) For instance, the period of Spanish colonialism in Latin America, for example.

36. Which of the following is the best revision of sentence 4?

    (A) The land of Latin American natives was confiscated by European settlers. In fact, the rights of the natives to own land was violated and repressed.
    (B) European settlers in Latin America have seized the land and the natives had repressed the right to own property.
    (C) The colonial rulers confiscated the natives' property and denied them the right to own land.
    (D) Having their rights violated, the natives of Latin America had their land taken away. Then the European settlers repress their right to own any land at all.
    (E) The rights of the Latin American natives were violated and repressed. For example, they took their land and they prohibited them from owning land.

GO ON TO NEXT PAGE ▶

37. In the context of paragraph 3, which is the best revision of sentences 8 and 9?

(A) Forcing them to collectivize their farmlands, Stalin confiscated their private property.

(B) One of the ways by which Stalin violated their rights was by forcing people to collectivize their farmlands, thus causing them to lose their right to hold private possessions.

(C) One way in which the kulaks had their rights violated was Stalin forcing them to collectivize their farmlands and therefore, surrender private property.

(D) Having lost the right to own private property, Stalin collectivized the kulaks' farmland.

(E) The loss of private property and the collectivization of farmland was one way by which Stalin violated their rights.

38. Considering the content of the entire essay, which revision of the underlined segment of sentence 13 below provides the best transition between paragraphs 3 and 4?

About the history of human rights violations, the Serbs in the former Yugoslavia and the leaders of Communist China should know that they can't go on forever.

(A) In conclusion,

(B) Finally,

(C) Last but not least,

(D) Based on the history of international agreements on human rights,

(E) If the experience of Latin America and the Soviet Union means anything,

39. On the basis of the essay as a whole, which of the following describes the writer's intention in the last paragraph?

(A) To draw a conclusion based on the evidence in the passage

(B) To prepare readers for the future

(C) To instruct readers about the past

(D) To offer solutions to the problem posed by the essay

(E) To give an example

IF YOU FINISH IN LESS THAN 30 MINUTES, YOU MAY CHECK YOUR WORK ON THIS SECTION ONLY. DO NOT TURN TO ANY OTHER SECTION IN THE TEST.

STOP

Answer Key

Section 1 Critical Reading

1. *D*	10. *C*	19. *D*
2. *E*	11. *C*	20. *C*
3. *A*	12. *A*	21. *D*
4. *D*	13. *E*	22. *B*
5. *B*	14. *B*	23. *E*
6. *C*	15. *B*	24. *E*
7. *D*	16. *A*	
8. *E*	17. *E*	
9. *C*	18. *B*	

Section 2 Mathematics

1. *C*	8. *A*	15. *B*
2. *C*	9. *C*	16. *C*
3. *D*	10. *A*	17. *A*
4. *B*	11. *D*	18. *D*
5. *C*	12. *A*	19. *E*
6. *D*	13. *D*	20. *A*
7. *B*	14. *B*	

Section 3 Critical Reading

25. *A*	33. *B*	41. *E*
26. *C*	34. *A*	42. *C*
27. *C*	35. *B*	43. *B*
28. *A*	36. *E*	44. *D*
29. *E*	37. *B*	45. *D*
30. *C*	38. *D*	46. *C*
31. *E*	39. *B*	47. *E*
32. *D*	40. *A*	48. *A*

Section 4 Mathematics

21. *D*	24. *C*	27. *B*
22. *B*	25. *C*	28. *C*
23. *D*	26. *B*	

or *15/2*

or *1.87*
or *1.88*

37.
```
1  3  /  5
```
or *2.6*

38.
```
         1
```

Section 5 Writing Skills

1. A	14. B	27. D
2. C	15. E	28. B
3. D	16. A	29. E
4. B	17. D	30. E
5. C	18. D	31. D
6. C	19. C	32. C
7. A	20. E	33. C
8. B	21. E	34. E
9. C	22. A	35. C
10. D	23. B	36. C
11. C	24. C	37. A
12. E	25. B	38. E
13. A	26. C	39. A

Scoring Chart—Model Test F

Critical Reading Sections

Section 1: 24 Questions (1–24)

Number correct	_____	(A)
Number omitted	_____	(B)
Number incorrect	_____	(C)
$\frac{1}{4}$ (C)	_____	(D)
(A) − (D)	_____	Raw Score I

Section 3: 24 Questions (25–48)

Number correct	_____	(A)
Number omitted	_____	(B)
Number incorrect	_____	(C)
$\frac{1}{4}$ (C)	_____	(D)
(A) − (D)	_____	Raw Score II

Total Critical Reading Raw Score

Raw Scores I + II   _____

Mathematics Sections

Section 2: 20 Questions (1–20)

Number correct	_____	(A)
Number omitted	_____	(B)
Number incorrect	_____	(C)
$\frac{1}{4}$ (C)	_____	(D)
(A) − (D)	_____	Raw Score I

Section 4: First 8 Questions (21–28)

Number correct	_____	(A)
Number omitted	_____	(B)
Number incorrect	_____	(C)
$\frac{1}{4}$ (C)	_____	(D)
(A) − (D)	_____	Raw Score II

Section 4: Next 10 Questions (29–38)

Number correct   _____ Raw Score III

Total Mathematical Raw Score

Raw Scores I + II + III   _____

NOTE: In each section (A) + (B) + (C) should equal the number of questions in that section.

Writing Skills Section

Section 5: 39 Questions (1–39)

Number correct	_____	(A)
Number omitted	_____	(B)
Number incorrect	_____	(C)
$\frac{1}{4}$ (C)	_____	(D)

Writing Skills Raw Score

(A) − (D)   _____

Evaluation Chart

Study your score. Your raw score is an indication of your probable achievement on the PSAT/NMSQT. As a guide to the amount of work you need or want to do with this book, study the following.

Raw Score			Self-rating
Critical Reading	*Mathematics*	*Writing*	
42–48	35–38	33–39	Superior
37–46	30–34	28–32	Very good
32–36	25–29	23–27	Good
26–35	21–24	17–22	Above average
20–25	17–20	12–16	Average
12–19	10–16	7–11	Below average
less than 12	less than 10	less than 7	Inadequate

Answer Explanations

Section 1 Critical Reading

1. *D* Fast-food restaurants are growing more popular in France. The traditional café is therefore growing less popular (falling "victim to the growing popularity" of McBurgers) and is slowly *becoming extinct* (vanishing, disappearing; dying out).

2. *E Although* signals a contrast. You would expect the coach to be *jubilant* (extremely joyful) about her team's victory. Instead, she was *disheartened* (discouraged).

3. *A Bantering* or joking remarks are clearly *inappropriate* in a serious speech.

4. *D* People uncomfortable with math would be likely to think the field should be *left to* those gifted in such an *esoteric* (hard to understand; known only to a chosen few) subject.

5. *B* A writer whose work was universally acclaimed or applauded and whose reputation was not yet *tarnished* or stained would be at the *zenith* or high point of her career.

6. *C* The passage contrasts the image of Nightingale, the night nurse carrying a lamp as she walked the wards, with the image of Nightingale, the hospital authority. What is more, it states that Nightingale "came into her own as the world's most renowned authority on hospital reform." To come into one's own is to achieve one's potential, to become fulfilled. According to the author, Nightingale did not reach her full potential until she became a recognized authority on hospital reform. To the author, therefore, *her greatest accomplishments were in improving hospital planning and administration.*

7. *D* When Nightingale addressed these aspects of hospital construction and management, she *dealt with* them thoroughly and in great detail.

8. *E* In this passage, the author celebrates the return into print of Green's novels and makes a case for her as the mother of detective fiction. Thus, the author's purpose is most likely to *reclaim* Green, *a forgotten literary pioneer*, from a century's worth of neglect, in process restoring her reputation.

9. *C* The publication of *The Leavenworth Case* marked or *denoted* (signaled) the first appearance of Inspector Gryce.

10. *C* The entire passage examines Bethune's beliefs in the ultimate victory of racial justice and in the possibility of winning whites to her cause.

In addition, it clearly shows Bethune, in her work to get her people represented in all public problems, having an impact on her people's progress.

11. *C* You can arrive at the correct answer by the process of elimination.

Williams assisted Bethune in influencing the advancement of blacks within the NYA. Therefore, you can eliminate Choices B and D. The opening sentence of the first paragraph indicates Williams was one of Bethune's white friends; references to him in the second paragraph suggest he was a liberal. Therefore, you can eliminate Choice A. Nothing in the passage suggests Williams was religious. Therefore, you can eliminate Choice E. Only Choice C is left. It is the correct answer.

12. *A* Bethune's success in getting Dickerson's appointment is a clear example of her impact.

Choice B is incorrect. The author is stressing how helpful Bethune was to Dickerson, not how different Bethune's career was from Dickerson's. Choice C is incorrect. Dickerson is not the subject of the paragraph that follows. Choice D is incorrect. The author brings up Bethune's belief in the "New Negro" well after he mentions her assistance to Dickerson. He draws no connection between Dickerson and the "New Negro." Choice E is incorrect. The author is making a point about Bethune, not about Dickerson.

13. *E* Bethune was the intermediary who helped arrange for Dickerson's new position. She was instrumental or *helpful* in gaining this end.

14. *B* By leading America to a "full realization of its democratic ideas," the New Negro would be *helping America accomplish its egalitarian goals.*

15. *B* The author compares and contrasts Bethune with her white liberal friends. The author directly quotes the wording of Bethune's 1944 appeals for black representation. The author gives concrete examples of the ways in which Bethune remained a black partisan champion of the New Deal. The author constantly reiterates the idea that Bethune had an ongoing influence on black progress during the Roosevelt years. However, the author uses figurative language only minimally and never develops an extended metaphor.

16. *A* Dickens implies that Gradgrind is so peremptory (absolute; dogmatic) about facts that he would insist upon the fact that his given name was, in fact, Thomas.

17. *E* Gradgrind carries scales and a rule in his pocket to "weigh and measure any parcel of human na-

ture." Though Dickens plays upon several meanings of *rule* here, the word basically refers to a ruler or measuring stick.

18. *B* As he walks home, Gradgrind is in "a state of considerable satisfaction." He is pleased with himself and with the school he has created; his mood is clearly one of *complacency* or smugness.

19. *D* Dickens is poking fun at Gradgrind's teaching methods and is thus *broadly satirical* (full of ridicule).

20. *C* Gradgrind never introduces his pupils to nursery rhymes or to fantasy creatures such as ogres. This suggests that he rejects from his curriculum anything that is in the least *fanciful* or imaginative.

21. *D* Dickens has written the passage from the point of view of an omniscient narrator, *an observer who knows all about Gradgrind's thoughts and feelings.* The narrator knows all about Gradgrind's emotional state, his goals as headmaster, his manner of speech. In short, he knows Gradgrind through and through.

22. *B* The little Gradgrinds, having studied the Great Bear and Charles's Wain, had never "known wonder on the subject of stars." This suggests that the Great Bear and the Wain are constellations, or *groupings of stars*.

23. *E* Gradgrind's main idea is to fill his pupils full of *facts*, particularly facts about *science* (statistics, constellations, graminivorous quadrupeds, etc.).

24. *E* The famous cow with the crumpled horn ("The House That Jack Built") and the yet more famous cow who swallowed Tom Thumb in the folk tale are legendary *fictional characters* with whose celebrity the young Gradgrinds are unacquainted.

Section 2 Mathematics

For many problems, the explanation provides a reference to one or more **KEY FACTS** from Chapter 9. These are the mathematical facts that you need to solve that problem. If a solution refers to **KEY FACT J2**, for example, the solution depends on the second **KEY FACT** discussed in Section J of Chapter 9.

For some problems, an alternative solution, indicated by two asterisks (**), follows the first solution. When this occurs, usually one of the solutions is the direct mathematical one and the other is based on one of the tactics discussed in Chapters 8 and 9.

1. *C* $35 = (7 - 2)(7 - m) = 5(7 - m) = 35 - 5m \Rightarrow 5m = 0 \Rightarrow m = 0.$

2. *C* Since the sum of the measures of the three angles of a triangle is 180° (**KEY FACT J1**) then
$$40 + 2a + 3a = 180 \Rightarrow 40 + 5a = 180 \Rightarrow$$
$$5a = 140 \Rightarrow a = 28.$$

Use **TACTIC 8-6. If you trust the diagram, there are many ways to go. If *a* were 45, 2*a* would be 90, which is clearly wrong. Likewise, if *a* were 10, 2*a* would be 20, which is also way off. In fact, ∠*S* appears to be *about* a 90° angle. So, $3a \approx 90$, which means $a \approx 30$. Choose 28.

3. *D* To convert 225 minutes to hours, divide by 60: the quotient is 3 and the remainder is 45. Therefore, 225 minutes from 10:05 A.M. is 3 hours and 45 minutes from 10:05 A.M., which is 1:50 P.M.

**If you divide 225 by 60 on your calculator, you get 3.75, and then you have to convert 0.75, or $\frac{3}{4}$, of an hour to 45 minutes.

4. *B* The easiest solution is to quickly reduce, by repeatedly dividing each side by 9:
$$(9)(9)(9)n = \frac{\overset{3}{\cancel{(27)}}{}^{1}(27)^{3}}{n}. \text{ So } n = \frac{1}{n} \Rightarrow n = 1.$$

**Of course, you can rewrite the equation as $n^2 = \frac{(27)(27)}{(9)(9)(9)}$ and use your calculator: $n^2 = 1.$

5. *C* Since the two angles, *x* and *y*, form a straight line, $x + y = 180$ (**KEY FACT I2**). Also, it is given that $x = y + 140.$ Therefore,
$$(y + 140) + y = 180 \Rightarrow 2y + 140 = 180 \Rightarrow$$
$$2y = 40 \Rightarrow y = 20.$$

Use **TACTIC 8-1 and backsolve. Start with 20, Choice C. If $y = 20$, then
$x = 140 + 20 = 160$, and $20 + 160 = 180$; so it works. The answer is Choice C.

6. *D* If $x^2 = 10$, then $x^6 = x^2 \cdot x^2 \cdot x^2 = 10 \times 10 \times 10 = 1000.$

**Use your calculator: $x = \sqrt{10}$, and $(\sqrt{10})^6 = 1000.$

7. *B* The average of four consecutive integers is the average of the middle two and so is always 0.5 more than an integer: the average of 1, 2, 3, and 4 is 2.5; the average of 10, 11, 12, and 13 is 11.5; and the average of 98, 99, 100, and 101 is 99.5. Only II is true.

8. *A* Calculate each 1995 salary by multiplying each 1985 salary by (1 + the percent change). Ann had the highest 1995 salary:
$$\$4200(1.06) = \$4452.$$

9. *C* For some number x, the measures of the angles are x, $2x$, and $3x$; so $180 = x + 2x + 3x = 6x \Rightarrow x = 30$. Therefore, the triangle is a 30-60-90 triangle, and the ratio of the sides is $1:\sqrt{3}:2$.

10. *A* The formula for the area of a circle is: $A = \pi r^2$.
Divide both sides by π: $r^2 = \frac{A}{\pi}$
Take the square root of each side: $r = \sqrt{\frac{A}{\pi}}$.
The diameter is twice the radius: $d = 2r = 2\sqrt{\frac{A}{\pi}}$.

**Let the radius of the circle be 1. Then, the area is π, and the diameter is 2. Which of the five choices is equal to 2 when $A = \pi$? Only $2\sqrt{\frac{A}{\pi}}$.

11. *D* Draw diagrams. *A, B, C could be* the vertices of a right triangle (I is true). If *A, B, C* were the vertices of a square, then $AC = \sqrt{2}AB$ (II is false). *A, B, C could* all lie on a circle. In fact, the only way they couldn't would be if they all were on the same line (III is true). Statements I and III only are true.

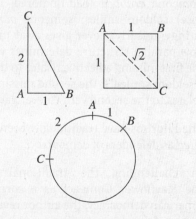

12. *A* On the first painting, Ross made a 20% profit; so if he bought it for x dollars and sold it for \$1200,
$1200 = x + .20x = 1.2x \Rightarrow$
$x = 1200 \div 1.2 = 1000$. His profit was \$200.
On the second painting, Ross lost 20%; so if he bought it for y dollars and sold it for \$1200,
$1200 = y - .20y = .80y \Rightarrow$
$y = 1200 \div .80 = 1500$. His loss was \$300.
In all, he lost exactly \$100.

13. *D* Draw a picture. The minute hand, of course, is pointing right at 6. The hour hand, however, is *not* pointing at 3. It was pointing at 3 at 3:00, half an hour ago. The hour hand is now one-half of the way between the 3 and 4. So there are 15° between the hour hand and 4 and another 60° between 4 and 6, a total of 75°.

**If you can't figure the answer out exactly, guess. From the picture, you should see that the angle definitely measures more than 60° and less than 90°. Eliminate Choices A, B, and E.

14. *B* Check each statement. The only factors of 15 are ±1, ±3, ±5, and ±15. If m is any of these, $\frac{15}{m}$ is an odd integer. (I is false.) Eliminate Choices A and D. Could $\frac{m}{15}$ be an even integer? Sure, it could be *any* even integer; for example, if $m = 30$, $\frac{m}{15} = 2$; if $m = 150$, $\frac{m}{15} = 10$. (II is true.) Eliminate Choice C. Could $15m$ be prime? No, $15m$ is divisible by 15. (III is false.) II is the only true statement.

15. *B* Since 1, 2, 3, and 6 are each divisors of 6, the remainder is 0 when they are divided into 6. The only nonzero remainders occur when 6 is divided by 4, in which case the remainder is 2, and when 6 is divided by 5, in which case the remainder is 1. The sum of the remainders is 3.

16. *C* Since $a < b$, when a is divided by b, the quotient is 0 and the remainder is a; so $a*b = a$. When *any* number is divided by a, the remainder must be less than a, and so the maximum value of $b*a$ is $a - 1$. Therefore, the greatest possible value of $a*b + b*a$ is $a + (a - 1) = 2a - 1$.

Use **TACTIC 8-2: plug in numbers. Let $a = 2$ and $b = 3$. When 2 is divided by 3, the quotient is 0 and the remainder is 2:
$$2 = 0(3) + 2. \text{ So } 2*3 = 2.$$
When 3 is divided by 2, the quotient is 1 and the remainder is 1:
$$3 = 1(2) + 1. \text{ So } 3*2 = 1.$$
$2*3 + 3*2 = 2 + 1 = 3$. Which choice equals 3 when $a = 2$ and $b = 3$? Only $2a - 1$.

17. *A* Use **TACTIC 9-G4**: When you have more than two equations, add them

$$x + y = 10$$
$$y + z = 15$$
$$+\ x + z = 17$$
$$2x + 2y + 2z = 42$$

Divide by 2: $x + y + z = 21$
To get the average,
divide the sum by 3: $\dfrac{x + y + z}{3} = \dfrac{21}{3} = 7$

(*Note:* you *could* solve for *x*, *y*, *z*, but you shouldn't.)

18. *D* Check each choice. (A) If $x = 5$, $\sqrt{x - 1} = 2$. (B) This one is more difficult; the only possibility is $x = 1$, in which case $\sqrt{x^2 - 1} = 0$. If you don't see that immediately, keep Choice B under consideration, and test the rest. (C) If $x = 1$, $\frac{1}{x} = 1$. (D) For positive *x*, $\frac{x + 2}{x + 1}$ is always greater than 1 but less than 2; $\frac{x + 2}{x + 1}$ cannot be an integer—that's it. If you didn't reason that out, check Choice E. $\frac{7}{x + 1}$ is an integer if $x = 6$. You should have eliminated at least Choices A, C, and E.

19. *E* Any odd number is the sum of two consecutive integers: $6 + 7 = 13$ and $7 + 8 = 15$. Eliminate Choices B and D. Next try the sum of three consecutive integers: $3 + 4 + 5 = 12$. Eliminate Choice A. Now try four consecutive integers: $2 + 3 + 4 + 5 = 14$. Eliminate Choice C. The answer must be 16.

20. *A* If *p* painters can complete a job in *d* days, then 1 painter will take *p* times as long: it would take 1 painter *pd* days to complete the job and $\frac{1}{4}pd = \frac{pd}{4}$ days to complete 25% of the job. Finally, if the work is divided up among *q* painters it would take $\frac{pd}{4} \div q = \frac{pd}{4q}$ days.

Use TACTIC 8-2: plug in easy-to-use numbers. If 2 painters can complete the job in 4 days, it would take them 1 day to complete 25% of the job. It would take 1 painter twice as long—2 days. Which choice is equal to 2, when $p = 2$, $d = 4$, and $q = 1$? Only $\frac{pd}{4q}$. Remember: Test each choice with your calculator and eliminate a choice as soon as it is clear that it is not equal to 2.

Section 3 Critical Reading

25. *A* Because it can now be grown successfully in America, the once-rare fruit is now *accessible* or readily available to American consumers.

26. *C* Someone always searching for new ways to do things is by definition *an innovator* (someone who introduces changes into the existing ways of doing things).

27. *C* A trip to France, with all the chances for conversing in French it would provide, would be a practical or *pragmatic* test of how much you had learned of conversational French.

28. *A* Since Cherokee society already granted certain rights to women, it did not break with or *violate* Cherokee custom to allow women their rights.

29. *E* Though scientists might be upset by *erroneous* (faulty) or *derivative* (unoriginal) work, the scientific community would be most shocked by *fraudulent* or faked research that was intentionally *deceptive* or deceitful.

30. *C* The key phrase "of few words" indicates that Eastwood's characters are *laconic*, untalkative types.

31. *E* *Insipid* (flavorless; dull and uninteresting) is a term that applies equally well to food and to conversations.

32. *D* Someone *crabbed* (bad-humored; harsh; morose) seldom smiles; someone *parsimonious* (stingy; miserly) never gives away money. Note how parallel structure determines word order: the first missing adjective relates to the first verb ("seldom smiled"); the second missing adjective relates to the second verb ("never gave away").

33. *B* The Pilgrims have traditionally been held up or *cited* as defenders of democracy.

34. *A* In challenging the traditional image of the Mayflower Compact as a cornerstone of American democracy, the author reveals himself to be a *debunker*, one who exposes false claims or attacks established beliefs.

35. *B* All of the aunt's comments belittle the father: he lives on dreams; a would-be actor, he never plays a leading role (he only gets to carry a spear); his wife marries him only for his looks. Throughout, her tone is *disparaging*.

36. *E* The ever-changing body of honorary aunts and uncles is the *collective group* of unrelated adults sharing the communal house with the narrator and his mother (and occasionally his father).

37. *B* In extending the pilot's control of the plane and making extreme actions (loops, sudden swerves, dives, etc.) comfortable, acrobatic flying *extends a pilot's range of capabilities*.

38. *D* The medium of the air is the *environment* in which flying creatures function.

39. *B* In the course of doing a loop, you lose sight of the horizon and must tilt your head backward to catch sight of the horizon line again. Thus, to pick up the horizon line is to *spot it visually*.

40. *A* Earlier in the passage, the author describes the experience of doing a loop as being "as far outside instinctive human behavior as you can go." In grabbing at the sides of the cockpit during the loop, the author is reverting to *instinctive*, involuntary behavior.

Choice B is incorrect. The experience of doing a loop was terrifying; grabbing the sides of the cockpit was not. Choice C is incorrect. It was not essential for the author to grab the sides of the cockpit; his seat belt was strong enough to keep him from falling out of the plane. Choice D is incorrect. The author did not wind up making a habit of grabbing the sides of the cockpit; he did it only that once. Choice E is incorrect. The experience of doing a loop may have seemed life threatening; grabbing the sides of the cockpit was not.

41. *E* In saying the belt held, the author means that it did not slip or come unfastened; instead, it *maintained its grasp*, keeping him safe.

42. *C* The instructor tells the author to put his arms out of the cockpit so that he can learn to have confidence in his seat belt's ability to hold him in the plane. He does so, *relying totally on his seat belt to keep him safe*.

43. *B* By stressing the terror that went into learning how to fly a loop, the author makes you feel that *satisfying* is an extremely mild word to describe the exhilaration of overcoming such an extreme fear and mastering such an unnatural skill. It is clearly an *understatement*.

44. *D* The author was not a fan of stunt flying; she was reluctant to pay attention to the aerial display. Therefore, this particular aerial display must have been unusually *captivating* to capture her attention.

45. *D* The author describes the audience's longing for a particular effect in the stunt-flying demonstration ("a certain kind of roll or climb, or a return to a certain portion of the air"). This is akin to a reader's longing for a particular effect in a poem—for example, a certain kind of image or rhyme or the return of an earlier refrain. Poets, however, play with their readers' expectations, sometimes varying exact end-rhymes with an occasional assonance or consonance (*slant* rhymes), as when Emily Dickinson unexpectedly rhymes *came* with *home*. Thus, in saying that Rahm "fulfilled your hope slantingly, like a poet," the author means that he *refused to satisfy your expectations directly* but gave you something unexpected instead.

46. *C* By "moving back the boundaries of the humanly possible" the author is talking about becoming aware *of new potentials for humanity*. This new knowledge leaves her gladdened and *exhilarated*.

47. *E* Passage 1 is both descriptive and informative. In recounting the story of the flying lesson, it is anecdotal. However, in comparison with Passage 2, it is not particularly poetic or *lyrical*.

48. *A* The author of Passage 1 talks about how useful acrobatic flying is in improving the skills of pilots. The author of Passage 2, however, looks on acrobatic flying as *an aesthetic experience*: she responds to Rahm's aerial demonstration as a new form of beauty, a performance that engages her aesthetically. Therefore, she would most likely consider the assessment of aerial flying in Passage 1 *too utilitarian* (concerned with practical usefulness) to be appropriate for an aesthetic experience.

Section 4 Mathematics

For many problems, the explanation provides a reference to one or more **KEY FACTS** from Chapter 9. These are the mathematical facts that you need to solve that problem. If a solution refers to **KEY FACT J2**, for example, the solution depends on the second **KEY FACT** discussed in Section J of Chapter 9.

For some problems, an alternative solution, indicated by two asterisks (**), follows the first solution. When this occurs, usually one of the solutions is the direct mathematical one and the other is based on one of the tactics discussed in Chapters 8 and 9.

21. *D* $2x - 1 = 9 \Rightarrow 2x = 10 \Rightarrow 20x = 100 \Rightarrow$ $20x - 1 = 99$.

22. *B* Since $8 - (8 + w) = -w$, the equation becomes $-w = 8$. So, $w = -8$.

23. *D* Let the numbers be x and $\frac{1}{5}x$. Then
$$20 = x\left(\frac{1}{5}x\right) = \frac{1}{5}x^2 \Rightarrow x^2 = 100 \Rightarrow$$
$$x = 10 \text{ or } x = -10.$$

Since the numbers are positive, $x = 10$, $\frac{1}{5}x = 2$, and their sum is 12.

**You can avoid using algebra by just testing pairs of small numbers, where one number is 5 times the other: 1 and 5? No. 2 and 10? Yes.

24. *C* Let x be Mr. Riccardo's number.
Then $x + 3 = 3x \Rightarrow 3 = 2x \Rightarrow x = 1.5$.

Use **TACTIC 8-1 and backsolve. Start with Choice C:
$1.5 + 3 = 4.5$ and $1.5 \times 3 = 4.5$. It works.

25. *C* If a team lost l of the g games it played, it won the rest: $g - l$. The fraction is $\frac{g-l}{g}$.

Use **TACTIC 8-2 and choose easy-to-use numbers. If the team lost 1 of its 3 games, it lost $\frac{1}{3}$ of them and won $\frac{2}{3}$ of them. Only Choice C equals $\frac{2}{3}$ when $g = 3$ and $l = 1$.

26. *B* When 200 is divided by 7, the quotient is 28 and the remainder is 4. Therefore, 200 days is 4 days more than 28 weeks. Twenty-eight weeks after a Friday is again a Friday, and 4 days after that is Tuesday. (Note that it is irrelevant that the *date* was September 13, 1998; this problem concerned only the day of the week.)

27. *B* Since the area of the square is 20, each side is $\sqrt{20}$. The radius of each semicircle, therefore, is $\frac{\sqrt{20}}{2}$. The area of the two semicircles is equal to the area of a circle of radius $\frac{\sqrt{20}}{2}$:
$$\pi\left(\frac{\sqrt{20}}{2}\right)^2 = \pi\left(\frac{20}{4}\right) = 5\pi.$$

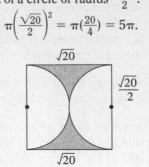

So the area of the shaded region is
$$20 - 5\pi = 5(4 - \pi).$$

28. *C* Adding the three equations, we get immediately that $a - d = 60$.

**Pick any number for d; say $d = 10$. Then $c = 40, b = 60$, and $a = 70$. Finally, $70 - 10 = 60$.

29. (7.5) $\triangle ABC$ is a right triangle; its area is given by $\frac{1}{2}(AB)(AC)$. Since $\overline{AB}$ is vertical, find its length by subtracting the y-coordinates: $AB = 4 - 1 = 3$. Similarly, since $\overline{AC}$ is horizontal, find its length by subtracting the x-coordinates: $BC = 6 - 1 = 5$. Then, area of $\triangle ABC = \frac{1}{2}(3)(5) = \frac{15}{2} = 7.5$.

30. (52.5) Since the sum of all the angles around a point is $360°$ (**KEY FACT I3**),
$$90 + a + a + 60 + a + a = 360 \Rightarrow$$
$$4a + 150 = 360 \Rightarrow 4a = 210 \Rightarrow a = 52.5.$$

31. $(360°)$ By **TACTIC 12-E1**, if the average of five numbers is 100, their sum is $5 \times 100 = 500$. The four given numbers add up to 140: $20 + 30 + 40 + 50 = 140$, so the fifth one, x, is $500 - 140 = 360$.

32. (50) Since 40% of the members of the club are boys, then 60% are girls. Let m be the number of members of the club.
Then $.60m = 30 \Rightarrow m = 30 \div .60 = 50$.

33. $\left(\frac{7}{12}\right)$ Use the slope formula (**KEY FACT N4**) to calculate the slope of line l: $\frac{7-3}{4-1} = \frac{4}{3}$. By **KEY FACT N6**, the slope of m is also $\frac{4}{3}$ and the slope of n is $-\frac{3}{4}$, the negative reciprocal of $\frac{4}{3}$. So the sum of the two slopes is $\frac{4}{3} + \left(-\frac{3}{4}\right) = \frac{7}{12}$.

34. (*67*) Write out enough terms of the sequence until you see a pattern.

$$1, 2, 3, 5, 8, 13, 21, 34, 55, \ldots$$

There are several patterns you might notice, but one observation is that the terms are

odd, even, odd, odd, even, odd, . . .

with the sequence odd, even, odd repeating indefinitely. The first 99 terms consist of 33 groups, with 2 odd numbers in each group, for a total of 66 odd numbers. The 100th number is the first number in the next group, which is odd. So there are 67 odd terms.

35. (*25*) $5(\sqrt{x} - 3) = 3\sqrt{x} - 5 \Rightarrow$

$5\sqrt{x} - 15 = 3\sqrt{x} - 5 \Rightarrow$

$2\sqrt{x} - 15 = -5 \Rightarrow$

$2\sqrt{x} = 10 \Rightarrow \sqrt{x} = 5 \Rightarrow x = 25.$

36. $\left(\frac{15}{8}\right)$ Use b, c, and t for "bangs," "clangs," and "tangs," respectively. Then the given equations are: $3b = 2c$ and $4b = 5t$. Multiply the first equation by 4 and the second by 3:

$12b = 8c$ and $12b = 15t$

So

$8c = 15t \Rightarrow c = \frac{15}{8}t$

So

$1 \text{ clang} = \frac{15}{8} \text{ tangs.}$

37. (*138*) Since 40% of 25 is 10, there are 10 girls and $25 - 10 = 15$ boys in the class. The total weight of the 10 girls is $10 \times 120 = 1200$ pounds and the total weight of the 15 boys is $15 \times 150 = 2250$. Therefore, the average weight of all 25 children is

$$\frac{1200 + 2250}{25} = \frac{3450}{25} = 138.$$

38. (*1*) By **KEY FACT K9**, the area of a square whose diagonal is d is $\frac{d^2}{2}$. So the area of the shaded region is the area of the large square minus the area of the middle square:

$$\frac{1}{2}(5^2) - \frac{1}{2}(4^2) = \frac{1}{2}(25) - \frac{1}{2}(16) =$$
$$12.5 - 8 = 4.5.$$

The striped region is a square whose diagonal is 3, and so its area is $\frac{1}{2}(3^2) = \frac{1}{2}(9) = 4.5$. Therefore, the two areas are equal, and so the ratio is 1.

Section 5 Writing Skills

1. *A* Sentence is correct.

2. *C* The two errors in diction (*imminent* for *eminent* and *stood* for *stayed*) are corrected in Choice C.

3. *D* This corrects the sentence fragment.

4. *B* Choice B corrects the run-on sentence.

5. *C* Choice C corrects the sentence fragment.

6. *C* Comma splice. Choice C corrects the run-on sentence and expresses the author's meaning directly and concisely. All other choices are indirect, ungrammatical, or do not retain the meaning of the original sentence.

7. *A* Sentence is correct.

8. *B* Error in coordination and subordination. Choice B corrects the conjunction *neither . . . nor* (not *neither . . . or*) and retains the meaning of the original sentence.

9. *C* Error in pronoun number agreement. Use *this kind of story* or *these kinds of stories*.

10. *D* The omission of the correct verb form is corrected in Choice D.

11. *C* Error in modification. The dangling participle construction is corrected in Choice C.

12. *E* Error in modification and word order. Choice E corrects the misplaced modifier and eliminates the unnecessary use of the passive voice.

13. *A* The use of the semicolon to separate the pair of clauses is correct.

14. *B* Choice B expresses the author's meaning directly and concisely. All other choices are indirect, ungrammatical, or do not retain the meaning of the original sentence.

15. *E* Double negative. Change *without scarcely a murmur* to *with scarcely a murmur*.

16. *A* Sentence is correct.

17. *D* Error in usage. Do not confuse *respectively* (singly in the order mentioned) and *respectfully* (politely and deferentially).

18. *D* Error in usage. The story is *incredible* or improbable; the jurors are *incredulous* (skeptical, disbelieving).

19. *C* Error in relative pronoun use. Relative pronouns are noun substitutes that serve to introduce subordinate clauses. Replace *which* with *a state of affairs that*.

20. *E* Dangling modifier. Ask yourself who is welding. Certainly not the goggles!

21. *E* Sentence is correct.

22. *A* Error in sequence of tenses. Change *has adopted* to *adopted*.

23. *B* Error in diction. Change *irregardless* to *regardless*.

24. *C* Error in subject-verb agreement. The subject *she and her staff* is plural; the verb should be plural—*are*.

25. *B* Error in diction. Change *or* to *nor*.

26. *C* Error in diction. Change *affect* to *effect*.

27. *D* Error in pronoun agreement. Change *his and her* to *their*.

28. *B* Error in pronoun case. Change *you* to *your*.

29. *E* Sentence is correct.

30. *E* Sentence is correct.

31. *D* Error in parallelism. Change *an increase in interest rates* to *interest rates increase*.

32. *C* Adjective and adverb confusion. Change *special prepared* to *specially prepared*.

33. *C* Error in tense. Change *been creating* to *created*.

34. *E* Sentence is correct.

35. *C* Choice A is a sentence fragment.
Choice B violates standard English idiom. The phrase *for example* should be followed by a noun, not by a prepositional phrase.
Choice C is a complete sentence and serves as an appropriate topic sentence for the second paragraph. It is the best answer.
Choice D serves neither as a good transition from the first to the second paragraph nor as an effective topic sentence for the second paragraph.

Choice E is a sentence fragment; also the phrases *for instance* and *for example* are redundant.

36. *C* Choice A contains an error in subject-verb agreement. The plural subject *rights* should have a plural verb, *were*.
Choice B shifts verb tenses from present perfect (*have seized*) to past perfect (*had repressed*). Confusion ensues.
Choice C succinctly and accurately revises the original sentence. It is the best answer.
Choice D is a confusion of verb tenses, which renders the sentence almost incomprehensible.
Choice E has a severe pronoun reference problem. It is unclear to whom the pronouns *they, their,* and *them* refer.

37. *A* Choice A clearly and succinctly explains the fate of the kulaks. It is the best answer.
Choice B is wordy and awkwardly expressed.
Choice C is wordy and contains a usage error. Because *forcing* is a gerund, *Stalin* should be possessive (*Stalin's*).
Choice D contains a dangling participle. It says that Stalin lost this right to own private property, an idea contrary to what the writer intended.
Choice E is not accurately expressed and contains an error in subject-verb agreement. The compound subject *loss* and *collectivization* requires a plural verb.

38. *E* Choices A, B, and C are trite and abrupt transitions. They should be avoided.
Choice D is not a good answer because the essay does not discuss international agreements on human rights.
Choice E accurately and smoothly provides a link between the content of the essay and the concluding paragraph. It is the best answer.

39. *A* Only Choice A accurately describes the function of the last paragraph. The conclusion—that people will eventually claim their rights—grows out of the discussion in paragraphs 1, 2, and 3. Therefore, Choice A is the best answer.

Index

A

Absolute value, 195
Acute angle, 233
Adjectives, 293
Adverbs, 293
Age-related word problems, 229
Algebra:
    inequalities, 224–228
    polynomials, 219–222
    solving equations, 224–228
Altitude of triangle, 239
Angles, 233–236
Arc, 251
Area of triangle, 246
Arithmetic:
    averages, 216–217
    decimals
        arithmetic operations with, 203–205
        comparing of, 203
        conversion to percents, 208
    fractions
        arithmetic operations with, 203–205
        comparing of, 203
        mixed numbers written as, 205–206
        multiplying of, 203–205
        simplifying of, 179
    percents, 208–210
    proportions, 212–214
    ratios, 212–214
Arithmetic sequence, 268
Averages, 216–217

B

Backsolving, 182
Bar graph, 271
Base, 198
Binomials, 219

C

Calculators, 14–16, 176
Center, 250
Central angle, 251
Central thought of a passage, 84–85
Chord, 250
Circle(s), 250–254
Circle graph, 273
Circumference, 251

Coefficient, 219
Consecutive integers, 197
Coordinate geometry, 259–264
Correlation, 274–275
Critical reading questions:
    abilities tested by, 80
    central thought of a passage, 84–85
    context of words, 80–81
    double passages, 79–80, 89–92
    paraphrasing, 82–83
    practice exercises, 92–105
    sample, 6–10
    strategy for, 78
    text
        applications of, 87–89
        implications from, 85–87
        inferences from, 85–87
        interpreting of, 82–83
        logic used in, 87–89
        techniques used in, 87–89
    tips for handling, 79–81
Cube, 255
Cylinder, 256–257

D

Data interpretation, 271–278
Decimals:
    arithmetic operations with, 203–205
    comparing of, 203
    conversion to percents, 208
Denominator, 205
Deviation, 216
Diagnostic test, 29–63
Diagonal, 256
Diagram:
    description of, 186–189
    scatter-plot, 274
Diameter, 250
Diction errors, 293
Difference, 195
Direct variation, 214
Distance-related word problems,
    229–230
Division:
    definition of, 195
    of polynomials, 221
Double passages, 79–80, 89–92

E

Edges, 255
Educated guessing, 25
Elements, 194
Equations:
    description of, 189–190
    linear, 226–227
    solution set of, 194
    solving of, 224–228
Equilateral triangle, 237
Event, 265
Exponent, 198–199
Exterior angle of triangle, 237

F

Faces, 255
Fractions:
    arithmetic operations with, 203–205
    comparing of, 203
    improper, 205
    mixed numbers written as, 205
    multiplying of, 203–205
    simplifying of, 179
Fragment, 292
Functions, 279–280

G

Geometric sequence, 268
Geometry:
    angles, 233–236
    circles, 250–254
    coordinate, 259–264
    lines, 233–235
    quadrilaterals, 244–249
    solid, 255–258
    triangles, 237–243
Grammar and usage errors, 291–294
Graphs:
    bar, 271
    circle, 273
    line, 271
Guessing, 24–26, 185–186
Guessing penalty, 25

H

Hypotenuse, 238

I

Idiom errors, 293
Improper fraction, 205
Inequalities, 224–228
Inferences, 85–87

Integers, 197–198
Interpreting of text, 82–83
Intersection of sets, 194
Inverse variation, 214
Isosceles triangle, 237

L

Least common denominator, 205
Least common multiple, 205
Like terms, 219
Linear equations, 226–227
Line graph, 271
Lines, 233–235
Lists, 190–191
Logical comparison errors, 292

M

Mathematical reasoning:
    algebra
        inequalities, 224–228
        polynomials, 219–222
        solving equations, 224–228
    averages, 216–217
    concepts regarding, 194–202
    data interpretation, 271–278
    decimals
        arithmetic operations with, 203–205
        comparing of, 203
        conversion to percents, 208
    directions for, 176–178
    fractions
        arithmetic operations with, 203–205
        comparing of, 203
        mixed numbers written as, 205–206
        multiplying of, 203–205
        simplifying of, 179
    geometry
        angles, 233–236
        circles, 250–254
        coordinate, 259–264
        lines, 233–235
        quadrilaterals, 244–249
        solid, 255–258
        triangles, 237–243
    grid-in questions for, 178–181
    introduction to, 175–181
    percents, 208–210
    probability, 265–267
    proportions, 212–214
    ratios, 212–214
    sample questions, 11–16
    sequences

arithmetic, 268
  geometric, 268
  repeating, 268–269
strategies for, 182–193
tactics for, 182–193
Median, 217
Merit Scholarships, 3
Mixed numbers:
  arithmetic operations with, 205–206
  as fractions, 205–206
  definition of, 179, 205
Mode, 217
Model tests, 305–508
Monomial, 219
Multiplication:
  definition of, 195
  of fractions, 203–205
  of polynomials, 220–221

N

Negative correlation, 274–275
Negative integers, 197
Negative numbers, 195
Nouns, 293
Numbers:
  choosing of, 184–185
  mixed
    arithmetic operations with, 205–206
    as fractions, 205–206
    definition of, 179, 205
  prime, 198
  signed, 195–197
  variables replaced with, 183–184

O

Obtuse angle, 233

P

Paragraphs, 290–291
Parallelism, 293
Parallel lines, 234
Parallelogram, 244
Paraphrasing, 82–83
Passages:
  central thought of, 84–85
  double, 79, 89–92
"PEMDAS," 200
Percent(s), 208–210
Percent decrease, 210
Percent increase, 210
Perfect squares, 198
Perimeter, 245–246

Perpendicular lines, 234
Pie chart, 273
Polynomials, 219–222
Positive correlation, 274–275
Positive integers, 197
Positive numbers, 195
Prefixes, 157–161
Prime numbers, 198
Probability, 265–267
Product, 195–196
Pronoun, 293
Pronoun-number agreement, 293
Proportions, 213–214
Pythagorean theorem, 238

Q

Quadrilaterals, 244–249
Quotient, 195

R

Radius, 250
Ratios, 212–214
Real number, 194
Reciprocal, 204
Rectangle, 245
Rectangular solid, 255
Remainder, 197
Repeating sequence, 268–269
Right angle, 233
Right triangle, 238
Roots:
  mathematical, 198–199
  square, 199
  of words, 161–170
Rounding off, 179
Run-on sentence, 291

S

Scatter-plot diagram, 274
Semicircles, 251
Sentence(s):
  errors in, 288–290
  improving of, 285–288
  run-on, 291
Sentence completion questions:
  description of, 67
  exercises, 70–77
  tips for handling, 67–70
Sentence fragment, 291
Sequences:
  arithmetic, 268
  geometric, 268

repeating, 268–269
Set, 194
Shaded regions, 189
Signed numbers, 195–197
Solid geometry, 255–258
Solution set, 194
Solving equations, 224–228
Square, 199, 245
Square root, 199
Straight angle, 233
Subject-verb agreement, 292
Subtraction:
  definition of, 195–196
  of mixed numbers, 206
  of polynomials, 220
Suffixes, 171–172
Sum, 195–196
Surface area of rectangular solid,
    256
Symbols, 175–176, 191
System of equations, 226–227

T
Tangent, 253
Test-taking tactics, 22–23
Text:
  applications of, 87–89
  implications from, 85–87
  inferences drawn from, 85–87
  inferences from, 85–87
  interpreting of, 82–83
  logic used in, 87–89
  techniques used in, 87–89
Topic sentences, 84
Transversal, 234
Triangles, 237–243
Trinomials, 219

U
Union of sets, 194

V
Verb tense, 292
Vertex, 233
Vertical angles, 234

Vocabulary building:
  strategy for, 106
  word lists
    basic types of, 109–156
    high-frequency, 107–108
    how to use, 107
  word parts
    prefixes, 157–161
    roots, 161–170
    suffixes, 171–172
Volume
  of cube, 255
  of cylinder, 256
  of rectangular solid, 255

W
Width of rectangular solid, 255
Word lists:
  basic types of, 109–156
  high-frequency, 107–108
  how to use, 107
Word order errors, 293
Word parts:
  prefixes, 157–161
  roots, 161–170
  suffixes, 171–172
Word problems, 229–232
Writing skills:
  grammar and usage errors, 291–294
  paragraphs, 290–291
  practice exercises, 294–302
  sample questions, 17–20
  sentence(s)
    description of, 67
    errors in, 288–290
    exercises, 70–77
    improving of, 285–288
    run-on, 291
    tips for handling, 67–70

X
x-coordinate, 259

Y
y-coordinate, 259

Notes

504 ABSOLUTELY ESSENTIAL WORDS, 5th Edition
$11.95, Can. $17.50 (0-7641-2815-9)
Builds practical vocabulary skills through funny stories and cartoons plus practice exercises.

1001 PITFALLS IN ENGLISH GRAMMAR, 3rd Edition
$12.95, Can. $18.95 (0-8120-3719-7)
Examines the most common errors in the English language.

1100 WORDS YOU NEED TO KNOW, 4th Edition
$12.99, Can. $18.99 (0-7641-1365-8)
This book is the way to master more than 1100 useful words and idioms taken from the mass media.

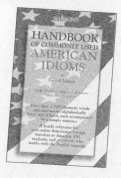

WORDPLAY: 550+ WORDS YOU NEED TO KNOW
CD Pkg. $19.95, Can. $28.95 (0-7641-7750-8)
Based on **1100 Words You Need to Know;** included are five CDs presented in comedy-drama form to add in the dimension of dialogue and the spoken word.

A DICTIONARY OF AMERICAN IDIOMS, 4TH EDITION
$14.95, Can. $21.95 (0-7641-1982-6)
Over 8,000 idiomatic words, expressions, regionalisms, and informal English expressions are defined and cross-referenced for easy access.

HANDBOOK OF COMMONLY USED AMERICAN IDIOMS, 4th Edition
$7.95, Can. $11.50 (0-7641-2776-4)
With 1500 popular idioms, this book will benefit both English-speaking people and those learning English as a second language.

BARRON'S EDUCATIONAL SERIES, INC.
250 Wireless Boulevard
Hauppauge, New York 11788
Canada: Georgetown Book Warehouse
34 Armstrong Avenue
Georgetown, Ont. L7G 4R9
www.barronseduc.com

Prices subject to change without notice. Books may be purchased at your bookstore, or by mail from Barron's. Enclose check or money order for total amount plus sales tax where applicable and 18% for postage and handling (minimum charge $5.95). New York, New Jersey, Michigan, Tennessee, and California residents add sales tax. Books listed are paperback editions.
$ = U.S. Dollars   Can. $ = Canadian Dollars

Notes

THERE'S ONLY ONE PLACE TO TURN FOR TOP SCORES...

Notes

Notes